YBM
실전토익
RC1000
1

YBM
실전토익
RC 1000 1

발행인   허문호
발행처   YBM

문항 개발   Marilyn Hook, 백주선
편집   김준하
디자인   김혜경, 이현숙, 이지현
마케팅   정연철, 박천산, 고영노, 박찬경, 김동진, 김윤하

개정판1쇄 발행   2019년 10월 1일
개정판6쇄 발행   2023년 6월 12일

신고일자   1964년 3월 28일
신고번호   제 300-1964-3호
주소   서울시 종로구 종로 104
전화   (02) 2000-0515 [구입문의] / (02) 2000-0436 [내용문의]
팩스   (02) 2285-1523
홈페이지   www.ybmbooks.com

ISBN 978-89-17-23213-4   978-89-17-95114-1 SET

토익 주관사가 제시하는 진짜 토익

YBM 실전토익 RC 1000 1을 발행하며

지난 30여 년간 우리나라에서 토익 시험을 주관하면서 토익 시장을 이끌고, 꾸준히 베스트셀러를 출간해온 YBM에서 〈YBM 실전토익 RC 1000 1〉을 출간하게 되었습니다.

YBM 토익은 이렇게 다릅니다!

YBM의 명성에 자부심을 가지고 개발했습니다!

YBM은 지난 1982년부터 우리나라의 토익 시험을 주관해온 토익 주관사로서, 지난 30여 년간 400여 권의 토익 베스트셀러를 출판해왔습니다. 그 오랜 시간 토익 문제를 분석하고 교재를 출판하면서 쌓아온 전문성과 실력으로 이번에 〈YBM 실전토익 RC 1000 1〉을 선보이게 되었습니다.

토익 주관사로서의 사명감을 가지고 개발했습니다!

토익 주관사로서 사명감을 갖고 신토익 최신 경향을 철저히 분석하여 〈YBM 실전토익 RC 1000 1〉을 개발하였습니다. 실제 시험과 가장 유사한 문제 유형을 반영하였고, 핵심 출제 포인트를 해설집에 상세히 담았습니다.

ETS 교재를 출간한 노하우를 가지고 개발했습니다!

출제기관 ETS의 토익 교재를 독점 출간하는 YBM은 그동안 쌓아온 노하우를 바탕으로 〈YBM 실전토익 RC 1000 1〉을 개발하였습니다. 본 책에 실린 1000개의 문항은 출제자의 의도를 정확히 반영하였기 때문에 타사의 어떤 토익 교재와도 비교할 수 없는 퀄리티를 자랑합니다.

YBM의 모든 노하우가 집대성된 〈YBM 실전토익 RC 1000 1〉은 최단 시간에 최고의 점수를 수험자 여러분께 약속 드립니다.

YBM 토익연구소

토익의 구성과 수험 정보

TOEIC은 어떤 시험인가요?

Test of English for International Communication(국제적 의사소통을 위한 영어 시험)의 약자로서, 영어가 모국어가 아닌 사람들이 일상생활 또는 비즈니스 현장에서 꼭 필요한 실용적 영어 구사 능력을 갖추었는가를 평가하는 시험이다.

시험 구성

구성	Part	내용		문항수	시간	배점
듣기 (L/C)	1	사진 묘사		6	45분	495점
	2	질의 & 응답		25		
	3	짧은 대화		39		
	4	짧은 담화		30		
읽기 (R/C)	5	단문 빈칸 채우기(문법/어휘)		30	75분	495점
	6	장문 빈칸 채우기		16		
	7	독해	단일 지문	29		
			이중 지문	10		
			삼중 지문	15		
Total	7 Parts			200문항	120분	990점

TOEIC 접수는 어떻게 하나요?

TOEIC 접수는 한국 토익 위원회 사이트(www.toeic.co.kr)에서 온라인 상으로만 접수가 가능하다. 사이트에서 매월 자세한 접수 일정과 시험 일정 등의 구체적 정보 확인이 가능하니, 미리 일정을 확인하여 접수하도록 한다.

시험장에 반드시
가져가야 할 준비물은요?

신분증 규정 신분증만 가능

(주민등록증, 운전면허증, 기간 만료 전의 여권, 공무원증 등)

필기구 연필, 지우개 (볼펜이나 사인펜은 사용 금지)

시험은 어떻게
진행되나요?

09:20 입실 (09:50 이후는 입실 불가)

09:30 – 09:45 답안지 작성에 관한 오리엔테이션

09:45 – 09:50 휴식

09:50 – 10:05 신분증 확인

10:05 – 10:10 문제지 배부 및 파본 확인

10:10 – 10:55 듣기 평가 (Listening Test)

10:55 – 12:10 독해 평가 (Reading Test)

TOEIC 성적 확인은
어떻게 하죠?

시험일로부터 12일 후 인터넷과 ARS(060-800-0515)로 성적을 확인할 수 있다. TOEIC 성적표는 우편이나 온라인으로 발급 받을 수 있다(시험 접수시, 양자 택일). 우편으로 발급 받을 경우는 성적 발표 후 대략 일주일이 소요되며, 온라인 발급을 선택하면 유효기간 내에 홈페이지에서 본인이 직접 1회에 한해 무료 출력할 수 있다. TOEIC 성적은 시험일로부터 2년간 유효하다.

TOEIC은
몇 점 만점인가요?

TOEIC 점수는 듣기 영역(LC) 점수, 읽기 영역(RC) 점수, 그리고 이 두 영역을 합계한 전체 점수 세 부분으로 구성된다. 각 부분의 점수는 5점 단위이며, 5점에서 495점에 걸쳐 주어지고, 전체 점수는 10점에서 990점까지이며, 만점은 990점이다. TOEIC 성적은 각 문제 유형의 난이도에 따른 점수 환산표에 의해 결정된다.

신토익 경향 분석

PART 1 사진 묘사 Photographs

총 6문제

사람 또는
사물 중심 사진
33%

1인
등장 사진
33%

PART 1
최신 출제 경향

사물/
배경 사진
17%

2인 이상
등장 사진
17%

1인 등장 사진
주어는 He/She, A man/woman 등이며 주로
앞부분에 나온다.

2인 이상 등장 사진
주어는 They, Some men/women/people, One
of the men/women 등이며 주로 중간 부분에 나온다.

사물/배경 사진
주어는 A car, some chairs 등이며 주로 뒷부분에
나온다.

사람 또는 사물 중심 사진
주어가 일부는 사람, 일부는 사물이며 주로 뒷부분에
나온다.

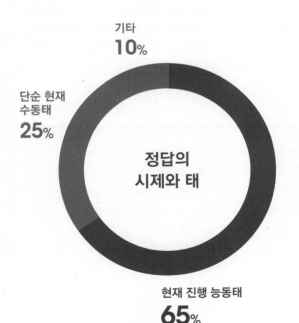

기타
10%

단순 현재
수동태
25%

정답의
시제와 태

현재 진행 능동태
65%

현재 진행 능동태
〈is/are + 현재분사〉 형태이며 주로 사람이 주어이다.

단순 현재 수동태
〈is/are + 과거분사〉 형태이며 주로 사물이 주어이다.

기타
〈is/are + being + 과거분사〉 형태의 현재 진행 수동태,
〈has/have + been + 과거 분사〉 형태의 현재 완료 수
동태, '타동사 + 목적어' 형태의 단순 현재 능동태, There
is/are와 같은 단순 현재도 나온다.

PART 2 질의 & 응답 Question-Response

총 25문제

평서문
질문이 아니라 객관적인 사실이나 화자의 의견 등을 나타내는 문장이다.

명령문
동사원형이나 Please 등으로 시작한다.

의문사 의문문
각 의문사마다 1~2개씩 나온다. 의문사가 단독으로 나오기도 하지만 What time ~?, How long ~?, Which room ~? 등에서처럼 다른 명사나 형용사와 같이 나오기도 한다.

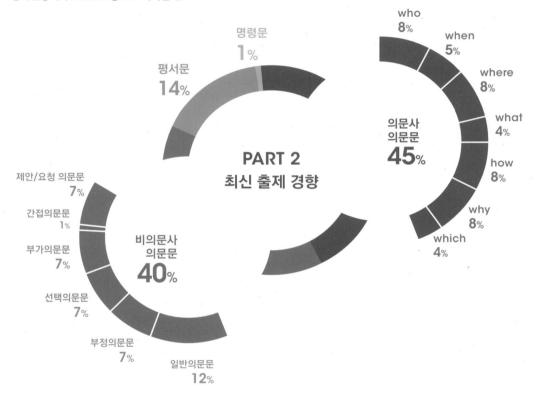

명령문 **1**%
평서문 **14**%
who **8**%
when **5**%
where **8**%
what **4**%
의문사 의문문 **45**%
how **8**%
why **8**%
which **4**%
제안/요청 의문문 **7**%
간접의문문 **1**%
부가의문문 **7**%
비의문사 의문문 **40**%
선택의문문 **7**%
부정의문문 **7**%
일반의문문 **12**%

PART 2 최신 출제 경향

비의문사 의문문
일반(Yes/No) 의문문 적게 나올 때는 한두 개, 많이 나올 때는 서너 개씩 나오는 편이다.
부정의문문 Don't you ~?, Isn't he ~? 등으로 시작하는 문장이며 일반 긍정 의문문보다는 약간 더 적게 나온다.
선택의문문 A or B 형태로 나오며 A와 B의 형태가 단어, 구, 절일 수 있다. 구나 절일 경우 문장이 길어져서 어려워진다.
부가의문문 ~ don't you?, ~ isn't he? 등으로 끝나는 문장이며, 일반 부정 의문문과 비슷하다고 볼 수 있다.
간접의문문 의문사가 문장 처음 부분이 아니라 문장 중간에 들어 있다.
제안/요청 의문문 정보를 얻기보다는 상대방의 도움이나 동의 등을 얻기 위한 목적이 일반적이다.

PART 3 짧은 대화 Short Conversations

총 13대화문 39문제 (지문당 3문제)

■ 3인 대화의 경우 남자 화자 두 명과 여자 화자 한 명 또는 남자 화자 한 명과 여자 화자 두 명이 나온다. 따라서 문제에서는 2인 대화에서와 달리 the man이나 the woman이 아니라 the men이나 the women 또는 특정한 이름이 언급될 수 있다.

■ 대화 & 시각 정보는 항상 파트의 뒷부분에 나온다.

■ 시각 정보의 유형으로 chart, map, floor plan, schedule, table, weather forecast, directory, list, invoice, receipt, sign, packing slip 등 다양한 자료가 골고루 나온다.

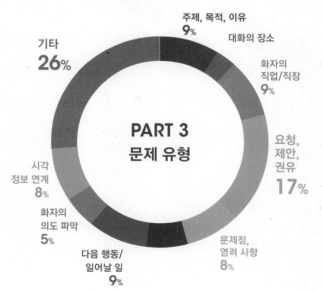

■ 주제, 목적, 이유, 대화의 장소, 화자의 직업/직장 등과 관련된 문제는 주로 대화의 첫 번째 문제로 나오며 다음 행동/일어날 일 등과 관련된 문제는 주로 대화의 세 번째 문제로 나온다.

■ 화자의 의도 파악 문제는 주로 2인 대화에 나오지만, 가끔 3인 대화에 나오기도 한다. 시각 정보 연계 대화에는 나오지 않고 있다.

■ Part 3 안에서 화자의 의도 파악 문제는 2개 나오고 시각 정보 연계 문제는 3개 나온다.

PART 4 짧은 담화 Short Talks

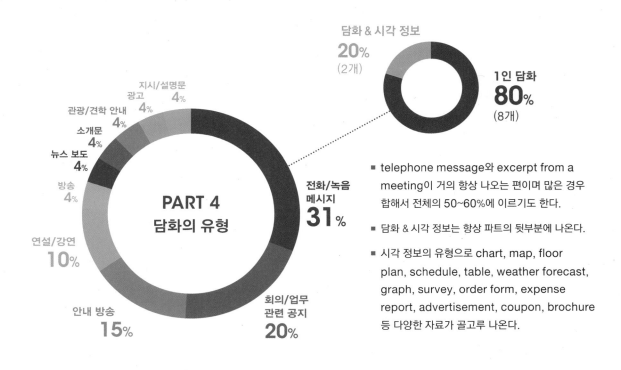

담화 & 시각 정보
20%
(2개)

1인 담화
80%
(8개)

지시/설명문
4%

광고 **4%**

관광/견학 안내
4%

소개문
4%

뉴스 보도
4%

방송
4%

연설/강연
10%

안내 방송
15%

PART 4
담화의 유형

전화/녹음
메시지
31%

회의/업무
관련 공지
20%

- telephone message와 excerpt from a meeting이 거의 항상 나오는 편이며 많은 경우 합해서 전체의 50~60%에 이르기도 한다.
- 담화 & 시각 정보는 항상 파트의 뒷부분에 나온다.
- 시각 정보의 유형으로 chart, map, floor plan, schedule, table, weather forecast, graph, survey, order form, expense report, advertisement, coupon, brochure 등 다양한 자료가 골고루 나온다.

주제, 목적, 이유
9%

담화의 장소
3%

화자의
직업/직장
13%

기타
35%

PART 4
문제 유형

요청,
제안, 권유
10%

문제점, 염려 사항
2%

특정한 시간/장소
7%

다음 행동/일어날 일
4%

시각 정보 연계
7%

화자의
의도 파악
10%

- 문제 유형은 기본적으로 Part 3과 거의 비슷하다.
- 주제, 목적, 이유, 담화의 장소, 화자의 직업/직장 등과 관련된 문제는 주로 담화의 첫 번째 문제로 나오며 다음 행동/일어날 일 등과 관련된 문제는 주로 담화의 세 번째 문제로 나온다.
- Part 4 안에서 화자의 의도 파악 문제는 3개 나오고 시각 정보 연계 문제는 2개 나온다.

PART 5 단문 빈칸 채우기 Incomplete Sentences

총 30문제

문법 문제

시제와 대명사와 관련된 문법 문제가 2개씩, 한정사와 분사와 관련된 문법 문제가 1개씩 나온다. 시제 문제의 경우 능동태/수동태나 수의 일치와 연계되기도 한다. 그 밖에 한정사, 능동태/수동태, 부정사, 동명사 등과 관련된 문법 문제가 나온다.

어휘 문제

동사, 명사, 형용사, 부사와 관련된 어휘 문제가 각각 2~3개씩 골고루 나온다. 전치사 어휘 문제는 3개씩 꾸준히 나오지만, 접속사나 어구와 관련된 어휘 문제는 나오지 않을 때도 있고 3개가 나올 때도 있다.

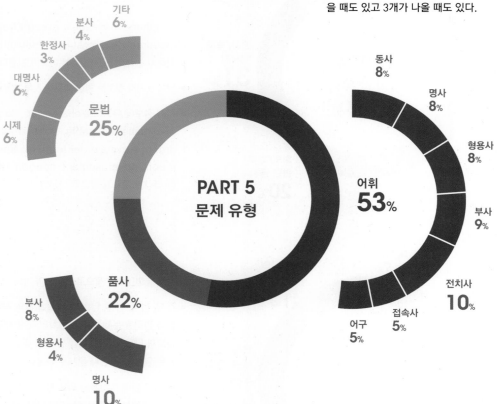

품사 문제

명사와 부사와 관련된 품사 문제가 2~3개씩 나오며, 형용사와 관련된 품사 문제가 상대적으로 적은 편이다.

PART 6 장문 빈칸 채우기 Text Completion

한 지문에 4문제가 나오며 평균적으로 어휘 문제가 2개, 품사나 문법
문제가 1개, 문맥에 맞는 문장 고르기 문제가 1개 들어간다.
문맥에 맞는 문장 고르기 문제를 제외하면 문제 유형은 기본적
으로 파트 5와 거의 비슷하다.

어휘 문제
동사, 명사, 부사, 어구와 관련된 어휘 문제는
매번 1~2개씩 나온다. 부사 어휘 문제의 경우
therefore(그러므로)나 however(하지만)처럼
문맥의 흐름을 자연스럽게 연결해 주는 부사가
자주 나온다.

문맥에 맞는 문장 고르기
문맥에 맞는 문장 고르기 문제는 지문당 한 문제씩 나
오는데, 나오는 위치의 확률은 4문제 중 두 번째 문제,
세 번째 문제, 네 번째 문제, 첫 번째 문제
순으로 높다.

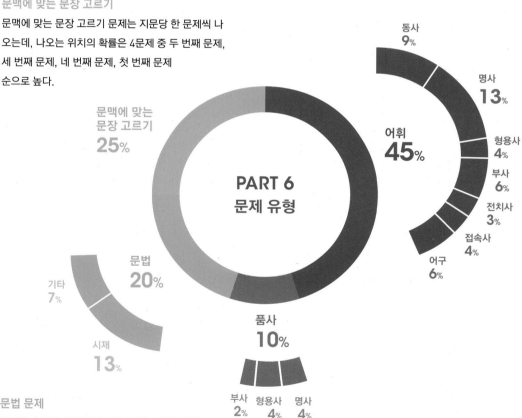

PART 6
문제 유형

동사 9%
명사 13%
형용사 4%
부사 6%
전치사 3%
접속사 4%
어구 6%
어휘 45%

품사 10%
부사 2% 형용사 4% 명사 4%

문맥에 맞는 문장 고르기 25%

문법 20%
기타 7%
시제 13%

문법 문제
문맥의 흐름과 밀접하게 관련이 있는 시제 문제
가 2개 정도 나오며, 능동태/수동태나 수의 일치
와 연계되기도 한다. 그 밖에 대명사, 능동태/수
동태, 부정사, 접속사/전치사 등과 관련된 문법
문제가 나온다.

품사 문제
명사나 형용사 문제가 부사 문제보다 좀 더
자주 나온다.

신토익 경향 분석

PART 7 독해 Reading Comprehension

지문 유형	지문당 문제 수	지문 개수	비중 %
단일 지문	2문항	4개	약 15%
	3문항	3개	약 16%
	4문항	3개	약 22%
이중 지문	5문항	2개	약 19%
삼중 지문	5문항	3개	약 28%

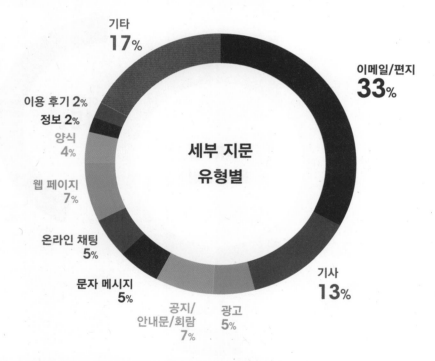

■ 이메일/편지, 기사 유형 지문은 거의 항상 나오는 편이며 많은 경우 합해서 전체의 50~60%에 이르기도 한다.

■ 기타 지문 유형으로 agenda, brochure, comment card, coupon, flyer, instructions, invitation, invoice, list, menu, page from a catalog, policy statement, report, schedule, survey, voucher 등 다양한 자료가 골고루 나온다.

(이중 지문과 삼중 지문 속의 지문들을 모두 낱개로 계산함 – 총 23지문)

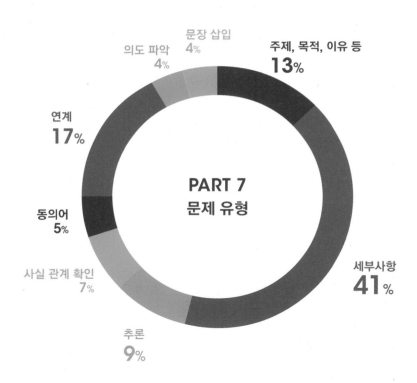

문장 삽입
4%

의도 파악
4%

주제, 목적, 이유 등
13%

연계
17%

동의어
5%

사실 관계 확인
7%

PART 7
문제 유형

세부사항
41%

추론
9%

- 동의어 문제는 주로 이중 지문이나 삼중 지문에 나온다.
- 연계 문제는 일반적으로 이중 지문에서 한 문제, 삼중 지문에서 두 문제가 나온다.
- 의도 파악 문제는 문자 메시지(text-message chain)나 온라인 채팅(online chat discussion) 지문에서 출제되며 두 문제가 나온다.
- 문장 삽입 문제는 주로 기사, 이메일, 편지, 회람 지문에서 출제되며 두 문제가 나온다.

점수 환산표

LISTENING Raw Score (맞은 개수)	LISTENING Scaled Score (환산 점수)	READING Raw Score (맞은 개수)	READING Scaled Score (환산 점수)
96-100	480-495	96-100	460-495
91-95	435-490	91-95	410-475
86-90	395-450	86-90	380-430
81-85	355-415	81-85	355-400
76-80	325-375	76-80	325-375
71-75	295-340	71-75	295-345
66-70	265-315	66-70	265-315
61-65	240-285	61-65	235-285
56-60	215-260	56-60	205-255
51-55	190-235	51-55	175-225
46-50	160-210	46-50	150-195
41-45	135-180	41-45	120-170
36-40	110-155	36-40	100-140
31-35	85-130	31-35	75-120
26-30	70-105	26-30	55-100
21-25	50-90	21-25	40-80
16-20	35-70	16-20	30-65
11-15	20-55	11-15	20-50
6-10	15-40	6-10	15-35
1-5	5-20	1-5	5-20
0	5	0	5

* 이 환산표는 본 교재에 수록된 Test용으로 개발된 것이다. 이 표를 사용하여 자신의 실제 점수를 환산 점수로 전환하도록 한다. 즉, 예를 들어 Listening Test의 실제 정답 수가 61~65개이면 환산 점수는 240점에서 285점 사이가 된다. 여기서 실제 정답 수가 61개이면 환산 점수가 240점이고, 65개이면 환산 점수가 285점임을 의미하는 것은 아니다. 본 책의 Test를 위해 작성된 이 점수 환산표가 자신의 영어 실력이 어느 정도인지 대략적으로 파악하는 데 도움이 되긴 하지만, 이 표가 실제 TOEIC 성적 산출에 그대로 사용된 적은 없다는 사실을 밝혀 둔다.

CONTENTS

RC

TEST 1

READING TEST

In the Reading test, you will read a variety of texts and answer several different types of reading comprehension questions. The entire Reading test will last 75 minutes. There are three parts, and directions are given for each part. You are encouraged to answer as many questions as possible within the time allowed.

You must mark your answers on the separate answer sheet. Do not write your answers in your test book.

PART 5

Directions: A word or phrase is missing in each of the sentences below. Four answer choices are given below each sentence. Select the best answer to complete the sentence. Then mark the letter (A), (B), (C), or (D) on your answer sheet.

101. The store's opening celebration has been ------- scheduled for the first day of a local festival.

(A) strategically
(B) strategizing
(C) strategy
(D) strategic

102. Employees should remember to log out of ------- work e-mail accounts before leaving for the day.

(A) that
(B) whose
(C) their
(D) its

103. Mr. Biden asked his supervisor ------- the deadline for this quarter's expense reports.

(A) extend
(B) will extend
(C) had extended
(D) to extend

104. ------- this afternoon's business seminar ends, Mr. Kane will have his staff clean the conference hall.

(A) Since
(B) When
(C) Why
(D) Should

105. According to our research, music streaming is the Clink smart speaker's most well-known -------.

(A) function
(B) destination
(C) style
(D) rating

106. To apply for the Web designer position, send us an e-mail ------- the appropriate job vacancy code in the subject line.

(A) with
(B) from
(C) where
(D) upon

107. All Bousquet Garments products, including accessories, ------- by us using priority post.

(A) shipped
(B) being shipped
(C) are shipped
(D) shipping

108. Penvex Group was able to offer more services and expand into new territories after ------- with Taron Bank.

(A) merged
(B) merging
(C) has merged
(D) merger

109. A common characteristic of global analysts is a willingness to go on ------- business trips overseas.
(A) frequently
(B) frequent
(C) frequency
(D) frequents

110. Baugh Entertainment's most recent video game ------- nearly $50 million in sales in just one month.
(A) released
(B) ranked
(C) depicted
(D) generated

111. Under this warranty, the performance of your Dorell-brand refrigerator is guaranteed ------- Byrnton Appliances.
(A) until
(B) for
(C) to
(D) by

112. The board of directors announced that it will ------- find a replacement for the outgoing CEO.
(A) usually
(B) extremely
(C) definitely
(D) formerly

113. Mr. Johnson is ------- to apply for the job at MindTek, Inc., as he lacks experience in the field of robotics.
(A) hesitation
(B) hesitant
(C) hesitated
(D) hesitantly

114. Rondel Plumbing Company offers a ------- range of apprenticeship opportunities for enthusiastic individuals.
(A) lasting
(B) several
(C) durable
(D) diverse

115. The director of tonight's play asks that theatergoers ------- refrain from taking pictures while the performance is taking place.
(A) closely
(B) kindly
(C) newly
(D) deeply

116. Customers of Dillon's Furniture can view an ------- delivery date on the checkout page when placing an order online.
(A) estimated
(B) estimating
(D) estimation
(D) estimate

117. Krush Juice & Smoothies is downsizing its operations and plans to ------- many of its current menu choices.
(A) reimburse
(B) purchase
(C) discontinue
(D) determine

118. The parking ------- in this neighborhood were introduced to enable the free movement of road traffic at all times.
(A) restricts
(B) restriction
(C) restrictions
(D) restricted

119. Part-time telephone operators will be hired to help deal with the ------- number of customer calls that is expected.
(A) overwhelmingly
(B) overwhelming
(C) overwhelmed
(D) overwhelms

120. Members of the accounting department are discouraged from taking vacations ------- tax preparation season.
(A) as
(B) about
(C) during
(D) without

GO ON TO THE NEXT PAGE

121. The marketing director believes that the Burton Hotel and Willoughby Restaurant are ------- suitable venues for the year-end banquet.
(A) equals
(B) equally
(C) equaled
(D) equality

122. ------- its greater durability, the Ruizon 180R has no clear advantages over our existing telescopes.
(A) Along with
(B) Owing to
(C) Rather than
(D) Apart from

123. Customer service staff have reported that computer software errors are occurring with increasing -------.
(A) regularized
(B) regular
(C) regularly
(D) regularity

124. Residents of Ikebukuro have ------- concern that the construction of the proposed shopping mall will raise noise pollution levels.
(A) opposed
(B) entailed
(C) assigned
(D) expressed

125. As the head of the personnel department, Mr. Murphy is ------- for ensuring the happiness and welfare of all company employees.
(A) likely
(B) sincere
(C) responsible
(D) conclusive

126. Employees at Tripoint Engineering are rewarded each year for perfect ------- and timekeeping.
(A) attendants
(B) attendance
(C) attended
(D) attends

127. The ------- bid for the property at 525 Eglington Road was much lower than the final price after negotiations.
(A) identical
(B) numerous
(C) initial
(D) versatile

128. Full details about the ------- of the security manager position can be found on the recruitment page on our Web site.
(A) batches
(B) objects
(C) trends
(D) duties

129. There is no need to respond to media inquiries about this matter, as we have ------- issued a statement that sufficiently explains our viewpoint.
(A) others
(B) already
(C) better
(D) long

130. ------- production costs have not significantly decreased, Matrox Chemicals has noted a sharp fall in its monthly expenditures.
(A) Although
(B) In addition to
(C) Either
(D) As well as

PART 6

Directions: Read the texts that follow. A word, phrase, or sentence is missing in parts of each text. Four answer choices for each question are given below the text. Select the best answer to complete the text. Then mark the letter (A), (B), (C), or (D) on your answer sheet.

Questions 131-134 refer to the following instructions.

Thank you for purchasing the Mercroft 6-Shelf Bookcase. Please follow the instructions and diagrams provided in this manual to construct the product. The shipping box serves as an ideal work surface for this process.

Save all packaging until the bookshelf is complete to avoid ------- discarding smaller parts. Prior to
131.
-------, use the parts and hardware lists to identify and separate each of the pieces included.
132.

Do not fully tighten all bolts until all parts are in place. Failure to follow these instructions may -------
133.
the bolts to become misaligned. If using power tools while putting the product together, please take
caution. -------.
134.

131. (A) mistake
(B) mistaken
(C) mistaking
(D) mistakenly

132. (A) delivery
(B) repair
(C) assembly
(D) manufacture

133. (A) expose
(B) cause
(C) risk
(D) hinder

134. (A) They can damage the wood when used without care.
(B) They have been recommended by technicians.
(C) They are too large to be easily misplaced.
(D) They should be disposed of in the appropriate bins.

Pelletier Arts Update

By Vicky Stevenson

After several weeks of preparation, the city ------- new murals under Mosser Bridge on Saturday.
135.
Citizens and tourists are invited to come down to Pelletier Canal to join in the daylong celebration,

which is to include games and refreshments.

The murals were conceived of and painted onto the brick undersides of the bridge by local artist

Preston Gilbert. The north side features images of animals, while the south presents famous works

of art. ------- are designed to provide onlookers with fun photo opportunities. -------, on the north side,
136.   137.
visitors will be able to take a picture in which it appears they are shaking hands with a friendly

gorilla.

------- .
138.

135. (A) was unveiling
(B) had unveiled
(C) unveiled
(D) will unveil

136. (A) Each
(B) Both
(C) Much
(D) Another

137. (A) Nonetheless
(B) Additionally
(C) Instead
(D) For instance

138. (A) For details about the event, visit
www.pelletiercanal.com.
(B) The bridge is also expected to ease traffic
along the waterway.
(C) Finally, Mr. Gilbert gave a short speech
about the murals.
(D) Those interested can call 555-0147 to
submit a suggestion.

Questions 139-142 refer to the following e-mail.

From: <k.chalmers@rybecks.com>
To: <s.underhill@me-mail.net>
Date: October 25
Subject: Order #6622

Dear Ms. Underhill,

We appreciate your choosing Rybeck's for your home furnishing needs. Unfortunately, when you ------- your order, our Web site was being updated. -------. In particular, the cushions that you wish to
139.   140.
purchase are actually not currently in stock. -------, we do have a similar set of cushions available.
141.
They are the same design and price as the ones you ordered, but a slightly different shade.

I have attached a picture of these items. If you are happy with their -------, they can be shipped to
142.
you immediately.

I look forward to receiving your reply.

Sincerely,

Kevin Chalmers
Rybeck's Home Furnishings

139. (A) place
(B) placed
(C) will place
(D) are placing

140. (A) Such routine maintenance ensures your data security.
(B) Please check back in a few hours to register your account.
(C) Because of this, some of the information on it was incorrect.
(D) Fortunately, all of our offline stores are operating normally.

141. (A) Therefore
(B) Besides
(C) Occasionally
(D) However

142. (A) appearance
(B) dimensions
(C) appraisals
(D) texture

GO ON TO THE NEXT PAGE

From: <d_wang@statecentral.edu>
To: <professionalspanishlist@statecentral.edu>
Date: January 14
Subject: Additional section added

Dear all,

Because our Introduction to Spanish for Professionals class at 10:00 A.M. on Saturday mornings has grown so ------, we have decided to add a second section of it to our schedule for the upcoming
143.
semester. The new class ------ on the same day and time, but across the hall in room 224.
144.
Professor Jorge Casilla of the Spanish Language and Literature Department, an experienced instructor, has agreed to teach it.

------. If you later become unable to attend, please cancel your ------ at least 12 hours in advance to
145.   146.
make room for other interested students.

Delia Wang
Extension Coordinator, State Central University

143. (A) popular
     (B) popularity
     (C) popularize
     (D) popularly

144. (A) will be meeting
     (B) was meeting
     (C) has met
     (D) met

145. (A) Intermediate French has also been
         cancelled.
     (B) Please turn in late assignments before this
         date.
     (C) Log in to the student portal to sign up.
     (D) The cafeteria is a short walk away.

146. (A) development
     (B) withdrawal
     (C) appointment
     (D) enrollment

PART 7

Directions: In this part you will read a selection of texts, such as magazine and newspaper articles, e-mails, and instant messages. Each text or set of texts is followed by several questions. Select the best answer for each question and mark the letter (A), (B), (C), or (D) on your answer sheet.

Questions 147-148 refer to the following form.

Portwin Business Association (PBA)

Seminar Registration Form (May Program)
Solihull Conference Center Rooms 210-212

Name: Amelie Giroud **Occupation:** Production Line Supervisor **Company:** Bixby Manufacturing, Inc. **Seminar Name:** Balancing Quantity & Quality **Seminar Number:** 13 **Seminar Location:** Room 212 **PBA Member** _____ **Non-member** __X__	_____ Cash Enclosed _____ Bill My Credit Card __X__ Bill My Company *Individuals who are not currently members of the Portwin Business Association are required to pay an additional £5 administration fee for the processing of their registration documents.

147. What is indicated about the PBA?

(A) It organizes seminars on an annual basis.
(B) It is funded by Bixby Manufacturing.
(C) It will hold talks in various rooms.
(D) It publishes a monthly newsletter.

148. What is implied about Ms. Giroud?

(A) She has attended a PBA seminar in the past.
(B) She has provided her credit card details.
(C) She will be reimbursed by her company.
(D) She will need to pay a processing charge.

GO ON TO THE NEXT PAGE

Especially For You

Is your company planning a large corporate banquet or retirement dinner? Perhaps you are hosting a small-scale gathering such as a shareholders' meeting or product launch?

Especially For You has more than a decade of experience in providing the finest foods and beverages for such corporate events. We employ a serving team of twenty-five, including our three highly experienced event managers. In addition to our delicious offerings, we can also arrange and provide live entertainment, and decorations such as lovely floral centerpieces.

Please visit www.especially4uco.com to view our full range of dishes and services and to request a free price quote. Hospitality & Service Association (HSA) certification held in the states of California, Nevada, Arizona, and Utah.

149. What kind of business is being advertised?

(A) A furniture store
(B) A recruitment agency
(C) A catering company
(D) A public relations firm

150. What is mentioned about the business?

(A) It operates in many countries.
(B) It charges a small fee for estimates.
(C) It has recently enlarged its workforce.
(D) It is certified in several states.

Questions 151-152 refer to the following online chat discussion.

Keiji Yamashita [3:00 P.M.]
Hi, Brittany. I just got approval to go to the ERS Manufacturing Trade Show in Melbourne. Could you get me plane tickets departing on the afternoon of 21 May and returning on the morning of 24 May, plus a hotel near the venue?

Brittany Jansson [3:01 P.M.]
I'm sure that can be arranged. But you'll need to make a formal request via e-mail. Don't you remember the memo we posted about that policy change?

Keiji Yamashita [3:01 P.M.]
Oh, I thought the point was to make requests in writing. Isn't a chat message good enough?

Brittany Jansson [3:02 P.M.]
Ah, no. We want to use e-mail specifically, so that there's an easily accessible record of requests.

Keiji Yamashita [3:03 P.M.]
Got it. I'll take care of that now.

---

151. What is most likely true about Ms. Jansson?

(A) She handles a company's travel planning.
(B) She recently asked Mr. Yamashita for a progress report.
(C) She is in charge of lending out exhibition equipment.
(D) She went to a trade show last year.

152. At 3:03 P.M., what does Mr. Yamashita most likely mean when he writes, "Got it"?

(A) He was able to make a reservation.
(B) He understands the purpose of a policy.
(C) He feels sufficiently prepared for an event.
(D) He has received an e-mail.

GO ON TO THE NEXT PAGE

Questions 153-154 refer to the following notice.

Winterton Rock Festival
Twin River Campgrounds
August 4-6

To all music lovers:

Join us at the Twin River Campgrounds this summer for the second annual
Winterton Rock Festival. It will be held from August 4 to August 6. We once again
have a star-studded lineup that is sure to be a delight for people young and old. In
addition to the two main stages, there will be a number of refreshment tents and
arts and crafts vendors. Also, Winterton's own local radio station WXO 97.9 will be
broadcasting live from the festival all weekend long. This year's lineup includes:

The Autumn Empire – Reunion of Carson City's '90s alternative rock icons
Three Dragons – Critically adored 3-piece rock band from Daytown
Summer Haze – Winterton's own famed progressive-rock outfit
The Amazing Randy – Famous children's performer and TV star from Mayville

For the full schedule and ticketing information, please visit our Web site at
www.wintertonrocks.com.

153. What is true about the music festival?

(A) It is free for Winterton residents.
(B) It will last for only two days.
(C) It takes place twice a year.
(D) It is intended for people of all ages.

154. Who most likely is a local band?

(A) The Autumn Empire
(B) Three Dragons
(C) Summer Haze
(D) The Amazing Randy

NEWFIELD (February 27)—With cupcake bakeries popping up on every corner, it can be difficult to decide where to purchase your favorite sweets. The treats at CupCakeCake, however, stand out because of their simplicity. While other bakeries create dozens of flavors, CupCakeCake focuses on perfecting only a handful: vanilla, chocolate, lemon, red velvet, and carrot. Their cupcakes are light, moist, and fluffy, with frosting that is rich without being overly sweet.

Proprietor and chef Stephen Evans takes pride in his creations. "People like to say that cupcakes are just a short-term trend," he says, "but here at CupCakeCake we try to avoid unusual flavors in favor of classic, comforting cupcakes that are perfect to celebrate a special occasion—or just because." Evans opened his bakery after serving as La Fontaine's pastry chef for five years. His love of casual baking, though, began in his parents' kitchen. "They always let me mess around," he says. This time, however, he has created something more than a mess.

CupCakeCake is located at 10471 Hall Street and operates Monday through Friday, 9:00 a.m. to 8:00 p.m., and Saturday and Sunday, 10:00 a.m. to 5 p.m. Prices range from $1.75 to $3.00 per cupcake.

155. What is the main purpose of the article?

(A) To analyze an industry trend
(B) To promote a business
(C) To encourage tourism to a city
(D) To report on a construction process

156. According to the article, how is CupCakeCake different from its competitors?

(A) Its recipes are publicly available.
(B) It has no indoor seating.
(C) It sells only a few flavors of cupcake.
(D) Its cupcakes do not contain sugar.

157. What does the article indicate about Stephen Evans?

(A) He has created new types of cupcake.
(B) He first started baking as an adult.
(C) He used to manage a café.
(D) He has years of experience with making desserts.

GO ON TO THE NEXT PAGE

Bruntley Tire and Auto Service

Bruntley Tire and Auto Service has been serving the Linsfield area with dedication for over a decade. We sell, service, and offer customization for tires for cars, trucks, RVs, and trailers. — [1] —. A variety of general auto services are also available, from engine repair to the installation of climate control systems. We are a family-owned business that is also a Certified Carlyle Auto Care Center (CCACC). — [2] —. Still not convinced we are a great place to get your vehicle repaired or serviced? Visit us on the Web at www.bruntleytas.com or in person between 8:00 A.M. and 6:00 P.M. from Monday to Friday to learn more. — [3] —.

Seasonal Special: Until November 30, customers can take advantage of amazing discounts on tires from major brands like Boriso and Traxxest. Those who purchase two or more tires from any brand will also receive a complimentary oil change. — [4] —. And don't forget to ask about our senior citizen discount, available year round!

158. What is NOT mentioned about Bruntley Tire and Auto Service?

(A) It is owned by a family.
(B) It was established more than 10 years ago.
(C) It has an online presence.
(D) It is open for part of the weekend.

159. How can customers get a free service during a promotion?

(A) By buying multiple tires
(B) By mentioning the advertisement
(C) By registering for a loyalty program
(D) By being over a certain age

160. In which of the positions marked [1], [2], [3], and [4] does the following sentence best belong?

"That is why our customers enjoy not just attentive service but also top-notch technical skills."

(A) [1]
(B) [2]
(C) [3]
(D) [4]

Questions 161-163 refer to the following Web page.

http://www.bengalheaven.co.uk

| ABOUT | MENU | LOCATIONS | **SPECIALS** |

Since opening three years ago, Bengal Heaven has enjoyed much success in downtown Birmingham. Our fantastic range of curries, including our famous Vindaloo, have been a big hit with all of our diners. To celebrate being in business for three years, we will be discounting several items throughout this month and another three items next month in October!

THIS MONTH!

Tikka Masala	Regular Price: $12	Special Price: $10
Jalfrezi	Regular Price: $15	Special Price: $13
Vindaloo	Regular Price: $14	Special Price: $12

NEXT MONTH!

Tandoori	Regular Price: $16	Special Price: $14
Korma	Regular Price: $14	Special Price: $12
Rogan Josh	Regular Price: $12	Special Price: $10

Throughout September and October, we will also be offering a free dessert to parties of more than four people. Regardless of what you order or how much you spend, each diner will get a dessert absolutely free.

161. Why is Bengal Heaven lowering its prices?

(A) It is introducing a new menu item.
(B) It is celebrating its founding.
(C) It is preparing to close a location.
(D) It is opening its third restaurant.

162. What menu item will cost $12 in October?

(A) Tikka Masala
(B) Vindaloo
(C) Korma
(D) Rogan Josh

163. According to the Web page, who can receive a complimentary item?

(A) Members of a large group of customers
(B) The first customer of each day
(C) Customers who order a specific dish
(D) Customers who spend over a certain amount

GO ON TO THE NEXT PAGE

Questions 164-167 refer to the following e-mail.

E-Mail message

From:	<fdunger@sunspearind.com>
To:	<galina_popova@rl-mail.net>
Date:	Monday, June 5, 2:29 P.M.
Subject:	SMS Information

Dear Ms. Popova,

Thank you for inquiring into Sunspear Industries' new Solar Module System (SMS). I would like to apologize that we cannot provide you with the information you requested; we are currently printing out new brochures that we will send you very soon. Until then, allow me to fill you in on some of the new features available with the SMS.

Developed for normal houses, this system is designed to give consumers a cost-effective and environmentally-friendly alternative to traditional sources of energy. The improved panels absorb the sun's rays with 30% more efficiency than our previous models. Furthermore, it has a battery system that automatically stores excess energy for later use. The battery contains enough energy to power the average home for up to two days in case of unfavorable weather conditions. Also, next to no maintenance is required.

Before introducing the SMS to the energy market, the independent Monterey Energy Research Center (MERC) led an eighteen-month, in-depth study of the SMS. It found that the improved design is drastically more efficient and could save consumers up to $100 per month in electricity bills.

If you have any questions about the SMS, please don't hesitate to contact me. As you mentioned in your previous e-mail, the SMS could indeed prove to be a worthwhile purchase for you. In the meantime, you can expect a detailed brochure to be delivered to your door.

Sincerely,

Florian D. Unger
Sunspear Industries

---

164. What is suggested about Sunspear Industries?

(A) It is temporarily unable to provide bills online.
(B) It recently operated a booth at a conference.
(C) It is currently updating some printed materials.
(D) Its research and development team is highly respected.

165. For whom is the SMS specifically designed?

(A) Motorists
(B) Homeowners
(C) Business owners
(D) Scientists

166. What is NOT indicated about the SMS?

(A) It can help its users save money.
(B) It has a powerful battery.
(C) It was created less than one year ago.
(D) It is simple to maintain.

167. What is most likely true about Ms. Popova?

(A) She is seeking investment opportunities.
(B) She is the spokesperson of an environmental association.
(C) She works for Sunspear Industries.
(D) She is considering purchasing a Sunspear product.

Questions 168-171 refer to the following text-message chain.

1:16 P.M.
James: I'm really looking forward to Felicia's party tonight. Do you know if everyone in our department is going to come?

1:17 P.M.
Aicha: Well, some of us are. Jessica and Nikos had other plans that they couldn't change.

1:18 P.M.
James: That's too bad. I know it's hard to free up a Saturday night, but Felicia's only going to turn 50 years old once. And I think it's going to be quite an event.

1:19 P.M.
Kate: Me too. I've never been to the Westbright Restaurant before. Actually, I was wondering what we should wear. Would normal clothing be OK, or should it be something kind of formal?

1:20 P.M.
James: Casual clothes will be alright. I actually asked Felicia that question a few days ago, and that's what she said.

1:21 P.M.
Kate: Oh, good. That will be easy.

1:23 P.M.
Aicha: This reminds me of something. There was a card going around the office yesterday for Felicia. We were hoping to give it to her tonight. Did you two sign it?

1:24 P.M.
Kate: I did.

1:25 P.M.
James: No, I was at the printer's all day. I'll have to try to sign it tonight.

| | Send |

---

168. What will Felicia most likely do today?

(A) Participate in a performance
(B) Take potential clients out for a meal
(C) Open a new branch of a company
(D) Celebrate her birthday

169. At 1:17 P.M., what does Aicha most likely mean when she writes, "Well, some of us are"?

(A) The number of attendees from their group will be limited.
(B) No one from another department will attend.
(C) She thinks James should change his plans.
(D) She wants James to send her some information.

170. What does Kate ask about an event?

(A) Where its venue is
(B) How to dress for it
(C) Who will be its host
(D) When it will likely end

171. What is suggested about James?

(A) He is a new employee.
(B) He ate lunch with Kate today.
(C) He was not in the office yesterday.
(D) He works in a different building.

GO ON TO THE NEXT PAGE

Questions 172-175 refer to the following e-mail.

From:	Gregory Chapman <greg.chapman@tgo-mail.com>
To:	Parveen Mirza <p.mirza@taylorchemistmanchester.co.uk>
Date:	4 March
Subject:	Application for the Pharmacist Position
Attachment:	📎 Chapman CV

Dear Ms. Mirza,

Alban Campbell, Managing Pharmacist at Taylor Chemist of Manchester's Hulme Street branch and former coworker of mine, suggested I get in touch with you about the Pharmacist opening at the Thomas Street location. I am very interested in the position and have attached my CV for your perusal.

As you will see in the education and experience sections on my CV, I am a fully qualified pharmacist. — [1] —. My daily tasks there include supplying prescription medication, providing advice to customers, and maintaining appropriate stock levels. I carry out these activities in a safe manner that emphasizes efficiency. — [2] —. This past year, I was even able to streamline our inventory procedure so that it takes nearly 30% less time than before, and earned special recognition from my manager for this accomplishment.

Additionally, I have long admired Taylor's focus on customer care, as that is my priority as well. After all, making people feel better is a pharmacist's main mission. — [3] —. This must be achieved not just through medication but also through kindness, patience, and communication. I work hard to create excellent relationships with customers and provide the help that they need. It would be a pleasure to exercise my skills as part of a business with such similar values.

In short, I believe that I am an ideal candidate for the post. I would be delighted to attend an interview and can be contacted at this e-mail address or at 03069-990621 on most afternoons. — [4] —.

Thank you for your consideration. I look forward to hearing from you.

Yours sincerely,

Gregory Chapman

172. How did Mr. Chapman most likely find out about a job opening?

   (A) From an acquaintance
   (B) From an industry journal
   (C) From a freelance recruiter
   (D) From a job search Web site

173. What recent achievement does Mr. Chapman mention?

   (A) He improved the speed of a process.
   (B) He earned a skill certification.
   (C) He managed some interns.
   (D) He designed a successful advertisement.

174. What is suggested about Taylor Chemist of Manchester?

   (A) It offers especially high salaries.
   (B) It prioritizes customer service.
   (C) Its branches are located within hospitals.
   (D) It requires job applicants to take an exam.

175. In which of the positions marked [1], [2], [3], and [4] does the following sentence best belong?

   "I have worked for the last four years at APK Pharmacy in Stockport."

   (A) [1]
   (B) [2]
   (C) [3]
   (D) [4]

GO ON TO THE NEXT PAGE

Questions 176-180 refer to the following Web page and online form.

http://www.bufordherald.com/home

Try *Sports Digest*, our new publication!

The Buford Herald is delighted to announce that we will soon launch a brand-new publication that is designed to specifically appeal to all sports fans. Starting from May 7, a brand-new edition of *Sports Digest* will be delivered to subscribers on every first and third Saturday of the month. The new publication will cover football, baseball, basketball, and more. It will include in-depth descriptions of games that have been played, discussions with the stars of top teams, and full details of all teams' wins, losses, and current form. For a limited time only, subscribers to *The Buford Herald* can subscribe to *Sports Digest* for the discounted rate of $45 per year. That means you can enjoy a savings of $25!

Sign up for *Sports Digest* before May 1 to take advantage of this special offer. On May 1, the price of an annual subscription will increase to the standard price of $70.

www.bufordherald.com/subscriptions/38843#

The Buford Herald is grateful for your patronage. We are delighted to confirm your transaction is complete.

Name:	Lorenzo Moretti
Address:	40 Ramirez Road, Trenton, NJ 08625
Phone Number:	555-0126
E-mail Address:	lmoretti@fab-mail.net
Date of Transaction:	April 23
Amount Paid:	$45.00

To print this receipt of payment, please **CLICK HERE**.
An electronic version of this document will also be sent to the address entered above.

For up-to-date sporting news, including game schedules, results, and special offers on game tickets, remember to check our dedicated sports page by clicking the link **HERE**.

176. What is NOT mentioned as a feature of
Sports Digest?

(A) Interviews with famous players
(B) Reports on completed games
(C) Schedules for sports broadcasts
(D) Statistics on teams' performances

177. How often will a new issue of *Sports Digest*
be published?

(A) Once a week
(B) Twice a week
(C) Once a month
(D) Twice a month

178. When will Mr. Moretti most likely get his first
issue of *Sports Digest*?

(A) On April 23
(B) On April 24
(C) On May 1
(D) On May 7

179. What is indicated about Mr. Moretti?

(A) He does not currently subscribe to *The
Buford Herald*.
(B) He paid a reduced price for a
subscription.
(C) He will receive *Sports Digest* at his
workplace.
(D) He previously sent an e-mail to *The
Buford Herald*.

180. What will Mr. Moretti receive via e-mail?

(A) A payment confirmation
(B) A baseball game ticket
(C) A discount voucher
(D) A stadium map

GO ON TO THE NEXT PAGE

Questions 181-185 refer to the following e-mails.

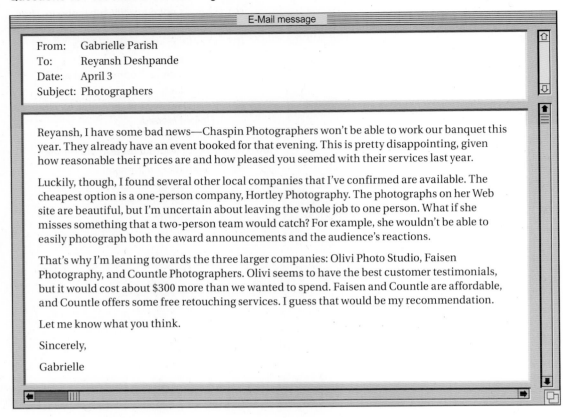

E-Mail message

From: Gabrielle Parish
To: Reyansh Deshpande
Date: April 3
Subject: Photographers

Reyansh, I have some bad news—Chaspin Photographers won't be able to work our banquet this year. They already have an event booked for that evening. This is pretty disappointing, given how reasonable their prices are and how pleased you seemed with their services last year.

Luckily, though, I found several other local companies that I've confirmed are available. The cheapest option is a one-person company, Hortley Photography. The photographs on her Web site are beautiful, but I'm uncertain about leaving the whole job to one person. What if she misses something that a two-person team would catch? For example, she wouldn't be able to easily photograph both the award announcements and the audience's reactions.

That's why I'm leaning towards the three larger companies: Olivi Photo Studio, Faisen Photography, and Countle Photographers. Olivi seems to have the best customer testimonials, but it would cost about $300 more than we wanted to spend. Faisen and Countle are affordable, and Countle offers some free retouching services. I guess that would be my recommendation.

Let me know what you think.

Sincerely,

Gabrielle

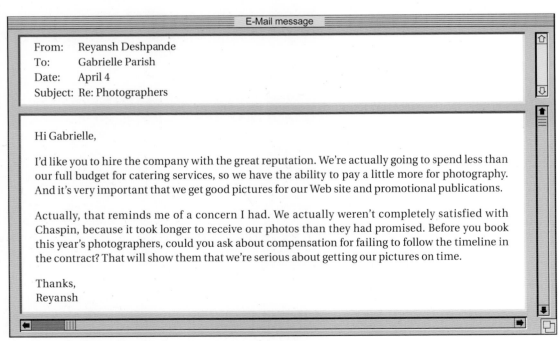

E-Mail message

From: Reyansh Deshpande
To: Gabrielle Parish
Date: April 4
Subject: Re: Photographers

Hi Gabrielle,

I'd like you to hire the company with the great reputation. We're actually going to spend less than our full budget for catering services, so we have the ability to pay a little more for photography. And it's very important that we get good pictures for our Web site and promotional publications.

Actually, that reminds me of a concern I had. We actually weren't completely satisfied with Chaspin, because it took longer to receive our photos than they had promised. Before you book this year's photographers, could you ask about compensation for failing to follow the timeline in the contract? That will show them that we're serious about getting our pictures on time.

Thanks,
Reyansh

181. Why is Ms. Parish unable to recommend hiring Chaspin Photographers?

(A) It has another engagement.
(B) It no longer offers off-site services.
(C) Its prices have risen since last year.
(D) The quality of its photographs has fallen.

182. What kind of event is Ms. Parish most likely involved in planning?

(A) A charity banquet
(B) A retirement party
(C) An awards dinner
(D) A graduation ceremony

183. Which company will Ms. Parish most likely contact?

(A) Hortley Photography
(B) Olivi Photo Studio
(C) Faisen Photography
(D) Countle Photographers

184. What does Mr. Reyansh indicate has changed about the event?

(A) The theme of its decorations
(B) The distribution of its budget
(C) The ordering of its schedule
(D) The method of its promotion

185. What does Mr. Reyansh instruct Ms. Parish to ask a photography company?

(A) Whether its staff are members of a professional association
(B) Why one of its previous customers was dissatisfied
(C) How long it will take to edit some photographs
(D) What will happen if an agreement is violated

GO ON TO THE NEXT PAGE

http://www.schorrpublishing.com/newauthors

Schorr Publishing — a leading independent publisher

<u>New Authors</u>

If you are interested in having your book published, we would like to hear from you.

We request submission of the following:
* Your contact information, personal résumé, and Web site (if any)
* A title and brief description of the work, along with a table of contents
* A storyboard and at least one sample of a finished sketch (children's books only)
* A description of the book's readership – age, education level, interests, etc.
* Any ideas giving weight to your work's marketing plan – What makes it different from other books on the topic?

Please send a package with the above information to: Proposals, Schorr Publishing, 5 Valley Road, Somerset, PA 19030. *If there is interest in your proposal, we will contact you to speak to you further.*

Schorr Publishing
5 Valley Road
Somerset, PA 19030

February 2

Ramon Notario
c/o Notario Automotive
12 Bay Street
Cicero, Il 61108

Dear Mr. Notario,

It was a pleasure speaking with you over the phone. After further consideration, we have decided to go ahead with the publication of your proposed book, *Vehicles of the Future*.

We were all very impressed with your proposal package. Our designers especially liked the storyboard and two sketches you submitted.

Enclosed you will see a set of instructions for using our manuscript editing software. I look forward to speaking with you in person when I visit your region in late July. Please feel free to contact me or my assistant, Erica Lien, with any questions you may have at any time.

Sincerely,

Nancy Dey
Nancy Dey, Chief Editor

Enclosure

```
═══════════════════ E-Mail message ═══════════════════
┌──────────┬────────────────────────────────────────────┐
│ From:    │ Nancy Dey <dey@schorr.com>                 │
├──────────┼────────────────────────────────────────────┤
│ To:      │ All Editorial Staff                        │
├──────────┼────────────────────────────────────────────┤
│ Date:    │ February 20                                │
├──────────┼────────────────────────────────────────────┤
│ Subject: │ Planning meeting                           │
└──────────┴────────────────────────────────────────────┘
```

Dear All,

I'd like to hold a planning meeting this Thursday at 2 P.M. We will brainstorm ways to promote our promising batch of upcoming releases, so come ready with ideas.

Also, please be sure to introduce yourselves to Karen Jun. She is a former intern and began taking over Erica Lien's role yesterday.

Regards,

Nancy

---

186. What are aspiring authors NOT asked to submit?

(A) A description of target readers
(B) A list of references
(C) A table of contents
(D) A personal résumé

187. In the Web page, the word "weight" in line 8 is closest in meaning to

(A) measurement
(B) pressure
(C) impact
(D) burden

188. What is implied about *Vehicles of the Future*?

(A) It is a children's book.
(B) It contains articles from a Web site.
(C) It will be published in two volumes.
(D) It will be sold in an electronic version.

189. What will most likely happen in July?

(A) A bookstore will hold a special promotion.
(B) A software program will be upgraded.
(C) Mr. Notario's book will be released.
(D) Ms. Dey will meet Mr. Notario.

190. Who most likely is Ms. Jun?

(A) A freelance designer
(B) An employee of Mr. Notario's
(C) An assistant to a chief editor
(D) An owner of a marketing firm

GO ON TO THE NEXT PAGE ▶

Questions 191-195 refer to the following Web page, e-mail, and information.

http://www.anstolf.org/tourism/events

| About the City | Government Services | Business | Tourism |

Upcoming Events in Anstolf

<u>Anstolf Home & Garden Expo</u> (May 4–6) — A three-day celebration of the art of home improvement. Visitors can attend educational seminars, tour garden landscapes made especially for the event, and buy top-quality home improvement products.

<u>Laskin Kings Bass Tournament</u> (June 23–24) — The Laskin Kings Fishing Club is set to host its twentieth annual bass fishing tournament. Top finishers will receive shares of the $50,000 in cash donated by generous local sponsors.

<u>Tocco Jazz Festival</u> (July 14–15) — Jazz music lovers won't want to miss this tribute to Roxanne Tocco, who was born and raised in Anstolf. Musicians from across the country will play her most famous songs.

<u>Anstolf Fireworks Show</u> (August 25) — Anstolf-based financial services company Fargess Group sponsors this two-hour spectacular each year. Come to Anstolf City Park or any other place with clear views of Laskin Lake to take in a brilliant display.

From:	Mark Neale <m.neale@npi-mail.com>
To:	<contact@anstolftours.com>
Date:	June 2
Subject:	Tour inquiry

Hello,

I'm traveling to Anstolf at the end of this month for a local event, and I was hoping to take the opportunity to do some sightseeing within the city. A friend who used to live there recommended your agency. I didn't find your Web site very helpful, so I decided to contact you directly.

Let me describe my situation and what I'm looking for. I'm going to arrive in Anstolf on a Friday morning, and I'd like to sign up for a tour that goes out that afternoon. I don't want anything longer than two hours, and I'd like to keep the price below $25. I don't mind walking or biking. Do you have something that fits those conditions? Please let me know.

Thanks,

Mark Neale

28

Anstolf Tours

Land tours offered in high season (May through October):

Name	Days Available	Departure Times	Length	Price
Anstolf by Bus	Daily	10 A.M., 1 P.M.	3 hours	$15
Pyve Manor Visit	Tuesday, Thursday	2 P.M.	2.5 hours	$23
Old Town Walking Tour	Daily except Sunday	4 P.M., 7 P.M.	1.5 hours	$12
A Taste of Anstolf	Thursday, Friday, Saturday	5 P.M.	2 hours	$34

191. In the Web page, what is NOT indicated about Anstolf?

(A) It is situated near a lake.
(B) It has a large public garden.
(C) It is the hometown of a celebrity.
(D) It is the site of a yearly competition.

192. What is Mr. Neale most likely interested in?

(A) Home improvement
(B) Bass fishing
(C) Jazz music
(D) Fireworks displays

193. How did Mr. Neale first hear of Anstolf Tours?

(A) From a former resident of Anstolf
(B) From the results of an Internet search
(C) From an employee of a government agency
(D) From a flyer distributed at an event

194. What does the information suggest about the tours?

(A) Some of them require advance registration.
(B) Their availability varies according to the time of year.
(C) Their departure times have temporarily changed.
(D) The maximum number of people allowed on any of them is 34.

195. Which tour will most likely be recommended to Mr. Neale?

(A) Anstolf by Bus
(B) Pyve Manor Visit
(C) Old Town Walking Tour
(D) A Taste of Anstolf

GO ON TO THE NEXT PAGE

Dalemont City Times

DALEMONT CITY (September 8) — The long-awaited Dalemont Plaza shopping mall is now about 70 percent rented out. Its developer, Laranic Properties, wants to fill the remaining space by offering reduced rent rates to new tenants. "We aim for full occupancy by December," said rental manager Brian Putney. "We are especially interested in attracting small, independent stores."

The mall's two floors of stores are arranged around a central dining area. Its west wing of shops faces the Dalemont River, and its east wing faces the main parking area in the rear.

Local retailer David Olson, who moved his shop into the mall's largest space, likes his new location. "I'm expanding," he said. "I may even bring on more store associates. It depends on how busy we get."

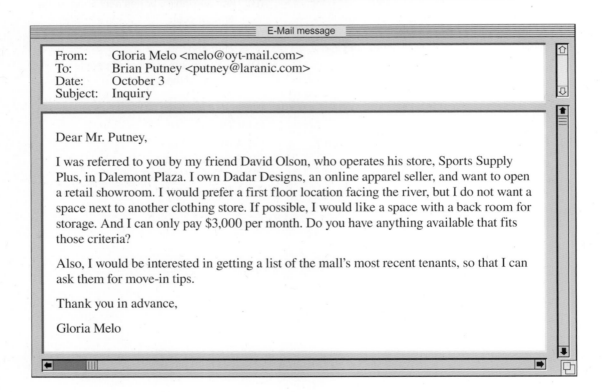

E-Mail message

From: Gloria Melo <melo@oyt-mail.com>
To: Brian Putney <putney@laranic.com>
Date: October 3
Subject: Inquiry

Dear Mr. Putney,

I was referred to you by my friend David Olson, who operates his store, Sports Supply Plus, in Dalemont Plaza. I own Dadar Designs, an online apparel seller, and want to open a retail showroom. I would prefer a first floor location facing the river, but I do not want a space next to another clothing store. If possible, I would like a space with a back room for storage. And I can only pay $3,000 per month. Do you have anything available that fits those criteria?

Also, I would be interested in getting a list of the mall's most recent tenants, so that I can ask them for move-in tips.

Thank you in advance,

Gloria Melo

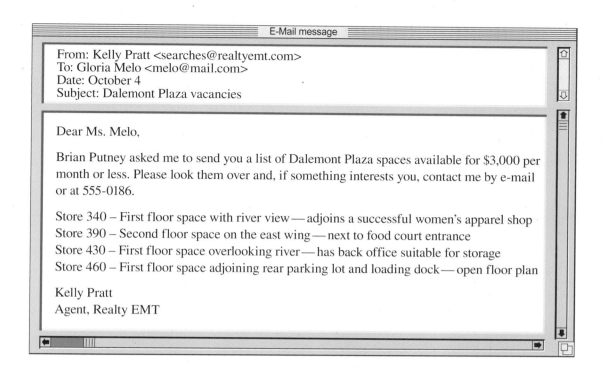

E-Mail message

From: Kelly Pratt <searches@realtyemt.com>
To: Gloria Melo <melo@mail.com>
Date: October 4
Subject: Dalemont Plaza vacancies

Dear Ms. Melo,

Brian Putney asked me to send you a list of Dalemont Plaza spaces available for $3,000 per month or less. Please look them over and, if something interests you, contact me by e-mail or at 555-0186.

Store 340 – First floor space with river view — adjoins a successful women's apparel shop
Store 390 – Second floor space on the east wing — next to food court entrance
Store 430 – First floor space overlooking river — has back office suitable for storage
Store 460 – First floor space adjoining rear parking lot and loading dock — open floor plan

Kelly Pratt
Agent, Realty EMT

196. What is indicated about Dalemont Plaza?

(A) It will be expanded to include four floors.
(B) It can be reached by public transportation.
(C) Its dining area will be renovated in December.
(D) Its new tenants will receive rent reductions.

197. In the article, the phrase "bring on" in paragraph 3, line 2, is closest in meaning to

(A) hire
(B) quicken
(C) serve
(D) produce

198. What is suggested about Sports Supply Plus?

(A) It has two entrances.
(B) It plans to relocate in October.
(C) Its main product category is clothing.
(D) It occupies a shopping mall's largest space.

199. What does Ms. Melo request from Mr. Putney?

(A) A list of new tenants
(B) A sample leasing contract
(C) A building's floor plan
(D) An estimate for moving costs

200. Which space will Ms. Melo most likely inquire about?

(A) Store 340
(B) Store 390
(C) Store 430
(D) Store 460

Stop! This is the end of the test. If you finish before time is called, you may go back to Parts 5, 6, and 7 and check your work.

GO ON TO THE NEXT PAGE

TEST 2

READING TEST

In the Reading test, you will read a variety of texts and answer several different types of reading comprehension questions. The entire Reading test will last 75 minutes. There are three parts, and directions are given for each part. You are encouraged to answer as many questions as possible within the time allowed.

You must mark your answers on the separate answer sheet. Do not write your answers in your test book.

PART 5

Directions: A word or phrase is missing in each of the sentences below. Four answer choices are given below each sentence. Select the best answer to complete the sentence. Then mark the letter (A), (B), (C), or (D) on your answer sheet.

101. Ms. Vardy's trip to China had to be canceled suddenly because her visa was issued too -------.

(A) lately
(B) latest
(C) lateness
(D) late

102. Ishida Transportation intends ------- its entire fleet of vans with environmentally-friendly electric vehicles.

(A) to replace
(B) are replaced
(C) replacement
(D) replacing

103. Assembly line workers must put on their safety helmets ------- vests prior to entering the factory floor.

(A) and
(B) both
(C) so
(D) as

104. Ms. Jacobson explained that ------- created the advertising campaign in an effort to reach younger consumers.

(A) hers
(B) her
(C) herself
(D) she

105. At this year's International Film Awards Show, acceptance speeches will be ------- to three minutes.

(A) commenced
(B) restricted
(C) allowed
(D) eliminated

106. Company policy requires all associates who interact with clients to dress as ------- as possible.

(A) neatly
(B) warmly
(C) directly
(D) steadily

107. Ms. Choi spoke most passionately ------- reforming the pension system, though her lecture also covered other topics.

(A) about
(B) amid
(C) by
(D) plus

108. Hiring experts to write certain entries would make the online reference guide's content more -------.

(A) reliably
(B) relying
(C) reliable
(D) reliability

109. Common ------- offered to executives by Botrego Corporation include stock options and subsidized housing.

(A) referrals
(B) applications
(C) procedures
(D) benefits

110. Inclement weather necessitated the postponement ------- the Stovintgon Charity Golf Tournament.

(A) against
(B) of
(C) with
(D) into

111. The chief technician will visit the plant at 2 P.M. today to ------- the damage caused to the packing machine.

(A) prevent
(B) withstand
(C) coordinate
(D) assess

112. Out of all of next year's -------, we should primarily focus on reducing our expenditures by 15 percent.

(A) target
(B) targets
(C) being targeted
(D) targeted

113. The Boutville City Council has introduced tax incentives for entrepreneurs in order to ------- the local economy.

(A) stimulate
(B) enforce
(C) grant
(D) resolve

114. A recent journal article indicates that conducting on-the-job training ------- helps to keep employees productive and alert.

(A) repeat
(B) repeated
(C) repeatedly
(D) repetition

115. Unfortunately, those who ------- Nairn Manufacturing within the past month will not be eligible for the Employee of the Quarter Award.

(A) are joined
(B) will be joining
(C) have joined
(D) would join

116. In addition to being ------- to division manager, Mr. Smalling will also be given a company car.

(A) promoting
(B) promoted
(C) promotion
(D) promote

117. The quality assurance team uses a process ------- of several methodical steps.

(A) attached
(B) consisting
(C) effective
(D) associated

118. Along with enjoying excellent seating inside the arena, holders of VIP tickets receive special parking -------.

(A) techniques
(B) privileges
(C) achievements
(D) expenditures

119. As expected, Pistone Technology Group's latest quarterly figures ------- surpassed the previous quarter's earnings.

(A) easily
(B) ease
(C) easy
(D) eased

120. *Digital Digest Magazine* has given its highest ------- in technical performance to the Mobium 6 smartphone.

(A) hesitation
(B) profile
(C) rating
(D) prevalence

GO ON TO THE NEXT PAGE

121. We are asking ------- who is a fan of Trident Audio products to participate in our marketing focus group.

(A) every
(B) individual
(C) person
(D) anyone

122. During the renovation of the reception area, visitors must access the building through the east wing entrance ------- the main entrance.

(A) as long as
(B) in case of
(C) as opposed to
(D) in response to

123. This equipment is to be operated ------- as directed by your fitness instructor.

(A) overly
(B) only
(C) barely
(D) longingly

124. For ------- purposes, guests must permit the hotel's front desk staff to make a copy of their passports.

(A) secured
(B) secures
(C) securely
(D) security

125. Preliminary research says that language barriers will make it impossible to sell most of our ------- toys abroad.

(A) educate
(B) educated
(C) educational
(D) educationally

126. Ms. Dennings was unable to finish her proposal ------- schedule because of an unexpected increase in her workload.

(A) ahead of
(B) so that
(C) except for
(D) in advance

127. Harvond Grocery does not ------- the New Year's Day holiday and thus will be open for business on January 1.

(A) observe
(B) verify
(C) anticipate
(D) redeem

128. Ms. Winth would like text to be added to the new pamphlets ------- Winth Enterprises' history and business practices.

(A) since
(B) similarly
(C) these
(D) regarding

129. ------- volunteers to clean the staff break room on Friday afternoon will be allowed to go home one hour earlier than usual that day.

(A) Whatever
(B) Another
(C) Whoever
(D) Someone

130. Ablent Sports prefers to make its in-store signs from soft fabric rather than the more ------- materials that most retailers use.

(A) perishable
(B) rigid
(C) fluent
(D) transparent

PART 6

Directions: Read the texts that follow. A word, phrase, or sentence is missing in parts of each text. Four answer choices for each question are given below the text. Select the best answer to complete the text. Then mark the letter (A), (B), (C), or (D) on your answer sheet.

Questions 131-134 refer to the following article.

The Springtown Gazette

Business Focus

Harrison Ashfield — A Story of Success

Harrison Ashfield's rise at Bitz-Marks, Inc., is a story that serves to inspire all budding business owners and entrepreneurs. Mr. Ashfield, ------- just a sales representative who sold products door to
131.
door, is now the head of the European Sales Division at the company.

Mr. Ashfield ------- to the position after displaying not only his impressive sales skills, but also his
132.
ability to manage employees and adapt to trends in domestic and continental telecommunications markets.

-------. However, the ambitious businessperson has larger goals to achieve. -------, he has publicly
133.   **134.**
stated that he hopes to establish a global sales department at Bitz-Marks, Inc., and help the company to become an international leader in the telecommunications market.

131. (A) still
     (B) once
     (C) soon
     (D) much

132. (A) will be appointed
     (B) is appointing
     (C) had appointed
     (D) was appointed

133. (A) Mr. Ashfield helped them all rise from such humble beginnings.
     (B) Mr. Ashfield's ultimate aim is to set up a sales department.
     (C) It seems like they were born to be leaders in the industry.
     (D) It may appear as if Mr. Ashfield has reached the top of his field.

134. (A) At first
     (B) Despite that
     (C) In fact
     (D) Instead

HEAVENLY CAKES CAN SWEETEN YOUR SPECIAL DAY!

Heavenly Cakes, Inc. is a Boston-based bakery ------ in fancy wedding cakes. As part of our
135.
expansion, we have recently opened our first branch in New York City.

------. They range from simple white cakes with black ribbons to elaborate, multi-colored creations
136.
covered with real flowers. You can also ------ your cake by choosing the frosting, the filling, the
137.
decorations, and the message.

Our New York City bakery ------ at 1123 West 12th Street, just across the road from the Odoner
138.
Theater.

Contact us at 555-0176 to make an order, or view our cake designs online at www.
heavenlycakesinc.com.

---

135. (A) specializes
     (B) is specializing
     (C) specializing
     (D) has specialized

136. (A) We are very proud of our top-notch
         pastry bakers.
     (B) We have developed more than 50
         different cake designs.
     (C) Plans to open more branches
         throughout the city are under way.
     (D) There are 120,000 customers
         registered in our rewards program.

137. (A) alternate
     (B) customize
     (C) conserve
     (D) distribute

138. (A) is located
     (B) will be located
     (C) being located
     (D) was located

September 27

Arnetta Wiseman
880 Desert Drive, Apt. 401
Mangault, KY 40171

Dear Ms. Wiseman,

This letter serves as notification that I will ------- Apartment 202 on Saturday, October 23. I have
                                                139.
accepted a job in Coombs and will be moving to that area. I will provide you with a forwarding

address shortly.

I plan to pay the full rental fee for the month of October. I hope that this, ------- my history as a
                                                                            140.
reliable tenant, will persuade you not to charge me a penalty for giving less than thirty days' notice.

-------. Consequently, I would like to know when I can expect my security deposit of $500 to be
141.
returned.

Please call me at 555-0126 to confirm ------- of this letter and discuss the abovementioned issues.
                                       142.

Sincerely,

Rodney Glover

---

139. (A) inspect
(B) vacate
(C) remodel
(D) buy

140. (A) together with
(B) in that
(C) such as
(D) prior to

141. (A) In addition, the wallpaper in the living room
is unattractive.
(B) Other tenants have carried out their own
improvements.
(C) Also, you will find the apartment to be in
excellent condition.
(D) I have been told that I will need to provide
a letter of reference.

142. (A) recipient
(B) received
(C) receive
(D) receipt

GO ON TO THE NEXT PAGE

From: Kyungjin Pyo <kpyo@fitmaster.com>
To: Catherine Elder <celder@evermail.net>
Date: February 12
Subject: ProPower Cyclemaster N50

Dear Ms. Elder,

------. I'm afraid that the ProPower Cyclemaster N50 you purchased will take longer to ship than
143.

originally expected. Although we promised seven-day shipping, I do not think the item will

arrive ------ the beginning of March.
144.

Please accept my sincerest apologies for this unfortunate ------. If you would like to request a full
145.

refund, I completely understand.

However, I hope you will choose to be patient and wait for the item to be delivered, as you

purchased a high-quality product at an ------ price.
146.

Kind regards,

Kyungjin Pyo
Fitmaster Exercise Equipment

143. (A) In comparison to the others, the one
          you ordered is quite popular.
     (B) First of all, the shipment of your order
          will take as many as seven days.
     (C) Sadly, some of those featured products
          have been discontinued.
     (D) I am writing to update you on the order
          you placed through our Web site.

144. (A) until
     (B) from
     (C) without
     (D) under

145. (A) cancellation
     (B) breakage
     (C) interference
     (D) delay

146. (A) afforded
     (B) afford
     (C) affordable
     (D) affording

PART 7

Directions: In this part you will read a selection of texts, such as magazine and newspaper articles, e-mails, and instant messages. Each text or set of texts is followed by several questions. Select the best answer for each question and mark the letter (A), (B), (C), or (D) on your answer sheet.

Questions 147-148 refer to the following text message.

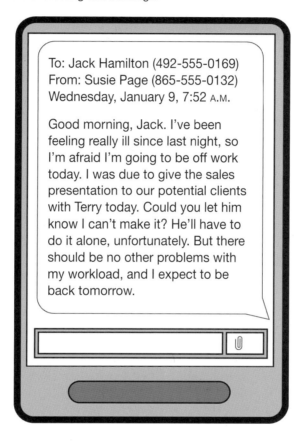

To: Jack Hamilton (492-555-0169)
From: Susie Page (865-555-0132)
Wednesday, January 9, 7:52 A.M.

Good morning, Jack. I've been feeling really ill since last night, so I'm afraid I'm going to be off work today. I was due to give the sales presentation to our potential clients with Terry today. Could you let him know I can't make it? He'll have to do it alone, unfortunately. But there should be no other problems with my workload, and I expect to be back tomorrow.

147. Why did Ms. Page send the message?

(A) To share a revised travel itinerary
(B) To describe a computer problem
(C) To report an absence
(D) To complain about a workload

148. What does Ms. Page ask Mr. Hamilton to do?

(A) Edit a document
(B) Speak to a colleague
(C) Entertain some clients
(D) Reschedule a presentation

GO ON TO THE NEXT PAGE

Our birthday gift to you!

To celebrate our fifth year of operations, Claude Clothing is offering a coupon for free delivery to our loyal customers on orders of $40 or more.* Claude Clothing is rapidly becoming famous for providing quality garments at affordable prices. We expect our winter catalog to be our most popular yet, and urge you to take advantage of this fantastic offer. This coupon may only be used when placing an order via telephone, our Web site, or postal order.

*One usage per customer. Visit our Web site for terms and conditions.

149. What is mentioned as a requirement for usage of the coupon?

(A) A form of identification
(B) A downloaded mobile app
(C) A customer account number
(D) A minimum purchase

150. Which means of placing an order is the coupon NOT valid for?

(A) In a shop
(B) Over the phone
(C) By post
(D) Online

questions 151-152 refer to the following information.

Congratulations on purchasing Boraldie eyeglasses from Sandoval Eyewear. Whether in your workplace or your home, you will now be able to use your computer or mobile device for long periods of time with less eye strain.

To keep your eyeglasses in top condition, make sure to clean the lenses regularly using the cleaning spray and microfiber cloth included in the provided case. Using other products for this purpose may result in scratched lenses. Should your eyeglasses' screws or nose pads need adjusting or replacing at any point, stop by any Sandoval Eyewear location to receive free maintenance service.

151. What is suggested about Boraldie eyeglasses?

(A) They are made of environmentally-friendly materials.

(B) They are intended to be worn while playing sports.

(C) They can protect wearers' eyes from hazardous chemicals.

(D) They reduce discomfort caused by looking at electronic screens.

152. According to the information, how can wearers avoid damage to their eyeglasses?

(A) By carrying them in a certain case

(B) By constantly adjusting their fit

(C) By caring for them with special products

(D) By having them checked at a store regularly

GO ON TO THE NEXT PAGE

Questions 153-154 refer to the following text-message chain.

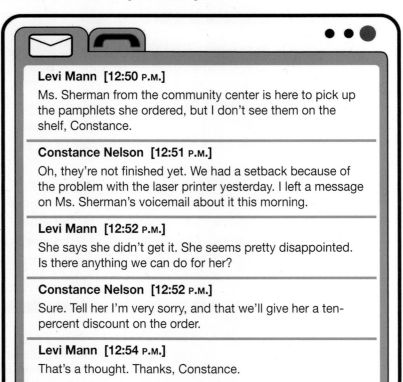

Levi Mann [12:50 P.M.]

Ms. Sherman from the community center is here to pick up the pamphlets she ordered, but I don't see them on the shelf, Constance.

Constance Nelson [12:51 P.M.]

Oh, they're not finished yet. We had a setback because of the problem with the laser printer yesterday. I left a message on Ms. Sherman's voicemail about it this morning.

Levi Mann [12:52 P.M.]

She says she didn't get it. She seems pretty disappointed. Is there anything we can do for her?

Constance Nelson [12:52 P.M.]

Sure. Tell her I'm very sorry, and that we'll give her a ten-percent discount on the order.

Levi Mann [12:54 P.M.]

That's a thought. Thanks, Constance.

153. What does Ms. Nelson mention that she did earlier today?

(A) Called a customer
(B) Reorganized some shelves
(C) Folded some pamphlets
(D) Fixed a printer

154. At 12:54 P.M., what does Mr. Mann most likely mean when he writes, "That's a thought"?

(A) A machine is working properly again.
(B) A vendor has accepted his coupon.
(C) Ms. Sherman might be no longer upset.
(D) He has found an order.

Questions 155-157 refer to the following memo.

To: Beniston Employees
From: Bradley Weekston, Product Manager
Date: June 2
Subject: Product line

As many of you will be aware, our engineering team has been developing a new line of kitchen appliances to be launched this fall. This range of merchandise has now been finalized. As such, several training workshops will be held in August to familiarize you with the features of the new products. Staff must tell their manager by the end of the week which workshop they are able to attend. All employees will be paid at the overtime rate for participating in this training.

We realize this is a transitional time for our company as we embrace a new product line that will hopefully enable us to become the number one supplier of kitchen appliances in the country. We assure you that the workshops will provide you with all the information you need in order for you to perform your sales role effectively. If you have any concerns after completing the training, please e-mail me at b.weekston@benistonstores.com. I will be happy to answer your questions.

155. What is the memo mainly about?

(A) The upgrading of office appliances
(B) The opening of a new store
(C) A new range of merchandise
(D) A change in staff pay rates

156. What are employees being asked to do?

(A) Read a set of guidelines
(B) Suggest some product ideas
(C) Apply for administrative positions
(D) Attend a training workshop

157. Who are employees instructed to contact with their concerns?

(A) The product manager
(B) The engineering team
(C) A sales representative
(D) The payroll department

E-Mail message

To:	Eli Ollinger
From:	Toronto Friends Group Management
Subject:	Welcome!
Date:	September 13

Dear Mr. Ollinger,

Thank you for joining the Toronto Friends Group on Your-Groups.com. We are Toronto citizens and visitors who want to make new friends while learning, teaching, and practicing language skills. — [1] —. Our most popular languages are English, Spanish, French, Korean, and Japanese, but it is often possible to find a native speaker or fellow learner of other languages as well. Our gatherings are held at the Springwood Café in Etobicoke on Tuesday evenings and Sunday afternoons. — [2] —.

Please take a few minutes to set up your member profile page, which lets other members know about you and your language interests. — [3] —. Then, see this page for an explanation of how our gatherings usually work and how to prepare for them. Please note that members must RSVP at least one hour in advance for all gatherings. Also, if you RSVP "yes" but do not attend the event you signed up for, you will not be allowed to participate in future gatherings for one month. — [4] — It is important that all of our members are enthusiastic and reliable.

We hope to see you soon.

Sincerely,

The Management Team

---

158. What happens at Toronto Friends Group gatherings?

(A) Board game tournaments
(B) Language exchange
(C) Cooking practice
(D) Arts and crafts activities

159. What will most likely cause a member to not be able to attend a gathering?

(A) Not submitting payment in advance
(B) Not possessing a required skill level
(C) Not including certain details in a member profile
(D) Not fulfilling a promise to go to a previous gathering

160. In which of the positions marked [1], [2], [3], and [4] does the following sentence best belong?
"A map with directions and parking information for this venue can be found here."

(A) [1]
(B) [2]
(C) [3]
(D) [4]

NEW HORIZONS, INC. TO EXPAND OPERATIONS

April 2—Director Diane Mosley announced at a press conference yesterday that New Horizons is to expand into Europe and the Middle East. Speaking to reporters, the director claimed that the time was right to explore new, untapped markets and that she was confident that the firm would be successful in competing with rival sporting attire manufacturer Speedigrab in these regions. Renowned within the industry for being a fierce negotiator, Ms. Mosley went on to declare that she would relocate to Germany to personally oversee the transition. Once there, she will work to make European customers just as enthusiastic about her company's range of sports clothing as American consumers are.

The Diane Mosley story is a classic example of the American dream. Coming from a working-class family in North Carolina, she took her first job at automobile manufacturer Typhoon at the age of sixteen. From there, she spent a few years working for real estate developer Home Comforts. Her potential was quickly recognized, and by the age of 30, Ms. Mosley had become a vice president in the organization. She finally made the move to New Horizons last year in order to explore her passion for outdoor activities.

161. According to the article, what is Ms. Mosley known for?

(A) Her negotiation style
(B) Her background in product development
(C) Her understanding of consumer behavior
(D) Her willingness to take risks

162. What type of business most likely is New Horizons, Inc.?

(A) An automobile firm
(B) A real estate developer
(C) A sportswear company
(D) A housewares manufacturer

163. At which company did Ms. Mosley begin her career?

(A) New Horizons, Inc.
(B) Home Comforts
(C) Typhoon
(D) Speedigrab

164. What happened during Ms. Mosley's time at Home Comforts?

(A) She was presented with an award.
(B) She became a company executive.
(C) She devised a new packaging method.
(D) She managed a marketing campaign.

Vellis Fitness Center
Registration Form

Explanation of Membership Types

Regular membership comes with access to all areas of the center except the sauna, a dedicated locker, and an introductory hour-long personal training session.

Premium membership comes with access to all areas of the center, a dedicated locker, monthly hour-long personal training sessions, and entrance to any fitness class.

Membership Fee

Length of Membership	Membership Type	
	Regular	Premium
1 month	$80	$110
3 months	$180	$210
6 months	$300	$340
12 months	$500	$550

Type selected: 6-month regular membership
Start / End date: April 12 / October 11

Terms and Conditions

- The entire membership fee is due upon registration. Canceling a membership does not entitle the member to a refund of fees paid unless it is done within 14 days of the membership start date.

- Members who are temporarily unable to use the fitness center may freeze their memberships for a minimum of one month and maximum of three months. An administrative surcharge of $10 per month, due in advance, will be charged for this.

- The member must abide by the rules for safe and courteous use of the fitness center. Failure to do so may result in membership being revoked.

I have read and understood the above information.

Name: Craig Barton   **Signature:** *Craig Barton*   **Date:** April 12

165. What benefit do both regular and premium memberships include?

(A) Usage of a private storage space
(B) Access to a bathing area
(C) The ability to join group classes
(D) Repeated appointments with a personal trainer

166. How much will Mr. Barton pay for his membership?

(A) $180
(B) $210
(C) $300
(D) $340

167. According to the form, what would Mr. Barton be charged an extra fee for?

(A) Suspending his membership for a short time
(B) Cancelling his membership after a certain date
(C) Violating fitness center safety regulations
(D) Bringing a guest to the fitness center

Questions 168-171 refer to the following online chat discussion.

Russo & Koziol Advertising Company Messenger

Lucek Koziol, 11:36 A.M. Do you two have a minute to chat? I wanted to check on how the Storling juice account is coming along.

Josh Pronsky, 11:37 A.M. Sure. It's going well. Account Planning is finished with the target audience research. They said they'll have the report to us by the end of the week.

Lucek Koziol, 11:38 A.M. Good. So when can Creative expect your brief?

Sabrina Beck, 11:38 A.M. On May 20, as scheduled.

Lucek Koziol, 11:39 A.M. All right. Any problems working with Storling so far?

Josh Pronsky, 11:40 A.M. Just that it takes them a long time to reply when we e-mail them. We've had to follow up with phone calls a couple of times.

Lucek Koziol, 11:41 A.M. I see. Well, tell me if that gets serious. Is there anything else I should know about?

Sabrina Beck, 11:42 A.M. Nothing that's related to this account. But we'd like to ask something about submitting expense reports.

Lucek Koziol, 11:43 A.M. Go ahead.

Sabrina Beck, 11:44 A.M. Finance is saying that all expense reports from Account Services need your approval before they're turned in. Is that right? We've never had to do that before.

Lucek Koziol, 11:45 A.M. That's a new policy and it only applies to certain accounts. Didn't you get the e-mail about it? I'll forward it to you now.

[|]   [**SEND**]

---

168. Why does Mr. Koziol begin the chat?

(A) To obtain a progress update
(B) To request some documents
(C) To explain a policy change
(D) To offer some feedback

169. What does Mr. Pronsky indicate is difficult about working with Storling employees?

(A) They do not have clear aims for a project.
(B) They are slow to respond when contacted.
(C) Their office is far away.
(D) Their desired budget is too low.

170. At 11:43 A.M., what does Mr. Koziol most likely mean when he writes, "Go ahead"?

(A) Ms. Beck should submit a report.
(B) Ms. Beck may ask a question.
(C) Ms. Beck can give an estimate.
(D) Ms. Beck must make a phone call.

171. What department do Mr. Pronsky and Ms. Beck most likely work in?

(A) Account Planning
(B) Creative
(C) Finance
(D) Account Services

Ogami and Ryan Centre to Partner Up

BRISBANE (3 February) — Today, rising start-up Ogami, Inc. announced that it has formed a partnership with the renowned Ryan Centre. — [1] —. The centre, a hub for sustainable energy technology, will make its considerable resources available to Ogami for the continued development of the Ogami-X wind turbine.

"The opportunity to work with such an excellent group of scientists and engineers in this cutting-edge facility is very exciting for us," said Mary Flynn, president and CEO of Ogami. "Their expertise in the field of wind energy will help advance our development program more quickly and perhaps in ways that we don't expect." — [2] —.

Situated deep within the University of Brisbane's main campus, the Ryan Centre has a world-class reputation for research and education. — [3] —. As a pioneer in collaborations between universities and industry, it employs more than 200 engineers and scientists with extensive knowledge of solar, wind, and geothermal power.

Dr. Elias Martin will lead the effort at the Ryan Centre to build on Ogami's initial model and continue to refine the product's design. — [4] —. At Ogami's first development meeting held at the centre, he expressed hope that the Ogami-X would be ready for market within a year and added, "What we create here could have a noticeable positive impact on the world."

172. What is the research focus of the Ryan Centre?

(A) Medical equipment
(B) Renewable energy
(C) Telecommunications
(D) Flight technology

173. What does Ms. Flynn suggest about the partnership?

(A) It may have unexpected results.
(B) It is likely to last for a long time.
(C) It receives financial support from the government.
(D) It is similar to another partnership that Ogami, Inc. is part of.

174. What is indicated about the Ryan Centre?

(A) It has fewer than 200 employees.
(B) Ms. Flynn used to work there.
(C) The Ogami-X was created there.
(D) It sits on a university's property.

175. In which of the positions marked [1], [2], [3], and [4] does the following sentence best belong?
"His team will start by focusing on specifications such as blade shape and rotor construction."

(A) [1]
(B) [2]
(C) [3]
(D) [4]

Orbital Office Furniture Supplies

Unit 9 Business Park, Cincinnati, OH 94932

Dispatch date: March 30
To Be Delivered To: Ergomath Consulting

Customer Account No: 70670532
Order Number: #DR4032

Item Code	Quantity	Price per unit	Total price
#C43	18	$49.95	$ 899.10
#H503	4	$159.95	$ 639.80
#X110	1	$279.99	$ 279.99
#D60	5	$24.95	$ 124.75
Balance Due:			**$ 1943.64**

Payment will be automatically processed 7 days after the dispatch date.
Thank you for your patronage.

E-Mail message

To:	William Mobile <wmobile@orbitaloffice.net>
From:	Betty Controlle <bcontrolle@ergo-math.com>
Date:	April 5
Subject:	Order number: DR4032

Dear Mr. Mobile,

We received our order of new office furniture late yesterday afternoon, and I'm afraid to report that it's not satisfactory. The invoice clearly states that we have been billed $899.10 for the office chairs, which seems far too high. Looking at your catalog here, the unit price of this item is just $29.95. We expect that you will credit our account for the difference as soon as possible. In addition, the height of the large boardroom table that we ordered is too short. After setting it up, we noticed that the chairs do not fit underneath it at all. When I spoke to you about its dimensions on the phone last week, you assured me that it was more than suitable for our purposes.

As you can imagine, I am extremely disappointed. These furniture items were purchased in good time for our directors' meeting on Friday, and so this situation needs to be rectified before then. As I am going out of town on a business trip for the next two days, I have passed your details to my colleague, Wayne Rollings. He has agreed to phone you this afternoon to discuss arrangements for picking up the table and delivering a larger one. We hope that such mistakes will not happen in the future so that we may continue our mutually beneficial business arrangement.

Sincerely,

Betty Controlle
Assistant Regional Manager
Ergomath Consulting

176. What is true about the invoice?

    (A) It alerts the customer to a special offer.
    (B) It states that a shipment will be sent to Cincinnati.
    (C) It indicates that a payment will be processed in April.
    (D) It describes how to contact the delivery company.

177. For what product was Ergomath Consulting most likely billed incorrectly?

    (A) #C43
    (B) #H503
    (C) #X110
    (D) #D60

178. What does Ms. Controlle mention about the table she ordered?

    (A) It was delivered to the wrong address.
    (B) The setup instructions were not included with it.
    (C) She was misinformed about its size.
    (D) It was damaged in transit.

179. What will Mr. Rollings most likely talk about with Mr. Mobile?

    (A) Adjusting some uncomfortable furniture
    (B) Exchanging an unsatisfactory product
    (C) Arranging a visit from repair personnel
    (D) Correcting an error in a catalog

180. In the e-mail, the word "passed" in paragraph 2, line 4, is closest in meaning to

    (A) exceeded
    (B) overlooked
    (C) transmitted
    (D) declined

GO ON TO THE NEXT PAGE

❧ **Job Opening** ❧

Job Title: Technical Designer

Location: Base-Solutions, 18 Carver Street, Albuquerque. Role to begin June 2.

Role: As an experienced technical designer, you will be working closely with coworkers to produce high-quality, sophisticated architectural designs that adhere to current citywide planning guidelines. You will be responsible for liaising with clients in order to determine the specifications they require. You will use the Cityscape computer program to output your designs.

Requirements:

- A four-year degree from a university or equivalent

- Extensive knowledge of the Cityscape computer software and 2+ years of experience using this program are essential

- A strong work ethic and an ability to work well within a team; robust communication skills are also desirable, along with a friendly and personable demeanor

Application process: Please visit www.base-solutionsco.com/apply and fill out the online application form by February 27. Successful candidates will be invited to attend an interview on March 11.

---

http://www.base-solutionsco.com/apply/form

Base-Solutions
Job Application Form

Position Applied For: Technical Designer   **Date Completed:** February 2
Name: Nathan Bridges
Address: 402 Greenacre Road, Albuquerque, NM 87119   **Tel. no.:** 555-0115
E-mail: nathanb@ubn-mail.com

Academic qualifications:
Four-year degree in architectural design from the University of Albuquerque

Experience:
- Amuna Architects   Junior Designer
- Cutting Edge Design   Design Assistant
- Maxifun Bike Rental Store   Assistant

Additional comments:
I consider myself a very hard-working and enthusiastic individual, who has the ability to work well both as part of a team and individually. I have almost 18 months of experience using Cityscape at my most recent job as a junior designer, and I feel that I have a solid understanding of the program. I also believe myself to be a friendly and approachable person, maintaining good working relationships with all of my colleagues. I would also like to mention that I am contracted to my current company through mid-May.

181. What is NOT a stated duty of the job?

(A) Meeting with clients
(B) Using a specific computer program
(C) Following city planning regulations
(D) Selecting contractors

182. What is the deadline for application submissions?

(A) February 2
(B) February 27
(C) March 11
(D) June 2

183. At which company is Mr. Bridges currently employed?

(A) Base-Solutions
(B) Amuna Architects
(C) Cutting Edge Design
(D) Maxifun Bike Rental Store

184. Why might Mr. Bridges be considered unsuitable for the job?

(A) He does not have sufficient experience with some software.
(B) He does not hold a university qualification.
(C) He has never worked as part of a team before.
(D) He will be on vacation on the interview date.

185. What does Mr. Bridges indicate will take place in May?

(A) His employment contract will expire.
(B) His department will be restructured.
(C) He will host a conference call.
(D) He will complete a certification course.

GO ON TO THE NEXT PAGE

Questions 186-190 refer to the following e-mail, advertisement, and online review.

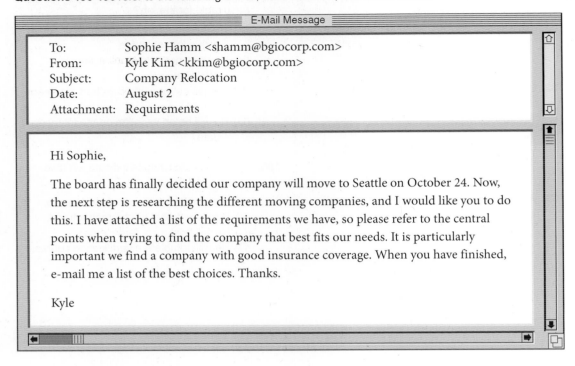

E-Mail Message

To: Sophie Hamm <shamm@bgiocorp.com>
From: Kyle Kim <kkim@bgiocorp.com>
Subject: Company Relocation
Date: August 2
Attachment: Requirements

Hi Sophie,

The board has finally decided our company will move to Seattle on October 24. Now, the next step is researching the different moving companies, and I would like you to do this. I have attached a list of the requirements we have, so please refer to the central points when trying to find the company that best fits our needs. It is particularly important we find a company with good insurance coverage. When you have finished, e-mail me a list of the best choices. Thanks.

Kyle

Crane Movers

With over 300 locations all over the country, Crane Movers offers the best moving services available. Our team is committed to ensuring your belongings are taken safely from one place to another. And we now provide a free tracking system for cross-country moves so you know where your items are at all times.

Residential Package: Whether individuals or families are moving to the next town or across the country, our movers will carefully pack belongings and transport them safely to their destination. Crane Movers wants to help college students during the month of August. Show a form of student identification and receive a free Tyrell Bookstore gift certificate after your move.

Corporate Package: Is your company relocating? Our professionals are prepared to help you and your employees transfer to a new place of business. We'll take great care of your business's machinery, documents, and other goods. Crane Movers is also offering 10% off corporate moves in September.

International Package: Moving to Madrid? Relocating to Singapore? Our experts are here to help make any move abroad go as smoothly as possible. Crane Movers offers a wide range of services from assisting with visa and immigration forms to picking the best mode of international transportation.

Please contact us at 1-800-555-0184 to speak to one of our representatives and get a free price quotation on any of our packages.

Testimonials

| HOME | MENUS | **REVIEWS** | LOCATIONS |

Written by: Sophie Hamm
Date: October 30

Our company used Crane Movers one week ago when our office relocated. The move could not have gone more smoothly. We were so pleased with their professional service. We were able to track all our boxes in transit, and everything was delivered in great shape. I would definitely recommend the corporate package to other companies.

---

186. What is the purpose of the e-mail?

(A) To arrange a board meeting
(B) To give some instructions
(C) To approve a proposal
(D) To recommend a business

187. In the e-mail, the word "central" in paragraph 1, line 3, is closest in meaning to

(A) middle
(B) nearby
(C) convenient
(D) key

188. What is part of the Residential Package?

(A) Handling of oversized furniture
(B) A special rate for families
(C) Transport of pet animals
(D) A free cost consultation

189. What is most likely true about Crane Movers?

(A) It offers moving insurance.
(B) Its headquarters are in Seattle.
(C) October is its busiest month.
(D) It uses recyclable packing supplies.

190. What is implied about Ms. Hamm?

(A) She applied for a Singaporean work visa.
(B) She frequently visits Tyrell Bookstore.
(C) Her company received a discounted service.
(D) Her company moved across the country.

GO ON TO THE NEXT PAGE

```
╔══════════════════ E-Mail message ══════════════════╗
║  ┌──────────────┐ ┌──────────────────────────────────────────────┐ ║
║  │ From:        │ │ Laurie Olson <laurie@grayfinecatering.com>     │ ║
║  └──────────────┘ └──────────────────────────────────────────────┘ ║
║  ┌──────────────┐ ┌──────────────────────────────────────────────┐ ║
║  │ To:          │ │ Darren Gregory <d.gregory@gil-mail.com>        │ ║
║  └──────────────┘ └──────────────────────────────────────────────┘ ║
║  ┌──────────────┐ ┌──────────────────────────────────────────────┐ ║
║  │ Subject:     │ │ Catering Menu                                  │ ║
║  └──────────────┘ └──────────────────────────────────────────────┘ ║
║  ┌──────────────┐ ┌──────────────────────────────────────────────┐ ║
║  │ Date:        │ │ October 29                                     │ ║
║  └──────────────┘ └──────────────────────────────────────────────┘ ║
║  ┌──────────────┐ ┌──────────────────────────────────────────────┐ ║
║  │ Attachment:  │ │ 📎 Gregory Menu Proposal                        │ ║
║  └──────────────┘ └──────────────────────────────────────────────┘ ║
╚══════════════════════════════════════════════════════╝
```

Dear Mr. Gregory,

As promised, I am sending you the proposed menu for your parents' wedding anniversary celebration. You will see that Grayfine Catering's expert chefs have taken care to craft a unique assortment of delicious dishes. They have also provided alternative options in case the initial offerings are not to your liking. Please review the attachment and let us know your decisions.

Once you do, we will create a contract specifying the number of staff that will be working your event, the hours we will work, the tasks we will be responsible for, and other matters. Please know that finalizing these details in advance will allow you to relax and have fun at your party, which is our chief aim. We will then require a 50% deposit to put your event on our official production calendar and begin scheduling preparatory events like the food tasting.

I look forward to hearing from you.

Sincerely,

Laurie Olson
Associate Manager
Grayfine Catering

Proposed Menu

First Course (Appetizers)	*Alternative:*
Chicken and Spinach Puffs ($8)	Salmon Cakes with Aioli Sauce ($10)
Second Course (Soup or Salad)	*Alternative:*
Cauliflower Soup with Seared Scallops ($13)	Mixed Greens Salad with Goat Cheese ($10)
Third Course (Entrée)	*Alternative:*
Balsamic Glazed Lamb Chops with Mashed Potatoes ($22)	Sautéed Filet Mignon with Roasted Mushrooms ($20)
Fourth Course (Dessert)	*Alternative:*
Cherry Almond Tart ($7)	Mint Chocolate Parfait ($7)

```
════════════════════════ E-Mail message ════════════════════════
┌──────────┐ ┌────────────────────────────────────────────────────┐
│ From:    │ │ Darren Gregory                                      │
└──────────┘ └────────────────────────────────────────────────────┘
┌──────────┐ ┌────────────────────────────────────────────────────┐
│ To:      │ │ Laurie Olson                                        │
└──────────┘ └────────────────────────────────────────────────────┘
┌──────────┐ ┌────────────────────────────────────────────────────┐
│ Subject: │ │ Re: Catering Menu                                   │
└──────────┘ └────────────────────────────────────────────────────┘
┌──────────┐ ┌────────────────────────────────────────────────────┐
│ Date:    │ │ November 7                                           │
└──────────┘ └────────────────────────────────────────────────────┘
```

Dear Ms. Olson,

Thank you for sending me the proposed menu. I apologize for not responding sooner. As I mentioned, I hadn't yet determined a site for the party when we met. I had to get that taken care of before moving on to the next steps, and finding a suitable venue turned out to be more difficult than I thought. But now we're all set—I've reserved the patio of the Lovana Hotel.

As for the menu, it looks great! Well done. The only change I would like you to make is to swap out the cauliflower soup for the mixed greens salad. I'm afraid the meal will feel a little heavy otherwise. Please move forward with this revised version of the menu.

Thanks,

Darren Gregory

191. What is indicated in the first e-mail about Mr. Gregory?

(A) He plans to invite 50 guests to a celebration.
(B) He has tasted samples of Grayfine Catering's food.
(C) He is throwing a party for some family members.
(D) He has spoken with a professional cook.

192. What does Ms. Olson say is Grayfine Catering's main goal?

(A) To provide unusual menu options
(B) To remain within the budget
(C) To enable the host to enjoy the event
(D) To build a positive reputation in the community

193. Why was Mr. Gregory unable to write to Ms. Olson earlier?

(A) He had to resolve another party-planning issue first.
(B) He found it difficult to make a menu decision.
(C) He had other tasks to do for his regular job.
(D) He did not notice her e-mail for several days.

194. Which course will be affected by the change Mr. Gregory requests?

(A) The first course
(B) The second course
(C) The third course
(D) The fourth course

195. What will Ms. Olson most likely do next?

(A) Add an entry to a calendar
(B) Ask a chef to suggest another dish
(C) Send a bill for an initial deposit
(D) Draw up a work agreement

GO ON TO THE NEXT PAGE

Symon Botanical Gardens

Symon Botanical Gardens opened over 40 years ago and currently has over 20 gardens on a 250-acre plot of land in the center of Symon City. It is open throughout the year Tuesday through Sunday from 7 A.M. to 7 P.M. Exceptions can be made for special exhibitions, previews, and events causing early or late closures of specific areas. For individual and group ticket prices, click <u>HERE</u>.

Areas to visit in July:

Water Lilies Pond: Starting in mid-July, these beautiful pink, yellow, and purple water lilies bloom and can be seen gracing the pond across from the Heath Gallery.

Ted Forest: After years of restoration, the forest has finally reopened to the public. Visitors can trek through it on guided paths to see trees, smaller plants, and animals.

Gold Lawn: There will be live performances that are free for all guests every Thursday night. Some special performers include The Falcons Jazz Band and Symon City Orchestra.

For more information about upcoming and current exhibits as well as our permanent and seasonal gardens, click <u>HERE</u>.

Symon Botanical Gardens
Permit Application for Filming

Name: _Cassandra Wiley_

Production Company Name: _Plent Film Productions_

Phone Number: _555-0194_

Type of Film: _Documentary_

Requested Location for Filming: _Orchid Place_

Requested Date for Filming: _August 28_

Requested Time for Filming: _5 A.M.–2 P.M._

Number of People: _20_

Equipment List: _Cameras, tripods, microphones, lighting stands_

Special Requests: _Our production team noticed a greenhouse in the northwest corner of Orchid Place and wanted to know if we could have permission to film near and inside it._

Notice

This area will be temporarily closed for a film production on August 28. Access will be limited to all visitors until 2 P.M. We kindly ask all guests to keep the volume of their voices to a minimum so as not to disrupt filming. In the meantime, please visit all our other great exhibits and gardens.

-Symon Botanical Gardens

196. What is indicated about Symon Botanical Gardens?

(A) It has longer hours on Tuesdays.
(B) It is operated by the Symon City government.
(C) All of its special exhibits are held indoors.
(D) Some of its gardens are accessible year-round.

197. What is NOT listed as available at Symon Botanical Gardens in July?

(A) Musical acts
(B) A flower display
(C) A gallery tour
(D) Walking trails

198. What did Ms. Wiley most likely request Symon Botanical Gardens do?

(A) Hire some entertainers for a performance
(B) Open an area earlier than its usual time
(C) Unload some equipment near a greenhouse
(D) Give a ticket discount for a group of 20 people

199. Where most likely is the notice posted?

(A) At Water Lilies Pond
(B) At Ted Forest
(C) At Gold Lawn
(D) At Orchid Place

200. In the notice, the word "volume" in paragraph 1, line 3, is closest in meaning to

(A) edition
(B) strength
(C) amount
(D) weight

Stop! This is the end of the test. If you finish before time is called, you may go back to Parts 5, 6, and 7 and check your work.

TEST 3

READING TEST

In the Reading test, you will read a variety of texts and answer several different types of reading comprehension questions. The entire Reading test will last 75 minutes. There are three parts, and directions are given for each part. You are encouraged to answer as many questions as possible within the time allowed.

You must mark your answers on the separate answer sheet. Do not write your answers in your test book.

PART 5

Directions: A word or phrase is missing in each of the sentences below. Four answer choices are given below each sentence. Select the best answer to complete the sentence. Then mark the letter (A), (B), (C), or (D) on your answer sheet.

101. Ms. Salem ------- her first management position at a fashion magazine three months ago.

(A) started
(B) starts
(C) will start
(D) start

102. Should the alarm fail to turn off when the authorization code is entered, contact ------- immediately.

(A) us
(B) our
(C) ours
(D) ourselves

103. Please recycle the ------- box in which the television was delivered.

(A) urgent
(B) total
(C) empty
(D) willing

104. Employees need a ------- form of transportation in order to consistently arrive at work on time.

(A) depended
(B) dependable
(C) dependability
(D) dependably

105. Ardary Associates has promised to ------- a few of its old computers to community organizations every year.

(A) donate
(B) conserve
(C) collect
(D) install

106. Mummings Group's business advisors have experience ------- a wide variety of industries.

(A) to
(B) on
(C) as
(D) in

107. Readers of the original *Cooking with Maximo* will appreciate the ------- revised version's updates and extra recipes.

(A) usually
(B) newly
(C) lastly
(D) nearly

108. After the commission structure was introduced, the sales staff began working ------- than they had previously.

(A) fastness
(B) fast
(C) faster
(D) fastest

109. Do not shut down the printer ------- any page of a document is still printing.
(A) before
(B) but
(C) if
(D) whether

110. Following a few hours of discussion, the contract ------- by the representatives yesterday afternoon.
(A) signing
(B) was signed
(C) to sign
(D) signed

111. Chiba Heating and Cooling's furnace maintenance services are guaranteed to ------- the life of your unit.
(A) convert
(B) expose
(C) offset
(D) prolong

112. It was fortunate that the outdoor music festival was held on ------- a sunny and breezy day.
(A) passing
(B) when
(C) such
(D) else

113. Because the licensing agreement was so important, the ------- for Redbud Media spent a lot of time preparing his proposals for it.
(A) negotiation
(B) negotiated
(C) negotiator
(D) negotiating

114. The guidebook reported that each room in Dovetail Inn is ------- decorated in a different theme.
(A) attractively
(B) attractive
(C) attraction
(D) attracted

115. Many delegates were late for the conference ------- the traffic congestion near the convention hall.
(A) yet
(B) since
(C) along with
(D) due to

116. Yambor Toys ------- a legal expert prior to releasing a product that was similar to that of its competitor.
(A) recognized
(B) consulted
(C) encouraged
(D) developed

117. The ------- of his absences from work caused Mr. Antonio to receive poor ratings on his employee evaluation.
(A) movement
(B) termination
(C) compliance
(D) frequency

118. Created with the help of a professional graphic designer, Newark Industries' new logo ------- its corporate values.
(A) depicts
(B) to depict
(C) depicting
(D) depict

119. Environmental scientists confirmed that the wildlife in Houston Lake could be ------- affected should a chemical plant be built nearby.
(A) doubtfully
(B) evenly
(C) mutually
(D) adversely

120. As the IT office was already closed, Ms. Seo had to make the repairs to the copy machine -------.
(A) she
(B) herself
(C) hers
(D) her

GO ON TO THE NEXT PAGE

121. The performance will last for around two hours, and audience members may meet the director -------.

(A) somewhat
(B) afterward
(C) instead
(D) beyond

122. Thanks to the ------- earned from the sale of its former manufacturing site, the company had surplus funds.

(A) salary
(B) account
(C) revenue
(D) payroll

123. Through decades of research, Dr. Carter has become the leading ------- on natural pain relief techniques.

(A) authoritatively
(B) authorities
(C) authority
(D) authoritative

124. The award will be given to the call center representative who is judged to be the most ------- to customer service.

(A) dedicated
(B) accomplished
(C) respected
(D) advanced

125. Our airline is pleased to offer several amenities designed to ensure passenger -------.

(A) comfort
(B) comforted
(C) comfortably
(D) comfortable

126. ------- the latest blockbusters, the cinema also routinely screens independent and classic films.

(A) Considering
(B) Besides
(C) Except
(D) For

127. Participants will be asked to put any mobile devices on silent mode ------- the seminar is in session.

(A) during
(B) so
(C) even
(D) while

128. The strongest economic ------- suggest that the currency's value will increase steadily this quarter.

(A) indicators
(B) merits
(C) alternates
(D) degrees

129. ------- the misspelling of the interviewee's name was discovered, the article had already been published.

(A) Suddenly
(B) By the time
(C) Now that
(D) Until

130. Ashe Cosmetics launched a popular skincare line ------- the moisturizing effects of aloe and coconut oil.

(A) combines
(B) combine
(C) combining
(D) combined

PART 6

Directions: Read the texts that follow. A word, phrase, or sentence is missing in parts of each text. Four answer choices for each question are given below the text. Select the best answer to complete the text. Then mark the letter (A), (B), (C), or (D) on your answer sheet.

Questions 131-134 refer to the following article.

March 16 — The Rosewood City Council is considering a measure to increase funding for the Parks and Recreation Department by 12%. The eighteen sites under the department's management ------- **131.** by residents of all ages for recreation and relaxation. Supporters of the proposal argue that the current amount of funding is not enough. " ------- we need is additional financial support for facility **132.** improvements," says Council Member Dena Walters.

The ------- will be discussed at a council meeting on March 28 at 7 P.M. All Rosewood residents are **133.** invited to attend, and those who wish to secure seating are urged to arrive early. -------. **134.**

131. (A) will use
    (B) had been used
    (C) are used
    (D) would have used

132. (A) What
    (B) Whichever
    (C) That
    (D) Anyone

133. (A) achievement
    (B) selection
    (C) matter
    (D) setback

134. (A) Departmental budgets are adjusted annually.
    (B) This includes a short public comment period.
    (C) Higher than usual attendance is expected.
    (D) Each council member serves a two-year term.

GO ON TO THE NEXT PAGE

Questions 135-138 refer to the following information.

Caring for Your Oakfirth Tent

You can ------- extend the life of your Oakfirth-brand camping tent by following these guidelines.
135.

First, make sure it is clean before putting it into storage for more than a few days. -------. If the tent
136.

must be washed, do not expose it to detergents or other cleaning fluids that contain ------- chemicals.
137.

Instead, obtain a specially-made tent-cleaning liquid or mix mild powdered soap with cold water.

Gently scrub the inner and outer surfaces of the tent with a sponge. Then, allow it to -------
138.

completely before packing it in the provided bag.

---

135. (A) signify
    (B) significant
    (C) significance
    (D) significantly

136. (A) Some types of tents may be more difficult
        to set up.
    (B) A piece of flat, soft ground makes an ideal
        campsite.
    (C) Use a cloth to wipe away small amounts of
        dirt.
    (D) These can be repaired with adhesive tape
        or patches.

137. (A) steep
    (B) harsh
    (C) timely
    (D) automated

138. (A) dry
    (B) cool
    (C) fill
    (D) harden

Questions 139-142 refer to the following letter.

Tyrone Berry
941 Joy Lane
Burbank, CA 91502

Dear Mr. Berry,

On behalf of the Small Business Owners Association (SBOA), I would like to invite you to our annual leadership workshop. This year, we have selected Kansas City as the host city because of its ------- 139. location. The event will be held at the Jenkins Center. If you are traveling from out of town, please see the enclosed details regarding -------. 140. SBOA has arranged for these hotels to offer discounted rates to our participants.

This workshop is an excellent way to ------- your business management skills. Space is limited, so if 141. you are interested in taking part in this event, be sure to register by the August 10 deadline. -------. 142.

Sincerely,

Shannon Payne
Event Coordinator, SBOA

139. (A) accessible
(B) accessibly
(C) accesses
(D) accessibility

140. (A) accommodations
(B) fees
(C) presentations
(D) requirements

141. (A) enforce
(B) observe
(C) enhance
(D) pursue

142. (A) Unfortunately, registration for that particular workshop has closed.
(B) We hope you had as much fun as we did at last year's gathering.
(C) We may decide that a larger venue is more suited to our needs.
(D) This will enable us to guarantee that a place is reserved for you.

GO ON TO THE NEXT PAGE

From: Jasmine Woods, CEO
To: All staff
Subject: Exciting news
Date: May 11

I am happy to announce that Plinkson, Inc. will begin maintaining free pantries for employees as a way to show our appreciation for your hard work. They will be stocked with fruit, snack bars, juices, and other treats, all ------- for their healthiness and good taste.
                                              143.

Two important notes:

— In order to avoid confusion with items brought in by and for individual employees, pantry goods will ------- be available in special pantry cupboards. These will be installed this week.
        144.

— The sole rule for the pantries' use is that employees may not take more food or drink than they will consume immediately. -------. Employees ------- this rule can expect to have their pantry
                                  145.   **146.**
privileges suspended.

143. (A) chosen
     (B) choosing
     (C) choice
     (D) choose

144. (A) now
     (B) only
     (C) again
     (D) hardly

145. (A) I will circulate the full list of rules as soon as it has been approved.
     (B) Items should not be stored in desks or transported out of the office.
     (C) Moreover, used dishes are to be washed promptly, not left in the sink.
     (D) Several staff members have reported instances of this behavior.

146. (A) broke
     (B) will break
     (C) are breaking
     (D) who break

PART 7

Directions: In this part you will read a selection of texts, such as magazine and newspaper articles, e-mails, and instant messages. Each text or set of texts is followed by several questions. Select the best answer for each question and mark the letter (A), (B), (C), or (D) on your answer sheet.

Questions 147-148 refer to the following form.

PC SOLUTIONS
1958 Tyler Avenue, 248-555-0171

Date: March 20   **Order accepted by:** Anna Bernard
Customer name: David Pierce   **Phone number:** 248-555-0174

Model: Viex Co. R-20 Tablet   **Serial number:** 3967285001
Description of issues: Cracked screen
Scheduled completion date: March 22   **Technician:** Jason Crawford

---

Special instructions / notes: Customer has paid in full for screen replacement and application of scratch-resistant coating. A 15% new customer discount was applied. No additional work should be undertaken without receiving customer's approval in advance. Customer will retrieve the item at 4 P.M. on the scheduled completion date.

---

147. What is Mr. Crawford most likely responsible for?

(A) Delivering packages
(B) Making repairs
(C) Taking orders
(D) Processing payments

148. What is suggested about Mr. Pierce?

(A) He purchased a carrying case for his device.
(B) He presented a coupon for the services.
(C) He is using PC Solutions for the first time.
(D) He will pick up an item on March 20.

GO ON TO THE NEXT PAGE

E-Mail message	
To:	Elias Kinnard <e.kinnard@valley-fashion.com>
From:	Jeanette Aguayo <aguayoj@wpamanufacturing.com>
Date:	January 8
Subject:	Details

Dear Mr. Kinnard,

It was a pleasure meeting with you to discuss the feasibility of Valley Fashion using our facility to produce the jeans for your new product line. I know you considered our initial offer too high, so I have discussed the issue with our fabrication team. Considering you would require a bulk order, we have adjusted the figures as below. Please note that this is the best offer we can provide.

Valley Fashion: Production Cost Summary	
	Updated January 7
Category	**Cost per item**
Labor	$2.91
Fabric	$3.21
Button, zipper, rivets	$1.24
Distressed finish	$0.84
Factory overhead	$0.39
Total	$8.59

The rate may be slightly higher than those of our competitors, but our company has the fewest on-site accidents of any facility in the region. Many socially conscious consumers pay attention to this factor when making purchasing decisions, and this would reflect positively on your company.

Sincerely,

Jeanette Aguayo
WPA Manufacturing

149. Why did Ms. Aguayo write to Ms. Kinnard?

(A) To request additional funds
(B) To provide a potential budget
(C) To propose a cost-saving measure
(D) To explain a billing error

150. What does Ms. Aguayo suggest about WPA Manufacturing?

(A) It has an excellent safety record.
(B) It is the largest factory in the area.
(C) It has especially low labor prices.
(D) It is popular on social media.

Questions 151-152 refer to the following Web page.

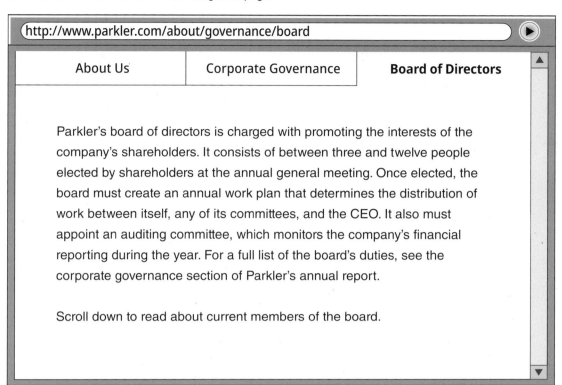

http://www.parkler.com/about/governance/board

| About Us | Corporate Governance | **Board of Directors** |

Parkler's board of directors is charged with promoting the interests of the company's shareholders. It consists of between three and twelve people elected by shareholders at the annual general meeting. Once elected, the board must create an annual work plan that determines the distribution of work between itself, any of its committees, and the CEO. It also must appoint an auditing committee, which monitors the company's financial reporting during the year. For a full list of the board's duties, see the corporate governance section of Parkler's annual report.

Scroll down to read about current members of the board.

151. What is NOT mentioned as a responsibility of the board of directors?

(A) Seeking benefits for investors
(B) Forming a team to oversee financial affairs
(C) Dividing tasks among the company's leadership
(D) Appointing the company's chief executive officer

152. What can most likely be found further down on the Web page?

(A) Biographical details about some people
(B) A list of the company's official rules
(C) A summary of a yearly report
(D) The schedule for a shareholder meeting

GO ON TO THE NEXT PAGE

Questions 153-154 refer to the following text-message chain.

Salvo Trevisano   3:08 P.M.
Are you still at the Strickland Street property?

Jaromir Nowak   3:14 P.M.
Yes. What's up?

Salvo Trevisano   3:15 P.M.
The supplier will deliver some materials around four, and I'd like some help unloading the truck. Will you be able to get back here by then?

Jaromir Nowak   3:16 P.M.
Probably not.

Salvo Trevisano   3:18 P.M.
Really? I thought it was only supposed to be a short job.

Jaromir Nowak   3:20 P.M.
It was supposed to be, but it turns out that some of the pipe is starting to wear away and needs to be replaced to stop the sink from leaking.

Salvo Trevisano   3:21 P.M.
OK. I understand.

153. At 3:16 P.M., what does Mr. Nowak mean when he writes, "Probably not"?

(A) He does not have enough materials.
(B) He does not think a truck has free space.
(C) He will be unable to assist Mr. Trevisano.
(D) He may have trouble finding Strickland Street.

154. What is Mr. Nowak currently doing?

(A) Reviewing some building plans
(B) Fixing a plumbing problem
(C) Organizing some supplies
(D) Replacing a light fixture

To: All Staff   September 30

With Summit Spa's plans to extend its business hours, the management team has been conducting interviews of applicants for a massage therapist position. We are pleased to announce that we have found someone to join our team: Angela Thorpe.

Ms. Thorpe is a state-certified massage therapist who received her initial training from the Grundy Institute in Sacramento. She first worked at the day spa at Jasper Hotel in Santa Barbara. During her time there, she started the Stress Reduction Association (SRA), a charity committed to teaching others about healing through relaxation techniques. She then moved to Oakland and started working at the Laurel Center, where she was awarded Employee of the Year. Because of the Laurel Center's upcoming closure, she was searching for similar work. Ms. Thorpe's skills cover a wide range of techniques, so we are excited to have her with us. Her first day here will be Monday, October 7. Please make an effort to make her feel welcome.

155. What is the purpose of the memo?

(A) To introduce an employee
(B) To compare some job candidates
(C) To publicize a retirement celebration
(D) To announce a promotion

156. What did Ms. Thorpe do in Santa Barbara?

(A) She founded a community service organization.
(B) She received a professional certification.
(C) She developed a new therapy technique.
(D) She won an annual award from her workplace.

157. The word "cover" in paragraph 2, line 10, is closest in meaning to

(A) protect
(B) hide
(C) publish
(D) include

GO ON TO THE NEXT PAGE

Questions 158-160 refer to the following article.

Kroft Koffee's New Grocery Store Line Struggles

NASHVILLE, June 15 — With its mismatched sofas and armchairs, contemporary artwork, and soft folk music, Kroft Koffee has become known internationally for being the perfect meeting place for a cozy afternoon with friends. But now the company has made a move to bring its products to consumers' homes as well. — [1] —. CEO Diego Cardoso, who recently took over for Isabelle Hammond, had a vision for stocking Kroft Koffee products in stores.

The new line of drinks, sold under the name Kroft Koffee Express, launched last week and is being sold exclusively at the Birchtree grocery store chain. — [2] —. The line consists of chilled versions of the business's lattes, cappuccinos, and americanos. "We're pleased to be partnering with Birchtree," Cardoso said. "Its shoppers and ours are alike, so we believed it was a perfect match."

However, while Kroft Koffee itself has had strong sales over the past year, the Express line appears to have drawn little consumer interest so far. — [3] —. This is despite Kroft Koffee's heavy investment in marketing campaigns for television and social media. Even the most optimistic analysts say the goods may be pulled from shelves within a few months. — [4] —.

158. What is implied about Kroft Koffee?

(A) It has branches inside Birchtree stores.
(B) It is under new management.
(C) It varies its menu seasonally.
(D) It has recently expanded overseas.

159. According to the article, why was Birchtree selected by Kroft Koffee?

(A) For its reasonable pricing
(B) For its brand recognition
(C) For its similar customer base
(D) For its stable distribution network

160. In which of the positions marked [1], [2], [3], and [4] does the following sentence best belong?

"Most stores reported selling just a few of the drinks in the entire first week that the product was offered."

(A) [1]
(B) [2]
(C) [3]
(D) [4]

Questions 161-163 refer to the following information.

Thank you for purchasing a Tetrex Freshwater Aquarium. To get started on enjoying the relaxing hobby of keeping fish, follow the steps below.

1. Wash the interior of the tank with warm, soapy water. Rinse the sides of the tank carefully so that no residue remains, as this can be toxic to fish.

2. Cover the bottom of the tank with pebbles or decorative gravel and fill the tank about 75% full. Add any live or plastic plants. Handle the roots of live plants gently, and make sure they are completely covered. Fill the rest of the tank with water.

3. Hang the filter on the side of the tank, ensuring that the filter is submerged. Allow the filter to soak for at least 20 minutes before turning on its pump.

4. Check that the water is room temperature. Add fish to the tank one by one.

If you are missing parts, please call our customer service line at 1-800-555-0166. For a duplicate warranty card, e-mail Patrick Davis at pdavis@tetrexaq.com.

161. What is the information mainly about?

(A) Setting up fish care equipment
(B) Selecting animals to have as pets
(C) Cleaning a home aquarium
(D) Growing underwater plants

162. What are users instructed to avoid doing?

(A) Overfilling the tank with water
(B) Getting electrical components wet
(C) Leaving soap on tank surfaces
(D) Exposing plant roots to the air

163. What can users do by e-mailing the address provided?

(A) Order special accessories
(B) Make a warranty claim
(C) Request a missing part
(D) Get a copy of a document

GO ON TO THE NEXT PAGE

Questions 164-167 refer to the following text-message chain.

Colin Gray, 1:56 P.M.
Eula, we have a problem. Mr. Hughes can't find his passport. It looks like he and I will need to stay here for a while to talk to the museum officials.

Eula Warren, 1:58 P.M.
OK. I'll go ahead with the rest of the group. Send me updates when you can. If it doesn't turn up, we'll need to take him to apply for a replacement so he can fly home as planned on Saturday.

Colin Gray, 1:58 P.M.
Right. They're checking the gift shop now.

Colin Gray, 2:24 P.M.
We're in luck! Mr. Hughes now has his passport in hand. We'll meet you at the restaurant for dinner.

Eula Warren, 2:25 P.M.
That's a relief. But actually—the tour bus has run into some light traffic. I think that if you two get on the subway right now, you'll be able to catch up with us.

Colin Gray, 2:26 P.M.
Oh, that's great. We'll do that. Did you let our contact from Fleming's Adventures know?

Eula Warren, 2:26 P.M.
I'll do that now.

Eula Warren, 2:27 P.M.
Tabitha, we're running late today. I don't think we're going to get to the pier until 3:15.

Tabitha Perry, 2:31 P.M.
Hi, Eula. That's all right. We're not very busy today. I just hope you arrive early enough that your group can finish our full course before the sea gets rough in the evening.

| I | Send |

164. What is Mr. Hughes most likely scheduled to do on Saturday?

(A) Explore a museum
(B) Check in to some lodgings
(C) Take a class on a water sport
(D) Depart the country

165. At 2:24 P.M., what does Mr. Gray most likely mean when he writes, "We're in luck"?

(A) An application was granted.
(B) A store sells a special type of merchandise.
(C) A business will accept a form of identification.
(D) A misplaced item has been located.

166. What will Mr. Hughes do differently from the rest of the tour group today?

(A) He will use another means of transportation.
(B) He will not participate in the next activity.
(C) He will eat dinner at a later time.
(D) He will see an attraction for free.

167. What kind of business does Ms. Perry most likely work for?

(A) A seaside hotel
(B) A boat tour company
(C) A campground operator
(D) An outdoor restaurant

GO ON TO THE NEXT PAGE

E-Mail message

To:	Undisclosed Recipients
From:	Taylor Diehl <diehlt@brantleyinc.com>
Date:	March 2
Subject:	Hello

On behalf of Brantley, Inc., I would like to welcome you all on board. We strive for accuracy and efficiency in the testing and analysis of laboratory samples, and you will play an important role in this regard. Your individual team leaders will soon be providing further orientation materials, which will help you to have a sound understanding of our policies and expectations. In the meantime, I'd like to summarize some of the key sites in our multi-building complex.

All of you will be stationed in Delano Tower, the center of our operations. Additional equipment can be procured from the warehouse in the Stokes Building, but a request must be made in advance. If you experience any safety issues, there is an on-site nurse available in the Elliot Building, which is also the home of our security office. Questions regarding payroll and benefits are handled by our finance department, which is located in Vine Hall (ext. 300).

If you plan on driving to work, you'll need a pass to leave your vehicle in one of the on-site lots. These are available at no cost, pending availability, and can be obtained from Steven Reiter (ext. 251). All employees must wear a photo ID badge at all times. You should get one from the security office as soon as you arrive on your first day.

Please feel free to contact me with questions at any time. I look forward to getting to know you all.

Taylor Diehl
HR Director, Brantley, Inc.

---

168. Who most likely are the recipients of the e-mail?

(A) Visiting inspectors
(B) Lab technicians
(C) Warehouse workers
(D) Job applicants

169. The word "sound" in paragraph 1, line 4, is closest in meaning to

(A) positive
(B) thorough
(C) durable
(D) noisy

170. Where should the recipients go upon arrival at the complex?

(A) To Delano Tower
(B) To the Stokes Building
(C) To the Elliot Building
(D) To Vine Hall

171. What is Mr. Reiter responsible for doing?

(A) Distributing orientation materials
(B) Answering payroll questions
(C) Issuing parking permits
(D) Performing safety training

NILLET (January 31)—Residents of one section of Mills Street are complaining about the effects that the popular navigation app "Navega" is having on their neighborhood.

Darlene Reed, one of the homeowners affected, spoke about the situation at yesterday's city council meeting. She explained that the app is sending drivers onto Mills Street during rush hour without warning them that it passes over a steep hill with sharp inclines. — [1] —.

Ms. Reed claimed that there has been a car-related problem on the street nearly once a week since the app was released in November. "Part of my fence was knocked down, and my neighbors' mailboxes have been hit," she said.

Though it is less famous than other steep Nillet roads like Tucker Street or Harwell Drive, Mills Street is in fact one of the city's steepest. — [2] —. The crest of its hill is also very short, which means that drivers stopped at the intersection at its peak cannot clearly see the area they are about to enter.

Ms. Reed said that the street's residents have tried contacting Chavisy, the company that developed Navega, about the problem, but their complaints were ignored. — [3] —. Therefore, she and the other homeowners are asking the city to take action. One option she suggested was making Mills Street a one-way street heading west, thus discouraging its use as a shortcut to Newman Avenue. — [4] —.

Council members promised to direct the Department of Transportation to look into the issue.

172. Why was the article written?

(A) To give an overview of a politician's career
(B) To describe an upcoming city project
(C) To bring attention to a local issue
(D) To promote a technological advance

173. According to the article, what did Ms. Reed mention at a city council meeting?

(A) She has been to Chavisy's headquarters.
(B) She frequently checks Navega when driving.
(C) Her neighbors oppose a transportation proposal.
(D) Her private property was recently damaged.

174. What is suggested about the city of Nillet?

(A) It is built on land that features multiple hills.
(B) Its traffic levels have increased since November.
(C) Some of its major roads are one-way streets.
(D) It is famous for having efficient city services.

175. In which of the positions marked [1], [2], [3], and [4] does the following sentence best belong?
"Another was banning left turns onto it from Cedar Road during peak commuting hours."

(A) [1]
(B) [2]
(C) [3]
(D) [4]

GO ON TO THE NEXT PAGE

http://www.charterantiques.com/aboutus

Charter Antiques

About Us

Owned and operated by Roger Litchfield for over two decades, Charter Antiques has one of the largest collections of competitively priced antique furniture on the East Coast. Our inventory is constantly changing, so we encourage you to visit the store regularly.

Antique Sales: We offer free delivery on all orders. If you're not satisfied with your purchase, you may return it for a full refund within 30 days. Please note that the item must be returned in the same condition and at the customer's expense.

Antique Refurbishments: If you have an old item that you love, we can bring it back to its original condition.

Sell Your Antiques: Send photos and a description to Roger (roger@charterantiques.com) and he can give you an estimate of its worth (a final offer will be made once the item is seen in person).

E-mail

To:	Charter Antiques <inquiries@charterantiques.com>
From:	Ye Chao <chaoye@premium-inbox.com>
Date:	May 20
Subject:	Antique desk

To Whom It May Concern:

I bought a mahogany writing desk at your store on May 15, and it was delivered to my home yesterday. While I think it's a lovely piece, and it's the perfect size for my home office, I'm afraid I need to return it. Unfortunately, the shade of its wood does not match the floorboards as well as I had expected.

Please e-mail me back to let me know what I need to do next. I'd like to get the item returned by May 24 if possible because that's when the replacement desk I ordered will arrive, and I don't really have space for both pieces in the room.

Sincerely,

Ye Chao

176. What is NOT mentioned about Charter Antiques?

(A) It advertises in a regional magazine.
(B) It has existed for twenty years.
(C) Its stock changes regularly.
(D) It offers furniture restoration services.

177. What is indicated about Charter Antiques' owner?

(A) He posts photos of the merchandise on a Web site.
(B) He purchased the business from someone else.
(C) He can assess the value of furniture.
(D) He wants to open another location.

178. What is implied about Mr. Chao?

(A) He is a long-time customer of Charter Antiques.
(B) He will have to pay some shipping costs.
(C) He is not eligible for a full refund.
(D) He has a large collection of antiques.

179. What does Mr. Chao find dissatisfactory about the item he bought?

(A) Its condition
(B) Its shape
(C) Its size
(D) Its color

180. Why does Mr. Chao want a transaction to be completed quickly?

(A) To settle an issue before a trip
(B) To facilitate a move into a new home
(C) To make room for some guests
(D) To prepare for another delivery

GO ON TO THE NEXT PAGE

Questions 181-185 refer to the following e-mail and information.

To:	Hamid Kasun <h.kasun@fast-mail.com>
From:	Wright Communications <accounts@wrightcomm.com>
Date:	March 10
Subject:	RE: Account #49506

Dear Mr. Kasun,

We have received your request to transfer your Wright Communications services from 672 Franco Street to 1051 Orleans Avenue on March 28. The request has been officially made on your account, and no further action is needed from you at this time.

The final day of service at your current residence will be March 27, and the new service will begin on March 28. Because there will be no break in service, you will be billed the usual amount ($49.99) for your package. Regarding your inquiry, your billing cycle will not change. It will still be from the fifth day of each month to the fourth day of the following month.

You also mentioned that you might want to add a mobile phone to your package sometime next month after you turn in the one from your company. This is very easy to do, and I have attached information about our packages for your convenience.

Thank you for being a Wright Communications customer!

Sincerely,

Nando Deleon
Accounts Agent, Wright Communications

Wright Communications Packages

Package	Services	Monthly Charge
Basic	Internet Only	$39.99
T-Basic	Internet + Cable	$49.99
P-Basic	Internet + Phone	$54.99
Premium	Internet + Cable + Phone	$89.99

Bills will be issued five days after the final day of the billing cycle. Customers can make payments by credit card on our Web site at www.wrightcomm.com or by sending a check to Wright Communications Billing Office, P.O. Box 1385, Bloomington, IN 47408. Please note that you must add a $2.99 processing fee to all check payments.

181. What is the purpose of the e-mail?

(A) To ask for an overdue payment
(B) To introduce a new service
(C) To explain a policy revision
(D) To confirm a change of address

182. Which package is Ms. Kasun currently using?

(A) Basic
(B) T-Basic
(C) P-Basic
(D) Premium

183. What is suggested about Mr. Kasun?

(A) He was dissatisfied with the answer to an inquiry.
(B) He and another customer have a joint account.
(C) He is considering downgrading his package.
(D) He currently has a work-issued phone.

184. When most likely will Mr. Kasun's next bill be issued?

(A) On March 31
(B) On April 4
(C) On April 9
(D) On April 30

185. What is indicated about payments?

(A) They are more expensive if made by check.
(B) They may take a few days to process.
(C) They can be electronically refunded.
(D) They will incur a fee if received late.

GO ON TO THE NEXT PAGE

EMPLOYEE NOTICE: CHANGES AT FORTUNA RESTAURANT

March 5

Fortuna Restaurant will undergo a construction project to add an outdoor patio to the property. The patio will wrap around two sides of the restaurant. It will have a regular section on Parson Avenue and a VIP section on the south side of the building with views of Canterbury Lake.

The work will begin next week and the patio's grand opening is tentatively scheduled for May 26, though this is subject to change depending on the construction's progress. The work will mainly entail pulling up the bushes that surround the building, laying a stone floor, and erecting a metal railing. During construction, the rear section of the dining room will be closed off.

Thank you for your cooperation.

To:	Undisclosed Recipients
From:	Vinay Narang <v.narang@fortunarest.com>
Date:	June 12
Subject:	Fortuna Restaurant

On behalf of Fortuna Restaurant, I would like to invite you all to the grand opening of our restaurant's outdoor patio. We believe this change to our business will be of interest to your readers, and we would be happy to give you a tour on the event day and tell you more about the change. The event will take place on Friday, June 18 at 11 A.M. There will be free food and opportunities to take pictures, and we even expect an appearance by a few city officials, including Mayor Stephanie Gonzalez.

Please reply to this e-mail address to reserve your seat. I hope to see you all there!

Vinay Narang
General Manager, Fortuna Restaurant

Dining in Style

By Joel Gossett

Summer is in full swing, and it's the perfect weather for some outdoor dining all around town.

Linda's Café: 922 Ingram Road, 555-0196
For casual meals on a budget, Linda's Café is a great summer hotspot. I dined in their rooftop section, which features tables with large umbrellas for shade.

Fortuna Restaurant: 613 Parson Avenue, 555-0122
I loved the beautiful view of Canterbury Lake when dining on Fortuna Restaurant's new patio. The menu has a wide selection of economical appetizers and entrées.

Pearl: 1705 Elk Street, 555-0164
Excellent service and exotic dishes make Pearl a wonderful choice for special occasions. The sophisticated atmosphere makes it one of my top choices for fine dining.

Marchini's: 1806 16th Street, 555-0134
Specializing in Italian cuisine, Marchini's has large portions for a low price. Outdoor balcony tables should be reserved in advance to avoid disappointment.

186. What is NOT mentioned as part of the remodeling project?

    (A) Extending a building's roof
    (B) Installing stone flooring
    (C) Putting up a barrier
    (D) Removing some plants

187. Who most likely was the e-mail sent to?

    (A) New restaurant staff
    (B) Members of the press
    (C) Local city officials
    (D) Construction crew workers

188. What is implied about the remodeling project?

    (A) It took place in two phases.
    (B) It caused a temporary road closure.
    (C) It experienced some delays.
    (D) Its results can be seen in pictures online.

189. What is suggested about Mr. Gossett?

    (A) He sat in the VIP section of Fortuna Restaurant.
    (B) He visited Fortuna Restaurant with a friend.
    (C) He called 555-0122 to reserve a table.
    (D) He currently works near Parson Avenue.

190. Which restaurant is probably the most expensive?

    (A) Linda's Café
    (B) Fortuna Restaurant
    (C) Pearl
    (D) Marchini's

Questions 191-195 refer to the following e-mail, instructions, and form.

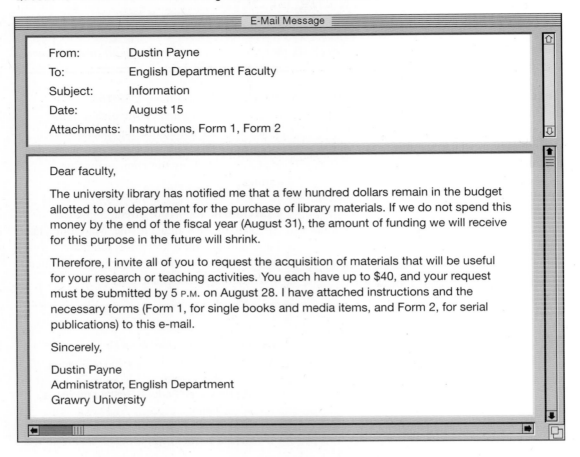

E-Mail Message

From: Dustin Payne
To: English Department Faculty
Subject: Information
Date: August 15
Attachments: Instructions, Form 1, Form 2

Dear faculty,

The university library has notified me that a few hundred dollars remain in the budget allotted to our department for the purchase of library materials. If we do not spend this money by the end of the fiscal year (August 31), the amount of funding we will receive for this purpose in the future will shrink.

Therefore, I invite all of you to request the acquisition of materials that will be useful for your research or teaching activities. You each have up to $40, and your request must be submitted by 5 P.M. on August 28. I have attached instructions and the necessary forms (Form 1, for single books and media items, and Form 2, for serial publications) to this e-mail.

Sincerely,

Dustin Payne
Administrator, English Department
Grawry University

GRAWRY UNIVERSITY LIBRARY
INSTRUCTIONS FOR FACULTY ACQUISITIONS REQUESTS

1. Confirm that the library does not already possess the item you want by searching our catalog from our Web site.

2. Download the correct request form at www.grawrylibrary.com/acquisitions/forms.

3. Fill out the form. Include as much information as possible about the desired item. If you are making a rush request, please explain why in the "Comments" box.

4. Submit the form to the member of your department's staff who has been designated as the library liaison. He or she will review it before passing it on to the library.

* *Inquiries about this process can be directed to the library's acquisitions coordinator.* *

GRAWRY UNIVERSITY LIBRARY FACULTY
ACQUISITIONS REQUEST FORM 1 (BOOKS AND MEDIA)

Requested by: Audrey Medina   **Submitted to:** Jean Bowers

Department: English   **Date:** August 27

E-mail address: a.medina@grawry.edu

Title*: Psychological Approaches to Poetry   **Publication year:**

Author*: Lee Dixon   **Publisher:** Portero Books

Edition/Series: First edition   **List price:** $43.00

Number of copies: 1

Rush request: Yes ☐   No ■

Comments: I found the price above on www.norris-rare-books.com. Perhaps you can find a better one on another site.

*Required fields

191. Why was the e-mail written?

    (A) To solicit suggestions for resolving a problem
    (B) To clarify the recipients' job responsibilities
    (C) To encourage recipients to use a resource
    (D) To announce improvements to a process

192. In the instructions, what are faculty members asked to do?

    (A) Confirm that some funding is available
    (B) Download a special software program
    (C) Visit the Web sites of several booksellers
    (D) Conduct a search of the library's collection

193. What is implied about Ms. Medina?

    (A) She did not meet a deadline.
    (B) She filled out the wrong document.
    (C) Her form is missing required information.
    (D) Her request exceeds a spending limit.

194. Who most likely is Ms. Bowers?

    (A) An employee of the English Department
    (B) The library's acquisitions coordinator
    (C) A sales associate at a bookstore
    (D) The author of a book

195. In the form, the word "better" in paragraph 2, line 7, is closest in meaning to

    (A) more affordable
    (B) more skilled
    (C) healthier
    (D) tidier

GO ON TO THE NEXT PAGE

Most recent films by director Louis Bryant

Across the Sea: Based on the novel of the same name, *Across the Sea* is one of the highest-grossing action movies to date. Set in the late seventeenth century, the film stars Corey Underwood as a mischievous pirate who tries to win the king's favor.

Dawn at Sornhill: This quiet, critically acclaimed historical drama set in the Elizabethan period follows one family's struggle with poverty. Bryant sought advice from leading scholars of English history to ensure accuracy in all aspects of the film.

The Icy Pavement: Starring Corey Underwood, this action film follows a 1920s detective as he tries to catch a criminal who is threatening the elites of New York. The film received rave reviews from critics and numerous awards.

We Were There: Depicting army life during the time of the Spanish Civil War (1936–1939), *We Were There* offers action-packed scenes alongside thought-provoking dialogue. The main roles are masterfully played by Corey Underwood and Pat Avis, winning them Best Actor and Best Supporting Actor, respectively.

Benito Giordano, owner

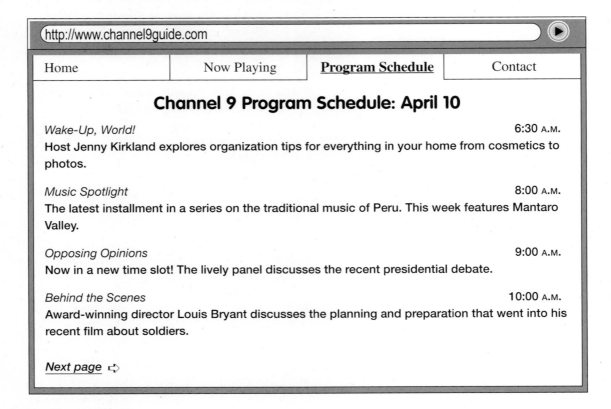

http://www.channel9guide.com

| Home | Now Playing | **Program Schedule** | Contact |

Channel 9 Program Schedule: April 10

Wake-Up, World! 6:30 A.M.
Host Jenny Kirkland explores organization tips for everything in your home from cosmetics to photos.

Music Spotlight 8:00 A.M.
The latest installment in a series on the traditional music of Peru. This week features Mantaro Valley.

Opposing Opinions 9:00 A.M.
Now in a new time slot! The lively panel discusses the recent presidential debate.

Behind the Scenes 10:00 A.M.
Award-winning director Louis Bryant discusses the planning and preparation that went into his recent film about soldiers.

Next page ⇨

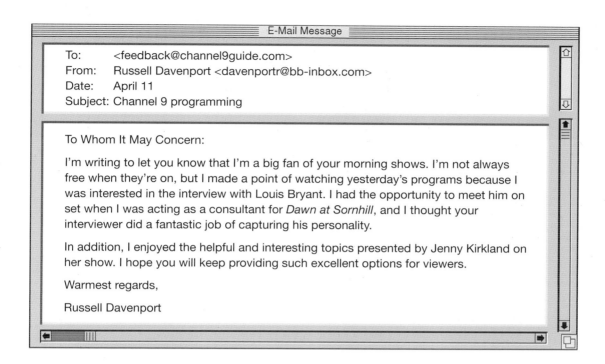

E-Mail Message

To: <feedback@channel9guide.com>
From: Russell Davenport <davenportr@bb-inbox.com>
Date: April 11
Subject: Channel 9 programming

To Whom It May Concern:

I'm writing to let you know that I'm a big fan of your morning shows. I'm not always free when they're on, but I made a point of watching yesterday's programs because I was interested in the interview with Louis Bryant. I had the opportunity to meet him on set when I was acting as a consultant for *Dawn at Sornhill*, and I thought your interviewer did a fantastic job of capturing his personality.

In addition, I enjoyed the helpful and interesting topics presented by Jenny Kirkland on her show. I hope you will keep providing such excellent options for viewers.

Warmest regards,

Russell Davenport

---

196. What do all of Mr. Bryant's recent films have in common?

(A) They were all praised by critics.
(B) They are all set in the past.
(C) They all star the same actor.
(D) They are all action movies.

197. Which film was discussed on Channel 9 on April 10?

(A) *Across the Sea*
(B) *Dawn at Sornhill*
(C) *The Icy Pavement*
(D) *We Were There*

198. In the Web page, what is indicated about Channel 9's programs?

(A) The host of *Wake-Up, World!* has recently changed.
(B) The latest episodes of *Music Spotlight* share a theme.
(C) *Opposing Opinions* features politicians as guests.
(D) *Behind the Scenes* has the longest time slot.

199. In the e-mail, the word "keep" in paragraph 2, line 2, is closest in meaning to

(A) preserve
(B) continue
(C) hold
(D) control

200. What is most likely true about Mr. Davenport?

(A) He has met Ms. Kirkland before.
(B) He watches Channel 9 daily.
(C) He is an expert on English history.
(D) His book was made into a movie.

Stop! This is the end of the test. If you finish before time is called, you may go back to Parts 5, 6, and 7 and check your work.

RC

TEST 4

READING TEST

In the Reading test, you will read a variety of texts and answer several different types of reading comprehension questions. The entire Reading test will last 75 minutes. There are three parts, and directions are given for each part. You are encouraged to answer as many questions as possible within the time allowed.

You must mark your answers on the separate answer sheet. Do not write your answers in your test book.

PART 5

Directions: A word or phrase is missing in each of the sentences below. Four answer choices are given below each sentence. Select the best answer to complete the sentence. Then mark the letter (A), (B), (C), or (D) on your answer sheet.

101. Mr. Willick opened a small bakery with ------- own savings last year.

(A) he
(B) his
(C) him
(D) himself

102. The client has agreed to ------- mail the contract to us or send a scanned copy by next Wednesday at the latest.

(A) neither
(B) some
(C) either
(D) anyone

103. The coupon can be used for any Crestview Housewares merchandise ------- custom-made items.

(A) regarding
(B) except
(C) toward
(D) at

104. Although the Jeong collection is one of the museum's most famous, exhibitions of its works are -------.

(A) rare
(B) urgent
(C) mistaken
(D) wide

105. Northland Rail sells hot drinks and sandwiches ------- most of its trains.

(A) into
(B) down
(C) on
(D) as

106. The attached brochure will ------- you with the information you requested about Baske Printing's services.

(A) outline
(B) remind
(C) introduce
(D) supply

107. Breet Furniture's newest offerings ------- blend traditional and modern design elements.

(A) skill
(B) skillful
(C) skillfully
(D) skillfulness

108. In negotiations, a delicate ------- between strength and flexibility brings about the best outcome.

(A) balance
(B) balances
(C) balanced
(D) to balance

109. Construction of the new branch of Dalton Insurance will ------- be completed.

(A) soon
(B) timely
(C) ever
(D) highly

110. According to the weather report, the severe storm warning will stay in ------- until midnight.

(A) opposition
(B) practice
(C) contact
(D) effect

111. Analysts say the difference in quality between the two brands has become more ------- over time.

(A) notices
(B) noticeable
(C) noticeably
(D) noticing

112. Today's baseball game is likely to cause delays for commuters ------- routes take them past the stadium.

(A) their
(B) who
(C) whose
(D) they

113. Nambot Electronics customers are ------- to retain all receipts throughout the life of the product's warranty.

(A) advisors
(B) advisable
(C) advising
(D) advised

114. To ensure that correct payment is given, payroll guidelines state that employees' work hours must be tracked -------.

(A) namely
(B) accurately
(C) importantly
(D) enormously

115. The funds that the charity raises go toward the ------- goal of providing clean water to developing countries.

(A) admirable
(B) admiring
(C) admiration
(D) admirably

116. The table is made from a ------- material so that it can withstand the weight of most everyday objects.

(A) mandatory
(B) durable
(C) grateful
(D) frequent

117. *Ms. Olson*, a comedy from director Alan Coronado, has received favorable ratings from ------- in the film industry.

(A) criticisms
(B) criticism
(C) critics
(D) critical

118. All confidential information is kept in ------- stored files in the headquarters building.

(A) securing
(B) security
(C) secures
(D) securely

119. Once the city sets aside enough money for the project, the library will ------- extensive renovations.

(A) commit
(B) establish
(C) accompany
(D) undergo

120. Investment giant Bedera Holdings has made a £200 million ------- to buy Westel Creek, a condominium development in Dansley.

(A) quote
(B) fine
(C) bid
(D) audit

GO ON TO THE NEXT PAGE

121. Updated spreadsheets will be available in the shared folders on Tuesday, ------- a schedule for the software seminar.
(A) along with
(B) notwithstanding
(C) other than
(D) during

122. Merrimack Media executives are hesitant to ------- the partnership because it has been so profitable.
(A) terminate
(B) enable
(C) surpass
(D) misplace

123. Many patients in the drug trial reported that taking the medicine gave them ------- relief from their symptoms.
(A) signified
(B) signifying
(C) significant
(D) significance

124. An informal poll found that retailers across the country ------- strong sales over the long holiday weekend.
(A) to expect
(B) expectations
(C) expectantly
(D) expect

125. ------- the food at Garden Bistro is delicious, its small portion sizes do not justify the high prices.
(A) In spite of
(B) While
(C) In order that
(D) Otherwise

126. Phelps Automotive has gained a reputation for reliability because it follows ------- standards for road safety testing.
(A) contrary
(B) rigorous
(C) vague
(D) fluent

127. In an effort to recruit the most talented chemists in the field, Goldex Pharmaceuticals offers generous ------- to its staff.
(A) compensate
(B) compensated
(C) compensatory
(D) compensation

128. ------- the short time allowed for the creation of the advertising campaign, it is no surprise that its results have been disappointing.
(A) Given
(B) Prior to
(C) Though
(D) In case

129. Mr. Parker brought a gift for the CEO on her birthday, but the other managers did not consider doing -------.
(A) yet
(B) likewise
(C) still
(D) instead

130. Patrons of Rutland Bank ------- up to $1,000 from this machine without paying a fee.
(A) may withdraw
(B) withdrawing
(C) can be withdrawn
(D) has withdrawn

PART 6

Directions: Read the texts that follow. A word, phrase, or sentence is missing in parts of each text. Four answer choices for each question are given below the text. Select the best answer to complete the text. Then mark the letter (A), (B), (C), or (D) on your answer sheet.

Questions 131-134 refer to the following instructions.

Follow these easy instructions to brew the perfect cup of coffee with the Knapp Co. coffee maker.

Fill the water reservoir to the desired level, as indicated by the number of cups along the side. ------- .
                                                                                              131.

This will help you to avoid impurities, and it will also improve the taste of the coffee. The green

button will blink ------- until the water is heated to the correct temperature. Remove the plastic basket
                   132.

and add into it one scoop of ground coffee for each cup you intend to make. Then ------- the basket
                                                                                  133.

to its place. The brewing process will begin ------- a few seconds. If this does not happen, check that
                                             134.

the basket is clicked into place all the way.

131. (A) Be careful not to get the power cord wet.
    (B) Place the device a few inches from the wall.
    (C) Always use bottled or filtered water.
    (D) You can select from two to ten cups.

132. (A) continuous
    (B) continuously
    (C) continual
    (D) continue

133. (A) return
    (B) label
    (C) discard
    (D) empty

134. (A) near
    (B) upon
    (C) beside
    (D) within

GO ON TO THE NEXT PAGE →

Mayor Rick Webb
City Hall, Suite #302
Twillingate, NL A0G 4M0

Dear Mayor Webb,

I would like to bring an important matter to your attention. The town's recent tourism campaign ------- many people to our town and its beautiful coastal scenery. However, visitors to the seaside are throwing litter on the ground, building unauthorized campfires, and not cleaning up after their dogs. These ------- are making the area unpleasant for everyone. I have enclosed a list of ways to resolve **136.** these problems, one of ------- is simply adding more trash cans. This would not cost the city much at **137.** all. -------. I hope you will consider my ideas. **138.**

Sincerely,

Libby Geiger
Twillingate Resident

Encl.

---

135. (A) has attracted
(B) attracting
(C) to attract
(D) is being attracted

136. (A) shortages
(B) obligations
(C) behaviors
(D) occupants

137. (A) what
(B) that
(C) which
(D) this

138. (A) For example, broken glass bottles are washing up on shore.
(B) Several city council members have even visited the area.
(C) Either way, it results in an unfair burden on residents.
(D) In fact, one of the local businesses might donate them.

NOTICE OF NEW POLICY

Scoul Financial will adopt a new policy on work space personalization as of September 1. Its main purposes will be to protect company property and ensure that our offices make positive ------- on
139.
clients and other visitors. ------- , employees will be asked to avoid modifying their work spaces in
140.
ways that damage the furniture or walls. Steps should also be taken to minimize -------. Work-related
141.
materials should be organized neatly when possible, and no more than 20% of the space in your office or cubicle should be taken up by personal items. ------- .
142.

The full policy was sent to your company e-mail account on August 22. Please review it carefully. Questions may be addressed to erika.strong@scoulfinancial.com

---

139. (A) impresses
(B) impressed
(C) impressively
(D) impressions

140. (A) Therefore
(B) Nevertheless
(C) Additionally
(D) Rather

141. (A) mess
(B) conflict
(C) lateness
(D) spending

142. (A) With luck, we will be able to reach 30% by the end of the year.
(B) These include photographs, decorative statues, posters, etc.
(C) Your supervisor will then guide you to your new work space.
(D) Putting these electronic devices on "energy saver" mode is also helpful.

To: Murphy Suites Tenants <alltenants@murphysuites.net>
From: Kevin Yoshida <k_yoshida@murphysuites.net>
Date: May 18
Subject: Renovations

Dear Tenants,

Murphy Suites intends to undertake much-needed renovations this summer to make your living space more comfortable and enjoyable. We have selected several items from a list of ------- **143.** requested by tenants. Mainly, we ------- the community lounge by changing the carpet and painting **144.** the walls. This project is scheduled for May 20–23. -------. Another project planned for the summer **145.** is the repainting of the pool. The work has not been scheduled yet, as it is being done ------- by a **146.** different company. Thank you for your patience.

Sincerely,

Kevin Yoshida

143. (A) shipments
     (B) improvements
     (C) regulations
     (D) transactions

144. (A) had upgraded
     (B) upgraded
     (C) upgrade
     (D) will upgrade

145. (A) We appreciate the feedback you provided to us afterward.
     (B) The lounge is commonly used for group gatherings and meetings.
     (C) While it is underway, tenants will not be allowed access to the room.
     (D) Accordingly, some tenants will be signing new lease agreements.

146. (A) separately
     (B) previously
     (C) consistently
     (D) urgently

PART 7

Directions: In this part you will read a selection of texts, such as magazine and newspaper articles, e-mails, and instant messages. Each text or set of texts is followed by several questions. Select the best answer for each question and mark the letter (A), (B), (C), or (D) on your answer sheet.

Questions 147-148 refer to the following information.

http://www.vepnexbank.com/about/3

Vepnex Bank is glad to cooperate with media requests for information under the following conditions. Inquiries must come from an employee of a media organization and include the name of the submitter and the organization with which he or she is affiliated. Please submit them via e-mail to our communications department at communications@vepnexbank.com. The communications department is staffed during the bank's hours of operation (Monday through Friday, 8 A.M. to 5 P.M.) and is generally able to respond in two business days.

Please note that the communications department does not provide customer support. To obtain customer service, please visit this page.

147. For whom is the information intended?

(A) Potential vendors
(B) Members of the press
(C) Existing customers
(D) Bank employees

148. What is indicated about Vepnex Bank?

(A) It is in a partnership with a local organization.
(B) It recently created a new department.
(C) It has a live chat support service.
(D) It is not open on weekends.

GO ON TO THE NEXT PAGE

Questions 149-150 refer to the following online chat discussion.

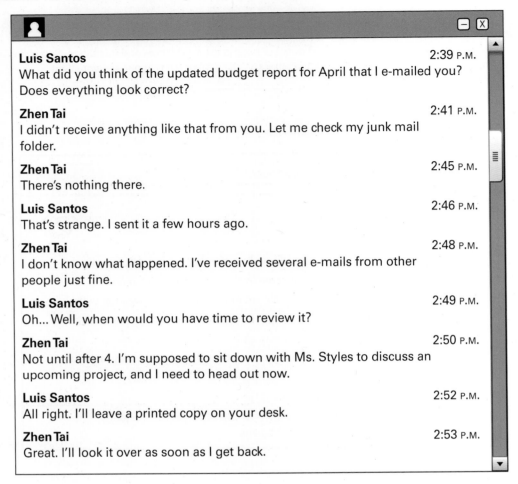

Luis Santos   2:39 P.M.
What did you think of the updated budget report for April that I e-mailed you?
Does everything look correct?

Zhen Tai   2:41 P.M.
I didn't receive anything like that from you. Let me check my junk mail
folder.

Zhen Tai   2:45 P.M.
There's nothing there.

Luis Santos   2:46 P.M.
That's strange. I sent it a few hours ago.

Zhen Tai   2:48 P.M.
I don't know what happened. I've received several e-mails from other
people just fine.

Luis Santos   2:49 P.M.
Oh... Well, when would you have time to review it?

Zhen Tai   2:50 P.M.
Not until after 4. I'm supposed to sit down with Ms. Styles to discuss an
upcoming project, and I need to head out now.

Luis Santos   2:52 P.M.
All right. I'll leave a printed copy on your desk.

Zhen Tai   2:53 P.M.
Great. I'll look it over as soon as I get back.

149. At 2:46 P.M., what does Mr. Santos most
     likely mean when he writes, "That's strange"?

   (A) He does not know why a file has been
       deleted.
   (B) He thinks an e-mail message should
       have arrived.
   (C) He is confused by the contents of a
       document.
   (D) He is having trouble accessing his e-mail
       account.

150. What will Ms. Tai most likely do next?

   (A) Go to a meeting
   (B) Review a financial report
   (C) Search a desk drawer
   (D) Turn on a printer

MEMO

From: Ye-Won Oh
To: All employees
Re: Announcement
Date: September 19

All employees are hereby notified that Ruby Miller has been voluntarily reassigned from the information technology department to the marketing department. In her new position as "Marketing Innovation Specialist," Ruby will be responsible for researching new marketing technologies and overseeing their adoption as necessary. She will also provide dedicated technical support for marketing activities including market research and product launch campaign planning.

This change will take place on September 26. The information technology department has already begun the search for Ruby's successor and expects to fill the role by the end of October. Until that time, Seth Fleming will handle her former responsibilities, as well as his own. We ask for everyone's patience and support during this transition period.

---

151. What is the main purpose of the memo?

(A) To publicize a departmental transfer
(B) To advertise a job opening
(C) To profile the winner of a staff award
(D) To provide an update on a marketing campaign

152. According to the memo, what will Mr. Fleming do?

(A) Assist with a recruitment process
(B) Begin working from home occasionally
(C) Carry out additional duties temporarily
(D) Travel to another branch in October

GO ON TO THE NEXT PAGE

Questions 153-154 refer to the following advertisement.

Apartment for Rent

Edington Realty is pleased to offer **a spacious three-bedroom apartment** in Crossett Tower. The apartment is on the fifth floor, and it comes with modern appliances, air conditioning, and a video intercom system. Crossett Tower is located in the popular suburb of Bingham Heights, just a few blocks from Amarillo Station. The building features underground parking, a rooftop garden, and a ground-floor gym for tenants.

The apartment may be rented on a one- or two-year lease, with further renewal possible. Interested parties should complete an application form—downloadable from the Edington Realty Web site (www.edingtonrealty.com)—and submit it with an accompanying statement from a current or previous landlord verifying the applicant's good character.

153. What is indicated about Crossett Tower?
(A) It is located opposite a train station.
(B) Its apartments come in three sizes.
(C) It has an on-site fitness facility.
(D) It is a five-story building.

154. What should applicants send to Edington Realty?
(A) A letter of reference
(B) A housing deposit
(C) A desired rent price
(D) A bank statement

Questions 155-157 refer to the following schedule.

Meadowview Cinema

Weekly Schedule: Friday, April 14 – Thursday, April 20

Title	Genre	Matinee (Sat. & Sun. Only)	Evening Show (Daily)	Night Show (Daily)
*The Quiet Calling**	Thriller	–	7:20	9:35
*Chicago Chase**	Action	3:15	7:05	9:20
Alien Adventure	Family	3:30	7:10	–
The Whipple Brothers	Comedy	3:20	–	9:15

*Patrons under 13 will not be admitted.

Our box office opens on weekdays at 6:00 P.M. and weekends at 1:30 P.M. Tickets may be purchased for shows up to one week in advance. We accept exchanges of tickets up to 24 hours before the show. We do not offer refunds on tickets.

155. What is implied in the schedule?

(A) Two of the films share the same genre.
(B) *The Whipple Brothers* is not shown every day.
(C) Some of the films start at the same time.
(D) Children are not allowed to see *Chicago Chase*.

156. Which film is not screened at night?

(A) *The Quiet Calling*
(B) *Chicago Chase*
(C) *Alien Adventure*
(D) *The Whipple Brothers*

157. What is indicated about tickets?

(A) They cannot be exchanged on the day of the show.
(B) They must be reserved ahead of time.
(C) They are priced differently depending on the patron's age.
(D) They can be refunded only with a manager's approval.

GO ON TO THE NEXT PAGE

Questions 158-160 refer to the following e-mail.

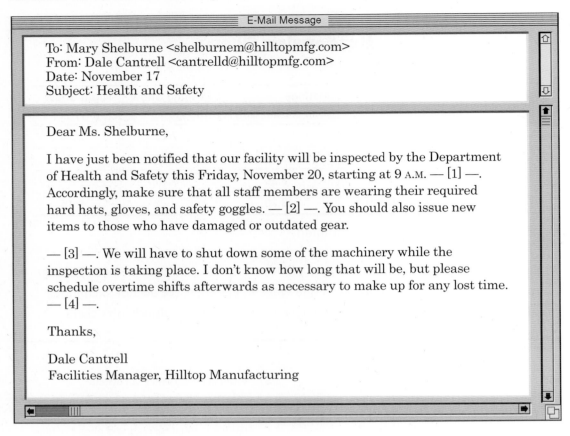

E-Mail Message

To: Mary Shelburne <shelburnem@hilltopmfg.com>
From: Dale Cantrell <cantrelld@hilltopmfg.com>
Date: November 17
Subject: Health and Safety

Dear Ms. Shelburne,

I have just been notified that our facility will be inspected by the Department of Health and Safety this Friday, November 20, starting at 9 A.M. — [1] —. Accordingly, make sure that all staff members are wearing their required hard hats, gloves, and safety goggles. — [2] —. You should also issue new items to those who have damaged or outdated gear.

— [3] —. We will have to shut down some of the machinery while the inspection is taking place. I don't know how long that will be, but please schedule overtime shifts afterwards as necessary to make up for any lost time. — [4] —.

Thanks,

Dale Cantrell
Facilities Manager, Hilltop Manufacturing

158. Why did Mr. Cantrell send the e-mail?

(A) To inquire about a safety record
(B) To assign tasks to an employee
(C) To schedule a safety inspection
(D) To announce a training session

159. What is Mr. Cantrell unsure about?

(A) How much time a process will take
(B) Whom to address some questions to
(C) Where to order some goods
(D) Who will give a presentation

160. In which of the positions marked [1], [2], [3], and [4] does the following sentence best belong?

"The inspector will check that all regulations are being followed correctly by employees."

(A) [1]
(B) [2]
(C) [3]
(D) [4]

Questions 161-164 refer to the following text-message chain.

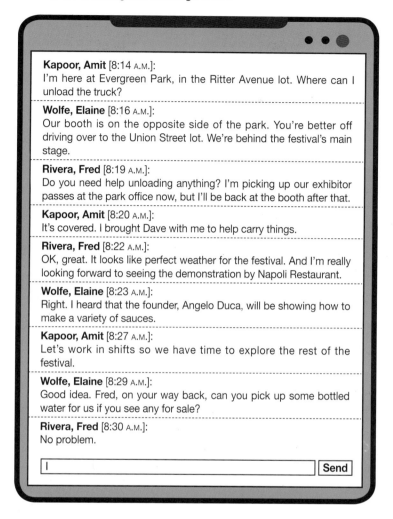

Kapoor, Amit [8:14 A.M.]:
I'm here at Evergreen Park, in the Ritter Avenue lot. Where can I unload the truck?

Wolfe, Elaine [8:16 A.M.]:
Our booth is on the opposite side of the park. You're better off driving over to the Union Street lot. We're behind the festival's main stage.

Rivera, Fred [8:19 A.M.]:
Do you need help unloading anything? I'm picking up our exhibitor passes at the park office now, but I'll be back at the booth after that.

Kapoor, Amit [8:20 A.M.]:
It's covered. I brought Dave with me to help carry things.

Rivera, Fred [8:22 A.M.]:
OK, great. It looks like perfect weather for the festival. And I'm really looking forward to seeing the demonstration by Napoli Restaurant.

Wolfe, Elaine [8:23 A.M.]:
Right. I heard that the founder, Angelo Duca, will be showing how to make a variety of sauces.

Kapoor, Amit [8:27 A.M.]:
Let's work in shifts so we have time to explore the rest of the festival.

Wolfe, Elaine [8:29 A.M.]:
Good idea. Fred, on your way back, can you pick up some bottled water for us if you see any for sale?

Rivera, Fred [8:30 A.M.]:
No problem.

| Send

161. What is most likely true about the location of the writers' booth?

(A) It is far from the Ritter Avenue parking area.
(B) It was difficult to obtain a permit for.
(C) It is behind the park office.
(D) It was changed unexpectedly.

162. At 8:20 A.M., what does Mr. Kapoor most likely mean when he writes, "It's covered"?

(A) He believes that the booth is protected from bad weather.
(B) He has already paid the exhibitor fee.
(C) He does not need assistance from Mr. Rivera.
(D) He has already made a schedule of work shifts.

163. What is suggested about Mr. Duca?

(A) He attended the festival last year.
(B) He used to be the writers' coworker.
(C) He owns Napoli Restaurant.
(D) He will demonstrate decorating techniques.

164. What is Mr. Rivera asked to do?

(A) Move a truck
(B) Buy some beverages
(C) Unload some boxes
(D) Pick up some maps

GO ON TO THE NEXT PAGE

http://www.uniquehomeinteriors.co.uk

Unique Home Interiors

"Unique Home Interiors makes remodeling fun and easy!"
—Pam Morgan, Professional Designer

Unique Home Interiors is the nation's most popular quarterly magazine on interior design. Our contributors are experts in the industry, and each issue is packed with useful information and creative design ideas you won't find anywhere else. You can find out about the hottest color schemes as well as how to upgrade your space on a budget. Each issue comes with templates for wall painting that you can download and print for a great DIY look. The magazine also features subscriber-only bargains on furniture, paint, home accessories, and more.

Get your one-year subscription today!

Trial digital issue for free!*	[SELECT]
Print version only for £14.95	[SELECT]
Digital version only for £9.95	[SELECT]

Our best offer! Print and digital version for £16.95 [SELECT]

*Available for download until the end of this month. A valid e-mail address is required.

165. How many issues of *Unique Home Interiors* are published each year?

(A) Four
(B) Six
(C) Twelve
(D) Fifty-two

166. What is NOT mentioned as available in *Unique Home Interiors*?

(A) Exclusive discount offers
(B) Color trend information
(C) Printable patterns
(D) Interviews with professionals

167. According to the Web page, what is true about *Unique Home Interiors*?

(A) Subscriptions can be canceled at any time.
(B) A sample edition can be accessed for a limited time.
(C) Renewed subscriptions are cheaper than new ones.
(D) New subscribers are eligible for a bonus gift.

Questions 168-171 refer to the following article.

ROSSEIN (May 22)—The Rossein City Parks and Recreation Department is holding a contest to give names to two birds that were recently born in the bell tower of the city hall building.

The birds are peregrine falcons, a species famous for its ability to reach speeds of over 200 miles per hour when diving through the air to catch the small animals it eats. Though its population dropped dangerously low in the mid-twentieth century due to the influence of harmful agricultural chemicals, environmental groups made a successful effort to increase its numbers to safe levels by providing more places for the birds to nest.

The nesting platform in the bell tower is an example of how this campaign has protected the birds in our local area. In the decades since it was installed, several pairs of adult falcons have nested there. Eiji Nakajima, a bird researcher who works for the department, says the current two have returned there annually for the past three years. He explains, "They live here in the summer and fly south in late fall." The pair, nicknamed "Jack" and "Jill," produced one male and one female chick this year.

Community members are encouraged to go to www.rosseinfalcons.com to see pictures of the young birds and submit their name suggestions. Submissions will be accepted until May 31, after which five finalist pairs will be chosen. Then, community members are encouraged to visit the site again to cast a vote for their favorite pair between June 3 and June 9. The winning names will be announced on June 10.

168. What is the purpose of the current project discussed in the article?

(A) To obtain funding to modernize an environmental laboratory
(B) To learn why a type of bird is behaving a certain way
(C) To decide what some young animals should be called
(D) To educate members of a community about nature

169. What is stated about the species of bird being discussed?

(A) It lives in the same area year-round.
(B) It can move very fast.
(C) It hunts for food underwater.
(D) It is currently classified as endangered.

170. According to the article, what happened many years ago in Rossein?

(A) Mr. Nakajima was hired to oversee a program.
(B) The use of some chemicals was forbidden.
(C) A city building was damaged by birds.
(D) Some homes for birds were built.

171. What is suggested about a Web site?

(A) It will not be updated after May 31.
(B) It features photographs of a promotional event.
(C) It is run by a local government.
(D) It lists teams of people chosen to participate in a contest.

Super Spin Laundromat
Clean clothes are our passion!

Super Spin Laundromat is the best place to get your laundry done. Our washers and dryers use state-of-the-art technology to clean and dry your clothes in a way that avoid causing wear and tear and enables them to last up to three times longer than those laundered in traditional machines. — [1] —.

If you're in a hurry, leave the items with us for our full-service wash, which includes washing, drying, and folding the clothes. — [2] —. The clothes can be delivered to your home or office for a small additional fee.

If you'd like a more economical option, there are machines on site so you can do your laundry yourself. We also sell a wide variety of detergents, fabric softeners, and dryer sheets. Do you have an article of clothing that needs extra attention? — [3] —. Our staff is available to give you advice on getting rid of discolorations caused by food, cosmetics, and more. We also have sinks for washing delicate items by hand.

Super Spin Landromats are now open 24 hours a day for your convenience, and our waiting areas have a television, a vending machine, and free magazines to read.

We have five locations throughout the city. — [4] —. We hope to see you soon at Super Spin Laundromat!

172. What is suggested about the appliances at Super Spin Laundromat?

(A) They are simple to use.
(B) They can be operated with coins.
(C) They are gentle on clothes.
(D) They have longer cleaning cycles.

173. What can customers get from Super Spin Laundromat's employees?

(A) A delivery schedule
(B) Explanations of handwashing techniques
(C) An Internet connection password
(D) Tips on stain removal

174. What has Super Spin Laundromat recently done?

(A) Extended its business hours
(B) Added more machines
(C) Started a dry cleaning service
(D) Opened a new location

175. In which of the positions marked [1], [2], [3], and [4] does the following sentence best belong?

"To find the one nearest to you, visit our Web site at www.s-spin.com and view the complete list."

(A) [1]
(B) [2]
(C) [3]
(D) [4]

GO ON TO THE NEXT PAGE

Test 4

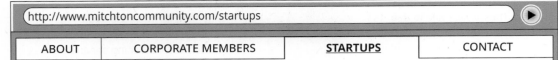

http://www.mitchtoncommunity.com/startups

ABOUT	CORPORATE MEMBERS	**STARTUPS**	CONTACT

The Niles Kern Corporation believes that a vibrant startup culture is the key to a city's long-term financial health. That's why it founded our Mitchton Community to provide support services to a select group of promising Shenna startups each year. We offer expert business consulting, free office space and cloud data storage if needed, and—most importantly—introductions to major corporations headquartered in Shenna. In addition to our founder, Niles Kern, we count Dottam Industries and Minand Hotels among our corporate members. On average, nearly a third of our startups end up making lucrative deals to provide services and equipment to such businesses.

Application Details

Applications are accepted in December of each year. All applicant organizations must be located within the greater Shenna area and engaged in developing innovative products or services in one of the following categories:

- A – Finance
- B – Marketing
- C – Medicine
- D – Renewable energy

Click here to download an application for the upcoming year.

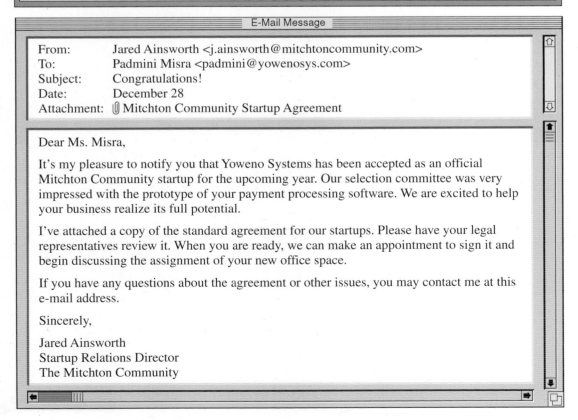

E-Mail Message

From:	Jared Ainsworth <j.ainsworth@mitchtoncommunity.com>
To:	Padmini Misra <padmini@yowenosys.com>
Subject:	Congratulations!
Date:	December 28
Attachment:	Mitchton Community Startup Agreement

Dear Ms. Misra,

It's my pleasure to notify you that Yoweno Systems has been accepted as an official Mitchton Community startup for the upcoming year. Our selection committee was very impressed with the prototype of your payment processing software. We are excited to help your business realize its full potential.

I've attached a copy of the standard agreement for our startups. Please have your legal representatives review it. When you are ready, we can make an appointment to sign it and begin discussing the assignment of your new office space.

If you have any questions about the agreement or other issues, you may contact me at this e-mail address.

Sincerely,

Jared Ainsworth
Startup Relations Director
The Mitchton Community

176. What is indicated about Mitchton Community startups?

(A) They submit a final report at the end of the year.
(B) They are expected to collaborate with each other.
(C) They are often acquired by bigger firms.
(D) They are based in a particular region.

177. What is NOT mentioned as a benefit of becoming a Mitchton Community startup?

(A) Guidance from experts
(B) A large sum of money
(C) Complimentary digital storage
(D) Connections to established companies

178. Which category did Yoweno Systems most likely apply under?

(A) A
(B) B
(C) C
(D) D

179. What is probably true about Yoweno Systems?

(A) It has experienced a change in leadership.
(B) It wishes to vacate its current office.
(C) Its application included a video demonstration of a device.
(D) Its staff members have yearlong employment contracts.

180. What is Ms. Misra instructed to do?

(A) Begin writing a draft of a document
(B) Set up a meeting with Mr. Ainsworth
(C) Provide an electronic signature
(D) Contact a business's attorney

GO ON TO THE NEXT PAGE

Questions 181-185 refer to the following Web page and online form.

http://www.customsol.com

Custom Solutions

Get exactly what you want. No job is too big or too small!

Custom Solutions is the area's leading provider of made-to-order apparel. We print your text and/or company logo on garments to help you promote your business, create a unique gift, prepare uniforms for a sports team, and more. Place an order online, call us at 623-555-0192 or stop by the store in person at 226 Willow Drive, St. Cloud, MN 56303. We highly recommend in-person visits for complicated orders.

We offer the following options for basic white T-shirts (Item #238). Please see our Pricing page for a full list of merchandise.
- One-color printing, front only: $9.50
- Two-color printing, front only: $10.00
- One-color printing, front and back: $11.50
- Two-color printing, front and back: $12.00

You will be required to pay a 25% deposit at the time of placing the order. The remainder of the balance is due at the time of pick-up or delivery.

Customer Name: Eva Ferguson
Order Date: May 25
Item Number: 238

Contact Number: 623-555-0127
Expected Delivery Date: June 18

Please complete all applicable fields. Write an *X* in fields that are not needed.

FRONT	BACK
Line 1: Hendrix Children's Hospital **Size:** Small **Color:** Navy Blue	**Line 1:** Every penny counts! **Size:** Medium **Color:** Forest Green
Line 2: 5th Annual Charity Fun Run **Size:** Large **Color:** Forest Green **Image:** hendrix.jpg **Image Position:** Center, below text	**Line 2:** June 30, Abrams Park **Size:** Small **Color:** Navy Blue **Image:** X **Image Position:** X

Special Instructions: In order to show participants what they will receive, I would like a photograph of one of the finished items at least one week before delivery, if possible.

Continue to sizes and delivery information ➪

181. What does Custom Solutions sell?

(A) Furniture
(B) Stationery
(C) Clothing
(D) Signage

182. What is indicated about merchandise orders?

(A) They must exceed a minimum number of items.
(B) Full payment must be made before shipment.
(C) Their fees include design services.
(D) They can be placed in several different ways.

183. What will Ms. Ferguson most likely use the items for?

(A) A fund-raising event
(B) An employee retreat
(C) A sports training camp
(D) A grand opening

184. How much will Ms. Ferguson most likely pay per item?

(A) $9.50
(B) $10.00
(C) $11.50
(D) $12.00

185. What does Ms. Ferguson specially ask Custom Solutions to do?

(A) Combine multiple images
(B) Send a photo in advance
(C) Expedite a delivery
(D) Save leftover materials

GO ON TO THE NEXT PAGE

Questions 186-190 refer to the following Web page, form, and e-mail.

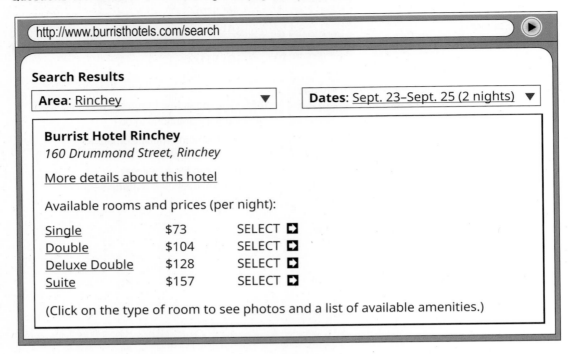

http://www.burristhotels.com/search

Search Results

Area: Rinchey ▼   **Dates**: Sept. 23–Sept. 25 (2 nights) ▼

Burrist Hotel Rinchey
160 Drummond Street, Rinchey

More details about this hotel

Available rooms and prices (per night):

Single	$73	SELECT ▶
Double	$104	SELECT ▶
Deluxe Double	$128	SELECT ▶
Suite	$157	SELECT ▶

(Click on the type of room to see photos and a list of available amenities.)

Burrist Hotels

Guest Feedback Form

Please let us know what you liked about your stay and how we can improve.

Guest name: Jodi Marlow   **Contact:** j.marlow@viopind.com
Hotel location: Rinchey

Comments: I visited this hotel at the end of last month and was satisfied with my experience overall. At just over $70 a night, my room was a good deal. I especially want to express my appreciation for Ms. Freitas at the front desk. I had a minor medical issue during my stay, and she kindly helped me find a pharmacy with delivery service. However, there was one problem that I'd like to mention. Your Web site says that this hotel is five minutes from Royt Convention Center by shuttle, but my shuttle took nearly twenty-five minutes to get there. I don't think you should engage in that kind of false advertising.

```
┌──────────────────────────────────────────────────────────────────┐
│ ═══════════════════════ E-Mail message ═══════════════════════     │
│ ┌────────────────────────────────────────────────────────────────┐ │
│ From:      │  <august.blair@burristhotels.com>                     │
│ To:        │  <j.marlow@viopind.com>                               │
│ Subject:   │  Response to feedback                                 │
│ Date:      │  October 4                                            │
│ └────────────────────────────────────────────────────────────────┘ │
└──────────────────────────────────────────────────────────────────┘
```

Dear Ms. Marlow,

Thank you for taking the time to fill out the feedback form.

I would like to address the problem you raised. When you were here, the road our hotel is located on was actually being resurfaced. The work site was up the street, so you may not have noticed it. Because of the resulting closure, as well as all the one-way streets in Rinchey, the shuttle was required to take a long, circuitous route to the convention center. I am sorry that the shuttle driver did not explain this situation to you and the other passengers, and I hope it did not cause you too much inconvenience.

Also, thank you very much for sharing that story about Ms. Freitas. I will make a note of your praise in her employee file.

Please do not hesitate to contact me if I can be of further assistance.

Sincerely,

August Blair
Customer Service Associate, Burrist Hotel Rinchey

Test 4

---

186. Which type of room did Ms. Marlow most likely stay in?

(A) Single
(B) Double
(C) Deluxe Double
(D) Suite

187. What complaint does Ms. Marlow make?

(A) She was charged for a service she did not ask for.
(B) Information on the hotel's Web site was inaccurate.
(C) A transportation worker made a series of mistakes.
(D) The hotel did not have some basic medical supplies.

188. In the e-mail, the word "raised" in paragraph 2, line 1, is closest in meaning to

(A) increased
(B) pointed out
(C) cared for
(D) erected

189. What is most likely true about Drummond Street?

(A) It is always closed to vehicles on certain days of the week.
(B) It is the site of a large conference space.
(C) It recently underwent roadwork.
(D) It only allows traffic to move in one direction.

190. What does Mr. Blair indicate that he will write?

(A) A formal letter of apology to some guests
(B) An instructional memo for shuttle bus operators
(C) A positive message in a personnel record
(D) A warning notice to be posted on a Web page

GO ON TO THE NEXT PAGE

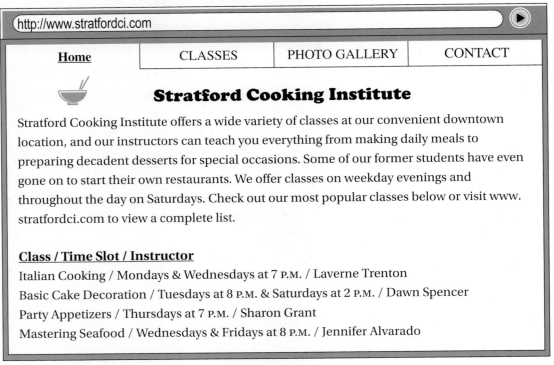

http://www.stratfordci.com

| **Home** | CLASSES | PHOTO GALLERY | CONTACT |

Stratford Cooking Institute

Stratford Cooking Institute offers a wide variety of classes at our convenient downtown location, and our instructors can teach you everything from making daily meals to preparing decadent desserts for special occasions. Some of our former students have even gone on to start their own restaurants. We offer classes on weekday evenings and throughout the day on Saturdays. Check out our most popular classes below or visit www.stratfordci.com to view a complete list.

Class / Time Slot / Instructor

Italian Cooking / Mondays & Wednesdays at 7 P.M. / Laverne Trenton

Basic Cake Decoration / Tuesdays at 8 P.M. & Saturdays at 2 P.M. / Dawn Spencer

Party Appetizers / Thursdays at 7 P.M. / Sharon Grant

Mastering Seafood / Wednesdays & Fridays at 8 P.M. / Jennifer Alvarado

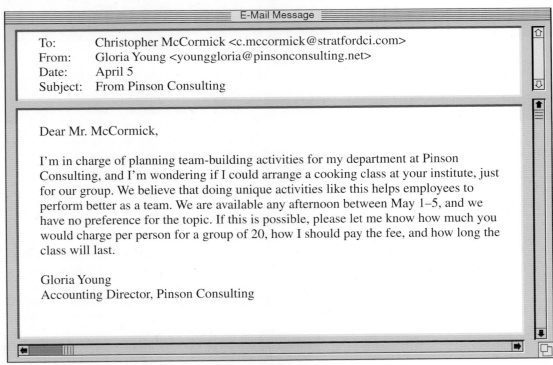

E-Mail Message

To:	Christopher McCormick <c.mccormick@stratfordci.com>
From:	Gloria Young <younggloria@pinsonconsulting.net>
Date:	April 5
Subject:	From Pinson Consulting

Dear Mr. McCormick,

I'm in charge of planning team-building activities for my department at Pinson Consulting, and I'm wondering if I could arrange a cooking class at your institute, just for our group. We believe that doing unique activities like this helps employees to perform better as a team. We are available any afternoon between May 1–5, and we have no preference for the topic. If this is possible, please let me know how much you would charge per person for a group of 20, how I should pay the fee, and how long the class will last.

Gloria Young
Accounting Director, Pinson Consulting

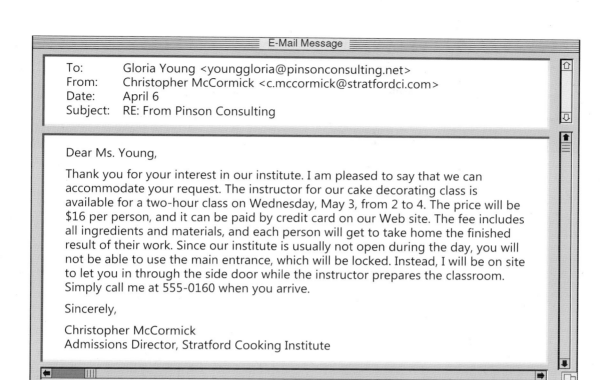

E-Mail Message

To: Gloria Young <younggloria@pinsonconsulting.net>
From: Christopher McCormick <c.mccormick@stratfordci.com>
Date: April 6
Subject: RE: From Pinson Consulting

Dear Ms. Young,

Thank you for your interest in our institute. I am pleased to say that we can accommodate your request. The instructor for our cake decorating class is available for a two-hour class on Wednesday, May 3, from 2 to 4. The price will be $16 per person, and it can be paid by credit card on our Web site. The fee includes all ingredients and materials, and each person will get to take home the finished result of their work. Since our institute is usually not open during the day, you will not be able to use the main entrance, which will be locked. Instead, I will be on site to let you in through the side door while the instructor prepares the classroom. Simply call me at 555-0160 when you arrive.

Sincerely,

Christopher McCormick
Admissions Director, Stratford Cooking Institute

191. What is mentioned about the Stratford Cooking Institute?

(A) It is the most popular institute of its kind.
(B) It conducts classes seven days a week.
(C) It is affiliated with a restaurant.
(D) It is located in the city center.

192. What is the purpose of Ms. Young's e-mail?

(A) To organize a private class
(B) To request a group discount
(C) To accept an invitation
(D) To confirm changes to a plan

193. In the first e-mail, the word "perform" in paragraph 1, line 4, is closest in meaning to

(A) observe
(B) achieve
(C) entertain
(D) function

194. What information does Mr. McCormick give that was NOT requested by Ms. Young?

(A) The duration of the class
(B) The cost per person
(C) The payment method
(D) The entrance to use

195. Who most likely will teach a daytime class on May 3?

(A) Ms. Trenton
(B) Ms. Spencer
(C) Ms. Grant
(D) Ms. Alvarado

GO ON TO THE NEXT PAGE

Questions 196-200 refer to the following report, e-mail, and article.

Energy Efficiency Audit Overview: Sternberg Manufacturing
Conducted by Mistral Energy Services (MES), September 4

An energy efficiency audit was carried out by the MES team at the Sternberg Manufacturing site in Bedford. This site was chosen among Sternberg's thirteen facilities throughout the country because it was the first factory built for Sternberg Manufacturing and has the most potential for improvement.

Five optimization opportunities were identified, and concrete suggestions were formulated for each. First, solar panels from Perales Co. should be added to sections of the rooftop to generate sustainable energy that could be used on site or sold back to the grid. Second, the packaging equipment should be replaced with energy-efficient machines designed by Forsyth, Inc. Third, skylights should be installed by Verne Enterprises to provide free natural light. Fourth, the exterior walls should be insulated by Webster Construction to reduce heat loss. Finally, employees should undergo training provided by Sternberg itself to learn about ways they can contribute to a reduction in energy usage.

E-mail

To:	Debra Lyon <d.lyon@sternbergmfg.com>
From:	Mitchell Thorpe <m.thorpe@sternbergmfg.com>
Date:	September 20
Subject:	Upcoming training

Dear Ms. Lyon,

I have reviewed the training proposals presented by the various shift managers, and I believe that your training would be the most suitable for the company's needs. The handouts you prepared highlight our goals clearly, and they will help employees to see exactly what needs to be done. We've tried other initiatives for energy conservation in the past, but despite these measures, the ratio of power consumed by non-core tasks still holds steady at 24%, which is above the industry average. By working together, I hope we can reduce this figure.

Sincerely,

Mitchell Thorpe

120

Sternberg Manufacturing Monthly Newsletter
October Edition

New Energy Conservation Efforts Underway

Sternberg Manufacturing is seeking to reduce its energy usage both to cut overhead expenses and to reduce the company's environmental impact. Based on recommendations made by Mistral Energy Services (MES) last month, the company will undertake four major projects. The first among them is scheduled to be carried out by Webster Construction in November. The others will follow next year, as funding allows. In addition, the human resources director has chosen Debra Lyon to administer employee training regarding conservation techniques. A schedule for the training has not been set yet.

196. Why was Sternberg Manufacturing's Bedford location selected for the audit?

(A) It received a high inspection score.
(B) It is the company's oldest facility.
(C) It is close to the headquarters of MES.
(D) It is the company's largest building.

197. What will be installed in November?

(A) Solar panels
(B) New packaging equipment
(C) Skylights
(D) Wall insulation

198. What is indicated about Ms. Lyon's training materials?

(A) They were the only ones submitted.
(B) They should be shortened.
(C) They are easy to understand.
(D) They contain a lot of technical information.

199. In the e-mail, the word "holds" in paragraph 1, line 6, is closest in meaning to

(A) arranges
(B) grasps
(C) remains
(D) occupies

200. What is implied about Mr. Thorpe?

(A) He will send Ms. Lyon some guidelines.
(B) He recommended hiring MES.
(C) He is the head of Human Resources.
(D) He plans to visit Sternberg Manufacturing's other sites.

Stop! This is the end of the test. If you finish before time is called, you may go back to Parts 5, 6, and 7 and check your work.

TEST 5

READING TEST

In the Reading test, you will read a variety of texts and answer several different types of reading comprehension questions. The entire Reading test will last 75 minutes. There are three parts, and directions are given for each part. You are encouraged to answer as many questions as possible within the time allowed.

You must mark your answers on the separate answer sheet. Do not write your answers in your test book.

PART 5

Directions: A word or phrase is missing in each of the sentences below. Four answer choices are given below each sentence. Select the best answer to complete the sentence. Then mark the letter (A), (B), (C), or (D) on your answer sheet.

101. Health benefits, vacation time, and bonus payments ------- employees to work hard.

    (A) to encourage
    (B) encouraging
    (C) are encouraged
    (D) encourage

102. Orders placed ------- 5:00 P.M. will be processed the next business day.

    (A) into
    (B) after
    (C) between
    (D) on

103. Though Ms. Klein stepped down two months ago, Gondol Industries has not ------- named a new finance director.

    (A) yet
    (B) much
    (C) always
    (D) either

104. The annual report should explain the lack of ------- made toward reaching our energy saving goals.

    (A) progress
    (B) progressively
    (C) progressive
    (D) progressed

105. It has been confirmed that Whistan Enterprises will ------- a new CEO to lead the business through its upcoming merger.

    (A) decide
    (B) assemble
    (C) establish
    (D) appoint

106. Yesterday's scheduled broadcast of *Chatting with Donna* was postponed ------- the preceding program ran over its time.

    (A) due to
    (B) because
    (C) following
    (D) by

107. Ms. Shim is our official spokesperson, so any media inquiries should be passed on to ------- immediately.

    (A) herself
    (B) her
    (C) hers
    (D) she

108. Making timely deliveries will require ------- efforts on the parts of the production and distribution teams.

    (A) cooperatively
    (B) cooperates
    (C) cooperator
    (D) cooperative

109. Several unsuccessful ------- were made to deliver the package to its intended recipient.

(A) receipts
(B) conclusions
(C) opportunities
(D) attempts

110. The best way to handle a ------- client is to apologize and assure them that you will take action to remedy the problem.

(A) disappoint
(B) disappointed
(C) disappointingly
(D) disappointment

111. The survey showed that managers would choose to open stores earlier in the morning ------- close them later at night.

(A) rather than
(B) in spite of
(C) regarding
(D) whereas

112. Please inform the staff that we will become fully ------- once we finish updating our equipment.

(A) operate
(B) operational
(C) operation
(D) operated

113. When searching for work, do not ------- for a position until you have researched the company offering it.

(A) submit
(B) approve
(C) consider
(D) apply

114. Be sure to respond ------- to complaints and address them in a professional manner.

(A) rarely
(B) namely
(C) promptly
(D) heavily

115. The number of laws regulating the travel industry has increased ------- over the past decade, particularly in relation to safety.

(A) dramatic
(B) dramatize
(C) dramatized
(D) dramatically

116. The X-R70 Thermometer, which is ------- to even slight changes in temperature, is a must-have item for laboratories.

(A) committed
(B) impressive
(C) perceptive
(D) sensitive

117. Save 5% on every delivery order from Greg's Green Grocer ------- by registering for our customer loyalty program.

(A) simplicity
(B) simplify
(C) simpler
(D) simply

118. If we leave the office at noon, we ------- at the station in plenty of time to catch the train to Chicago.

(A) would have arrived
(B) arrived
(C) will arrive
(D) arriving

119. Zantmarket.com shoppers can now see their past purchases ------- the new "My History" section of their accounts.

(A) in
(B) among
(C) except
(D) of

120. At the New England campus, international student ------- has risen over the last few years.

(A) enrollment
(B) enrolls
(C) enroll
(D) enrolled

GO ON TO THE NEXT PAGE

121. For a variety of reasons, detailed statistics on tourists and other visitors from abroad are ------- on a regular basis.

    (A) compiled
    (B) undergone
    (C) attracted
    (D) convened

122. Ever since Mr. Ka has become head of marketing, the company's revenues have grown at a ------- of nearly 10% per quarter.

    (A) rate
    (B) height
    (C) measurement
    (D) figure

123. The clients ------- with the architect's final sketches and would like to begin construction right away.

    (A) were satisfying
    (B) satisfied
    (C) were satisfied
    (D) had satisfied

124. ------- you are not attending the conference, the manager would still like you to help your team with its preparations for the event.

    (A) Whether
    (B) Even if
    (C) Before
    (D) As soon as

125. Scholars found that a direct ------- of the text from Chinese to English resulted in a loss of the author's intentions.

    (A) translatable
    (B) translate
    (C) translation
    (D) translated

126. The free seven-day trial period is a one-time offer available ------- to new customers of Cypress TV.

    (A) expensively
    (B) thoroughly
    (C) exclusively
    (D) respectively

127. Meeting participants will be asked to discuss ------- they find inconvenient about the current time sheet system.

    (A) anything
    (B) especially
    (C) where
    (D) many

128. Rayo Hotel is perfect for those who want affordable accommodations just minutes ------- the beach.

    (A) further
    (B) besides
    (C) away from
    (D) as far

129. The seller, Ms. Thompson, ------- agreed to accept a lower offer on the house since it had been on the market for a long time.

    (A) fluently
    (B) adversely
    (C) reluctantly
    (D) unanimously

130. The play features ------- costumes that must have taken its crew weeks of painstaking work to create.

    (A) vigorous
    (B) courteous
    (C) elaborate
    (D) eventful

PART 6

Directions: Read the texts that follow. A word, phrase, or sentence is missing in parts of each text. Four answer choices for each question are given below the text. Select the best answer to complete the text. Then mark the letter (A), (B), (C), or (D) on your answer sheet.

Questions 131-134 refer to the following information.

Thank you for purchasing a Renaust electric beard trimmer. To begin using your new trimmer, remove the ------- plastic coating that covers the blade. If you purchased the Renaust Deluxe
          131.
Toiletries package, your trimmer came pre-loaded with two AA batteries. If you did not, you must

insert such batteries into the ------- at the back of the device.
                              132.

Make sure to clean the trimmer after each use. -------. Also, store the device in a dry place and -------
                                               133.   134.
children from playing with it. Following these instructions will keep your trimmer in good condition for

many years.

131. (A) protector
     (B) protections
     (C) protective
     (D) protectively

132. (A) warranty
     (B) description
     (C) power
     (D) compartment

133. (A) Your request will be processed
         immediately.
     (B) The diagram below depicts other popular
         styles.
     (C) After all, coating made from paper is more
         eco-friendly.
     (D) The provided brush can remove hair from
         the blades.

134. (A) prohibit
     (B) is prohibiting
     (C) prohibited
     (D) will prohibit

Questions 135-138 refer to the following letter.

April 22

Dear Mr. Fred,

Congratulations on opening your new restaurant, Schnitzels & Such! Now that you are a Humbont County business owner, I would like to ------ invite you to join the Humbont County Chamber of
135.
Commerce (HCCOC). The HCCOC was founded 82 years ago to promote the county's business interests. ------.
136.

Our organization ------ local businesses in several ways. For example, members benefit from
137.
community exposure in our monthly newsletter. ------, they receive invitations to participate in
138.
community events. To learn more, please visit our headquarters on Lehman Street or our Web site at www.hccoc.com.

Sincerely,

Susan Cain
Humbont County Chamber of Commerce

135. (A) formal
(B) formally
(C) formalize
(D) formality

136. (A) Thank you for serving on our advisory
board.
(B) We have been striving to fulfill this aim
ever since.
(C) Therefore, we have decided to host a food
festival.
(D) Each of our members must agree to these
rules.

137. (A) assists
(B) investigates
(C) reorganizes
(D) surpasses

138. (A) However
(B) In addition
(C) In contrast
(D) Originally

---

http://www.lattlerapparel.com/recycling

Lattler Apparel

Clothing Recycling Program

Contributing to the sustainability of the fashion industry is one of Lattler Apparel's ------- objectives.
139.
This is why we are proud to operate a clothing recycling program in ------- with Dilline Services.
140.
Under this program, customers can drop off their used Lattler clothing at any of our stores. Dilline
Services then collects the items and sorts them according to their condition. Garments with relatively
little wear or damage ------- to secondhand stores for resale. At the same time, recycling plants turn
141.
the rest into textile fibers. -------. Lattler Apparel customers can thus be sure that their unwanted
142.
clothes will continue to be useful to other consumers in the future.

---

139. (A) prime
(B) fragile
(C) remote
(D) eligible

140. (A) impact
(B) authority
(C) supplement
(D) conjunction

141. (A) were distributed
(B) are distributed
(C) distributing
(D) distribute

142. (A) The recycling method varies depending on the material.
(B) Then, place your unwanted clothes in the green bin by the door.
(C) These can be used to make products like furniture padding.
(D) We are currently preparing to build a new one outside of Toronto.

GO ON TO THE NEXT PAGE

Questions 143-146 refer to the following e-mail.

From: Dorothy Squires
To: Rudy Nakayama
Subject: Revised lobby design
Date: September 17
Attachments: Set A, Set B

Dear Rudy,

I have attached two sets of mock-ups of the revised design for your lobby. ------. In both sets, I have
143.
added the seating you asked for and replaced the light fixtures with less noticeable options.

You will also find that in Set B, I did not change the flooring ------ you requested. To ------, the
144.   145.
original flooring seems much more suited to the lobby's overall design. I will, of course, accept your
decision, but I urge you to compare the two sets carefully when you make it.

We are scheduled to finish the design phase of this project on September 20. I hope you will get
back to me by ------.
146.

Thanks,

Dorothy Squires
Squires Interior Design

143. (A) You will see that most of the issues you
        raised have been resolved.
    (B) The renovation process may be frustrating
        for your staff and clients.
    (C) It has caused the building to become a
        local architectural landmark.
    (D) There are extra designs on the "Portfolio"
        page of my Web site.

144. (A) so
    (B) as
    (C) what
    (D) beyond

145. (A) them
    (B) him
    (C) her
    (D) me

146. (A) quickly
    (B) such
    (C) far
    (D) then

Directions: In this part you will read a selection of texts, such as magazine and newspaper articles, e-mails, and instant messages. Each text or set of texts is followed by several questions. Select the best answer for each question and mark the letter (A), (B), (C), or (D) on your answer sheet.

Questions 147-148 refer to the following memo.

MEMORANDUM

CONWAY ACCOUNTING

TO: All staff
FROM: Sandra Bruna, Director
DATE: January 4
RE: January 12 closure

The city is conducting repairs on our water lines next Tuesday, and instead of asking everyone to avoid using water that day, the office will close. As far as pay is concerned, this will be treated like a regular day of work. You will not be called upon to work from home, unless you are working on a deadline-driven project. In particular, the team leaders working on the Akins account should complete and e-mail me their reports—I need them Wednesday morning before the conference.

Sandra Bruna

---

147. Why will the office close on Tuesday?

(A) Work on the Akins account has been completed.
(B) A city celebration will cause some disruptions.
(C) Employees will go to a conference.
(D) Some pipes require maintenance.

148. What does Ms. Bruna ask some team leaders to do?

(A) Discourage water usage
(B) Issue paychecks early
(C) Send her an e-mail
(D) Lock the office doors

GO ON TO THE NEXT PAGE

Carluzzi's Diner

55 51st Street, New York City, NY 10019

Come to Carluzzi's Diner to enjoy rich, authentic Italian cuisine.
Whether it's freshly baked garlic bread, pasta with olive oil, or our thin crust pizza,
our dishes feature flavors straight from Napoli!
Our lunch menu includes specials on classic deli sandwiches.

Tuesday Special! Save money on drinks and desserts!
All large-size beverages are just $1 and all dessert combination plates are just $3.
Kids ages six and under eat for free!

Lunch
11:00 A.M. to 3:00 P.M.

Dinner
4:00 P.M. to 10:00 P.M.
(We are closed between 3:00 P.M. and 4:00 P.M.)

"Tastes like my grandma's cooking... 4/5 stars!"
- Nicole Rossi, writer for the famous food blog *Taste of New York*

For dinner reservations, please call:
202-555-0189

149. What can customers do only once a week?

(A) Order a dessert for free
(B) Pay a lower price for beverages
(C) Make a reservation for dinner
(D) Get a private dining room

150. What is mentioned about the restaurant by a reviewer?

(A) It imports ingredients from Italy.
(B) Its deli sandwiches are custom-made.
(C) Its dishes are prepared quickly.
(D) Its food tastes homemade.

Questions 151-152 refer to the following text-message chain.

Julie Bayu   1:34 P.M.
Sorry that I missed your call, but it's too loud to talk anyway. Are you almost here? The game is in the second inning, and you've already missed a home run.

Hank Lowe   1:38 P.M.
I just arrived at the stadium. There's a lot of traffic today! It looks like there are several entrance gates. Which one should I go to?

Julie Bayu   1:39 P.M.
You have your ticket, right?

Hank Lowe   1:40 P.M.
Oh, I see. OK, I'll be there in a few minutes. Want anything from the snack bar? I'm going to get a hot dog.

Send

151. Where most likely is Ms. Bayu?

(A) On a bus tour
(B) In an art gallery
(C) At a sporting event
(D) At an outdoor concert

152. At 1:39 P.M., what does Ms. Bayu most likely mean when she writes, "You have your ticket, right"?

(A) Mr. Lowe should keep his ticket as a souvenir.
(B) Mr. Lowe bought his ticket himself.
(C) The ticket can be used to get a discount.
(D) The ticket contains some useful information.

GO ON TO THE NEXT PAGE

Test 5

Questions 153-155 refer to the following information.

Alppit Industries

Chef's Mate 480

Alppit Industries' new Chef's Mate 480 meat thermometer and kitchen timer consists of a sharp, six-inch probe attached to a sturdy electronic base unit by a long mesh cable. At $18.99, it's a gourmet-quality product at fast food prices!

Features:

 ◆ Measures temperatures between -50 and 300 degrees Celsius (°C)

 ◆ Offers pre-set recommended temperatures for common types of meat

 ◆ Base unit's large LCD display allows for easy reading

 ◆ Timer can count down from or up to 50 hours

 ◆ Probe and cable can withstand temperatures of up to 380 °C

 ◆ Runs for weeks powered by just one AAA battery

153. What is one function of the Chef's Mate 480?

 (A) Keeping track of time
 (B) Warming up food
 (C) Sharpening cooking tools
 (D) Improving kitchen sanitation

154. What is indicated about the Chef's Mate 480's cable?

 (A) It supplies power to the base unit.
 (B) It can endure intense heat.
 (C) It is removable.
 (D) Its length can be adjusted.

Questions 156-157 refer to the following schedule.

5th Annual American Hospitality Association (AHA) Workshop in Mason

Aldrich Convention Center – May 23

Session	Topic
9:30 A.M. – 10:45 A.M.	Using New Technology – Learn about the latest gadgets, including tablet computers that can be used for taking orders.
11:00 A.M. – 12:00 P.M.	Maintaining Your Appearance – As a member of the service industry, it is important to look professional. Learn how to look your best at all times.
1:30 P.M. – 3:15 P.M.	Dealing with Customers – Find out how to speak to dissatisfied customers. Topics will include explaining issues clearly and suggesting solutions.
3:30 P.M. – 4:45 P.M.	Speeding Up Service – Learn how to serve diners more quickly without lowering the standard of service.

Attendees should present their registration receipts upon arrival at the convention center in order to receive a token that can be redeemed for lunch in the cafeteria during the break. Parking is available on a first-come, first-served basis. Additional parking spaces may be found in the nearby Willis Shopping Mall parking area.

Please visit www.masonaha.com/workshop/info for further information.

155. For whom is the workshop most likely intended?

(A) Hotel clerks
(B) Transportation workers
(C) Clothing store staff
(D) Restaurant employees

156. When will workshop attendees learn about communication skills?

(A) At 9:30 A.M.
(B) At 11:00 A.M.
(C) At 1:30 P.M.
(D) At 3:30 P.M.

157. What is stated about the workshop?

(A) Attendees will need a parking permit.
(B) A meal will be provided to attendees.
(C) Its schedule may be changed.
(D) It will take place in a shopping mall.

Test 5

City Provides Loan for Expansion of Dorry's Fashions

MEARA—The City of Meara has made a loan available to Dorry's Fashions as part of its Business Development Loan Program. The new loan will allow Dorry's to create two new jobs, expand their production capacity, and increase sales.

Dorry's has become famous in Meara and surrounding areas for its elegant women's blouses, skirts, and dresses. — [1] —. Owner Dorry Saunders, who started the business two years ago, is a graduate of Vanden Fashion Institute. She expressed gratitude for the loan and said it would be used to buy machinery and hire a dressmaking assistant and a salesperson, bringing the number of store employees up to five. — [2] —. "It's going to allow me to spend more time on design and get clothes into the store more quickly," she explained.

Business Development Loan Program official Bart Southcott said, "We feel that Dorry's Fashions has the potential to become a valuable part of the Meara business community. — [3] —. If the results of this project are as outstanding as we expect, the next step could be another loan to facilitate large-scale manufacturing of the clothing by contracting with a factory." He added that the program is seeking additional recipients for the current year and asked those interested to contact him at 555-0175. — [4] —.

158. What is indicated about Ms. Saunders?

(A) She grew up in Meara.
(B) She specializes in menswear.
(C) She has studied fashion academically.
(D) She is currently the store's only staff member.

159. What does Mr. Southcott say a future loan might be used for?

(A) Purchasing real estate for a new retail location
(B) Increasing the scale of marketing campaigns
(C) Hiring a mass production facility
(D) Creating and maintaining an online shop

160. In which of the positions marked [1], [2], [3], and [4] does the following sentence best belong?

"Designed and made in-house, these items are prized for their unique style."

(A) [1]
(B) [2]
(C) [3]
(D) [4]

Questions 161-163 refer to the following e-mail.

```
═══════════════════ E-Mail message ═══════════════════
From:      Hisoka Ito <hisoka@me-zoom.com>

To:        Rosen County Animal Protection Society <contact@rcaps.org>

Subject:   Web site problem

Date:      July 30
```

Hi,

I'm writing to report a problem with your Web site. I want to contribute to your fund-raising drive to buy care supplies for animals, so I went to the RCAPS site and clicked the link for it. On the next page, I provided all the requested payment details in the boxes. But when I clicked "Submit," the sentence "Missing required information" appeared in red next to several of the boxes. I reloaded the page and reentered my information, but the same thing happened again.

I was very moved by the poster for your drive that I saw in my veterinarian's office, and I would really like to be a part of it. I hope you can get this problem fixed soon.

Sincerely,

Hisoka Ito

161. Why did Mr. Ito visit RCAPS's Web site?

(A) To donate to a charity effort
(B) To subscribe to a mailing list
(C) To learn about volunteer opportunities
(D) To read evaluations of pet care supplies

162. What problem did Mr. Ito encounter?

(A) A computer program's sudden shutdown
(B) A link to an unavailable Web page
(C) Slow uploading speeds
(D) Inaccurate error messages

163. What is indicated about RCAPS?

(A) It is a branch of a national organization.
(B) It advertises at a medical clinic for animals.
(C) It recently moved into a new office building.
(D) It gives out posters as thank-you gifts.

GO ON TO THE NEXT PAGE

TEST 5   **137**

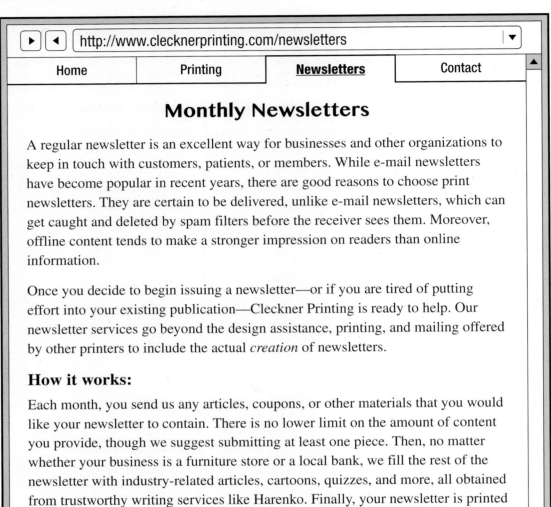

http://www.clecknerprinting.com/newsletters

| Home | Printing | **Newsletters** | Contact |

Monthly Newsletters

A regular newsletter is an excellent way for businesses and other organizations to keep in touch with customers, patients, or members. While e-mail newsletters have become popular in recent years, there are good reasons to choose print newsletters. They are certain to be delivered, unlike e-mail newsletters, which can get caught and deleted by spam filters before the receiver sees them. Moreover, offline content tends to make a stronger impression on readers than online information.

Once you decide to begin issuing a newsletter—or if you are tired of putting effort into your existing publication—Cleckner Printing is ready to help. Our newsletter services go beyond the design assistance, printing, and mailing offered by other printers to include the actual *creation* of newsletters.

How it works:

Each month, you send us any articles, coupons, or other materials that you would like your newsletter to contain. There is no lower limit on the amount of content you provide, though we suggest submitting at least one piece. Then, no matter whether your business is a furniture store or a local bank, we fill the rest of the newsletter with industry-related articles, cartoons, quizzes, and more, all obtained from trustworthy writing services like Harenko. Finally, your newsletter is printed on high-quality paper and mailed out on the date you specify.

164. What is mentioned about e-mail newsletters?

(A) They are inexpensive.
(B) They can be distributed quickly.
(C) They may not display correctly when opened.
(D) They may not reach the intended recipients.

165. According to the Web page, how is Cleckner Printing different from its competitors?

(A) It uses special paper.
(B) It offers an extra service.
(C) It has a physical store.
(D) It charges fewer fees.

166. What type of business is Harenko in?

(A) Print
(B) Finance
(C) Content creation
(D) Stationery manufacturing

167. What is NOT suggested as an activity that a newsletter recipient could do?

(A) Enter a mail-in contest
(B) Take a short written test
(C) Redeem a discount voucher
(D) Enjoy humorous drawings

GO ON TO THE NEXT PAGE

Test 5

Questions **168-171** refer to the following online chat discussion.

👤 **Abrival Company Messenger**

Sofia Alvelo [9:40 A.M.]   Does anybody know where Stanley is? He's not answering his phone.

Duane Sibley [9:42 A.M.]   Oh, he had to take some time off to help his mother. She's having some health problems.

Sofia Alvelo [9:43 A.M.]   I'm sorry to hear that. Do you know when he'll be back? An issue has come up with Zamexon, Inc.

Anwei Chao [9:44 A.M.]   He'll be away at least until May 14, but I've been put in charge of many of his tasks. What's going on?

Duane Sibley [9:44 A.M.]   I don't know anything about Zamexon. I'll leave you two to it.

<Duane Sibley has exited the chat room.>

Sofia Alvelo [9:45 A.M.]   I got word from Zamexon that another company has offered a bigger contract for the time period that we're hoping to reserve.

Anwei Chao [9:46 A.M.]   So they want to take the other company's offer?

Sofia Alvelo [9:47 A.M.]   Right. I need to know if we can make a higher offer or not. If we can do it, we should, because it would be difficult for us to find another manufacturer at this stage.

Anwei Chao [9:48 A.M.]   I'll have to look over the budget.

Sofia Alvelo [9:49 A.M.]   OK, but I think we should hurry before their deal with the other company is finalized. Could you get back to me with your conclusions by the end of the day?

Anwei Chao [9:50 A.M.]   I'll do my best.

[   ] **SEND**

---

168. What does Mr. Sibley mention that Stanley is doing?

(A) Taking a vacation abroad
(B) Caring for a family member
(C) Attending a training program
(D) Visiting potential clients

169. Why does Mr. Sibley most likely leave the chat room?

(A) He is not involved in the issue being discussed.
(B) He will bring some materials to Ms. Alvelo.
(C) He is already aware of some news.
(D) He must make a phone call to Stanley.

170. What is implied about Zamexon, Inc.?

(A) It is based in another country.
(B) It has finalized a deal with Abrival.
(C) It will make a decision on May 14.
(D) It is a manufacturing company.

171. At 9:48 A.M., what does Ms. Chao most likely mean when she writes, "I'll have to look over the budget"?

(A) She cannot answer a question right now.
(B) She thinks some calculations may be incorrect.
(C) Ms. Alvelo is not qualified to perform a task.
(D) Ms. Alvelo should start a meeting without her.

GO ON TO THE NEXT PAGE

==================== E-Mail message ====================

From:	Sasha Woods <sasha.woods@yoplexholdings.com>
To:	All employees
Date:	April 9
Subject:	Social media policy

Because of recent issues caused by violations of our social media policy, Yoplex Holdings would like to refresh employees' memory about its main points. Please read the following carefully. — [1] —.

- The term "social media" here refers to blogs, message boards, chat rooms, social networking sites, and similar sites and services.
- When using social media in reference to the company, employees must adhere to the codes of conduct set out in the <u>Employee Handbook</u>. — [2] —.
- Yoplex may seek out writings and images that employees have made public on social media in order to ensure that they are not harmful to the company. — [3] —.
- Do not disclose confidential information about company procedures, clients, finances, etc.
- Company duties must take priority over social media usage during working hours. Spending more than a few minutes of company time per day on such activities is unwise.
- In the case that a social media interaction related to the company turns into a conflict, disengage from the situation and notify the Public Relations department. Any inquiries received through social media about the company should also be referred there. — [4] —.

The full list of rules can be seen <u>here</u>. Failure to follow them may result in penalties being imposed by management.

You may contact me by e-mail if you have any questions about these points. Thank you.

Sincerely,

Sasha Woods
Human Resources Coordinator

172. Why was this e-mail sent?

(A) Some rules have not been followed.
(B) Some changes have been made to the policy.
(C) A similar e-mail is sent each year at this time.
(D) The information was requested by employees.

173. What is NOT one of the directives given to employees?

(A) Do not reveal company secrets.
(B) Never use social media in the workplace.
(C) Pass on inquiries received to publicity specialists.
(D) Comply with general Employee Handbook guidelines.

174. Why would an employee most likely contact Ms. Woods?

(A) To report a conflict on a social media site
(B) To obtain the complete list of rules
(C) To dispute a previous penalty
(D) To ask for clarification about the policy

175. In which of the positions marked [1], [2], [3], and [4] does the following sentence best belong?

"If such material is found, the employee may be asked to delete it."

(A) [1]
(B) [2]
(C) [3]
(D) [4]

Questions 176-180 refer to the following notice and form.

Ranch Hands Seeks Tasters

Ranch Hands Food Company, famous for its delicious cooking ingredients, will enter the frozen foods market in the first quarter of next year. Ranch Hands is looking for groups to give feedback on the flavor and palatability of new ready-to-eat meals. The meals should appeal to adults and teenagers, so a family of 3 to 4 people with teenage children would be an ideal test group. If you would like to apply, please contact the customer outreach coordinator, Rick Malone, at (270) 555-0165. He will give you an application form to fill out and conduct a brief interview. Applicants who subscribe to our weekly newsletter will automatically be entered into a drawing for $100 in Ranch Hands gift certificates.

- The tasting will be at the Ranch Hands satellite facility on Winthrop Lane.
- The tasting will take one hour.
- The tasting will be videotaped.
- The videotape might be used for promotional purposes.

Tasting Group Application

Group affiliation:
We are in a marketing class together at Green Back University.

Group members:

Name	Age	Occupation
Pika Kualana	*29*	*Graduate student*
Evelyn Ra	*31*	*Graduate student*
Marina Lyubov	*24*	*Research Assistant*
Dinh Thanh	*41*	*Professor*

Do you eat Ranch Hands foods regularly? If yes, how frequently?
Yes, about twice a week

Contact information:
Phone   *(270) 555-0106*
E-mail   *kualana@greenbackuniversity.edu*
Address   *111 Davies St., Owensboro, KY 42303*

Would you like to receive our weekly newsletter at the provided mailing address?
☑ Yes   ☐ No

176. What most likely is a featured aspect of the food products being tested?

(A) Their inexpensive price
(B) Their unusual flavor
(C) Their healthiness
(D) Their convenience

177. In the notice, the word "conduct" in paragraph 1, line 7, is closest in meaning to

(A) hold
(B) steer
(C) transmit
(D) collect

178. What is true about the tasting?

(A) It will take an entire evening to finish.
(B) It will be at a corporate headquarters.
(C) It will be recorded for advertisements.
(D) It will gather data for a university.

179. Why would Mr. Kualana's application most likely be rejected?

(A) All of the members of his group are adults.
(B) A member of his group has worked for Ranch Hands.
(C) Some members of his group have food allergies.
(D) His group does not have enough members.

180. What is suggested about Mr. Kualana?

(A) He has never eaten Ranch Hands food.
(B) He will be registered in a lottery for gift cards.
(C) He is a research assistant in an academic program.
(D) He has participated in tasting tests before.

Test 5

From:	Shirley Hill
To:	Randall Kwak
Subject:	Checking in
Date:	November 6

Hi Randall,

I hope you're enjoying your time off. Here's what's going on at the shop:

First, we've gotten a few more e-mail applications for the junior technician position. I'll print them out and leave them in a folder on your desk for you to look at on Monday.

Second, I'm ordering some supplies from Irving Wholesale Auto Supply tomorrow morning. We're running out of polishing pads and lens repair tape. And I'm going to get a bottle of that environmentally-friendly cleaner you heard about so that we can try it out. Is there anything else we need? You know Irving stocks almost anything you could want. If so, let me know by the end of the day.

Shirley Hill
Office Manager
Sandiston Auto Repair

Irving Wholesale Auto Supply

4200 Rowell Drive
Plaskin, NC 27009
www.irving-was.com

INVOICE

Customer: Sandiston Auto Repair
Account #: 340691
Billing/Shipping address: 460 Palmer Street
Sandiston, MO 63030

Order #: 12773
Order date: November 7
Estimated ship date: November 9
Payment due: December 6

Item #	Description	Quantity	Unit Price	Amount
T3207	Auto lens repair tape	2 cases	$16.00	$32.00
F1843	Grease removal fluid	1 bottle	$35.00	$35.00
M6215	No-slip floor mat	1 item	$57.00	$57.00
P5033	Polishing pads	5 packs	$28.00	$140.00
Notes: As you requested, all of your items will be grouped into a single shipment. Note that this may result in a delay.			Subtotal	$264.00
			Tax	$18.48
			Shipping	$13.20
			Total	**$295.68**

181. What is one purpose of the e-mail?

(A) To give some updates
(B) To make some comparisons
(C) To point out a personnel problem
(D) To request repair advice

182. According to the e-mail, what will Mr. Kwak have access to on Monday?

(A) An electronic device
(B) A desk calendar
(C) Some documents
(D) Some sample goods

183. What does Ms. Hill indicate about Irving Wholesale Auto Supply?

(A) It was first recommended to her by a friend.
(B) It has been in business for many years.
(C) It offers an expedited shipping option.
(D) It sells a wide selection of products.

184. Which product is Sandiston Auto Repair most likely ordering for the first time?

(A) T3207
(B) F1843
(C) M6215
(D) P5033

185. What is mentioned in the invoice about the order?

(A) All of the items in it will be sent at the same time.
(B) It will be paid for via automatic bank transfer.
(C) It was taxed more heavily than previous orders.
(D) Some of the items in it cannot be returned.

GO ON TO THE NEXT PAGE

www.gerarduniversity.edu/facultyprofiles

Faculty

Annabelle Parker is a visiting professor at Gerard University. She received a BS in Computer Science at Port Bright College and an MBA at Knightstown School of Business.

Ms. Parker is the current CEO of Spiegel Technologies. She started working there seventeen years ago in the product development department. Since becoming CEO, she is credited with steadily increasing Spiegel's revenue and making it one of the most popular and trusted technology companies in the nation.

Prior to joining Spiegel, Ms. Parker worked at the San Francisco-based Stamos and Company. She was in charge of creating many of the company's computer software programs. She also started its internship program, Excel Entrepreneurs Program (EEP). It runs every summer and helps students learn about the technology industry from actual Stamos and Company employees.

Ms. Parker will teach a twelve-week course called "The Digital Age" in the upcoming fall semester. The course will be open to master's program students only.

Gerard University Newsletter

December 28—Annabelle Parker's long list of impressive job titles, which includes CEO, has now expanded to include one more—visiting professor.

Ms. Parker taught a course at Gerard this past semester based on her early career at Stamos and Company. She explained the different aspects of making computer software programs, such as brainstorming and evaluating ideas, working collaboratively with other people, overcoming technical limitations, and more.

Ms. Parker also gave advice and inspiration to her students. One student explained, "She shared some of the trials and hardships she faced when she first started her career. It was really encouraging to know she overcame the same struggles I'm dealing with today."

So will Ms. Parker teach another class? Although she has no immediate plans to return, she says not to rule it out.

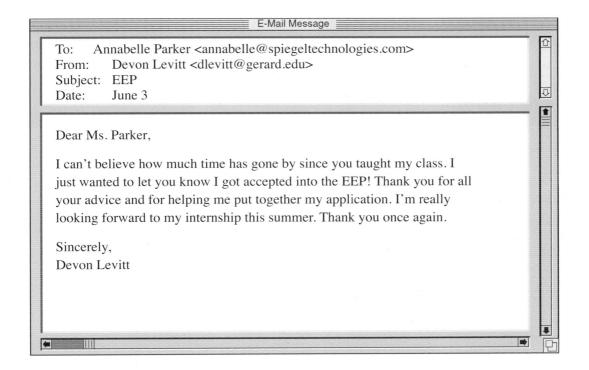

E-Mail Message

To: Annabelle Parker <annabelle@spiegeltechnologies.com>
From: Devon Levitt <dlevitt@gerard.edu>
Subject: EEP
Date: June 3

Dear Ms. Parker,

I can't believe how much time has gone by since you taught my class. I just wanted to let you know I got accepted into the EEP! Thank you for all your advice and for helping me put together my application. I'm really looking forward to my internship this summer. Thank you once again.

Sincerely,
Devon Levitt

186. What is indicated about Ms. Parker?

(A) She completed a summer internship.
(B) She oversaw the merger of two companies.
(C) She attended two higher educational institutions.
(D) She established a research and development department.

187. What did "The Digital Age" mainly focus on?

(A) Marketing products online
(B) Developing software programs
(C) Evaluating data security systems
(D) Raising funds for new technology businesses

188. In the article, the word "faced" in paragraph 3, line 2, is closest in meaning to

(A) preserved
(B) experienced
(C) opposed
(D) watched

189. Who most likely is Mr. Levitt?

(A) Ms. Parker's former student
(B) The Stamos and Company CEO
(C) An intern at Spiegel Technologies
(D) A Port Bright College professor

190. What will Mr. Levitt most likely do in the summer?

(A) Purchase a new computer
(B) Launch a Web site
(C) Meet Ms. Parker
(D) Work in San Francisco

GO ON TO THE NEXT PAGE

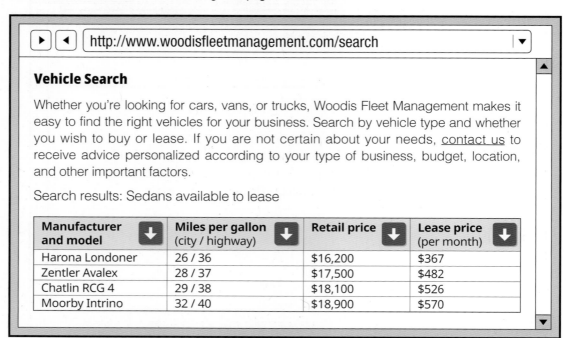

http://www.woodisfleetmanagement.com/search

Vehicle Search

Whether you're looking for cars, vans, or trucks, Woodis Fleet Management makes it easy to find the right vehicles for your business. Search by vehicle type and whether you wish to buy or lease. If you are not certain about your needs, contact us to receive advice personalized according to your type of business, budget, location, and other important factors.

Search results: Sedans available to lease

Manufacturer and model	Miles per gallon (city / highway)	Retail price	Lease price (per month)
Harona Londoner	26 / 36	$16,200	$367
Zentler Avalex	28 / 37	$17,500	$482
Chatlin RCG 4	29 / 38	$18,100	$526
Moorby Intrino	32 / 40	$18,900	$570

E-Mail message

From:	Etsuko Satou <e.satou@isiomassociates.com>
To:	Daniel Jefferson <daniel.jefferson@woodisfm.com>
Subject:	Inquiry
Date:	September 8

Hi Daniel,

Let me start by assuring you that we're very happy with Woodis's vehicles and fleet management services. In nearly six months of leasing from you, we haven't had any major problems. In fact, I'd like to compliment your Sparnley maintenance center. One of our sales representatives recently got into a minor traffic accident nearby, and he says the center's employees provided excellent assistance.

However, we're having an issue on our end that I'm hoping you can help with. Our employees have learned about the vehicle tracking devices that are installed in each car, and they are expressing privacy-related concerns about it. As you know, we don't actually use the devices, but the employees have asked that they be uninstalled. Would you be able to do that? Please let me know.

Thanks,

Etsuko Satou
Operations Specialist
Isiom Associates

```
┌─────────────────────────────────────────────────────────────────┐
│ ════════════════════════ E-Mail message ════════════════════════ │
│                                                                    │
│  From:     │ Tracy Yount <t.yount@isiomassociates.com>            │
│                                                                    │
│  To:       │ Etsuko Satou <e.satou@isiomassociates.com>           │
│                                                                    │
│  Subject:  │ Re: Update                                            │
│                                                                    │
│  Date:     │ September 21                                          │
└─────────────────────────────────────────────────────────────────┘
```

Etsuko,

Thanks for the updates on the company car program. I'm glad to hear that Boyd Snell's accident repairs were taken care of efficiently, and that Woodis is responsive to special requests. Also, on a personal note—I think it's great that we chose to lease Intrinos for our fleet. I like to see them in the parking lot.

Like you, however, I'm concerned about the fact that some drivers haven't been submitting their mileage records on time. It's important that we get prompt, accurate information about their use of the cars for business and personal reasons so that we can reimburse them properly for gas used on business trips. I'd like to meet with you to discuss this issue. Do you have time tomorrow?

–Tracy

191. What special service is mentioned on the Web page?

(A) Driver safety training
(B) Resale of used vehicles
(C) On-site maintenance work
(D) Customized consulting

192. What does Ms. Satou ask Woodis Fleet Management to do?

(A) Remove equipment from some automobiles
(B) Extend the length of some lease agreements
(C) Increase a type of insurance coverage
(D) Upgrade some tracking software

193. How much does Isiom Associates pay to lease each of its vehicles?

(A) $367
(B) $482
(C) $526
(D) $570

194. Who most likely is Mr. Snell?

(A) An account manager at Woodis Fleet Management
(B) An auto mechanic at Woodis Fleet Management
(C) A salesperson at Isiom Associates
(D) An executive at Isiom Associates

195. In the second e-mail, what is indicated about Isiom Associates?

(A) It is digitizing some administrative records.
(B) It pays some fuel costs incurred by employees.
(C) It recently expanded its parking area.
(D) It has clients in overseas locations.

---

http://www.wander-tg.nl/eng/day

Day Trips with Wander Tour Group

Now that you've seen Amsterdam, take a day trip and see other picturesque sights of the Netherlands!

Bike Tour: This five-hour tour takes place in a rural area outside of Amsterdam. Bikers will have a chance to see a range of beautiful Dutch landscapes from the wetlands to the plains. Although the tour is open to adults and children, participants are required to have a reasonable level of fitness and biking skills.

Flower Tour: Take a walk through the world's largest open-air flower garden with over seven million flower bulbs. Visitors will also be able to enjoy a picnic lunch (for an additional fee) in the middle of a colorful flower bed. This tour is only available in the spring when the flowers are in bloom.

Crafts and Windmills Tour: This tour makes two stops at quaint rural towns to allow visitors to get a feel for traditional Dutch life. Visitors will be able to buy Dutch handicrafts and even learn to make some themselves. Afterwards, they will see old windmills that are still running today.

Reserve a spot on any of our tours today by calling us at 555-0122 or sending an e-mail to reservations@wander-tg.nl.

Receipt for Reservation #4623

Name: Caroline Braxton
Date Purchased: 3 March

Tour	Date	Guest	Price
Flower Tour (Lunch included)	18 April	1	€40
Crafts and Windmills Tour	20 April	1	€80
		Total Amount Paid:	€120

- -

For bookings that are cancelled more than one week prior to the start of a tour, an 80% refund will be given. For bookings that are cancelled less than a week before the start of a tour, a 50% refund will be given. For bookings that are cancelled on the day before a tour begins, a 10% refund will be given.

```
┌─────────────────────────────────────────────────────────────┐
│ ══════════════════════════ E-Mail message ══════════════════ │
│ ┌──────┬────────────────────────────────────────────────┐    │
│ │ To:  │ <customersupport@wander-tg.nl>                 │    │
│ ├──────┼────────────────────────────────────────────────┤    │
│ │From: │ <caroline22@jrmail.com>                        │    │
│ ├──────┼────────────────────────────────────────────────┤    │
│ │Date: │ 19 April                                       │    │
│ ├──────┼────────────────────────────────────────────────┤    │
│ │Subject:│ Cancellation                                 │    │
│ └──────┴────────────────────────────────────────────────┘    │
└─────────────────────────────────────────────────────────────┘
```

Hello,

First, let me assure you that I thoroughly enjoyed my Wander Tour Group tour yesterday. The places we visited were beautiful, and it was a pleasure to listen to my guide, Alex, who was very knowledgeable and conducted the tour in Dutch and English.

However, I'm sorry to say that I got sick this morning. I will not be able to make my tour tomorrow, so I would like a refund. My reservation number is 4623.

Caroline Braxton

Test 5

196. According to the Web page, what is true about the day trips?

(A) They take place in Amsterdam.
(B) They are centered around outdoor activities.
(C) They have a minimum age limit.
(D) They do not operate on Sundays.

197. In the Web page, the word "spot" in paragraph 5, line 1, is closest in meaning to

(A) point
(B) stain
(C) view
(D) seat

198. What is suggested about Ms. Braxton?

(A) She took advantage of a temporary price reduction.
(B) She is not interested in traditional Dutch culture.
(C) She signed up for a seasonal tour.
(D) She frequently rides a bike.

199. What does Ms. Braxton imply about Wander Tour Group?

(A) Its Web site is misleading.
(B) Its tour groups are too large.
(C) It has bilingual tour guides.
(D) It carries out feedback surveys.

200. What percent of a tour's price will be refunded to Ms. Braxton?

(A) 10%
(B) 50%
(C) 80%
(D) 100%

Stop! This is the end of the test. If you finish before time is called, you may go back to Parts 5, 6, and 7 and check your work.

TEST 6

In the Reading test, you will read a variety of texts and answer several different types of reading comprehension questions. The entire Reading test will last 75 minutes. There are three parts, and directions are given for each part. You are encouraged to answer as many questions as possible within the time allowed.

You must mark your answers on the separate answer sheet. Do not write your answers in your test book.

PART 5

Directions: A word or phrase is missing in each of the sentences below. Four answer choices are given below each sentence. Select the best answer to complete the sentence. Then mark the letter (A), (B), (C), or (D) on your answer sheet.

---

101. Laverne Airlines allows bags weighing ------ eight kilograms to be carried onto aircraft as hand luggage.

(A) on
(B) across
(C) between
(D) under

102. ------- candidate demonstrated a strong understanding of how to use the required software programs.

(A) Neither
(B) Especially
(C) Few
(D) Almost

103. The company's sales results from the previous quarter will be shared ------- with the public.

(A) open
(B) opens
(C) openly
(D) opened

104. Barb Salonen's speeches on economic development consistently leave her audiences with favorable -------.

(A) impresses
(B) impressed
(C) impressions
(D) impressing

105. Employees should not ------- to more than one volunteer project during the year.

(A) commit
(B) participate
(C) lead
(D) afford

106. The use of mobile apps for international calls is a ------- that is likely to continue while services remain free.

(A) setting
(B) trend
(C) record
(D) quote

107. The park's renovation has finally given local tennis enthusiasts a space of -------, separate from the basketball courts.

(A) them
(B) their
(C) their own
(D) themselves

108. Community groups' ------- efforts persuaded the town council to approve construction of the statue.

(A) to collaborate
(B) collaboratively
(C) collaborate
(D) collaborative

109. Carson City has announced that it will begin a three-year-long ------- to install solar panels on all city buildings.
(A) election
(B) initiative
(C) comment
(D) industry

110. State fishing regulations are strictly ------- at Visk Wildlife Refuge, limiting visitors to ten fish per visit.
(A) enforcement
(B) enforcing
(C) enforced
(D) enforce

111. The 20th anniversary party will be held outside at Hutchinson Gardens ------- the weather becomes inclement.
(A) rather than
(B) despite
(C) unless
(D) because

112. Valute Corporation's merger with Stanford Partners impacted the majority of investors -------.
(A) positively
(B) positive
(C) positivity
(D) more positive

113. Binnis Auto Shop's mechanics always obtain ------- from customers before performing repair work.
(A) authorization
(B) opportunity
(C) supervision
(D) demand

114. If ------- fail to notify the agency of a change of address within one month of moving, a fine will be issued.
(A) registrants
(B) register
(C) registered
(D) registering

115. The packet includes a list of ------- tour participants will need.
(A) most
(B) much
(C) anywhere
(D) everything

116. The decades Ms. Wang has spent at Harford One Tire Company guarantee her a ------- pension.
(A) skillful
(B) substantial
(C) loyal
(D) numerous

117. Since the implementation of the new safety standards, Wiltshire Towers has undergone ------- inspections several times.
(A) randomly
(B) random
(C) randomize
(D) to randomize

118. VirafTech's latest high-definition camcorder debuted at a ------- high price compared to similar models.
(A) diligently
(B) productively
(C) relatively
(D) tightly

119. Light snacks and beverages will be available to attendees ------- today's seminar.
(A) along
(B) throughout
(C) such as
(D) among

120. The outcome of an external laboratory's test of the vitamin formula matched Dr. Chan's initial -------.
(A) analytical
(B) analyzes
(C) analyzed
(D) analysis

GO ON TO THE NEXT PAGE

121. Sudip Banerjee ------- to a new post in India, where he is expected to grow our business network.
    (A) assigned
    (B) will assign
    (C) has assigned
    (D) has been assigned

122. ------- many senior directors, Mr. Nguyen started his career in research.
    (A) Although
    (B) Until
    (C) Except
    (D) Unlike

123. Famous for its cosmetics, Rosalita's Necessaries ------- carries medicinal and therapeutic skin care products as well.
    (A) actual
    (B) actually
    (C) actuality
    (D) actualize

124. ------- your letter of request, North Ridge Suites is pleased to offer use of our main ballroom at a reduced rate to the Iduwe Society.
    (A) On behalf of
    (B) In response to
    (C) Now that
    (D) In case

125. Zalbi has not revealed its motives for acquiring RipChat, but experts are ------- that it is related to the latter firm's large collection of consumer data.
    (A) attributing
    (B) investigating
    (C) convincing
    (D) speculating

126. Stacy's Candy Store customers ------- accumulate enough annual rewards points to earn a free box of chocolates.
    (A) unusually
    (B) slightly
    (C) rarely
    (D) sparsely

127. New Imij Share members will receive confirmation by e-mail ------- their application is approved.
    (A) thereby
    (B) at least
    (C) once
    (D) regardless of

128. Exhibitors ------- about security at the fair may contact the Exhibitor Services Team at 555-0162.
    (A) concerned
    (B) concerns
    (C) concern
    (D) concerning

129. Many scientific terms were ------- deleted from the article in order to make it easier for the general public to understand.
    (A) enormously
    (B) intentionally
    (C) domestically
    (D) alternatively

130. In keeping with policy, only those responsibilities and credentials deemed ------- to the position will be mentioned in the job posting.
    (A) essential
    (B) flexible
    (C) accustomed
    (D) competent

PART 6

Directions: Read the texts that follow. A word, phrase, or sentence is missing in parts of each text. Four answer choices for each question are given below the text. Select the best answer to complete the text. Then mark the letter (A), (B), (C), or (D) on your answer sheet.

Questions 131-134 refer to the following Web page.

http://www.rhodes-mr.com

Rhodes Mountain Retreat

Rhodes Mountain Retreat is a cozy hotel and spa boasting spectacular views of the mountain. ------ . Our 25-room hotel combines artful décor ------ excellent guest services. It regularly appears
131.   **132.**

on the *Rhodes Mountain Journal*'s list of top places to ------ in the area. Likewise, our spa offers the
133.

finest in beauty and wellness treatments. ------ can enjoy a simple sports massage after a long day
134.

on the mountain slopes, or choose an inclusive package with additional services such as a facial or

pedicure.

Visit this page to learn more about our spa offerings, or contact us to make a reservation.

---

131. (A) More and more of them have visited the mountain in recent years.
(B) The Chamber of Commerce publishes a helpful business directory.
(C) Special rates are available for children below the age of 12.
(D) It is perfect for skiers, snowboarders, and those who just want to relax.

132. (A) for
(B) into
(C) with
(D) about

133. (A) work
(B) dine
(C) shop
(D) stay

134. (A) They
(B) You
(C) We
(D) I

Make Your Résumé Come to Life

This is a tough time for job hunters. Competition is so stiff that hundreds of equally ------- applicants
135.
are sending in their résumés for the same positions.

Career counselor Hiroshi Tanaka explains that, in this situation, the key to getting organizations
to notice you is to make sure you stand out. "Job applicants should no longer consider an
application a plain list of achievements," he explains. " -------, view this process as an opportunity to
136.
tell your unique story." Don't merely inform HR personnel that you have "good organizational skills."
Describe a career challenge you have experienced and how you ------- utilized these abilities to
137.
solve it. ------- .
138.

---

135. (A) extensive
(B) unbiased
(C) qualified
(D) beneficial

136. (A) Instead
(B) Similarly
(C) Nevertheless
(D) Finally

137. (A) successfully
(B) succeeding
(C) succeeded
(D) succeed

138. (A) After all, such difficulties are very common.
(B) The career counselor will then make any
necessary edits.
(C) They must be confirmed by the certifying
organization.
(D) This will be more memorable to a reader.

To: Toasty Oats Advertising Team
From: Jan Ortega
Date: October 29
Subject: Additional meeting

Hi team,

Due to some unexpected changes, there will be an additional meeting regarding our winter advertising campaign for Toasty Oats cereal. All members of the team should ------- to the

139.

conference room tomorrow at 9:30 A.M.

The following two items will be on the -------. First, there has been a dramatic increase in advertising

140.

costs at the television network. Second, there is a possible copyright violation involving the use of the Toasty Oats mascot. These complications must be discussed and resolved before the ad package can be launched.

Please ------- that the meeting is expected to take three hours. -------.

141.   **142.**

Thanks,

Jan

Test 6

139. (A) report
(B) accompany
(C) consolidate
(D) seek

140. (A) invoice
(B) agenda
(C) questionnaire
(D) cover

141. (A) have advised
(B) advisably
(C) to advise
(D) be advised

142. (A) You may also postpone it to later in the day.
(B) If it goes longer, lunch will be provided.
(C) We have to celebrate this major accomplishment.
(D) Most of this time will be used for taste-testing.

Questions 143-146 refer to the following letter.

April 4

Patricia Schafer
450 Durden Way
Artis, GA 39851

Dear Ms. Schafer,

As you may know, Artis Community Center is currently renovating its swimming pool facilities. The planned ------- include a better filtration system and additional changing rooms. Unfortunately, we **143.** have now discovered that the project will require more work than ------- expected. -------. In order to **144.** **145.** pay for this, we ------- for your support. If every member of the community center donates $100 **146.** today, we will be able to reopen this wonderful community resource without a major delay. To contribute, please fill out the enclosed form and return it to us with your donation. Thank you.

Sincerely,

Alan Kenney
Director, Artis Community Center

Encl.

---

143. (A) improvingly
(B) improvements
(C) improving
(D) improves

144. (A) originally
(B) considerably
(C) separately
(D) gradually

145. (A) The majority of the pool's users are elderly residents of Artis.
(B) The pool is scheduled to remain open until construction begins.
(C) It turns out that the foundation of the pool's deck must be replaced.
(D) Jenk Community Center has agreed to let our patrons access its pool.

146. (A) would have asked
(B) asked
(C) are asking
(D) will be asked

Directions: In this part you will read a selection of texts, such as magazine and newspaper articles, e-mails, and instant messages. Each text or set of texts is followed by several questions. Select the best answer for each question and mark the letter (A), (B), (C), or (D) on your answer sheet.

Questions 147-148 refer to the following building directory.

Building Directory

1st Floor
Information Desk
Building Services
Main Lobby
Café

2nd Floor
Robinto Pharmacy
Wheatly Health Services
Orea Grocers & Vitamins

3rd Floor
Law Offices of Smith & Hesson
Ohmes Consulting
Misel Global Trading, Inc.
Pretton Press

4th Floor
Nera Marketing Advantage
Rapido Personal Trainers
GSB Films

5th Floor
The Western Rooftop
The Wheatly Vine
Ajani's Caribbean Kitchen
Mary's Burgers and Fries

Elevators can be accessed from the north entrance of the lobby.

Leasing services provided by Wheatly Square (202) 555-0198

147. On what floor would visitors most likely find personal care products?

(A) The 1st floor
(B) The 2nd floor
(C) The 3rd floor
(D) The 4th floor

148. Whom should visitors contact to rent office space?

(A) Misel Global Trading, Inc.
(B) Ohmes Consulting
(C) Building Services
(D) Wheatly Square

GO ON TO THE NEXT PAGE

Test 6

Questions 149-150 refer to the following notice.

Attention, Customers:

From March 1, Gregorel Market will charge $0.10 for each single-use plastic carrier bag issued at checkout. This charge is mandated by a new city ordinance and cannot be waived under any circumstances.

To avoid the charge, customers are encouraged to bring or buy reusable bags in which to carry their purchases. Cloth bags are already available for sale in front of each checkout counter.

The charge is intended to reduce the amount of difficult-to-recycle waste produced in Keeling City. Gregorel Market and Keeling City ask for your support for this worthy cause.

---

149. What is the main purpose of the notice?

(A) To announce a recycling project
(B) To publicize the launch of new merchandise
(C) To explain the closure of some checkout counters
(D) To warn shoppers about a new fee

150. What is indicated about a change?

(A) It will only be in effect temporarily.
(B) It is required by a local law.
(C) It was motivated by customer feedback.
(D) It does not affect every branch of Gregorel Market.

```
========================= E-Mail message =========================

From:      Readthrough Customer Service <service@readthrough-app.com>

To:        Chibuzo Iheme <grover123@aeg-mail.com>

Date:      March 30

Subject:   Account confirmation
```

Dear Mr. Iheme,

Welcome to Readthrough! Now that you have created an account with us, you will be able to borrow and listen to our vast catalog of fiction and nonfiction audiobooks absolutely free through the Readthrough app. — [1] —.

If this is your first time using Readthrough, you may want to start by viewing the short clip we made to explain the app's features. — [2] —. It should pop up when you open the app. If it does not, you can also find it through the "Help" menu. — [3] —.

Also, we see that you have chosen not to receive promotional e-mail notifications. — [4] —. From now on, we will only e-mail you when we have important information about your account. Alternatively, you may change this setting to learn about new services and books as soon as they become available.

Happy listening!

–The Readthrough Team

---

151. What has Mr. Iheme signed up to receive access to?

(A) Audio content
(B) News updates
(C) Reviews of books
(D) Language translation services

152. What is Mr. Iheme encouraged to do in an app?

(A) Adjust a display setting
(B) Submit a help request
(C) Watch a video tutorial
(D) Try out a new feature

153. In which of the positions marked [1], [2], [3], and [4] does the following sentence best belong?

"Rest assured that this preference will be respected."

(A) [1]
(B) [2]
(C) [3]
(D) [4]

Questions 154-155 refer to the following text-message chain.

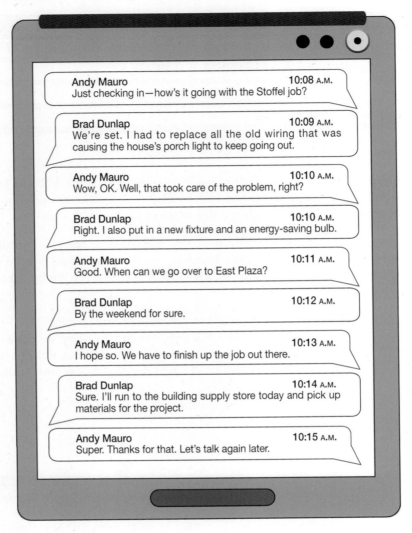

Andy Mauro	10:08 A.M.
Just checking in—how's it going with the Stoffel job?	
Brad Dunlap	10:09 A.M.
We're set. I had to replace all the old wiring that was causing the house's porch light to keep going out.	
Andy Mauro	10:10 A.M.
Wow, OK. Well, that took care of the problem, right?	
Brad Dunlap	10:10 A.M.
Right. I also put in a new fixture and an energy-saving bulb.	
Andy Mauro	10:11 A.M.
Good. When can we go over to East Plaza?	
Brad Dunlap	10:12 A.M.
By the weekend for sure.	
Andy Mauro	10:13 A.M.
I hope so. We have to finish up the job out there.	
Brad Dunlap	10:14 A.M.
Sure. I'll run to the building supply store today and pick up materials for the project.	
Andy Mauro	10:15 A.M.
Super. Thanks for that. Let's talk again later.	

154. According to Mr. Dunlap, what was the problem?

(A) A construction material was out of stock.

(B) A light was not functioning properly.

(C) A kitchen was missing an appliance.

(D) A building's access code was unavailable.

155. At 10:11 A.M., what does Mr. Mauro most likely mean when he writes, "When can we go over to East Plaza?"

(A) He wants to praise Mr. Dunlap for his work.

(B) He needs directions to a site.

(C) He is asking for permission to buy supplies.

(D) He is reminding Mr. Dunlap about a task's urgency.

MEMO

February 4

To: All Departments
From: Financing and Accounts
Re: Expenses and Reimbursements

Due to the frequency of expense reports being submitted beyond the deadline, we will be changing the due date for submission. Starting February 20, all personal expense reports must be received within three business days of the expenditure. Please include on your expense log all expenses you wish to have reimbursed as well as the time and date each one was incurred.

From that same date onward, we will accept expense reports via company e-mail only. All paper receipts should be provided on the next working day.

As a reminder, personal expenses that can be reimbursed include dinners with clients, travel for business, and other unexpected spending related to the company. If you have any questions related to the personal expenses policy, please contact Ms. Sheffield.

156. What is the main purpose of the memo?

(A) To urge staff to limit their spending
(B) To inform staff of policy changes
(C) To describe a department's new duty
(D) To give an overview of recent expenditures

157. What is suggested about the expense reports?

(A) Physical copies are currently accepted.
(B) They often have calculation inaccuracies.
(C) Receipts must be submitted at the same time.
(D) They are due once per quarter.

Every Car Club

Every Car Club is one of the top car sharing clubs in the country and has been trusted by customers for over 20 years. With over 800 vehicles for you to rent morning, noon, and night, you can always find a car when you need one. Choose among our sedans, trucks, hybrids, and more. Whichever kind of vehicle you need, it is available to you 24/7.

* We have over 30 locations at airports and cities across the country. Drop off and pick up your rental car wherever you are. Use the CarFinder app on your smartphone to locate the closest pick-up point, see what cars are available, and at what time, without having to speak to a representative. It can't get any easier than this!

* Pay a simple monthly fee. Membership starts at $10/month—insurance and servicing charges included. Save hundreds on car ownership fees per year!

Please call or reserve online one hour before your journey.
Phone: 503-555-0194
www.everycarclub.com

158. What is required to join Every Car Club?

(A) A reference from an existing member
(B) Special driving insurance
(C) Payment of a membership charge
(D) A purchase of a new car

159. What is NOT mentioned as something Every Car Club customers can do?

(A) Rent a vehicle from multiple locations
(B) Reduce maintenance costs
(C) Hire a driver for short trips
(D) Obtain a car any day of the week

160. According to the advertisement, what is the most efficient way to use Every Car Club?

(A) Contacting a vehicle owner
(B) Visiting a Web site
(C) Going to a rental office
(D) Using a mobile app

City of Tobeko Study

The Chrysalis outdoor pool and adjoining park are being demolished, and proposals for a new facility are being considered. We would like to ask you, the residents of our local area, to answer the following questions in order to help us understand how we can best service the community with this new facility.

1. Would you prefer an indoor pool or outdoor pool (June/July/August operation only)?
   (a) Indoor pool ☐   (b) Outdoor pool ■

2. Please indicate which two of the following facilities you would like to be included in the facility.
   (a) Soccer field ☐   (b) Baseball field ■
   (c) Football field ☐   (d) Basketball court ☐
   (e) Tennis court ■

3. During what time period will you most likely use the facility?
   (a) Early mornings (6 A.M.–9 A.M.) ☐   (b) Mornings (9 A.M.–11 A.M.) ☐
   (c) Afternoons (12 P.M.–5 P.M.) ☐   (d) Evenings (6 P.M.–9 P.M.) ■

4. Do you think priority parking passes should be provided to city residents who pay a membership fee?
   (a) Yes ☐   (b) No ☐
   (c) Other (Please specify in comments) ■

Comments: I work a day shift in an office, and I plan on using the facility on weekdays. It's in my neighborhood, which is already a busy part of town. With more visitors coming to use the facility, there's going to be a serious influx of drivers into our area. How is this issue being accounted for?

---

161. What kind of facility is the survey about?

   (A) A public sports complex
   (B) A local government office
   (C) A history museum
   (D) A retail center

162. When will the survey respondent most likely visit the facility?

   (A) Before work
   (B) After work
   (C) During lunch breaks
   (D) On weekends

163. What is the survey respondent concerned about?

   (A) Construction noise
   (B) Traffic congestion
   (C) Short opening hours
   (D) Obstructed views

GO ON TO THE NEXT PAGE

Questions 164-167 refer to the following text-message chain.

Ginger Sims [11:23 A.M.] Harold, I've been called out of the office by a client. It looks like I won't be able to take part in the interviews we scheduled for this afternoon.

Harold Byrd [11:24 A.M.] I see. Well, I'd like to avoid postponing them, but I don't feel like I know enough about computer programming to manage that part of the interviews by myself. Do you have any ideas?

Ginger Sims [11:25 A.M.] Yes—I've been training Gustav as a backup interviewer for just this kind of situation. Let me see if he's available.

Ginger Sims [11:26 A.M.] Gustav, can you assist Harold with interviews with some programmer candidates from two to five this afternoon? You'd be discussing the results of the candidates' coding tests, like we've talked about.

Gustav Axelsson [11:26 A.M.] Sure. I'm not working on anything urgent right now.

Ginger Sims [11:27 A.M.] Great. I'll e-mail you the test files right now. I've already written my comments in them, so you can base your questions on those. And of course ask follow-up questions as needed.

Gustav Axelsson [11:27 A.M.] Will do.

Harold Byrd [11:28 A.M.] Thanks, Gustav. I really appreciate it.

Gustav Axelsson [11:29 A.M.] Well, it's important to hire skilled programmers! Let me know if there's anything else I need to be aware of beforehand.

| Send

164. Why is Mr. Byrd hesitant to conduct the interviews alone?

(A) Because he is new to the company
(B) Because his job rank is somewhat low
(C) Because he lacks some technical expertise
(D) Because he knows some of the job candidates personally

165. What are the numbers that Ms. Sims mentions to Mr. Axelsson?

(A) Room numbers
(B) Sizes of groups
(C) Test scores
(D) Times of day

166. What does Ms. Sims indicate about some computer files?

(A) Mr. Axelsson should share them with Mr. Byrd.
(B) She has made notes in them.
(C) She has printed them out.
(D) They are too large to send by e-mail.

167. At 11:29 A.M., what does Mr. Axelsson most likely mean when he writes, "it's important to hire skilled programmers"?

(A) Mr. Byrd's gratitude is unnecessary.
(B) Mr. Byrd should prepare carefully.
(C) He wants to give additional tests.
(D) He will ask Ms. Sims for advice.

GO ON TO THE NEXT PAGE

FOR IMMEDIATE RELEASE   *March 5*

COLMOR CITY—The city's historic single-screen Harledic Theater will reopen on Friday, March 13 after two months of renovation work. The newly-remodeled theater boasts a larger screen and an all-new digital projection and sound system. Interior renovations include wider aisles and bigger, more comfortable seats. — [1] —.

Devoted film fans will be happy to hear that the theater is keeping one of its vintage movie projectors so that it can continue to screen older films. Twice a month, on Thursday evenings, the theater also gives the public the rare chance to see films made by students at Colmor Arts College. As in the past, foreign films will be showcased every Sunday. — [2] —.

The theater's owner, Don Gresch, is especially excited about this year's weeklong classic film festival, scheduled to begin on the first Monday in May. As a result of popular demand, the event will once again open with a screening of a fully-restored version of the epic film *Treasure of Kanpur*. — [3] —.

Also, starting this year, the festival will be called "Classic Cinema Week" to better reflect its programming content. It was previously called the "Harledic Film Society Festival". The event, now in its 14th year, attracts about 5,000 patrons each year. — [4] —.

168. What is suggested about the Harledic Theater?

(A) It is under new management.
(B) It plans to raise its ticket prices.
(C) It had new equipment installed.
(D) It has more than one screen.

169. What can Harledic Theater patrons do twice per month?

(A) View amateur filmmakers' work
(B) Listen to scholarly analyses
(C) Attend midnight screenings
(D) Bring along young children

170. According to the press release, what was given a new name?

(A) A feature film
(B) A movie theater
(C) A city street
(D) A film festival

171. In which of the positions marked [1], [2], [3], and [4] does the following sentence best belong?

"To complement these updates, the concession stand has been expanded as well."

(A) [1]
(B) [2]
(C) [3]
(D) [4]

GO ON TO THE NEXT PAGE

Steel & Concrete

July 12

Dorian Herring
Eason Lake Construction
756 Fourth Street
Eason Lake, AZ 87524

Dear Mr. Herring,

Steel & Concrete is a monthly magazine that has been providing its readers with the latest news and thoughtful insight into the commercial building industry for over forty years. We count top architectural, engineering, construction, and property development companies including Slosten Engineering and Kresswist among our loyal subscribers.

Because it has come to our attention that you recently established a construction firm, we wanted to reach out and make you and your partners aware of the many benefits of subscribing to *Steel & Concrete*. Whether you are hoping to expand rapidly or simply to provide superior, cost-effective service to your clients, we can help.

Steel & Concrete comes in both print and digital formats, and we offer digital-only and print-plus-digital subscriptions. Both types include a copy of *The Year in Figures*, our yearly compilation of numerical data on the building industry, as well as discounts on admission to S&C Nights, the industry-related lectures we began hosting in cities across the country this year.

As a new subscriber, you would be eligible to receive a yearlong print-plus-digital subscription—a $136 value—for the amazing price of $99. Simply fill out and return the enclosed subscription card or use the code NEWSUMMER at sandc-mag.com/subscribe to take advantage of this offer and begin accessing invaluable information and opinions.

Sincerely,

Danita Orlando
Editor-in-Chief

Encl.

---

172. Why is Ms. Orlando writing to Mr. Herring?

(A) To offer him a freelance writing assignment
(B) To invite him to begin subscribing to a magazine
(C) To describe the benefits of advertising in a magazine
(D) To persuade him to renew a subscription

173. What is indicated about Mr. Herring?

(A) He is a member of an industry association.
(B) He made an inquiry over the Internet.
(C) He recently started a business.
(D) He was referred to Ms. Orlando by his coworker.

174. According to the letter, what did Ms. Orlando's company recently begin offering?

(A) A digital version of its magazine
(B) A series of live talks
(C) Directories for certain cities
(D) Branded clothing

175. What is suggested about Kresswist?

(A) It is an architectural firm.
(B) It has access to product discounts.
(C) It used to publish *Steel & Concrete*.
(D) It has received a statistical report.

GO ON TO THE NEXT PAGE

Questions 176-180 refer to the following announcement and letter.

Announcement

Starting on January 4, all guests and members of Wiffle Athletic Club will be required to wear wristbands when engaged in aquatic activities.

- Blue wristbands will be worn by adults over the age of 18.
- Yellow wristbands will be worn by all children under 5.
- Children ages 5 and over may take a water safety test to wear a blue wristband.

Permanent wristbands may be obtained at the front desk for $5. This new policy applies to the swimming pools at both our Downtown location and our Crossroads location. We hope that it gives peace of mind to our members and staff as we move forward in serving the larger community.

Sign up now for the spring racquetball tournament! Winter results are posted on the Member Bulletin Board near the weightlifting rooms.

Wiffle Athletic Club

Dear Members,

We have received some questions about the new aquatics safety measures that we recently implemented.

Here is the background for installing these measures. It was recommended by risk management professionals and inspectors that we initiate more stringent aquatic safety policies, install a security camera system, and increase staffing. We understand that change is difficult and frustrating. However, it can improve the service we bring to you.

Now that we've had a full month to test out the policy, we want to respond to your feedback. It is clear that the overriding issue is the difficulty of wearing the silicone band in any form while lap swimming. It is also clear that the safety goal will be compromised if the band is not used at all times except in a class setting which includes an instructor with no more than eight students.

Therefore, we have determined that there will no longer be a fee charged for the first band, and two sizes will be available. Please understand that this requirement is not a way to burden our members, but rather a plan that will soon become a common practice in all aquatic facilities.

Sincerely,

Wiffle Athletic Club Management

176. According to the announcement, why most likely would people visit a front desk?

(A) To make a purchase
(B) To sign up for some lessons
(C) To return some gear
(D) To see a policy

177. What does the announcement indicate about Wiffle Athletic Club?

(A) It has only one aquatic facility.
(B) It has changed the colors of its logo.
(C) It holds seasonal competitions.
(D) It offers free swimming lessons.

178. In the letter, the word "form" in paragraph 3, line 2, is closest in meaning to

(A) style
(B) paperwork
(C) symptom
(D) object

179. Who most likely is NOT required to wear a wristband while swimming?

(A) Adults who have passed a test
(B) Children younger than 5 years old
(C) Those taking a group class
(D) All long-term members of the club

180. When most likely was the letter sent?

(A) In December
(B) In January
(C) In February
(D) In March

GO ON TO THE NEXT PAGE

Test 6

VOLUNTEER APPLICATION

Thank you for your interest in volunteering for the Juniper Community Assistance Center! Our volunteers assist us in providing high-quality services to the thousands of new residents who come through our doors every year. Please tell us a little bit about yourself by completing this application. Volunteer applications must be received by December 10 to be considered for the session beginning January 15.

Date of Application: _October 15_

Personal Information

Name: _Singh_   _Gregory_   _F._
     (Last)   (First)   (Middle Initial)

Mailing Address: _203 Crescent Blvd_   _Juniper_   _MD_   _48392_
     (Street Address or PO Box) (City)   (State)   (ZIP)

Phone Numbers: _321-555-0182_   _283-555-0169_
     (Home)   (Mobile)

E-mail Address: _gregory.singh@rpoglobal.com_

Volunteering Interests

Tell us about your previous volunteer experience (if any).
I have worked as a volunteer interpreter for the Juniper Medical Center and led a 10-week English conversation group at the Juniper Public Library.

Why would you like to volunteer at the center?
I received services from the center when I first moved to the United States a decade ago and would like to give back to the community. With six years of professional experience as an accountant, I would be particularly interested in assisting clients with tax forms.

Please return this volunteer application, along with references, in the envelope provided.

To:	Gregory Singh <gregory.singh@rpoglobal.com>
From:	Rajesh Amir <ramir@communityasst.org>
Date:	October 17
Subject:	Your volunteer application

Dear Mr. Singh,

Thank you for applying to volunteer at the Community Assistance Center.

Over the next week, we are conducting interviews with volunteers to determine the best way to leverage their experience. Please let me know if you are free any day next week between the hours of 10 A.M. and 2 P.M. We would love to schedule you for a 15-minute conversation with Jessa Flint, our Financial Services Coordinator (FSC). Based on your work experience, she is the person whom you would most likely assist.

I look forward to hearing back from you. Thank you again for your application!

Sincerely,

Rajesh Amir
Volunteer Coordinator
Juniper Community Assistance Center

181. What does the application notify applicants of?

(A) A potential expense
(B) A training requirement
(C) A submission deadline
(D) A staffing shortage

182. What is mentioned about Mr. Singh?

(A) He is a medical doctor.
(B) He does not own a mobile phone.
(C) He has never been to the center.
(D) He used to live in another country.

183. What does Mr. Amir ask Mr. Singh to do?

(A) Send a certification
(B) Indicate his availability
(C) Read some guidelines
(D) Sign an agreement

184. What will most likely happen next week?

(A) Mr. Singh will meet with a center employee.
(B) Mr. Singh will begin his volunteer position.
(C) Mr. Amir will give a short demonstration.
(D) Ms. Flint will resign from her job.

185. What most likely is one of the activities that the FSC offers assistance with?

(A) Renewing a work visa
(B) Securing a loan from a bank
(C) Making health insurance claims
(D) Preparing tax documents

GO ON TO THE NEXT PAGE

Test 6

========== E-Mail message ==========

From:	Lloyd Kim
To:	Naomi Turner
Subject:	Changes
Date:	August 13
Attachment:	⬓ Notice

Naomi,

A representative from the convention center just called to say the air conditioning for part of the second floor has broken down and won't be back in working order until noon tomorrow. Given the hot weather, we'll need to move some of the conference's morning sessions. Luckily, there aren't many other events going on then, so the representative was able to assign us to some rooms on the same floor that aren't affected.

I'll notify the speakers myself, but I need you to do two things. First, please print out copies of the attached notice explaining the changes and add one to the front of each information packet for attendees. Second, the representative said that sometimes visitors have trouble locating Room 207, so please stand in the hallway nearby tomorrow to direct people to it. Try to get there about ten minutes before the session in that room is scheduled to start.

Thanks,

Lloyd

NOTICE

- Room Changes for August 14 Morning Sessions -

Time	Session and Speaker Name	Original Room	Updated Room
9:45–11:00 A.M.	"Creative Employee Recognition Methods" (Akari Sano)	201	205
9:45–11:00 A.M.	"Integrating International Employees" (Theresa Rice)	202	207
11:15 A.M.–12:30 P.M.	"Using Big Data in Recruiting" (Brigid Pollack)	203	206
11:15 A.M.–12:30 P.M.	"Telecommuting and Teamwork" (Elmo Fairley)	201	205

Please be aware that, because of these changes, the sessions involved may begin slightly later than stated. We appreciate your patience with this inconvenience.

From:	Faye Harrison
To:	Troy Munoz
Subject:	Idea
Date:	August 14

Hi Troy,

I heard a great lecture at the Chapman Human Resources Conference this morning. The speaker, Brigid Pollack, is an expert in big data, and she explained how to use it for hiring. Not only was the subject useful, but Ms. Pollack is an engaging lecturer. She had the whole audience paying close attention. Now, I kept the very helpful handout to share with the team, but how would you feel about inviting her to our office to speak instead? I think it would be the best way to get started with this promising technology. Let me know your thoughts when you get a chance.

Thanks,

Faye

186. Why were the room changes made?

(A) Another event is taking place on the second floor.
(B) A speaker was dissatisfied with a room assignment.
(C) There is a mechanical problem at the convention center.
(D) A large number of people registered for the conference.

187. What time did Ms. Turner most likely stand in a hallway?

(A) Shortly before 9:45 A.M.
(B) Shortly before 11:00 A.M.
(C) Shortly before 11:15 A.M.
(D) Shortly before 12:30 P.M.

188. What does the notice ask readers to do?

(A) Tolerate some noise
(B) Avoid taking up excessive space
(C) Keep conference rooms clean
(D) Expect some delays

189. In which room did Ms. Harrison attend the conference session?

(A) Room 202
(B) Room 203
(C) Room 205
(D) Room 206

190. What does Ms. Harrison NOT praise a conference speaker for?

(A) Her session's group activities
(B) Her presentation materials
(C) Her choice of topic
(D) Her speaking ability

GO ON TO THE NEXT PAGE

Questions 191-195 refer to the following summary, e-mail, and newsletter article.

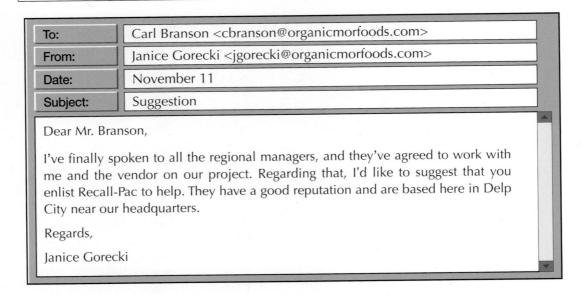

Responding to records management issues: Summary

This report details the results of an inquiry performed by Denovac Business Consultants (DBC) at the request of Organic-Mor Foods. The goal of the study was to determine whether the company's personnel records could be streamlined and more effectively managed. It was carried out via statistical analysis and interviews with relevant personnel. The responses of the local district supervisors indicate the need for a timely solution, as employee records pass through their hands on a daily basis. Two key findings were:

- 82% of the respondents reported that managing employee records is time consuming.
- 74% of the respondents expressed concern about cost burdens related to managing employee records.

This report is divided into three sections: a detailed overview of the client company's business strategy involving strategic mergers and regional expansions, an in-depth presentation of DBC's survey findings, and a proposed solution to be implemented by the client company's management.

To:	Carl Branson <cbranson@organicmorfoods.com>
From:	Janice Gorecki <jgorecki@organicmorfoods.com>
Date:	November 11
Subject:	Suggestion

Dear Mr. Branson,

I've finally spoken to all the regional managers, and they've agreed to work with me and the vendor on our project. Regarding that, I'd like to suggest that you enlist Recall-Pac to help. They have a good reputation and are based here in Delp City near our headquarters.

Regards,

Janice Gorecki

A Recall-Pac Solution for a Natural Food Retailer

With nearly 200 stores and 15,000 staff associates, Organic-Mor Foods has become a major natural food retailer. However, its new store openings have produced significant amounts of paper personnel records. Managing this documentation has, in turn, increased operational costs. Based on a recommendation provided by its consulting firm, the company decided to digitize its documents. Realizing that the process would involve complex decisions, Organic-Mor Foods management turned to Recall-Pac to supervise the entire project. Our specialists helped the company eliminate its paper personnel documents, and now its managers can access associates' files via computer. This has ultimately saved time and valuable resources.

191. Why most likely did DBC speak to district supervisors?

(A) They conduct new staff training programs.
(B) They are in charge of hiring consulting firms.
(C) They select displays for company stores.
(D) They work directly with personnel records.

192. What is most likely included in DBC's report?

(A) Criteria for employee promotions
(B) Advice for designing consumer surveys
(C) Details about merger deals
(D) Price comparisons for organic foods

193. What is implied about Mr. Branson?

(A) He was interviewed for the newsletter article.
(B) He followed Ms. Gorecki's suggestion.
(C) He is no longer based in Delp City.
(D) He is a former regional manager.

194. What did DBC probably recommend that Organic-Mor Foods do?

(A) Convert paper documents to electronic files
(B) Reduce staffing at certain locations
(C) Increase the security of a computer system
(D) Allocate more funding for storage facilities

195. In the newsletter article, the word "significant" in paragraph 1, line 5, is closest in meaning to

(A) contemporary
(B) meaningful
(C) necessary
(D) sizable

FOR IMMEDIATE RELEASE (April 9) — The District Arts Council (DAC) is gearing up to hold its Town Arts Festival on Saturday, July 7 at Belten City Park. While entry fees from artists competing for the Best Local Artist award will cover some of the costs of staging the festival, the DAC still seeks corporate funding. There are four sponsorship options:

Headline — The company name and logo will be displayed on the homepage of the Town Arts Festival Web site, and on all T-shirts sold at the festival. $5,000

Platinum – The company name and logo will appear on all posters at the festival. $3,000

Appearance – An overview of the company will appear in the festival's 48-page souvenir magazine. $1,000

Supporter – The sponsor will receive four vouchers for lifetime memberships to the Town Art Museum. $500

CONTACT: Lou Kenner, DAC Fund-raising Director, at 555-0108

E-Mail message	
From:	Dina Fallon <fallon@bilesky-designstudio.com>
To:	Amit Mohile <mohile@bilesky-designstudio.com>
Date:	June 23
Subject:	Donation

Dear Amit,

The DAC has just received our sponsorship donation. For bookkeeping purposes, please record it as "Arts Festival."

I will submit a digital copy of our company logo to the DAC so they can print it onto the official event T-shirts. Their designers can accommodate a wide range of fonts, so ours shouldn't be a problem.

There's more news. I accepted the DAC's invitation to present the Best Local Artist awards at the festival. It will be a great opportunity to represent all of us at Bilesky Design Studio.

Regards,

Dina Fallon, President

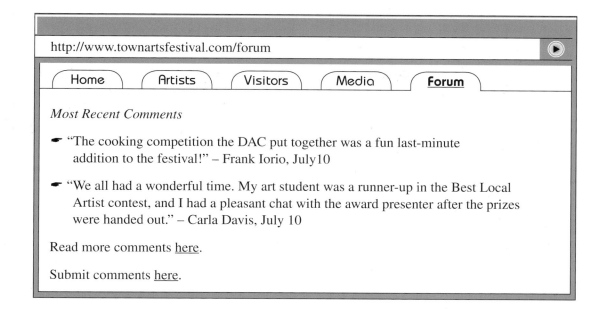

http://www.townartsfestival.com/forum

| Home | Artists | Visitors | Media | **Forum** |

Most Recent Comments

☛ "The cooking competition the DAC put together was a fun last-minute addition to the festival!" – Frank Iorio, July10

☛ "We all had a wonderful time. My art student was a runner-up in the Best Local Artist contest, and I had a pleasant chat with the award presenter after the prizes were handed out." – Carla Davis, July 10

Read more comments <u>here</u>.

Submit comments <u>here</u>.

196. What is indicated about the Town Arts Festival?

(A) It is an annual celebration.
(B) It lasted for two days.
(C) It took place in a city park.
(D) It was free for participants to enter.

197. In the e-mail, the word "accommodate" in paragraph 2, line 2, is closest in meaning to

(A) contain
(B) handle
(C) regulate
(D) lend

198. What sponsorship option did Bilesky Design Studio most likely choose?

(A) Headline
(B) Platinum
(C) Appearance
(D) Supporter

199. What is mentioned on the online message board about the DAC?

(A) It was founded by a local entrepreneur.
(B) It recently organized a cooking contest.
(C) It postponed the starting date of an event.
(D) It has begun holding weekly arts classes.

200. What most likely is true about Ms. Davis?

(A) She will be profiled in a newspaper article.
(B) She was responsible for a printing job.
(C) She met Ms. Fallon after a ceremony.
(D) She is employed at a bookkeeping firm.

Stop! This is the end of the test. If you finish before time is called, you may go back to Parts 5, 6, and 7 and check your work.

Test 6

RC

TEST 7

READING TEST

In the Reading test, you will read a variety of texts and answer several different types of reading comprehension questions. The entire Reading test will last 75 minutes. There are three parts, and directions are given for each part. You are encouraged to answer as many questions as possible within the time allowed.

You must mark your answers on the separate answer sheet. Do not write your answers in your test book.

PART 5

Directions: A word or phrase is missing in each of the sentences below. Four answer choices are given below each sentence. Select the best answer to complete the sentence. Then mark the letter (A), (B), (C), or (D) on your answer sheet.

101. Comments for Ziller Supermarket management may ------- at any checkout counter.

(A) leaving
(B) be left
(C) leave
(D) be leaving

102. Ms. Irving is sorry to be departing Gamel Industries ------- excited to take on a new challenge.

(A) nor
(B) also
(C) but
(D) like

103. To obtain a copy of ------- score report, please submit a request in writing.

(A) yourself
(B) yours
(C) you
(D) your

104. Sign here to certify that ------- information provided in this document is true and correct.

(A) total
(B) all
(C) full
(D) every

105. The "About Us" page on our corporate Web site includes a ------- of each department head.

(A) profile
(B) profiled
(C) to profile
(D) profiler

106. The inspector will point out any issues with the structure that must be examined more ------- by a specialist.

(A) commonly
(B) thoroughly
(C) eventually
(D) fortunately

107. Payment must be made to the main office by Wednesday to ------- a spot in the course.

(A) compete
(B) surround
(C) secure
(D) remain

108. Imperfect merchandise is sold at a ------- discount to secondhand stores, where it is advertised as new.

(A) steepest
(B) steep
(C) steeply
(D) more steeply

188

109. Mr. Dunn was employed at Lakeside Grill from its launch ------- its closure two years ago.
(A) until
(B) across
(C) into
(D) by

110. Homes in the Ramsill metropolitan area stay on the ------- for an average of 90 days before they are sold.
(A) industry
(B) neighborhood
(C) utility
(D) market

111. ------- Mr. Treat has an excellent academic record, Ms. Ma has valuable hands-on experience.
(A) According to
(B) On top of
(C) Should
(D) Whereas

112. Buffalo Aquarium will renovate its sea lion habitat in keeping with the Wildlife Council's ------- recommendations.
(A) revise
(B) revised
(C) to revise
(D) revises

113. Hayes Club members are entitled to bring one guest ------- month to the fitness center.
(A) with
(B) except
(C) per
(D) as

114. The adoption of FaverQuick technology ------- production at the Farmingham factory by nearly 9% over the past year.
(A) increasing
(B) will increase
(C) increased
(D) increases

115. Owners of historic houses on Bronti Street must receive approval from the Preservation Committee for any paint -------.
(A) choices
(B) choose
(C) chooses
(D) chose

116. ------- meet demand, Ailanthus Design Co. has begun recruiting additional interior design professionals.
(A) Because of
(B) In order to
(C) As soon as
(D) Not only

117. Dunlass Apparel sincerely apologizes for the technical difficulties you ------- while using our mobile app.
(A) undertook
(B) surrendered
(C) encountered
(D) accompanied

118. The software program we have developed is capable of ------- processing large quantities of statistical data.
(A) rapid
(B) rapider
(C) rapidness
(D) rapidly

119. Although media coverage tends to focus on the few success stories, the ------- of Internet start-up companies fail.
(A) majority
(B) amount
(C) variety
(D) extent

120. Plants such as potted palms can bring a lively atmosphere to ------- boring office buildings.
(A) otherwise
(B) however
(C) much
(D) else

GO ON TO THE NEXT PAGE

121. The high-efficiency machinery we bought from Shibata Solutions has been ------- the substantial sum we paid for it.
(A) designated
(B) related
(C) worth
(D) due

122. Research has shown that children do better if given ------- feedback instead of general praise.
(A) specifically
(B) specifies
(C) specify
(D) specific

123. ------- one indicator suggests that the economy is beginning to recover from its recent downturn.
(A) Apart from
(B) At least
(C) Even if
(D) Now that

124. Athlete Maurice Vickers ------- Troy's new community activity center for a ribbon-cutting ceremony when it opens.
(A) has visited
(B) visited
(C) will visit
(D) will be visited

125. Employees ------- wish to schedule vacation time must notify Human Resources two weeks in advance.
(A) who
(B) some
(C) their
(D) whose

126. The Lakeham Web design suite gives its users the tools to craft impressive Web sites and requires only basic ------- of computing.
(A) know
(B) knowingly
(C) knowledge
(D) known

127. Concerned about reports of flaws, the city asked a third party to conduct an ------- review of the plans for the new bridge.
(A) ambiguous
(B) occupied
(C) abundant
(D) external

128. To attract and retain talented staff, Corak Associates offers employee benefits ------- those available at other companies.
(A) beyond
(B) since
(C) through
(D) than

129. Attendance at this part of the convention is limited to ------- with significant authority in member organizations.
(A) patents
(B) debates
(C) expenditures
(D) delegates

130. While the economic value of hiring an assistant is disputable, the extra help will ------- improve morale.
(A) assure
(B) assuredly
(C) assurance
(D) assured

PART 6

Directions: Read the texts that follow. A word, phrase, or sentence is missing in parts of each text. Four answer choices for each question are given below the text. Select the best answer to complete the text. Then mark the letter (A), (B), (C), or (D) on your answer sheet.

Questions 131-134 refer to the following letter.

Regina Aramid
907 Marshall Lane
Gaborne, OK 73415

Dear Ms. Aramid,

It has been one year since your last eye exam, and the Association of Optometrists recommends that all adults have ------- checkups regardless of whether their eyesight needs correction. We hope
        131.
you visit our office soon to ensure the health of your -------.
                                                      132.

Also, you may not be aware that we opened a second branch at 38 South Meadow Street in June. If this location is ------- to your residence, we encourage you to begin going there. The enclosed card
                 133.
contains contact information for both of our offices. -------.
                                                      134.

And remember — we care about your eye health!

Zane Weatherall, M.D.

131. (A) fluent
     (B) grateful
     (C) vacant
     (D) annual

132. (A) diet
     (B) vision
     (C) hearing
     (D) breathing

133. (A) nearer
     (B) nearly
     (C) neared
     (D) nearness

134. (A) Note that they will expire at the end of the month.
     (B) It will be stored securely along with your patient history.
     (C) We appreciate your kindness in pointing out this mistake.
     (D) Please schedule an appointment at either one soon.

GO ON TO THE NEXT PAGE

Questions 135-138 refer to the following e-mail.

From: <jhartmann@molinacity.gov>
To: <nskeane@molinacity.gov>
Date: July 28
Subject: Q2 Reports
Attachment: report_april; report_may; report_june

Dear Mr. Keane,

Here are the reports you requested. Please let me know if you require anything else.

The contents of this e-mail and its attachments may include ------- information. For this reason, only
                                                              135.
the person to whom it is addressed is authorized to read it. If you are not the intended recipient of

this e-mail, please understand that the distribution of any information in it is ------- prohibited by
                                                                              136.
Chapter 3, Section 4.1 of the city code. -------. If you have received this e-mail in error, please notify
                                         137.
the sender by replying, and then ------- it immediately.
                                 138.

Thank you,

Jason Hartmann

---

135. (A) predictable
(B) confidential
(C) outdated
(D) diverse

136. (A) expressive
(B) expressed
(C) expressly
(D) express

137. (A) Simply click the "share" icon on the Web
site.
(B) Construction regulations are covered in
Chapter 4.
(C) Its text can be viewed at www.molinacity.
gov/code.
(D) The city recommends bringing a copy to
meetings.

138. (A) interrupt
(B) withdraw
(C) delete
(D) waive

From: Abe Ferguson
To: Managers
Subject: Announcement
Date: January 29

Hi Managers,

I was just informed that our CEO, Pearl Griffith, is going to visit our offices late next week. ------.
   139.
In preparation for this, please relay the following information to your employees.

First, Ms. Griffith will take a tour of the office at some point. ------, employees should keep their
                                                                   140.
workspaces tidy throughout her visit. Second, a reception will be held at 5 P.M. on Thursday in the

large conference room ------ Ms. Griffith. As this is after business hours, employees' presence will
                      141.
not be ------. Still, we hope that many will attend.
       142.

Over the next few days, I'll send individual messages to anyone scheduled to be more involved in

the visit.

- Abe

139. (A) Though it is sad to see her go, she has
         had a great career.
     (B) She will meet with senior management
         and look over our operations.
     (C) We should find a way to congratulate her
         on this achievement.
     (D) From what I have read, she is the perfect
         candidate for the job.

140. (A) Accordingly
     (B) Nevertheless
     (C) Furthermore
     (D) Rather

141. (A) welcomes
     (B) welcomed
     (C) should welcome
     (D) to welcome

142. (A) costly
     (B) allowed
     (C) particular
     (D) mandatory

GO ON TO THE NEXT PAGE

Infovo

An Invaluable Tool for Jobseekers

Infovo shares information about tens of thousands of companies that is collected from ordinary employees and job applicants, not public relations departments. That's ------- millions of
143.
professionals use our site to make career decisions. Our users can read honest reviews of businesses' corporate cultures as they consider where to apply, and find out what questions to expect ------- going in for an interview.
144.

Infovo also provides ------- insights based on analyses of our data. Have you been offered a position,
145.
but are unsure whether the proposed salary is reasonable? -------.
146.

What are you waiting for? Stop by www.infovo.com today to put your career on the fast track.

143. (A) why
(B) often
(C) when
(D) around

144. (A) before
(B) despite
(C) among
(D) plus

145. (A) broaden
(B) broadly
(C) broadness
(D) broad

146. (A) Upload your résumé so that potential employers can find you.
(B) We can show you the typical range for similar positions in your area.
(C) We verify that reviews are posted by actual current or former employees.
(D) Our listings are updated the most frequently of any jobseeking site.

Directions: In this part you will read a selection of texts, such as magazine and newspaper articles, e-mails, and instant messages. Each text or set of texts is followed by several questions. Select the best answer for each question and mark the letter (A), (B), (C), or (D) on your answer sheet.

Questions 147-148 refer to the following notice.

Help us conserve energy and water!

We will change your linens every morning during your stay. If you wish for your linens to be changed less frequently to conserve the resources required to wash them, please leave this card on the bed.

The thermostat will sense when you are away and switch off the heater or air conditioning. Please press the green button as you leave if you would like it to stay on.

Thank you for your patronage! The Grand is dedicated to providing excellent customer service. Please contact the front desk if anything about your stay is less than exceptional.

147. What most likely is The Grand?

(A) A movie theater
(B) An art gallery
(C) A restaurant
(D) A hotel

148. What is indicated about the thermostat?

(A) It is behind a help desk.
(B) It only affects the heating.
(C) It has automatic controls.
(D) It must be reset each morning.

GO ON TO THE NEXT PAGE

14th Laketown Cosmetics Expo

The Laketown Cosmetics Expo will be held from 9:00 A.M. to 4:00 P.M. on June 27–28, at the Laketown Convention Center at 1145 Center Street. This yearly gathering of industry professionals is one of Laketown's biggest events!

• Watch a documentary on the history of cosmetics
• See and try out the newest trendy products
• Talk directly with representatives from all the major cosmetics companies as well as independent developers
• Explore a display of vintage cosmetics on loan from the Laketown County Museum and private collectors

The event is open to the public all day on Sunday, June 28. Adults $7; children $4. Your ticket purchase buys you entry into a raffle for a $100 gift certificate to Polliard's, your local source for high-quality cosmetics and skin-care products.

For more information, please visit our Web site, www.laketowncosmeticsexpo.com.

149. What activity is mentioned in the advertisement?

(A) Exploring a historic building
(B) Seeing a nonfiction film
(C) Listening to a lecture
(D) Eating special food

150. What is suggested about the Laketown Cosmetics Expo?

(A) It is held every other year.
(B) It is open only to members of the industry.
(C) It takes place at two locations.
(D) It begins on a Saturday.

YOU'RE INVITED!

The Swinton Club of Western Pennsylvania cordially invites you to a social event for local business owners. Come out and get to know your neighbors! Attendees will also have the chance to learn more about the Swinton Club and how to become involved in service projects like last weekend's river cleanup.

Date: Friday, February 27
Time: 5:30–7:30 p.m.
Location: Sweet Life Bakery & Deli, 431 Elmer St., Springfield

Reserve your space by e-mailing Julie Walker at j.walker@swintonclub.com by Monday, February 23. For general inquiries, please e-mail Vice President Molly Fields at m.fields@swintonclub.com.

151. Who most likely would be receiving this invitation?

(A) A professional athlete
(B) A store owner
(C) A university student
(D) A local politician

152. What is implied about Ms. Fields?

(A) She manages Sweet Life Bakery & Deli.
(B) She is an officer in the Swinton Club.
(C) She will organize a cleanup of a waterway.
(D) She is responsible for handling reservations.

Test 7

Questions 153-155 refer to the following e-mail.

```
═══════════════════ E-Mail message ═══════════════════

To:      Thomas Gunther <thomas_gunther@gmsmail.com>

From:    Susan Guo <susan.guo@boardgamesunltd.com>

Re:      Your questions

Date:    May 13
```

Dear Mr. Gunther,

Greetings! Based on the information you provided in the contact form on our Web site, I'm reaching out to familiarize you with our company.

Board Games Unlimited is a board game manufacturer based in Guangzhou, China with over a decade of experience in printing and packaging board games for a range of companies. All the printing and assembly is done in-house, and you can rely on our sourcing team to find the highest-quality accessories, including cards, dice, coins, and customized parts in any material you desire. You can see samples of our games on our Web site, as you may know from your earlier visit. Many of them have earned accolades and awards, including the prestigious Panzac Medal.

We are committed to crafting a proposal that offers you the best combination of quality and cost, enabling you to launch your game within any budget you set. Please let me know when you would like to schedule a phone call to discuss your needs in more detail.

Best Regards,

Susan Guo

Board Games Unlimited
Add: Rm. 802-804, 1500 Nong Zhongshan 6 Road
        Guangzhou, Guangdong, 102108, PR China
Mob: +86 555 1609 4291
Tel: +86 55 51696158

153. What is the main purpose of the e-mail?

(A) To introduce a company
(B) To finalize an agreement
(C) To revise a schedule
(D) To publicize a new service

154. What is suggested about Mr. Gunther?

(A) He would like to create a board game.
(B) He is employed by Board Games
        Unlimited.
(C) He has met Ms. Guo before.
(D) He will travel to China soon.

155. What is NOT mentioned about Board Games Unlimited?

(A) It has made award-winning products.
(B) It produces accessories in-house.
(C) It was founded more than 10 years ago.
(D) Its Web site shows examples of its work.

Questions 156-157 refer to the following text-message chain.

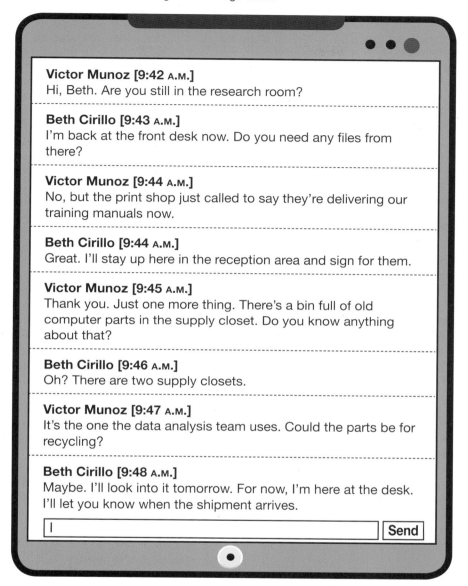

Victor Munoz [9:42 A.M.]
Hi, Beth. Are you still in the research room?

Beth Cirillo [9:43 A.M.]
I'm back at the front desk now. Do you need any files from there?

Victor Munoz [9:44 A.M.]
No, but the print shop just called to say they're delivering our training manuals now.

Beth Cirillo [9:44 A.M.]
Great. I'll stay up here in the reception area and sign for them.

Victor Munoz [9:45 A.M.]
Thank you. Just one more thing. There's a bin full of old computer parts in the supply closet. Do you know anything about that?

Beth Cirillo [9:46 A.M.]
Oh? There are two supply closets.

Victor Munoz [9:47 A.M.]
It's the one the data analysis team uses. Could the parts be for recycling?

Beth Cirillo [9:48 A.M.]
Maybe. I'll look into it tomorrow. For now, I'm here at the desk. I'll let you know when the shipment arrives.

| Send

156. What does Ms. Cirillo offer to do today?

(A) Accept a delivery
(B) Print some files
(C) Proofread a manual
(D) Lead a facility tour

157. At 9:46 A.M., what does Ms. Cirillo most likely mean when she writes, "There are two supply closets"?

(A) A department ordered too many supplies.
(B) She is concerned about the time a task will take.
(C) She needs additional clarification.
(D) There is enough space for some items.

GO ON TO THE NEXT PAGE

Arlin Plaza

From: Arlin Plaza management
To: All tenants
Re: IMPORTANT: Parking policy
Date: February 3

To ensure that there is sufficient parking for actual patrons of our shopping mall at all times, we have decided to institute a new parking policy. Prior to reading further, please note that an official press release announcing the new policy will be sent out tomorrow. — [1] —.

From March 1, use of the mall's parking area will be free only for the first 90 minutes, after which visitors will be charged $2 an hour. — [2] —. To enforce this policy, parking booths to be operated by Holloway Parking Company will be constructed at the parking area's entrances and exits. — [3] —.

Of course, all employees of Arlin Plaza and its tenant businesses will still be allowed to park for free. To enable this, all staff must visit www.hollowayparking.com/arlin to register for a permit. Please do so well before the change is implemented. — [4] —.

---

158. What is suggested about Arlin Plaza's parking area?

(A) A second exit gate was recently added to it.
(B) A newspaper reported on issues with its security.
(C) It is used by people who are not customers.
(D) Its hours of operation will be extended.

159. According to the memo, what should employees of Arlin Plaza tenants do in February?

(A) Submit a form to a city official
(B) Attend some all-staff training sessions
(C) Avoid some construction sites
(D) Sign up for a parking pass

160. In which of the positions marked [1], [2], [3], and [4] does the following sentence best belong?
"We ask that you do not discuss this matter with your staff or others before its publication."

(A) [1]
(B) [2]
(C) [3]
(D) [4]

Information on StarGlint
for employees of Rowlant Associates

StarGlint is an innovative tool that increases productivity and builds a positive atmosphere in the workplace. Employees that feel undervalued take more sick leave and communicate less effectively with their coworkers. Rowlant Associates has invested in StarGlint to combat these problems by offering an easy way to thank and receive thanks from others.

StarGlint is incredibly simple to use. To give a "gold star" to another person, simply click the red button labeled "Give a Star" and enter the information requested. Make certain to write a short description of the recipient's praiseworthy actions so that Human Resources can also understand the situation. Then, hit "Send" to submit.

To see the gold stars you have received, click the blue button labeled "See My Stars." Once you have earned ten gold stars, click "Redeem" to exchange them for a gift certificate from one of Rowlant Associates' local partner shops and restaurants.

We hope all members of the Rowlant Associates family will use StarGlint frequently but wisely to encourage each other.

---

161. What is StarGlint used for?

(A) Requesting time off of work
(B) Altering shared files remotely
(C) Expressing appreciation to coworkers
(D) Reporting problems with machinery

162. What are employees specially asked to do when making a submission?

(A) Include an explanation
(B) Save a record of it
(C) Choose a category from a list
(D) Double-check the recipient's name

163. What is indicated about Rowlant Associates?

(A) It is a family-owned company.
(B) It issues training certificates to employees.
(C) It is expanding its human resources department.
(D) It has special relationships with retail businesses.

GO ON TO THE NEXT PAGE

Test 7

Questions 164-167 refer to the following letter.

Stanello Logistics
3400 Austin Street
Meer Park, CT 06002

January 12

Guadalupe Martino
Morvan Solutions
1650 Green Ave.
Vanson, CT 06016

Dear Ms. Martino,

I am writing in response to your request for a reference for Stewart Glover, an applicant for the position of warehouse manager at your organization.

As a warehouse manager myself, I did not have much contact with Mr. Glover when he joined us four years ago as an entry–level package handler. However, when a supervisory position opened up after a year, Mr. Glover's own supervisor strongly recommended promoting him into it. I accepted that suggestion, and I am glad I did.

Over the past three years, I have observed that Mr. Glover is a natural leader who delivers excellent support and guidance to the people he supervises. He has also frequently found ways to improve our operations. For example, he proposed replacing our previous workbenches with height–adjustable ones to better accommodate our staff. When we did, our productivity rose 8%.

In light of my experiences with Mr. Glover, and having studied the job listing that you kindly provided, I can confidently recommend that you hire him.

Sincerely,

Pauline Massey
Warehouse Manager, Meer Park Location
Stanello Logistics

---

164. What does Ms. Massey mention about Mr. Glover's career at Stanello Logistics?

(A) He has had three different job titles.
(B) He was hired based on a recommendation.
(C) She was initially unimpressed by his performance.
(D) She did not work closely with him at first.

165. The word "observed" in paragraph 3, line 1, is closest in meaning to

(A) noticed
(B) investigated
(C) commemorated
(D) obeyed

166. How did Stanello Logistics improve a warehouse's productivity?

(A) By replacing out-of-date software
(B) By offering financial incentives to staff
(C) By supplying customizable equipment
(D) By changing the layout of a storage area

167. What does Ms. Massey indicate that she has reviewed?

(A) A description of a position
(B) The results of an inspection
(C) Guidelines for formatting a document
(D) A request for some production figures

Questions 168-171 refer to the following online chat discussion.

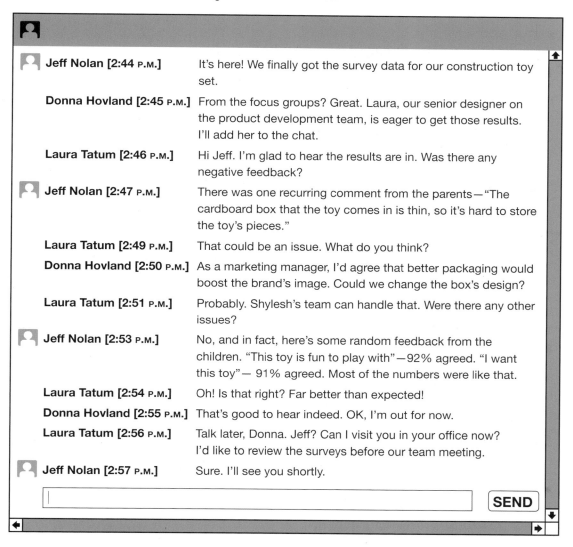

Jeff Nolan [2:44 P.M.] It's here! We finally got the survey data for our construction toy set.

Donna Hovland [2:45 P.M.] From the focus groups? Great. Laura, our senior designer on the product development team, is eager to get those results. I'll add her to the chat.

Laura Tatum [2:46 P.M.] Hi Jeff. I'm glad to hear the results are in. Was there any negative feedback?

Jeff Nolan [2:47 P.M.] There was one recurring comment from the parents—"The cardboard box that the toy comes in is thin, so it's hard to store the toy's pieces."

Laura Tatum [2:49 P.M.] That could be an issue. What do you think?

Donna Hovland [2:50 P.M.] As a marketing manager, I'd agree that better packaging would boost the brand's image. Could we change the box's design?

Laura Tatum [2:51 P.M.] Probably. Shylesh's team can handle that. Were there any other issues?

Jeff Nolan [2:53 P.M.] No, and in fact, here's some random feedback from the children. "This toy is fun to play with"—92% agreed. "I want this toy"—91% agreed. Most of the numbers were like that.

Laura Tatum [2:54 P.M.] Oh! Is that right? Far better than expected!

Donna Hovland [2:55 P.M.] That's good to hear indeed. OK, I'm out for now.

Laura Tatum [2:56 P.M.] Talk later, Donna. Jeff? Can I visit you in your office now? I'd like to review the surveys before our team meeting.

Jeff Nolan [2:57 P.M.] Sure. I'll see you shortly.

SEND

168. Who most likely is Ms. Tatum?

(A) A product developer
(B) A marketing manager
(C) A Web designer
(D) An accounting executive

169. What does Ms. Hovland suggest doing?

(A) Lowering a product's price
(B) Redesigning some packaging
(C) Rewriting a question
(D) Conducting follow-up interviews

170. At 2:54 P.M., what does Ms. Tatum most likely mean when she writes, "Is that right"?

(A) She is uncertain about some survey procedures.
(B) She is surprised by some survey results.
(C) She thinks some data must be incorrect.
(D) She wants to confirm some participants' ages.

171. What will Mr. Nolan probably do next?

(A) Lead a focus group session
(B) Review a press release
(C) Meet with Ms. Tatum
(D) Contact the IT team

GO ON TO THE NEXT PAGE

City News

December 22

Grocery store included on Great Workplaces list

MELLVIEW—A local supermarket chain, Dalesatt Ltd., has once again been recognized as a great place to work.

The company is ranked number three on this year's list of Great Workplaces, up two places from last year. — [1] —.

Headquartered in Mellview, Dalesatt Ltd. operates 107 supermarkets across the Lumisedo region. The shops offer a wide selection of natural foods, including nuts, crackers, and dried fruit marketed under the "Dalesatt" brand.

The Great Workplaces awards program is run by Top Companies Group, a major publisher of business magazines. — [2] —. To get the recognition, participating companies go through a two-part evaluation process. They earn up to 80 points based on the results of an employee satisfaction survey and up to 20 points from a review of their workplace policies and management philosophy. — [3] —. As of now, most area companies take part in the assessment program; a few small firms do not yet participate.

In its report, Top Companies Group praised Dalesatt Ltd. for acting on its employees' ideas. Partly in response to feedback from its staff, the chain unveiled a new concept at its recently-opened Branden Road location. — [4] —. The store features hot and cold sandwiches, a salad bar, and a tray service that lets customers eat at tables inside the store. "This change demonstrates our staff's pioneering spirit," said Dalesatt Ltd.'s Vice President, Emily Wang.

172. What is mentioned about Dalesatt Ltd.?

(A) It is more than 100 years old.
(B) It sells its own line of snack foods.
(C) It was bought by a magazine publisher.
(D) It plans to relocate its headquarters.

173. What is suggested about the Great Workplaces program?

(A) It gives out awards once a quarter.
(B) It has a separate category for small firms.
(C) Cash prizes are presented to its top firms.
(D) Participation in it is voluntary.

174. According to the article, what new feature did Dalesatt Ltd. recently introduce?

(A) In-store dining options
(B) Home delivery services
(C) Self-checkout machines
(D) Uniforms for its staff

175. In which of the positions marked [1], [2], [3], and [4] does the following sentence best belong?

"The combined scores determine the final rankings."

(A) [1]
(B) [2]
(C) [3]
(D) [4]

GO ON TO THE NEXT PAGE

Test 7

Questions 176-180 refer to the following chart and letter.

Olivard Apartment Complex Waste Disposal Guide

Type of Material	Bin Color	Notes
Paper	Yellow	- DOES NOT include facial tissue - Should be dry and free of matter such as food
Plastic	Blue	- DOES NOT include styrofoam - Should be free of excess liquid and matter such as food - Labels do not need to be removed
Metal	Purple	- DOES NOT include small appliances or batteries - Should be free of excess liquid and matter such as food - Place metal lids inside cans
Glass	White	- DOES NOT include mirrors or ceramics - Rinse before placing in the bin - Labels do not need to be removed
Food Waste	Green	- DOES NOT include bones or shells
Others	Black	- Includes all other small, non-hazardous items

Olivard Apartment Complex

June 1

Dear Resident,

Please be advised of the following changes related to waste disposal at the complex:

- As of June 10, waste that requires special pick-up (such as furniture and appliances) should be left 20 yards north of the West Entrance instead of right next to it. Look for the sign that says "Large Item Disposal."

- Thanks to the city's efforts to streamline recycling for citizens, from this month we no longer need to recycle paper and plastic separately. Please begin putting both types of materials in the bin that we have been using for paper recyclables.

In addition, the complex's owners have determined that the amount of trash regularly left on the playground has become excessive. They are considering raising the fine for littering on complex property to $25. You have until June 30 to register your opinion on this matter at the management office.

Sincerely,

Damon Brooks
Apartment Complex Manager

176. According to the chart, what should people do before recycling glass items?

(A) Eliminate all liquid from them
(B) Remove product stickers from them
(C) Cleanse them with water
(D) Sort them by color

177. What can be placed in the purple bin?

(A) A flattened cardboard box
(B) A broken rice cooker
(C) A used battery cell
(D) An empty beverage can

178. From June, which color bin should recyclable plastic be placed in?

(A) Yellow
(B) Blue
(C) White
(D) Black

179. Why most likely has a recycling policy changed?

(A) The complex's residents complained.
(B) The complex's owners hope to lower costs.
(C) A new technology became available.
(D) A local authority relaxed a regulation.

180. What is indicated about Olivard Apartment Complex?

(A) It has four main entrances.
(B) It has an outdoor recreational facility.
(C) It operates a furniture donation program.
(D) It imposes fines for putting recyclables in trash bins.

GO ON TO THE NEXT PAGE

http://www.marblerock.city.gov/council

Marble Rock City Council Meetings

The city council convenes on the first and third Tuesday of each month. All meetings are held at the town hall on 93 E. Clover St.

Meetings begin at 6:30 P.M. with an executive committee session that is not open to the public. However, the minutes of the closed session are made available after the meeting.

Doors open to the community at 7:15, and the open session is called to order at 7:30 P.M. Each open session begins with a comment portion, during which community members are allowed to speak for no more than five minutes each.

Each meeting's agenda is posted on this Web site and published in the *Clover Street Herald* on the Sunday prior to the meeting.

City Council Minutes

City Council Minutes

Date: June 14

Members Present: Ted Lunst, Carrie Honigbaum, Phil Preston, George Masters

Closed Session
Meeting called to order at 6:30 P.M.
 1. **Approval of minutes.** Minutes approved with corrections. Abstention: Phil Preston
 2. **Budget discussion.** City treasurer presented a budget draft. Budget was discussed and several changes proposed. Treasurer agreed to revise budget. A special meeting was scheduled for July 27 for review.
Meeting dismissed at 7:10 P.M.

Open Session
Meeting called to order at 7:30 P.M.
 1. Minutes approved.
 2. Bill Brady requested an update on the status of the sidewalk replacement in the Falls River neighborhood. Council agreed to publish updates on its Web site.
 3. Three property development firms presented proposals for the empty school building on Catoga Street. Proposals will be posted in the town hall lobby for three weeks, after which community will vote on them.
 4. Council approved the banning of vehicles from Main Street between Chestnut and Maple Streets on Friday, October 3 between 6:30 P.M. and 9:30 P.M. for the Lights of Autumn lantern festival.
Meeting dismissed at 8:15 P.M.

181. According to the Web page, when should a member of the executive committee arrive?

(A) By 6:30 P.M.
(B) By 7:15 P.M.
(C) By 7:30 P.M.
(D) By 8:00 P.M.

182. In the Web page, the word "portion" in paragraph 3, line 2, is closest in meaning to

(A) division
(B) period
(C) setting
(D) share

183. What will be discussed at a special meeting of the executive committee?

(A) The corrected minutes
(B) An amended financial plan
(C) Proposals for an empty building
(D) The outcome of a vote

184. Who most likely is Mr. Brady?

(A) An employee of a property development firm
(B) A reporter for the *Clover Street Herald*
(C) The city treasurer
(D) A resident of Marble Rock

185. What does the council agree to do for a festival?

(A) Provide extra security personnel
(B) Remove a noise restriction
(C) Advertise on its Web site
(D) Close a roadway to traffic

GO ON TO THE NEXT PAGE

ENNIS & LEONE ACCOUNTING

From: Sean Gustafson
To: All Staff
Re: Cleaning reminder
Date: April 17

As I notified you in March, I have scheduled appointments for a deep cleaning of our offices on Saturday, April 25 and Monday, April 27. Now that the appointments are drawing near, I would like to explain our plans. On the preceding Friday afternoon, we will move furniture from one half of the office into the other half, so that part of the office can be cleaned on Saturday. On Monday, we will reverse the process. Therefore, we ask you to report to the office on Monday morning and then complete your regular tasks from home after lunch.

The only action I need you to take beforehand is to let me know details (location, substance, etc.) about any stains you would like the cleaners to try to remove. They need that information by 5 P.M. on April 23 so that they can prepare the necessary supplies. On April 24, 27, and 28 simply come to the office dressed in comfortable clothes and ready to move furniture or help out in other ways.

E-Mail message

From:	Madeline Bey <m.bey@porcaro-cc.com>
To:	Sean Gustafson <sean.gustafson@ennis-leone.com>
Subject:	Cleaning services
Date:	April 28
Attachment:	⬚ Invoice

Dear Mr. Gustafson,

Attached you will find the invoice for our services rendered on April 25 and 27.

Also, the leader of the crew sent to your office asked me to pass some comments along to you. First, he hopes that Mr. Kahn is satisfied with their work on the coffee stain near his desk. If not, he has offered to treat it one more time for free. Second, he believes you could avoid needing to have all of the break room chairs professionally cleaned again by buying washable covers for them.

Thank you again for choosing Porcaro Commercial Cleaners.

Sincerely,

Madeline Bey
Customer Service Representative

Porcaro Commercial Cleaners

602 Garland St.
Fairfax, VA 22030
(571) 555-0182

Client: Ennis & Leone Accounting
Service date(s): April 25, April 27

Payment due: May 31

Service	Number /Square ft.	Unit Price	Subtotal
Carpet washing	1450	$0.40	$580.00
Window washing	14	$3.00	$42.00
Furniture cleaning	4	$15.00	$60.00
Ceiling cleaning	1850	$0.40	$740.00
		Total	$1422.00

186. What does Mr. Gustafson ask recipients of the memo to do on April 27?

(A) Oversee a cleaning process during the morning
(B) Attend a meeting in the morning
(C) Work off-site during the afternoon
(D) Clear an area of furnishings in the afternoon

187. In the memo, the word "drawing" in paragraph 1, line 2, is closest in meaning to

(A) sketching
(B) attracting
(C) coming
(D) matching

188. What is implied about Mr. Kahn?

(A) He did not receive a notification in March.
(B) His desk was moved by Ms. Bey.
(C) His workspace was cleaned on April 25.
(D) He alerted Mr. Gustafson to a problem in advance.

189. What does Ms. Bey suggest about Porcaro Commercial Cleaners?

(A) It has more than one work crew member.
(B) It only accepts credit card payments.
(C) It will begin serving Ennis & Leone Accounting regularly.
(D) It can install protective floor coverings.

190. Which amount on the invoice does Ms. Bey mention could be saved in the future?

(A) $42.00
(B) $60.00
(C) $580.00
(D) $740.00

www.gosilconationalpark.com/info/trails ▶

| HOME | **INFO** | NEWS | CONTACT |

Info ➤ Trails

Gosilco National Park's trails range from easy to difficult, self-guided to guided, and half-day to two-day courses. Note that all visitors participating in multi-day hikes are required to book campsite accommodations before they start their hikes. Also, any of our trails may be closed without prior notice due to weather conditions.

Sylvan Trail: This 24-kilometer walk is the perfect way to see Gosilco's natural beauty. It takes hikers through a forest and by a river, and ends at Sylvan Waterfall. Hikers must be accompanied by a guide.

Lake Pep Way: Take a leisurely walk along the south shore of Lake Pep. This 8-kilometer path is smooth and flat. It has many entrances and exits so visitors are not required to start and finish at one point.

Carby Hill Trail: This self-guided trail ends at the top of Carby Hill, where there are stunning views of Lake Pep. Hikers should wear hiking boots for its mostly-uphill 11-kilometer track. The Carby Hill Trail is only available during peak season.

Daisy Lane: This 14-kilometer intermediate trail takes hikers through Daisy Forest. It is the only place in Gosilco people can catch a glimpse of the rare janeto bird. The trail can be hiked alone or with a guide.

MEMO

To: Department Managers
From: Portia Woodard
Subject: Trip
Date: 14 April

For Hutchings Pharmaceuticals' yearly hiking trip, we will head to Gosilco National Park on 18 May. I will e-mail everyone a detailed description of the event tonight. Please encourage anyone interested to join us. If we have more than 20 hikers sign up, Hutchings Pharmaceuticals will qualify for a special hike for big groups with two private guides. Please send me a list of participants by 28 April.

HOME	**INFO**	NEWS	CONTACT

Reviewed by: Juliet Campos

Date: 21 May

I visited Gosilco National Park with my Hutchings Pharmaceuticals coworkers a few days ago and had a wonderful time. Since there were so many of us, we participated in a special group hike. Our guides, Ken and Lisa, pointed out native plants and explained the geology of the land. We were even lucky enough to see two janeto birds! I highly recommend making a trip out to Gosilco.

191. What is indicated about Gosilco National Park?

(A) It has overnight campsites.
(B) It is inaccessible during winter.
(C) Its staff conduct research on endangered species.
(D) Visitors must register to hike on its trails.

192. What information is NOT given about Carby Hill Trail?

(A) The recommended gear for it
(B) Its length
(C) Its starting point
(D) The view it offers hikers

193. In the memo, the word "head" in paragraph 1, line 2, is closest in meaning to

(A) direct
(B) go
(C) act
(D) think

194. What is most likely true about Hutchings Pharmaceuticals' hiking trip?

(A) It was targeted at photography enthusiasts.
(B) It was postponed by several days.
(C) It was organized by Ms. Campos.
(D) It had more than 20 participants.

195. Which trail did Ms. Campos most likely hike?

(A) Sylvan Trail
(B) Lake Pep Way
(C) Carby Hill Trail
(D) Daisy Lane

Test 7

GO ON TO THE NEXT PAGE

Questions 196-200 refer to the following Web page, online form, and schedule.

---

http://www.safa.org/events/conference ▶

| Home | About | Membership | Resources | **Events** |

Southern Association of Flight Attendants
25th Conference

Perrietta Convention Center, October 5–6

As we celebrate a quarter century of informative and inspiring gatherings, SAFA has decided to honor our profession's past by holding this year's conference in Perrietta, the location of one of the first training centers for flight attendants. In addition, Bessie Allen, a long-time SAFA officer, will give the keynote address on the changes she has seen over her career.

However, the conference will also have plenty to offer to those focused on the present and future of our industry. Participants can expect stimulating presentations, enjoyable meet-and-greet opportunities, and vendor booths stocked with cutting-edge in-flight products.

Click here to purchase a two-day conference pass that includes breakfasts, lunches, and dinners, or a single-day pass that allows scheduling flexibility. SAFA members receive a 20% discount on both types.

---

http://www.safa.org/events/conference/reg ▶

25th Conference
Registration Form

Name:	Heath Weiss
Organization:	Wasken Airlines
Position:	Junior Flight Attendant
Are you a member of SAFA?	Yes ☒ No ☐
Member ID:	04329
Address:	5660 Sand Street, Apt. 202, Tulsa, OK, 74120
Contact phone:	(918) 555-0174
E-mail:	h.weiss@waskenair.com
Type of pass:	Two-day ☒ Single-day Oct. 5 ☐ Oct. 6 ☐

Please help us organize later events by telling us why you are attending this conference:
As someone just starting out in this field, I'm hoping to learn more about my future options and make some professional connections.

Submit →

(You will be asked to enter your payment details on the next page.)

Southern Association of Flight Attendants
25th Conference

Schedule for October 5

Time	Event	Location
8–9 A.M.	**Breakfast**	Cafeteria
9–10:30 A.M.	**"From the Other Side"** (Hannah Sadler, DeBaun University) – Based on her research on passenger experiences, Ms. Sadler will give advice on improving in-flight service.	Room 102
10:45 A.M. –12:15 P.M.	**"Are You Prepared?"** (Chao Yang, Algrain Consulting) – Mr. Yang will introduce common medical situations faced in the air and explain how to deal with them.	Room 104
12:15–1:15 P.M.	**Lunch**	Cafeteria
1:30–3 P.M.	**"The Best Fare"** (Kyle Zahn, Gustina Events) – Mr. Zahn will pass on tips gained from decades spent making, transporting, and serving great food in every kind of location.	Room 103
3:30–5 P.M.	**"Planning Your Journey"** (Deidre Fitzgerald, LinkWest Airlines) – Ms. Fitzgerald will discuss professional development opportunities and career paths open to flight attendants.	Room 104
6–8 P.M.	**Closing Banquet**	Ballroom

196. Why is the conference being held in Perrietta?

(A) Because the city has historical significance
(B) Because the city is centrally located
(C) Because the city has excellent transportation services
(D) Because the city is the new location of SAFA's headquarters

197. What is NOT mentioned in the Web page as part of the conference?

(A) Networking events
(B) A speech by a SAFA official
(C) A field trip to a nearby site
(D) Displays of merchandise

198. What is implied about Mr. Weiss?

(A) He is not eligible for a registration discount.
(B) He will pay for his meals before the conference.
(C) He will not need sleeping accommodations.
(D) His employer will reimburse an expense.

199. Who most likely is Mr. Zahn?

(A) A medical professional
(B) A baggage handler
(C) An event caterer
(D) An airline pilot

200. Whose presentation will Mr. Weiss probably be most interested in?

(A) Ms. Sadler's
(B) Mr. Yang's
(C) Mr. Zahn's
(D) Ms. Fitzgerald's

Stop! This is the end of the test. If you finish before time is called, you may go back to Parts 5, 6, and 7 and check your work.

TEST 8

READING TEST

In the Reading test, you will read a variety of texts and answer several different types of reading comprehension questions. The entire Reading test will last 75 minutes. There are three parts, and directions are given for each part. You are encouraged to answer as many questions as possible within the time allowed.

You must mark your answers on the separate answer sheet. Do not write your answers in your test book.

PART 5

Directions: A word or phrase is missing in each of the sentences below. Four answer choices are given below each sentence. Select the best answer to complete the sentence. Then mark the letter (A), (B), (C), or (D) on your answer sheet.

101. Unstable fuel prices make it challenging to set appropriate shipping ------- for our products.

(A) rates
(B) facilities
(C) supervisors
(D) evaluations

102. The editor was able to make an immediate ------- to the online version of the article.

(A) correct
(B) correction
(C) correctly
(D) corrected

103. Because the VIP seats in the front row are already occupied, some esteemed guests will have to sit -------.

(A) otherwise
(B) instead
(C) elsewhere
(D) even

104. Hundreds of passengers are waiting to rebook flights after ------- were cancelled due to a computer system error.

(A) them
(B) their
(C) theirs
(D) themselves

105. Clark Catering has provided ------- food services to the local community for 25 years.

(A) exceptionally
(B) exceptional
(C) exception
(D) excepting

106. The last train to Lanetown ------- from the city center at 11:17 P.M. yesterday.

(A) departed
(B) departs
(C) is departing
(D) will be departing

107. After Mr. Jeffries moves ------- the east office, there will be room for all of the engineers to work on the same floor.

(A) during
(B) without
(C) into
(D) between

108. Mr. Ishida ------- his findings to the board at the regular meeting in October.

(A) collaborated
(B) announced
(C) invested
(D) acquired

218

109. Managers should write annual reviews ------- so that employees may receive prompt feedback.
(A) suddenly
(B) rather
(C) forward
(D) quickly

110. Mr. Henderson's previous accounting experience makes him ------- to the team.
(A) value
(B) values
(C) valuing
(D) valuable

111. ------- the production department set a quarterly record, all of its members earned a bonus.
(A) When
(B) Neither
(C) Whether
(D) Then

112. All citizens holding a ------- passport are eligible to register for the national government's Traveler Safety Alert Program.
(A) sizable
(B) valid
(C) willing
(D) steady

113. The pamphlets will introduce gallery visitors to the artist ------- this wonderful series of paintings.
(A) both
(B) therefore
(C) behind
(D) while

114. This year's Worldwide Tech Summit, featuring talks from leaders in the defense technology field, will begin at ------- 12 P.M.
(A) exact
(B) exacted
(C) exactness
(D) exactly

115. The contract renewal negotiation with Palliam Corporation failed ------- serious attempts to reach a compromise.
(A) by
(B) against
(C) despite
(D) regarding

116. The Roland World amusement park operates -------, opening for the year in May and closing in September.
(A) seasonally
(B) gradually
(C) especially
(D) absolutely

117. Notwithstanding opposition from neighborhood residents, the north end of Cherry Street has been rezoned to allow commercial -------.
(A) builder
(B) buildings
(C) build
(D) built

118. Buyers are sure to drive away happy with West Norwich Cars' ------- financing and competitive pricing.
(A) reasons
(B) reasoning
(C) reasonable
(D) reason

119. The vice president of marketing, Ms. Park, launched a social media campaign ------- nearly tripled online engagement.
(A) where
(B) everyone
(C) that
(D) who

120. Although the sales ------- needs a new director, the human resources manager has not yet filled the job opening.
(A) illustration
(B) pressure
(C) division
(D) outcome

GO ON TO THE NEXT PAGE

121. Cross Country Airlines ------- a $25 fee per checked bag, with an extra $5 for any bags over 50 pounds.

    (A) instituted
    (B) patterned
    (C) dominated
    (D) motivated

122. The staff of the *Ruffine Tribune* won a journalism prize for its in-depth ------- of changes in Ruffine's farming industry.

    (A) cover
    (B) covered
    (C) coverable
    (D) coverage

123. ------- the electricians are coming this morning to fix a switch in the lobby, the receptionist is working in the conference room.

    (A) Including
    (B) Since
    (C) However
    (D) From

124. Ms. Zhu has a busy schedule, so all appointment requests and inquiries must be ------- to her assistant.

    (A) directs
    (B) directing
    (C) directly
    (D) directed

125. Kenneth Page, the head of product development, is on vacation, but he can answer ------- questions by e-mail.

    (A) unequal
    (B) honorary
    (C) resolved
    (D) urgent

126. The organizers of the Seipel Music Festival have assembled a remarkable ------- of talented performers.

    (A) array
    (B) pace
    (C) role
    (D) option

127. Local businesses raised so much money for the city park fund that the garden can be ------- maintained for the next three years.

    (A) complete
    (B) completes
    (C) completing
    (D) completely

128. The rapid speed at which technology becomes ------- makes it even more important to find a cost-effective way to recycle outdated electronic devices.

    (A) persistent
    (B) obsolete
    (C) separate
    (D) crucial

129. For greater accessibility, the link to the page containing our company's contact details ------- closer to the top of the homepage.

    (A) should be placed
    (B) to be placed
    (C) are being placed
    (D) will be placing

130. HyView's newest entry in its line of curved-screen monitors ------- a high-definition, 70-inch display.

    (A) boasts
    (B) aims
    (C) excels
    (D) appeals

PART 6

Directions: Read the texts that follow. A word, phrase, or sentence is missing in parts of each text. Four answer choices for each question are given below the text. Select the best answer to complete the text. Then mark the letter (A), (B), (C), or (D) on your answer sheet.

Questions 131-134 refer to the following letter.

Dear Customer,

After 15 years of serving the Greendale community, we are sorry to notify you that the Maple Street location of Fitness Unlimited ------- its doors. Our last day of public operation is scheduled for next
131.
Friday, March 31.

We have enjoyed sponsoring local events and helping our community meet fitness goals, and we hope to make this transition as easy as possible. ------- you are storing any personal belongings in
132.
the lockers on our premises, please remove them by March 31. Those who have paid for a membership beyond the end of March should contact our front desk about ------- their membership
133.
to the Route 7 branch.

134.

Sincerely,

Bob Jackson, Owner

131. (A) will be shutting
(B) will have shut
(C) has shut
(D) shuts

132. (A) Among
(B) Until
(C) But
(D) If

133. (A) transferred
(B) transferable
(C) transferring
(D) transfers

134. (A) Members who reach these goals earn prizes.
(B) Thank you for 15 years of patronage.
(C) Finally, towels may be rented for a small fee.
(D) Stop by soon to try them out for yourself.

Questions 135-138 refer to the following article.

Donut Ads Charm Viewers

Ezell's Donuts' latest series of television advertisements have won over viewers across the country. The ads star actress Virginia Conti as "Cheryl," a baker at one of the franchise's locations. In them, Cheryl delights her coworkers and the shop's customers with her ideas for creative new ------ of 135. donuts. Once the ------ ads began appearing, Ezell's Donuts received a flood of praise through 136. social media and enjoyed a noticeable boost in sales. ------, it has revealed plans to produce 137. several more ads featuring Ms. Conti over the coming year. ------. 138.

---

135. (A) phases
(B) approaches
(C) majorities
(D) varieties

136. (A) likably
(B) likable
(C) liking
(D) like

137. (A) Nevertheless
(B) As a result
(C) For example
(D) In other words

138. (A) The first is expected to air in early March.
(B) All visitors to Ezell's Donuts will receive one.
(C) Fans have expressed concern about the change.
(D) The effects of television advertising have been similar.

Nunaley Industries' Rupp 5 is a fixed-wing drone that has been ------- designed for use by farmers
139.
and others in the agriculture industry. Monitoring the condition of crops or livestock spread out over
a large area has never been so easy. Thanks to its high-powered battery, the Rupp 5 can ------- for
140.
55 minutes on a single charge. While in the air, its camera and other sensors capture a range of
data that can be uploaded upon landing to any ------- brand of FMIS (farm management information
141.
system) software. Simple, fast, and reliable, the Rupp 5 is the perfect choice for your farm. -------.
142.

139. (A) special
(B) specially
(C) specialty
(D) specialized

140. (A) ring
(B) roll
(C) dig
(D) fly

141. (A) ideal
(B) repeated
(C) major
(D) eager

142. (A) Call 555-0176 for pricing, set-up times, and other specifications.
(B) Please note that cleanup and restoration services are not included.
(C) Photos of the plants are available for download on our Web site.
(D) This offer applies only to farm holdings of 500 acres or fewer in size.

Test 8

Questions 143-146 refer to the following e-mail.

From: Jack Lawler <j.lawler@fivelive-software.com>
To: Evelyn Moretz <e.moretz@addigitalware.com>
Date: 17 April
Subject: Request

Dear Ms. Moretz,

------. I recently had the pleasure of interviewing Alan Naylor, one of your ------ employees. He
143.   144.
informed me that you were his team leader during his time at AD Digital Ware, Inc.

Mr. Naylor has applied for a lead programmer position at our company, and he listed you as one
of his references on his résumé. I ------ your feedback regarding this promising candidate. In
                                 145.
particular, I am interested in ------ Alan's contribution was to the various projects he worked on
                               146.
under you.

Please let me know a few dates and times in the next week when you might be available to have
a 15-minute phone call on this topic. Thank you for your consideration.

Yours truly,

Jack Lawler
FiveLive Software

---

143. (A) I am writing about the possibility of
         engaging your design services.
     (B) I am sorry to notify you that our project
         has encountered a delay.
     (C) I am a student hoping to learn more
         about the field of programming.
     (D) I am a personnel manager involved in
         hiring at FiveLive Software.

144. (A) former
     (B) new
     (C) future
     (D) permanent

145. (A) appreciated
     (B) would appreciate
     (C) am appreciating
     (D) have appreciated

146. (A) it
     (B) each
     (C) what
     (D) another

224

Directions: In this part you will read a selection of texts, such as magazine and newspaper articles, e-mails, and instant messages. Each text or set of texts is followed by several questions. Select the best answer for each question and mark the letter (A), (B), (C), or (D) on your answer sheet.

Questions 147-148 refer to the following advertisement.

New Student Special

For the month of June, students new to Adah's Lotus Yoga get their first class free! They can also buy class packages at discounted prices:

- 3 classes: $45
- 5 classes: $60
- 12 classes: $100

Access this deal by registering at our Web site, www.adahlotusyoga.com/newstudent. This offer is good only for students who have never visited the studio before. Each student is allowed a single package at the discount price.

147. What is being advertised?

(A) Language classes
(B) Exercise classes
(C) Cooking classes
(D) Music classes

148. How many discounted packages can be purchased by one new student?

(A) One
(B) Three
(C) Five
(D) Twelve

GO ON TO THE NEXT PAGE

Questions 149-150 refer to the following text-message chain.

Myrtle Coleman, 12:08 P.M.
Levi, are you going to be working on your report for much longer? If so, I'll head downstairs first to wait in the lobby.

Levi Hines, 12:09 P.M.
Oh no! I've already left. I forgot that we were supposed to have lunch together today. I'm really sorry, Myrtle.

Myrtle Coleman, 12:09 P.M.
It's OK. Should we cancel, then?

Levi Hines, 12:10 P.M.
Well, I just sat down at Reve's Grill, but I haven't ordered yet. What do you think?

Myrtle Coleman, 12:11 P.M.
I don't like Reve's, but I wouldn't mind going to that Mexican restaurant next door to it.

Levi Hines, 12:11 P.M.
That sounds great. I'll see you there.

149. What is probably true about Ms. Coleman?

(A) She works in the same building as Mr. Hines.
(B) She took public transportation this morning.
(C) She does not like Mexican food.
(D) She is waiting to read a report.

150. At 12:10 P.M., what does Mr. Hines most likely mean when he writes, "I haven't ordered yet"?

(A) He is behind schedule.
(B) He can still change his plans.
(C) He wants Ms. Coleman to recommend a dish.
(D) He is emphasizing that Reve's Grill is very busy.

Ivory Serenity Opening at Woodfield Mall

Woodfield Mall is proud to advertise the grand opening of a new business at the west end of the mall complex. This addition fills the vacancy left by the departure of MegaBooks last spring.

Ivory Serenity will open its elegant doors on Saturday, October 15, and will offer a wide range of services to keep the community feeling pampered and peaceful. Salon services will include haircuts, hair coloring, manicures, and pedicures, all offered by certified aestheticians. In the attached spa, clients can receive massages, facials, body scrubs, and more.

An entire menu of services is available on the Ivory Serenity Web site at www.ivoryserenity.com/services.

151. What is indicated about MegaBooks?

(A) It will open a new branch in October.
(B) It is located next to Ivory Serenity.
(C) Its owner also runs Ivory Serenity.
(D) It is no longer part of Woodfield Mall.

152. Why most likely would a customer visit Ivory Serenity?

(A) To learn artistic techniques
(B) To enjoy beauty treatments
(C) To get decorating supplies
(D) To buy healthy snacks

Test 8

http://www.moyandville-ha.org/internships

Internships with the Moyandville Housing Agency

The internship program at the Moyandville Housing Agency (MHA) is structured to provide advantages to both the students who participate in it and the MHA. While working on projects under the guidance of MHA staff, interns gain experience in the field of affordable housing services and earn a generous hourly wage. The MHA benefits from contact with young, diverse voices and the future increase in skilled workers who require less training when they enter the field after graduation.

Internships begin in early June and last approximately three months, during which interns work twenty-hour weeks (either 8 A.M. to 12 P.M. or 1 P.M. to 5 P.M., Monday to Friday). Only those enrolled full-time at the University of Moyandville or Moyandville State University may apply. However, students from any academic discipline are welcome, as there are positions available across several departments. Each position is advertised separately on the online job boards of the eligible universities, so those interested in applying should check those services regularly.

153. What is indicated about internships at the MHA?

(A) They include low-cost lodgings.
(B) They are 20 weeks long.
(C) They have flexible hours.
(D) They are paid positions.

154. According to the Web page, who is eligible for the internships?

(A) Students who study certain subjects
(B) Students who attend certain institutions
(C) Students who have a high grade point average
(D) Students who have completed two years of university

155. What are potential applicants instructed to do?

(A) Monitor postings on a Web site
(B) Contact a department in their university
(C) Collect some official documents
(D) Read an MHA publication

From:	Cormi <customerservice@cormi-co.com>
To:	Clint Baldwin <drbaldwin@pv-dc.com>
Date:	January 27
Subject:	Code from Cormi

Dear Mr. Baldwin,

Your authentication code is 06178. Please sign in to your Cormi account and enter the code when prompted to prove that you are the owner or manager of Pask Valley Dental Clinic.

Once you have done this, you will gain control over the Cormi listing for your business. You will be able to add, update, and delete most of the information about it that Cormi visitors are shown when they search for relevant service providers in your city. We recommend including as much detail as possible for the convenience of potential customers.

Please note that changes may take up to 48 hours to appear on your listing. Also, you will not be able to change or delete reviews of your business posted by Cormi users, though you can write short responses to them.

For assistance using Cormi, please start by visiting the "Help" page on our Web site.

Cormi Customer Service

156. What is the purpose of the e-mail?

(A) To facilitate verification of a person's identity
(B) To confirm that an order has been received
(C) To respond to a user's complaint
(D) To reset an account password

157. What does Cormi do?

(A) Supply equipment to medical clinics
(B) Maintain e-mail lists for use by advertisers
(C) Provide information about businesses to the public
(D) Assist with the recruitment of short-term workers

Test 8

GO ON TO THE NEXT PAGE

City News

EAST CITY (September 2)—The East City Farmers Market's return from Hardar Plaza to its old site at Courtway Square, where it began its operations nearly 15 years ago, has led to "steadily increasing" attendance, says market organizer Linda Lee. — [1] —.

"A lot of residential construction took place around Courtway Square in the years the market was gone," Ms. Lee explains. "This development has brought in more customers." The market operates every Saturday from May to November, from 7 A.M. to 4 P.M. — [2] —. Visitor numbers can vary on a given day, but its overall attendance from June to August was up 27% from last year. On one sunny day in August, a record 600 people visited. — [3] —.

Organizers have also received mostly encouraging feedback about the site itself. "Visitors are really pleased with the market's patio area, which offers plenty of places to sit down in the shade," Ms. Lee says. She notes, though, that her team is actively addressing the issue of parking shortages. Street parking is often scarce around Court Street, where the market begins. — [4] —.

Although the market has no Web site of its own, it is listed on the neighborhood's site, www.courtway-sq.com.

158. What is mentioned about the East City Farmers Market?

(A) It is sponsored by a real estate company.
(B) It stopped operating for several years.
(C) It moved back to its original location.
(D) It experienced record attendance in June.

159. What does Ms. Lee say that visitors like about the market?

(A) Its opening hours
(B) Its delivery service
(C) Its online presence
(D) Its outdoor seating

160. In which of the positions marked [1], [2], [3], and [4] does the following sentence best belong?

"For now, visitors are advised to park two or three blocks west of that area."

(A) [1]
(B) [2]
(C) [3]
(D) [4]

From: Office Manager
To: All staff
Subject: Announcement and policies
Date: May 22

This message is to alert you that the second floor break room will undergo renovations starting on Monday, May 29. The process is scheduled to take five days and will involve the installation of deluxe flooring and modern countertops, and the replacement of the sink, microwave, and refrigerator.

To prepare the room, please remove anything that you've been storing in the refrigerator. Anything left behind will be discarded at 5 P.M. on Friday, May 26. During construction, employees will be able to store their lunches in the refrigerator on the fifth floor, but please note that space will be limited.

As a reminder, these are the break room policies:

* All food that is kept in the refrigerator must be labeled with the owner's name and the date.
* Everyone is responsible for throwing out his or her own trash or expired food.
* However, each department should designate a break room representative who will be responsible for enforcing this policy.
* The inside of the microwave must be wiped thoroughly with a cleaning agent after use.
* No dirty dishes should be left in the sink.
* Any dishes that you've washed should be taken out of the drying rack at the end of the day.
* The sink should be wiped thoroughly after use. *Note: This is a new policy.*

We hope that everyone will enjoy the new break room and that these policies will keep it clean and useful for years to come.

161. What is one topic of the memo?

(A) The timing of staff rest breaks
(B) Conserving some resources
(C) Improvements to an office amenity
(D) Complaints about a janitorial crew

162. What will happen on May 26 ?

(A) A meal time will be shorter than usual.
(B) An appliance will be emptied.
(C) Some policies will go into effect.
(D) Some representatives will be elected.

163. What recommended action has been added to the break room policies?

(A) Wiping the microwave regularly
(B) Cleaning the sink after each use
(C) Removing dishes from the drying rack daily
(D) Labeling items stored in the refrigerator

164. The word "limited" in paragraph 2, line 4, is closest in meaning to

(A) restricted
(B) cautious
(C) imperfect
(D) secret

GO ON TO THE NEXT PAGE

Questions 165-168 refer to the following Web page.

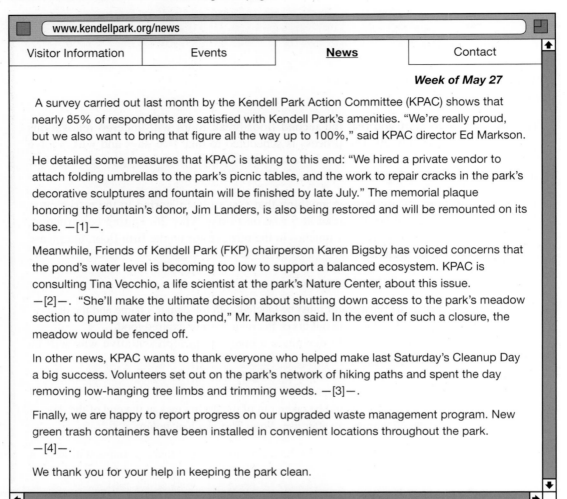

www.kendellpark.org/news

| Visitor Information | Events | **News** | Contact |

Week of May 27

A survey carried out last month by the Kendell Park Action Committee (KPAC) shows that nearly 85% of respondents are satisfied with Kendell Park's amenities. "We're really proud, but we also want to bring that figure all the way up to 100%," said KPAC director Ed Markson.

He detailed some measures that KPAC is taking to this end: "We hired a private vendor to attach folding umbrellas to the park's picnic tables, and the work to repair cracks in the park's decorative sculptures and fountain will be finished by late July." The memorial plaque honoring the fountain's donor, Jim Landers, is also being restored and will be remounted on its base. —[1]—.

Meanwhile, Friends of Kendell Park (FKP) chairperson Karen Bigsby has voiced concerns that the pond's water level is becoming too low to support a balanced ecosystem. KPAC is consulting Tina Vecchio, a life scientist at the park's Nature Center, about this issue. —[2]—. "She'll make the ultimate decision about shutting down access to the park's meadow section to pump water into the pond," Mr. Markson said. In the event of such a closure, the meadow would be fenced off.

In other news, KPAC wants to thank everyone who helped make last Saturday's Cleanup Day a big success. Volunteers set out on the park's network of hiking paths and spent the day removing low-hanging tree limbs and trimming weeds. —[3]—.

Finally, we are happy to report progress on our upgraded waste management program. New green trash containers have been installed in convenient locations throughout the park. —[4]—.

We thank you for your help in keeping the park clean.

165. What did KPAC most likely do recently?

(A) It conducted a survey.
(B) It appointed a new director.
(C) It raised an entry fee.
(D) It hosted a science conference.

166. What feature of the park is NOT mentioned on the Web page?

(A) Public artwork
(B) Picnic facilities
(C) Walking trails
(D) Parking areas

167. Who most likely will make a final decision on closing part of the park?

(A) Mr. Markson
(B) Mr. Landers
(C) Ms. Bigsby
(D) Ms. Vecchio

168. In which of the positions marked [1], [2], [3], and [4] does the following sentence best belong?

"Two of them have been placed prominently near the park's west entrance."

(A) [1]
(B) [2]
(C) [3]
(D) [4]

GO ON TO THE NEXT PAGE

Questions 169-171 refer to the following memo.

MEMO

TO: Certainty Bank Employees
FROM: Jesse Audubon, Director of Human Resources
RE: Staff Recognition Awards
DATE: December 1

As we bring another successful year to a close at Certainty Bank, the Human Resources Department will soon begin accepting nominations for the following staff recognition awards:

- Branch Manager of the Year
- Teller of the Year
- Community Volunteer of the Year

It is our goal to recognize staff members who go above and beyond their normal duties to serve our customers and communities. If you would like to nominate someone, go to the main page of the Certainty Bank Web site and click on the "Recognize an Employee" link. Please advertise this opportunity to Certainty Bank patrons as well, as we would also like to receive their feedback on outstanding employees.

Nominations will be accepted from December 14 through December 31. We expect to reveal the winners by January 31, and awards will be presented at a banquet the following week. Thank you for your cooperation in this important initiative.

169. What is indicated about the staff recognition awards?

(A) They are chosen by a companywide vote.
(B) They are divided into two categories.
(C) The winners receive bonus pay.
(D) They are given out annually.

170. According to the memo, what should readers do to nominate an employee?

(A) Go to a dinner
(B) Submit a comment card
(C) Send an e-mail
(D) Visit a Web page

171. When can a nomination be made?

(A) On December 1
(B) On December 14
(C) On January 31
(D) On February 7

Questions 172-175 refer to the following text-message chain.

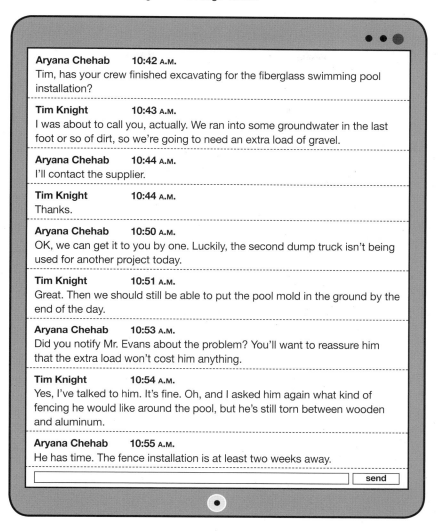

Aryana Chehab   10:42 A.M.
Tim, has your crew finished excavating for the fiberglass swimming pool installation?

Tim Knight   10:43 A.M.
I was about to call you, actually. We ran into some groundwater in the last foot or so of dirt, so we're going to need an extra load of gravel.

Aryana Chehab   10:44 A.M.
I'll contact the supplier.

Tim Knight   10:44 A.M.
Thanks.

Aryana Chehab   10:50 A.M.
OK, we can get it to you by one. Luckily, the second dump truck isn't being used for another project today.

Tim Knight   10:51 A.M.
Great. Then we should still be able to put the pool mold in the ground by the end of the day.

Aryana Chehab   10:53 A.M.
Did you notify Mr. Evans about the problem? You'll want to reassure him that the extra load won't cost him anything.

Tim Knight   10:54 A.M.
Yes, I've talked to him. It's fine. Oh, and I asked him again what kind of fencing he would like around the pool, but he's still torn between wooden and aluminum.

Aryana Chehab   10:55 A.M.
He has time. The fence installation is at least two weeks away.

send

172. What problem does Mr. Knight describe?

(A) A swimming pool is leaking.
(B) Some soil naturally contains water.
(C) It is currently raining at a work site.
(D) A digging machine has damaged some pipes.

173. What does Ms. Chehab indicate will happen by 1 P.M.?

(A) A shipment will be delivered.
(B) A vehicle will be repaired.
(C) A contract will be created.
(D) A revised schedule will be issued.

174. Who most likely is Mr. Evans?

(A) A member of a construction crew
(B) A residential plumber
(C) The owner of a property
(D) The representative of a supplier

175. At 10:55 A.M., what does Ms. Chehab most likely mean when she writes, "He has time"?

(A) Mr. Evans will be able to help with a task.
(B) A destination is only a short distance away.
(C) She is frustrated that Mr. Evans has not contacted her.
(D) A decision does not need to be made yet.

GO ON TO THE NEXT PAGE

Adur-Networking

99 Pattenson Street
Boston, MA 20039
Phone: (222) 555-0199
Fax: (222) 555-0167

Date: December 10
Invoice number: 1122334
Customer ID: 4532

BILL TO
Andrews Hair Care Supplies
22 Fawn Street
Ottawa, ON Canada K2L 1B6

Description	Taxed	Amount
Base Rate		$0.10
Ad Size: Medium		$0.03
Ad Type: Pop-up		$0.10
Additional Requests		$0.04
Total charge per click:		$0.27

$0.27 x 25,304 clicks = $6,832.08
Total Due: $6,832.08

Comments:
1. Total payment is due in 30 days.
2. Printed receipts will only be issued if you have requested them.
3. "Online Marketing Services" will appear on the receipt.
4. If you have any questions, please e-mail Patricia Hawk (pathawk@adurnet.com).
5. To receive priority placement, include a payment for $2,150.00 (sum calculated according to your current ad criteria).
6. Ads are automatically renewed.

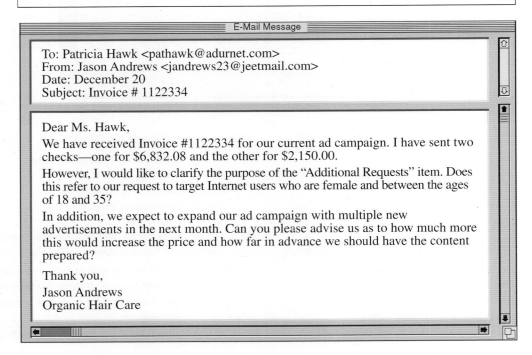

E-Mail Message

To: Patricia Hawk <pathawk@adurnet.com>
From: Jason Andrews <jandrews23@jeetmail.com>
Date: December 20
Subject: Invoice # 1122334

Dear Ms. Hawk,

We have received Invoice #1122334 for our current ad campaign. I have sent two checks—one for $6,832.08 and the other for $2,150.00.

However, I would like to clarify the purpose of the "Additional Requests" item. Does this refer to our request to target Internet users who are female and between the ages of 18 and 35?

In addition, we expect to expand our ad campaign with multiple new advertisements in the next month. Can you please advise us as to how much more this would increase the price and how far in advance we should have the content prepared?

Thank you,

Jason Andrews
Organic Hair Care

176. What is most likely featured in an advertisement?

    (A) A hairstylist training program
    (B) Hair care products
    (C) Hair salon services
    (D) A hairstyling magazine

177. What is suggested about the type of advertisement the customer ordered?

    (A) It appears on-screen suddenly.
    (B) It includes a video clip.
    (C) It is the largest size available.
    (D) It expires after one month.

178. What is indicated about the billing arrangement?

    (A) The advertising company has reduced a price.
    (B) The customer is billed by the number of clicks.
    (C) The amount owed is the same each month.
    (D) The invoice total is calculated on a weekly basis.

179. Why is Mr. Andrews sending two checks?

    (A) To pay the next month's base rate
    (B) To start funding a second marketing effort
    (C) To obtain greater visibility for an advertisement
    (D) To settle a past overdue bill

180. What does Mr. Andrews NOT ask about?

    (A) The successfulness of a campaign
    (B) The fee for targeting specific consumers
    (C) The cost of additional advertisements
    (D) The time needed to process new advertisements

Director of County Transportation Commission to Retire

by Ellen Gibson

MINAHAN (September 8)—Andreas Ruiz, who has headed the Boivin County Transportation Commission (BCTC) for 11 years, has revealed his intention to step down from the position at the end of this year. A search is currently being conducted for his successor.

Mr. Ruiz began his career at the Rohr Heights Department of Transportation, where he worked his way up to head of the Project Delivery Group. He considers the highlight of his 23 years there to be the installation of several miles of bicycle lanes, a project that succeeded in its goal of decreasing the number of pollution-causing vehicles on the city's roads.

Since being appointed as the director of the BCTC, Mr. Ruiz has mainly focused on improving the agency's existing services. He converted some buses into express buses during the county's rush hours, built a transfer station in Tavenette, and expanded the weekend service hours of all bus lines. In addition, he has been responsible for some new offerings, such as a popular free transportation service for residents over the age of 65.

Mr. Ruiz said he is proud of what the BCTC has accomplished during his tenure, explaining, "I feel like we've made life better for Boivin residents." Along with spending time with his family at his home in West Summell, he hopes to continue helping the community during his retirement through consulting work.

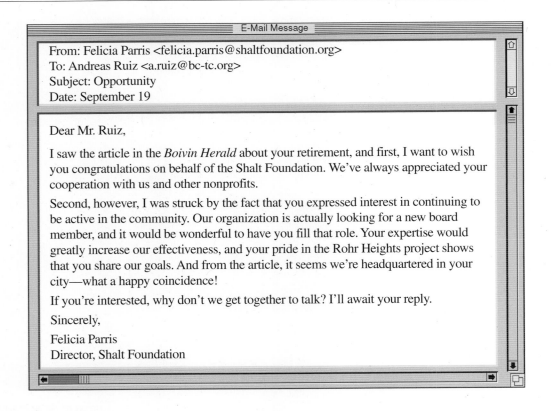

E-Mail Message

From: Felicia Parris <felicia.parris@shaltfoundation.org>
To: Andreas Ruiz <a.ruiz@bc-tc.org>
Subject: Opportunity
Date: September 19

Dear Mr. Ruiz,

I saw the article in the *Boivin Herald* about your retirement, and first, I want to wish you congratulations on behalf of the Shalt Foundation. We've always appreciated your cooperation with us and other nonprofits.

Second, however, I was struck by the fact that you expressed interest in continuing to be active in the community. Our organization is actually looking for a new board member, and it would be wonderful to have you fill that role. Your expertise would greatly increase our effectiveness, and your pride in the Rohr Heights project shows that you share our goals. And from the article, it seems we're headquartered in your city—what a happy coincidence!

If you're interested, why don't we get together to talk? I'll await your reply.

Sincerely,

Felicia Parris
Director, Shalt Foundation

181. What is mentioned about the BCTC?

(A) It consists of 11 appointed officials.
(B) It has named Mr. Ruiz's successor.
(C) It offers a special service for the elderly.
(D) All Boivin County residents may attend its meetings.

182. What is listed as one of Mr. Ruiz's accomplishments?

(A) Expanding the routes of some buses
(B) Preventing rises in passenger fares
(C) Enabling faster commutes for bus riders
(D) Converting a structure into a transfer station

183. What is one purpose of the e-mail?

(A) To ask Mr. Ruiz to become part of an organization
(B) To suggest a new project for the BCTC
(C) To report a problem with a community service
(D) To invite Mr. Ruiz to a party held by the Shalt Foundation

184. What is most likely true about the Shalt Foundation?

(A) It promotes environmentally-friendly transportation.
(B) It is concerned with the affordability of public transit.
(C) It provides support to people with disabilities.
(D) It attempts to improve road safety.

185. Where is the main office of the Shalt Foundation?

(A) In Minahan
(B) In Rohr Heights
(C) In Tavenette
(D) In West Summell

GO ON TO THE NEXT PAGE

MEMO

To: All Employees
From: Henrietta Drake, Human Resources Director
Re: Employee activity clubs
Date: March 20

Aglan Medical Technologies has decided to begin sponsoring employee activity clubs. By providing this support, we hope to foster social relationships, improve wellness, and increase opportunities for employees to learn from each other.

If you would like to start a club, please fill out the attached application form and return it to my department. Note that you must find at least one other staff member to assist with the club's operation. We will review the form and, if necessary, send it to the accounting or legal department to check for budget or liability issues, respectively. Once the application has been approved, you may begin recruiting members through company communications channels.

E-Mail message

From:	Connor Hayes
To:	Henrietta Drake
Subject:	Employee activity clubs
Date:	June 2

Dear Ms. Drake,

I was very interested to see your announcement about the employee activity clubs program, and I'd like to apply to start a club. However, I've been busy with a work project since the announcement was made, and I'm worried that I may have missed my chance. Could you confirm for me that there is still some funding left for new clubs? Also, I am most interested in starting a basketball club, so I wanted to check whether anyone has already applied to do that. If so, I will look into other activities.

Thanks,

Connor Hayes

APPLICATION TO START AN EMPLOYEE ACTIVITY CLUB

Applicant Information

Name: _Connor Hayes_   Department: _Sales_   Position: _Sales Consultant_

Extension No.: _493_   E-mail address: _c.hayes@aglanmt.com_

Secondary applicant name: _Camille Ingram_   Extension No.: _448_

Club Information

Name: _Hiking Club_

Proposed activities: _Weekend hikes on area trails, once per month_

Proposed budget: _$50 per month_

Comments: _The money would be used for snacks, water, and gas._

- -

HUMAN RESOURCES DEPARTMENT USE ONLY

Application received: _June 3_

Reviewed by: _Hachiro Kato_

Approved: Yes ___ No ___   Requires further review _X_ (Budget ___ Liability _X_)

Signature (if approved): _____

---

186. What is NOT a stated purpose of the employee activity clubs program?

(A) To enhance employees' health
(B) To stimulate friendships between employees
(C) To encourage employees to share knowledge
(D) To provide new experiences to employees

187. According to the memo, what does an employee need in order to start a club?

(A) The administrative support of a coworker
(B) The approval of a department head
(C) A list of potential club members
(D) A background in the relevant activity

188. Why did Mr. Hayes write the e-mail?

(A) To inquire about a rejection
(B) To confirm the steps of a process
(C) To seek updated information
(D) To point out a problem

189. What is implied about the employee activity clubs program?

(A) It has received a request to start a basketball club.
(B) It is most popular among sales department staff.
(C) Its activities always take place on weekends.
(D) Its budget has already been fully spent.

190. Which department will the form be sent to next?

(A) Human Resources
(B) Accounting
(C) Legal
(D) Sales

GO ON TO THE NEXT PAGE

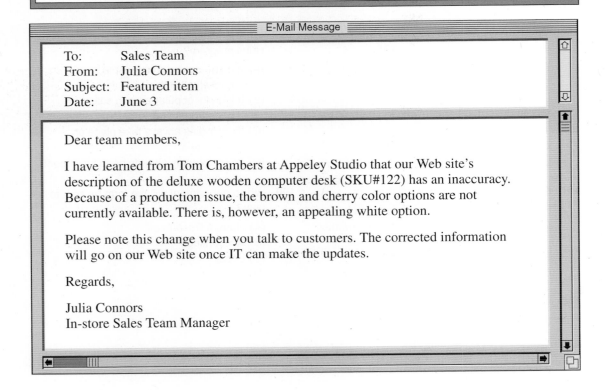

http://www.schumofffurniture.com

ALE **Schumoff Furniture**

A fixture on Alton Street for more than a century, Schumoff Furniture is proud to be the region's most trusted retailer of handmade wooden furniture. We do not display all of our items on this Web site, so please visit our showroom to view our current selection of furniture.

FEATURED ITEM SALE – June 4 to June 21

- ☙ SKU#122 Deluxe wooden computer desk with four storage drawers – $685
- ☙ Colors available: Black, brown, and cherry
- ☙ Upgrade options: – *with fold-out table and bookcase with three adjustable shelves – $865*
                       – *two-piece set with fabric armchair – $895*
                       – *two-piece set with leather-backed executive chair – $935*

This is a special-edition piece from a local woodworking studio.

Last updated: June 1

E-Mail Message

To: Sales Team
From: Julia Connors
Subject: Featured item
Date: June 3

Dear team members,

I have learned from Tom Chambers at Appeley Studio that our Web site's description of the deluxe wooden computer desk (SKU#122) has an inaccuracy. Because of a production issue, the brown and cherry color options are not currently available. There is, however, an appealing white option.

Please note this change when you talk to customers. The corrected information will go on our Web site once IT can make the updates.

Regards,

Julia Connors
In-store Sales Team Manager

Customer Reviews Plus

Business Reviewed: Schumoff Furniture   **By:** Maggie Clarkson   **On:** July 12

I visited Schumoff Furniture on the first day of its "featured item" sale to purchase a special-edition wooden computer desk. I really like it. Thanks to its handy folding table and bookshelf, it functions as an all-in-one workstation. In fact, I was able to get just the look I had wanted for my home office — I couldn't have asked for a better fit. The sales clerk who handled my purchase, Jerry Hinde, was very knowledgeable about all the showroom's handmade furniture. All in all, I strongly recommend both the desk and the store.

191. What is indicated about Schumoff Furniture?
(A) It manufactures handmade furnishings.
(B) It lists its products in a paper catalog.
(C) It has been in business for over 100 years.
(D) It is closed part of the year.

192. What color options are now available for the desk?
(A) Tan and cherry
(B) Black and white
(C) Brown and black
(D) White and tan

193. How much did Ms. Clarkson most likely pay for her desk?
(A) $685
(B) $865
(C) $895
(D) $935

194. What most likely is true about Mr. Hinde?
(A) He has read Ms. Clarkson's review.
(B) He met Ms. Clarkson in person.
(C) He works in a call center.
(D) He assembled a desk.

195. In the customer review, the word "just" in paragraph 1, line 3, is closest in meaning to
(A) barely
(B) possibly
(C) precisely
(D) recently

GO ON TO THE NEXT PAGE

Questions 196-200 refer to the following e-mails and schedule.

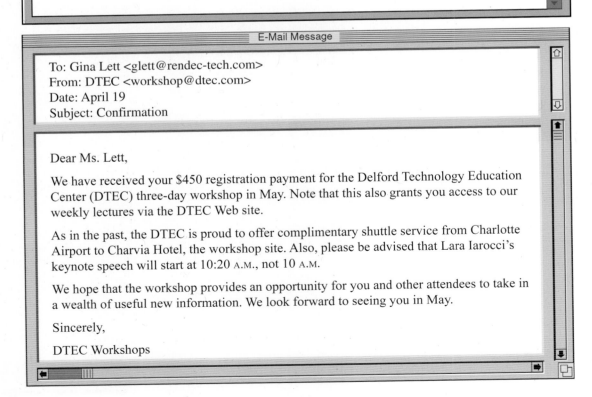

E-Mail message

To: Gina Lett <glett@rendec-tech.com>

From: Mia Ortiz <mortiz@rendec-tech.com>

Date: April 17

Subject: Card

Dear Ms. Lett,

The accounting department is processing your application for our company's credit card, the RCT Payment Card. To complete the process, we need proof of one of the following:

* At least five monthly commutes to our Tech Campus in Lodi, NJ

* Payment of conference or workshop fees totaling $400 or more

* A manager's approval to spend at least $200 on entertaining out-of-town clients

Also, once you receive your card, please ensure that you follow these RCT corporate travel policies:

— Car rentals must be reserved through our in-house travel department.

— Lodging must be arranged through our designated travel agency, TZAD Travel.

— Paper receipts must be obtained for all taxi travel to and from airports.

— Up to $75 per day in cash advances may be taken only on trips lasting five or more days.

Best regards,

Mia Oritz, Accounting Team, Rendec Center of Technology (RCT)

E-Mail Message

To: Gina Lett <glett@rendec-tech.com>
From: DTEC <workshop@dtec.com>
Date: April 19
Subject: Confirmation

Dear Ms. Lett,

We have received your $450 registration payment for the Delford Technology Education Center (DTEC) three-day workshop in May. Note that this also grants you access to our weekly lectures via the DTEC Web site.

As in the past, the DTEC is proud to offer complimentary shuttle service from Charlotte Airport to Charvia Hotel, the workshop site. Also, please be advised that Lara Iarocci's keynote speech will start at 10:20 A.M., not 10 A.M.

We hope that the workshop provides an opportunity for you and other attendees to take in a wealth of useful new information. We look forward to seeing you in May.

Sincerely,

DTEC Workshops

Schedule for: <u>Gina Lett</u>

May 2
- 9 A.M. Transfer to Charvia Hotel (booking #181, by TZAD Travel) via DTEC shuttle
- 2 P.M.-5 P.M. Attend workshop led by Dr. Ron Yun

May 3
- 10 A.M.-3:40 P.M. Group discussions
- 4 P.M. Job interview with Dr. Ron Yun, hotel meeting room

May 4
- 10 A.M.-5 P.M. Hands-on sessions
- 5:30 P.M. Closing remarks and reception

May 5
- 8 A.M. Transfer to airport via DTEC shuttle

---

196. Why most likely will Ms. Lett receive an RCT Payment Card?

(A) She commutes to the Tech Campus frequently.
(B) She will entertain visiting clients in May.
(C) She paid over $400 for an industry event.
(D) She was promoted to a management position.

197. What is indicated about the DTEC?

(A) It gives discounts to RCT staff.
(B) It operates its own hotel chain.
(C) It was founded by Ms. Iarocci.
(D) It shares talks on its Web site.

198. In the second e-mail, the phrase "take in" in paragraph 3, line 1, is closest in meaning to

(A) provide housing to
(B) be composed of
(C) shorten
(D) absorb

199. What is suggested about Ms. Lett?

(A) She will transfer to another job site.
(B) She will interview a workshop instructor.
(C) She will miss a closing address.
(D) She will have a long layover at the airport.

200. What corporate travel policy most likely applies to Ms. Lett's trip?

(A) The policy about vehicle rentals
(B) The policy about taxi receipts
(C) The policy about hotel arrangements
(D) The policy about cash advances

Stop! This is the end of the test. If you finish before time is called, you may go back to Parts 5, 6, and 7 and check your work.

TEST 9

READING TEST

In the Reading test, you will read a variety of texts and answer several different types of reading comprehension questions. The entire Reading test will last 75 minutes. There are three parts, and directions are given for each part. You are encouraged to answer as many questions as possible within the time allowed.

You must mark your answers on the separate answer sheet. Do not write your answers in your test book.

PART 5

Directions: A word or phrase is missing in each of the sentences below. Four answer choices are given below each sentence. Select the best answer to complete the sentence. Then mark the letter (A), (B), (C), or (D) on your answer sheet.

101. The cleaning staff will finish work early today in ------- of a national holiday.

(A) observe
(B) observers
(C) observing
(D) observance

102. In order to be well-prepared for her interview at the firm, Ms. Adams did some research on ------- in advance.

(A) its
(B) it
(C) itself
(D) its own

103. The county courthouse ------- at 2:00 P.M. tomorrow due to the Historic Homes Festival.

(A) closed
(B) will close
(C) was closing
(D) to close

104. The orientation for new employees is scheduled to be held on Sunday, April 26 in the office ------- from the break room.

(A) inside
(B) above
(C) beside
(D) across

105. There is some debate as to ------- we should revise the budget now or wait for Ms. Gwon's report.

(A) whether
(B) everything
(C) since
(D) merely

106. The Stability Recline line of lounge chairs is ------- available at Quinn Department Store.

(A) exclusion
(B) exclusive
(C) excluding
(D) exclusively

107. The WXI reporter recommended that drivers take the Dill Court Expressway to ------- avoid traffic from the parade.

(A) newly
(B) heavily
(C) loudly
(D) fully

108. Happy Village Bank would like to apologize to those customers ------- by the service outages.

(A) affected
(B) classified
(C) referred
(D) prevented

109. The new version of the smartphone is ------- on sale in four different colors.
    (A) extremely
    (B) previously
    (C) already
    (D) highly

110. Apartment construction has continued to increase throughout Kastar City ------- urban planners' efforts to create more public recreation spaces.
    (A) steadily
    (B) except
    (C) far enough
    (D) in spite of

111. Gift certificate ------- are refillable via the Swankson Web site.
    (A) markets
    (B) balances
    (C) descriptions
    (D) regulations

112. Overseas shipping is available at multiple price points ------- by weight, speed of delivery, and insurance amount.
    (A) determine
    (B) determines
    (C) determined
    (D) determination

113. ------- the advice of environmental experts, the city has approved a proposal to build a golf course in Wend Hills.
    (A) Against
    (B) Until
    (C) Among
    (D) Near

114. Ms. Hughes plans to take a long-term leave of absence, ------- Mr. Dowell is being trained to handle her reception duties.
    (A) how
    (B) so
    (C) in that
    (D) depending on

115. Exports of fruit and other foods are expected to decline after a poor ------- due to an unusually long rainy season.
    (A) region
    (B) fuel
    (C) harvest
    (D) resource

116. Once the commenters finished speaking, Mr. Fujii thanked them for their ------- remarks on his study.
    (A) usefully
    (B) useful
    (C) used
    (D) use

117. The "Platinum Pass" grants the holder ------- to all of Maddrington's major museums.
    (A) admittedly
    (B) admitting
    (C) admission
    (D) admit

118. Recent demand for more ------- organic produce has brought about mass-production opportunities for organic farmers.
    (A) affordable
    (B) accurate
    (C) enthusiastic
    (D) effective

119. Becoming an official partner of the Tachibana Society would ------- our brand with the positive values that the charity represents.
    (A) associate
    (B) gain
    (C) cooperate
    (D) emphasize

120. ------- devices can be exchanged at the point of sale within two years of the purchase date.
    (A) Ambitious
    (B) Prospective
    (C) Intermittent
    (D) Malfunctioning

GO ON TO THE NEXT PAGE

121. In order to provide better insulation, the single-pane glass in this window ------- with double-pane glass next year.
    (A) will replace
    (B) has replaced
    (C) will be replaced
    (D) has been replaced

122. The cafeteria, ------- offers inexpensive lunch and dinner options for employees, is located on the second floor.
    (A) who
    (B) when
    (C) where
    (D) which

123. There are very few cracks in the stone used in Hendrilon countertops, and the ones that do exist are ------- noticeable in the final product.
    (A) seldom
    (B) exactly
    (C) ever
    (D) hard

124. Company guidelines state that only ------- technical problems with unknown causes should be brought to the IT department.
    (A) lasted
    (B) lastly
    (C) lasts
    (D) lasting

125. Aspiring mail carriers must pass a written ------- exam to qualify for employment with the postal service.
    (A) enterable
    (B) entrance
    (C) entered
    (D) enters

126. Supply chain interruptions that may reduce the factory's productivity must be reported ------- they arise.
    (A) at first
    (B) because of
    (C) as soon as
    (D) whatever

127. Rondstone Financial is waiting ------- for the perfect candidate to submit an application.
    (A) patient
    (B) more patient
    (C) patiently
    (D) patience

128. Clarifent bleach pens promise to remove even the most ------- stains from neckties and other apparel.
    (A) elegant
    (B) stubborn
    (C) hesitant
    (D) practical

129. If the contractor had notified us of the construction issue, we ------- our engineers to assist with finding a solution.
    (A) could have sent
    (B) were sending
    (C) have sent
    (D) send

130. To ------- a smooth transition into the new office, a relocation specialist has been assigned to each department.
    (A) assume
    (B) facilitate
    (C) encompass
    (D) distribute

PART 6

Directions: Read the texts that follow. A word, phrase, or sentence is missing in parts of each text. Four answer choices for each question are given below the text. Select the best answer to complete the text. Then mark the letter (A), (B), (C), or (D) on your answer sheet.

Questions 131-134 refer to the following Web page.

Belfort Shop Online   → Out of stock items

Belfort Shop does its best to ensure product availability. ------. When a product is shown as "out of
                                        131.
stock," it is currently unavailable. Because we try to order more of such products promptly, we

recommend checking our Web site ------ to see if the item is back in stock. Additionally, sometimes
                                 132.
a product's ------ cannot be increased during the check-out process. This means there is a
            133.
restriction on the number of units—e.g., no more than four—of the item that we can ship to you at

present. In this case, you will not be able to purchase more than this ------.
                                                                        134.

131. (A) Furthermore, these coupons offer real
        value.
    (B) As a result, it has been tested
        thoroughly in advance.
    (C) However, we may run out of certain
        popular items.
    (D) In particular, production costs are an
        important factor.

132. (A) consecutively
    (B) periodically
    (C) formerly
    (D) briefly

133. (A) discount
    (B) manual
    (C) quantity
    (D) feedback

134. (A) limit
    (B) limits
    (C) limitedly
    (D) limited

Important notice to all employees about our holiday energy conservation program

Aldaric Industries Ltd. will make efforts to minimize energy usage ------- the upcoming holiday
135.
season. In the staff kitchen, small appliances such as the microwave, coffeemakers, and toaster will
be turned off and unplugged.

Also, management asks staff to help by turning off and unplugging the ------- equipment in each
136.
office. This includes printers, scanners, and photocopiers that are ------- used by all the employees in
137.
your work section. -------. Similarly, all windows and doors should be closed and locked.
138.

---

135. (A) only
(B) over
(C) then
(D) almost

136. (A) portable
(B) safety
(C) shared
(D) defective

137. (A) normally
(B) normalizing
(C) normality
(D) normal

138. (A) Sections usually consist of between five
and ten people.
(B) These upgrades will greatly reduce energy
consumption.
(C) Environmentally-friendly ink can be found
in the storage room.
(D) This task can be assigned to a designated
employee.

DINSER (September 12)—Holter Airlines is now offering a flight route ------- Dinser Airport to
    139.
Reaveton International Airport.

Gloria Lugo, Dinser's director of aviation, says that the decision was prompted by airline statistics.
"Holter was seeing a lot of travelers traveling between Dinser and Reaveton via Wenwater. They
approached us about offering ------- flights instead," she explains. She also points out that the high
    140.
volume of traffic between the two cities is likely due to their economic similarities. -------.
    141.

The first flights will take off on October 15. Initially, flights ------- each direction will be operated once
    142.
a day, though the frequency may increase later.

139. (A) should connect
     (B) it connects
     (C) that connects
     (D) of connection

140. (A) direct
     (B) night
     (C) international
     (D) commercial

141. (A) The congestion has led to delays on
         weekends and holidays.
     (B) Both are home to branches of major
         insurance firms.
     (C) They are roughly eight hours apart by car.
     (D) Reaveton's finances, however, have
         improved in recent years.

142. (A) aboard
     (B) under
     (C) with
     (D) in

GO ON TO THE NEXT PAGE

Questions 143-146 refer to the following e-mail.

From: Delora Stockton <d.stockton@nqy-mail.com>
To: <jobs@rendonsystems.com>
Subject: Application
Date: April 17

Dear Mr. Messer,

I am writing to apply for the position of German language specialist at Rendon Systems.

Looking at your ad on www.language-jobs.com, I am confident that I ------- the abilities and
                                                                        143.
experience needed to succeed in the role. As stated on my attached résumé, I am a native speaker
of English and have a master's degree in German translation. I have worked continuously as a
freelance translator for the past three years. During that time, I ------- to several app translation and
                                                                     144.
localization efforts like yours. ------- you request them, I can provide letters of reference from the
                                  145.
clients involved.

-------. You may reach me at this e-mail address or 555-0198. Thank you for your consideration.
146.

Sincerely,

Delora Stockton

---

143. (A) possess
     (B) resemble
     (C) occupy
     (D) fulfill

144. (A) contribute
     (B) will contribute
     (C) am contributing
     (D) contributed

145. (A) Unless
     (B) Regarding
     (C) Should
     (D) Shortly

146. (A) Rendon Systems is an industry leader with
         a great reputation.
     (B) Finally, I have a good command of all
         variations of the language.
     (C) It is difficult for foreign firms to compete in
         German-speaking countries.
     (D) I would love to talk with you further about
         my qualifications.

PART 7

Directions: In this part you will read a selection of texts, such as magazine and newspaper articles, e-mails, and instant messages. Each text or set of texts is followed by several questions. Select the best answer for each question and mark the letter (A), (B), (C), or (D) on your answer sheet.

Questions 147-148 refer to the following text message.

From: Jeff Milton, 555-0194
To: Nana Dragoti

Hi, Nana. We're preparing the small vintage fountain for shipment to the buyer, Mr. Yu. It looks like we'll have to pack and ship the sculpture part of the fountain separately from its water pump so that they don't damage each other during shipping. Could you e-mail Mr. Yu to let him know that's the way the item will go out? Thanks! I'm about to leave the warehouse and drive back to the main office now.

147. What is Ms. Dragoti asked to do?

(A) Alert staff about an upcoming policy change
(B) Modify a price list for some items
(C) Buy additional packing supplies
(D) Notify a customer about a shipping method

148. What will Mr. Milton probably do next?

(A) Repair some plumbing
(B) Set up some shelves
(C) Return to an office
(D) Phone a delivery driver

GO ON TO THE NEXT PAGE

The Brindon Dessert Festival is back!

Following the success of last year's inaugural event, the Brindon Dessert Festival is coming back to Brindon Park from Friday, May 9 through Sunday, May 11, 2 P.M. to 8 P.M. each day.

- *Admission ($8 per person) includes souvenir drinking glass, canvas tote bag, and a voucher for two sample desserts!*
- *Sample locally-made cakes, tarts, pastries, pies, and more!*
- *Great lineup of live entertainment each day!*

Brindon Park's main entrance is located across from Wheldon Drive. There will be ample vehicle parking at nearby city parking facilities. To avoid paying a fee, simply show your ticket stub to the parking attendant.

---

149. What is mentioned about the festival?

(A) It is being held for the third time.
(B) It will have free parking available.
(C) Its organizers are seeking performers.
(D) Its Sunday hours have been extended.

150. What is NOT included with admission?

(A) A glass
(B) A carrying bag
(C) A food coupon
(D) A beverage

Questions 151-152 refer to the following text-message chain.

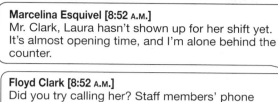

Marcelina Esquivel [8:52 A.M.]
Mr. Clark, Laura hasn't shown up for her shift yet. It's almost opening time, and I'm alone behind the counter.

Floyd Clark [8:52 A.M.]
Did you try calling her? Staff members' phone numbers are listed in the back room.

Marcelina Esquivel [8:53 A.M.]
I called her mobile phone twice, but she didn't answer. What should I do? I don't know how to make all of our specialty coffee drinks yet.

Floyd Clark [8:54 A.M.]
I can come in for the first hour, but then I have to leave for a family event. I'll send out a group text to see if anyone can work the rest of the shift.

Marcelina Esquivel [8:54 A.M.]
Oh, great. But what happens if someone orders a drink I can't make before you get here?

Floyd Clark [8:55 A.M.]
I'm only ten minutes away. But just in case—say the drink is temporarily unavailable and give them a 20% discount voucher. There are a few in the drawer under the cash register.

151. Where do the writers work?

(A) At a café
(B) At a library
(C) At a factory
(D) At a clothing store

152. At 8:55 A.M., what does Mr. Clark most likely mean when he writes, "I'm only ten minutes away"?

(A) Ms. Esquivel should wait to take a break.
(B) Ms. Esquivel is unlikely to encounter a problem.
(C) He does not mind making a trip.
(D) He needs a task to be done quickly.

GO ON TO THE NEXT PAGE

WEEKEND SUBWAY DELAYS

Construction work on the C and F lines will cause scheduled delays for the next two weeks. This project will improve transport safety by replacing old tracks and installing special emergency lights.

C-line trains: From 2:00 A.M. on Saturday, May 1, until 4:00 A.M. on Monday, May 3, the C line will be using only the southbound track between the Van Houten and Newbury stops while the northbound track undergoes work.

F-line trains: From 2:00 A.M. on Saturday, May 8, until 4:00 A.M. on Monday, May 10, the F line will be using only the eastbound track between the Whitehurst and Canberry stops while the westbound track undergoes work.

Rerouted service maps are available on all train platforms. Thank you for your patience as we work to keep our tracks safe.

153. Why are delays scheduled?

(A) A terminal is being expanded.
(B) A new line is being constructed.
(C) Damage is being repaired.
(D) Upgrades are being performed.

154. When will work on the F line end?

(A) On May 1
(B) On May 3
(C) On May 8
(D) On May 10

155. According to the notice, where can special maps be obtained?

(A) On trains
(B) At stations
(C) On the Internet
(D) At city newsstands

Questions 156-158 refer to the following e-mail.

```
================= E-Mail message =================

From:        Alexis Kurtz

To:          Eric Guo

Subject:     Research results

Date:        October 5

Attachment:  📎 Report
```

Hi Eric,

My team has completed focus group testing for the packaging design of the Deriche snack crackers. The full report of our results is attached, but I'll summarize the main points for you here.

As you'll recall, we had narrowed down the packaging options to two designs. The first, "Option 1," is green and has a drawing of a farm on the front, while the second, "Option 2," is blue and shows a photograph of the crackers on a plate. The focus groups gave the options equally high marks in the category of attractiveness, but after they actually tried the crackers, more than 80% of the participants said that Option 1 better represented the taste. It seems that once they realized that our crackers were modeled after Karpiec Foods' Temptos line, they felt that our packaging should be, too.

Therefore, we recommend Option 1. Please let me know if we have your authorization to proceed to the production stage.

Thanks,

Alexis

156. Why did Ms. Kurtz send the e-mail to Mr. Guo?

(A) To request his approval
(B) To prepare him for a meeting
(C) To inform him of a revision to a plan
(D) To apologize to him for a mistake

157. What information is given about the packaging options?

(A) The dates their designs were completed
(B) The expected cost of producing them
(C) The materials they are made of
(D) The images featured on them

158. What is suggested about the Deriche snack crackers?

(A) They are similar to a competitor's product.
(B) They have been in development for a long time.
(C) They are targeted at young adults.
(D) They come in two flavors.

GO ON TO THE NEXT PAGE

Questions 159-160 refer to the following Web page.

Kaldac Tools, Inc.   *Home>>Support>>Warranty*

<u>Warranty and Return Policy</u>

The terms and conditions of our warranties vary depending on which type of Kaldac product you own. To view a specific warranty, please go to <u>Warranty by Product Type</u> and follow the prompts. All warranty returns must be accompanied by a Warranty Authorization Number (WAN). The WAN can be obtained by e-mailing service@kaldac.com and will include a return packing slip for your package. Note that a fee will be charged to ship the product back to you. If you have a specific question about your warranty coverage, please call our Customer Service Department at 555-0135.

Special note to consumers: Under its "Cutting Edge" guarantee, Kaldac Tools, Inc. will sharpen the blades of any of its cutting tools for free, whether or not they are under warranty. To request this service, please e-mail the Lifetime Product Support Center (LPSC) at support@kaldac.com.

159. What is indicated about Kaldac Tools, Inc.'s warranties?

(A) They differ according to the product.
(B) They are sold separately from the product.
(C) They are only valid in a single country.
(D) They cover all shipping charges.

160. Why most likely would a consumer contact the LPSC?

(A) To get details about a warranty guarantee
(B) To make a large purchase
(C) To arrange a free service
(D) To dispute a decision

From:	April Mackey <a.mackey@lawning.edu>
To:	Joseph Witt <joseph.witt@jwittauthor.com>
Subject:	Lawning University PSP
Date:	June 30

Dear Mr. Witt,

Hello. My name is April Mackey, and I am part of the organizing committee for Lawning University's Politics and Society Program (PSP). I recently read your book *Digital Citizens* and found your arguments fascinating. — [1] —. I would like you to come to our campus next semester to give a talk about your research as a PSP event.

The PSP is funded by the university's Graduate School of Social Sciences, and our mission is to promote academic exchange between political science researchers and those in other disciplines. — [2] —. I am sure you can see why your book, as an analysis of the ways that modern technology is changing what it means to be a citizen, is appealing to us.

We would hope to schedule your visit for October 11. Your talk would be an hour long, and would be followed by a half-hour Q&A session. We cannot pay you a speaking fee, but we would cover all your travel costs. — [3] —. I would be happy to give more details upon request.

I look forward to hearing from you. — [4] —.

Regards,

April Mackey
Professor of Political Science

161. What is the purpose of the e-mail?

(A) To announce the establishment of a committee
(B) To propose collaborating on a book
(C) To issue a speaking invitation
(D) To apply for funding for a study

162. What does Ms. Mackey indicate is the goal of the PSP?

(A) To encourage communication among scholars in different fields
(B) To discover problems with existing research techniques
(C) To increase public participation in politics
(D) To reliably predict future technological trends

163. In which of the positions marked [1], [2], [3], and [4] does the following sentence best belong?
"These would include taxi fare from the airport and lodging at a hotel near campus."

(A) [1]
(B) [2]
(C) [3]
(D) [4]

GO ON TO THE NEXT PAGE

Storage company exhibits at the Spaces-Plus Expo

ROODEPOORT—Last week, Storage-Tec Ltd. became the first storage company to exhibit at the Spaces-Plus Expo, an annual trade fair that is open to the public. — [1] —.

The expo, held at the Horizon Convention Center, ran from August 11 to 14 and centered on trends in decorating interior spaces. According to its brochure, it featured more than 600 exhibitors, including décor specialists, remodeling contractors, and decoration suppliers. — [2] —.

Storage-Tec Ltd.'s booth included a 3.3-meter wide walk-in storage unit similar to those it rents at its facilities. During the expo, the company had daily drawings for prizes it had on display, including a refrigerator and a microwave. All visitors to its booth received a paper voucher for discounts on storage services. — [3] —.

Headquartered in Durban, Storage-Tec Ltd. operates 32 self-storage facilities in seven South African cities. It recently acquired Upsal Self-Storage's six facilities and has plans to rebrand these properties with the Storage-Tec Ltd. name. Visitors to the company's Web site, www.storage-tec.com, can browse a full range of storage unit sizes, get pricing information, and read customer testimonials. — [4] —.

164. What is NOT suggested about this year's Spaces-Plus Expo?

(A) It was focused on a specific theme.
(B) It charged vendors extra fees for storage space.
(C) It had booths that were at least three meters wide.
(D) It included a new type of exhibitor.

165. What is most likely true about Storage-Tec Ltd.?

(A) Its head office is in Roodepoort.
(B) It acquired a moving company.
(C) It gave away appliances at a trade fair.
(D) It intends to change its name in the future.

166. According to the newsletter article, what is featured on Storage-Tec Ltd.'s Web site?

(A) Virtual tours of its facilities
(B) Comments from customers
(C) Details about its corporate history
(D) Lists of available storage units

167. In which of the positions marked [1], [2], [3], and [4] does the following sentence best belong?

"An online update to the handout stated that more than 50,000 people attended the event."

(A) [1]
(B) [2]
(C) [3]
(D) [4]

Questions 168-171 refer to the following online chat discussion.

Michael Manno [10:11 A.M.]   Hi, all. Did you see the scarves I brought in? They're the product samples I picked up from a potential supplier — Tex-Garmm in Shenzhen.

Tom Lopez [10:12 A.M.]   Yes. I was surprised at how good-looking they are.

Sue Dalhart [10:13 A.M.]   Me too. My colleagues really liked their variety of colors.

Michael Manno [10:14 A.M.]   I agree! And the thick-knit fabric is a plus.

Tom Lopez [10:15 A.M.]   How about the manufacturing cost?

Michael Manno [10:15 A.M.]   It's $5 per unit. So, yes, Tex-Garmm would be more expensive than our other suppliers.

Tom Lopez [10:16 A.M.]   Hmm… it's more than we had anticipated.

Sue Dalhart [10:17 A.M.]   That's true. The products are attractive, though. With a good marketing plan, we could make a profit on them.

Tom Lopez [10:18 A.M.]   What's Tex-Garmm's minimum order total?

Michael Manno [10:19 A.M.]   It's 500 scarves. Why don't we put in an order for that amount? We can then test-market the scarves in stores as limited edition items.

Sue Dalhart [10:20 A.M.]   Great. I'll have my team come up with some marketing ideas during our afternoon meeting. Tom? I'd like you to sit in on our discussion.

Tom Lopez [10:21 A.M.]   Sure.

Michael Manno [10:22 A.M.]   Good plan. OK, let's keep each other updated.

`[                    ]` **SEND**

---

168. What is mentioned about some product samples?

(A) They come in a variety of sizes.
(B) They have a pleasing appearance.
(C) They are made of waterproof fabric.
(D) They were produced quickly.

169. At 10:17 A.M., what does Ms. Dalhart most likely mean when she writes, "That's true"?

(A) She understands others' concerns about costs.
(B) She agrees that a timeline is unreasonable.
(C) She expects a supplier to accept a proposal.
(D) She is disappointed with her firm's recent sales.

170. What does Mr. Manno suggest?

(A) Reducing staff numbers
(B) Visiting an industrial complex
(C) Placing the smallest order allowed
(D) Opening some stores abroad

171. What does Ms. Dalhart ask Mr. Lopez to do?

(A) Cancel a site inspection
(B) Form a project team
(C) Join a brainstorming meeting
(D) Draft a marketing report

GO ON TO THE NEXT PAGE

Bonuses may be money awarded in addition to employees' regular salary payments, but that does not mean that the employees eligible for them do not consider them important. This is what Gollit Hotels, Inc. was reminded of this week when employees across the country reacted strongly to an announcement that it would soon be changing its bonus program for the first time in over two decades.

Currently, the highest-performing 30% of Gollit's full-time employees in each job category receive quarterly bonuses of up to $500. Under the new system, the hotel chain would give bonuses on a yearly basis to just 10% of employees chosen at random through a lottery. However, the payments would be much larger, ranging between $5,000 and $20,000. The company's management claims that the plan will make the process of awarding bonuses more exciting; critics say it is mostly intended to cut costs.

The new plan was communicated to employees on Monday morning via a companywide memo. As well as causing a surge of posts on Gollit's internal forums, the news became a topic of public discussion that afternoon when individual employees began mentioning it on social media. While a small number of employees and outside commentators support the lottery system because it would give bonuses to people who had not received them before, most agree that it is unfair because its payments are not tied to employee performance.

Because of this controversy, the decision is expected to be reversed eventually.

172. What is one purpose of the article?

(A) To suggest strategies for recruiting staff
(B) To explain a special characteristic of the hospitality industry
(C) To describe a difficulty facing a corporation
(D) To praise a new type of incentive program

173. The word "regular" in paragraph 1, line 2, is closest in meaning to

(A) natural
(B) recurring
(C) average
(D) classic

174. What do critics suggest about the management of Gollit Hotels, Inc.?

(A) Its structure is inefficient.
(B) It intends to shut down some forums.
(C) Its approach to employee compensation is outdated.
(D) It wants to lower expenses.

175. According to the article, what do most people dislike about the lottery system?

(A) It does not reward employees for doing good work.
(B) Employees must complete an entry form to participate.
(C) It awards bonuses less frequently than other systems.
(D) The names of winners are publicly announced.

GO ON TO THE NEXT PAGE

Test 9

Questions 176-180 refer to the following announcement and letter.

DeSoto Fellowship

The DeSoto Foundation Media Center, located in Los Angeles, solicits applications from mid-career professionals in the arts and media fields to pursue projects that combine technology and the humanities.

The fellowship is a two-year residential award that comes with a stipend equal to 80% of the recipient's salary, up to $70,000 per year. It is intended to replace the awardee's salary during the two-year period so that his or her employer can hire a temporary replacement while the awardee completes the fellowship project.

Applicants should submit:
- A 1,500-word project proposal
- A 500-word personal/professional profile
- Three letters of recommendation
- Portfolio of related work (optional)

The deadline for applying is October 12. Finalists will be notified by January 1, at which point interviews will be arranged. Interviews will be conducted in Denver and New York City.

Applications are reviewed by an independent board of industry professionals and university faculty. To read about previous recipients and view their fellowship projects, please visit www.desotofellowship.com/recipients.

DeSoto Foundation Media Center

March 23

Ms. Grace Sun
302 Orange Grove Lane
Orlando, FL 29438

Dear Ms. Sun,

Congratulations! We are delighted to inform you that you have been selected to receive this year's DeSoto Fellowship. In their decision, our interviewers particularly cited your enthusiasm for and commitment to using film in order to interface between the tech industry and the public.

As you know, this fellowship requires a two-year residency at the DeSoto Foundation Media Center. Relocation agents are available to assist you and your family in the moving process. We are truly pleased to welcome you as one of a select and special group. We look forward to seeing you in September.

Sincerely,

Peter Gallant

DeSoto Foundation Media Center
Fellowship Coordinator

176. Who would be eligible to receive a DeSoto Fellowship?

(A) A computer programmer
(B) A medical doctor
(C) A structural engineer
(D) A film director

177. What is NOT listed as a required part of the application?

(A) Recommendation letters
(B) A description of an idea
(C) Samples of work
(D) A biography

178. In the e-mail, what is suggested about Ms. Sun?

(A) She is passionate about her work.
(B) She is the only recipient of the fellowship this year.
(C) She is a highly paid professional.
(D) She has applied for the fellowship multiple times.

179. Where will Ms. Sun be moving?

(A) To Los Angeles
(B) To Denver
(C) To New York
(D) To Orlando

180. When will Ms. Sun begin her fellowship?

(A) In January
(B) In March
(C) In September
(D) In October

GO ON TO THE NEXT PAGE

For immediate release

Contact: Dean Smyth,
d.smyth@burleys.com.au

SYDNEY (1 March)—Burley's Pizza will no longer automatically provide plastic drinking straws to eat-in customers. By making this change, the chain hopes to decrease the amount of trash generated at its restaurants.

Though made of recyclable plastic, straws' small size makes them impossible to sort at recycling plants. Most end up in landfills, or travel through sewer systems to the ocean, where they cause harm to the ecosystem.

A sticker will be affixed to the restaurants' beverages list to inform customers that waitstaff will supply plastic straws only upon request. Additionally, the chain's southeastern locations will sell reusable metal straws made by Kreble Industries. Burley's locations across Australia will do the same as soon as the straws can be manufactured on a larger scale.

The practice will be the latest of Burley's Pizza's environmentally-friendly initiatives, which also include sourcing most of its ingredients domestically and composting its food waste. CEO Ciara Krauss says, "We believe that it is our responsibility as members of the global community to contribute to our planet's sustainability."

From:	Mark Duran
To:	All waitstaff
Subject:	Meeting
Date:	2 March

Hi, everyone,

You may have heard that corporate just made a public announcement that will affect us. (If you don't know what I'm talking about, see this press release.) Please arrive 15 minutes early for at least one shift this week so that the manager on duty can explain it and give you some instructions on dealing with customer inquiries and promoting our new product. Your shift manager can also handle any questions you may have.

Thanks,

Mark Duran
Head Manager, Neagle Branch
Burley's Pizza

181. What is the press release mainly about?

(A) An event to celebrate a company milestone
(B) A partnership between two businesses
(C) A policy regarding restaurant safety
(D) An effort to reduce waste production

182. According to the press release, how will customers most likely be notified of a change?

(A) By a sign hung in a front window
(B) By a note attached to a menu
(C) By a statement made by staff
(D) By a pamphlet offered in a waiting area

183. What is indicated about straws made by Kreble Industries?

(A) They are manufactured domestically.
(B) They have a special shape.
(C) They are made of recycled plastic.
(D) They are meant to be used repeatedly.

184. Why does Mr. Duran ask employees to come in early?

(A) To receive some training
(B) To put up some decorations
(C) To check a shift schedule
(D) To submit paperwork to a manager

185. What is implied about the Neagle branch of Burley's Pizza?

(A) It recently opened.
(B) Ms. Krauss will visit it.
(C) It is in the southeastern part of Australia.
(D) It received special recognition from company headquarters.

GO ON TO THE NEXT PAGE

Test 9

Questions 186-190 refer to the following e-mail, advertisement, and review.

E-Mail message

To:	Alby Tran <atran@castlerockelectronics.com>
From:	Dorothy Connors <dconnors@castlerockelectronics.com>
Date:	October 3
Subject:	Request

Dear Alby,

The shipment of the new Systemax 7 that Storrey Appliances released last month has arrived in our warehouse. I think it will be popular, so I'd like you to replace the current washing machine that is on display in our store with one of these. It should be set up at the front of Aisle 9. Could you make the arrangements for this to happen by Wednesday of next week? Thanks.

Dorothy
Manager, Castle Rock Electronics

Castle Rock Electronics

--Featured Washing Machines in November--

XM332
The XM332, one of the biggest consumer washing machines, is able to accommodate large loads of blankets or other bulky items. It also allows water temperature adjustments to suit different types of fabrics.
Price: $475

Systemax 7
With an LED display and touchscreen controls, the Systemax 7 has a sleek, modern look. It is now offered in dark green, which sets it apart even more from the usual black and white washers.
Price: $425

Washen 3.0
The Washen 3.0 specializes in reducing the vibrations that make other washing machines so loud. It operates so quietly that users may wonder if the machine is truly on.
Usual price: $425
Sale price: $350 (Valid until November 30)

Tron T40
The Tron T40 will finish your laundry in no time! Its wash cycle can clean clothes in 30 minutes, no matter whether it is a heavy or delicate load.
Price: $375

This month only!

Castle Rock Electronics is offering free delivery and installation of washing machines priced at $450 and above.

Consumer Reviews Online

Reviewer: Caroline Ackley

Date: November 11

I purchased the Washen 3.0 washing machine yesterday at Castle Rock Electronics. My salesperson was extremely helpful, and I got a great deal. Mostly, I am impressed with how quiet the machine is. I used to hear my old washing machine running throughout the entire apartment, but this one barely makes any noise at all.

186. What does Ms. Connors ask Mr. Tran to do?

(A) Unload a shipment from a vehicle
(B) Put merchandise on display
(C) Replace a broken machine
(D) Clean a store aisle thoroughly

187. What is emphasized about a Storrey Appliances washing machine?

(A) Its new color
(B) Its large capacity
(C) Its quietness
(D) Its speed

188. Which machine is Castle Rock Electronics offering to install for free?

(A) XM332
(B) Systemax 7
(C) Washen 3.0
(D) Tron T40

189. What is most likely true about Ms. Ackley's washing machine?

(A) It has water temperature controls.
(B) It will stop being sold in December.
(C) She bought it at a special price.
(D) She can operate it by tapping on a screen.

190. In the review, the word "running" in paragraph 1, line 3, is closest in meaning to

(A) rushing
(B) supervising
(C) spreading
(D) functioning

Test 9

December 12—After five years, singer Tatiana Newton has finally released her new album, *River Flows*. It has received rave reviews and is expected to have high record sales.

The Los Angeles native says she took a lot of time writing this album because she was busy managing Pink Artists, Inc., a Nashville-based record label she launched three years ago. "Starting my own music company has been difficult yet extremely rewarding," Ms. Newton shares. "I've learned so much about the business side of the music industry."

Although Ms. Newton is now the head of a record label, she wants to continue to be a successful singer as well. This is why she is in the middle of preparing a nationwide tour. She plans to begin it with one performance at Jarcher Arena in Los Angeles in May. "I've been living in Nashville for the past couple of years, so I think it would be special to come back and play in my hometown for a night," Ms. Newton says.

Jarcher Arena

Weekly Events

May 23 6:00 P.M.	May 24 7:00 P.M.	May 25 9:00 A.M.	May 26 9:00 A.M.	May 27 8:00 P.M.	May 28 7:00 P.M.	May 29 7:00 P.M.
Lightning vs. Gladiators	Bike World	Tysonfest	Tysonfest	Mya Wade Live	Tatiana Newton	Tatiana Newton
Event Type: Sports	Event Type: Other live performance	Event Type: Exhibition	Event Type: Exhibition	Event Type: Comedy	Event Type: Music	Event Type: Music

www.jarcherarena.com/guestservices/FAQ ▶

Jarcher Arena

Frequently Asked Questions

Q: Can I bring a camera?
A: Yes, small cameras and mobile phones are allowed. However, all professional cameras with lens that are over 35 millimeters are not permitted. Those attending exhibition events are exempt from this restriction. Please click <u>here</u> for more details.

Q: Can I bring food and drinks?
A: No. Food and beverages can be purchased from vendors inside Jarcher Arena. Exceptions can be made for guests with special dietary needs. Please contact Masao Harada at guestservices@jarcherarena.com.

Q: Can I bring a bag?
A: Yes, but all bags must be small enough to fit under a seat. Oversized bags, backpacks, suitcases, etc. will not be permitted. Please click <u>here</u> for size details.

191. What is mentioned about Ms. Newton?

(A) She founded a company.
(B) She has released her fifth album.
(C) She will move to Los Angeles.
(D) She has completed a worldwide tour.

192. What does the calendar indicate about Jarcher Arena?

(A) It has an outdoor space.
(B) It hosts comedy acts.
(C) Its office opens at 8 A.M.
(D) It can seat 20,000 people.

193. What most likely has changed about Ms. Newton's tour plans for Jarcher Arena?

(A) She will perform for more than two hours.
(B) There are more shows than originally planned.
(C) It is no longer the first stop of her tour.
(D) She has raised her ticket prices.

194. For which event could a guest bring a professional camera?

(A) Lightning vs. Gladiators
(B) Bike World
(C) Tysonfest
(D) Mya Wade Live

195. According to the Web page, why should someone contact Mr. Harada?

(A) To become an arena vendor
(B) To get permission to bring a large bag
(C) To locate a lost item
(D) To make a food request

Test 9

Questions 196-200 refer to the following e-mails and excerpt from a brochure.

```
═══════════════════════ E-Mail message ═══════════════════════

From:     Jay Russell

To:       Claudia Sanchez, Dustin Butler, Elana Tinsley

Subject:  Company brochure

Date:     January 10
```

Hello all,

I'm now gathering necessary information for the company brochure you asked me to make. To that end, I need each of you, as our top executives, to give me any details about your position or career that you'd like included in a short paragraph describing you. Or, if you want, you can write the paragraph yourself, as long as it's under 50 words. Once I get the pieces I need, I'll put them together on a template and send it back for you all to approve.

Thanks,

Jay Russell
Marketing Communications Manager
Lebbar, Inc.

Our Management Team

Claudia Sanchez
President

Dustin Butler
Vice President of Sales and Marketing

Elana Tinsley
Vice President of Operations

Ms. Sanchez started Lebbar, Inc. after leaving Blakin Industries, where she was the director of operations for 10 years. She determines Lebbar's overall business strategy and provides guidance to the vice presidents and other senior executives.

Mr. Butler has been a valued member of the Lebbar team since its establishment. He is responsible for formulating and implementing plans to expand the business by finding new distributors and developing existing retail accounts.

Ms. Tinsley oversees the development and production of Lebbar, Inc.'s innovative floor, table, and desk lamps. After joining the company as a junior engineer, she rose through its ranks thanks to her hard work and dedication to quality.

Page 3

```
═══════════════════ E-Mail message ═══════════════════
From:      Claudia Sanchez

To:        Jay Russell

Subject:   Re: Company brochure mock-up

Date:      January 22
```

Hi Jay,

Thanks for sending me the mock-up of the company brochure. After looking over it, I can say that I'm mostly very pleased. I like the clean, simple design you chose. In fact, I only have one small change to request as far as the style goes. On the "Our Management Team" page, please use italic font for the second line of each piece of writing so that there's more contrast between it and the paragraph that follows.

However, I do have some concerns about the content on page 2 (the page headed "About Lebbar, Inc."). There is quite a lot of detail about our work processes there that seems unnecessary to me. Could you explain why you thought this information should be in the brochure? If there isn't a particularly good reason, it would be better to delete it and insert a graphic instead.

-Claudia

196. What is the main purpose of the first e-mail?

(A) To show gratitude for an opportunity
(B) To ask for some personal information
(C) To remind the recipients about a restriction
(D) To gather responses to a proposal

197. What is implied about Mr. Butler?

(A) He joined Lebbar, Inc. before Ms. Sanchez.
(B) He chose not to write a paragraph about himself.
(C) He holds a newly-created position.
(D) He is Mr. Russell's boss.

198. What kind of company is Lebbar, Inc.?

(A) A lighting installation firm
(B) A furniture distributor
(C) An appliance manufacturer
(D) A building materials supplier

199. Which phrase in the brochure will be affected by the change Ms. Sanchez requests?

(A) "Claudia Sanchez"
(B) "President"
(C) "Lebbar, Inc."
(D) "10 years"

200. What does Ms. Sanchez ask Mr. Russell to do regarding page 2 of the brochure?

(A) Add an explanation of a graphic
(B) Reconsider the wording of a heading
(C) Increase the speed of the editing process
(D) Justify the inclusion of some content

Stop! This is the end of the test. If you finish before time is called, you may go back to Parts 5, 6, and 7 and check your work.

RC

TEST 10

READING TEST

In the Reading test, you will read a variety of texts and answer several different types of reading comprehension questions. The entire Reading test will last 75 minutes. There are three parts, and directions are given for each part. You are encouraged to answer as many questions as possible within the time allowed.

You must mark your answers on the separate answer sheet. Do not write your answers in your test book.

PART 5

Directions: A word or phrase is missing in each of the sentences below. Four answer choices are given below each sentence. Select the best answer to complete the sentence. Then mark the letter (A), (B), (C), or (D) on your answer sheet.

---

101. Over the past decade, the Shenke Foundation ------- in a variety of activities to promote sustainable development.

(A) has engaged
(B) is engaged
(C) engages
(D) engaging

102. Large items such as furniture should be left ------- the waste bins for convenient pick-up by disposal services.

(A) beside
(B) from
(C) until
(D) out

103. Gathering information about all of the products in one place will make it easy to ------- them.

(A) argue
(B) resume
(C) compare
(D) determine

104. Gillas Catering used to serve a lot of corporate customers, but it has not had any -------.

(A) nearly
(B) primarily
(C) lately
(D) personally

105. Mr. Okada's ------- about this week's weather has turned out to be mostly accurate.

(A) predicted
(B) predicts
(C) predictably
(D) prediction

106. Ayelt's Siolon smartphone is compatible with most headphones, but using ------- will ensure maximum sound quality.

(A) we
(B) our
(C) ours
(D) ourselves

107. The contractor suggested adding a row of trees ------- several planters along the front walkway.

(A) so
(B) yet
(C) or
(D) since

108. The lead entertainer who performed on the cruise ship had an ------- attitude when he took the stage.

(A) energetic
(B) energy
(C) energies
(D) energetically

109. To avoid delays in processing, fill out the form
------- when making a refund request.
(A) careful
(B) carefulness
(C) most careful
(D) carefully

110. If the address on the package does not state
a specific employee's name, it will be taken
------- the mail room.
(A) away
(B) as
(C) on
(D) to

111. Despite the ------- overtime pay rate, it is
often difficult to persuade workers to accept
additional shifts in busy periods.
(A) lengthy
(B) generous
(C) infrequent
(D) intensive

112. The departments whose staff members -------
one another usually have a high level of
productivity.
(A) cooperate with
(B) qualify for
(C) refrain from
(D) contribute to

113. The event coordinator made a few
announcements ------- the break between the
two sessions.
(A) whenever
(B) during
(C) while
(D) then

114. ------- included on lists of the city's top tourist
sites, the Lambert neighborhood offers
beautiful, diverse architecture.
(A) Increases
(B) Increasing
(C) To increase
(D) Increasingly

115. After Mr. Drake expertly handled a -------
between two of his colleagues, he was
offered a promotion.
(A) disputes
(B) disputable
(C) disputed
(D) dispute

116. Ms. Cooper fixed the computer problem that
------- down transactions all last weekend.
(A) slows
(B) will be slowing
(C) had slowed
(D) will slow

117. Government officials support measures to
double the country's supply of wind power
and reduce ------- on oil from overseas.
(A) reliance
(B) congestion
(C) dissatisfaction
(D) attendance

118. In the future, marketing materials should
emphasize that our office electronics are
------- for small businesses.
(A) affording
(B) affordability
(C) affordable
(D) affords

119. Ms. Mayes was given a discount on the
produce she bought at the farmers' market
because it was ------- bruised.
(A) closely
(B) actively
(C) slightly
(D) briefly

120. In accordance with county noise -------,
outdoor concerts at Cold Creek Pavilion must
end by 10:00 P.M.
(A) regulate
(B) regulations
(C) regulator
(D) regulates

GO ON TO THE NEXT PAGE

121. Flavor of India's head chef creates dishes with a ------- blend of herbs and spices.
    (A) remote
    (B) countless
    (C) wealthy
    (D) delicate

122. Two months after its projected completion date, construction of the escalator at Exit 2 is ------- ongoing.
    (A) still
    (B) far
    (C) well
    (D) soon

123. A great deal of interest in the film ------- by the director's comments on social media yesterday.
    (A) generated
    (B) was generated
    (C) will generate
    (D) to be generated

124. Please suggest three keywords that describe your study but ------- do not already appear in the title of your paper.
    (A) preferably
    (B) preferred
    (C) preferable
    (D) preferences

125. ------- the snow has been cleared from the roadways, motorists are advised to drive slowly this morning.
    (A) Ahead of
    (B) So that
    (C) Even though
    (D) In case

126. Vince's Autos promises to give a fair trade-in price on any vehicle, ------- of the condition it is in.
    (A) regards
    (B) regarding
    (C) regarded
    (D) regardless

127. The team has an excellent chance of winning the championship ------- Jody Shin has recovered from her injury.
    (A) after all
    (B) instead of
    (C) due to
    (D) now that

128. All of the items in the warehouse ------- crates marked with a red sticker must be unpacked by lunchtime.
    (A) except
    (B) apart
    (C) onto
    (D) prior to

129. Employees of Armida International receive reimbursement for any expenses ------- in the course of their professional duties.
    (A) proceeded
    (B) incurred
    (C) nominated
    (D) attained

130. It is important that visitors take certain ------- before entering the factory's production floor.
    (A) accomplishments
    (B) precautions
    (C) malfunctions
    (D) incidents

PART 6

Directions: Read the texts that follow. A word, phrase, or sentence is missing in parts of each text. Four answer choices for each question are given below the text. Select the best answer to complete the text. Then mark the letter (A), (B), (C), or (D) on your answer sheet.

Questions 131-134 refer to the following article.

BERLIN (5 September)—VCF Automotive is moving forward with plans to make its vehicle manufacturing plants more environmentally-friendly.

A spokesperson for the company said that the ------- can be achieved through a few major changes.
                                            131.
First, the need for outside electricity will be reduced by ------- rooftop solar panels. The panels will
                                                                 132.
enable the plants to generate their own clean energy. The company also wants to ------- reduce the
                                                                                  133.
amount of matter it releases into the air. Therefore, filters will be added to all exterior vents. Finally,

there are plans to move distribution centers closer to dealerships. -------.
                                                                    134.

Consumers have reacted favorably to the news and are praising VCF's efforts to minimize its environmental impact.

131. (A) objective
     (B) revenue
     (C) technique
     (D) facility

132. (A) to install
     (B) installing
     (C) installs
     (D) install

133. (A) sharpening
     (B) sharpen
     (C) sharply
     (D) sharp

134. (A) This will result in less pollution from transportation.
     (B) Otherwise, the impact would be even more significant.
     (C) The centers track their inventory using sophisticated equipment.
     (D) Customers can thus experience the benefits for themselves.

Cunningham Library provides an impressive collection of books and periodicals to the community. Extensively renovated to restore it to its ------- condition, this historical building is appreciated for its
135.

beautiful woodwork, classic design, and cozy atmosphere. Patrons can ------- the rare and out-of-
136.

print books in the Research Room and borrow contemporary books for up to two weeks at a time. There are plenty of events for library visitors as well. A weekly lecture is conducted every Tuesday

evening. -------.
137.

There are also special ------- just for writers. These include academic journals, textbooks, grammar
138.

checking software, and more. The library is open on weekdays from 10:00 A.M. to 8:30 P.M.

135. (A) origin
(B) originate
(C) originally
(D) original

136. (A) browse
(B) publish
(C) conserve
(D) edit

137. (A) We have several openings for part-time library assistants.
(B) Topics cover everything from economics to literature.
(C) Make sure to prepare your recipes for this in advance.
(D) Most communities of our size have a smaller library.

138. (A) awards
(B) resources
(C) workshops
(D) organizations

To: Jeffrey Curtis <jeffrey@jcurtisdesign.com>
From: Edward Wilcox <e.wilcox@conceptmedia.com>
Date: November 20
Subject: Concept Media Submission

Dear Mr. Curtis,

I am pleased to inform you that Concept Media's Web site relaunch will include the background image that you submitted. Please sign and return the attached consent form ------. **139.** As you know, we do not pay for submissions. ------, **140.** we do offer a link to your Web site, which could be excellent exposure for your business. If our steady growth continues, we ------ **141.** 800 daily unique visitors by the end of the year. Once I have finalized the design for the relaunch, I will let you know. ------. **142.**

All the best,
Edward Wilcox

139. (A) strictly
(B) promptly
(C) consistently
(D) largely

140. (A) Besides
(B) In other words
(C) For instance
(D) However

141. (A) were reaching
(B) had reached
(C) will have reached
(D) reached

142. (A) You will also get notification of the relaunch if you are on our mailing list.
(B) Everyone here is excited that you will be joining our team.
(C) I thought your color scheme recommendations were especially helpful.
(D) Please choose a day and time that work best for you.

GO ON TO THE NEXT PAGE

Questions 143-146 refer to the following notice.

We're Moving!

Locklear Dental Center is moving to a new location. From Monday, June 13, our address will be 1200 Byrd Street, Locklear. All of our other contact details, as well as our hours of operation, will remain ------.
143.

The major reason for this decision is that the Byrd Street space is larger than our current offices. Occupying it ------ us to better serve our patients.
144.

Unfortunately, the transition will not be without inconvenience ------ some of you. The moving
145.
process will take place from June 6 to June 11. ------. If you have an appointment scheduled for that
146.
period, we will call you to reschedule it for a different week. We ask for your patience with this disruption.

---

143. (A) competitive
     (B) confidential
     (C) unchanged
     (D) visible

144. (A) allowed
     (B) should allow
     (C) is allowing
     (D) has allowed

145. (A) through
     (B) about
     (C) for
     (D) of

146. (A) Our physicians' shift schedule is the same each week.
     (B) Last year, that duration was considerably shorter.
     (C) Staff will be paid at regular intervals throughout this time.
     (D) On these dates, we will be unable to see patients.

Directions: In this part you will read a selection of texts, such as magazine and newspaper articles, e-mails, and instant messages. Each text or set of texts is followed by several questions. Select the best answer for each question and mark the letter (A), (B), (C), or (D) on your answer sheet.

Questions 147-148 refer to the following coupon.

Amazing Art Supplies
889 Cook Street

We hope you enjoyed learning how to paint at our Saturday session. Please visit us for another learning opportunity in the future. In the meantime, stock up on art supplies for your home with this coupon.

10% Off Watercolor Paints
20% Off Paintbrushes

Both discounts may be applied if used within the same purchase. Offer valid until April 1. Coupon can only be used for products available in the store at the time of purchase. No cash value.

147. What is suggested about Amazing Art Supplies?

(A) It sells books about painting.
(B) It displays its customers' artwork.
(C) It has recently relocated.
(D) It holds a class on the weekend.

148. What is stated about the coupon?

(A) It cannot be used with other offers.
(B) It has an expiration date.
(C) It can be applied to only one item.
(D) It is limited to certain brands.

GO ON TO THE NEXT PAGE

Test 10

Questions 149-150 refer to the following Web page.

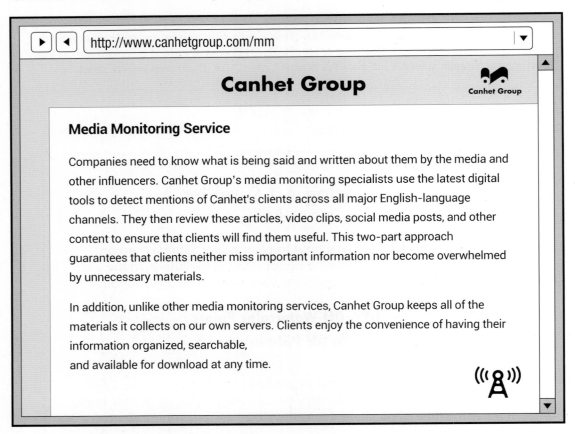

http://www.canhetgroup.com/mm

Canhet Group

Canhet Group

Media Monitoring Service

Companies need to know what is being said and written about them by the media and other influencers. Canhet Group's media monitoring specialists use the latest digital tools to detect mentions of Canhet's clients across all major English-language channels. They then review these articles, video clips, social media posts, and other content to ensure that clients will find them useful. This two-part approach guarantees that clients neither miss important information nor become overwhelmed by unnecessary materials.

In addition, unlike other media monitoring services, Canhet Group keeps all of the materials it collects on our own servers. Clients enjoy the convenience of having their information organized, searchable,
and available for download at any time.

149. What is indicated about some Canhet Group employees?

(A) They invented a new digital search tool.
(B) They have contacts in the media field.
(C) They judge the value of collected information.
(D) They each specialize in monitoring a different industry.

150. What is mentioned as a special feature of Canhet Group's media monitoring service?

(A) Electronic storage of files
(B) Fast delivery of materials
(C) Translation of foreign languages
(D) Coverage of offline news sources

Questions 151-152 refer to the following text-message chain.

Tessa Kirkland   2:23 P.M.
It doesn't look like I'm going to get back to the office in time to ride with you to the lecture at the Rockmond Center. I'm planning on going anyway, though.

Jason Yong   2:25 P.M.
Where are you now?

Tessa Kirkland   2:26 P.M.
I'm at the Hartford Building, negotiating the contract with Averill Communications. We're taking a short break now, but I think it's going to be another hour. I thought I'd be done by now.

Jason Yong   2:27 P.M.
I don't mind driving to the Hartford Building to pick you up.

Tessa Kirkland   2:27 P.M.
I appreciate that, but it's out of your way. I'll just take public transportation instead and see you there.

Jason Yong   2:28 P.M.
You're right. That would be easier. If I get there first, I'll save you a seat.

Tessa Kirkland   2:29 P.M.
Thanks. I'll text you when I arrive.

| | Send |

151. What problem does Ms. Kirkland mention?

(A) A discussion is taking longer than expected.
(B) Her vehicle has broken down.
(C) A building was difficult to locate.
(D) She needs assistance with a negotiation.

152. At 2:28 P.M., what does Mr. Yong most likely mean when he writes, "That would be easier"?

(A) He will take public transportation to the Hartford Building.
(B) He is agreeing to meet at the Rockmond Center.
(C) He wants to attend the lecture on Ms. Kirkland's behalf.
(D) He will pick Ms. Kirkland up in an hour.

Test 10

GO ON TO THE NEXT PAGE

Questions 153-154 refer to the following notice.

Public Notice

In an effort to make the building more easily accessible to wheelchair users, the Daltonville Post Office will be adding an exterior ramp. The construction work will begin on June 4 and end on June 5. A portion of the current stairs leading to the Holly Street entrance will be removed and replaced with a ramp and metal railing. Throughout this time, the Bennett Avenue entrance—the one facing Gardenia Mall—will remain open to the public. For a complete list of planned changes to the building, visit our Web site or check the bulletin board near the elevator.

153. For whom is the notice most likely intended?
   (A) Apartment complex tenants
   (B) Shopping mall visitors
   (C) Postal service customers
   (D) Hotel guests

154. Where will some construction work take place?
   (A) At the Holly Street entrance
   (B) At the Bennett Avenue entrance
   (C) Near the elevators
   (D) On an interior staircase

Questions 155-157 refer to the following advertisement.

CRUISE THE MISSISSIPPI RIVER WITH BIG M TOURS!

Make your next special occasion memorable by holding it on the Mississippi River. For fifteen years, Big M Tours has been renting out boats for private parties. We have an excellent safety record, and all of our captains have ten to twenty years of experience. Customers may select one of our three luxury boats, each with a distinct appearance and features. They are available every day and can accommodate groups as large as eighty people. Our reasonable basic rate includes an experienced crew, light snacks, and parking near the docking site. We also offer the following services for an additional fee:

↘ Catered meals
↘ Live musical entertainment
↘ Wireless Internet service

To make a reservation, call 555-0113. Be prepared to tell us how many people will be taking the boat trip. Please note that weekends fill up quickly, so we recommend early reservations.

155. What is mentioned about Big M Tours?

(A) It only operates on the weekends.
(B) All of its boats are different from each other.
(C) Some of its crew members are history experts.
(D) It also conducts tours on land.

156. What is covered in the basic fee?

(A) A performance by a musician
(B) Wireless access to the Internet
(C) Shuttle service from a parking area
(D) A small amount of refreshments

157. According to the advertisement, what information should people provide when they call?

(A) The number of passengers
(B) The preferred method of payment
(C) The name of the person who gave a referral
(D) The desired departure point

Mahlon Bank Credit Card Services Survey

Thank you for completing this survey. Your feedback is valuable to us. To show our appreciation for your time, you will be entered to win state-of-the-art noise-cancelling headphones from Viva Music. Be sure to include your e-mail address so that you may be contacted in case you are the winner.

Name: Anthony Jordan   **E-mail Address:** ajordan@quickmail.net

How often do you use credit cards?
[X] Daily   [ ] Weekly   [ ] Monthly   [ ] Less than once a month

What do you usually purchase with credit cards (check all that apply)?
[ ] Online goods   [X] Groceries   [X] Gas   [X] Other   Clothing

Please rate the following credit card features from most important (1) to least important (5):

     2   Annual fees

     5   Connected mobile app

     3   Credit limit

     1   Interest rate

     4   Point-/Reward-earning opportunities

Is there any other information that you think would be helpful for us to know?

When choosing a credit card, the safety of my data is also important to me. I don't use your mobile app because I'm worried about this issue. I wish you offered stronger safeguards against this and other security risks.

---

158. What is Mahlon Bank offering to the survey participants?

(A) Entry into a prize drawing
(B) A free gift certificate
(C) Credit at a music store
(D) A discount on electronics

159. What is indicated about Mr. Jordan?

(A) He hopes to enroll in a better rewards program.
(B) He is most concerned about how much interest he pays.
(C) He usually does some of his grocery shopping online.
(D) He does not use his credit card very often.

160. What does Mr. Jordan want Mahlon Bank to provide?

(A) A helpline with a well-trained customer service team
(B) The option of changing his credit limit frequently
(C) Improved security protections for his credit card
(D) The ability to check his account from his mobile phone

Questions 161-163 refer to the following memo.

MEMO

From: Nia Gaskin
To: All laboratory employees
Re: Pipetting robots
Date: February 22

As many of you know, the majority of problems related to the use of a pipette in research laboratories are the result of human error. — [1] —. What's more, manual pipetting for long periods of time can cause staff to seek medical treatment for strain injuries. To resolve these problems, I've ordered several "Sarfines," new pipetting robots made by Halcomb Bioscience. — [2] —. I feel certain that using them will help us devise and refine new household cleaners more quickly and conveniently.

Because the Sarfine comes with complex software, though, you will all need to take a training session online to learn to use it. To do so, log on to the laboratory Web site and click on the "Sarfine Training" button on the top right-hand side. — [3] —. The training should take about one hour. Please complete it by Friday, March 5. — [4] —.

---

161. What is a purpose of the memo?

(A) To inform the recipients of a requirement
(B) To apologize for inconveniencing the recipients
(C) To explain the reason for a refusal
(D) To seek solutions to a problem

162. What does Ms. Gaskin's laboratory most likely do?

(A) Facilitate research by university students
(B) Conduct tests for medical clinics
(C) Develop commercial products
(D) Monitor conditions in an outdoor area

163. In which of the positions marked [1], [2], [3], and [4] does the following sentence best belong?

"They can be programmed to automatically perform tasks such as plate filling and serial dilution."

(A) [1]
(B) [2]
(C) [3]
(D) [4]

Lauren Talbert
2147 Briarhill Lane
Kinston, NC 28501

Dear Ms. Talbert,

I am the president of the Wooster Gardening Association (WGA), a club dedicated to gardening and plant care. We do community projects about four times a year, and as you are the head of the city's Parks and Recreation Department, I am writing to you to ask if our group can assist with some work at Valley Park. We are aware that the park was closed for a few weeks after the storm passed through the area. We visited it when it reopened, and noticed that several flower beds were torn up, in addition to the fallen trees and other issues. We would love the opportunity to replant some of these flowers to help restore the park to its former condition.

Derek Nava of Wooster Greenhouse, a regular donor to our projects, has verbally agreed to donate enough flowers, plants, and small shrubs to fill the three flower beds at the northern end of the park. And of course, we wouldn't charge anything for the labor. Therefore, the project could be completed at no cost to the city.

Please call me at 555−0185 to let me know if you are interested in going forward with this. I look forward to hearing from you.

Sincerely,

Matthew Holloway

Matthew Holloway

164. What is the purpose of the letter?

(A) To request contributions to a project
(B) To encourage Ms. Talbert to join a club
(C) To offer some volunteer services
(D) To present an idea for a fund-raiser

165. What is implied about Valley Park?

(A) It is the region's largest park.
(B) It is currently closed for safety reasons.
(C) It was damaged by weather conditions.
(D) It has been the site of WGA events.

166. What is suggested about Mr. Holloway?

(A) He lives near Valley Park.
(B) He recently visited City Hall.
(C) He works at Wooster Greenhouse.
(D) He has spoken with Mr. Nava.

167. What does Mr. Holloway emphasize about a plan?

(A) The speed at which it could be implemented
(B) Its compliance with city laws
(C) Its lack of expense to the city
(D) The ease with which it could be modified

GO ON TO THE NEXT PAGE

Questions 168-171 refer to the following online chat discussion.

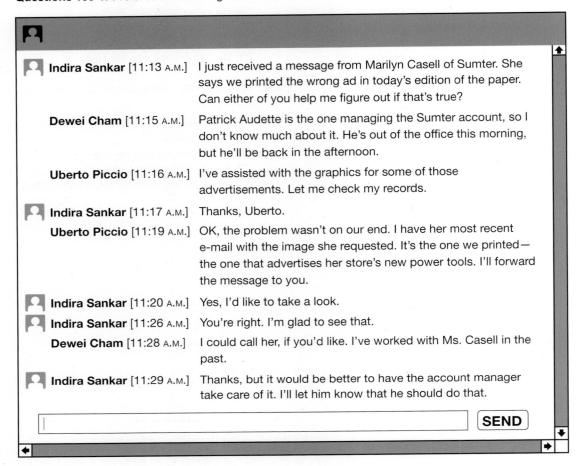

Indira Sankar [11:13 A.M.]	I just received a message from Marilyn Casell of Sumter. She says we printed the wrong ad in today's edition of the paper. Can either of you help me figure out if that's true?
Dewei Cham [11:15 A.M.]	Patrick Audette is the one managing the Sumter account, so I don't know much about it. He's out of the office this morning, but he'll be back in the afternoon.
Uberto Piccio [11:16 A.M.]	I've assisted with the graphics for some of those advertisements. Let me check my records.
Indira Sankar [11:17 A.M.]	Thanks, Uberto.
Uberto Piccio [11:19 A.M.]	OK, the problem wasn't on our end. I have her most recent e-mail with the image she requested. It's the one we printed— the one that advertises her store's new power tools. I'll forward the message to you.
Indira Sankar [11:20 A.M.]	Yes, I'd like to take a look.
Indira Sankar [11:26 A.M.]	You're right. I'm glad to see that.
Dewei Cham [11:28 A.M.]	I could call her, if you'd like. I've worked with Ms. Casell in the past.
Indira Sankar [11:29 A.M.]	Thanks, but it would be better to have the account manager take care of it. I'll let him know that he should do that.

168. What does Ms. Sankar ask for assistance with?

(A) Revising an advertisement
(B) Investigating a complaint
(C) Relaying a message
(D) Preparing a proposal

169. Where does Ms. Casell probably work?

(A) At a graphic design firm
(B) At a marketing agency
(C) At a newspaper company
(D) At a hardware store

170. At 11:26 A.M., what does Ms. Sankar most likely mean when she writes, "I'm glad to see that"?

(A) She approves of the printing layout that was suggested.
(B) She likes the image that Mr. Cham created.
(C) She is pleased that her company is not at fault.
(D) She is relieved that a project was completed on time.

171. Who will most likely contact Ms. Casell?

(A) Mr. Audette
(B) Mr. Cham
(C) Mr. Piccio
(D) Ms. Sankar

GO ON TO THE NEXT PAGE

PHILADELPHIA (December 29)—Despite being the mind behind one of the most popular new lines of accessories of recent years, Ji-Ae Wang does not think of herself as a fashion expert. "This isn't what I trained for, so I have a lot to learn even now," she laughs, sitting in the Philadelphia offices of Poselet, the company she co-founded. — [1] —.

Ms. Wang was a corporate attorney until four years ago, when she learned at a doctor's visit that the pain she had been having in one shoulder was likely caused by the heavy briefcase she carried. — [2] —. The doctor recommended that she try wearing a backpack instead, but when Ms. Wang looked around for one suitable for her conservative profession, she learned that there were few choices available.

This is where Ira Douglas, her former school friend and current business partner, came in. Mr. Douglas was working as a designer for Cattaneo Group when Ms. Wang contacted him with a proposal to collaborate on a line of backpacks for women in white collar jobs. — [3] —. They got to work designing and planning, and Poselet soon began selling its first backpacks online.

Made of fine leather and boasting elegant designs and comfortable straps, the items were an instant hit. Poselet now offers backpacks in six styles, but Ms. Wang says they may not make many more. Instead, the company will likely begin manufacturing other types of useful accessories, such as belts. — [4] —.

172. What is indicated about Ms. Wang?

(A) She consulted a medical professional for design advice.
(B) She plans to open some offline stores soon.
(C) She first met Mr. Douglas four years ago.
(D) She does not have a background in fashion.

173. For whom are Poselet backpacks intended?

(A) Schoolchildren
(B) Office workers
(C) Hikers
(D) Tourists

174. What is NOT mentioned as an advantage of Poselet backpacks?

(A) The attractiveness of their appearance
(B) The physical comfort they offer to wearers
(C) The high-quality material they are made of
(D) The range of styles they are available in

175. In which of the positions marked [1], [2], [3], and [4] does the following sentence best belong?

"He liked the idea immediately."

(A) [1]
(B) [2]
(C) [3]
(D) [4]

GO ON TO THE NEXT PAGE

Test 10

Industrial Arts Back on Track at Plansell High School

By Hope Ortega, Staff Writer

PLANSELL (March 2)—The efforts of some Plansell residents to save the Plansell High School industrial arts program have met with success. The school reports that introductory classes in carpentry and automotive technology are at capacity for the second semester in a row.

Yet just one year ago, the program was nearly eliminated when its longtime teacher, Samuel Reeves, announced his retirement.

Luckily, Mr. Reeves mentioned the uncertainty of the program's future to Vince Brower, a graduate of Plansell High School and the owner of Brower's Auto Repair. Mr. Brower explains, "Auto shop classes show students a potential career path they might not have considered. I've been hiring the program's graduates for years. So I couldn't stand back and let it shut down." He started a social media group to raise awareness of the program's difficulties and gather support for it.

The peak of the group's campaign came when forty of its members attended a school board meeting last April. Their passionate arguments convinced the board to continue the program and even increase its budget. The school was able to hire a replacement for Mr. Reeves, Leslie Greene, and buy some new equipment. Also, Mr. Brower and other local business leaders visited classrooms to promote industrial arts to students.

Letters to the Editor
Keyward Herald
3011 Fisher Lane
Keyward, ND 58003

March 4

Dear Editor,

I would like to express my gratitude to you and Ms. Hope Ortega for her article "Industrial Arts Back on Track at Plansell High School." I was one of the forty people who stepped forward to save the program last year, and I am pleased that our efforts have been recognized.

Also, as a current employee of Mr. Brower's, I agree with him that the industrial arts program is important from a vocational perspective. However, I would like to offer another reason why it is necessary. When I was a student at Plansell High School ten years ago, my industrial arts classes taught me that being good with your hands is another type of intelligence as well as a valuable skill. The self-confidence and discipline that I gained through them allowed me to perform better in my other classes. I hope your readers will keep this benefit in mind.

Sincerely,

Allen Murray

176. In the article, what is indicated about the industrial arts program?

(A) It is divided into three subjects.
(B) Its classes are currently full.
(C) Its participants take off-campus trips.
(D) It requires two semesters to complete.

177. According to the article, why was a social media group founded?

(A) To save an educational program
(B) To connect graduates of a high school
(C) To discuss trends in technical industries
(D) To organize a teacher's retirement party

178. What is a purpose of the letter?

(A) To express disagreement with an opinion
(B) To correct some misinformation
(C) To suggest a topic for another article
(D) To provide additional support for an argument

179. Who most likely is Mr. Murray?

(A) A journalist
(B) An auto mechanic
(C) A schoolteacher
(D) A carpenter

180. What is implied about Mr. Murray?

(A) He went to a school board meeting.
(B) He used to be Ms. Greene's student.
(C) He gave a speech to some current students.
(D) He sold some equipment to the school.

GO ON TO THE NEXT PAGE

To:	Casey Irvine <casey@bluewavespa.co.uk>
From:	Lillian Blais <lillian@bluewavespa.co.uk>
Date:	January 10
Subject:	Please read

Dear Casey,

Let me fill you in on what you missed at our spa's annual planning meeting. We mainly discussed Ms. Gould's idea of offering more treatments and, in particular, how to determine which ones would be best. In preparation for the meeting, I had looked into hiring a professional research company. Iris Kelm, whom I used to work with at Calvin Hotel, had suggested using Starks Research. In the end, though, given their high fees, I decided that it would be better to perform the research ourselves.

To that end, we've decided to hold an event called "Exploratory Week" from February 2 to 8. We'll specially invite regular customers to come in on those days and receive unique treatments from outside specialists at no charge. In exchange, the customers will provide us with feedback on the treatments. We'll then make the most popular one permanently available. We can have a maximum of forty people participate, unless Ms. Gould releases some extra funds.

Let me know if you have any questions about this plan.

Lillian

Summary Report of Exploratory Week at Blue Wave Spa

Prepared by: Raymond Biscoe   Submitted to: Maya Gould (Owner)

A total of 63 clients—44 women and 19 men—participated in the event. Each participant received between one and three treatments, depending on his or her schedule and preferences. Their evaluations of the treatments are summarized below.

Treatment	Average Customer Rating (1=poor, 5=excellent)
Cell Rejuvenation Facial	4.2
Crystal Body Massage	4.8
Oxygen Boost	3.9
Whipped Cocoa Bath	3.7

181. Why did Ms. Blais send the e-mail?

(A) To respond to a question
(B) To ask for some feedback
(C) To provide an update
(D) To schedule a meeting

182. How did Ms. Blais initially learn about Starks Research?

(A) By receiving a publication in the mail
(B) By listening to comments during a staff debate
(C) By getting a former coworker's recommendation
(D) By performing an online search

183. What is NOT true about Exploratory Week?

(A) It involves free services.
(B) It takes place annually.
(C) It is for frequent clients only.
(D) Temporary workers are engaged for it.

184. What is suggested about Blue Wave Spa?

(A) It signed a consulting contract with Starks Research.
(B) It is located inside the Calvin Hotel.
(C) Its clients requested a wider variety of treatments.
(D) Its owner allotted additional funds for an event.

185. Which treatment will Blue Wave Spa probably begin offering permanently?

(A) Cell Rejuvenation Facial
(B) Crystal Body Massage
(C) Oxygen Boost
(D) Whipped Cocoa Bath

GO ON TO THE NEXT PAGE

Questions 186-190 refer to the following information, e-mail, and review.

Events at Valdosta Plaza, August 9–15

Sunday, August 9, 9 A.M.–4 P.M. — **Flower Spectacular**

It's not too late to add beautiful blooms to your garden! The Regional Nature Association is sponsoring this sale to raise funds for community parks.

Tuesday, August 11, 8 P.M.–10 P.M. — **City Glow**

This lantern parade's route will start at Becker Park, run through the business district, and end at the plaza, where lanterns will be available for purchase.

Friday, August 14, 10 A.M.–5 P.M. — **Walk through Time**

You won't want to miss the largest antiques market in the area, complete with furniture, dishes, and artwork. Get one-of-a-kind items to complement your home décor.

Saturday, August 15, 8 A.M.–11 A.M. — **Dazzle Dash**

Participants and spectators dress up in their brightest clothing for this 10K race. Event T-shirts are free for participants and $8 for spectators. Participants must sign up on the city's Web site by August 12.

E-Mail message	
To:	Undisclosed recipients
From:	Akane Mori
Date:	August 4
Subject:	Plaza security

Hi everyone,

It seems there is some confusion regarding security next week at the plaza. We are trying a new system in which we appoint a head of security for each event. If you need to change your shift, please don't e-mail me. You must e-mail the head of the event and also find your own replacement for the shift. The assignments for next week are as below:

Date	Head of Security	# of Security Personnel
Aug. 9	Marty Harris	3
Aug. 11	Edgar Foster	18
Aug. 14	Helen Clarke	3
Aug. 15	Daniel Langston	10

Sincerely,

Akane Mori
Manager of Operations, Valdosta Security Service

302

Destination: Valdosta
Rating: 5/5 stars

Posted August 20 by Bethany Engel
Travel Dates: August 9–14

I traveled to Valdosta with my husband and daughter recently, and we had a wonderful time. I was especially impressed with the organization of the City Glow parade at Valdosta Plaza. The area was very crowded, and I ended up accidentally getting separated from my handbag. Fortunately, event security staff were able to help me locate it almost immediately. On the final day of our trip, we stopped by the plaza for another special event, and I got some great souvenirs to take home. I would definitely visit Valdosta again!

186. What is mentioned about Dazzle Dash?

(A) Its winner receives a trophy.
(B) People must pay to participate.
(C) It attracts thousands of spectators.
(D) It requires advance registration.

187. Which event was assigned the most security personnel?

(A) Flower Spectacular
(B) City Glow
(C) Walk through Time
(D) Dazzle Dash

188. In the e-mail, the word "find" in paragraph 1, line 4, is closest in meaning to

(A) supply
(B) observe
(C) discover
(D) achieve

189. Why did Ms. Engel require assistance from security personnel?

(A) She felt ill.
(B) She lost a personal item.
(C) She could not locate a landmark.
(D) She became separated from a family member.

190. What did Ms. Engel most likely purchase as souvenirs?

(A) Some plants
(B) Some lanterns
(C) Some antiques
(D) Some clothing

GO ON TO THE NEXT PAGE

MEMO

From: Oliver Russell
To: All Hesnik Technology Staff
Re: Software training
Date: November 25

Hello, everyone.

As head of the human resources department, it is my pleasure to announce that we have acquired Switzer Sync, a new software tool that will make Hesnik Technology's vacation scheduling process easier and faster.

We hope to adopt Switzer Sync companywide on January 1. In order to do this, employees will need to receive training on it. We believe that a two-hour session led by Randall Grantham of the information technology department will be enough to teach you all of its features.

Please look up your department's training session on the attached schedule. If you'll need to attend a different one, your manager must notify me by December 3. Also, you can expect a feedback request from me the day after your session. Please take the time to answer it.

Oliver Russell
Director of Human Resources

Attached: Switzer Sync Training Schedule

Switzer Sync Training Schedule

Sessions will be held from 10 A.M. to 12 P.M. in Conference Room 1.

Date	Department
December 8	Information Technology
December 9	Human Resources
December 10	Production
December 11	Accounting
December 12	Sales and Marketing

```
┌─────────────────────────────────────────────────────────────┐
│══════════════════════ E-Mail message ══════════════════════ │
│                                                               │
│  From:      Darla Adkins                                      │
│                                                               │
│  To:        Oliver Russell                                    │
│                                                               │
│  Subject:   RE: Software training                             │
│                                                               │
│  Date:      December 15                                       │
│                                                               │
│  ┌──────────────────────────────────────────────────────┐   │
│  │ Hi Mr. Russell,                                        │   │
│  │                                                        │   │
│  │ My training session last week was good. I especially   │  │
│  │ appreciated the practice part.                         │   │
│  └──────────────────────────────────────────────────────┘   │
└─────────────────────────────────────────────────────────────┘
```

Hi Mr. Russell,

My training session last week was good. I especially appreciated the practice part. Once I actually tried using Switzer Sync, I realized that I hadn't understood some of its functions very well just from the explanation. I liked that I was able to catch those problems when the instructor was there to help me, instead of later when I tried to use the software by myself.

At the same time, I have some less positive feedback on the software. The program itself is fine, but actually any computer-based system can be difficult for people in the production department. It just isn't as easy for us to access a company computer. When I talked with the rest of my department after our session, we agreed that we'd like the company to take that factor into account in the future.

Sincerely,
Darla Adkins

191. What is mentioned about Switzer Sync?

(A) It will be used to plan employee leave.
(B) It is intended to make a process more secure.
(C) It was developed by Mr. Grantham's team.
(D) It now includes several new features.

192. What does the memo indicate about the schedule?

(A) It does not apply to department managers.
(B) It displays the first of two rounds of training.
(C) Mr. Russell has not yet finalized one of the dates.
(D) Staff could go to another department's session.

193. What did Mr. Russell most likely do on December 12 ?

(A) He sent requests to Accounting.
(B) He gave a talk to Sales and Marketing.
(C) He posted reminder notices in a conference room.
(D) He missed a regular morning gathering.

194. What does Ms. Adkins want Hesnik Technology to do?

(A) Look for ways to improve its other systems
(B) Relay some positive feedback to an instructor
(C) Give her more time to practice using some software
(D) Show consideration for her department's situation

195. On what date did Ms. Adkins attend a training session?

(A) December 8
(B) December 9
(C) December 10
(D) December 11

GO ON TO THE NEXT PAGE

Test 10

NOTICE TO SHIMMER JEWELRY CUSTOMERS

After nearly two decades of service to the Huntsville community at its Powley Street location, Shimmer Jewelry will be going out of business on April 30. It has been a pleasure serving you over the years, and we are honored that we have been a part of so many weddings, anniversaries, birthdays, and other celebrations. Although our jewelry repair services will no longer be available, you will continue to be able to purchase some of the styles created by our jewelry designers. Susan Marlow plans to start her own jewelry Web site, and Amy Sabo will open a small shop on Custer Avenue. We hope you will support their endeavors. Thank you for your patronage.

Thank you for your patronage.

Mercedes Chenoweth
Owner, Shimmer Jewelry

E-mail

To:	Mark Reese <reesem@stylerealty.net>
From:	Aaron Salazar <asalazar@bid-co.com>
Date:	May 4
Subject:	Viewing

Dear Mr. Reese,

Thanks for showing me the former Shimmer Jewelry space today. It is definitely much larger than the Mayfield Street property I viewed last week. However, I'm concerned about how profitable my business would be in that location. I thought there would be a lot of foot traffic in the area, but there wasn't. You mentioned that there is another site on Wright Avenue that will be available from next month. I'm wondering if we could schedule a time to see it together.

Many thanks,

Aaron Salazar

Downtown Businesses Struggle to Stay Afloat

May 25—Grand City's downtown shopping district, once a bustling area of activity, is suffering due to skyrocketing rents. Rental fees in the neighborhood have risen by nearly 30% over the last few years, driving small businesses out. For example, local business owner Mercedes Chenoweth said her store went out of business because of these conditions. Another shop owner, Gloria Lohman, said she relocated to the Clifton Mall, where rents are nearly half the price.

On the other hand, City Manager Kyle Trevino said, "Rent is just part of the equation." He pointed out that a 2% increase in sales tax, approved by voters last fall, is also putting pressure on businesses. He also believes that "if we plan more activities in the area, we can bring in more business." The number of festivals, live performances, and other events held in the district has declined dramatically in recent years. The local business community is looking into addressing this and other issues to keep the economy moving in downtown Grand City.

196. What is implied about the owner of Shimmer Jewelry?

(A) She has been in business for over 20 years.
(B) She moved her store to a shopping mall.
(C) She will begin selling jewelry online.
(D) She was affected by rent increases.

197. Where did Mr. Salazar view a building on May 4 ?

(A) On Powley Street
(B) On Custer Avenue
(C) On Mayfield Street
(D) On Wright Avenue

198. What concerns Mr. Salazar about the retail space he saw on May 4 ?

(A) The lack of parking near it
(B) The poor condition of its flooring
(C) The limited size of its showroom
(D) The small number of people walking by it

199. In the article, the word "driving" in paragraph 1, line 6, is closest in meaning to

(A) forcing
(B) urging
(C) transporting
(D) powering

200. What does Mr. Trevino express support for?

(A) Forming a business association
(B) Voting again on a proposal
(C) Hosting more events downtown
(D) Granting leases on city-owned property

Stop! This is the end of the test. If you finish before time is called, you may go back to Parts 5, 6, and 7 and check your work.

ANSWER SHEET

YBM 실전토익 RC 1000

성명 한글 / 한자 / 영자

수험번호

응시일자 : 20   년   월   일

Test 01 (Part 5~7)

101	102	103	104	105	106	107	108	109	110	111	112	113	114	115	116	117	118	119	120

121	122	123	124	125	126	127	128	129	130	131	132	133	134	135	136	137	138	139	140

141	142	143	144	145	146	147	148	149	150	151	152	153	154	155	156	157	158	159	160

161	162	163	164	165	166	167	168	169	170	171	172	173	174	175	176	177	178	179	180

181	182	183	184	185	186	187	188	189	190	191	192	193	194	195	196	197	198	199	200

Test 02 (Part 5~7)

101	102	103	104	105	106	107	108	109	110	111	112	113	114	115	116	117	118	119	120

121	122	123	124	125	126	127	128	129	130	131	132	133	134	135	136	137	138	139	140

141	142	143	144	145	146	147	148	149	150	151	152	153	154	155	156	157	158	159	160

161	162	163	164	165	166	167	168	169	170	171	172	173	174	175	176	177	178	179	180

181	182	183	184	185	186	187	188	189	190	191	192	193	194	195	196	197	198	199	200

ANSWER SHEET

YBM 실전토익 RC 1000

수험번호

응시일자 : 20   년   월   일

성명
| 한글 |
| 한자 |
| 영자 |

Test 03 (Part 5~7)

101–120, 121–140, 141–160, 161–180, 181–200

Test 04 (Part 5~7)

101–120, 121–140, 141–160, 161–180, 181–200

ANSWER SHEET

YBM 실전토익 RC 1000

수험번호

응시일자 : 20   년   월   일

성명
한글
한자
영자

Test 05 (Part 5~7)

Test 06 (Part 5~7)

ANSWER SHEET

YBM 실전토익 RC 1000

수험번호

응시일자 : 20   년   월   일

성명
한글
한자
영자

Test 07 (Part 5~7)

101	102	103	104	105	106	107	108	109	110	111	112	113	114	115	116	117	118	119	120
121	122	123	124	125	126	127	128	129	130	131	132	133	134	135	136	137	138	139	140
141	142	143	144	145	146	147	148	149	150	151	152	153	154	155	156	157	158	159	160
161	162	163	164	165	166	167	168	169	170	171	172	173	174	175	176	177	178	179	180
181	182	183	184	185	186	187	188	189	190	191	192	193	194	195	196	197	198	199	200

Test 08 (Part 5~7)

101	102	103	104	105	106	107	108	109	110	111	112	113	114	115	116	117	118	119	120
121	122	123	124	125	126	127	128	129	130	131	132	133	134	135	136	137	138	139	140
141	142	143	144	145	146	147	148	149	150	151	152	153	154	155	156	157	158	159	160
161	162	163	164	165	166	167	168	169	170	171	172	173	174	175	176	177	178	179	180
181	182	183	184	185	186	187	188	189	190	191	192	193	194	195	196	197	198	199	200

ANSWER SHEET

YBM 실전토익 RC 1000

성명
- 한글
- 한자
- 영자

수험번호

응시일자 : 20 년 월 일

Test 09 (Part 5~7)

101 102 103 104 105 106 107 108 109 110 111 112 113 114 115 116 117 118 119 120
121 122 123 124 125 126 127 128 129 130 131 132 133 134 135 136 137 138 139 140
141 142 143 144 145 146 147 148 149 150 151 152 153 154 155 156 157 158 159 160
161 162 163 164 165 166 167 168 169 170 171 172 173 174 175 176 177 178 179 180
181 182 183 184 185 186 187 188 189 190 191 192 193 194 195 196 197 198 199 200

Test 10 (Part 5~7)

101 102 103 104 105 106 107 108 109 110 111 112 113 114 115 116 117 118 119 120
121 122 123 124 125 126 127 128 129 130 131 132 133 134 135 136 137 138 139 140
141 142 143 144 145 146 147 148 149 150 151 152 153 154 155 156 157 158 159 160
161 162 163 164 165 166 167 168 169 170 171 172 173 174 175 176 177 178 179 180
181 182 183 184 185 186 187 188 189 190 191 192 193 194 195 196 197 198 199 200

YBM
실전토익
RC1000
1

TEST 1

101 (A)	**102** (C)	**103** (D)	**104** (B)	**105** (A)
106 (A)	**107** (C)	**108** (B)	**109** (B)	**110** (D)
111 (D)	**112** (C)	**113** (B)	**114** (D)	**115** (B)
116 (A)	**117** (C)	**118** (C)	**119** (B)	**120** (C)
121 (B)	**122** (D)	**123** (D)	**124** (D)	**125** (C)
126 (B)	**127** (C)	**128** (B)	**129** (B)	**130** (A)
131 (D)	**132** (C)	**133** (B)	**134** (A)	**135** (D)
136 (B)	**137** (D)	**138** (A)	**139** (B)	**140** (C)
141 (D)	**142** (A)	**143** (A)	**144** (A)	**145** (C)
146 (D)	**147** (C)	**148** (D)	**149** (C)	**150** (D)
151 (A)	**152** (B)	**153** (D)	**154** (C)	**155** (B)
156 (C)	**157** (D)	**158** (D)	**159** (A)	**160** (B)
161 (B)	**162** (C)	**163** (A)	**164** (C)	**165** (B)
166 (C)	**167** (D)	**168** (B)	**169** (A)	**170** (B)
171 (C)	**172** (A)	**173** (A)	**174** (B)	**175** (A)
176 (C)	**177** (D)	**178** (D)	**179** (B)	**180** (A)
181 (A)	**182** (C)	**183** (B)	**184** (B)	**185** (D)
186 (B)	**187** (C)	**188** (B)	**189** (D)	**190** (C)
191 (B)	**192** (B)	**193** (A)	**194** (B)	**195** (C)
196 (D)	**197** (A)	**198** (D)	**199** (A)	**200** (C)

PART 5

101 부사 자리 _ 동사 수식

해설 빈칸은 현재 완료 수동태의 동사구를 수식하는 부사 자리로, 정답은 (A) strategically이다. 동사구 사이에는 현재분사 (B) strategizing, 명사 (C) strategy, 그리고 형용사 (D) strategic은 품사상 적합하지 않다.

번역 상점 개업식은 전략적으로 지역 축제 첫째 날에 맞춰 잡혔다.

어휘 opening celebration 개업식, 개관 기념식 be scheduled for ~로 예정되다 local 지역의 festival 축제 strategically 전략적으로 strategize 전략을 짜다 strategy 전략 strategic 전략적인

102 소유격 대명사

해설 명사 앞에 올 수 있는 대명사는 소유격이 유일하다. 그와 동시에 이 문제에서는 복수 명사 employees를 받아야 하기 때문에 (D) its는 정답이 될 수 없다. 따라서 정답은 (C) their이다.

번역 직원들은 퇴근하기 전에 그들의 업무 이메일 계정에서 로그아웃할 것을 기억해야 한다.

어휘 account 계정 leave for the day 퇴근하다

103 동사 / 준동사 구분

해설 한 문장에 동사는 하나만 있어야 한다. 이 문장에는 이미 동사(asked)가 있기 때문에 더 이상의 동사는 존재하면 안 된다. 따라서 준동사(to부정사)인 (D) to extend가 정답이다.

번역 바이든 씨는 상사에게 이번 분기의 지출품의서 마감 기한을 연장해 달라고 요청했다.

어휘 supervisor 감독관, 관리자 deadline 마감 기한 quarter (사)분기 expense report 지출품의서 extend 연장하다, 늘리다

104 부사절 접속사 자리

해설 이 문장은 문장 맨 앞이 빈칸이고, 중간에 콤마(,)로 연결된 두 개의 문장으로 구성되어 있다. 따라서 빈칸은 두 문장을 연결할 부사절 접속사 자리임을 알 수 있다. (C) Why는 부사절을 이끌지 못하므로 정답에서 제외되며, (A) Since는 '~하기 때문에'라는 뜻의 접속사로 쓰일 수 있지만 문맥에 맞지 않다. (D) Should가 도치 구문으로 쓰이려면 뒤에 오는 동사는 원형이 되어야 하는데 현재형이므로 정답은 (B) When(~할 때)이다.

번역 오늘 오후 사업 세미나가 끝나면 케인 씨는 그의 직원들이 회의장을 청소하도록 할 것이다.

어휘 conference hall 회의장

105 명사 어휘

해설 주어인 음악 스트리밍을 보어인 '클링크 스마트 스피커의 가장 잘 알려진 _____'라고 설명하는 내용으로, 가장 잘 알려인이라는 형용사 다음에는 '기능'이라는 말이 가장 적절하다. 따라서 정답은 (A) function(기능)이다.

번역 조사에 따르면 음악 스트리밍은 클링크 스마트 스피커의 가장 잘 알려진 기능이다.

어휘 according to ~에 따르면 research 연구, 조사 well-known 잘 알려진 function 기능 destination 목적지 rating 순위, 등급

106 전치사 어휘

해설 이메일을 보낼 때 코드를 '함께(포함해서)' 보내라는 의미를 나타낼 수 있는 전치사를 고르는 문제이다. '~을 포함해서, ~와 함께'라는 의미를 가진 전치사 (A) with가 정답이다.

번역 웹디자이너 직에 지원하시려면 제목란에 해당 공석 코드를 넣어 이메일을 보내 주십시오.

어휘 apply for ~에 지원하다 appropriate 적절한, 알맞은 vacancy 결원, 공석 subject line 제목란

107 동사 자리 _ 수동태

해설 한 문장에 동사는 반드시 하나만 있어야 한다. 하지만 이 문장에는 동사가 없기 때문에 빈칸은 동사가 들어가야 하는 자리이다. 주어가 All ~ products이고, 빈칸 뒤에 by가 있는 것으로 보아, 동사의 형태는 수동태가 들어가야 한다. 따라서 정답은 (C) are shipped(선적되다, 출하되다)이다. (B), (D)는 동사의 형태가 아니며, (A)는 능동형이므로 답이 될 수 없다.

번역 부대 용품을 포함한 부스케 가먼츠 제품 일체는 우선 취급 우편으로 출하된다.

어휘 accessory 부대 용품 priority 우선

108 동명사 자리 _ 전치사의 목적어

해설 전치사(after) 뒤에는 명사(구)나 동명사(구)가 들어갈 수 있으므로, 동명사인 (B) merging과 명사인 (D) merger가 정답으로 가능하다. merger는 가산명사이므로 앞에 관사가 있어야 하는데, 빈칸 앞에는 관사가 없으므로, 정답은 동명사인 (B) merging이다.

번역 펜벡스 그룹은 테런 은행과의 합병 이후 더 많은 서비스를 제공하고 새로운 영역으로 확장할 수 있었다.

어휘 offer 제공하다 expand into ~로 확장하다 territory 영역, 영토 merge 합병하다 merger 합병

109 형용사 자리 _ 명사 수식

해설 빈칸 뒤에 명사가 있으므로, 빈칸에는 명사를 수식하는 형용사가 들어가는 것이 가장 적절하다. go on a business trip은 '출장을 가다'라는 의미로, 여기서는 빈칸에 형용사 (B) frequent(빈번한, 잦은)가 들어가면 '잦은 출장을 가다', 즉 '출장을 자주 가다'라는 말이 된다. 따라서 정답은 (B)이다.

번역 글로벌 분석가의 공통된 특성은 기꺼이 잦은 해외 출장을 가고자 하는 의향이다.

어휘 characteristic 특성 analyst 분석가 willingness 의향, 기꺼이 하는 마음 business trip 출장 overseas 해외로 frequently 자주 frequency 빈도

110 동사 어휘

해설 주어인 최신 비디오 게임(Baugh ~ video game)과 목적어인 거의 5천만 달러(nearly $50 million)라는 내용과 잘 어울리는 동사를 고르는 어휘 문제이다. '매출을 만들어 내다'라는 의미로 정답은 (D) generated(창출했다)이다.

번역 보 엔터테인먼트의 최신 비디오 게임은 한 달 만에 거의 5천만 달러의 매출을 창출했다.

어휘 recent 최근의 nearly 거의 sales 판매, 매출 release 출시하다, 발표하다 rank 순위를 매기다 depict 묘사하다

111 전치사 어휘

해설 문장의 동사가 수동태이고 주어인 냉장고의 성능이 번튼 어플라이언스에 의해 보장된다는 내용이므로, 수동태에서 '~에 의해'라는 의미로 행위자를 나타내는 (D) by가 정답이다.

번역 품질 보증 기간 동안 귀하의 도렐 냉장고 성능은 번튼 어플라이언스에 의해 보장됩니다.

어휘 under warranty 품질 보증 기간 중인 performance 성능 refrigerator 냉장고 be guaranteed 보장되다

112 부사 어휘

해설 동사 find를 수식할 수 있는 부사의 의미를 구분하는 문제이다. (A) usually(보통), (B) extremely(극도로), (C) definitely(분명히, 반드시), (D) formerly(이전에) 각각의 의미를 볼 때, 문맥상 후임자를 '반드시' 찾겠다는 표현이 가장 적절하다. 따라서 정답은 (C)이다.

번역 이사회는 물러나는 CEO의 후임자를 반드시 찾겠다고 발표했다.

어휘 board of directors 이사회 announce 공표하다 find a replacement for ~를 대신할 사람을 찾다, ~의 후임을 찾다 outgoing 물러나는

113 형용사 자리 _ be동사의 보어

해설 be동사는 보어를 취하는 동사로서 주어와 동격인 경우에는 명사를, 상태를 설명해 주는 경우에는 형용사를 보어로 쓴다. 여기에서는 명사(hesitation)가 동격이 아니기 때문에 올 수 없다. 따라서 '주저하는' 상태를 설명해 주는 형용사 (B) hesitant가 어울린다. 또는 'be hesitant to + 동사원형(~하는 것을 주저하다)'라는 표현을 알고 있다면 바로 답을 고를 수 있을 것이다.

번역 존슨 씨는 로봇공학 분야에 대한 경험이 부족하기 때문에 마인드텍 주식회사의 그 직종에 지원하는 것을 주저하고 있다.

어휘 apply for ~에 지원하다 lack 부족하다 in the field of ~의 분야에서 robotics 로봇공학 hesitation 주저, 망설임 hesitantly 머뭇거리며

114 형용사 어휘

해설 빈칸을 사이에 두고 a range of라는 표현이 보인다. '다양한'이라는 의미는 a wide range of(광범위한)의 형태로 많이 쓰인다. 보기 중에서 wide와 비슷한 의미로 (D) diverse(다양한)가 있다. 따라서 정답은 (D)이다. 참고로 range 대신 variety를 쓰는 경우도 많다.

번역 론델 배관 회사는 열정 있는 사람들을 위해 다양한 범위의 견습 기회를 제공한다.

어휘 plumbing 배관 offer 제공하다 range 범위 apprenticeship 견습 enthusiastic 열정적인 individual 개인 lasting 지속적인 several 몇몇의 durable 내구성이 있는

115 부사 어휘

해설 주어와 동사 사이가 빈칸이므로 동사를 수식하는 부사가 들어갈 자리이다. 기분이 나쁠 수 있는 상황이거나 윗사람에게 '정중하게' 부탁을 할 때는 kindly라는 표현을 쓴다. 따라서 정답은 (B) kindly이다.

번역 오늘 밤 연극의 감독은 관객들에게 공연 중 사진 찍는 것을 삼가달라고 부탁한다.

어휘 director 감독 theatergoer 관객 refrain from ~을 삼가다 performance 공연 take place (행사가) 열리다, 행해지다

116 형용사(분사) 자리 _ 명사 수식

해설 관사와 명사 사이가 빈칸이므로 명사를 수식하는 형용사가 들어갈 자리이다. 보기 중에 형용사와 같은 역할을 하는 과거분사 (A) estimated와 현재분사 (B) estimating이 있다. '예상되는 배송 날짜'라는 의미가 자연스러우므로 정답은 (A) estimated(예상되는)이다.

번역 딜런스 가구 고객들은 온라인 주문을 할 때 체크아웃 페이지에서 예상 배송 일자를 볼 수 있다.

어휘 delivery date 배송 일자 place an order 주문하다 estimation 견적, 평가 estimate 추정, 견적서; 추정하다

117 동사 어휘

해설 빈칸 앞부분에 '영업을 축소한다'는 내용이 나오고 and로 연결되어 있기 때문에 같은 맥락의 내용이 나와야 한다. 따라서 현재 메뉴 중 여러 개의 생산을 '중단할' 것이라는 내용이 가장 적절하다. 따라서 정답은 (C) discontinue(중단하다)이다.

번역 크러쉬 주스 앤 스무디즈는 사업을 축소하고 있으며 현재의 메뉴 중 여러 개를 없앨 것이다.

어휘 downsize (사업체가 비용 절감을 위해 규모를) 줄이다, 축소하다 operation 사업, 운영 current 현재의 reimburse 변제하다 purchase 구매하다; 구매 determine 결정하다

118 명사 자리 _ be동사의 주어

해설 빈칸은 동사 'were introduced'의 주어이므로 명사가 들어갈 자리이다. 이 경우 단수 명사인 (B) restriction과 복수 명사인 (C) restrictions 둘 중 be동사 were와 어울릴 수 있는 것은 복수 명사이므로 정답은 (C) restrictions(제한 규정)이다.

번역 이 근방의 주차 제한 규정은 교통이 항상 원활할 수 있도록 하기 위해 도입됐다.

어휘 parking restrictions 주차 제한 규정 neighborhood 인근, 근방 introduce 도입하다, 소개하다 enable 가능하게 하다 movement 움직임 road traffic 교통 at all times 항상 restrict 제한하다

119 형용사 자리 _ 명사 수식

해설 관사(the)와 명사(number) 사이에 들어가서 명사를 수식하는 형용사를 고르는 문제이다. 형용사 형태는 없지만 분사인 (B) overwhelming(압도적인)과 (C) overwhelmed(압도된)가 가능하다. 여기에서는 '압도적인 숫자'라는 의미가 자연스러우므로 (B)가 정답이다.

번역 예상되는 엄청난 수의 고객 전화를 처리하는 데 도움이 되도록 시간제 전화 교환원들이 채용될 것이다.

어휘 telephone operator 전화 교환원 deal with ~를 다루다, 처리하다 overwhelmingly 압도적으로

120 전치사 어휘

해설 빈칸 뒤에 온 명사구 'tax preparation season'과 어울리는 전치사를 찾는 문제이다. 기간을 나타내는 명사와 어울리는 전치사를 찾아야 하며 또한 문장에서 이 기간 동안에는 휴가 사용을 금지한다고 하였으므로 (C) during(~ 동안)이 정답이다.

번역 회계부서 직원들은 세금 준비 기간 동안 휴가를 쓸 수 없다.

어휘 accounting department 경리부서, 회계부서 discourage 막다, 말리다 take a vacation 휴가를 얻다 tax 세금 preparation 준비

121 부사 자리 _ 형용사 수식

해설 빈칸은 be동사와 형용사(suitable) 사이에서 형용사를 수식하는 부사 자리이다. 따라서 부사인 (B) equally(똑같이, 동등하게)가 정답이다.

번역 마케팅 이사는 버튼 호텔과 윌러비 레스토랑이 공히 송년 만찬을 위해 똑같이 적합한 장소라고 확신한다.

어휘 suitable 적합한 venue (행사 등을 위한) 장소 year-end 연말의 banquet 연회, 만찬 equal 똑같은, 동등한 equality 평등, 균등

122 전치사 어휘

해설 빈칸은 더 좋은 내구성이라는 명사 목적어와 함께, 문장 전체 해석에 어울리는 전치사를 찾는 문제이다. '기존 망원경에 비해 내구성 말고는 뚜렷한 장점이 없다'는 내용이 가장 적절하므로 정답은 (D) Apart from(~ 이외에는, ~ 말고는)이 정답이다.

번역 루이즌 180R은 내구성이 더 좋은 점 외에는 기존 망원경에 비해 뚜렷한 장점이 없다.

어휘 durability 내구성 clear 뚜렷한 advantage 장점 existing 기존의, 현재 사용되는 telescope 망원경 along with ~와 함께 owing to ~ 때문에 rather than ~보다는

123 명사 자리 _ 전치사의 목적어

해설 빈칸 앞에 전치사(with)와 현재분사(increasing)가 있으므로 빈칸에는 명사가 들어가는 것이 가장 자연스럽다. 따라서 정답은 명사형인 (D) regularity(규칙성, 규칙적임)이다. (B)의 regular가 원래는 형용사로 '규칙적인', '정규적인'이라는 의미이지만, '단골'이라는 의미의 명사로 쓰일 수도 있다. 하지만, 이 경우 regular가 가산 명사인데 빈칸 앞에 관사가 없으므로 정답이 될 수 없다.

번역 고객 서비스 부서 직원들은 컴퓨터 소프트웨어 오류가 점점 더 규칙적으로 발생하고 있다고 보고했다.

어휘 customer service 고객 서비스 occur 발생하다 regularize 합법화하다 regularly 규칙적으로, 정기적으로

124 동사 어휘

해설 빈칸 뒤에 온 명사 concern과 잘 어울리는 동사를 고르는 어휘 문제이다. 토익에 잘 나오는 express를 이용한 표현에는 '감사를 표하다(express one's gratitude)', '우려를 표하다(express one's concern)'가 있다. 따라서 정답은 (D) expressed이다.

번역 이케부쿠로 주민들은 제안된 쇼핑몰 건립이 소음 공해 수준을 높일 것이라는 우려를 표했다.

어휘 resident 거주민 concern 우려 noise pollution 소음 공해 oppose 반대하다 entail 수반하다 assign 맡기다

125 형용사 어휘

해설 be responsible for(~에 대한 책임이 있다)라는 표현을 알고 있다면 금방 답을 찾을 수 있는 문제로 정답은 (C)이다. 이 표현을 모르고 있었다면, 보기의 형용사를 하나하나 대입시켜 의미를 파악해 보아야 한다. (A) likely는 'be likely+to부정사'의 형태로 '~할 것 같다'라는 의미로 주로 쓰인다. (B) sincere(진실된), (D) conclusive(결정적인)는 의미상 어색하다.

번역 머피 씨는 인사부장으로서 전 직원의 행복과 복지를 보장할 책무가 있다.

어휘 personnel department 인사부 ensure 보장하다 welfare 복지

126 명사 자리 _ 전치사의 목적어

해설 전치사(for) 뒤에 위치한다는 점과 등위접속사 and로 이어지므로 and 뒤의 명사(timekeeping)와 같은 품사여야 한다는 점을 고려하면 명사가 들어갈 자리이다. 명사는 (A) attendants(종업원, 안내원)와 (B) attendance(출석, 참석) 두 개인데, 보상을 받는 이유에 대한 것이고, timekeeping(시간 엄수)과 대등한 의미를 가져야 하므로 (B) attendance가 정답이다.

번역 트라이포인트 엔지니어링 직원들은 개근과 시간 엄수에 대해 매년 포상을 받는다.

어휘 be rewarded 포상을 받다 perfect attendance 개근 timekeeping 시간 엄수 attend 참석하다

127 형용사 어휘

해설 bid(입찰가, 호가)라는 단어 앞에 올 수 있는 형용사 어휘 문제이다. 문장 뒷부분을 보면 비교급 구문으로, than the final price가 문제 해결의 단서이다. 처음 입찰가와 실제 최종 가격을 비교하는 내용이므로, 정답은 (C) initial(처음의)이다.

번역 에글링턴 로드 525번지 부동산의 처음 입찰가는 협상 후 최종 가격보다 훨씬 낮았다.

어휘 bid 입찰가, 호가 property 부동산 negotiation 협상 identical 동일한, 똑같은 numerous 많은 versatile 다재다능한; 다용도의

128 명사 어휘

해설 보안 관리자 직(the security manager position)의 _____에 대한 것을 웹사이트 채용 페이지에서 볼 수 있다는 내용이므로, 그 직책의 '직무'라는 말이 가장 적절하다. 따라서 정답은 (D) duties(직무)이다.

번역 보안 관리자 직의 직무에 대한 세부 사항은 당사 웹사이트의 채용 페이지에서 찾을 수 있다.

어휘 full details 세부 항목 security 보안, 안전 recruitment 채용 batch 집단; 한 회분 object 목표

129 부사 자리

해설 빈칸은 현재완료 동사 사이에 들어가는 부사 자리이다. 이유를 나타내는 접속사 as를 중심으로 앞뒤 두 문장의 해석을 보면, 이미 의견을 충분히 설명한 성명을 발표했기 때문에 대응 필요성이 없다는 내용이므로, 정답은 (B) already(이미, 벌써)이다.

번역 우리측 견해를 충분히 설명한 성명을 이미 발표했으니, 이 사안에 관한 매체의 질문에 대응할 필요가 없습니다.

어휘 respond to ~에 대응하다, 응답하다 inquiry 질문, 조사 matter 문제 issue a statement 성명을 발표하다 sufficiently 충분히 explain 설명하다 viewpoint 관점, 시각

130 접속사 자리

해설 문장 두 개가 연결되어 있는 구조이므로 빈칸에는 접속사가 들어가야 한다. 문맥상 '비록 ~이지만'이라는 양보의 의미가 어울리므로 정답은

(A) Although(비록 ~이지만)이다. (B) In addition to(~에 더하여)는 전치사구이고, (D) As well as(~에 더하여)는 접속사나 전치사로 쓰일 수 있지만 문맥에 맞지 않다. (C) Either는 다양한 품사로 쓰일 수 있지만 문법과 문맥상 어울리지 않는다.

번역 생산비가 크게 줄지는 않았지만 매트록스 케미컬즈는 월 지출이 급격히 줄어든 것에 주목했다.

어휘 production cost 생산비 significantly 상당히, 꽤 note 주목하다 a sharp fall 급격한 하락 monthly expenditure 월 지출

PART 6

131-134 설명서

> 머크로프트 6단 책장을 구매해 주셔서 감사합니다. 제품을 조립하시려면 본 설명서에 제공된 설명 및 도표를 따르십시오. 발송된 상자는 이 절차에 이상적인 작업대 역할을 할 것입니다.
>
> 작은 부품을 **131잘못해서** 버리는 일이 없도록 책장이 완전히 구성될 때까지 포장재 일체를 남겨 두십시오. **132조립**에 앞서, 들어 있는 각 부품을 확인하고 분리하기 위해 부품 및 하드웨어 목록을 사용하십시오.
>
> 모든 부품이 자리를 잡을 때까지 볼트 일체를 완전히 조이지 마십시오. 이 지침을 따르지 않을 경우 볼트가 어긋나는 일이 **133발생**할 수 있습니다. **134제품 조립 시 전동 공구를 사용할 경우 유의하십시오.** 사용 시 주의하지 않으면 나무를 손상시킬 수 있습니다.

> **어휘** purchase 구매하다 bookcase 책장 instruction 설명, 지시 사항 diagram 도표, 도형 construct 구성하다 shipping box 배송 상자 ideal 이상적인 work surface 작업대 process 절차 packaging 포장재 avoid 피하다 discard 버리다 identify 확인하다 separate 분리하다 tighten 조이다 be in place 제자리에 놓이다 misaligned 어긋난 power tool 전동 공구 take caution 주의를 기울이다

131 부사 자리

해설 빈칸 앞의 to avoid의 목적어는 동명사 discarding이므로 빈칸은 부사가 들어갈 자리이다. 따라서 정답은 (D) mistakenly(잘못해서)이다.

어휘 mistake 실수, 잘못 mistaken 잘못 알고 있는

132 명사 어휘

해설 이 지문은 책장을 조립하는 과정을 담은 매뉴얼이다. 빈칸 뒤의 내용을 보면, 부품 목록을 보면서 부품들이 다 있는지 확인하라는 말이 나온다. '조립'하기 전에 이런 것을 하라는 지침으로 보는 것이 자연스럽다. 따라서 정답은 (C) assembly(조립)이다. (A) delivery는 '배송', (B) repair는 '수리', (D) manufacture는 '제조'라는 의미이다.

133 동사 어휘

해설 이러한 지침(these instructions)을 따르지 않는다면 다음과 같은 결과를 '야기할' 수 있다는 의미가 되는 것이 가장 자연스럽다. 'cause A + to 부정사'는 'A가 ~하도록 야기하다'라는 뜻으로 정답은 (B) cause(야기하다, 초래하다)이다. (A) expose(노출시키다), (C) risk(위태롭게 하다)는 바로 뒤에 목적어가 오고, (D) hinder는 'hinder A from -ing'와 같은 구조로 'A가 ~을 못하게 하다'라는 뜻으로 쓰여 어법상 적절치 않다.

134 문맥에 맞는 문장 고르기

번역 (A) 사용 시 주의하지 않으면 나무를 손상시킬 수 있습니다.
(B) 기술자들이 그것들의 사용을 권장합니다.
(C) 잘못된 곳에 두기에는 너무 큽니다.
(D) 알맞은 쓰레기통에 폐기되어야 합니다.

해설 바로 앞 문장에서 조심하라는 얘기가 나오기 때문에 그 뒤에 이어질 문장은 그 내용을 곧바로 받을 수 있는 연관된 문장이 나와야 한다. 조심하지 않으면 어떤 일이 일어날 수 있는지 알려 주는 문장이기 때문에 (A)가 정답으로 가장 적절하다.

135-138 기사

> **펠레티어 아트 새 소식**
> 글: 비키 스티븐슨
>
> 시에서는 수 주의 준비를 거쳐 토요일에 모서 브리지 아래 새로운 벽화를 **135공개할 예정입니다.** 시민과 관광객은 펠레티어 운하를 찾아 온종일 계속되는 기념 행사에 참여할 수 있습니다. 기념 행사에서는 각종 경기와 다과가 마련됩니다.
>
> 벽화는 지역 화가인 프레스턴 길버트가 기획하고 벽돌로 된 다리 아래쪽에 그린 것입니다. 북쪽에는 동물이, 남쪽에는 유명 미술작품이 그려져 있습니다. **136두 곳 모두** 관람객들이 재미있는 사진을 찍을 기회를 갖도록 기획된 것입니다. **137예를 들어** 북쪽에서 방문객들은 다정다감한 고릴라와 악수를 하는 것처럼 보이는 사진을 찍을 수 있습니다.
>
> **138행사에 관한 더 자세한 소식은 www.pelletiercanal.com에서 확인할 수 있습니다.**
>
> ---
>
> **어휘** preparation 준비 mural 벽화 citizen 시민 tourist 관광객 daylong 온종일 계속되는 celebration 기념 행사, 축하 refreshments 다과 conceive 마음속에 품다, 상상하다 brick 벽돌 underside 아래쪽 local 지역의 feature 특징으로 삼다, 특별히 포함하다 present 보여주다, 나타내다 design 고안하다 provide 제공하다 onlooker 구경꾼 opportunity 기회 take a picture 사진을 찍다 appear ~인 것 같다, ~처럼 보이다 shake hands with ~와 악수하다

135 동사 시제

해설 빈칸은 동사 자리로 시제를 묻고 있다. 첫 번째 문장에서 몇 주의 준비 끝에(After several weeks of preparation)라는 말과 두 번째 문장에서 지역 주민과 관광객들을 초대한다(are invited)는 내용이 있으므로 미래를 나타내는 시제가 적절함을 알 수 있다. 따라서 정답은 (D) will unveil (공개할 것이다)이다. (A)와 (C)는 과거시제이고, (B)는 과거완료이므로 정답이 될 수 없다.

어휘 unveil 덮개를 벗기다, 공개하다

136 대명사

해설 이 문장에서 빈칸 주어는 관람객들이 재미있는 사진을 찍을 기회를 갖도록 기획되었다는 내용이다. 주어 동사 수 일치의 경우 (A) Each와 (D) Another는 단수 명사이고 (C) Much는 셀 수 없는 명사이므로 모두 복수 동사 are 앞에 올 수가 없다. 그러므로 앞 문장의 북쪽과 남쪽, 장소 두 곳을 나타내는 (B) Both가 정답이다.

어휘 each 각각 both 둘 다 another 다른 것[사람]

137 부사 어휘

해설 접속 부사 문제이다. 북쪽에서는 고릴라와 악수를 하는 것처럼 보이는 사진을 찍을 수도 있다는 예를 들어 앞 문장에서 언급한 재미있는 사진 촬영의 기회에 대한 추가 설명을 하고 있으므로 정답은 (D) For instance(예를 들어)이다. (A) Nonetheless(그럼에도 불구하고), (B) Additionally (추가로), (C) Instead(대신에)는 의미상 적합하지 않다.

138 문맥에 맞는 문장 고르기

번역 (A) 행사에 관한 더 자세한 소식은 www.pelletiercanal.com에서 확인할 수 있습니다.
(B) 다리는 수로를 따라 교통을 원활하게 해 줄 것으로 예상됩니다.
(C) 마침내 길버트 씨가 벽화에 관한 짧은 연설을 했습니다.
(D) 관심 있는 사람은 555-0147로 전화해 제안사항을 전달할 수 있습니다.

해설 두 번째 단락에서 북쪽에는 동물이, 남쪽에는 유명 미술작품이 있고 관람객들이 재미있는 사진을 찍을 수 있으며, 특히 빈칸 앞 문장에서 고릴라와 악수를 하는 것처럼 보이는 사진을 찍을 수 있다고 하였다. 그러므로 이에 관한 더 자세한 소식을 확인할 수 있다는 것이 문맥상 자연스러우므로, 정답은 (A)이다.

어휘 details 세부 사항 be expected to + 동사원형 ~할 것으로 기대되다, 예상되다 ease 완화하다 traffic 교통 waterway 수로 finally 결국, 마침내 give a speech 연설하다 submit 말하다, 제출하다 suggestion 제안

139-142 이메일

> 발신: ⟨k.chalmers@rybecks.com⟩
> 수신: ⟨s.underhill@me-mail.net⟩
> 날짜: 10월 25일
> 제목: 주문 번호 6622
>
> 언더힐 씨께,
>
> 귀하의 실내 장식을 위해 라이벡스를 선택해 주셔서 감사합니다. 안타깝게도 귀하께서 **139주문을 하셨을** 때 저희 웹사이트가 업데이트 중이었습니다. **140이 때문에** 일부 잘못된 정보가 있었습니다. 특히 구매하고자 하신 쿠션은 현재 재고가 없는 상태입니다. **141그러나** 저희에게 비슷한 쿠션 세트가 있습니다. 주문하신 상품과 디자인과 가격은 동일하나 색상이 약간 다릅니다.
>
> 이 상품의 사진을 첨부했습니다. **142모습이** 마음에 드신다면 바로 배송해 드릴 수 있습니다.

답신 기다리겠습니다.

케빈 차머스
라이벡스 홈 퍼니싱

> **어휘** appreciate 감사하다 home furnishing 실내 장식
> needs 요구 unfortunately 안타깝게도, 유감스럽게도 in
> particular 특히 purchase 구매[구입]하다 actually 실제로,
> 사실 currently 현재 not in stock 재고가 없는 similar 유사한
> available 이용 가능한 slightly 약간 shade 색조 attach
> 첨부하다 immediately 즉시

139 동사 시제

해설 place an order는 '주문을 하다'라는 표현이다. 특별한 경우가 아니라면
주절과 종속절의 시제는 일치시키는 것이 원칙이다. 뒤의 주절의 시제가
과거 시제(was being updated)이므로 정답은 (B) placed이다.

140 문맥에 맞는 문장 고르기

번역 (A) 이런 정기적인 정비는 데이터 보안을 보장해 줍니다.
(B) 몇 시간 후 계정이 등록되었는지 다시 확인하십시오.
(C) 이 때문에 일부 잘못된 정보가 있었습니다.
(D) 다행히 저희 오프라인 매장은 모두 정상 영업 중입니다.

해설 앞 문장에서 업데이트가 있었다는 내용과 뒤 문장에서 구매하려던 쿠션이
재고가 없다는 내용을 토대로, 업데이트 하는 도중에 주문을 하여 약간의
오류가 있었다는 내용이 들어가면 적절할 것이다. 따라서 정답은 (C)이다.

141 부사 어휘

해설 문맥에 맞는 접속부사를 고르는 문제이다. 빈칸 앞에서 '재고가 없다'라고
말한 뒤, 빈칸 뒤에서 '비슷한 것은 있다'라고 했으므로 그 사이에는 이전
내용을 반대로 전개시킬 수 있는 부사가 들어가야 한다. 정답은 앞뒤 내용
을 반대로 전개시킬 수 있는 접속부사인 (D) However(그러나)이다.

어휘 therefore 그러므로 besides 게다가 occasionally 가끔

142 명사 어휘

해설 첫 번째 단락 마지막 문장에서 '디자인과 가격은 동일하지만 약간 다
른 색상(shade)을 가지고 있다'고 했다. 따라서 문맥상 빈칸은 shade
와 동일한 의미를 가진 단어가 들어가는 것이 적절하므로 정답은
(A) appearance(모습, 외관)이다.

어휘 dimension 치수 appraisal 평가, 판단 texture 질감

143-146 이메일

> 발신: ⟨d_wang@statecentral.edu⟩
> 수신: ⟨professionalspanishlist@statecentral.edu⟩
> 날짜: 1월 14일
> 제목: 추가 강좌 개설

여러분,

토요일 아침 10시에 있는 저희 '전문인을 위한 스페인어 입문' 강좌의 **143**인기
가 높아져서 다음 학기에는 일정에 두 번째 강의를 추가하기로 결정했습니다. 새
강좌는 같은 요일과 시간에 **144**열리지만 장소는 홀 건너편 224호입니다. 강의
경력이 있는 스페인어문학과의 호르헤 카실라 교수가 강의를 맡기로 했습니다.

학생 포털에 접속하여 등록하십시오. **145**추후 출석이 불가능할 경우, 다른 관심
있는 학생들의 좌석을 확보하기 위해 최소 12시간 전 미리 **146**등록을 취소해 주
십시오.

딜리아 왕
사회교육원 코디네이터, 주립 센트럴 대학교

> **어휘** introduction to ~ 입문 upcoming 곧 다가오는
> semester 학기 attend 출석하다 in advance 미리 make
> room for ~를 위해 자리를 만들다 extension (대학교 부설)
> 사회교육원

143 형용사 자리 _ 보어를 취하는 동사 뒤

해설 become처럼 grow도 보어를 취하는 동사다. 주어와의 관계가 동격이 아
니라 상태를 나타내기 때문에 형용사가 와야 한다. 부사 so가 수식하면서
'매우 인기가 있는'이라는 뜻이 되는 (A) popular(인기 있는)가 정답이다.

144 동사 시제

해설 바로 앞 문장에서 다음 학기(the upcoming semester)에 강의를 추가
하기로 했다는 말이 나왔다. 빈칸이 있는 이 문장에서는 그 새로운 수업에
대한 이야기를 하고 있으므로 시제는 미래 시제가 되어야 한다. 따라서 정
답은 (A) will be meeting이다.

145 문맥에 맞는 문장 고르기

번역 (A) 중급 프랑스어 역시 취소되었습니다.
(B) 해당 날짜 전까지 밀린 과제물을 제출하십시오.
(C) 학생 포털에 접속하여 등록하십시오.
(D) 카페테리아는 걸어서 가까운 거리에 있습니다.

해설 빈칸 뒤 문장을 보면, 추후 출석이 불가능할 경우, 다른 학생들이 등록할
수 있도록 미리 등록을 취소해 달라는 말이 나온다. 따라서 빈칸에는 첫 번
째 단락에서 말한 새로운 수업에 대한 등록 이야기가 나와야 함을 알 수 있
다. 따라서 정답은 (C)이다.

146 명사 어휘

해설 앞 문장에서 '등록'과 관련된 내용이 이미 나왔고 만약 추후 출석이 불
가능하다면 그 '등록'을 12시간 전에 미리 취소하라는 의미가 되어야 하
므로 정답은 (D) enrollment(등록)이다. (A) development(개발),
(B) withdrawal(철수), (C) appointment(약속)는 의미상 맞지 않다.

PART 7

147-148 양식

포트원 비즈니스 협회 (PBA)

세미나 신청서 (5월 프로그램)

147솔리헐 컨퍼런스 센터 210-212호

이름: <u>아멜리에 지루</u>	____ 현금 동봉
직업: <u>생산라인 관리자</u>	____ 신용카드 청구
회사: <u>빅스비 매뉴팩처링 주식회사</u>	X 회사에 청구
세미나명: <u>물량과 품질 간 균형 유지</u>	***148**현재 포트원 비즈니스 협회의 회원이 아니신 분은 등록 서류 처리를 위한 추가 수수료 5파운드를 납부하셔야 됩니다.
세미나 번호: <u>13</u>	
세미나 장소: <u>212호</u>	
PBA 회원 ____ **148**비회원 <u>X</u>	

어휘 association 협회 registration form (등록) 신청서 occupation 직업 supervisor 관리자, 감독 balance 균형을 잡다 enclosed 동봉된 individual 개인 currently 현재 be required to+동사원형 ~하도록 요구되다 administration fee 수수료 processing 처리

147 사실 관계 확인

번역 PBA에 대해 명시된 것은?
(A) 일년 단위로 세미나를 조직한다.
(B) 빅스비 매뉴팩처링의 후원을 받는다.
(C) 여러 개의 회의실에서 세미나를 열 것이다.
(D) 월간 소식지를 발행한다.

해설 표 바로 위에 솔리헐 컨퍼런스 센터 방 번호가 210-212호까지 언급되었기 때문에 정답이 (C)라는 것을 알 수 있다.

148 추론 / 암시

번역 지루 씨에 대해 추론할 수 있는 것은?
(A) 이전에 PBA 세미나에 참석한 적이 있다.
(B) 자신의 신용카드 상세 정보를 제공했다.
(C) 회사로부터 비용 정산을 받을 것이다.
(D) 수수료를 지불해야 한다.

해설 Non-member에 체크가 되어 있고, 마지막 부분을 보면, 회원이 아닌 경우, 등록 서류 처리를 위해 추가 수수료 5파운드를 내야 한다고 했다. 이를 토대로 정답이 (D)라는 것을 알 수 있다.

149-150 광고

이스페셜리 포 유

귀사는 회사 대연회나 퇴직 기념 만찬을 준비하고 있습니까? 주주 회의나 제품 런칭 행사와 같은 소규모 모임을 주최할 예정이십니까?

이스페셜리 포 유는 그와 같은 **149**기업 행사를 위한 최상의 식음료를 제공하는 데 10년 이상의 경험을 보유하고 있습니다. 경험이 풍부한 세 명의 행사 관리자를 비롯해 25명으로 구성된 서빙팀을 고용하고 있습니다. 맛있는 식사 제공 이외에도 라이브 공연이나 예쁜 테이블 꽃장식과 같은 장식을 준비해서 제공해 드

릴 수 있습니다.

www.especially4uco.com을 방문하셔서 저희 음식과 서비스 전체를 살펴보시고 무료 견적을 요청해 보세요. **150**캘리포니아, 네바다, 애리조나, 유타 주에서 접객 서비스 협회(HAS) 인증을 받은 업체입니다.

어휘 corporate 기업의 banquet 연회, 만찬 retirement 퇴직 host 주최하다 gathering 모임 shareholder 주주 highly experienced 경험이 풍부한 offering 제공하는 것 arrange 주선하다 live entertainment 라이브 공연 decoration 장식 centerpiece (테이블 등의) 중앙부 장식 a full range of 폭넓은 ~ price quote 견적서 hospitality 접대 certification 인증

149 세부 사항

번역 어떤 종류의 사업을 광고하고 있는가?
(A) 가구점
(B) 채용 대행사
(C) 출장 연회 서비스 업체
(D) 홍보 회사

해설 두 번째 단락 첫 줄에 보면, '기업 행사를 위해 식음료를 제공한다(providing finest foods and beverages)'는 말이 나온다. 따라서 출장 연회 서비스를 하는 회사임을 알 수 있으므로 정답은 (C)이다.

150 사실 관계 확인

번역 이 업체에 대해 명시된 것은?
(A) 여러 국가에서 운영한다.
(B) 견적을 내는 데 약간의 수수료를 청구한다.
(C) 최근 종업원 수를 늘렸다.
(D) 여러 주에서 인증을 받았다.

해설 지문 마지막 문장을 보면, 캘리포니아, 네바다, 애리조나, 유타 주에서 인증을 받았다는 말이 나온다. 따라서 정답은 (D)이다. (A)와 (C)에 대한 언급은 없으며, 마지막 단락에서 무료 견적(a free price quote)을 해 준다고 했으므로 (B)도 오답이다.

151-152 온라인 채팅

케이지 야마시타 [오후 3:00]

안녕하세요, 브리타니 씨. 방금 멜버른에서 열리는 ERS 제조산업 박람회 참석에 관한 승인을 받았어요. **151**5월 21일 오후에 떠나서 5월 24일 오전에 돌아오는 비행기표와 행사장 근처 호텔을 구해주실 수 있을까요?

브리타니 잰슨 [오후 3:01]

처리할 수 있을 겁니다. 단, 이메일을 통해 정식 요청을 해야 합니다. **152**정책 변경에 관해 게시한 메모를 기억하고 계시지 않나요?

케이지 야마시타 [오후 3:01]

152아, 서면으로 요청을 하라는 뜻이라고 생각했습니다. 채팅 메시지로 충분하지 않나요?

브리타니 잰슨 [오후 3:02]

152아, 아닙니다. 정확히 이메일을 사용해서 요청 기록을 쉽게 열람할 수 있도록 하려고 해요.

케이지 야마시타 [오후 3:03]

<u>알겠습니다.</u> 지금 처리할게요.

어휘 approval 승인 manufacturing 제조업 trade show 무역박람회 depart 출발하다, 떠나다 return 돌아오다 venue 장소 arrange 처리하다, 주선하다 make a request 요청하다 formal 공식적인, 정식의 post 게시하다 policy 정책 in writing 서면으로 specifically 분명히, 정확하게 accessible 접근 가능한, 이용 가능한 record 기록 take care of ~를 처리하다

151 사실 관계 확인

번역 잰슨 씨에 관해 가장 사실인 것은?
(A) 회사의 출장 계획을 처리한다.
(B) 최근 야마시타 씨에게 경과 보고서를 요청했다.
(C) 전시 장비 대여를 책임지고 있다.
(D) 작년에 무역박람회에 참석했다.

해설 야마시타 씨가 잰슨 씨에게 오후 3시 보낸 메시지에서 방금 멜버른에서 열리는 ERS 제조산업 박람회 참석에 관한 승인을 받았다라는 내용이 있었고 바로 이어서 출장에 관련된 비행기표와 행사장 근처의 호텔 예약을 요청하였으므로 정답은 (A)이다.

어휘 handle 처리하다 recently 최근 progress report 중간 보고서, 경과 보고서 in charge of ~를 맡아 lend out 빌려주다 exhibition 전시 equipment 장비

152 의도 파악

번역 오후 3시 3분에 야마시타 씨가 "알겠습니다."라고 쓸 때, 그 의도는 무엇인가?
(A) 예약을 할 수 있었다.
(B) 정책의 의도를 이해했다.
(C) 행사 준비를 충분히 했다고 생각한다.
(D) 이메일을 받았다.

해설 3시 1분에 젠슨 씨는 정책 변경을 얘기하였고 야마시타 씨는 서면 요청을 얘기했으며, 3시 2분 젠슨 씨가 이메일을 사용한 요청의 목적으로 설명하자 야마시타 씨가 알겠습니다(God it)라고 표현을 했으므로 정답은 (B)이다. 참고로 Got it.은 I understand. 또는 I see.와 같은 의미이다.

어휘 make a reservation 예약하다 purpose 의도 sufficiently 충분히 prepared for ~에 준비가 된 receive 받다

153-154 공지

원터튼 록 페스티벌
트윈리버 캠핑장
8월 4일-6일

음악 애호가 여러분께,

올 여름 트윈리버 캠핑장에서 열리는 제2회 원터튼 연례 록 페스티벌에 참가하세요. 8월 4일부터 6일까지 개최될 예정입니다. 화려한 출연진이 다시 찾아와 153노소를 불문하고 여러분께 큰 즐거움을 선사해 드립니다. 두 번의 본무대 이외에도 많은 다과 천막과 미술 및 공예품 판매자들이 있습니다. 또한 원터튼의 자체 지역 라디오 방송국 WXO 97.9가 주말 내내 페스티벌을 생중계할 예정입니다. 올해 출연진을 소개합니다.

The Autumn Empire – 카슨 시티의 90년대 얼터너티브 록 아이콘의 재결합
Three Dragons – 비평가들의 호평을 받은 데이타운 출신의 3인조 록 밴드

154Summer Haze – 원터튼의 유명한 프로그레시브 록 밴드
The Amazing Randy – 메이빌 출신의 유명한 아동 공연가이자 TV 스타

전체 일정과 매표 정보를 보시려면 웹사이트 www.wintertonrocks.com을 방문하세요.

어휘 campground 야영지, 캠핑장 star-studded 스타들이 대거 출연하는 lineup 구성, 출연진 be sure to + 동사원형 반드시 ~하다 delight 기쁨, 즐거움 in addition to ~에 더하여 refreshment 다과 crafts 공예 vendor 판매자, 상인 broadcast live 실황 방송을 하다 all weekend long 주말 내내 reunion 재결합 critically adored 비평가들의 호평을 받은 famed 매우 유명한 outfit (함께 작업하는) 팀, 그룹

153 사실 관계 확인

번역 음악 페스티벌에 대해 사실인 것은?
(A) 원터튼 주민은 무료이다.
(B) 이틀 동안만 열린다.
(C) 일 년에 두 차례 열린다.
(D) 모든 연령대의 사람들을 위한 것이다.

해설 첫 번째 단락 세 번째 문장을 보면 나이와 상관없이 즐길 수 있다(a delight for people young and old)는 내용이 나온다. 따라서 이를 바탕으로 정답은 (D)이다.

▸▸ Paraphrasing   지문의 for people young and old
→ 정답의 for people of all ages

154 세부 사항

번역 지역 출신 밴드는 누구일 것 같은가?
(A) The Autumn Empire
(B) Three Dragons
(C) Summer Haze
(D) The Amazing Randy

해설 지문에서 소개하는 행사는 원터튼 록 페스티벌이며, 지문 중간 아래 소개된 출연진을 살펴보면 세 번째의 Summer Haze라는 팀이 원터튼 출신의 프로그레시브 록 밴드라고 나와 있다. 따라서 정답은 (C)이다.

155-157 기사

뉴필드(2월 27일) – 컵케이크 전문점이 여기저기 생겨나는 가운데 가장 좋아하는 과자를 살 곳을 정하기가 어려울 수 있다. 155그러나 컵케이크케이크의 특별한 과자들은 단순함 덕에 돋보인다. 156다른 과자점들이 수십 가지의 맛을 만들어 내는 데 반해, 컵케이크케이크는 바닐라, 초콜릿, 레몬, 레드벨벳, 당근 등 몇 가지 맛만을 완벽하게 구현해 내는 데 집중한다. 이 컵케이크들은 지나치게 달지 않으면서도 풍부한 맛을 내는 프로스팅을 입혀 가볍고 촉촉하면서도 부드럽다.

가게 주인이자 요리사인 스티븐 에반스 씨는 자신의 작품에 자부심이 있다. "사람들은 컵케이크가 단기적인 유행에 불과하다고 말하지만 우리 컵케이크케이크에서는 특이한 맛을 지양하고 특별한 날을 기념하기에 딱 맞는, 혹은 평상시에도 그냥 먹고 싶은 전통적이고 위안이 되는 컵케이크를 추구합니다."라고 그는 말한다. 157에반스 씨는 5년간 라폰테인의 파티시에로 일한 후 자신의 가게를 열었다. 그러나 그의 격식을 차리지 않는 베이킹 사랑은 부모님의 부엌에서 시작

됐다고 한다. "부모님은 제가 난장판을 만들어 놓아도 그냥 내버려 두셨습니다." 라고 그는 설명한다. 하지만 지금 그는 난장판 이상의 무엇인가를 창조해 냈다.

컵케이크케이크는 홀 스트리트 10471에 위치하며 월요일~금요일은 오전 9시부터 저녁 8시까지, 토요일과 일요일은 오전 10시부터 오후 5시까지 문을 연다. 컵케이크 개당 가격은 1.75~3달러이다.

> **어휘** pop up 불쑥 나타나다 every corner 구석구석 treat 특별한 것, 선물 stand out 두드러지다 simplicity 간결함 flavor 맛, 풍미 a handful 소수, 소량 moist 촉촉한 fluffy 푹신푹신한, 부드러운 frosting 당의를 입히는 것 overly 과도하게 take pride in ~을 자랑으로 여기다 short-term 단기의 avoid 피하다 in favor of ~를 지지하여 comforting 위안이 되는 special occasion 특별한 경우 mess around (함부로) 손대다, (만지작거리며) 느긋하게 즐기다 range from A to B 범위가 A에서 B 사이다

155 주제 / 목적

번역 기사의 주된 목적은 무엇인가?
(A) 업계 동향을 분석한다.
(B) 한 업체를 홍보한다.
(C) 어느 도시를 관광해 볼 것을 권한다.
(D) 한 건설 프로젝트를 보도한다.

해설 '컵케이크케이크'라는 과자점을 홍보하고 있으므로 정답은 (B)이다.

156 세부 사항

번역 기사에 따르면, 컵케이크케이크는 경쟁업체들과 어떻게 다른가?
(A) 조리법이 공개되어 있다.
(B) 실내 좌석이 없다.
(C) 단지 몇 가지 맛의 컵케이크만을 판매한다.
(D) 컵케이크에 설탕이 들어 있지 않다.

해설 첫 번째 단락 중간쯤 보면, 다른 과자점들은 수십 가지의 맛을 만들어 내는 데 반해, 컵케이크케이크는 '몇 가지 맛 만을 완벽하게 구현해 내는 데 집중한다(focuses on perfecting only a handful)'는 내용이 나온다. 이것을 토대로 정답이 (C)라는 것을 알 수 있다.

> ▶ **Paraphrasing** 지문의 **focuses on perfecting only a handful** → 정답의 **sells only a few flavors of cupcake**

157 사실 관계 확인

번역 기사에서 스티븐 에반스에 대해 명시한 것은?
(A) 새로운 종류의 컵케이크를 만들었다.
(B) 성인이 되었을 때 베이킹을 처음 시작했다.
(C) 카페를 운영했었다.
(D) 디저트를 만드는 데 수년간의 경험이 있다.

해설 두 번째 단락에서 스티븐 에반스에 대해 말하고 있는데, 중간쯤 보면, 5년 동안 파티시에로 일한 뒤에 자신의 제과점을 열었다는 말이 나온다. 파티시에가 하는 일이 과자나 케이크 같은 디저트류를 만드는 일이므로 정답은 (D)이다.

158-160 광고

> ### 브런틀리 타이어 앤 오토 서비스
>
> 158(B)브런틀리 타이어 앤 오토 서비스는 린스필드 지역에서 10년 이상 헌신을 다해 서비스를 제공해왔습니다. 저희는 자동차, 트럭, 레저용 자동차, 트레일러 등을 위한 타이어를 판매, 서비스, 주문 제작합니다. 엔진 수리에서 실내 온도 조절 시스템 설치에 이르기까지 160다양한 일반 자동차 서비스도 제공합니다. 158(A), 160가족 운영 사업체로서 공인된 칼라일 오토 케어 센터(CCACC)이기도 합니다. 이것이 바로 고객께서 배려 깊은 서비스와 최상의 기술력을 누릴 수 있는 이유입니다. 귀하의 차량 수리 또는 서비스를 받기에 적합한 곳이라는 확신이 아직 들지 않으십니까? 158(C)저희 웹사이트 bruntleytas.com을 방문하시거나 월~금요일 오전 8시~오후 6시 사이에 매장을 직접 방문하셔서 더 자세한 내용을 알아보세요.
>
> 시즌 특별 할인: 11월 30일까지 보리소나 트랙시스트 등 주요 브랜드의 타이어에 대해 놀라운 할인 혜택을 받으실 수 있습니다. 159어떤 브랜드든 타이어를 두 개 이상 구매하신 분은 무료 오일 교환 서비스도 해드립니다. 일년 내내 받으실 수 있는 경로 할인도 잊지 말고 문의하세요.

> **어휘** with dedication 헌신을 다해 customization 주문제작 RV 레저용 자동차(= recreational vehicle) a variety of 다양한 installation 설치 climate control system 실내 온도 조절 시스템 family-owned 가족이 운영하는 be convinced 확신하다 in person 직접, 몸소 seasonal 계절적인 take advantage of ~를 이용하다 amazing 놀라운 complimentary 무료의 senior citizen discount 경로 할인 year round 연중 내내

158 사실 관계 확인

번역 브런틀리 타이어 앤 오토 서비스에 대해 명시되지 않은 것은?
(A) 가족이 소유하고 있다.
(B) 10년도 더 전에 설립됐다.
(C) 인터넷 홈페이지가 있다.
(D) 주말에 일부 문을 연다.

해설 (A)는 첫 번째 문단 중간쯤 가족 운영 사업체라는 내용이 나오며, (B)는 첫 문장에 린스필드 지역에서 10년 이상 서비스를 제공해왔다고 나온다. 웹사이트 주소가 있으므로 (C)도 맞는 내용이다. (D)는 지문의 내용만으로는 알 수 없는 사항이므로 정답은 (D)이다.

159 세부 사항

번역 고객들은 프로모션 기간 중 어떻게 무료 서비스를 받는가?
(A) 다수의 타이어를 구매
(B) 광고에 대해 언급
(C) 로열티 프로그램에 등록
(D) 특정 연령 이상

해설 두 번째 문단 두 번째 문장을 확인해 보면 타이어를 두 개 이상 구입하면 무료로 엔진 오일 교환을 해 준다는 내용(purchase two or more tires ~ a complimentary oil change)이 나온다. 이를 토대로 정답이 (A)라는 것을 알 수 있다.

> ▶ **Paraphrasing** 지문의 **a complimentary oil change** → 정답의 **a free service**
> 지문의 **two or more tires** → 정답의 **multiple tires**

160 문장 삽입

번역 [1], [2], [3], [4]로 표시된 곳 중에서 다음 문장이 들어가기에 가장 적합한 곳은?

"이것이 바로 고객께서 배려 깊은 서비스와 최상의 기술력을 누릴 수 있는 이유입니다."

(A) [1]
(B) [2]
(C) [3]
(D) [4]

해설 해당 문장 앞에는 '서비스'와 '기술력'에 관한 내용이 언급되어야 한다. [2]번 앞 문장을 살펴보면 '서비스'는 다양한 일반 자동차 서비스 제공(A variety of general auto services)이라는 내용으로, '기술력'은 공인된 칼라일 오토 케어 센터(CCACC)라는 점을 언급하고 있기 때문에 [2]번에 위치하는 것이 가장 적절하다. 따라서 정답은 (B)이다.

161-163 웹페이지

http://www.bengalheaven.co.uk

소개	메뉴	위치	**특별 이벤트**

벵갈 헤븐은 3년 전 문을 연 이래 버밍햄 시내에서 큰 성공을 거두고 있습니다. 명성 높은 빈달루를 포함해 무척 다양한 커리 메뉴들은 모든 손님들께 큰 인기를 끌었습니다. **161개업 3주년을** 기념하기 위해 이번 달 내내 몇 개의 품목을, 다음 달 10월에도 다른 세 개 품목을 할인해 드릴 예정입니다.

이번 달!

티카 마살라	정상가: 12달러	특별가: 10달러
잘프레지	정상가: 15달러	특별가: 13달러
빈달루	정상가: 14달러	특별가: 12달러

다음 달!

탄두리	정상가: 16달러	특별가: 14달러
162코르마	정상가: 14달러	**특별가: 12달러**
로간 조쉬	정상가: 12달러	특별가: 10달러

1639월, 10월 내내 네 명 이상 단체께 무료 디저트를 제공합니다. 주문하시는 품목과 지불하시는 가격에 상관없이 모든 손님께서는 완전히 무료로 디저트를 드실 수 있습니다.

어휘 big hit 대성공 diner (식당에서) 식사하는 사람, 손님
discount 할인하다 throughout this month 이번 달 내내
regular price 정상가 party 일행, 단체 regardless of ~에 관계없이 absolutely 전적으로

161 세부 사항

번역 벵갈 헤븐은 왜 가격을 낮추는가?
(A) 새로운 메뉴를 선보이고 있다.
(B) 창립을 기념하고 있다.
(C) 지점을 닫으려고 준비 중이다.
(D) 세 번째 레스토랑을 개장한다.

해설 첫 번째 단락 마지막 부분에서 개업 3주년을 기념하기 위해서(To celebrate being in business for three years) 할인 행사를 한다고 언급했다. 따라서 정답은 (B)이다.

▶▶ **Paraphrasing** 지문의 **To celebrate being in business** → 정답의 **celebrating its founding**

162 세부 사항

번역 10월에는 어떤 메뉴가 12달러일 것 같은가?
(A) 티카 마살라
(B) 빈달루
(C) 코르마
(D) 로간 조쉬

해설 다음 달이 10월이기 때문에 Next Month!에서 Special Price 중 12달러를 고르면 된다. 3주년 기념 할인 행사이므로 왼쪽 칸에 있는 Regular Price가 아니라 오른쪽 칸에 있는 Special Price에서 골라야 한다. 따라서 정답은 (C)이다.

163 세부 사항

번역 웹페이지에 따르면, 무료 상품을 받을 수 있는 사람은?
(A) 단체 손님
(B) 매일 첫 번째 손님
(C) 특정 상품 구매 손님
(D) 특정 금액 이상을 지불한 손님

해설 마지막 단락 첫 번째 문장에서 4명 이상 단체(parties of more than four people)에게 무료 디저트를 제공한다는 내용을 토대로 정답이 (A)라는 것을 알 수 있다.

164-167 이메일

발신: ⟨fdunger@sunspearind.com⟩
수신: ⟨galina_popova@rl-mail.net⟩
날짜: 6월 5일 월요일 오후 2:29
제목: SMS에 관한 정보

포포바 씨께,

선스피어 인더스트리즈의 새로운 솔라 모듈 시스템(SMS)에 대해 문의해 주셔서 감사합니다. 요청하신 정보를 제공해 드릴 수 없는 점 사과 드립니다. **164현재 새 안내 책자를 인쇄하고 있으니 곧 보내 드리겠습니다.** 그때까지 SMS로 사용 가능한 신규 기능 일부에 대해 알려 드리고자 합니다.

165일반 가정용으로 개발된 본 시스템은 소비자들에게 전통적인 에너지원에 대해 비용 효율적이고 환경친화적인 대안을 제공하도록 고안되었습니다. 개선된 패널은 이전 모델에 비해 30% 더 높은 효율성으로 태양 광선을 흡수합니다. 또한 과잉 에너지를 추후 사용할 수 있도록 자동 저장하는 배터리 시스템이 있습니다. 배터리는 **165, 166(B)일반 가정에 간혹 좋지 않은 기상 조건일 때 최대 이틀까지 전력을 공급하기에 충분한 에너지를 갖고 있습니다.** **166(D)아울러 유지 보수가 거의 필요하지 않습니다.**

독립 기관인 몬트레이 에너지 연구 센터(MERC)는 SMS를 에너지 시장에 선보이기 전 18개월간 SMS 심층 연구를 이끌었습니다. 연구 결과, 개선된 설계가 훨씬 더 효율적이며 소비자들에게 **166(A)매월 전기 요금을 최대 100달러까지 절약해 준다는 것이 밝혀졌습니다.**

SMS에 대해 궁금한 점이 있으시면 주저없이 저에게 연락해 주십시오. 이전 이메일에서 언급하신 대로 **167**SMS는 귀하께 무척 가치 있는 구매가 될 것입니다. 그 사이에 댁으로 자세한 안내 책자가 배달될 것입니다.

플로리안 D. 웅거
선스피어 인더스트리즈

어휘 inquire 문의하다 apologize 사과하다 fill ~ in on ~에게 새로운 정보를[자세한 지식을] 알리다 feature 기능 be designed to+동사원형 ~하도록 고안되다 cost-effective 비용 효율적인 environmentally-friendly 환경친화적인 alternative to ~에 대한 대안[대체제] absorb 흡수하다 efficiency 효율성 previous 이전의 furthermore 게다가 automatically 자동으로 excess 과잉, 초과량 contain 함유하다 occasionally 가끔 unfavorable 형편이 나쁜 weather condition 기상 상태[조건] next to 거의 maintenance 유지 보수 independent 독자적인, 독립된 in-depth 심층의, 면밀한 drastically 대폭 electricity bill 전기 요금 hesitate 망설이다 indeed 참으로 worthwhile ~할 가치가 있는 in the meantime 그동안

164 추론 / 암시

번역 선스피어 인더스트리즈에 대해 암시된 것은?
(A) 일시적으로 온라인으로 청구서를 제공할 수 없다.
(B) 최근에 한 컨퍼런스에서 부스를 운영했다.
(C) 현재 일부 인쇄 자료를 업데이트하고 있다.
(D) 연구 개발팀이 높게 평가된다.

해설 첫 번째 단락 두 번째 문장의 '새 안내 책자를 인쇄하고 있다(we are ~ printing out new brochures)'는 내용을 바탕으로 정답이 (C)라는 것을 알 수 있다. 다른 보기들은 지문에서 언급하지 않은 내용이다.

▸▸ Paraphrasing 지문의 new brochures
→ 정답의 some printed materials

165 세부 사항

번역 SMS는 누구를 위해 특별히 고안되었는가?
(A) 자동차 운전자
(B) 주택 소유주
(C) 사업주
(D) 과학자

해설 두 번째 단락 맨 처음에 '일반 가정용으로 개발되었다(Developed for normal houses)'는 말이 나오고, 그 단락 후반부에도 '일반 가정에 전력을 공급하는(to power the average home)'이라는 말이 나온다. 이를 통해 SMS는 일반 가정을 위해 고안된 것임을 알 수 있다. 따라서 정답은 (B)이다.

166 사실 관계 확인

번역 SMS에 대해 명시되지 않은 것은?
(A) 사용자들이 돈을 절약할 수 있게 도와 준다.
(B) 강력한 배터리를 가지고 있다.
(C) 개발된 지 1년이 채 되지 않았다.
(D) 유지 보수가 간단하다.

해설 (A)는 세 번째 단락 후반부의 '전기 요금을 한 달에 최대 100달러까지 줄일 수 있다'는 말에서, (B)는 두 번째 단락 후반부의 '최대 이틀까지 전력을 공급한다'는 말에서, (D)는 두 번째 단락 후반부의 '유지 보수가 거의 필요 없다'는 말에서 확인할 수 있다. (C)는 심층 연구기간이 18개월이라고 했으므로 이메일의 내용과 일치하지 않는다. 따라서 정답은 (C)이다.

167 사실 관계 확인

번역 포포바 씨에 관해 사실일 것 같은 것은?
(A) 투자할 기회를 찾는 중이다.
(B) 환경 협회의 대변인이다.
(C) 선스피어 인더스트리즈에서 일한다.
(D) 선스피어 제품 구매를 고려하고 있다.

해설 마지막 단락의 '귀하께서 구매할 만한 가치가 있다(a worthwhile purchase for you)'라는 말을 통해서 포포바 씨가 책자를 요청한 것은 해당 제품 구매를 고려하기 위해서임을 알 수 있다. 따라서 정답은 (D)이다.

168-171 문자 메시지

오후 1:16
제임스: **168**오늘 밤 펠리시아를 위한 파티가 정말 기대돼요. 우리 부서 전원이 올 건지 아세요?

오후 1:17
아이샤: 음, 우리 중 몇 명이 가요. **169**제시카와 니코스는 변경하지 못할 다른 일이 있대요.

오후 1:18
제임스: 아쉽군요. **168**토요일 밤에 시간을 내는 게 어렵다는 건 알지만 펠리시아가 50세가 되는 날은 한 번이잖아요. 그리고 굉장한 행사가 될 것 같은데 말이죠.

오후 1:19
케이트: 저도 그래요. 전에 웨스트브라이트 레스토랑은 가 본 적이 없어요. **170**사실 뭘 입어야 하는지 궁금했어요. 평상복이 괜찮을까요, 아니면 다소 격식을 차린 옷이어야 할까요?

오후 1:20
제임스: 캐주얼한 복장도 괜찮을 겁니다. 사실 며칠 전 펠리시아에게 물어봤는데 그녀가 그렇게 말했어요.

오후 1:21
케이트: 아, 잘됐군요. 그럼 간단하죠.

오후 1:23
아이샤: 그러고 보니 생각나네요. 어제 사무실에서 펠리시아를 위한 카드를 돌렸어요. 오늘 밤 펠리시아에게 주고 싶어서요. 두 분 다 서명했나요?

오후 1:24
케이트: 저는 했어요.

오후 1:25
제임스: 아니오, **171**저는 하루 종일 인쇄소에 있었어요. 오늘 밤에 해야겠군요.

어휘 look forward to+명사/-ing ~를 고대하다 free up 시간을 내다 formal 격식을 차린 remind A of B A에게 B를 상기시키다 the printer's 인쇄소(= the printer's shop)

168 세부 사항

번역 펠리시아는 오늘 무엇을 할 것 같은가?
(A) 공연에 참가하기
(B) 잠재 고객들에게 식사 대접하기
(C) 회사의 신규 지점 열기
(D) 생일 축하하기

해설 제임스의 첫 번째 대사에서 '오늘 밤 펠리시아를 위한 파티가 정말 기대된다'는 말을 통해 정답이 (D)임을 알 수 있다.

169 의도 파악

번역 오후 1시 17분에 아이사가 "음, 우리 중 몇 명이 가요"라고 쓴 의도는 무엇이겠는가?
(A) 그 그룹 중에서 참석하는 사람의 수가 한정되어 있다.
(B) 다른 부서에서는 아무도 참석하지 않을 것이다.
(C) 그녀는 제임스가 일정을 바꿔야 한다고 생각한다.
(D) 그녀는 제임스가 자신에게 정보를 보내기를 바란다.

해설 바로 앞에서 '모든 사람이 참석하는지' 물어본 것에 대한 답변이면서 곧바로 뒤에 두 명이 참석하지 못하는 것을 언급하고 있으므로 정답은 (A)이다.

170 세부 사항

번역 케이트는 행사에 대해 무엇을 물어보는가?
(A) 행사 장소가 어디인지
(B) 옷을 어떻게 입어야 하는지
(C) 행사 주최자가 누구인지
(D) 언제 행사가 끝날 것 같은지

해설 1시 19분에 케이트가 언급한 내용을 살펴보면 복장에 관한 질문이 나온다. 따라서 정답은 (B)이다.

▶▶ **Paraphrasing** 지문의 **what we should wear**
→ 정답의 **how to dress**

171 추론 / 암시

번역 제임스에 대해 암시된 것은?
(A) 새로 온 직원이다.
(B) 오늘 케이트와 점심을 먹었다.
(C) 어제 사무실에 없었다.
(D) 다른 건물에서 일한다.

해설 1시 23분 대화에서 어제 사무실에서 펠리시아를 위한 카드를 돌렸는데, 1시 25분 제임스의 대화를 보면 어제 하루 종일 인쇄소에 있었다는 내용이 나온다. 이를 종합해 보면 제임스는 어제 사무실에 없어서 카드를 함께 쓰지 못했다는 것을 알 수 있다. 따라서 정답은 (C)이다.

172-175 이메일

발신: 그레고리 채프먼 〈greg.chapman@tgo-mail.com〉
수신: 파르빈 미르자 〈p.mirza@taylorchemistmanchester.co.uk〉
날짜: 3월 4일
제목: 약사직 지원서
첨부: ⓪ 채프먼 이력서

미르자 씨께,

맨체스터 테일러 케미스트 홈 스트리트 지점의 부장 약사이자 **172저의 예전 동료였던 앨번 캠벨 씨가 토마스 스트리트에서 개점하는 약국과 관련해 귀하께 연락을 취해 보라고 하셨습니다.** 저는 해당 직에 큰 관심을 갖고 있어 검토하실 수 있도록 제 이력서를 첨부했습니다.

제 이력서의 학력 및 경력란에서 보시는 대로 저는 자격을 모두 갖춘 약사입니다. 지난 4년 동안 스톡포트에 있는 APK 약국에서 근무했습니다. **175그곳에서 저의 일상 직무는 처방약을 제공하고 손님들에게 조언을 하며 알맞은 재고 수준을 유지하는 일 등이었습니다.** 저는 효율성을 강조하는 안전한 방식으로 이런 업무를 완수합니다. **173지난해 저는 재고 정리 절차를 간소화하여 전보다 30% 가까이 시간을 줄일 수 있었고 이러한 성과에 대해 관리자로부터 특별히 인정을 받았습니다.**

174아울러 테일러 사가 고객 서비스에 중점을 두는 것을 오랫동안 존경해왔는데, 그것은 저의 최우선 순위이기도 하기 때문입니다. 결국 사람들의 병을 낫게 하는 것이 약사의 주요 임무일 것입니다. 이는 약을 통해서뿐만 아니라 친절, 인내, 소통 등을 통해 이뤄져야 합니다. 저는 고객들과 아주 좋은 관계를 맺고 그들이 필요로 하는 도움을 제공하기 위해 열심히 일합니다. 이렇게 비슷한 가치관을 가진 회사의 일원으로 제 역량을 발휘할 수 있다면 좋겠습니다.

요컨대 제가 해당 직책에 이상적인 지원자임을 확신합니다. 면접의 기회가 주어진다면 기쁘겠습니다. 오후에는 대부분 제 이메일 주소나 03069-990621번으로 연락 가능합니다.

감사합니다. 답신 기다리겠습니다.

그레고리 채프먼

어휘 pharmacist 약사, 약국 branch 지점 former 이전의 coworker 동료 get in touch with ~와 연락을 취하다 attach 첨부하다 CV 이력서(= curriculum vitae) perusal 정독, 숙독 qualified 자격이 있는 daily 일상적인, 매일의 task 직무 prescription 처방전 medication 약 maintain 유지하다 appropriate 적절한 stock 재고 carry out 수행하다 in a safe manner 안전한 방식으로 emphasize 강조하다 efficiency 효율성 streamline 간소화하다 inventory 재고, 물품 목록 procedure 절차 recognition 인정 accomplishment 성취, 업적 additionally 게다가 priority 우선 순위 after all 결국 relationship 관계 exercise one's skill 수완을 발휘하다 candidate 지원자 post 직책 delighted 기쁜

172 추론 / 암시

번역 채프먼 씨는 구인 건에 대해 어떻게 알았을 것 같은가?
(A) 지인을 통해
(B) 업계 간행물을 통해
(C) 프리랜서 모집자를 통해
(D) 구직 웹사이트를 통해

해설 채프먼이라는 이름을 찾아보니 편지의 발신인이다. 그리고 지문 맨 처음 부분에 '예전 동료가 연락을 해 보라고 했다'는 내용이 나온다. 따라서 정답은 (A)이다.

▶▶ **Paraphrasing** 지문의 **former coworker of mine**
→ 정답의 **an acquaintance**

173 세부 사항

번역 채프먼 씨가 언급한 최근의 성과는 무엇인가?

    (A) 업무 처리 속도를 개선했다.
    (B) 기술 자격증을 받았다.
    (C) 인턴 사원 몇 명을 관리했다.
    (D) 성공적인 광고를 디자인했다.

해설 두 번째 단락 후반부를 보면 '재고 정리 절차를 간소화하여 시간을 줄였다'는 말이 나온다. 따라서 정답은 (A)이다.

> ▸▸ **Paraphrasing** 지문의 **streamline our inventory procedure** → 정답의 **improved the speed of a process**

174 추론 / 암시

번역 맨체스터 테일러 케미스트에 대해 암시된 것은?

    (A) 특별히 높은 급여를 제공한다.
    (B) 고객 서비스를 우선시한다.
    (C) 지점들이 병원 내에 위치해 있다.
    (D) 구직자들에게 시험을 치르도록 한다.

해설 세 번째 단락 첫 번째 문장에 테일러 사가 고객 서비스에 중점을 둔다는 말이 나온다. 따라서 정답이 (B)라는 것을 알 수 있다.

> ▸▸ **Paraphrasing** 지문의 **focus on customer care** → 정답의 **prioritizes customer service**

175 문장 삽입

번역 [1], [2], [3], [4]로 표시된 곳 중에서 다음 문장이 들어가기에 가장 적합한 곳은?
"지난 4년 동안 스톡포트에 있는 APK 약국에서 근무했습니다."

    (A) [1]
    (B) [2]
    (C) [3]
    (D) [4]

해설 삽입문이 들어가는 곳 바로 뒤에는 그 약국에서 근무했던 경력의 내용이 나와야 할 것이다. [1]번 뒤 문장을 보면 My daily duties there라는 말로 시작하는데, 여기서 there가 바로 그 약국을 의미한다고 볼 수 있다. 따라서 가장 적절한 곳은 (A)이다.

176-180 웹페이지+온라인 양식

---

http://www.bufordherald.com/home

저희 신간 〈스포츠 다이제스트〉를 구독해 보세요

〈뷰포드 헤럴드〉는 모든 스포츠 팬들을 위해 특별히 기획된 신간 출판물을 곧 선보인다는 소식을 전해 드리게 되어 기쁩니다. **178**5월 7일부터 〈스포츠 다이제스트〉 신간은 **177**매월 첫째 주와 셋째 주 토요일에 구독자에게 배달될 것입니다. 신규 발행물에서는 축구, 야구, 농구, 그 외 다양한 스포츠를 다룹니다. **176** 진행됐던 경기에 대한 심층 해설, 최고의 팀들의 스타 선수들과의 대화, 모든 팀의 승패 및 현재 상황에 대한 자세한 내용 등이 포함됩니다. 〈뷰포드 헤럴드〉 정

기 구독자들은 한시적으로 〈스포츠 다이제스트〉를 **179**연 45달러의 할인된 가격에 정기 구독할 수 있습니다. 이렇게 하면 25달러의 비용을 절약할 수 있습니다.

5월 1일 전까지 〈스포츠 다이제스트〉를 등록하셔서 이번 특가 판매의 혜택을 누리세요. 5월 1일부로 연간 정기 구독료가 정상가인 70달러로 인상됩니다.

> **어휘** brand-new 새로운 publication 발행물 specifically 특별히 appeal to ~에게 호소하다 subscriber 구독자 in-depth 심층의 description 설명, 기술 current 현재의 for a limited time 제한된 시간 동안 discounted rate 할인 가격 savings 절약한 금액 take advantage of ~를 이용하다 special offer 특가 판매 annual 연간의 standard price 정상가

---

www.bufordherald.com/subscriptions/38843#

〈뷰포드 헤럴드〉는 여러분의 성원에 감사드립니다. 귀하의 거래 처리가 완료되었습니다.

이름: 로렌조 모레티
주소: 라미레즈 로드 40, 트렌트, NJ 08625
전화번호: 555-0126
이메일 주소: lmoretti@fab-mail.net
거래일자: 4월 23일
179지불액: 45달러

영수증을 인쇄하려면 **이곳을 클릭하십시오.**
180본 서류의 전자 버전도 위에 기입한 주소로 발송될 것입니다.

경기 일정, 결과, 경기 티켓 특가 판매 등 최신 스포츠 뉴스를 보시려면 **이곳을** 클릭하여 저희 스포츠 전용 페이지를 확인하십시오.

> **어휘** patronage 후원, 애용 confirm 확정하다 transaction 거래 receipt of payment 지불 영수증 electronic 전자의 up-to-date 최신의 dedicated 전용의

176 사실 관계 확인

번역 〈스포츠 다이제스트〉의 특집 기사로 언급되지 않은 것은?

    (A) 유명 선수들과의 인터뷰
    (B) 끝난 경기에 대한 보도
    (C) 스포츠 방송 일정
    (D) 팀들의 성적에 관한 통계 자료

해설 첫 번째 지문 중간에 나열된 내용을 토대로 정답을 확인할 수 있다. (A)는 '스타 선수들과의 대화(discussions with the stars)'에서, (B)는 '경기에 대한 심층 해설(in-depth descriptions of games)'에서, (D)는 '모든 팀의 승패 및 상황에 대한 내용(full details of all teams ~ form)'에서 확인할 수 있다. 글에서 언급하지 않은 것은 (C)이다.

> ▸▸ **Paraphrasing** 지문의 **discussions with the stars** → 보기의 **Interviews with famous players**
> 지문의 **in-depth descriptions of games** → 보기의 **Reports on completed games**

177 세부 사항

번역 〈스포츠 다이제스트〉 신간은 얼마나 자주 발행될 것인가?
(A) 주 1회
(B) 주 2회
(C) 월 1회
(D) 월 2회

해설 첫 번째 단락 두 번째 문장에서 확인할 수 있다. 매월 첫째, 셋째 토요일에 구독자에게 배달된다는 내용(will be delivered ~ the month)을 통해서 정답이 (D)라는 것을 알 수 있다.

▶▶ **Paraphrasing** 지문의 on every first and third Saturday of the month → 정답의 Twice a month

178 추론 / 암시

번역 모레티 씨는 〈스포츠 다이제스트〉 첫 호를 언제 받을 것 같은가?
(A) 4월 23일
(B) 4월 24일
(C) 5월 1일
(D) 5월 7일

해설 첫 번째 지문의 두 번째 문장을 보면 Starting from May 7로 시작되는데, 5월 7일부터 〈스포츠 다이제스트〉 신간이 배달될 것이라는 말이다. 따라서 정답은 (D)이다.

179 연계

번역 모레티 씨에 대해 명시된 것은?
(A) 현재 〈뷰포드 헤럴드〉를 정기 구독하고 있지 않다.
(B) 정기 구독을 신청할 때 할인가를 지불했다.
(C) 〈스포츠 다이제스트〉를 직장 주소로 받을 것이다.
(D) 전에 〈뷰포드 헤럴드〉로 이메일을 보냈다.

해설 첫 번째 첫 단락 마지막 부분을 보면 한정된 기간에 한해서 '45달러의 할인된 가격에 연간 구독을 할 수 있다'는 내용이 나온다. 그리고 두 번째 지문의 양식을 보면 모레티 씨가 지불한 금액이 45달러인 것을 알 수 있다. 따라서 정답은 (B)이다.

180 세부 사항

번역 모레티 씨는 이메일로 무엇을 받을 것인가?
(A) 지불 확인서
(B) 야구 경기 티켓
(C) 할인 쿠폰
(D) 경기장 지도

해설 두 번째 지문 후반부를 보면 위에 입력한 이메일 주소로 전자 서류를 보내줄 것이라는 내용을 확인할 수 있다. this document라는 것은 돈을 지불한 내역이 담긴 서류를 의미하기 때문에 정답은 (A)이다.

181-185 이메일+이메일

> 발신: 가브리엘 패리시
> 수신: 르얀쉬 데쉬판데
> 날짜: 4월 3일
> 제목: 사진 촬영업체

> **182**르얀쉬 씨, 좋지 않은 소식을 전합니다. 채스핀 포토그래퍼스가 올해는 저희 연회 작업을 할 수 없을 거라고 합니다. **181**그 날 저녁 이미 예약된 행사가 있다고 해요. 요금이 매우 합리적이고 작년 작업에 만족하신 걸 생각하면 꽤 실망스럽습니다.
>
> 하지만 다행히 제가 확인한 지역 업체 몇 곳이 가능합니다. 가장 저렴한 곳은 1인 업체인 호틀리 포토그래피입니다. 웹사이트에 게시된 사진들은 훌륭합니다만, 전체 작업을 한 명에게 맡기는 것에 대해 확신이 서지 않습니다. 2인조 작가들이 잡아낼 수 있는 무언가를 놓친다면 어쩌죠? **182**예를 들어 수상 발표와 청중의 반응 모두를 촬영하기가 쉽지 않을 테니까요.
>
> 그래서 저는 올리비 포토 스튜디오, 페이슨 포토그래피, 카운를 포토그래퍼스 등 규모가 더 큰 3개 업체 쪽으로 기울고 있습니다. **183**올리비는 고객평이 가장 좋아 보이지만 우리가 지출하려는 금액보다 300달러 정도 더 듭니다. 페이슨과 카운를은 가격이 적당한데, 카운를에서는 무료 리터칭 서비스도 제공해요. 그래서 저는 그 곳을 추천합니다.
>
> 의견을 알려 주세요.
>
> 가브리엘

어휘 photographer 사진작가 banquet 연회 book 예약하다 disappointing 실망스러운 given ~를 고려해 볼 때 reasonable 합리적인 several 몇몇의 local 지역의 confirm 확인하다 available 이용 가능한 option 선택 uncertain 확신이 없는, 잘 모르는 whole 전체의 miss 놓치다 award 상, 수여 announcement 발표 audience 청중 reaction 반응 lean towards ~ 쪽으로 마음이 기울다 testimonial 추천의 글 spend 소비하다 affordable (가격이) 적당한 offer 제공하다 recommendation 추천

> 발신: 르얀쉬 데쉬판데
> 수신: 가브리엘 패리시
> 날짜: 4월 4일
> 제목: Re: 사진 촬영업체

> 안녕하세요, 가브리엘 씨.
>
> **183**저는 평판이 좋은 업체를 고용하고 싶습니다. **184**사실 케이터링 서비스는 전체 예산보다 적게 쓸 예정이라서 사진 촬영에 조금 더 지불할 여력이 있습니다. 그리고 웹사이트와 홍보용 간행물에 쓸 좋은 사진이 나오는 것이 아주 중요해요.
>
> 그런데 한 가지 우려사항이 떠오릅니다. 사실 채스핀에 완전히 만족한 것은 아니었죠. 약속한 것보다 사진을 받는 데 더 오래 걸렸으니까요. **185**올해는 사진 촬영업체를 예약하기에 앞서, 계약서 상의 기한을 지키지 못했을 경우 손해배상에 관해 물어보실 수 있나요? 그렇게 하면 우리가 사진을 제때 받는 것을 중요히 여긴다는 걸 보여줄 수 있을 겁니다.
>
> 르얀쉬

어휘 hire 고용하다 reputation 평판, 명성 actually 사실, 실제로 budget 예산 promotional publication 홍보용 간행물 remind A of B A에게 B를 상기시키다 concern 우려, 걱정 completely 완전히 be satisfied with ~에 만족하다 compensation 보상, 손해배상 timeline 시각표 contract 계약 on time 시간을 어기지 않고

181 세부 사항

번역 패리시 씨가 채스핀 포토그래퍼스 고용을 추천하지 못하는 이유는?
(A) 다른 업무가 있다.
(B) 더 이상 외부 서비스를 제공하지 않는다.
(C) 작년 이후로 가격이 올랐다.
(D) 사진의 품질이 떨어졌다.

해설 첫 번째 이메일의 첫 번째 단락에서 좋지 않은 소식을 전한다고 하면서 채스핀 포토그래퍼스가 그 날 저녁에 이미 다른 예약이 있다고 하였으므로 정답은 (A)이다.

어휘 be unable to + 동사원형 ~할 수 없다 recommend 추천하다 engagement (시간 약속을 정해서 하는) 업무, 약속 off-site 부지 밖의 rise 오르다 quality 품질

182 추론 암시

번역 패리시 씨는 어떤 행사 기획에 관여하는가?
(A) 자선 연회
(B) 은퇴 기념파티
(C) 시상식 저녁 연회
(D) 졸업식

해설 첫 번째 이메일의 맨 앞부분에서 저녁 연회라는 내용을 언급하였고 두 번째 단락 다섯 번째 문장에서 수상 발표와 청중의 반응 모두를 촬영한다고 하여 이 연회는 시상식임을 알 수 있다. 따라서 정답은 (C)이다.

어휘 be involved in ~에 관여하다 charity 자선 retirement 은퇴 graduation ceremony 졸업식

183 연계

번역 패리시 씨는 어떤 업체에 연락하겠는가?
(A) 호틀리 포토그래피
(B) 올리비 포토 스튜디오
(C) 페이슨 포토그래피
(D) 카운틀 포토그래퍼스

해설 첫 번째 이메일의 세 번째 단락에서 올리비의 고객평이 가장 좋으나 비용이 더 든다는 내용이 있다. 두 번째 이메일 맨 앞 부분에서 패리시 씨는 평판이 좋은 업체를 고용하고 싶다고 하였으므로 정답은 (B)이다.

어휘 contact 연락하다

184 세부 사항

번역 르얀쉬 씨가 행사에 대해 변경되었다고 명시한 것은?
(A) 장식 주제
(B) 예산 배분
(C) 일정 순서
(D) 홍보 수단

해설 두 번째 이메일의 첫 번째 단락 두 번째 문장에서 르얀쉬 씨가 예산 관련하여 사진 촬영에 좀 더 지불할 능력이 있다고 하였으므로 정답은 (B)이다.

어휘 theme 주제, 테마 decoration 장식 distribution 분배 ordering 순서 method 방법, 수단 promotion 홍보

185 세부 사항

번역 르얀쉬 씨가 패리스 씨에게 사진 촬영업체에 물어보라고 지시한 것은?
(A) 직원들이 전문 협회 회원인지의 여부
(B) 이전 고객 중 한 명이 만족하지 못했던 이유
(C) 사진 편집에 소요되는 기간
(D) 계약 위반 시 발생하는 일

해설 두 번째 이메일 두 번째 단락 세 번째 문장에서 계약서 상의 기한을 지키지 못했을 경우 손해배상에 관해 물어봐 달라고 하였으므로 정답은 (D)이다.

어휘 professional 전문적인 association 협회 previous 이전의 dissatisfied 불만족한 edit 편집하다 agreement 계약 violate 위반하다

186-190 웹페이지+편지+이메일

---

http://www.schorrpublishing.com/newauthors

쇼어 퍼블리싱 – 앞서가는 독립 출판사

신예 작가 페이지

귀하의 책을 출판하는 데 관심이 있으시면 저희에게 말씀해 주십시오.

다음을 제출하셔야 합니다.
* 연락처, ^{186(D)}개인 이력서, 웹사이트 (있을 경우)
* 작품 제목 및 간략한 소개, ^{186(C)}목차 포함
* ¹⁸⁸스토리보드, 최소 1컷의 완성된 스케치 샘플 (아동용 도서만 해당)
* ^{186(A)}책의 독자층에 대한 설명 – 연령, 교육 수준, 관심사 등
* 작품의 마케팅 계획을 ¹⁸⁷강조하는 아이디어 – 같은 주제의 다른 책들과 차별화되는 점은 무엇인가?

위의 정보와 함께 다음으로 패키지를 보내 주십시오. – 제안서, 쇼어 퍼블리싱, 밸리로드 5, 서머셋, PA 19030 – 귀하의 제안서에 관심이 있을 경우 저희가 추후 연락 드리겠습니다.

어휘 leading 선도하는 independent 독립적인 publisher 출판사 request 요청하다 submission 제출 contact information 연락처 résumé 이력서 description 설명, 기술 along with ~와 함께 a table of contents 목차 at least 최소한 readership 독자 수, 독자층 give weight to ~를 강조하다, 비중을 두다 proposal 제안

쇼어 퍼블리싱
밸리로드 5
서머셋, PA 19030

2월 2일

하몬 노타리오
노타리오 오토모티브 내
베이 스트리트 12
키케로, Il 61108

노타리오 씨께,

전화로 말씀 나눠서 무척 기뻤습니다. 숙고한 끝에 귀하가 제안하신 도서 〈미래의 자동차들〉의 출판을 추진하기로 결정했습니다.

저희 모두 귀하의 제안서 패키지에 깊은 감명을 받았습니다. 특히 저희 디자이너들은 제출하신 **188스토리보드와 두 컷의 스케치를 마음에 들어 했습니다.**

동봉해 드린 저희 원고 편집 소프트웨어 사용 설명서를 보실 수 있을 겁니다. **1897월 말 계신 곳을 방문할 때 직접 뵙고 말씀 나누고 싶습니다. 190언제든** 궁금한 점이 있으시면 저나 제 비서 에리카 리엔에게 연락해 주시기 바랍니다.

낸시 데이, 편집장
동봉

어휘 over the phone 전화로 further 더 이상의 go ahead with ~를 추진하다 publication 출판 be impressed with ~에 감명 받다 instruction 설명, 지시 사항 manuscript 원고 editing 편집 in person 직접, 몸소 at any time 언제라도 chief editor 편집장

발신: 낸시 데이 〈dey@schorr.com〉
수신: 편집부원 일동
날짜: 2월 20일
제목: 기획 회의

여러분,

이번 주 목요일 오후 2시에 기획 회의를 열고자 합니다. 우리의 유망한 예정 신간들을 홍보할 방법을 자유롭게 제시해 볼 예정이니 아이디어를 준비해서 와 주십시오.

아울러 케런 준 씨에게 인사를 건네도록 하십시오. **190이전 인턴이었는데 어제 부로 에리카 리엔 씨의 담당 업무를 인계 받기 시작했습니다.**

낸시

어휘 editorial staff 편집부원 hold a meeting 회의를 열다 brainstorm 자유롭게 자기 생각을 제시하다 promote 홍보하다 promising 유망한 a batch of 한 묶음의 upcoming 곧 다가오는 release 출간 former 이전의 take over 인계 받다

186 사실 관계 확인

번역 잠재 저자들이 제출하도록 요청 받지 않은 것은?
(A) 타깃 독자층에 대한 설명
(B) 참고 문헌 목록
(C) 목차
(D) 개인 이력서

해설 첫 번째 지문에서 확인할 수 있다. (A)는 네 번째 항목에서, (C)는 두 번째 항목, (D)는 첫 번째 항목에서 확인할 수 있다. 참고 문헌 목록에 대한 언급은 없으므로 정답은 (B)이다.

187 동의어 찾기

번역 웹페이지에서 8행의 "weight"와 의미가 가장 가까운 것은?
(A) 측정
(B) 압력
(C) 영향력
(D) 부담

해설 give weight to라는 표현은 '~을 강조하다'라는 뜻이다. impact는 '영향력'이라는 뜻으로 give weight to 대신 give impact to라는 표현도 사용

할 수 있다. 따라서 정답은 (C) impact이다.

188 연계

번역 〈미래의 자동차들〉에 대해 암시된 것은?
(A) 아동용 도서이다.
(B) 웹사이트에 나온 기사들을 실었다.
(C) 두 권으로 출판될 예정이다.
(D) 전자책으로 판매될 예정이다.

해설 첫 번째 지문 세 번째 항목을 보면 어린이 대상으로 하는 책에 한해서만 스토리보드와 완성된 스케치 샘플을 제출해야 한다고 명시되어 있다. 그리고 두 번째 지문의 두 번째 단락을 살펴보면 제출한 스토리보드와 두 컷의 스케치가 마음에 들었다고 했다. 이것을 종합해 볼 때, 〈미래의 자동차들〉이라는 도서가 아동용이라는 것을 알 수 있다. 따라서 정답은 (A)이다.

189 추론 / 암시

번역 7월에 어떤 일이 일어날 것 같은가?
(A) 서점에서 특별 프로모션을 열 것이다.
(B) 소프트웨어 프로그램이 업그레이드될 것이다.
(C) 노타리오 씨의 책이 출간될 것이다.
(D) 데이 씨가 노타리오 씨를 만날 것이다.

해설 July가 나온 부분을 재빨리 찾아보도록 한다. 두 번째 지문인 편지의 후반부를 보면, 7월 말에 방문해서 직접 뵙고 얘기 나누자는 말이 나온다. 편지의 발신자인 데이 씨가 수신자인 노타리오 씨를 방문한다는 말이므로 정답은 (D)이다.

190 연계

번역 준 씨는 누구일 것 같은가?
(A) 프리랜서 디자이너
(B) 노타리오 씨 회사의 직원
(C) 편집장의 비서
(D) 마케팅 회사 소유주

해설 두 번째 지문 마지막 문장에서 에리카 리엔이 편집장 낸시 데이의 비서라는 사실을 알 수 있고, 세 번째 지문 마지막 단락에서 준 씨가 에리카 리엔 씨의 업무를 인계 받기 시작했다는 내용을 확인할 수 있다. 이를 토대로 준 씨가 편집장의 비서가 되었다는 것을 알 수 있다. 정답은 (C)이다.

191-195 웹페이지+이메일+정보문

http://www.anstolf.org/tourism/events

시 소개	정부 서비스	사업	관광

앤스톨프 향후 행사

앤스톨프 홈 앤 가든 엑스포 (5월 4-6일) - 3일간의 주택 개조 기념행사로, 교육 세미나 참석, 행사를 위해 특별 조성된 정원 조경 관람, 최고급 주택 개조 제품 구입 등이 가능하다.

192라스킨 킹스 농어 토너먼트 (6월 23-24일) - 191(D)라스킨 킹스 낚시 클럽이 제 20회 연례 농어 낚시 토너먼트를 개최한다. 우승자에게는 지역 후원업체가 기부한 5만 달러의 현금이 지급된다..

토코 재즈 페스티벌 (7월 14–15일) – **191(C)**앤스톨프 출신의 음악가 록산느 토코 헌정 재즈 페스티벌은 재즈 애호가라면 놓쳐서는 안 될 공연이다. 전국의 음악가들이 한데 모여 록산느 토코의 명곡을 연주한다.

앤스톨프 불꽃놀이 쇼 (8월 25일) – 앤스톨프에 기반을 둔 금융업체 파지스 그룹이 매년 후원하는 2시간짜리 화려한 쇼가 펼쳐진다. 멋진 불꽃놀이를 감상하려면 앤스톨프 시립공원 또는 **191(A)**라스킨호가 잘 보이는 장소를 찾으면 된다.

어휘 upcoming 다가오는 celebration 기념행사, 축하 home improvement 주택 개조 educational 교육의 landscape 풍경 bass 농어 be set to+동사원형 ~하기로 예정되어 있다 host 개최하다 annual 연례의, 매년 열리는 finisher (경주의) 마지막 주자 in cash 현금으로 donate 기부하다 generous 후한, 너그러운 sponsor 후원업체 miss 놓치다 tribute 헌사 raise 기르다 financial 금융의 spectacular 화려한 공연 brilliant 훌륭한, 멋진

발신: 마크 닐 〈m.neale@npi-mail.com〉
수신: 〈contact@anstolftours.com〉
192날짜: 6월 2일
제목: 투어 관련 질문

안녕하세요.

192저는 이번 달 말 지역 행사에 참여하기 위해 앤스톨프에 갑니다. 앤스톨프시에서 관광을 할 기회가 있었으면 합니다. **193**거기 살았던 제 친구가 귀사를 추천했습니다. 귀사 웹사이트는 그다지 도움이 되지 않았어요. 그래서 직접 연락을 드리기로 했습니다.

제 상황과 원하는 바를 말씀드리겠습니다. **195**저는 금요일 아침 앤스톨프에 도착할 예정이고, 그 날 오후 진행되는 투어를 신청하고 싶습니다. 2시간 이상은 원하지 않습니다. 가격은 25달러 미만이었으면 합니다. 도보나 자전거도 괜찮습니다. 이런 조건에 맞는 상품이 있나요? 알려주세요.

감사합니다.

마크 닐

어휘 local 지역의 opportunity 기회 sightseeing 관광 used to+동사원형 ~하곤 했다, 예전에는 ~했다 recommend 추천하다 directly 직접 describe 말하다, 서술하다 situation 상황 look for ~를 찾다 sign up for ~를 신청하다 mind 꺼리다 fit 맞다 condition 조건

앤스톨프 투어

194성수기에 제공되는 육상 투어 (5–10월):

이름	가능 요일	출발 시간	소요 시간	가격
앤스톨프 버스 투어	매일	오전 10시, 오후 1시	3시간	15달러
피비 저택 방문	화요일, 목요일	오후 2시	2시간 30분	23달러
195구시가지 도보 투어	일요일을 제외한 매일	오후 4시, 오후 7시	1시간 30분	12달러
앤스톨프 맛보기 투어	목요일, 금요일, 토요일	오후 5시	2시간	34달러

어휘 offer 제공하다 high season 성수기 available 이용 가능한 daily 매일 taste 맛, 짧은 경험

---

191 사실 관계 확인

번역 웹페이지에서 앤스톨프에 대해 명시되지 않은 것은?
(A) 호수 근처에 위치해 있다.
(B) 대규모 공공 정원이 있다.
(C) 유명 인사의 고향이다.
(D) 연례 대회 개최지이다.

해설 첫 번째 지문에 나열된 내용으로 확인할 수 있다. (A)는 네 번째 단락 라스킨 호수(Laskin Lake)에서, (C)는 세 번째 단락 앤스톨프 출신의 음악가(Roxanne Tocco, who was born and raised in Anstolf)에서, (D)는 두 번째 단락의 제20회 연례 농어 낚시 토너먼트(annual bass fishing tournament)에서 확인할 수 있다. 그러므로 정답은 (B)이다.

어휘 be situated 위치해 있다 public 공공의 hometown 고향 celebrity 유명 인사 yearly 매년 하는 competition 대회

---

192 연계

번역 닐 씨는 무엇에 관심을 갖겠는가?
(A) 주택 개조
(B) 농어 낚시
(C) 재즈 음악
(D) 불꽃놀이 쇼

해설 두 번째 지문에서 맨 처음에 닐 씨는 이번 달 말 지역 행사 참여로 앤스톨프에 간다고 했는데, 이메일 날짜를 보면 6월 2일이므로, 결국 닐 씨는 6월 말에 열리는 행사에 관심이 있음을 할 수 있다. 첫 번째 지문을 보면 6월 말에 열리는 행사는 라스킨 킹스 농어 토너먼트이므로 정답은 (B)이다.

어휘 be interested in ~에 관심이 있다

---

193 세부 사항

번역 닐 씨는 앤스톨프 투어에 대해 어떻게 처음 알았는가?
(A) 앤스톨프 예전 주민으로부터
(B) 인터넷을 검색해서
(C) 정부 기관 직원으로부터
(D) 행사에서 나눠준 전단을 보고

해설 두 번째 지문 첫 번째 단락 두 번째 문장에서 확인할 수 있다. 전에 앤스톨프에서 살았던 친구가 추천했다고 하였으므로 정답은 (A)이다.

어휘 former 이전의 resident 주민 search 검색 employee 직원 government agency 정부 기관 flyer 전단 distribute 나눠주다, 분배하다

---

194 추론 / 암시

번역 정보에서 투어에 대해 암시된 것은?
(A) 투어 중 일부는 사전 등록이 필요하다.
(B) 예약 가능 여부는 연중 시기에 따라 다르다.
(C) 출발 시간이 임시 변경됐다.
(D) 투어 참여 가능한 최대 인원은 34명이다.

해설 세 번째 지문 앤스톨프 투어 정보문의 제목에서 확인 할 수 있다. 성수기(5–10월)에 제공되는 육상 투어는 연중 시기에 따라 다르다는 것을 알 수 있으므로 정답은 (B)이다.

어휘 require 요구하다, 필요로 하다 advance 사전의 registration 등록 availability 가능성 vary 달라지다, 다르다 according to ~에 따라서 departure 출발 temporarily 임시로 maximum 최대의 allow 허락하다

195 연계

번역 닐 씨는 어떤 투어를 추천받겠는가?
(A) 앤스톨프 버스 투어
(B) 피비 저택 방문
(C) 구시가지 도보 투어
(D) 앤스톨프 맛보기 투어

해설 두 번째 지문 두 번째 단락에서 닐 씨는 원하는 투어의 시간(2시간 미만)과 비용(25달러 미만)을 언급하였고 세 번째 지문 육상 투어에서 이 두 조건을 모두 충족시키는 것은 구시가지 도보 투어이므로 정답은 (C)이다.

196-200 기사+이메일+이메일

데일몬트 시티 타임즈

데일몬트 시티 (9월 8일)–오래 기다려온 데일몬트 플라자 쇼핑몰이 현재 70 퍼센트 가량 임대된 상태다. 개발업체인 라라닉 프라퍼티스는 **196**새 임차인들에게 임대료를 할인해 줌으로써 남는 공실을 채우기를 바라고 있다. "12월까지 만실을 목표로 하고 있습니다."라고 임대 관리인 브라이언 퍼트니는 말한다. "우리는 매력적인 소형 독립 매장들에 특히 관심이 많습니다."

쇼핑몰 두 개 층 매장들은 중앙 식사 장소를 중심으로 배치됐다. 서관은 데일몬트강 쪽을 바라보고 있으며 동관은 뒤쪽 주요 주차 구역을 바라본다.

198매장을 쇼핑몰의 가장 큰 구역으로 옮긴 지역 소매업자 데이비드 올슨 씨는 새 위치를 마음에 들어한다. "확장 중입니다. 매장 동료들이 더 많이 **197**필요하게 될 수도 있습니다. 얼마나 바빠지느냐에 달려 있죠."라고 그는 설명한다.

어휘 long-awaited 오래 기다려온 developer 개발업체 offer 제공하다 reduced rate 할인된 가격 tenant 임차인 aim for ~를 목표로 하다 occupancy (건물, 방 등의) 사용 attract 끌어들이다 arrange 배치하다 wing 부속 건물 face ~을 마주보다[향하다] parking area 주차 구역 in the rear 뒤쪽[후방]에 local 지역의 retailer 소매업자 location 위치 expand 확장하다 bring on ~을 야기[초래]하다 associate (사업·직장) 동료 depend on ~에 달려 있다

발신 글로리아 멜로 〈melo@oyt-mail.com〉
수신 브라이언 퍼트니 〈putney@laranic.com〉
날짜 10월 3일
제목 문의

퍼트니 씨께,

198데일몬트 플라자에서 스포츠 서플라이 플러스라는 자신의 매장을 운영하는 제 친구 데이비드 올슨이 저에 대해 언급했을 것입니다. 저는 온라인 의류 판매업인 다다 디자인스를 소유하고 있으며 소매 쇼룸을 열고자 합니다. 저는 강을 바라 보는 1층의 위치가 좋지만 옆에 다른 옷 가게가 있는 장소는 원치 않습

니다. **200**가능하다면 보관을 위한 뒷방이 딸린 공간이 좋겠습니다. 그리고 저는 월세로 3000달러만 낼 수 있습니다. 이러한 기준에 알맞은 곳이 있으신가요?

199아울러 저는 쇼핑몰의 최근 임차인 목록을 받아서 전입 요령을 물을 수 있었으면 합니다.

감사합니다.

글로리아 멜로

어휘 be referred to ~에게 언급되다 apparel 의류 retail 소매 backroom 뒷방, 창고 storage 보관, 저장 criteria 기준

발신 켈리 프랫 〈searches@realtyemt.com〉
수신 글로리아 멜로 〈melo@mail.com〉
날짜 10월 4일
제목 데일몬트 플라자 공실

멜로 씨께,

브라이언 퍼트니가 저에게 귀하께 월세 3000달러 이하의 데일몬트 플라자의 공실 목록을 보내드리라고 하여 연락드립니다. 아래 목록을 살펴봐 주시고 마음에 드시는 곳이 있으시면 저에게 이메일이나 555-0186번으로 연락 주십시오.

매장 340 – 강물이 보이는 1층 공간 – 잘되는 여성 의류 매장과 인접함
매장 390 – 동관 2층 공간 – 푸드코트 입구 바로 옆
200매장 430 – 강이 내려다보이는 1층 공간 – 보관에 적합한 뒤쪽 사무실 있음
매장 460 – 뒤쪽 주차장 및 하역장에 인접한 1층 공간 – 탁 트인 설계

켈리 프랫
중개인, EMT 부동산

어휘 vacancy 빈 방, 공실 adjoin 인접하다 overlook 내려다보다 back office 백오피스 (손님에게 노출되지 않는 장소) suitable for ~에 적합한 rear 뒤쪽의 loading dock 하역장 agent 중개인, 대리인

196 사실 관계 확인

번역 데일몬트 플라자에 대해 명시된 것은?
(A) 네 개 층을 포함하도록 확장될 것이다.
(B) 대중교통으로 올 수 있다.
(C) 식사 장소는 12월에 개조할 예정이다.
(D) 신규 임차인들은 임대료 할인을 받을 것이다.

해설 첫 번째 지문 맨 앞 두 문장을 보면, 데일몬트 플라자가 70퍼센트 정도 임대된 상태이고, 나머지 공실은 임대료를 할인하여 채우고 싶어한다는 얘기가 나왔다. 따라서 정답은 (D)라는 것을 알 수 있다.

197 동의어 찾기

번역 기사에서 세 번째 단락 2행의 "bring on"과 의미가 가장 가까운 것은?
(A) 고용하다
(B) 빠르게 하다
(C) 제공하다
(D) 생산하다

해설 bring on의 사전적인 의미는 '~을 야기[초래]하다', '~을 데리고 오다'라는 뜻이다. 이 문장에서는 더 많은 매장 직원들을 '고용한다'는 의미가 가장 적절하다. 따라서 정답은 (A) hire이다.

198 연계

번역 스포츠 서플라이 플러스에 대해 암시된 것은?
(A) 입구가 두 개이다.
(B) 10월에 이전할 계획이다.
(C) 주요 제품은 의류이다.
(D) 쇼핑몰에서 가장 큰 공간을 차지하고 있다.

해설 첫 번째 지문 마지막 단락에서 데이비드 올슨 씨가 쇼핑몰의 가장 큰 공간으로 매장을 옮겼다는 내용이 나온다. 그리고 두 번째 지문 첫 번째 문장에서 데이비드 올슨 씨가 스포츠 서플라이 플러스를 운영한다는 것을 알 수 있다. 따라서 스포츠 서플라이 플러스가 쇼핑몰에서 가장 큰 공간을 차지하고 있다는 것을 알 수 있으므로, 정답은 (D)이다.

199 세부 사항

번역 멜로 씨는 퍼트니 씨에게 무엇을 요청하는가?
(A) 신규 임차인 목록
(B) 임대차 계약서 샘플
(C) 건물 도면
(D) 이사 비용 견적

해설 멜로 씨가 퍼트니 씨에게 보낸 첫 번째 이메일을 확인해야 한다. 마지막 단락에서 멜로 씨가 쇼핑몰의 최근 임차인 목록을 요청하고 있음을 확인할 수 있다(I would be interested in getting a list of the mall's most recent tenants). 따라서 정답은 (A)이다.

200 추론 / 암시

번역 멜로 씨는 어떤 공간에 대해 문의할 것 같은가?
(A) 매장 340
(B) 매장 390
(C) 매장 430
(D) 매장 460

해설 두 번째 지문 첫 번째 단락 후반부에서 멜로 씨가 원하는 공간에 대한 언급을 하고 있다. 강이 바라보이는 위치는 선호하지만 바로 옆에 의류 매장이 있는 것은 원치 않기에 (A)는 적절하지 않다. 대신에 보관 공간이 있었으면 좋겠다는 내용을 토대로 1층이면서 강이 보이고 보관 공간이 있는 (C)가 적절하다.

TEST 2

101 (D)	102 (A)	103 (A)	104 (D)	105 (B)
106 (A)	107 (A)	108 (C)	109 (D)	110 (B)
111 (D)	112 (B)	113 (A)	114 (C)	115 (C)
116 (B)	117 (B)	118 (B)	119 (A)	120 (C)
121 (D)	122 (C)	123 (B)	124 (D)	125 (C)
126 (A)	127 (A)	128 (D)	129 (C)	130 (B)
131 (B)	132 (D)	133 (D)	134 (C)	135 (C)
136 (B)	137 (B)	138 (A)	139 (B)	140 (A)
141 (C)	142 (D)	143 (D)	144 (A)	145 (D)
146 (C)	147 (C)	148 (B)	149 (D)	150 (A)
151 (D)	152 (C)	153 (A)	154 (C)	155 (C)
156 (D)	157 (A)	158 (C)	159 (D)	160 (B)
161 (A)	162 (B)	163 (C)	164 (B)	165 (A)
166 (C)	167 (A)	168 (C)	169 (D)	170 (B)
171 (D)	172 (B)	173 (A)	174 (C)	175 (D)
176 (C)	177 (A)	178 (C)	179 (D)	180 (C)
181 (D)	182 (B)	183 (B)	184 (A)	185 (A)
186 (B)	187 (D)	188 (D)	189 (A)	190 (D)
191 (C)	192 (C)	193 (A)	194 (C)	195 (D)
196 (D)	197 (C)	198 (B)	199 (D)	200 (B)

PART 5

101 부사 자리 _ 동사 수식

해설 빈칸은 수동형 동사 was issued(발급되었다)를 수식하는 부사 자리이며 의미상 '늦게 발급되었다'라는 뜻이 적합하므로 정답은 (D) late(늦게)이다. late은 형용사 '늦은'과 부사 '늦게'로 모두 쓰일 수 있는데 이 문장에서는 부사로 쓰인 것이다. (A) lately(최근에)도 부사로 쓰이지만 의미상 부적절하다. (B) latest(최신의)는 형용사이고 (C) lateness(늦음)는 명사이므로 동사를 수식할 수 없다.

번역 바디 씨의 중국 여행은 비자가 늦게 나와서 갑자기 취소되어야 했다.

어휘 be canceled 취소되다 suddenly 갑자기 be issued 발급되다

102 to부정사 자리 _ 목적어

해설 빈칸 앞에 동사가 있고 빈칸 뒤에는 명사구가 있다. 동사 intends의 목적어 역할을 하는 동시에 명사구를 목적어로 취할 수 있는 것은 to부정사이므로 정답은 (A) to replace이다. (B)는 수동태 동사이며 (C)는 명사, (D)는 동명사나 현재분사로 답이 될 수 없다.

번역 이시다 수송은 밴 전체를 환경친화적인 전기차량으로 교체하려고 한다.

어휘 intend to+동사원형 ~할 의도이다 entire 전체의 fleet (한 기관이나 개인이 소유한 차량, 배, 비행기 등의) 무리 environmentally-friendly 환경친화적인 electric vehicle 전기 자동차 replace 교체하다

103 접속사 어휘

해설 빈칸의 앞뒤로 동사구 put on의 목적어인 their safety helmets와 vests가 있는 구조이다. 따라서 두 개의 명사(구)를 연결해 주는 등위접속

사가 필요하므로 정답은 (A) and이다.

번역 조립 라인 작업자들은 작업장 안에 들어가기 전에 안전모와 조끼를 착용해야 한다.

어휘 assembly line 조립 라인 put on ~을 착용하다 safety helmet 안전모 vest 조끼 prior to -ing ~하기 전에

104 주어 자리 _ 주격 대명사

해설 이 문제는 〈접속사(that)+주어+동사(created)〉의 구조에서 주어가 빈칸 처리된 것이므로 정답은 (D) she이다. 다른 보기들은 모두 created의 주어가 될 수 없으므로 오답이다.

번역 제이콥슨 씨는 더 젊은 소비자들에게 다가가기 위해 그 광고 캠페인을 고안했다고 설명했다.

어휘 create 고안하다, 만들어 내다 advertising campaign 광고 캠페인 in an effort to + 동사원형 ~하기 위한 노력으로 reach ~에 닿다, 도달하다 consumer 소비자

105 동사 어휘

해설 어휘 문제를 풀 때는 문장 전체의 의미를 가장 자연스럽게 만들어 줄 단어를 선택해야 한다. 빈칸 뒤 three minutes와 결합해 '수상 소감이 3분으로 제한될 것이다'라고 하는 것이 의미상 자연스러우므로 정답은 (B) restricted(제한된)이다. 다른 보기들은 모두 의미상 부적절하다.

번역 올해 국제 영화제에서는 수상 소감이 3분으로 제한될 것이다.

어휘 international 국제적인 film awards show 영화제 acceptance speech 수상 소감 be restricted to ~로 제한되다 commence 시작하다 eliminate 제거하다

106 부사 어휘

해설 빈칸 앞의 to dress를 꾸미는 부사를 찾는 문제이다. 보기 (B) warmly(따뜻하게), (C) directly(곧장), (D) steadily(끊임없이) 각각의 의미를 볼 때, 문맥상 '깔끔하게' 옷차림을 한다는 표현이 가장 적절하다. 따라서 정답은 (A) neatly(깔끔하게)이다.

번역 회사 방침은 고객을 상대하는 모든 직원들이 가능한 깔끔하게 옷차림을 하라고 요구한다.

어휘 company policy 회사 방침 associate 직장 동료, 직원 client 고객 dress 옷차림을 하다

107 전치사 어휘

해설 동사 spoke와 같이 쓸 수 있는 전치사를 고르는 문제이다. 문맥상 '연금 제도 개혁에 관하여 말했다'라는 의미가 되어야 하므로 정답은 (A) about(~에 관하여)이다. 빈칸 뒤의 동명사를 보고 전치사 (D) by를 고르지 않도록 주의한다.

번역 최 씨는, 물론 그녀의 강의가 다른 주제들도 다루기는 했지만, 연금 제도 개혁에 대해 가장 열정적으로 말했다.

어휘 passionately 열정적으로 reform 개혁하다, 개선하다 pension system 연금 제도 cover 다루다, 포함시키다

108 형용사 자리 _ 목적격 보어

해설 빈칸은 5형식 동사 make의 목적격 보어 자리이므로, 빈칸에는 형용사가 명사가 가능하다. 그런데 목적격 보어 자리에 명사가 오는 경우에는 목적어와 같은 의미(the online reference guide's content)를 나타내야 하므로, 명사인 (D) reliability는 정답이 될 수 없다. 의미상 '온라인 참고 안내 자료의 내용을 신뢰할 수 있도록 만들다'라는 뜻이 되어야 하므로, 정답은 형용사인 (C) reliable(신뢰할 수 있는)이다.

번역 특정 항목들을 작성하기 위해 전문가를 고용하는 것은 온라인 참조 안내 자료의 내용을 보다 신뢰할 수 있게 해줄 것이다.

어휘 hire 고용하다 expert 전문가 entry (사전이나 참고 서적에 포함되는) 항목 reference guide 참조 안내서[안내 자료] content (책, 프로그램 등의) 내용 reliability 신뢰할 수 있음

109 명사 어휘

해설 목적어인 stock options와 subsidized housing이 회사에서 제공하는 혜택임에 주목한다. 따라서 빈칸에는 '혜택들'이라는 단어가 필요하므로 정답은 (D) benefits(혜택)이다. 다른 보기들은 모두 명사이지만 의미상 부적절하다.

번역 보트리고 사에서 이사들에게 제공하는 공통 혜택에는 스톡 옵션과 주거비 지원이 포함된다.

어휘 common 공통적인 offer 제공하다 executive 이사 corporation 회사, 법인 include 포함하다 stock option 스톡 옵션, (증자주에 대한 회사 임직원의) 주식 매입 선택권 subsidized housing 주거비 지원 referral 소개, 위탁 application 지원(서), 신청(서) procedure 절차

110 전치사 어휘

해설 빈칸 앞뒤의 명사를 이어주는 전치사를 고르는 문제다. postponement (연기) 뒤에 알맞은 전치사로는 '~의'를 뜻하는 (B) of가 가장 적절하다.

번역 악천후 때문에 스터빙턴 자선 골프 대회가 연기되었다.

어휘 inclement weather 악천후, 나쁜 날씨 necessitate ~을 필요하게 만들다 charity 자선 tournament 토너먼트, 대회

111 동사 어휘

해설 의미상 to ~ machine까지가 '포장 기계에 발생한 손상을 평가하기 위해'라는 뜻이 되어야 한다. 따라서 빈칸에는 '평가하다'라는 뜻의 동사가 필요하므로 정답은 (D) assess(평가하다)이다. (A) prevent(~을 막다), (B) withstand(견디다), (C) coordinate(조직화하다)는 의미상 부적절하다.

번역 포장 기계에 발생한 손상을 평가하려고 기능장이 오늘 오후 2시에 공장을 방문할 것이다.

어휘 chief technician 기능장, 최고 기술자 damage 손상 packing machine 포장 기계 prevent 방지하다, 막다 withstand 견디다, 버티다

112 명사 자리 _ 소유격 뒤

해설 빈칸이 next year's라는 소유격 뒤에 있으므로 빈칸에는 명사가 들어가

야 한다. 또한 all of 뒤에는 복수 명사를 써야 하므로 정답은 (B) targets이다. (A) target은 단수 명사이므로 정답이 될 수 없고, (C) being targeted와 (D) targeted는 명사가 아니므로 품사상 부적절하다.

번역 모든 내년도 목표들 가운데서 우리는 비용을 15% 줄이는 데 주로 집중해야 한다.

어휘 out of ~ 중에서, ~ 가운데서 primarily 주로 focus on ~에 집중하다, 초점을 맞추다 reduce 줄이다 expenditure 비용, 지출 target 목표

113 동사 어휘

해설 빈칸 뒤의 명사구(the local economy)와 잘 어울리는 동사를 고르는 문제다. '지역 경제를 활성화하기 위해'라는 뜻이 자연스러우므로 (A) stimulate(활성화시키다, 자극하다)가 정답이다. (B) enforce(강요하다), (C) grant(승인하다), (D) resolve(해결하다)는 의미상 어색하다.

번역 부트빌 시의회는 지역 경제를 활성화하기 위해 사업가들을 위한 세금 혜택 방침을 도입했다.

어휘 tax incentive 세금 혜택 entrepreneur 사업가

114 부사 자리 _ 동명사 수식

해설 문장 구조상 conducting부터 빈칸까지가 that절의 주어이며 의미상 '현장 직무 교육을 반복해서 실시하는 것'이란 뜻이 되어야 한다. 따라서 빈칸에는 '반복해서'라는 뜻으로 동명사 conducting을 수식하는 부사가 들어가야 하므로 정답은 (C) repeatedly이다. 다른 보기들은 모두 부사가 아니므로 품사상 정답이 될 수 없다.

번역 최근의 한 학술지 기사는 현장 직무 교육을 반복해서 실시하면 직원들이 생산성과 기민성을 유지하는 데 도움이 된다는 것을 보여 준다.

어휘 journal article 학술지 기사 indicate 보여 주다 conduct 실시하다 on-the-job training 현장 직무 교육 repeatedly 반복해서, 반복적으로 employee 직원 productive 생산적인 alert 기민한, 조심하는 repetition 반복

115 동사 시제 _ 현재완료

해설 보기는 모두 시제가 다른 동사 형태이므로, 시제를 알 수 있는 힌트를 찾아야 한다. within the past month라는 표현은 '지난 한 달 내에'라는 의미로, 한 달 전부터 지금까지를 의미하므로 현재완료 시제가 적절하다. 따라서 (C) have joined이다.

번역 유감스럽지만, 네이언 매뉴팩처링에 입사한 지 한 달이 되지 않은 사람들은 분기 우수 직원상을 받을 자격이 없을 것이다.

어휘 unfortunately 유감스럽게도 join 입사하다, 합류하다 be eligible for (조건이 맞아서) ~을 가질[할] 수 있다 Employee of the Quarter Award 분기 우수 직원상

116 형용사 / 분사 자리 _ 수동태

해설 이 문제는 'be promoted to + 직책(~로 승진하다)'을 적용시키는 문제이므로 정답은 (B) promoted이다. 누군가 승진을 하게 될 경우에 자신이 스스로 승진하는 것이 아니라 회사에 의해 승진이 되는 수동적 입장이므로 항상 'be promoted to + 직책'의 형태로 쓰인다는 점을 알아 두자.

번역 스몰링 씨는 부장 승진과 함께 회사 차도 받게 될 것이다.

어휘 in addition to ~에 더하여, ~ 외에도 division manager 부장 be promoted to ~로 승진하다 promotion 승진; 홍보 promote 승진시키다; 홍보하다

117 형용사 / 분사 자리 _ 명사 뒤에서 수식

해설 빈칸 뒤의 of와 결합해 '~으로 구성된'이란 뜻으로 명사 process 를 수식할 수 있는 분사가 필요하므로 정답은 (B) consisting이다. (A) attached(첨부된)는 전치사 to와 결합하고, (C) effective는 보통 effective of/from 뒤에 날짜와 함께 쓰여 '~부로 시행되는'이라는 뜻을 지니며, (D) associated(관련된)는 전치사 with와 결합해서 쓰이므로 정답이 될 수 없다.

번역 품질 보증 팀은 몇 가지 체계적인 단계로 구성된 공정을 활용한다.

어휘 quality assurance 품질 보증 process 공정, 과정, 절차 methodical 체계적인 step 단계 consist of ~로 구성되다 attached 부착된 effective 시행[발효]되는; 효과적인 associated 관련이 있는

118 명사 어휘 _ 복합 명사

해설 동사 receive의 목적어이며 special parking이라는 명사구와 함께 쓸 수 있는 명사를 찾는 문제이다. 특별 주차 권한을 받는다는 내용이므로 '특권'이라는 말이 가장 적절하다. 따라서 정답은 (B) privileges(특혜, 특권) 이다.

[**번역**] VIP 티켓 소지자는 경기장 내 좋은 자리를 차지하는 것 외에 특별한 주차 혜택도 받는다.

[**어휘**] along with ~와 더불어 seating 좌석 arena 경기장, 공연장 holder 소지자 expenditure 지출, 경비

119 부사 자리 _ 동사 수식

해설 빈칸에는 뒤의 동사 surpassed를 수식해 줄 부사가 들어가야 한다. 정답은 (A) easily(쉽게)이다.

번역 예상한 대로 피스톤 테크놀로지 그룹의 가장 최근 분기 수치가 이전 분기의 수익을 거뜬히 넘어섰다.

어휘 as expected 예상한 대로 latest 가장 최근의 quarterly figures 분기 수치 surpass 뛰어넘다, 능가하다 previous 이전의 earnings 수익

120 명사 어휘

해설 의미상 has given ~ performance가 '기술 성능 면에서 최고 등급을 주었다'라는 뜻이 되어야 자연스럽다. 따라서 빈칸에는 '등급'이란 명사가 필요하므로 정답은 (C) rating이다.

번역 〈디지털 다이제스트 매거진〉이 모비움 6 스마트폰에 기술 성능 면에서 최고 등급을 주었다.

어휘 technical performance 기술 성능 hesitation 망설임 profile 개요 prevalence 만연, 횡행

121 대명사 자리 _ 관계대명사의 선행사

해설 빈칸에는 관계대명사 who의 수식을 받을 수 있는 선행사가 필요하므로 정답은 (D) anyone(누구나)이다. (A) every(모든)는 형용사이므로 관계대명사 앞에서 선행사로 쓰일 수 없다. (B) individual(개인)과 (C) person(사람)은 모두 가산명사이므로 앞에 관사를 붙여야 하므로 정답이 될 수 없다.

번역 저희는 트라이던트 오디오 제품을 아끼는 모든 분들께 저희 시장 조사의 표적 집단에 참여해 주실 것을 요청합니다.

어휘 ask A(사람) to + 동사원형 A에게 ~하라고 요청하다 fan 팬, 애호가 focus group 표적 집단(시장 조사나 여론 조사를 위해 각 계층을 대표하도록 뽑은 소수의 사람들로 구성된 집단)

122 전치사구 어휘

해설 의미상 through ~ entrance가 '정문이 아니라 동쪽 부속 건물 출입구를 통해'라는 뜻이 되어야 한다. 따라서 빈칸에는 '~이 아니라'라는 표현이 들어가야 하므로 정답은 (C) as opposed to이다. instead of와 같은 뜻으로 쓰였다.

번역 접수 구역 개조 기간 동안에 방문객들은 정문이 아니라 동쪽 부속 건물 출입구를 통해 건물에 들어와야만 한다.

어휘 renovation 개조 reception area 접수 구역, 로비 access 접근하다, 들어가다 east wing 동쪽의 부속 건물 main entrance 정문 as long as ~하는 한 in case of ~일 경우 as opposed to ~이 아니라, ~와 반대로 in response to ~에 대응하여

123 부사 어휘

해설 빈칸부터 instructor까지가 의미상 '피트니스 강사의 지시대로만'이라는 뜻이 되어야 한다. 따라서 '단지, 오로지'라는 뜻의 부사가 빈칸에 들어가야 하므로 정답은 (B) only이다. 보기 (A), (C), (D)는 의미상 부적절하다.

번역 이 장비는 피트니스 강사가 지시한 대로만 사용해야 한다.

어휘 equipment 장비 as directed by ~가 지시한 대로 fitness instructor 피트니스 강사 overly 과도하게, 지나치게 barely 간신히, 가까스로, 거의 ~ 아니게 longingly 열망[갈망]하여

124 명사 자리 _ 복합 명사

해설 명사 purposes 앞에 빈칸이 있으므로 형용사가 들어가서 명사를 수식하거나, 명사가 들어가서 복합 명사를 이룰 수 있다. For ------- purposes는 '무슨 목적으로'라는 말이 되어야 하므로 뒤 문장의 의미를 봐야 한다. 호텔의 프런트 데스크 직원들이 여권을 복사한다고 하였으므로, 내용상 '보안 목적으로'라는 뜻이 되어야 자연스럽다. 따라서 purposes와 결합해 복합 명사를 이룰 수 있는 명사가 필요하므로 정답은 (D) security(보안)이다. '보안 목적'이라는 뜻의 복합 명사 security purposes는 토익에 자주 등장하므로 반드시 기억해 두자. (A) secured(확보된, 보증된)는 과거분사로 볼 수 있으나 purposes를 수식하기에는 의미상 부자연스럽다.

번역 보안을 위해 손님들은 그들의 여권을 호텔의 프런트 데스크 직원들이 복사하는 것을 허락해야 한다.

어휘 permit A to + 동사원형 A가 ~하도록 허용하다 make a copy of ~을 복사하다 passport 여권 secure 확보하다 securely 확실하게, 단단히, 안정적으로

125 형용사 자리 _ 명사 수식

해설 명사 toys를 수식할 수 있는 품사는 형용사이므로 정답은 (C) educational(교육용의, 교육적인)이 가장 적절하다. (B) educated(교육 받은)를 과거분사로 볼 경우 명사를 수식할 수 있으나 '교육 받은 장난감'이라는 의미는 부자연스러우므로 오답이다. (A) educate(교육시키다)는 동사이고 (D) educationally(교육적으로)는 부사이므로 명사 toys를 수식할 수 없어 오답이다.

번역 예비 조사를 보면 언어 장벽 탓에 우리의 교육용 장난감 대부분을 해외에서 판매할 수 없다고 나온다.

어휘 preliminary research 예비 조사, 사전 조사 language barrier 언어 장벽 most of ~의 대부분 educational toy 교육용 장난감 abroad 해외에서

126 전치사구 어휘

해설 이 문제는 '예정보다 앞서'라는 뜻의 ahead of schedule을 적용시키는 문제이므로 정답은 (A) ahead of이다. 참고로 behind schedule(예정보다 늦게)과 on schedule(예정대로)도 기억해 두자. 다른 보기들은 schedule과 결합해 관용적 표현을 이루지 못하므로 오답이다.

번역 데닝스 씨는 갑작스런 업무량 증가로 예정보다 앞서 제안서를 마무리할 수가 없었다.

어휘 be unable to+동사원형 ~할 수 없다 proposal 제안(서) because of ~ 때문에 unexpected 갑작스런, 예상치 못한 increase 증가 workload 업무량 except for ~을 제외하고 in advance 미리, 앞서

127 동사 어휘

해설 빈칸 뒤의 명사 목적어와 어울리는 동사를 찾는 문제이다. observe에는 '보다, 관찰하다'의 의미도 있지만 '(법률을) 준수하다'는 의미도 있다. '공휴일을 지킨다(observe the holiday)'는 토익에서 자주 등장하는 표현이니 알아둔다. 정답은 (A) observe(준수하다, 지키다)이다.

번역 하본드 식료품점은 신년 휴일을 지키지 않으므로 1월 1일에 영업을 합니다.

어휘 New Year's Day 새해 첫날 open for business 영업 중인 verify 확인하다, 입증하다 anticipate 예상하다, 예측하다 redeem 보완하다, 상쇄하다

128 전치사 자리

해설 빈칸 앞에는 완벽한 절이 있고 뒤에는 명사구가 있으므로 빈칸은 전치사 자리이다. '~에 관한'이라는 뜻을 지닌 전치사가 와야 하므로 정답은 (D) regarding이다. (A) since는 '~ 이래로', '~ 때문에'라는 의미의 전치사나 접속사, (B) similarly는 부사, (C) these는 대명사 또는 형용사로 쓰인다.

번역 윈스 씨는 윈스 엔터프라이지즈의 역사 및 사업 방식에 관한 새 팸플릿에 글을 포함하고 싶어 한다.

어휘 text 글, 본문 business practice 사업 방식, 사업 관행

129 주어 자리 _ 복합관계대명사

해설 이 문장의 주어는 빈칸부터 afternoon까지이며 동사는 will be allowed이다. 즉, 명사절이 주어가 되는 구조이므로 빈칸에는 명사절을 이끌 관계대명사가 들어가야 한다. 복합관계대명사인 (A) Whatever(무엇이든지)와 (C) Whoever(누구든지) 중에서 문맥상 '자원하는 사람은 누구든지'라는 의미가 되어야 하므로 정답은 (C) Whoever이다. 이 Whoever는 Anyone who로 바꿔 쓸 수 있다는 점도 알아 두어야 한다. 아울러 빈칸 뒤에 있는 volunteers는 명사절 안의 동사이지 명사가 아니라는 점에 주의해야 한다. (B) Another와 (D) Someone은 접속사 없이 명사절의 주어로 바로 쓰일 수 없으므로 정답이 될 수 없다.

번역 금요일 오후에 직원 휴게실을 자원해서 청소하는 사람은 누구든지 그 날 평소보다 한 시간 일찍 귀가하도록 허용될 것이다.

어휘 volunteer to+동사원형 자발적으로 ~하다 clean 청소하다 staff break room 직원 휴게실 be allowed to+동사원형 ~하도록 허용되다 earlier than usual 평소보다 일찍

130 형용사 어휘

해설 rather than 앞에는 '부드러운 직물'이라는 표현이 있고 빈칸 뒤로는 '좀 더 ~한 재료'라는 전체 의미를 파악해 보아야 한다. soft와 대비되는 개념인 (B) rigid(뻣뻣한)가 정답이다. (A) perishable(상하기 쉬운), (C) fluent(유창한), (D) transparent(투명한)는 의미상 어색하다.

번역 애블런트 스포츠는 대다수 소매상들이 이용하는 뻣뻣한 소재보다는 부드러운 직물로 매장 내 간판들을 만들기를 선호한다.

어휘 prefer 선호하다 in-store 매장 안의 fabric 직물 material 소재, 재료 retailer 소매상

Part 6

131-134 기사

스프링타운 가제트
업계 초점

해리슨 애시필드-성공신화

비츠-마크스 주식회사에서 해리슨 애시필드의 출세는 모든 신진 사업주와 기업가들에게 영감을 불어넣는 이야깃거리다. 애시필드 씨는 **131**한때 집집마다 돌아다니며 제품을 판매하는 외판원이었지만 지금은 회사의 유럽 담당 영업부장이다.

애시필드 씨는 인상적인 판매 기술뿐 아니라 직원들을 관리하고 국내와 대륙 통신 시장의 동향에 적응하는 능력까지 보여준 뒤 이 자리에 **132**임명되었다.

애시필드 씨가 자신의 분야에서 최고의 자리에 오른 것처럼 보일지도 모른다, **133**하지만 이 야심 많은 사업가에게는 성취해야 할 더 큰 목표들이 있다. **134**사실, 그는 비츠-마크스 주식회사에 세계적인 영업부를 설립해서 회사가 통신 시장에 서 국제적인 선두 주자가 되도록 돕고 싶다고 공언해왔다.

어휘 rise 부상, 출세 inspire 영감을 불어넣다 budding 신진, 신참 entrepreneur 기업가 sales representative 외판원, 판매 대리인 door to door 집집마다 sales division 영업부(= sales department) be appointed to ~로 임명되다 display 보이다,

전시하다 **not only A but also B** A뿐 아니라 B도 **manage**
관리하다 **employee** 직원, 종업원 **adapt to** ~에 적응하다
trend 동향, 추세 **domestic** 국내의 **continental** 대륙의
telecommunications market 통신 시장 **ambitious** 야심 찬,
의욕적인 **achieve** 성취하다 **publicly state** 공언하다 **establish**
설립하다 **global** 세계적인 **international** 국제적인 **leader**
지도자, 선발업체, 선두 주자

131 부사 어휘

해설 빈칸 다음 문장을 살펴보면, 해리슨 애시필드가 지금은 회사의 유럽 담당
영업부장(now the head of the European Sales Division at the
company)이라고 했다. 이에 비해 집집마다 돌아다니며 제품을 팔던 외
판원(a sales representative who sold products door to door)은
해리슨 애시필드의 과거 직책이었다. 따라서 '(과거) 한때'를 뜻하는 부사
가 빈칸에 들어가는 것이 의미상 적합하므로 (B) once(한때)가 정답이다.
(A) still(여전히), (C) soon(곧), (D) much(많이)도 모두 부사로 쓰일 수
있지만 의미상 부적절하다.

132 동사 시제 / 태

해설 의미상 주어인 애시필드가 영업부장의 자리에 임명된 수동적 입장이므로
수동태가 필요하다. 또한 빈칸 뒤 부분에 나오는 내용은 과거에 애시필드
가 승진을 할 수 있게 해준 능력에 대해 기술한 것이므로 시점 또한 과거가
되어야 한다. 따라서 빈칸에는 과거 수동태가 필요하므로 정답은 (D) was
appointed이다. (A) will be appointed는 수동태이긴 하지만 미래 시제
이므로 부적절하고, (B) is appointing과 (C) had appointed는 수동태
가 아니므로 정답이 될 수 없다.

133 문맥에 맞는 문장 고르기

번역 (A) 애시필드 씨는 그들이 모두 아주 초라하게 시작해서 출세하도록 도움을 주
었다.
(B) 애시필드 씨의 최종 목표는 영업부를 세우는 것이다.
(C) 그들은 그 산업의 타고난 리더인 것처럼 보인다.
**(D) 애시필드 씨가 자신의 분야에서 최고의 자리에 오른 것처럼 보일지도 모
른다.**

해설 빈칸 바로 다음 문장에서 역접의 접속부사 However를 써서 '야심 많
은 사업가에게는 성취해야 할 더 큰 목표들이 있다(However, the
ambitious businessperson has larger goals to achieve.)'고 했
다. 즉, '애시필드가 최고 자리에 오른 것처럼 보일 수도 있다. 그러나
(However) 그에게는 더 큰 목표들이 있다'고 이어지는 것이 의미상 자연
스러우므로 정답은 (D)이다.

134 부사 어휘

해설 빈칸 앞 문장에서 애시필드에게는 성취해야 할 더 큰 목표(larger goals
to achieve)가 있다고 했다. 그리고 빈칸 뒤에는 그의 향후 계획들이 제
시되어 있다. 그러므로 빈칸에는 앞서 한 말에 대해 구체적인 설명을 덧
붙일 때 쓰는 표현이 들어가야 하므로 (C) In fact(사실, 실제로)가 정
답이다. (A) At first(첫째로), (B) Despite that(그것에도 불구하고),
(D) Instead(대신)는 모두 의미상 부적절하다.

135-138 광고

어휘 **heavenly** 천상의, 천국의 **sweeten** 단맛을 더하다 **Boston-
based** 보스턴에 본사를 둔 **specializing in** ~을 전문으로 하는
fancy wedding cake 화려한 결혼 기념 케이크 **as part of** ~의
일환으로 **expansion** 확장, 확대 **recently** 최근에 **branch** 지점
develop 개발하다 **range from A to B** 범위가 A에서 B까지 이르다
elaborate 정교한 **multi-colored** 여러 가지 색깔의, 다채로운
creation 창작품 **covered with** ~로 덮여 있는 **customize** 맞춤
제작하다 **choose** 고르다, 택하다 **frosting** 프로스팅(케이크 표면의
당의) **filling** 속 **decoration** 장식 **be located at** ~에 자리 잡고
있다[위치하다] **theater** 극장 **contact** 연락하다 **make an order**
주문하다 **view** 보다 **online** 온라인으로, 인터넷으로

135 형용사 / 분사 자리 _ 명사 뒤에서 수식

해설 빈칸은 선행 명사인 Boston-based bakery를 수식하는 현재분사 자리
이므로 정답은 (C) specializing(전문으로 하는)이다. (A), (B), (D)는 모
두 동사인데 빈칸 앞쪽에 문장의 동사로 is가 있으므로 동사를 중복해서
쓸 수 없어 모두 오답이다.

136 문맥에 맞는 문장 고르기

번역 (A) 저희는 저희의 최고급 페이스트리 제과 장인들이 매우 자랑스럽습니다.
(B) 저희는 50여 가지의 서로 다른 케이크 디자인을 개발했습니다.
(C) 도시 전역에 더 많은 지점을 열려고 계획하고 있습니다.
(D) 저희의 보상 프로그램에는 12만 명의 고객이 등록되어 있습니다.

해설 빈칸 바로 다음 문장이 They로 시작하며 '검은 리본 장식이 달린 단순
한 백색 케이크부터 생화로 뒤덮인 다양한 색상의 정교한 창작품에 이르
기까지 다양하다(They range from simple white cakes ~ real
flowers.)'고 했다. 이 문장을 통해 They가 가리키는 것이 케이크의 다양
한 디자인(different cake designs)이라는 것을 알 수 있으므로 정답은
(B)이다.

137 동사 어휘

해설 빈칸 뒤에서 '고객이 프로스팅과 케이크 속 내용물, 장식품, 그리고 메시지
를 고를 수 있다(by choosing the frosting, ~ and the message)'

고 했다. 즉, 빈칸에는 고객이 케이크를 맞춤 제작할 수 있다는 의미가 들 어가야 하므로 정답은 (B) customize(맞춤 제작하다)이다. (A) alternate(교대하다), (C) conserve(보존하다), (D) distribute(유통시 키다)는 모두 의미상 부적절하다.

138 동사 시제 + 수동태

해설 의미상 뉴욕시 제과점(Our New York City bakery)은 웨스트 12번가 1123번지에 위치되어 있는 수동적 입장이고, 또한 현재의 위치를 공지하고 있는 것이므로 (A) is located가 정답이다. (B) will be located 와 (D) was located도 수동태이긴 하지만 시제가 적합하지 않으며, (C) being located는 동사의 역할을 할 수 없으므로 오답이다.

139 -142 편지

9월 27일

아네타 와이즈만
데저트 드라이브 880, 아파트 401호
멘골트, 켄터키주 40171

와이즈만 씨께,

이 편지는 10월 23일 토요일에 제가 아파트 202호를 **139비우게 됨**을 통지하기 위한 것입니다. 쿰스에 일자리를 얻게 돼서 그 지역으로 이사를 갈 예정입니다. 이사할 집 주소는 곧 알려 드리겠습니다.

10월 임대료는 전액 지불할 계획입니다. 믿을 만한 세입자라는 저의 이력과 **140더불어**, 제가 이렇게 하므로 30일 여유를 두지 못하고 통지 드린 데 대한 위약금 청구는 하지 않으시기를 바랍니다.

또한 아파트가 아주 훌륭한 상태임을 확인하시게 될 겁니다. **141그러니까**, 제 임대 보증금 500달러를 언제 돌려받을 수 있을지 알고 싶습니다.

555-0126번으로 제게 전화 주셔서 이 편지를 **142받으신 걸** 확인해 주시고 위에 말씀드린 문제를 논의할 수 있기를 바랍니다.

로드니 글로버

어휘 notification 통지, 알림 provide A with B A에게 B를 제공하다 forwarding address 이전지 주소(옛 주소로 오는 우편물을 재발송해줄 수 있는 새집 주소) shortly 곧 rental fee 임대료 reliable 믿을 만한 tenant 세입자 persuade 설득하다, 납득시키다 charge 청구하다 penalty 벌금, 위약금 notice 통지 consequently 그 결과 security deposit 임대 보증금 confirm 확인해 주다 abovementioned 앞서 말한

139 동사 어휘

해설 빈칸의 뒤 문장에서 '쿰스'라는 지역으로 이사를 갈 예정이라는 내용이 나온다. 그러므로 정답은 아파트를 비운다는 (B) vacate(비우다)이다.

어휘 inspect 검사하다 remodel 개조하다 buy 구입하다

140 전치사(구) 어휘

해설 빈칸이 있는 문장은 '믿을 만한 세입자라는 저의 이력'으로 위약금 청구

는 하지 말아 달라는 부탁의 내용이다. 따라서 빈칸 다음 명사와 함께 쓰일 수 있는 전치사 (A) together with(~와 함께)가 정답이다. (B) in that(~라는 점에서)은 접속사로 문법상 맞지 않고 (C) such as(그러한)와 (D) prior to(~ 이전에)는 전치사이지만 의미상 적합하지 않다.

141 문맥에 맞는 문장 고르기

번역 (A) 게다가 거실 벽지가 보기 안 좋습니다.
(B) 다른 세입자들은 자체적으로 개선을 했습니다.
(C) 또한 아파트가 아주 훌륭한 상태임을 확인하시게 될 겁니다.
(D) 제가 추천서를 내야 한다고 들었습니다.

해설 빈칸의 뒤 문장을 보면 보증금을 전액 돌려받고 싶다는 내용이 나온다. 그러므로 빈칸에는 아파트의 상태가 매우 훌륭하다는 이야기가 나와야 함을 알 수 있다. 따라서 정답은 (C)이다.

어휘 unattractive 매력적이지 않은 improvement 개선 a letter of reference 추천서

142 명사 자리

해설 빈칸의 앞에는 to부정사가 있고 뒤에는 전치사 of가 있다. 그러므로 빈칸은 명사 자리이다. (A) recipient는 '수령인'이라는 사람 명사이다. 또한, 편지의 수령을 확인하기 위하여 전화를 달라고 하였으므로 빈칸은 사물 명사 자리이다. 따라서 정답은 (D) receipt(수령)이다.

어휘 recipient 수령인 receive 받다, 수령하다

143 -146 이메일

발신: 표경진 〈kpyo@fitmaster.com〉
수신: 캐서린 엘더 〈celder@evermail.net〉
날짜: 2월 12일
제목: 프로파워 사이클마스터 N50

엘더 씨께,

귀하께서 저희 웹사이트에서 주문하신 상품의 최근 상황에 관해 알려 드리고자 이메일을 드립니다. 귀하께서 주문하신 프로파워 사이클마스터 N50이 원래 예상했던 것보다 배송에 시간이 더 걸릴 것 같습니다. 저희가 7일 배송을 약속 드렸으나 귀하께서 3월 초**144까지** 해당 물품을 수령하지 못하실 것 같습니다.

이런 유감스런 **145지연** 사태에 대해 저의 심심한 사과를 받아 주시기 바랍니다. 전액 환불을 원하신다 해도 전적으로 이해합니다.

하지만, 귀하께서 높은 품질의 제품을 **146저렴한** 가격에 구입하셨으니 인내심을 가지고 해당 물품이 배달되기를 기다려 주시기를 바랍니다.

표경진
피트마스터 운동 기구

어휘 purchase 구입하다 ship 배송하다 than originally expected 원래 예상했던 것보다 promise 약속하다 item 물품, 항목 sincerest apology 심심한[진심어린] 사과 unfortunate 유감스러운 would like to+동사원형 ~하고 싶다 full refund 전액 환불 completely 완전히, 전적으로 patient 인내하는, 참는 wait for ~을 기다리다 deliver 배달하다 high-quality 고급의

143 문맥에 맞는 문장 고르기

번역 (A) 다른 것들과 견줘 귀하께서 주문하신 상품은 꽤 인기가 좋습니다.
(B) 무엇보다, 귀하의 주문품은 배송하는 데 7일이나 걸릴 것입니다.
(C) 안타깝게도, 그 특별 제품들 중 일부가 단종되었습니다.
(D) 귀하께서 저희 웹사이트에서 주문하신 상품의 최근 상황에 관해 알려 드리고자 이메일을 드립니다.

해설 이메일 첫 문장에는 글의 목적이 나와야 한다. 따라서 최근에 주문한 물건에 대한 새로운 정보를 알리기 위해 이메일을 쓰고 있다(I am writing to update you on the order you placed)는 말이 글의 목적에 해당하므로 정답은 (D)이다.

어휘 update A on B A에게 B의 최근 상황을 알려 주다 order 주문품

144 전치사 어휘

해설 빈칸 뒤에 '3월 초(the beginning of March)'라는 시점이 있으므로 시점과 결합해 '~까지'라는 의미를 나타내는 전치사가 필요하다. 따라서 정답은 (A) until이다. (B) from(~부터), (C) without(~ 없이), (D) under(~ 밑에)는 의미상 부적절하다.

145 명사 어휘

해설 먼저 앞 문장에서 고객이 주문한 물건이 '원래 예상했던 것보다 배송에 시간이 더 걸릴 것(take longer to ship than originally expected)'이라고 했다. 그러므로 해당 문장의 의미는 '유감스런 지연 사태에 대해 심심한 사과를 받아 주십시오'라는 뜻이 되어야 한다. 따라서 '지연 (사태)'란 단어가 문맥상 적합하므로 정답은 (D) delay이다. (A) cancellation(취소), (B) breakage(파손), (C) interference(간섭, 개입)는 모두 의미상 부적절하다.

146 형용사 자리 _ 명사 수식

해설 빈칸이 명사 price 앞에 있으므로 명사를 수식할 수 있는 형용사가 필요하다. 또한 price와 결합해 의미상 '저렴한, 적당한'이란 뜻이 적합하므로 (C) affordable(저렴한, 적당한)이 정답이다. (A) afforded(제공된)와 (D) affording(제공하는)은 각각 과거분사와 현재분사로 볼 수는 있으나 의미상 부적절하고 (B) afford(~할 여유가 있다)는 동사이므로 품사상 오답이다.

Part 7

147-148 문자 메시지

수신: 잭 해밀턴 (492-555-0169)
발신: 수지 페이지 (865-555-0132)
1월 9일 수요일, 오전 7시 52분

안녕하세요, 잭. **147**어젯밤부터 몸이 정말 좋지 않아서 오늘 출근하지 못할 것 같아요. 제가 오늘 테리와 함께 우리의 잠재 고객들에게 제품 설명회를 하기로 되어 있는데요. **148**제가 참석하지 못한다고 그에게 알려 주시겠어요? 안됐지만 그가 혼자서 해야겠네요. 하지만 제 업무상 다른 문제는 없고 내일 복귀할 수 있

을 것 같아요.

어휘 be off work 결근하다 be due to+동사원형 ~할 예정이다 sales presentation 제품 설명회 potential client 잠재 고객 make it 참석하다, 가다 unfortunately 안됐지만, 유감스럽게도 workload 업무량

147 글의 주제 / 목적

번역 페이지 씨가 메시지를 보낸 이유는?
(A) 여행 일정 변경을 공유하려고
(B) 컴퓨터 문제를 설명하려고
(C) 결근 보고를 하려고
(D) 업무량에 대해 항의하려고

해설 메시지 초반부에서 '몸이 좋지 않아서 오늘 출근하지 못할 것 같다(I'm afraid I'm going to be off work today)'고 했으므로 정답은 (C)이다.

▶▶ **Paraphrasing** 지문의 **be off work** → 정답의 **an absence**

148 세부 사항

번역 페이지 씨는 해밀턴 씨에게 무엇을 해 달라고 요청하는가?
(A) 문서 편집하기
(B) 동료에게 말하기
(C) 일부 고객을 접대하기
(D) 설명회 일정 변경하기

해설 문자 메시지 중간쯤에 페이지 씨가 '자신이 참석하지 못한다는 것을 테리에게 전해달라(Could you let him know I can't make it?)'라고 해밀턴 씨에게 부탁하고 있으므로 정답은 (B)이다.

어휘 entertain (손님을) 접대하다, 즐겁게 해주다

▶▶ **Paraphrasing** 지문의 **let him know** → 정답의 **speak to a colleague**

149 -150 쿠폰

> ### 저희가 귀하께 드리는 생일 선물!
>
> 클로드 의류는 개업 5주년을 기념하여 단골 고객들께 **149**40달러 이상 주문 시 사용할 수 있는 무료 배송 쿠폰을 제공하고 있습니다.* 클로드 의류는 질 좋은 의상을 저렴한 가격에 제공하여 빠르게 유명해지고 있습니다. 저희는 겨울 카탈로그가 가장 많은 인기를 끌 것으로 예상하며, 고객님께서 이 멋진 기회를 이용하시길 적극 권장합니다. **150**이 쿠폰은 전화나 웹사이트, 우편으로 주문할 때만 사용하실 수 있습니다.
>
> *고객 1인당 1회 사용. 이용 약관을 보시려면 저희 웹사이트를 방문하세요.

어휘 celebrate 기념하다, 축하하다 operation 영업 clothing 의류 offer 제공하다, 제안하다 free delivery 무료 배송 loyal customer 단골 고객 order 주문(품) rapidly 빠르게 become famous for ~때문에 유명해지다 provide 제공하다, 공급하다 quality garment 질 좋은 의상 at affordable prices

저렴한[적당한] 가격에 expect 예상하다, 기대하다 popular 인기 있는 urge 촉구하다, 강력히 권하다 take advantage of ~을 활용하다 fantastic 멋진, 환상적인, 근사한 place an order 주문하다 via ~를 통해, ~으로 postal order 우편 주문 usage 사용 terms and conditions 이용 약관

149 사실 관계 확인

번역 쿠폰 사용에 관한 요건으로 언급된 것은 무엇인가?
(A) 신분증
(B) 휴대 전화 앱 다운로드
(C) 고객 계정 번호
(D) 최소 구매액

해설 지문 맨 처음에 클로드 의류는 개업 5주년을 기념하여 단골 고객들에게 40달러 이상 주문(orders of $40 or more)시 사용할 수 있는 무료 배송 쿠폰을 제공하고 있다고 했으므로 정답은 (D)이다.

▶▶ **Paraphrasing**   지문의 **orders of $40 or more**
→ 정답의 **a minimum purchase**

150 세부 사항

번역 쿠폰은 어떤 방법으로 주문할 때 유효하지 않은가?
(A) 점포에서 주문할 때
(B) 전화로 주문할 때
(C) 우편으로 주문할 때
(D) 인터넷으로 주문할 때

해설 첫 번째 단락 후반부에서 쿠폰은 전화나 웹사이트 또는 우편으로 주문할 때만 사용할 수 있다고 했다. 하지만 점포에서의 주문에 대한 언급은 없으므로 정답은 (A)이다.

151 -152 정보문

산도발 아이웨어에서 보럴디 안경을 구입하신 걸 축하드립니다. **151**이제 직장에서나 가정에서나 눈의 피로를 덜 받으면서 오랫동안 컴퓨터나 모바일 기기를 사용하실 수 있을 것입니다.

152고객님의 안경을 최선의 상태로 보관하려면 제공된 케이스 안에 들어 있는 분무 세정제나 극세사 천을 사용해 반드시 주기적으로 렌즈를 닦아 주셔야 합니다. 이 목적에 다른 제품을 사용하는 건 렌즈에 상처를 낼 수 있습니다. 언제든 안경의 나사나 코 받침 부분의 조절이나 교체가 필요하면 산도발 아이웨어 매장에 들르셔서 무료 관리 서비스를 받으십시오.

어휘 purchase 구매하다 eyeglasses 안경 mobile device 휴대 기기 eye strain 눈의 피로 make sure to+동사원형 반드시 ~하다 microfiber cloth 극세사 천 result in ~을 야기하다 scratched 긁힌 자국이 있는 screw 나사 nose pad (안경의) 코 받침 adjust 조절하다 replace 교체하다 stop by ~에 들르다 maintenance 유지, 관리

151 추론 / 암시

번역 보럴디 안경에 관해 암시된 것은?
(A) 환경친화적인 소재로 만들었다.
(B) 운동을 할 때 착용하도록 만들어졌다.
(C) 위험한 화학 물질로부터 착용자의 눈을 보호해 준다.
(D) 전자 화면을 바라볼 때 생기는 불편함을 줄여 준다.

해설 첫 번째 단락 두 번째 문장에 보면, 눈의 피로를 덜 받으면서 오랫동안 컴퓨터나 모바일 기기를 사용할 수 있을 것이라는 내용이 나온다. 따라서 정답은 (D)이다.

▶▶ **Paraphrasing**   지문의 **computer or mobile device**
→ 정답의 **electronic screens**

152 사실 관계 확인

번역 정보문에 따르면, 안경 착용자는 어떻게 안경 손상을 피할 수 있는가?
(A) 특정 케이스에 넣고 다녀서
(B) 맞도록 계속 조절해서
(C) 특정 제품으로 관리해서
(D) 안경점에서 정기적으로 점검을 받아서

해설 두 번째 단락 첫 문장을 보면, 분무 세정제나 극세사 천을 사용해 반드시 정기적으로 렌즈를 닦아 주어야 한다는 내용이 나온다. 따라서 정답은 (C)이다.

153 -154 문자 메시지

레비 만 [오후 12:50] 주민센터의 셔먼 씨가 주문한 팸플릿을 가지러 와 있는데 선반에 팸플릿이 안 보이네요, 콘스탄스.
콘스탄스 넬슨 [오후 12:51] 아, 그거 아직 안 끝났어요. 어제 레이저 프린터 문제 때문에 차질이 생겨서요. **153**오늘 아침 셔먼 씨 음성 메일에 그것에 관해 메시지를 남겼는데.
레비 만 [오후 12:52] 셔먼 씨는 못 받았다고 합니다. **154**굉장히 실망한 거 같은데. 우리가 뭐 해줄 수 있는 게 있을까요?
콘스탄스 넬슨 [오후 12:52] 그럼요. **154**제가 굉장히 죄송해한다고 전해 주시고 이 주문 건에 대해 10% 할인을 해드린다고 얘기해주세요.
레비 만 [오후 12:54] 그거 괜찮은 생각이네요. 고마워요, 콘스탄스.

어휘 pick up 찾아가다 setback 좌절, 차질 disappointed 실망한

153 세부 사항

번역 넬슨 씨는 아까 오전에 무엇을 했다고 말하는가?
(A) 고객에서 전화했다.
(B) 선반을 재정돈했다.
(C) 팸플릿을 접었다.
(D) 프린터를 수리했다.

해설 넬슨 씨의 처음 대화에서 오늘 아침에 고객인 셔먼 씨 음성 메일에 팸플릿에 관해 메시지를 남겼다고 했다. 따라서 (A)가 정답이다.

154 의도 파악

번역 오후 12시 54분에 만 씨가 "그거 괜찮은 생각이네요"라고 쓸 때, 그 의도는 무엇인가?
(A) 기계가 다시 제대로 작동하고 있다.
(B) 한 상인이 그의 쿠폰을 받았다.
(C) 셔먼 씨는 이제 마음이 풀릴 수 있을 것이다.
(D) 그가 주문품을 찾았다.

해설 바로 앞에서 넬슨 씨가 고객에게 사과와 함께 이 주문 건에 대해 10% 할인해 주자고 하자 만 씨는 그에 대해 고객인 셔먼 씨가 이제는 마음이 풀릴 수도 있는 '좋은 생각'이라는 의도로 언급하고 있으므로 정답은 (C)이다.

155-157 회람

수신: 베니스턴 직원들
발신: ¹⁵⁷브래들리 위크스턴, 제품 관리자
날짜: 6월 2일
제목: 제품군

여러분 중 다수가 알게 될 테지만 ¹⁵⁵우리 기술팀이 올 가을에 출시될 새로운 종류의 주방 용품들을 개발해왔습니다. 이 상품군이 이제 마무리되었습니다. 그에 따라 여러분이 신제품들의 기능에 익숙해지도록 8월에 교육 워크숍이 몇 차례 열릴 예정입니다. ¹⁵⁶직원들은 이번 주 말까지 관리자에게 어떤 워크숍에 참석할 수 있는지 알려 주셔야 합니다. 이번 교육에 참석하면 모든 직원이 초과 근무 수당을 받게 됩니다.

우리는 지금이 우리 회사로서는 과도기임을 알고 있습니다. 잘하면 우리가 전국 제일의 주방 용품 공급 업체가 될 수 있는 신제품군을 갖추는 시기이기 때문입니다. 단언컨대 여러분이 영업자의 역할을 효과적으로 수행하는 데 필요한 모든 정보를 워크숍이 제공해 줄 것입니다. ¹⁵⁷교육을 받은 후에 궁금한 점이 있으면 제게 b.weekston@benistonstores.com으로 이메일을 주시기 바랍니다. 기꺼이 여러분의 질문에 대답해 드리겠습니다.

어휘 product line 제품군 be aware 알다, 인식하다 engineering team 기술팀 develop 개발하다 kitchen appliances 주방 용품 launch 출시하다 merchandise 상품 be finalized 마무리되다 as such 그에 따라 training workshop 교육 워크숍 familiarize A with B A가 B에 익숙해지게 하다 feature 기능, 특징 by the end of ~말까지 be paid at the overtime rate 초과 근무 수당을 받다 participate in ~에 참석하다 transitional time 과도기 embrace 받아들이다, 아우르다 hopefully 바라건대, 잘하면 enable A(사람) to+동사원형 A가 ~할 수 있게 하다 supplier 공급 업체 provide A with B A에게 B를 제공하다 perform 수행하다 effectively 효과적으로

155 글의 주제 / 목적

번역 이 회람의 주된 내용은 무엇인가?
(A) 사무용 가전제품 업그레이드
(B) 신규 점포 개점
(C) 새로운 상품군
(D) 직원 급여율의 변동

해설 지문 초반부에서 '기술팀이 올 가을에 출시될 새로운 종류의 주방 용품들(a new line of kitchen appliances)을 개발해왔으며 이제 상품군이 마무리되었다'고 했다. 즉, 이 회람은 직원들에게 새로운 상품군 개발과 관련된 내용을 공지하고 있으므로 정답은 (C)이다.

▶▶ Paraphrasing 지문의 a new line of kitchen appliances
→ 정답의 a new range of merchandise

156 세부 사항

번역 직원들에게 무엇을 하라고 요청하는가?
(A) 일련의 지침을 읽으라고
(B) 제품 아이디어를 제안하라고
(C) 행정직에 지원하라고
(D) 교육 워크숍에 참석하라고

해설 첫 번째 단락에서 '직원들은 이번 주 말까지 관리자에게 어떤 워크숍에 참석할 수 있는지 알려 주어야 한다(Staff must tell ~ they are able to attend.)'고 했으므로 정답은 (D)이다.

157 세부 사항

번역 문의 사항이 있는 직원들은 누구에게 연락하라고 하는가?
(A) 제품 관리자
(B) 엔지니어링팀
(C) 판매 대리인
(D) 경리부

해설 이메일의 발신자가 제품 관리자인 브래들리 위크스턴이고 두 번째 단락 후반부에서 교육을 받은 후에 궁금한 점이 있으면 자신에게 이메일을 보내라고 했으므로, 정답은 (A)이다.

158-160 이메일

수신: 일라이 올린저
발신: 토론토 친구 그룹 운영진
제목: 환영합니다!
날짜: 9월 13일

올린저 씨께,

Your-Groups.com의 토론토 친구 그룹에 가입해 주셔서 감사합니다. ¹⁵⁸우리는 언어를 배우고, 가르치고, 연습하면서 새로운 친구들을 사귀고 싶어 하는 토론토 시민과 방문객들입니다. 우리 그룹에서 가장 인기 있는 언어들은 영어, 스페인어, 불어, 한국어, 일본어이지만 다른 언어들을 쓰는 원어민이나 동료 학습자들도 흔히 찾을 수 있습니다. ¹⁶⁰우리는 화요일 저녁과 일요일 오후에 이토비코크에 있는 스프링우드 카페에서 모입니다. 이곳의 약도와 주차 정보를 여기에서 찾을 수 있습니다.

몇 분만 시간을 내어 회원 정보 페이지를 설정해 주시기 바랍니다. 그러면 다른 회원들이 당신과 당신의 언어적 관심사에 관해 알 수 있습니다. 그런 다음, 우리 모임이 대개 어떻게 운영되는지, 모임을 어떻게 준비해야 할지를 설명한 이 페이지를 살펴보십시오. 회원들은 모든 모임에 대해 적어도 1시간 전에 참석 여부를 알려 줘야 한다는 점을 유념하시기 바랍니다. 또한, ¹⁵⁹·'참석한다'고 회신하고

등록하신 행사에 참석하지 않으면, 향후 한 달 동안 모임 참석이 허락되지 않습니다. 모든 회원들이 열의와 신뢰를 갖추는 것이 중요합니다.

곧 뵙기를 바랍니다.

운영진 드림

어휘 management 운영진, 경영진 join 가입하다, 합류하다 citizen 시민 make new friends 새 친구를 사귀다 practice 연습하다 popular 인기 있는 native speaker 원어민 fellow learner 동료 학습자 as well ~도, 또한 gathering 모임, 회합 set up 설정하다 member profile page 회원 정보 페이지 work 돌아가다, 작동하다 note 유념하다, 주목하다 RSVP (참석 여부를) 회신하다, 회답하다 at least 적어도 sign up for ~에 가입[등록]하다 be allowed to+동사원형 ~하도록 허용되다 participate in ~에 참여하다 enthusiastic 열의 있는, 열심인 reliable 믿을 수 있는, 신뢰가 가는

---

158 세부 사항

번역 토론토 친구 그룹 모임에서는 무슨 일이 일어나는가?
(A) 보드게임 대회
(B) 언어 교환
(C) 요리 실습
(D) 예술 및 공예 활동

해설 첫 번째 단락에서 자신들을 소개하길 언어를 배우고, 가르치고, 연습하면서 새로운 친구들을 사귀고 싶은 토론토 시민과 방문객들이라고 했다. 즉, 토론토 친구 그룹의 모임에서는 언어 교환을 한다는 것을 알 수 있으므로 정답은 (B)이다.

▶▶ **Paraphrasing** 지문의 learning, teaching, and practicing language skills
→ 정답의 language exchange

159 세부 사항

번역 회원이 모임에 참석할 수 없게 되는 원인은 무엇일 것 같은가?
(A) 회비를 미리 납부하지 않아서
(B) 필수적인 기술 수준에 도달하지 못해서
(C) 회원 정보에 특정 세부 정보를 포함하지 않아서
(D) 이전 모임에 참석하기로 한 약속을 지키지 못해서

해설 두 번째 단락 후반부에서 참석한다고 회신하고 등록한 행사에 참석하지 않으면 한 달 동안 모임에 참석할 수 없다고 했으므로 정답은 (D)이다.

▶▶ **Paraphrasing** 지문의 if you RSVP "yes" but do not attend the event
→ 정답의 not fulfilling a promise

160 문장 삽입

번역 [1], [2], [3], [4]로 표시된 곳 중에서 다음 문장이 가장 적합한 곳은?
"이곳의 약도와 주차 정보를 여기에서 찾을 수 있습니다."
(A) [1]
(B) [2]
(C) [3]
(D) [4]

해설 먼저 삽입문에 쓰인 this venue(이곳)에 주목해야 한다. [2]번 앞 문장에서 매주 화요일 저녁과 일요일 오후에 이토비코크에 있는 스프링우드 카페에서 모임이 있다고 했다. 문맥상 삽입문의 this venue는 바로 Springwood Café를 가리키는 것이라 볼 수 있다. 따라서 특정 장소와 그 장소에 대한 정보 제공 측면을 고려했을 때 삽입문이 [2]번에 들어가는 것이 가장 자연스러우므로 정답은 (B)이다.

161-164 기사

뉴 호라이즌스 주식회사 사업 확장

4월 2일—뉴 호라이즌스가 유럽과 중동으로 사업을 확장할 것이라고 다이앤 모슬리 이사가 어제 기자회견에서 발표했다. 이사는 기자들에게 새로운 미개척 시장들을 탐사할 적기라고 주장하며, 회사가 이 지역들에서 **162스포츠 의류 경쟁 업체인 스피디그랩과의 경쟁에서 성공할 수 있다는 자신감**을 드러냈다. **161업계 내에서 날카로운 협상가로 이름난 모슬리 씨**는 이어서 자신이 변화를 몸소 감독하기 위해 독일로 옮길 것이라고 선언했다. 일단 그곳에 가면 그녀는 유럽 고객들이 그녀의 회사의 다양한 스포츠 의류에 대해 미국 소비자들만큼 열광하도록 노력할 것이다.

다이앤 모슬리의 사연은 아메리칸 드림의 전형적인 예다. 노스캐롤라이나주 노동 계급 가정 출신인 **163그녀는 16세 때 자동차 제조업체인 타이푼에서 첫 직장을 구했다.** 그 후 그녀는 부동산 개발업체인 홈 컴포츠에서 몇 년 동안 일했다. **164그녀는 잠재력을 빠르게 인정받아 30세에 그 기관의 부사장이 되었다.** 작년에는 마침내 야외 활동을 좋아하는 자신의 열정을 탐구하기 위해 뉴 호라이즌스로 이직했다.

어휘 expand operation 사업을 확장하다 director 이사 announce 발표하다, 공표하다 press conference 기자회견 expand into ~로 확장하다 claim 주장하다 the time was right to+동사원형 ~할 적당한 시기 untapped market 미개척 시장 confident 자신감 있는, 확신하는 successful 성공적인 compete with ~와 경쟁하다 sporting attire manufacturer 스포츠 의류 제조업체 region 지역 renowned for ~로 유명한 fierce negotiator 치열한 협상가 go on to+동사원형 계속해서 ~하다 declare 선언하다 relocate to ~로 이주[이사, 이전]하다 personally 몸소, 개인적으로 oversee 감독하다 transition (다른 상태로의) 이행 enthusiastic 열광하는 consumer 소비자 a classic example 전형적인 예 working-class 노동 계급의 automobile manufacturer 자동차 제조업체 from there 그 후 spend+시간+-ing ~하느라 시간을 보내다 real-estate developer 부동산 개발 회사 potential 잠재력 make the move to ~로 옮기다, 이직하다 explore 탐구하다 passion 열정 outdoor activities 야외 활동

161 세부 사항

번역 기사에 따르면, 모슬리 씨는 무엇으로 유명한가?
(A) 협상 기술
(B) 제품 개발 경력
(C) 고객의 행동에 대한 이해
(D) 위험을 무릅쓰는 것

해설 첫 번째 단락에서 모슬리 씨는 '업계 내에서 날카로운 협상가로 유명하다(Renowned within the industry for being a fierce negotiator)'고 했으므로 정답은 (A)이다.

162 추론 / 암시

번역 뉴 호라이즌스는 어떤 종류의 회사일 것 같은가?
(A) 자동차 회사
(B) 부동산 개발회사
(C) 스포츠 의류 회사
(D) 가정용품 제조업체

해설 첫 번째 단락에서 뉴 호라이즌스의 이사인 모슬리 씨가 스포츠 의류 경쟁업체 스피디그랩(rival sporting attire manufacturer Speedigrab)과의 경쟁에서 성공할 수 있다고 했다. 이를 통해 뉴 호라이즌스는 스포츠 의류 회사임을 추론할 수 있으므로 정답은 (C)이다.

▶▶ **Paraphrasing** 지문의 **sporting attire manufacturer**
→ 정답의 **a sportswear company**

163 세부 사항

번역 모슬리 씨는 어떤 회사에서 경력을 시작했는가?
(A) 뉴 호라이즌스 주식회사
(B) 홈 컴포츠
(C) 타이푼
(D) 스피디그랩

해설 두 번째 단락에서 월시 씨의 첫 직장은 16살 때 자동차 제조업체인 타이푼이었다고 했으므로 정답은 (C)이다.

164 세부 사항

번역 모슬리 씨가 홈 컴포츠에 있는 동안 무슨 일이 일어났는가?
(A) 상을 받았다.
(B) 회사의 중역이 되었다.
(C) 새로운 포장 방법을 고안해냈다.
(D) 마케팅 캠페인을 관리했다.

해설 두 번째 단락에서 '그녀는 (홈 컴포츠에서) 잠재력을 빠르게 인정받아 30세에 부사장이 되었다(by the age of ~ a vice president in the orgnization)'고 했으므로 정답은 (B)이다.

▶▶ **Paraphrasing** 지문의 **a vice president**
→ 정답의 **a company executive**

165-167 양식

벨리스 피트니스 센터
등록 신청서

회원 유형 설명

165일반 회원은 사우나를 제외한 센터의 모든 구역, 전용 로커, 1시간짜리 입문용 개인 지도를 이용할 수 있습니다.
165고급 회원은 센터의 모든 구역, 전용 로커, 한 달간의 1시간 개인 지도, 피트니스 수업 참여 등을 이용할 수 있습니다.

회비

	회원 유형	
회원 자격 기간	일반	고급
1개월	80달러	110달러
3개월	180달러	210달러
1666개월	300달러	340달러
12개월	500달러	550달러

166선택한 유형: 6개월 일반 회원
시작일/종료일: 4월 12일 / 10월 11일

이용 약관

* 등록 시 회비 전액을 지불해야 한다. 회원 자격을 취소하는 경우, 자격 개시일 14일 이내에 하지 않는 한 납입한 회비에 대한 환불금을 받을 자격이 없다.
* 167일시적으로 피트니스 센터를 이용할 수 없는 회원은 최소 1개월에서 최대 3개월까지 회원 자격을 중단할 수 있다. 이에 대해서는 관리를 위한 추가 요금이 1개월당 10달러씩 부과되며, 사전에 지불해야 한다.
* 회원들은 피트니스 센터의 안전하고 올바른 이용 수칙을 준수해야 한다. 그렇지 못할 경우 회원 자격을 상실할 수 있다.

나는 위의 내용을 읽고 이해했습니다.

이름: 크레이그 바튼   서명: *Craig Barton*   날짜: 4월 12일

어휘 access 접근, 입장 dedicated 전용의 introductory 입문자를 위한 hour-long 1시간 걸리는 personal training 개인 지도 premium 고급의 entrance 입장 membership fee 회비 due 지불해야 하는 registration 등록 entitle 자격을 주다 refund 환불(금) temporarily 일시적으로 freeze 정지시키다 administrative 관리상의 surcharge 추가 요금 in advance 미리 charge 청구하다 abide by ~을 준수하다 courteous 정중한 failure to+동사원형 ~하지 못함 revoke 취소하다, 철회하다

165 세부 사항

번역 일반 및 고급 회원 자격 둘 다에 포함되는 혜택은 무엇인가?
(A) 개인 수납 공간 이용
(B) 목욕 공간 입장
(C) 그룹 지도 참여
(D) 개인 트레이너와 반복적인 만남

해설 첫 번째 단락 회원 유형 설명에서 일반 회원과 고급 회원의 공통 사항을 찾아보면 '전용 로커(a dedicated locker)'가 나오므로 정답은 (A)이다.

▶▶ **Paraphrasing** 지문의 **a dedicated locker** → 정답의 **a private storage space**

166 세부 사항

번역 바튼 씨는 회원 가입을 위해 얼마를 지불할 것인가?
(A) 180달러
(B) 210달러
(C) 300달러
(D) 340달러

해설 회비를 나타내는 표 아래에 보면 바튼 씨는 '6개월 동안 일반 회원(6-month regular membership)'으로 등록했음을 알 수 있다. 바튼 씨의 회비는 300달러이므로 정답은 (C)이다.

167 추론 / 암시

번역 양식에 따르면, 바튼 씨는 무엇에 대해 추가 요금이 청구될 수 있는가?
(A) 일시적인 회원 자격 정지
(B) 일정 날짜 이후 회원 자격 취소
(C) 피트니스 센터 안전 수칙 위반
(D) 손님을 동반한 피트니스 센터 방문

해설 이용 약관에 보면 회원은 자격을 중단할 수 있으며 이에 대해서는 관리를 위한 추가 요금이 1개월당 10달러씩 부과된다고 하였다. 따라서 정답은 (A)이다.

168-171 온라인 채팅

루소 앤 코지올 광고 회사 메신저

루섹 코지올 [오전 11:36]
두 사람 잠시 얘기 좀 할 수 있어요? 168스톨링 주스 건이 어떻게 되어가고 있는지 확인하고 싶었어요.

조시 프런스키 [오전 11:37]
물론이죠. 잘 진행되고 있어요. 기획부가 광고 대상자 조사를 끝냈어요. 주말까지 우리에게 보고서를 줄 거라고 했어요.

루섹 코지올 [오전 11:38]
잘됐네요. 그럼 제작부가 언제 당신의 브리핑을 기대할 수 있나요?

사브리나 벡 [오전 11:38]
일정대로 5월 20일에요.

루섹 코지올 [오전 11:39]
좋아요. 현재까지 스톨링과 작업하면서 문제는 없었나요?

조시 프런스키 [오전 11:40]
169우리가 이메일을 보내면 그들이 답장을 보내오는 데 시간이 오래 걸린다는 것 정도요. 우리가 나중에 따로 두어 번씩 전화를 해야만 했어요.

루섹 코지올 [오전 11:41]
그렇군요. 음, 심각해지면 내게 말하세요. 내가 알아야 할 게 또 있나요?

사브리나 벡 [오전 11:42]
이 건과 관련된 것은 없어요. 170하지만 지출품의서 제출에 관해 여쭤보고 싶어요.

루섹 코지올 [오전 11:43]
말해 보세요.

사브리나 벡 [오전 11:44]
171서비스관리부에서 나오는 지출품의서는 제출하기 전에 모두 당신의 결재를 받아야 한다고 경리부에서 이야기해요. 맞나요? 전에는 그렇게 한 적이 없거든요.

루섹 코지올 [오전 11:45]
그건 새로운 방침인데 특정 거래처만 해당돼요. 그에 관해 이메일을 못 받았나요? 지금 내가 전달해 줄게요.

어휘 Do you have a minute to+동사원형 ~? 잠시 ~할 수 있어요? check on ~을 확인하다 account 회사의 고객, 거래처 come along (원하는 대로) 되어 가다, 진행되다 go well 잘 진행되다, 잘되어가다 be finished with ~을 끝내다 target audience research 광고 대상자 조사 brief 브리핑, 요약 as scheduled 일정대로 so far 현재까지, 이제까지 reply 답장하다, 회신하다

follow up with phone calls 나중에 따로 전화하다 be related to ~와 관련이 있다 submit 제출하다 expense report 지출품의서, 경비 보고서 approval 결재, 승인 apply to ~에 적용되다 forward 전달하다

168 글의 주제 / 목적

번역 코지올 씨가 채팅을 시작한 이유는?
(A) 진척 상황에 관한 최신 정보를 얻으려고
(B) 몇몇 문서들을 요청하려고
(C) 정책 변화를 설명하려고
(D) 피드백을 주려고

해설 맨 처음 대화에서 코지올 씨가 '스톨링 주스 건이 어떻게 진행되고(how the Storling juice account is coming along) 있는지 확인하고 싶다'고 했으므로 정답은 (A)이다.

169 세부 사항

번역 프런스키 씨는 스톨링 직원들과 일할 때 힘든 점이 무엇이라고 지적하는가?
(A) 프로젝트의 명확한 목표가 없다.
(B) 연락할 때 응답이 느리다.
(C) 사무실이 멀리 떨어져 있다.
(D) 그들이 희망하는 예산이 너무 적다.

해설 오전 11시 40분에 프런스키 씨가 말하길 이메일을 보내면 '스톨링 측에서 답장을 보내는 데 시간이 오래 걸린다(it takes them a long time to reply)'고 했으므로 정답은 (B)이다.

▶▶ Paraphrasing   지문의 **takes them a long time to reply**
→ 정답의 **slow to respond**

170 의도 파악

번역 오전 11시 43분에 코지올 씨가 "말해 보세요"라고 쓴 의도는 무엇이겠는가?
(A) 벡 씨가 보고서를 제출해야 한다.
(B) 벡 씨가 질문을 해도 좋다.
(C) 벡 씨가 견해를 낼 수 있다.
(D) 벡 씨가 전화해야 한다.

해설 사브리나 벡이 11시 42분에 지출품의서 제출에 관해 질문이 있다고 했다. 이에 대해 코지올 씨가 Go ahead라고 응답한 것인데, 문맥상 이 말은 사브리나 벡에게 질문을 해도 좋다는 의미를 나타낸 것이므로 정답은 (B)이다.

171 추론 / 암시

번역 프런스키 씨와 벡 씨는 어떤 부서에서 일할 것 같은가?
(A) 기획부
(B) 제작부
(C) 경리부
(D) 서비스관리부

해설 11시 44분에 벡 씨가 경리부에서 말하길 서비스관리부의 지출품의서를 제출하기 전에 모두 코지올 씨의 결재를 받아야 한다는데 이것이 맞는지 물어보고 있다. 그러면서 '자신들은 전에는 그렇게 한 적이 없다(We've never had to do that before.)'고 했다. 이 말을 통해 프런스키 씨와 벡 씨가 서비스관리부에서 근무한다는 것을 추론할 수 있으므로 정답은 (D)이다.

172-175 보도 자료

오가미, 라이언 센터와 제휴

브리즈번 (2월 3일)—오늘, 떠오르는 신생기업 오가미 주식회사가 유명한 라이언 센터와 제휴를 맺었다고 발표했다. **¹⁷²지속 가능한 에너지 기술의 중추인 라이언 센터**는 오가미-X 풍력 터빈의 지속적인 개발을 위해 센터의 풍부한 자원을 오가미가 이용할 수 있게 할 것이다.

매리 플린 오가미 사장 겸 최고경영자는 "이토록 탁월한 과학자 및 공학자 집단과 이 첨단 시설에서 함께 일할 기회가 생겨서 우리는 매우 설렌다"면서 "풍력 에너지 분야에서의 이들의 전문성에 힘입어 우리의 개발 프로그램이 더 빠르게 그리고 ¹⁷³어쩌면 우리가 예상하지 못하는 방식으로 발전할 것"이라고 말했다.

¹⁷⁴브리즈번 대학교 본교 캠퍼스 내 깊숙한 곳에 위치한 라이언 센터는 세계 최고 수준의 연구와 교육으로 유명하다. 산학협동의 선구자로서 센터는 태양, 풍력, 지열 에너지에 관한 폭넓은 지식을 갖춘 공학자와 과학자들을 200명 이상 고용하고 있다.

¹⁷⁵라이언 센터에서는 엘리아스 마틴 박사가 오가미의 초기 모델을 발전시키고 해당 제품의 디자인을 계속해서 세련되게 다듬는 작업을 주도할 것이다. 그의 팀은 처음에는 날개 형태와 로터(회전자) 설계 같은 사양에 초점을 맞출 것이다. 센터에서 열린 오가미의 첫 개발 회의에서 그는 오가미-X가 1년 안에 시장에 나갈 준비가 되면 좋겠다는 바람을 밝히면서 "우리가 이곳에서 만드는 것이 세계에 뚜렷하고도 긍정적인 영향을 미칠 수도 있다"고 덧붙였다.

어휘 **partner up** 제휴하다, 동반자가 되다 **rising** 떠오르는, 부상하는 **start-up** 신생기업 **announce** 발표하다 **form a partnership with** ~와 제휴하다, 협력하다, 동반자가 되다 **renowned** 명망 있는 **hub** 중심, 중추 **sustainable energy technology** 지속 가능한 에너지 기술 **considerable** 많은, 상당한 **resources** 자원 **available** 이용할 수 있는 **continued development** 지속적인 개발 **wind turbine** 풍력 터빈 **opportunity** 기회 **excellent** 탁월한 **engineer** 공학자 **cutting-edge facility** 첨단 시설 **president and CEO** 사장 겸 최고경영자 **expertise** 전문성, 전문 지식 **wind energy** 풍력 에너지 **advance** 발전시키다 **situated deep within** ~내의 깊숙한 곳에 자리 잡은 **world-class reputation** 세계 최고 수준의 명성 **research** 연구 **education** 교육 **pioneer** 선구자, 개척자 **collaborations between universities and industry** 산학협동 **employ** 고용하다 **extensive knowledge** 광범위한 지식 **geothermal power** 지열 에너지 **lead** 이끌다, 주도하다 **build on** ~을 기반으로 쌓다 **initial model** 초기 모델 **refine** 세련되게 다듬다 **development meeting** 개발 회의 **express hope that** ~하면 좋겠다는 바람을 표하다 **be ready for market** 출시 준비가 되다 **add** 덧붙이다, 추가하다 **noticeable** 눈에 띄는, 뚜렷한 **positive impact on** ~에 대한 긍정적인 영향

172 세부 사항

번역 라이언 센터의 연구 초점은 무엇인가?
(A) 의료 장비
(B) 재생에너지
(C) 통신
(D) 비행 기술

해설 첫 번째 단락에서 라이언 센터를 '지속 가능한 에너지 기술의 중추(a hub for sustainable energy technology)'라고 설명했으므로 정답은 (B)이다.

▶▶ **Paraphrasing** 지문의 **sustainable energy** → 정답의 **Renewable energy**

173 추론 / 암시

번역 플린 씨가 제휴에 관해 암시하는 것은?
(A) 예상치 못한 결과가 생길 수도 있다.
(B) 오랫동안 지속될 것 같다.
(C) 정부로부터 재정 지원을 받는다.
(D) 오가미가 맺은 또 다른 제휴와 비슷하다.

해설 두 번째 단락에서 플린 씨가 탁월한 과학자와 공학자 집단과 이 첨단 시설에서 함께 일할 기회가 생겨서 매우 설렌다고 하면서 '풍력 에너지 분야에서의 이들의 전문성에 힘입어 개발 프로그램(our development program)이 더 빠르게 그리고 어쩌면 우리가 예상하지 못하는 방식으로 (in ways that we don't expect)발전할 수도 있다'고 했다. 이 말은 제휴 관계가 예상치 못한 결과를 가져올 수도 있다는 의미이므로 정답은 (A)이다.

174 사실 관계 확인

번역 라이언 센터에 관해 명시된 것은?
(A) 직원이 200명이 안 된다.
(B) 플린 씨가 그곳에서 일했다.
(C) 오가미-X가 그곳에서 만들어졌다.
(D) 대학교 안에 자리 잡고 있다.

해설 세 번째 단락에서 라이언 센터가 '브리즈번 대학교 본교 캠퍼스 내 깊숙한 곳에 위치해 있다(Situated deep within the University of Brisbane's main campus)'고 했으므로 정답은 (D)이다.

▶▶ **Paraphrasing** 지문의 **situated within** → 정답의 **sits on**

175 문장 삽입

번역 [1], [2], [3], [4]로 표시된 곳 중에서 다음 문장이 가장 적합한 곳은?
"그의 팀은 처음에는 날개 형태와 로터(회전자) 설계 같은 사양에 초점을 맞출 것이다."
(A) [1]
(B) [2]
(C) [3]
(D) [4]

해설 삽입문의 주어가 His team이므로 먼저 His가 가리키는 인물이 있는 문장을 찾아야 한다. [4]번 바로 앞 문장에서 '라이언 센터에서는 엘리아스 마틴 박사(Dr. Elias Martin)가 오가미의 초기 모델을 발전시키고 해당 제품의 디자인을 계속해서 세련되게 다듬는 작업을 주도할 것'이라고 했다. 문맥상 Dr. Elias Martin이 삽입문의 His에 해당하는 인물임을 알 수 있다. 따라서 특정 인물과 대명사의 관계를 고려하여 삽입문은 [4]번에 들어가야 하므로 정답은 (D)이다.

오비탈 오피스 가구용품

비즈니스 파크 9호, 신시내티, OH 94932

176발송일: 3월 30일   고객 계정 번호: <u>70670532</u>

배송지: 어고매스 컨설팅   주문 번호: <u>#DR4032</u>

품목 코드	수량	단가	전체 가격
#C43	18	**177**49.95달러	899.10달러
#H503	4	159.95달러	639.80달러
179#X110	1	279.99달러	279.99달러
#D60	5	24.95달러	124.75달러
미납액:			1943.64달러

176결제는 발송일로부터 7일 후에 자동으로 처리됩니다.

이용해 주셔서 감사합니다.

어휘 office furniture 사무용 가구 dispatch date 발송일 customer account no 고객 계정 번호 item code 물품 부호 quantity 수량 price per unit 단가 balance due 미불액, 미납금 be automatically processed 자동으로 처리되다 Thank you for your patronage. 이용해 주셔서 감사합니다.

수신: 윌리엄 모바일 (wmobile@orbitaloffice.net)

발신: 베티 컨트롤 (bcontrolle@ergo-math.com)

날짜: 4월 5일

제목: 주문 번호: DR4032

모바일 씨께,

우리가 주문한 새 사무용 가구를 어제 오후 늦게 받았는데, 만족스럽지 않다는 말씀을 드리게 되어 유감입니다. **177**송장에는 분명히 사무용 의자 가격으로 899.10달러를 청구한다고 나와 있는데, 액수가 지나치게 높아 보입니다. 여기 귀하의 카탈로그를 보니 이 품목은 개당 가격이 29.95달러에 불과합니다. 우리는 귀하가 가능한 한 빨리 차액을 우리 계좌로 입금해 주시기를 기대합니다. **178**더욱이, 우리가 주문한 대형 회의실 탁자의 높이도 너무 낮아 보입니다. 탁자를 설치하고 보니 그 아래에 의자들이 들어가지 않더군요. 제가 지난주에 전화로 탁자 **180**크기에 관해 말씀드렸을 때 귀하는 그것이 우리의 용도에 아주 적합하다고 장담했습니다.

상상하실 수 있듯이 저는 이만저만 실망한 게 아닙니다. 이 가구들은 금요일에 우리 이사회 회의가 열리는 시간에 늦지 않게 맞춰 구입한 것이라 그 전에 이런 상황을 바로잡아야만 합니다. 앞으로 이틀 동안 제가 타지로 출장을 갈 예정이라 귀하의 자세한 정보를 제 동료인 웨인 롤링스에게 넘겨주었습니다. **179**그가 오늘 오후 귀하에게 전화해 이 탁자를 가져다주고 더 큰 탁자를 배달하는 문제를 논의하겠다고 했습니다. 우리가 서로에게 유익한 사업 계약을 지속해 나갈 수 있도록 앞으로는 이와 같은 실수가 발생하지 않기를 바랍니다.

베티 컨트롤 드림

부지사장

어고매스 컨설팅

어휘 order 주문(품) report 통보하다, 보고하다 satisfactory 만족스러운 invoice 송장, 청구서 state 명시하다 bill 청구하다

어휘 catalog 카탈로그 unit price 개당 가격 credit one's account ~의 계좌로 입금하다 as soon as possible 가능한 한 빨리 in addition 게다가, 더욱이 height 높이 boardroom table 회의실 탁자 set up 설치하다 notice 알아차리다 fit 들어맞다 dimension 크기, 치수 assure 장담하다, 확언하다 more than suitable 아주 적합한 for one's purposes ~의 용도로, ~ 목적으로 extremely disappointed 몹시 실망한 purchase 구입하다 in good time for ~할 시간에 맞춰 늦지 않게 directors' meeting 이사회 회의, 중역 회의 situation 상황 rectify 바로잡다, 수정하다, 고치다 go out of town on a business trip 타지로[멀리] 출장을 가다 details 자세한 정보 colleague 동료 pick up 가져가다, 치우다 deliver 배달하다 mutually beneficial 서로에게 유익한 business arrangement 사업 계약 Assistant Regional Manager 부지사장

176 사실 관계 확인

번역 송장에 관해 사실인 것은?

(A) 고객에게 특별 할인을 알려 준다.

(B) 상품이 신시내티로 배송될 것이라고 나와 있다.

(C) 결제가 4월에 처리될 것으로 명시되어 있다.

(D) 배송 회사와 연락하는 방법이 나와 있다.

해설 송장인 첫 번째 지문 맨 마지막에 결제는 발송일로부터 7일 후(7 days after the dispatch date)에 자동으로 처리될 것이라고 했고 발송일이 3월 30일로 명시되어 있다. 따라서 결제는 4월 6일에 처리될 것이므로 정답은 (C)이다.

177 연계

번역 어고매스 컨설팅이 대금을 잘못 청구 받은 제품은 어느 것이겠는가?

(A) #C43

(B) #H503

(C) #X110

(D) #D60

해설 두 번째 지문 첫 번째 단락에서 송장에는 사무용 의자 가격으로 899.10달러를 청구한다고 나와 있는데, 액수가 지나치게 높은 것 같다고 하면서 회사 카탈로그에는 해당 품목의 단가(the unit price of this item)가 29.95달러로 나와 있다고 했다. 그리고 송장을 보면 #C43 품목에 해당하는 단가가 $49.95로 명시되어 있다. 즉, 어고매스 컨설팅이 #C43에 대해 잘못 청구 받은 것이므로 정답은 (A)이다.

178 사실 관계 확인

번역 컨트롤 씨는 자신이 주문한 탁자에 관해 뭐라고 언급하는가?

(A) 엉뚱한 주소로 배송되었다.

(B) 설치 설명서가 포함되어 있지 않았다.

(C) 크기에 관해 잘못 안내 받았다.

(D) 배송 도중 손상되었다.

해설 두 번째 지문 첫 번째 단락에서 주문한 대형 회의실 탁자의 높이가 너무 낮아 탁자를 설치하고 보니 그 밑으로 의자가 들어가지 않는다고 했다. 그러면서 지난주에 전화로 탁자 크기(its dimensions)에 대해 얘기했을 때 모바일 씨는 그 탁자가 용도에 아주 적합할 것이라고 컨트롤 씨에게 말했

다고 했다. 결국 컨트롤 씨는 탁자의 크기에 대해 잘못 안내 받은 것이므로 정답은 (C)이다.

▶▶ **Paraphrasing** 지문의 **its dimensions** → 정답의 **its size**

179 세부 사항

번역 롤링스 씨는 모바일 씨와 무엇에 관해 이야기하겠는가?
(A) 일부 불편한 가구 조정
(B) 불만족스러운 제품의 교체
(C) 수리 기사가 방문하도록 예약
(D) 카탈로그의 오류 수정

해설 두 번째 지문 두 번째 단락에서 웨인 롤링스 씨가 오늘 오후에 모바일 씨에게 전화해 탁자를 가져가고 더 큰 탁자를 배달하는 문제에 대해 논의할 것이라고 했다. 따라서 두 사람은 불만족스러운 제품의 교체를 논의할 것이므로 정답은 (B)이다.

180 동의어 찾기

번역 이메일에서 두 번째 단락 4행의 "passed"와 의미상 가장 가까운 것은?
(A) 초과했다
(B) 간과했다
(C) 전달했다
(D) 하락했다

해설 passed는 지문에서 '넘겨줬다', '전달했다'라는 뜻으로 쓰였다. 따라서 정답은 (C) transmitted이다.

어휘 exceed 초과하다 overlook 간과하다 decline 하락하다; 거절하다

181-185 광고+온라인 양식

채용 공고

직함: 기술 디자이너

위치: 베이스-솔루션즈, 카버 스트리트 18, 앨버커키. 6월 2일 근무 시작

역할: 기술 디자인 경력자로서 동료들과 긴밀히 협업하여 **181(C)현재 도시 전역에 적용되는 설계 지침에 충실한 고품질의 세련된 건축 디자인을 제작할 것입니다.** 고객들이 요구하는 설계 명세를 결정하기 위해 **181(A)고객들과의 연락을 담당하게 될 것입니다. 181(B)시티스케이프 컴퓨터 프로그램을 사용해 디자인 작업 결과물을 만들어 내야 합니다.**

자격 요건:
– 4년제 대학 졸업 또는 이와 동등한 학력
– **184시티스케이프 컴퓨터 소프트웨어에 대한 폭넓은 지식과 2년 이상 이 프로그램을 사용한 경험 필수**
– 투철한 직업 윤리와 팀 내에서 잘 어울려 일할 수 있는 능력. 친근하고 호감을 주는 태도와 더불어 탄탄한 의사소통 능력이 있으면 바람직함

지원 절차: 182www.base-solutionsco.com/apply에 방문하여 2월 27일까지 온라인 지원 양식을 작성해 주시기 바랍니다. 서류 합격자들은 3월 11일 면접에 참석하도록 초대됩니다.

어휘 job opening 일자리 job title 직함 experienced 경력이 있는, 경험 많은, 노련한 work closely with ~와 긴밀히 협력하다 coworker 동료 sophisticated 세련된, 정교한 architectural design 건축 설계, 건축물 디자인 adhere to ~에 충실하다, ~을 고수하다 current 현재의 planning guideline 계획 지침 be responsible for ~에 책임이 있다, ~을 담당하다 liaise with ~와 연락을 취하다 client 고객 determine 결정하다 specifications 설계 명세, 세목 output 출력하다 requirements 자격 요건 equivalent 동등한 것 extensive knowledge 광범위한 지식 essential 필수적인 work ethic 직업 윤리, 근무 윤리 robust 탄탄한, 활기찬 desirable 바람직한 along with ~와 더불어 personable demeanor 매력적인[품위 있는] 태도 application process 지원 절차 application form 지원서 양식 successful candidate 합격자

---

http://www.base-solutionsco.com/apply/form

베이스-솔루션즈
입사 지원서

지원 직책: 기술 디자이너 **작성일:** 2월 2일

성명: 네이선 브리지스

주소: 우편번호 87119 그린에이커 로드 402, 앨버커키, NM

전화번호: 555-0115

이메일: nathanb@ubn-mail.com

학력: 앨버커키 대학교 건축 디자인 학사

근무 경력:
– **183아뮤나 아키텍츠**   **주니어 디자이너**
– 커팅 에지 디자인   보조 디자이너
– 맥시펀 자전거 대여점   점원

특기 사항:
저는 제가 매우 근면하고 열정적인 사람이며, 팀에 소속되어서든 혼자서든 모두 일을 잘 할 수 있다고 생각합니다. **183,184가장 최근 직장에서는 주니어 디자이너로서 시티스케이프를 거의 18개월 동안 사용한 경험이 있으며, 제가 이 프로그램을 잘 이해하고 있다고 생각합니다.** 또한 저는 친근하고 다가가기 쉬운 사람으로서, 모든 동료들과 원만한 업무 관계를 유지하고 있다고 생각합니다. **183,185아울러 5월 중순까지 현재의 회사와 계약되어 있다는 사실도 말씀드리고 싶습니다.**

어휘 date completed 작성일 additional comment 특기 사항 enthusiastic 열의 있는, 열정적인 individual 개인 as part of a team 팀원으로서 individually 개인적으로 have a solid understanding of ~을 잘 이해하다 approachable 다가가기 쉬운 maintain good working relationships 좋은 업무 관계를 유지하다 colleague 동료 mention 언급하다, 말하다 be contracted to ~와 계약을 맺고 있다 current 현재의

181 사실 관계 확인

번역 언급된 직무가 아닌 것은 무엇인가?
(A) 고객과 만나기
(B) 특정한 컴퓨터 프로그램 사용하기
(C) 도시 설계 규정 따르기
(D) 도급 업자 선정하기

해설 첫 번째 지문의 역할(Role)부분을 보면 직무의 역할이 나온다. (A) 고객과 만나기(liaising with clients), (B) 특정 컴퓨터 프로그램 사용하기(use the Cityscape computer program), (C) 도시 설계 규정 따르기(adhere to current citywide planning guidelines)가 모두 언급되어 있다. 하지만 도급 업자 선정하기는 명시되어 있지 않으므로 정답은 (D)이다.

▶▶ Paraphrasing
지문의 liaising with clients
→ 보기의 Meeting with clients
지문의 use the Cityscape computer program → 보기의 Using a specific computer program
지문의 adhere to current citywide planning guidelines → 보기의 Following city planning regulations

182 세부 사항

번역 지원서 제출 기한은 언제인가?
(A) 2월 2일
(B) 2월 27일
(C) 3월 11일
(D) 6월 2일

해설 첫 번째 지문의 지원 절차(Application Process)에서 지원서를 2월 27일까지(by February 27)보내라고 했으므로 정답은 (B)이다.

183 세부 사항

번역 브리지스 씨가 현재 고용되어 있는 곳은 어디인가?
(A) 베이스-솔루션즈
(B) 아뮤나 아키텍츠
(C) 커팅 에지 디자인
(D) 맥시펀 자전거 대여점

해설 두 번째 지문 특기 사항(Additional comments)에서 브리지스는 가장 최근 직장에서 주니어 디자이너로서 시티스케이프를 거의 18개월 동안 사용한 경험이 있다고 했다. 그리고 근무 경력(Experience)을 보면 상단에 아뮤나 아키텍츠에서 주니어 디자이너로 근무한다고 명시되어 있으므로 정답은 (B)이다.

184 연계

번역 브리지스 씨가 이 일자리에 적합하지 않다고 여겨질 만한 이유는?
(A) 어떤 소프트웨어를 충분히 경험해 보지 않았다.
(B) 대학교 졸업 자격이 없다.
(C) 전에 팀원으로 일해 본 적이 없다.
(D) 면접일에 휴가 중일 것이다.

해설 첫 번째 지문의 자격 요건(Requirements)에서 시티스케이프 컴퓨터 소프트웨어에 대한 폭넓은 지식과 해당 프로그램을 2년 이상 사용한 경험이 필수라고 명시되어 있다. 그런데 두 번째 지문 특기 사항(Additional comments)에서 브리지스 씨는 이 프로그램을 18개월 정도(almost 18 months of experience using Cityscape)사용했다고 밝혔다. 즉, 2년 이상 해당 프로그램 사용이라는 요건을 충족시키지 못해 브리지스 씨는 적합한 지원자가 아니라고 추론할 수 있으므로 정답은 (A)이다.

185 사실 관계 확인

번역 브리지스 씨는 5월에 무슨 일이 있을 것이라고 명시하고 있는가?
(A) 그의 현재 고용 계약이 종료될 것이다.
(B) 그의 부서가 구조 조정될 것이다.
(C) 전화 회의를 주최할 것이다.
(D) 그가 자격증 수업을 마칠 것이다.

해설 두 번째 지문 특기 사항에서 5월 중순까지 현재의 회사와 계약되어 있다(contracted to my current company through mid-May)고 했다. 이를 통해 브리지스 씨의 고용 계약이 5월에 종료될 것임을 알 수 있으므로 정답은 (A)이다.

어휘 restructure 구조를 조정하다

186 -190 이메일+광고+온라인 후기

수신: 소피 함 〈shamm@bgiocorp.com〉
발신: 카일 킴 〈kkim@bgiocorp.com〉
제목: 회사 이전
날짜: 8월 2일
첨부 파일: 요구 사항

안녕하세요, 소피.

이사회가 마침내 10월 24일에 시애틀로 회사를 이전하기로 결정했어요. 이제, 다음 단계는 여러 이삿짐 센터들을 조사하는 것인데, **186나는 당신이 이 일을 해 줬으면 합니다.** 우리의 요구 사항을 적은 목록을 첨부했으니 우리 필요에 가장 잘 맞는 회사를 찾을 때 이 **187핵심 사항들을 참고하도록 하세요.** **189보험이 잘 되어 있는 회사를 찾는 게 특히 중요합니다.** 마무리되면 가장 좋은 회사들을 목록으로 뽑아서 내게 이메일로 보내 주세요. 고마워요.

카일

어휘 company relocation 회사 이전 the board 이사회 finally 마침내 move to ~로 이사하다 the next step 다음 단계 research 조사하다 moving company 이삿짐 회사 attach 첨부하다 requirements 요구 사항, 필수 사항 refer to ~을 참고하다 central points 핵심 사항 fit one's needs ~의 필요에 알맞다 insurance coverage 보험 보장 범위

크레인 무버스

전국 300여 곳에 지점을 둔 크레인 무버스는 최상의 이사 서비스를 제공합니다. 저희 팀은 귀하의 소유물을 한 장소에서 다른 장소로 안전하게 옮기는 데 매진하고 있습니다. **190그리고 저희는 지금 고객님께서 고객님의 물건이 어디에 있는지 항상 아실 수 있도록 전국 횡단 이사에 대해 무료 추적 시스템을 제공하고 있습니다.**

주택 이사 패키지: 개인이나 가족이 옆 도시로 이사를 하든지 국토를 가로질러 이사를 하든지 저희의 이사 도우미들은 소유물을 조심스럽게 포장해서 안전하게 목적지까지 가져옵니다. 크레인 무버스는 8월 한 달 동안 대학생들을 돕고 싶습니다. 학생증을 보여 주시고 이사가 끝난 후 타이렐 서점 상품권을 무료로 받아 가십시오.

기업 이사 패키지: 회사를 이전하시나요? 저희의 이사 전문가들은 귀하와 직원들이 새로운 영업 장소로 옮겨 가는 것을 도와드릴 준비가 되어 있습니다. 귀하의 사업장에 있는 기계류, 문서, 여타 물건들을 저희가 소중히 다루겠습니다. 크레인 무버스는 9월에 기업 이사 비용도 10% 할인해 드리고 있습니다.

국제 이사 패키지: 마드리드로 이사하시나요? 싱가포르로 이주하신다고요? 어떤 해외 이사라도 가능한 한 순조롭게 진행되도록 돕기 위해 저희 전문가들이 여기에 있습니다. 크레인 무버스는 비자 발급과 출입국 신고서 작성 지원부터 최상의 국제 운송 수단 선택에 이르기까지 폭넓은 서비스를 제공합니다.

1-800-555-0184번으로 전화하셔서 저희의 직원 중 한 명과 상담하시고 **188저희의 모든 이사 패키지에 대해 무료 견적을 받아보십시오.**

어휘 location 장소, 위치 moving service 이사 서비스 be committed to ~에 매진[헌신]하다 ensure 보장하다, 반드시 ~하게 하다 from one place to another 한 곳에서 또 다른 곳으로 free tracking system 무료 추적 시스템 at all times 항상 residential 주택의, 주거의 individual 개인 pack 짐을 싸다 belonging 소유물 destination 목적지, 행선지 student identification 학생증 gift certificate 상품권 corporate 회사의, 기업의 relocate 이사[이전]하다 professional 전문가 be prepared to+동사원형 ~할 준비가 되어 있다 transfer 옮기다, 이전하다 a new place of business 새로운 영업 장소 take great care of ~을 소중히 돌보다 machinery 기계류 document 문서, 서류 goods 재물, 소유물 international 국제적인 expert 전문가 as ~ as possible 가능한 한 a wide range of 폭넓은 immigration form 출입국 신고서 mode of international transportation 국제 운송 수단 contact 연락하다 representative 직원, 대리인 quotation 견적

이용 후기			
홈	메뉴	**후기**	지점

작성자: 소피 함
날짜: 10월 30일

189저희 회사가 일주일 전에 사무실을 이전하면서 크레인 무버스를 이용했습니다. 이사가 더할 나위 없이 순조로웠어요. 저희는 전문적인 서비스를 받아서 기분이 매우 좋았습니다. **190이동 중인 상자들을 모두 추적할 수 있었고,** 모든 게 아주 말끔한 상태로 배달되었습니다. 저는 이곳의 기업 이사 패키지를 다른 회사들에게 확실히 추천하겠습니다.

어휘 could not have gone more smoothly 더할 나위 없이 순조로웠다 be pleased with ~해서 기분이 좋다 professional service 전문 서비스 track 추적하다, 뒤쫓다 in transit 운송 중인 deliver 배달하다 in great shape 아주 말끔한 상태로 definitely 분명히, 확실히 recommend 추천하다

186 글의 주제 / 목적

번역 이메일의 목적은 무엇인가?
(A) 이사회를 준비하려고
(B) 지시 사항을 전달하려고
(C) 제안을 승인하려고
(D) 한 업체를 추천하려고

해설 이메일 초반부에서 발신자인 카일이 소피에게 다음에 할 일이 여러 이삿짐 센터들을 조사하는 것인데 이 일을 소피가 해주었으면 한다고 했다. 즉, 카일이 소피 함에게 업무 지시를 하기 위해 이메일을 쓴 것이므로 정답은 (B)이다.

187 동의어 찾기

번역 이메일에서 첫 번째 단락 3행의 "central"과 의미상 가장 가까운 것은?
(A) 중간의
(B) 가까운
(C) 편리한
(D) 중요한

해설 지문에서 refer to the central points는 '핵심 사항들을 참고하라'는 의미로 쓰인 것이다. 따라서 문맥상 central은 '중요한, 핵심적인'이란 뜻으로 쓰였으므로 정답은 (D) key이다.

188 세부 사항

번역 주택 이사 패키지에는 무엇이 포함되는가?
(A) 특대형 가구 처리
(B) 가족을 위한 특별 요금
(C) 애완동물 운송
(D) 무료 비용 상담

해설 두 번째 지문 맨 마지막에 모든 이사 패키지에 대해 무료 견적(a free price quotation)을 받아 보라고 했으므로 정답은 (D)이다.

▶▶ **Paraphrasing** 지문의 **a free price quotation** → 정답의 **A free cost consultation**

189 연계

번역 크레인 무버스에 관해 사실인 것은?
(A) 이사 보험을 제공한다.
(B) 시애틀에 본사가 있다.
(C) 가장 바쁜 이사철은 10월이다.
(D) 재활용할 수 있는 포장재를 사용하고 있다.

해설 첫 번째 지문 후반부에서 보험이 잘 되어 있는 회사(a company with good insurance coverage)를 찾는 게 특히 중요하다고 했다. 그리고 세 번째 지문 첫 문장에서 소피 함의 회사가 일주일 전에 사무실을 이전하면서 크레인 무버스를 이용했다고 했다. 즉, 소피 함이 크레인 무버스를 선택한 이유 중 하나는 그 회사가 이사 보험을 제공하기 때문일 것이므로 정답은 (A)이다.

190 연계

번역 함 씨에 관해 암시된 것은 무엇인가?
(A) 싱가포르 취업 비자를 신청했다.
(B) 타이렐 서점에 자주 간다.
(C) 그녀의 회사가 이사 비용을 할인 받았다.
(D) 그녀의 회사가 나라를 횡단하여 이전했다.

해설 두 번째 지문 첫 번째 단락에서 고객의 물건이 어디에 있는지 항상 알 수 있도록 전국 횡단 이사에 대해 무료 추적 시스템(a free tracking system for cross-country moves)을 제공한다고 했다. 그리고 세 번째 지문 중반부에서 함 씨는 이동 중인 상자들을 모두 추적할 수 있었다(track all our boxes in transit)고 했다. 즉, 함 씨의 회사는 전국 횡단 이사를 하면서 무료 추적 시스템을 이용한 것으로 추론할 수 있으므로 정답은 (D)이다.

191 -195 이메일+메뉴+이메일

발신: 로리 올슨 〈laurie@grayfinecatering.com〉
수신: 대런 그레고리 〈d.gregory@gil-mail.com〉
제목: 출장 연회 메뉴
날짜: 10월 29일
첨부: 그레고리 메뉴 제안

그레고리 씨께,

191약속 드린 대로 고객님 부모님의 결혼기념일 축하 행사를 위해 제안하는 메뉴를 보내드립니다. 고객님은 그레이파인 케이터링의 전문 셰프들이 심혈을 기울여 독특한 조합의 맛있는 요리들을 만들어 내는 걸 보시게 될 겁니다. 이들은 또한 처음 제공된 것이 마음에 들지 않을 경우를 위해 대안도 마련했습니다. 첨부 파일을 검토하시고 결정 사항을 알려 주십시오.

195일단 결정을 하시면, 저희는 행사 관련해 일할 직원의 수, 일하게 될 시간, 저희가 맡게 될 일, 그리고 기타 사안들을 명시한 계약서를 만들게 됩니다. 192이들 세부사항을 사전에 확정 지어야 고객께서 여유롭고 즐거운 시간을 보낼 수 있게 되고, 이는 곧 저희의 주요 목표라는 점을 기억해 주시기 바랍니다. 그 다음에 귀하의 행사를 저희 공식 생산 일정에 올리고 시식 등 예비 행사 일정을 잡기 위해 착수금 50%를 청구할 것입니다.

연락 주시기를 고대합니다.

로리 올슨
대리
그레이파인 케이터링

어휘 wedding anniversary 결혼기념일 celebration 축하 행사 craft 공들여 만들다 assortment 모음, 조합 alternative 대안이 되는 in case ~일 경우에 대비해 initial 처음의 offering 제공된 것, 내놓은 것 to one's liking ~의 기호에 맞는 contract 계약(서) specify 명시하다 finalize 마무리 짓다 detail 세부 사항 chief 주된 deposit 착수금, 보증금 schedule 일정을 잡다 preparatory 준비의 food tasting 시식

제안 메뉴

제1 코스 (전채 요리)	대안:
치킨과 시금치 퍼프 페이스트리 (8달러)	아이올리 소스를 얹은 연어 완자 (10달러)
194제2 코스 (수프 또는 샐러드) 겉만 구운 가리비를 곁들인 콜리플라워 수프 (13달러)	**194대안: 염소 젖 치즈를 넣은 야채 샐러드 (10달러)**
제3 코스 (주 요리) 발사믹 글레이즈를 넣은 램찹과 으깬 감자 (22달러)	대안: 살짝 구운 필레 미뇽에 버섯 구이를 곁들임 (20달러)
제4 코스 (후식) 체리 아몬드 타르트 (7달러)	대안: 민트 초콜릿 파르페 (7달러)

어휘 appetizer 에피타이저, 전채 요리 aioli sauce 아이올리 소스(마요네즈와 마늘로 만듦) sear (고기를) 강한 불에 표면만 재빨리 굽다 scallop 가리비 (mixed) green salad (상추가 주로 들어간) 야채 샐러드 entrée 앙트레, 주 요리 balsamic glazed 발사믹 글레이즈(발사믹 식초에 당분과 전분 등을 넣고 졸인 것)를 넣은 sautéed 살짝 볶은[구운] filet mignon 필레 미뇽, 안심 스테이크 roasted 구운

발신: 대런 그레고리
수신: 로리 올슨
제목: Re: 케이터링 메뉴
날짜: 11월 7일

올슨 씨께,

제안 메뉴를 보내주셔서 감사합니다. 좀 더 빨리 답을 드리지 못한 점 사과드립니다. 말씀드렸듯이, 저희가 만났을 때 파티 장소를 결정하지 못했었죠. **193다음 단계로 진행하기 전에 그 문제를 처리해야 했는데 적당한 행사 장소를 찾는 게 생각보다 어렵더군요.** 하지만 이제 준비가 다 됐습니다. 로바나 호텔 안뜰을 예약했습니다.

메뉴는 아주 훌륭해 보입니다! 수고하셨습니다. **194부탁드리고 싶은 유일한 변경 사항은 콜리플라워 수프를 야채샐러드로 바꿔달라는 겁니다.** 그렇지 않으면 식사가 좀 배가 부르지 않을까 싶어서요. **195이렇게 변경된 메뉴 안으로 진행해 주시기 바랍니다.**

감사합니다.

대런 그레고리

어휘 apologize 사과하다 take care of ~을 처리하다 venue 공연장, 행사장 turn out ~인 것으로 드러나다 be all set 모든 준비가 되다 patio 안뜰, 테라스 swap out 바꾸다 heavy (식사가) 양이 많은, 배가 부른 otherwise 그렇지 않으면 move forward 나아가다 revised 변경된

---

191 세부 사항

번역 첫 번째 이메일에서 그레고리 씨에 관해 알 수 있는 것은 무엇인가?
(A) 축하 행사에 손님 50명을 초대할 계획이다.
(B) 그레이파인 케이터링의 음식을 시식했다.
(C) 가족 구성원을 위해 파티를 열려고 한다.
(D) 전문 요리사와 얘기를 했다.

해설 첫 번째 지문 첫 문장을 보면 부모님의 결혼기념일 축하 행사를 위해 제안하는 메뉴 얘기가 나왔다. 따라서 정답은 (C)이다.

▶▶ **Paraphrasing** 지문의 **parents**
→ 정답의 **some family members**

---

192 세부 사항

번역 올슨 씨는 그레이파인 케이터링의 주요 목표가 무엇이라고 말하는가?
(A) 독특한 메뉴를 제공하는 것
(B) 예산을 초과하지 않는 것
(C) 행사 주최자가 행사를 즐길 수 있게 해주는 것
(D) 지역사회에서 긍정적인 평판을 쌓는 것

해설 첫 번째 지문 두 번째 단락에서 자사의 주요 목표는 고객이 여유롭고 즐겁게 시간을 보낼 수 있게 되는 것이라고 하였다. 따라서 정답은 (C)이다.

193 세부 사항

번역 그레고리 씨가 올슨 씨에게 좀 더 일찍 편지를 쓰지 못한 이유는 무엇인가?

(A) 다른 파티 계획 문제를 먼저 해결해야 해서
(B) 메뉴를 결정하는 것이 어려워서
(C) 정규 직업 때문에 다른 할 일이 있어서
(D) 며칠 동안 이메일을 확인하지 않아서

해설 세 번째 지문 첫 번째 단락 앞부분에서 적당한 행사 장소를 찾는 게 생각보다 어렵다고 했다. 그러므로 장소 섭외에 문제가 있었다는 것을 알 수 있으므로, 정답은 (A)이다.

194 연계

번역 그레고리 씨가 요청한 변경 사항 때문에 어떤 코스가 영향을 받게 되겠는가?

(A) 제1 코스
(B) 제2 코스
(C) 제3 코스
(D) 제4 코스

해설 세 번째 지문 마지막 부분에서 그레고리 씨가 콜리플라워 수프를 야채샐러드로 변경하여 달라고 했다. 두 번째 지문 메뉴를 보면 그 결과 제 2코스에 수프에서 샐러드로 변경 사항이 생겼음을 알 수 있다. 따라서 정답은 (B)이다.

195 연계

번역 올슨 씨는 다음에 무엇을 하겠는가?

(A) 일정표에 항목을 추가한다.
(B) 셰프에게 다른 음식을 제안해 달라고 요청한다.
(C) 최초 입금 고지서를 보낸다.
(D) 계약서를 작성한다.

해설 첫 번째 지문 두 번째 단락에서 일단 메뉴 결정이 되면 계약서를 만들게 된다고 하였고, 세 번째 지문 마지막 부분에서 변경된 메뉴 안으로 진행해 달라고 하였다. 이를 토대로 올슨 씨는 계약서 작성을 진행할 것임을 알 수 있다. 따라서 정답은 (D)이다.

196-200 웹페이지+양식+공지

사이먼 식물원

사이먼 식물원은 40여 년 전 문을 열었으며 현재 사이먼 시 한복판 250에이커의 대지에 20개가 넘는 정원을 구비하고 있습니다. **196,198**사이먼 식물원은 연중 내내 화요일부터 일요일까지 오전 7시부터 오후 7시까지 개장합니다. 특정 지역의 조기 또는 늦은 폐장을 유발하는 특별 전시와 시사회, 행사들이 있는 경우에는 예외를 둘 수도 있습니다. 개인 및 단체 입장권 가격을 보시려면 여기를 클릭하십시오.

7월에 방문할 만한 곳들:

수련 연못: **197(B)**7월 중순에 피기 시작하는 이 아름다운 분홍, 노랑, 보라색 수련들이 활짝 피어 히스 전시관 건너편에 있는 연못을 우아하게 장식하는 모습을 볼 수 있습니다.

테드 숲: 이 숲은 몇 년 동안 복원을 거친 끝에 드디어 대중에게 다시 개방되었습니다. **197(D)**방문객들은 가이드가 안내하는 산책로를 따라 나무와 작은 식물, 동물들을 보면서 숲속을 트레킹할 수 있습니다.

금잔디: **197(A)**매주 목요일 밤 모든 손님에게 무료로 제공되는 라이브 공연이 펼쳐집니다. 특별 연주자들 가운데에는 더 팰컨스 재즈 밴드와 사이먼 시립 교향악단도 포함되어 있습니다.

상설 및 계절 정원뿐 아니라 예정된 전시와 진행 중인 전시에 대해 더 알고 싶으시면 여기를 클릭하십시오.

어휘 botanical garden 식물원 currently 현재 throughout the year 연중 내내 exception 예외 special exhibition 특별 전시 preview 시사회 closure 폐장 specific 특정한 water lily 수련 bloom 활짝 피다 grace 우아하게 하다, 장식하다 restoration 복원 the public 일반 대중 trek 여행하다, 이동하다 guided 안내원이 있는[딸린] path 경로, 길, 산책로 live performance 라이브 공연 upcoming 다가오는, 곧 있을 exhibit 전시 A as well as B B뿐 아니라 A도 permanent 상설의, 영구적인 seasonal 계절성의

사이먼 식물원
영화 촬영 허가 신청서

성명: 카산드라 와일리
제작사명: 플렌트 영화사
전화번호: 555-0194
영화 종류: 다큐멘터리

199요청 받은 촬영 장소: 오키드 플레이스
199요청 받은 촬영 날짜: 8월 28일
198요청 받은 촬영 시간: 오전 5시–오후 2시

인원수: 20명
장비 목록: 카메라, 삼각대, 마이크, 조명 스탠드

특별 요청: 저희 촬영 팀이 오키드 플레이스 북서쪽 모퉁이에 있는 온실을 보았는데, 그 온실 안과 주변에서 촬영할 수 있게 허가를 받을 수 있는지 알고 싶습니다.

어휘 production company 제작사 equipment 장비 tripod 삼각대 production team 촬영 팀 notice 알아차리다 greenhouse 온실 have permission to+동사원형 ~할 수 있게 허가 받다

공지

199이 지역은 8월 28일 영화 촬영으로 인해 일시 폐쇄될 예정입니다. 오후 2시까지 모든 방문객의 접근이 제한됩니다. 모든 손님께서는 촬영에 방해가 되지 않도록 **200**목소리를 최대한 낮춰 주실 것을 정중히 부탁 드립니다. 그사이에, 저희 식물원의 다른 근사한 전시회와 정원들을 방문하시기 바랍니다.

– 사이먼 식물원

어휘 be temporarily closed 일시적으로 폐쇄되다 access 접근 be limited to ~에게 제한되다 kindly ask 정중히 요청하다 volume 음량 to a minimum 최소한으로 so as not to+동사원형 ~하지 않도록 disrupt 방해하다, 지장을 주다 in the meantime 그 사이에, 그러는 동안 exhibit 전시회

196 사실 관계 확인

번역 사이먼 식물원에 관해 명시된 것은?
(A) 화요일마다 개장 시간이 길다.
(B) 사이먼 시 정부에서 운영한다.
(C) 모든 특별 전시회는 실내에서 열린다.
(D) 일부 정원은 일년 내내 개방한다.

해설 첫 번째 지문 두 번째 문장에서 사이먼 식물원은 연중 내내(throughout the year) 화요일부터 일요일까지 오전 7시부터 오후 7시까지 개장한다고 나와 있으므로 정답은 (D)이다.

> ▶▶ Paraphrasing   지문의 **throughout the year**
> → 정답의 **year-round**

197 사실 관계 확인

번역 7월에 사이먼 식물원에서 이용할 수 없는 것은 무엇인가?
(A) 음악극
(B) 화훼 전시
(C) 전시관 투어
(D) 산책로

해설 첫 번째 지문에 언급된 7월에 방문할 만한 곳들(Areas to visit in July)를 보면 7월 금잔디(Gold Lawn) 행사에서 매주 목요일 밤에 (A) 음악 공연을 즐길 수 있다. 그리고 수련 연못(Water Lilies Pond)에는 7월 중순에 피기 시작하는 아름다운 분홍, 노랑, 보라색 수련들이 있으므로 (B) 화훼 전시 또한 볼 수 있다. 또한 테드 숲(Ted Forest)에서는 방문객들이 안내원과 함께 (D) 산책로를 걸을 수도 있다. 하지만 (C) 전시관 투어에 대한 언급은 없으므로 정답은 (C)이다.

198 세부 사항

번역 와일리 씨는 사이먼 식물원에 무엇을 요청했겠는가?
(A) 공연을 위해 연주자 몇 명을 고용하기
(B) 한 지역을 평소보다 일찍 개장하기
(C) 온실 근처에서 장비 내리기
(D) 20명 단체 관람객에게 입장권 할인해 주기

해설 두 번째 지문에서 와일리 씨가 요청한 영화 촬영 시간은 오전 5시에서 오후 2시이다. 그런데 첫 번째 지문에 사이먼 식물원의 개장 시간은 오전 7시에서 오후 7시까지로 명시되어 있다. 즉, 와일리 씨는 사이먼 식물원에 오키드 플레이스를 두 시간 일찍 개장해 달라고 요청했을 것이므로 정답은 (B)이다.

199 연계

번역 공지가 붙어 있을 만한 장소는 어디인가?
(A) 수련 연못
(B) 테드 숲
(C) 금잔디
(D) 오키드 플레이스

해설 두 번째 지문에서 영화 촬영을 요청한 장소는 오키드 플레이스이고 날짜는 8월 28일로 되어 있다. 그런데 세 번째 지문 첫 문장에서 이 지역은 8월 28일 영화 촬영으로 인해 일시 폐쇄될 예정이라고 했다. 따라서 이 두 정보를 종합하면 공지가 게시된 장소는 오키드 플레이스라는 것을 알 수 있으므로 정답은 (D)이다.

200 동의어 찾기

번역 공지에서 첫 번째 단락 3행의 "volume"과 의미상 가장 가까운 것은?
(A) 판
(B) 강도
(C) 양
(D) 무게

해설 지문에서 the volume of their voices는 '목소리의 강도'를 뜻한다. 즉, volume이 문맥상 '강도' 또는 '세기'라는 뜻으로 쓰인 것이므로 정답은 (B) strength이다.

TEST 3

101 (A)	102 (A)	103 (C)	104 (B)	105 (A)
106 (D)	107 (B)	108 (C)	109 (C)	110 (B)
111 (D)	112 (C)	113 (C)	114 (A)	115 (D)
116 (B)	117 (D)	118 (A)	119 (D)	120 (B)
121 (B)	122 (C)	123 (C)	124 (A)	125 (A)
126 (B)	127 (D)	128 (A)	129 (B)	130 (C)
131 (C)	132 (A)	133 (C)	134 (C)	135 (D)
136 (C)	137 (B)	138 (D)	139 (A)	140 (A)
141 (C)	142 (D)	143 (C)	144 (A)	145 (B)
146 (D)	147 (B)	148 (C)	149 (B)	150 (A)
151 (D)	152 (A)	153 (C)	154 (B)	155 (A)
156 (A)	157 (D)	158 (B)	159 (C)	160 (C)
161 (A)	162 (C)	163 (D)	164 (C)	165 (D)
166 (A)	167 (B)	168 (D)	169 (B)	170 (C)
171 (C)	172 (C)	173 (D)	174 (A)	175 (D)
176 (A)	177 (C)	178 (B)	179 (D)	180 (D)
181 (D)	182 (B)	183 (D)	184 (C)	185 (A)
186 (A)	187 (B)	188 (D)	189 (D)	190 (C)
191 (C)	192 (D)	193 (C)	194 (A)	195 (A)
196 (B)	197 (D)	198 (B)	199 (B)	200 (C)

PART 5

101 동사 시제 _ 과거 시제 + ago

해설 과거 시제를 나타내는 부사구 three months ago를 통해서 동사의 시제가 과거 시제가 되어야 한다는 것을 알 수 있다. 따라서 정답은 (A) started이다.

번역 세일럼 씨는 3개월 전 패션 잡지사에서 관리직 일을 처음 시작했다.

어휘 management position 관리직

102 목적격 대명사

해설 동사 contact 뒤에서 목적어 역할을 할 수 있는 대명사를 고르는 문제. (B)는 소유격, (D)는 재귀대명사이기 때문에 적절하지 않고, (C)는 소유대명사로 목적어 자리에 올 수는 있지만 의미상 '우리의 것'에 연락을 취할 수는 없기 때문에 올 수 없다. 따라서 목적격인 (A) us가 정답이다.

번역 인증 번호를 입력했을 때 경보 장치가 꺼지지 않으면 즉시 저희에게 연락하십시오.

어휘 authorization code 인증 번호 enter 입력하다

103 형용사 어휘

해설 명사 앞에는 명사를 수식하는 형용사가 와야 하므로 box와 어울리는 형용사를 찾아야 한다. '텅 빈 상자'가 내용상 가장 적절하기 때문에 (C) empty(텅 빈)가 정답이다. 보기 (A) urgent는 '급한', (B) total은 '전체의', (D) willing은 '기꺼이 하는'이라는 의미로 문맥상 적절하지 않다.

번역 텔레비전이 배송되고 남은 빈 상자는 재활용하십시오.

어휘 recycle 재활용하다 deliver 배송하다

104 형용사 자리 _ 명사 수식

해설 관사와 명사 사이에 들어갈 수 있는 품사는 형용사와 명사이다. 하지만 여기서는 '명사+ 명사' 형태의 복합명사가 되는 것이 의미상 적절하지 않기 때문에 형용사인 (B) dependable(믿을 수 있는)이 정답이다.

번역 직원들은 지속적으로 제시간에 회사에 도착하기 위해 믿을 만한 교통편을 필요로 한다.

어휘 a form of ~의 한 형태 transportation 운송 수단 consistently 지속적으로, 일관되게 work 회사, 직장 on time 시간을 어기지 않고, 제시간에 dependability 의존할 수 있음

105 동사 어휘

해설 빈칸 앞 동사와 다음에 나오는 명사 목적어와 함께 전체 의미가 어울리는 to부정사를 찾는 문제. 문맥상 '낡은 컴퓨터 몇 대를 기부하기로 약속했다'라는 의미가 자연스러우므로 정답은 (A) donate(기증하다)이다. 나머지 동사는 의미상 적합하지 않다.

번역 아더리 어소시에이츠는 매년 낡은 컴퓨터 몇 대를 지역사회 단체에 기부하기로 약속했다.

어휘 promise 약속하다 organization 단체 donate 기부하다 conserve 보존하다 collect 모으다, 수집하다 install 설치하다

106 전치사 어휘

해설 빈칸 뒤 목적어와 함께 '다양한 업계에서의 경력'이라는 의미가 어울리므로 '~에서(의)'라는 뜻의 전치사를 골라야 한다. 따라서 정답은 (D) in이다.

번역 머밍스 그룹의 사업 고문들은 매우 다양한 업계에서 경력을 지니고 있다.

어휘 advisor 고문 experience 경험 a wide variety of 매우 다양한 industry 산업, 업계

107 부사 어휘

해설 분사형 형용사 revised를 수식할 수 있는 부사의 의미를 구분하는 문제이다. (A) usually(보통), (C) lastly(마지막으로), (D) nearly(거의)는 문장 전체의 의미를 고려했을 때 어울리지 않는다. 따라서 정답은 (B) newly(새롭게)이다.

번역 〈맥시모와 함께 요리하기〉 원본의 독자들은 새롭게 개정된 판의 최신 정보들과 추가된 요리법들을 반길 것이다.

어휘 reader 독자 appreciate 고마워하다, 환영하다 revised 개정된

108 비교급

해설 비교의 대상이 되는 것을 나타낼 때 쓰이는 than이 나오면 반드시 그 앞에는 비교급이 나와야 한다. 빈칸을 제외하고는 비교급이 없기 때문에 빈칸이 비교급이 되어야 한다. 따라서 정답은 (C) faster이다.

번역 수수료 체계가 도입된 후 영업부 직원들은 전보다 더 빠르게 일했다.

어휘 commission (판매 대가로 받는) 수수료[커미션] structure 체계 introduce 도입하다 fastness 빠름

109 접속사 어휘

해설 빈칸 앞뒤로 완전한 문장이 두 개 있으므로 두 문장을 연결할 알맞은 접속사를 찾아야 한다. 문맥상 '~한다면'이라는 뜻의 조건 접속사 (C) if가 가장 잘 어울린다.

번역 어떤 문서가 계속 인쇄되는 중에는 프린터를 끄지 마시오.

어휘 shut down 끄다   document 문서   still 여전히

110 동사의 태 구분

해설 빈칸은 동사 자리이고, 계약(contract)은 '체결되는' 것이므로 동사의 형태는 수동태가 적절하다. 따라서 정답은 (B) was signed이다.

번역 몇 시간의 논의 끝에 어제 오후 대표들에 의해 계약이 체결되었다.

어휘 following ~ 후에   sign a contract 계약을 맺다   representative 대표(자)

111 동사 어휘_to부정사

해설 빈칸 다음의 명사 목적어와 어울리는 to부정사 어휘를 찾는 문제이다. 보기 (A) convert(전환하다), (B) expose(노출시키다), (C) offset(상쇄하다), (D) prolong(연장하다) 중에서 문맥상 제품 수명이 연장되는 것을 보장한다는 내용이 가장 적절하다. 따라서 정답은 (D) prolong이다.

번역 치바 냉난방의 보일러 유지 보수 서비스는 제품의 수명이 연장되는 것을 보장합니다.

어휘 furnace 보일러; 용광로   maintenance 유지 보수   be guaranteed to+동사원형 ~하는 것을 보장하다, 반드시 ~하게 되다

112 such+a(n)+형용사+명사

해설 such는 수식하는 명사가 단수 가산명사이면 관사(a/an) 앞에 쓰인다. 따라서 정답은 (C) such이다.

번역 야외 음악 축제가 그렇게 화창하고 산들바람 부는 날에 열려서 다행이었다.

어휘 fortunate 다행한, 운 좋은   outdoor 야외의   be held 개최되다   breezy 산들바람이 부는, 경쾌한   passing 일시적인, 지나가는   else 그 밖의 다른

113 명사 자리_관사 뒤

해설 빈칸 앞에 정관사 the가 있고 뒤에 전치사 for가 있으므로 빈칸은 명사가 들어갈 자리이다. 명사 (A)와 (C) 중 동사가 spend라는 것을 감안하면 주체가 사람이 되어야 한다. 따라서 정답은 (C) negotiator(교섭자)이다.

번역 라이선스 계약이 매우 중요했기 때문에 레드버드 미디어 측 교섭자는 제안서를 준비하는 데 많은 시간을 들였다.

어휘 licensing agreement 라이선스 계약   spend time -ing ~하는 데 시간을 보내다   negotiation 협상

114 부사 자리

해설 be동사와 과거분사 사이에서 과거분사를 수식해 주는 부사를 고르는 문제. 보기 중 부사는 (A) attractively(보기 좋게)밖에 없으므로 정답이다.

번역 안내서에는 도브테일 인의 객실마다 각기 다른 주제로 보기 좋게 꾸며져 있다고 나와 있었다.

어휘 guidebook 안내서   report 알리다   decorate 꾸미다, 장식하다   attractive 매력적인   attraction 끌림, 명소

115 전치사 어휘

해설 빈칸 앞을 보면 문장이 완벽하므로 빈칸 뒤와 이어질 말이 필요하다. 부사인 (A) yet(아직)은 품사상 맞지 않고, 전치사 (B) since(~ 이래로)와 전치사구 (C) along with(~에 덧붙여)와 (D) due to(~ 때문에)가 가능하다. 빈칸 뒷부분에서 늦은 이유를 설명하고 있기 때문에 정답은 (D) due to이다.

번역 회의장 근처의 교통 체증 때문에 많은 대표자들이 회의에 늦었다.

어휘 delegate 대표자   conference 회의   traffic congestion 교통 체증

116 동사 어휘

해설 제품 출시 전에 법률 전문가와 '상의했다'라는 문장이 되는 것이 문맥상 자연스럽다. 정답은 (B) consulted(상의하다)이다. (A) recognized는 '인식하다', (C) encouraged는 '격려하다', (D) developed는 '개발하다'라는 의미이다.

번역 얌브로 토이즈는 경쟁사 제품과 유사한 제품을 출시하기 전에 법률 전문가에게 자문을 구했다.

어휘 legal expert 법률 전문가   prior to ~ 전에   release a product 제품을 출시하다   similar to ~와 유사한   competitor 경쟁자, 경쟁사

117 명사 어휘

해설 직원 평가에서 등급이 낮았던 이유에 대한 내용이 와야 하기 때문에 주로로 '잦은 결근'이 오는 것이 의미가 적절하다. 따라서 정답은 (D) frequency(빈도, 잦음)이다. (A) movement는 '움직임', (B) termination은 '종료', (C) compliance는 '준수, 따름'라는 의미이다.

번역 안토니오 씨는 잦은 결근으로 인해 직원 평가에서 낮은 등급을 받았다.

어휘 absence from work 결근   poor ratings 저조한 평가 등급   employee evaluation 직원 평가

118 동사의 수 / 시제 일치

해설 빈칸은 단수 명사 new logo를 주어로 하는 본동사가 들어갈 자리이다. 준동사인 (B)와 (C)는 답이 될 수 없고, '기업 가치를 묘사하는' 것은 보편적 사실을 나타내므로 현재단수형인 (A) depicts가 정답이다.

번역 전문 그래픽 디자이너의 도움을 받아 만들어진 뉴어크 인더스트리즈의 새로운 로고는 그들의 기업 가치를 나타낸다.

어휘 **with the help of** ~의 도움으로 **professional** 전문적인 **corporate value** 기업 가치 **depict** 묘사하다, 그리다

119 부사 어휘

해설 affect라는 동사에는 '긍정적', '부정적'이라는 의미의 부사가 자주 함께 쓰인다. 이 문장에서는 '부정적으로' 영향을 받게 된다는 의미가 적절하다. 따라서 정답은 (D) adversely(불리하게)이다. 참고로 'positively/negatively+affect'의 조합이 시험에 자주 등장하기 때문에 알아두자. (A) doubtfully는 '미심쩍게', (B) evenly는 '고르게', (C) mutually는 '서로'라는 의미이다.

번역 환경과학자들은 화학 공장이 인근에 들어서면 휴스턴호의 야생동물들이 악영향을 받을 수 있다고 확인해 주었다.

어휘 **confirm** 확인하다 **wildlife** 야생동물 **affect** 영향을 주다 **chemical plant** 화학 공장 **nearby** 인근에

120 재귀대명사

해설 일단 빈칸이 문장 맨 뒤에 있다는 사실에 주목하자. 주어 자리는 될 수 없기에 (A) she는 우선 답에서 제외된다. 접속사가 있는 두 개의 문장인데, 콤마(,) 뒤의 문장을 보니 주어, 동사, 목적어까지 완벽히 갖춘 문장이다. 따라서 빈칸에 들어갈 수 있는 것은 재귀대명사뿐이므로 정답은 (B) herself이다. 재귀대명사는 이 문장에서처럼 강조하기 위해 쓰일 때는 생략해도 문장이 완벽히 성립한다.

번역 IT 사무실이 이미 문을 닫았으므로 서 씨는 복사기를 직접 수리해야 했다.

어휘 **make repairs** 수리하다 **copy machine** 복사기

121 부사 어휘

해설 콤마(,) 앞 문장과 뒤 문장은 순서대로 이어질 수 있는 관계이다. 공연이 있고 '그 이후에' 감독을 만날 것이라는 의미가 자연스럽다. 따라서 정답은 (B) afterward(그 후에)이다. 보기 (A) somewhat(다소), (C) instead (그 대신에)는 의미상 맞지 않는다. (D) beyond(~ 너머에, ~ 이후에)는 전치사나 부사로 쓰일 수 있지만 이 문장에서는 맞지 않는다.

번역 공연은 약 두 시간 동안 계속될 예정이며, 관객들은 그 후에 감독을 만날 수 있다.

어휘 **performance** 공연 **last** 지속되다 **audience** 관객, 청중

122 명사 어휘

해설 판매를 통해 얻을 수 있는 '무엇'이 들어가야 하는 자리이다. (C) revenue가 '수익'이라는 뜻으로 가장 적절하다. 보기는 모두 '돈'과 관련된 어휘이지만 (A) salary와 (D) payroll은 일한 대가로 받을 수 있는 '급여'를 의미하고 (B) account는 '계좌'라는 뜻이다.

번역 전 공장 부지 판매로 얻은 수익 덕분에 회사는 잉여 자금을 얻었다.

어휘 **earn** 벌다 **former** 이전의 **manufacturing site** 공장 부지 **surplus fund** 잉여 자금

123 명사 자리

해설 '관사 + 형용사' 뒤에는 명사가 들어가야 한다. 따라서 보기 중 부사인 (A), 형용사인 (D)는 제외된다. become은 보어를 취하는 동사이기 때문에 주어와 같은 의미일 때만 명사를 쓸 수 있다. 주어(Dr. Carter)가 사람 단수 명사이기 때문에 (C) authority(권위자)가 정답이다.

번역 카터 박사는 수십 년간의 연구를 통해 자연 통증 완화 기술을 선도하는 권위자가 되었다.

어휘 **decades of** 수십 년간의 **leading** 선도하는 **pain relief** 통증 완화 **authorities** (관계) 당국 **authoritative** 권위적인; 권위 있는

124 형용사 어휘

해설 빈칸 다음의 전치사 to와 명사 목적어에 어울리는 분사형 형용사를 찾는 문제이다. 보기 (A) dedicated(헌신적인), (B) accomplished(뛰어난), (C) respected(존경 받는), (D) advanced(선진의) 중에서 '고객 서비스에 가장 헌신적인'이라는 표현이 가장 적절하다. 따라서 정답은 (A) dedicated이다.

번역 그 상은 고객 서비스에 가장 헌신적이라고 판단되는 콜센터 직원에게 수여될 것이다.

어휘 **award** 상 **representative** 상담원 **be judged to** ~라고 판단되다 **dedicated to** ~에 헌신하는

125 복합 명사

해설 빈칸 앞의 명사 passenger를 눈여겨 보아야 한다. passenger는 셀 수 있는 명사이므로 단수라면 앞에 a가 와야 하고, 복수라면 뒤에 -s가 붙어야 한다. 하지만 a도 없고, -s도 붙지 않았다는 것은 빈칸에 명사가 와서 복합 명사를 만들어줘야 한다는 뜻이다. 따라서 보기 중 명사형인 (A) comfort(편의, 안락)가 정답이다.

번역 저희 항공사는 승객의 편안함을 보장하기 위해 설계된 몇 가지 편의 시설을 제공하게 되어 기쁩니다.

어휘 **airline** 항공(사) **be pleased to**+동사원형 ~해서 기쁘다 **offer** 제공하다 **amenities** 편의 시설 **design** 설계하다, 고안하다 **ensure** 보장하다, 반드시 ~하게 하다 **passenger** 승객 **comforted** 위로 받은 **comfortably** 편안하게, 안락하게 **comfortable** 편안한

126 전치사 어휘

해설 빈칸은 전체 문맥상 어울리는 의미의 전치사가 들어가야 하는 자리이다. 문장에서 '또한 정기적으로 상영한다'는 내용이 있으므로 '~ 이외에'의 의미를 가진 전치사 (B) Besides가 정답이다. (A) Considering(~을 고려하면), (C) Except(~을 제외하고), (D) For(~을 위하여)는 문맥상 어울리지 않는다.

번역 그 극장은 최신 블록버스터 외에도 독립 영화와 고전 영화 또한 정기적으로 상영한다.

어휘 **cinema** 극장 **routinely** 일상적으로, 정기적으로 **screen** 영화를 상영하다 **independent** 독립적인 **classic** 고전의

127 접속사 자리

해설 문장 두 개가 연결된 구조이므로 빈칸에는 접속사가 와야 한다. (A) during(~ 동안에)은 전치사, (B) so(그래서)는 접속사나 부사, (C) even(심지어)은 부사, (D) while(~하는 동안에)은 접속사이다. 따라서 접속사인 (D) while이 정답이다.

번역 세미나가 열리는 동안 참가자들은 모바일 기기를 무음 모드로 돌려두라는 요청을 받을 것이다.

어휘 participant 참가자   mobile device 모바일 기기   be in session 개최 중이다

128 명사 어휘

해설 형용사(economic)와 잘 어울리면서 that절의 내용을 '알려 줄 수 있는' 명사가 들어가야 하는 자리다. (A) indicators는 '지표', (B) merits는 '장점', (C) alternates는 '대체 요원', (D) degrees는 '정도'라는 의미인데, '경제 지표가 다음과 같은 내용을 알려 준다'는 의미가 적절하기 때문에 정답은 (A)이다.

번역 가장 강력한 경제 지표는 이번 분기에 통화 가치가 꾸준히 상승할 것임을 시사한다.

어휘 economic indicator 경제 지표   suggest 시사하다   currency 통화   value 가치   steadily 꾸준히   quarter 분기

129 접속사 어휘

해설 문장이 두 개이므로 두 문장을 연결해 줄 접속사가 있어야 한다. (A)는 부사로 품사상 틀리다. (C) Now that(~이므로)과 (D) Until(~할 때까지)은 의미상 맞지 않다. 문맥상 '잘못된 점이 발견될 때쯤엔 이미 발간돼 있었다'는 의미가 자연스럽기 때문에 정답은 (B) By the time이다.

번역 인터뷰 대상자 이름의 오자가 발견됐을 때는 이미 기사가 발간된 후였다.

어휘 misspelling 오자, 틀린 표기   interviewee 인터뷰 받는 사람   article 기사

130 동사 어형

해설 한 문장에 동사는 하나만 나와야 한다. 이 문장에는 이미 동사(launched)가 있기 때문에 접속사가 없다면 더 이상의 동사는 필요 없다. 따라서 (A), (B)는 답이 될 수 없다. 빈칸 앞의 명사 skincare line을 수식해 주는 능동 형태의 현재분사인 (C) combining이 정답이다.

번역 애쉬 코스메틱스는 알로에와 코코넛 오일의 보습 효과를 결합한 인기 있는 스킨케어 라인을 출시했다.

어휘 launch 출시하다   moisturizing effect 보습 효과   combine 결합하다

PART 6

131-134 기사

> 3월 16일 – 로즈우드 시의회는 공원 및 휴양국을 위한 자금을 12% 확대하는 정책을 고려하고 있다. 공원 및 휴양국 관리하에 있는 18개 부지는 전 연령대 거주자들의 휴양 및 휴식 목적으로 **131사용된다**. 이러한 변화를 지지하는 사람들은 현재 재원이 충분치 않다고 주장한다. "**132우리가 필요로 하는 것은** 시설 개선을 위한 재정적 지원입니다"라고 의회 의원 디나 월터스 씨는 말한다.
>
> 이 **133사안은** 3월 28일 저녁 7시에 시의회 회의에서 논의될 예정이다. 모든 로즈우드 주민은 회의에 참석할 수 있고 **134좌석에 앉기를 원하는 분은 일찍 도착해야 한다**. 평상시보다 높은 출석률이 예상된다.
>
> **어휘** City Council 시의회   measure 조치, 정책   funding 자금   recreation 휴양   site 부지, 장소   resident 주민, 거주자   of all ages 모든 연령의   relaxation 휴식   supporter 지지자   argue 주장하다   current 현재의   financial support 재정적 지원   facility 시설   improvement 개선, 향상

131 동사의 시제 / 태

해설 빈칸 뒤에 by가 나오고, 18개의 부지가 거주자들에 의해서 '사용되는' 것이기 때문에 수동태가 와야 한다. 보기 (B)와 (C)가 수동태인데, 문장 앞뒤를 보았을 때 현재 시제가 자연스러우므로 정답은 (C)가 되어야 한다.

132 접속사 어휘

해설 is 앞의 '------- we need'까지가 주어이기 때문에 명사절을 이끄는 접속사를 찾아야 한다. 또 한 가지, need 뒤에 빠져 있는 목적어까지 포함하는 접속사여야 하기 때문에 '우리가 필요한 것'이라는 의미를 만들어 주어야 한다. 그러한 명사절 접속사는 바로 (A) What이다.

133 명사 어휘

해설 앞 단락에서 변화를 위해 부족한 자금을 지원 받아야 한다는 내용이 나왔고, 그것을 회의 때 논의할 것이라는 말이 이어지는 것이 자연스럽다. (A) achievement는 '업적', (B) selection은 '선정된 것', (C) matter는 '문제, 사안', (D) setback은 '차질'이라는 의미로, 문맥상 '사안'이 가장 적절하다. 따라서 정답은 (C) matter이다. 참고로 이와 비슷한 issue, topic 등도 답이 될 수 있다.

134 문맥에 맞는 문장 고르기

번역 (A) 부서 예산은 매년 조정된다.
(B) 이는 짧은 의견 발표 시간을 포함한다.
(C) 평상시보다 높은 출석률이 예상된다.
(D) 각 의회 의원은 2년의 임기를 가진다.

해설 빈칸 바로 앞에서 '좌석에 앉기를 원하는 분은 일찍 도착해야 한다'고 했다. 뒤 문장에서 그 이유를 부연 설명해 주는 것이 적절하므로 정답은 (C)이다.

어휘 budget 예산   adjust 조정하다   attendance 출석률   serve 근무[복무]하다   term (정해진) 기간

135 -138 정보문

> ### 오크퍼스 텐트 관리
>
> 다음 지침 사항을 따르면 오크퍼스 캠핑 텐트의 수명을 **135**상당히 연장시킬 수 있습니다. 먼저 텐트를 **136**며칠 이상 창고에 보관하기 전에는 깨끗이 청소하세요. <u>적은 양의 먼지는 헝겊을 이용해 닦아 내십시오.</u> 텐트를 세척해야 할 경우, **137**유독성 화학 물질을 포함한 세제 또는 기타 액상 세제에 노출되지 않도록 하십시오. 대신에 특별 제조된 텐트 전용 세척액을 구하거나 순한 가루비누를 찬물에 섞어서 사용하세요. 텐트 안팎 표면을 스펀지로 부드럽게 문지르세요. 그런 다음 제공된 가방에 넣기 전에 완전히 **138**건조해 주십시오.
>
> **어휘** extend 연장하다 guideline 지침 make sure 확실하게 하다 storage 저장(고), 보관소 expose 노출시키다 detergent 세제 cleaning fluid 액상 세제 contain 함유하다 chemical 화학물질 instead 대신에 obtain 구하다, 입수하다 liquid 액체 powdered 가루로 된 scrub 문지르다 surface 표면 completely 완전히, 완벽하게

135 부사 자리

해설 빈칸 앞에는 조동사 can이 있고 빈칸 다음에는 동사 extend가 나오므로 빈칸은 동사를 꾸며주는 부사 자리이다. 따라서 정답은 (D) significantly(상당히)이다.

어휘 signify 의미하다 significant 중요한 significance 중요성, 의의

136 문맥에 맞는 문장 고르기

번역 (A) 몇몇 종류의 텐트는 설치하기가 더 어려울 수 있습니다.
(B) 평평하고 푹신한 땅은 캠핑장으로 이상적입니다.
(C) 적은 양의 먼지는 헝겊을 이용해 닦아 내십시오.
(D) 이러한 것들은 접착 테이프나 패치를 이용해 수리할 수 있습니다.

해설 빈칸 앞 문장을 보면 캠핑 텐트를 창고에 보관하기 전에 깨끗이 청소하라는 내용이 나왔다. 따라서 빈칸에는 청소 방법에 관한 내용이 들어가야 적절할 것이므로 정답은 (C)이다.

어휘 set up 설치하다 flat 평평한 ideal 이상적인 campsite 캠핑장 cloth 천, 헝겊 wipe away 닦아 내다 repair 수리하다 adhesive tape 접착 테이프

137 형용사 어휘

해설 빈칸 뒤에 있는 명사를 꾸며 주는 형용사를 고르는 문제이다. harsh chemicals가 '유독성 화학 물질'을 뜻함을 알고 있다면 쉽게 풀 수 있는 문제이다. (A) steep(가파른), (C) timely(시기적절한), (D) automated(자동화된)은 '화학 물질'과 어울리지 않는다. 따라서 정답은 (B) harsh(유독한)이다.

138 동사 어휘

해설 앞 문장에서 계속 캠핑 텐트의 '청소' 방법에 관한 내용이 나왔고 빈칸이 있는 문장이 그 마지막 단계임을 알 수 있다. 그러므로 전체 지문 내용으로 볼 때 빈칸에는 완전하게 '건조해야 한다'는 말이 나와야 한다. 따라서 정답은 (A) dry(건조하다)이다.

어휘 fill 채우다 harden 굳다

139 -142 편지

> 타이론 베리
> 조이 레인 941
> 버뱅크, 캘리포니아주 91502
>
> 베리 씨께,
>
> 영세 자영업자 협회(SBOA)를 대표하여 저희 연례 리더십 워크숍에 귀하를 초대하고자 합니다. 올해 저희는 **139**접근이 용이한 위치 때문에 캔자스시티를 개최 도시로 선정하였습니다. 행사는 젠킨스 센터에서 개최될 예정입니다. 다른 지역에서 오실 경우, **140**숙소에 관해 동봉한 세부 사항을 참조하십시오. SBOA가 참석자들을 위해 할인 요금으로 이 호텔들을 주선했습니다.
>
> 이번 워크숍은 귀하의 비즈니스 관리 역량을 **141**향상시킬 수 있는 좋은 방책이 될 것입니다. **142**<u>좌석이 한정되어 있으므로,</u> 본 행사에 참가를 원하실 경우 기한인 8월 10일까지 반드시 등록해 주십시오. <u>등록하시면 귀하를 위한 자리가 확보됨을 보장할 수 있습니다.</u>
>
> 섀넌 페인
> 행사 진행자, SBOA
>
> **어휘** on behalf of ~를 대표[대신]하여 small business 소규모 자영업 annual 연례의 host city 개최 도시 enclosed 동봉된 regarding ~에 관해 arrange 마련하다, 주선하다 discounted rate 할인 요금 participant 참석자 skill 기량 space 공간 be limited 한정되다 take part in ~에 참가하다 register 등록하다 deadline 기한

139 형용사 자리 _ 명사 수식

해설 대명사 소유격과 명사 사이에 들어갈 수 있는 품사는 형용사와 명사이다. 하지만 여기에서 명사 (D)는 연결이 부자연스럽기 때문에 형용사가 들어가서 '접근이 용이한'이라는 뜻이 되는 것이 자연스럽다. 따라서 정답은 (A) accessible(접근 가능한)이다.

140 명사 어휘

해설 빈칸 바로 앞에 캔자스시티 밖의 다른 지역에서 오는 사람들은 동봉된 세부 사항을 보라는 말이 나온다. 그 뒤 문장에서 이 호텔들을 할인 요금으로 주선했다는 말이 이어지는 것으로 보아 빈칸에 어울리는 말은 (A) accommodations(숙소)이므로 정답은 (A)이다. (B) fees는 '요금', (C) presentations는 '발표', (D) requirements는 '요구 사항'이라는 의미이다.

141 동사 어휘

해설 워크숍을 통해서 비즈니스 관리 역량을 어떻게 한다는 말이 들어가야 하는데 (A) enforce(강요하다; 시행하다), (B) observe(관찰하다), (D) pursue(추구하다)는 적절하지 않다. (C) enhance(향상시키다)가 들어가서 '워크숍은 자신이 가지고 있는 기량을 향상시킬 수 있는 좋은 자리'라고 하는 것이 의미상 적절하다. 따라서 정답은 (C)이다.

142 문맥에 맞는 문장 고르기

번역 (A) 안됐지만 그 워크숍 등록은 마감되었습니다.
(B) 지난해 모임에서만큼 즐거운 시간이 되셨기를 바랍니다.
(C) 우리에게 더 큰 장소가 적합하다고 결정할지도 모릅니다.
(D) 등록하시면 귀하를 위한 자리가 확보됨을 보장할 수 있습니다.

해설 바로 앞 문장에서 등록하라는 말이 나왔으므로, 등록과 관련된 내용이 연결되는 것이 자연스럽다. 등록과 관련된 문장은 (A), (D)이지만 (A)는 바로 앞부분에서 등록하라 말해 놓고 뒤이어 마감되었다고 말하는 것은 부적절하다. 따라서 정답은 (D)이다. 특히 앞부분에 나온 '좌석이 한정되어 있다(Space is limited)'는 문장을 통해서 정답을 더 확실하게 고를 수 있을 것이다.

143-146 회람

> 발신: 재스민 우즈, CEO
> 수신: 전 직원
> 제목: 희소식
> 날짜: 5월 11일
>
> 저희 플링크선 주식회사가 여러분의 노고에 감사를 표하고자 직원용 무료 탕비실 운영을 시작한다는 사실을 알리게 되어 기쁩니다. 건강과 맛을 고려해 **143선택된** 과일, 간식, 주스 및 기타 먹거리가 구비될 것입니다.
>
> 두 가지 중요한 사항이 있습니다.
>
> - 직원이 개인적으로 가져다 둔 물품과 혼동되는 일을 방지하기 위해 탕비실 물품은 탕비실 특별 **144보관장에서만** 이용할 수 있습니다. 보관장은 이번 주에 설치할 예정입니다.
> - **145탕비실 사용에 있어 유일한 규정은 직원들이 바로 먹을 수 있는 양 이상의 식음료를 가져가지 않아야 한다는 것입니다. 물품은 책상에 보관하거나 사무실 밖으로 가져가서는 안 됩니다.** 이 규정을 **146위반하는** 직원은 탕비실 이용 권한이 중지됩니다.

어휘 announce 발표하다, 알리다 maintain 유지하다 pantry 식료품 저장실, 탕비실 appreciation 감사 be stocked with ~가 구비되다 treat 대접, 한턱 healthiness 건강함 in order to +동사원형 ~하기 위해 avoid 피하다 confusion 혼동 individual 개별적인 available 이용 가능한 cupboard 찬장 install 설치하다 sole 유일한 consume 소비하다 immediately 즉시 privilege 특전, 특혜 suspend 중단하다

143 동사 형태 _ 분사형 형용사

해설 빈칸은 앞에 있는 대명사 all을 뒤에서 수식하는 형용사 자리이다. 빈칸이 있는 문장 앞에서 다양한 먹거리들을 언급했고 이 먹거리들(all)이 건강과 맛을 고려해 선택되었다는 내용이므로 정답은 (A) chosen(선택된)이다.

어휘 choice 선택 choose 선택하다

144 부사 어휘

해설 빈칸 앞에서 개인 물품과의 혼동을 방지하기 위하여 탕비실 물품은 전용 찬장에서만 이용 가능하다는 말이 나온다. 따라서 (B) only(유일한)가 정답이다. (A) now(지금), (C) again(한 번 더), (D) hardly(거의 ~않는)는 문맥상 available(가능한)과 어울리지 않는다.

145 문맥에 맞는 문장 고르기

번역 (A) 규정 목록이 승인되는 즉시 회람되도록 하겠습니다.
(B) 물품은 책상에 보관하거나 사무실 밖으로 가져가서는 안 됩니다.
(C) 아울러 사용한 접시는 싱크대에 두지 말고 즉시 씻어야 합니다.
(D) 직원 여러 명이 이러한 행위가 일어난 사례를 보고한 바 있습니다.

해설 바로 앞 문장에서 주의 사항에 관한 얘기가 나오기 때문에 그 뒤에 이어지는 문장에서도 연관된 내용이 나와야 한다. 물품을 책상에 보관하거나 외부로 유출하지 말아야 한다는 (B)가 정답으로 가장 적절하다.

어휘 circulate 회람하다, 알리다 approve 승인하다 store 보관하다 transport 이동시키다 moreover 게다가 promptly 즉시 report 보고하다 instance 사례 behavior 행위, 행동

146 동사의 시제 / 태

해설 빈칸 뒤에 동사 can expect가 있으므로 this rule을 목적어로 받으며 앞의 employees를 수식할 수 있는 '관계대명사+동사'가 와야 한다. 따라서 (D) who break가 정답이다.

어휘 break (법, 약속 등을) 어기다

PART 7

147-148 양식

> **PC 솔루션즈**
> 타일러 애비뉴 1958, 248-555-0171
>
> | 날짜: 3월 20일 | 주문 접수자: 안나 버나드 |
> |---|---|
> | 고객명: 데이비드 피어스 | 전화번호: 248-555-0174 |
>
> | 모델: Viex Co. R-20 태블릿 | 일련번호: 3967285001 |
> |---|---|
> | 문제점 설명: 스크린에 금이 감 | |
> | 완료 예정일: 3월 22일 | **147기사: 제이슨 크로포드** |
>
> 특별 지시/주의 사항: 고객은 스크린 교체 및 긁힘 방지 코팅을 위한 비용을 완불함. **148신규 고객 할인 15% 적용됨.** 고객의 동의 없이 추가 작업을 하지 말 것. 고객은 완료 예정일 오후 4시에 물건을 찾아갈 것임.

어휘 accept 수락하다, 응하다 description 설명, 명세 cracked 금이 간 completion 완료 technician 기사, 기술자 special instruction 특별 지시 사항 pay in full 전액 지불하다 replacement 교체 scratch-resistant 긁힘 방지 apply 적용하다 undertake 착수하다 retrieve 되찾아오다, 회수하다

147 세부 사항

번역 크로포드 씨는 무엇을 담당하는가?
(A) 소포 배송
(B) 수리
(C) 주문 접수
(D) 지불 처리

해설 양식에서 Technician이라고 나온 부분을 통해서 태블릿 PC를 수리를 한 '기사'라는 것을 알 수 있다. 따라서 정답은 (B)이다.

148 추론 / 암시

번역 피어스 씨에 대해 추론할 수 있는 것은?
(A) 기기 케이스를 구매했다.
(B) 서비스를 받기 위해 쿠폰을 제시했다.
(C) PC 솔루션즈를 처음 이용했다.
(D) 3월 20일에 제품을 찾아갈 것이다.

해설 하단에 A 15% new customer discount를 적용 받았다고 나오므로
(C)가 정답이다.

▶▶ **Paraphrasing** 지문의 **new** → 정답의 **for the first time**

149 -150 이메일

수신: 엘리아스 키너드〈e.kinnard@valley-fashion.com〉
발신: 쟈넷 아구아요〈aguayoj@wpamanufacturing.com〉
날짜: 1월 8일
제목: 세부 사항

키너드 씨께,

밸리 패션이 저희 설비를 이용하여 신규 제품 라인에 들어갈 청바지를 생산하고
자 하는 가능성에 대해 만나 뵙고 논의하게 되어 매우 기뻤습니다. 저희가 처음
제안한 가격이 너무 높다고 생각하신 것을 잘 알고 있습니다. 그래서 그 문제를
저희 제조팀과 상의했습니다. **149대량 발주를 하실 것을 감안하여 아래와 같이**
가격을 조정하였습니다. 이것이 저희가 드릴 수 있는 최선의 가격입니다.

밸리 패션: 제조 원가 요약

업데이트: 1월 7일

항목	개당 비용
공임	$2.91
천	$3.21
단추, 지퍼, 리벳	$1.24
낡은 것처럼 만드는 마감 처리	$0.84
공장 간접비	$0.39
합계	$8.59

가격은 경쟁 업체보다 약간 높을 수 있으나, **150저희 업체는 지역 내의 설비들 중**
현장 사고가 가장 적습니다. 사회적으로 의식이 있는 많은 고객들은 구매 결정 시
이러한 요인에 주목하며, 이 점이 귀사에 긍정적으로 작용하게 될 것입니다.

쟈넷 아구아요
WPA 매뉴팩처링

어휘 feasibility 실현 가능성 facility 설비, 시설 produce
생산하다 initial 최초의 offer 제안, 제안한 액수 fabrication
제작, 제조 considering ~을 감안하여 require 요구하다, 필요로
하다 bulk order 대량 발주 adjust 조정하다 figure 수치 as
below 아래와 같이 provide 제공하다 production cost 생산비,
제조 원가 cost per item 개당 비용 labor 노동력 fabric 직물, 천
distressed (옷을) 낡은 것처럼 만든 overhead 간접비 rate 가격
slightly 약간 competitor 경쟁자 on-site 현장의 socially
conscious 사회적으로 의식이 있는 pay attention to ~에 주목하다
factor 요인 make purchasing decision 구매 결정을 내리다
reflect 반영하다 positively 긍정적으로

149 글의 주제 / 목적

번역 아구아요 씨가 키너드 씨에게 이메일을 쓴 이유는 무엇인가?
(A) 추가 자금을 요청하기 위해
(B) 예상 비용을 알리기 위해
(C) 비용 절감 방안을 제안하기 위해
(D) 비용을 잘못 청구한 것을 설명하기 위해

해설 첫 번째 단락에서 '대량 주문을 감안해 가격을 조정했다'고 했으므로 관련
내용인 (B)가 정답인 것을 알 수 있다.

150 추론 / 암시

번역 아구아요 씨가 WPA 매뉴팩처링에 대해 암시한 것은?
(A) 훌륭한 안전 기록을 보유하고 있다.
(B) 지역 최대 규모의 공장이다.
(C) 공임이 특히 낮다.
(D) 소셜미디어에서 유명하다.

해설 제조 원가표 밑에 있는 단락의 첫 번째 줄의 내용을 살펴보면 지역 내에
서 현장 사고가 가장 적다는 내용을 확인할 수 있다. 이를 토대로 정답이
(A) 임을 유추할 수 있다. 나머지 보기들은 본문에서 언급되지 않았다.

▶▶ **Paraphrasing** 지문의 **the fewest on-site accidents**
→ 정답의 **an excellent safety record**

151 -152 웹페이지

http://www.parkler.com/about/governance/board

회사 소개	기업 지배 구조	이사회

151(A)파클러의 이사회는 회사 주주들의 이익을 증진시키는 임무를 맡고 있습
니다. 이사회는 주주 연례 총회에서 선출된 3~12명의 인원으로 구성됩니다.
151(C)이사회가 선출되면 이사회 및 하위 위원회와 CEO 간 업무 분장을 결정하
는 연례 업무 계획을 수립해야 합니다. **151(B)또한 감사위원회를 임명해야 합니**
다. 감사위원회는 1년 동안 회사의 재무 보고를 감사합니다. 이사회 책무 전체를
확인하시려면 파클러 연간 보고서의 기업 지배 구조 부분을 참조하십시오.

152현 이사회 위원들의 정보를 보시려면 화면을 아래로 내려 주세요.

어휘 corporate governance 기업 지배 구조 board of
directors 이사회 be charged with ~의 책임을 맡다 promote
증진하다 interests 이익 shareholder 주주 consist of ~로
구성되다 elect 선출하다 annual 연례의 general meeting
총회 determine 결정하다 distribution 분배 committee 위원
appoint 임명하다 auditing committee 감사위원회 monitor
감시하다 financial 재정의 duty 의무, 직무 scroll down 컴퓨터
화면을 아래로 움직이다 current 현재의

151 사실 관계 확인

번역 이사회의 책무로 언급되지 않은 것은?
(A) 투자자의 이익 추구
(B) 팀을 구성해 재무 감시
(C) 회사 지도부 내 업무 분장
(D) 회사 CEO 임명

해설 (A)는 첫 번째 단락의 첫 번째 줄에서 '이익을 증진시키는 임무'라는 말에서, (B)는 첫 번째 단락 끝부분에서 '재무 보고를 감시한다'는 말에서, (C)는 첫 번째 단락 중간에 '이사회 및 하위 위원회와 CEO 간 업무 분장'에서 확인할 수 있다. 따라서 정답은 (D)이다.

어휘 seek 추구하다 benefit 이득 form 구성하다 financial affairs 재무 divide 나누다 appoint 임명하다

152 추론 / 유추

번역 웹페이지 하단으로 더 내려가면 어떤 정보가 있겠는가?
(A) 일부 사람들의 약력
(B) 회사의 공식 규정 목록
(C) 연간 보고서 요약
(D) 주주회의 일정

해설 본문 맨 마지막에 '현 이사회 위원들의 정보'라는 말에서 확인할 수 있다. 따라서 정답은 (A)이다.

어휘 further 더 biographical 전기의 official 공식적인 yearly 연례의

153-154 문자 메시지

살보 트레비사노	오후 3:08
아직 스트릭랜드 가 부동산에 있어요?	
야로미르 노박	오후 3:14
네, 무슨 일이에요?	
살보 트레비사노	오후 3:15
공급 업체에서 4시 경에 얼마간의 자재를 배달할 거예요. ¹⁵³트럭에서 짐을 내리는 데 도움을 받고 싶은데, 그때까지 돌아올 수 있어요?	
야로미르 노박	오후 3:16
안 될 것 같은데요.	
살보 트레비사노	오후 3:18
정말요? 일이 금방 끝날 거라고 생각했어요.	
야로미르 노박	오후 3:20
¹⁵⁴그랬는데, 파이프 일부가 낡아서 물이 새지 않도록 교체해야 해서요.	
살보 트레비사노	오후 3:21
그래요. 알았어요.	

어휘 property 부동산 supplier 공급업자 deliver 배달하다 material 자재 unload (짐을) 내리다 by then 그때까지 be supposed to+동사원형 ~하기로 되어 있다 turn out ~인 것으로 밝혀지다 replace 교체하다 leak (액체, 기체가) 새다

153 의도 파악

번역 오후 3시 16분에 노박 씨가 "안 될 것 같은데요"라고 쓴 의도는 무엇이겠는가?
(A) 자재를 충분히 갖고 있지 않다.
(C) 트럭에 빈 공간이 있을 것이라고 생각하지 않는다.
(C) 트레비사노 씨를 도와줄 수 없다.
(D) 스트릭랜드 가를 찾는 것이 쉽지 않을 것 같다.

해설 트레비사노 씨가 '짐을 내리는 것을 도와줄 수 있냐'고 물은 것에 대한 답변으로 안 된다고 했기 때문에 정답은 (C)이다.

154 추론 / 암시

번역 노박 씨는 현재 무엇을 하고 있는가?
(A) 건설 계획을 검토하고 있다
(B) 배관 문제를 해결하고 있다
(C) 물품을 정리하고 있다
(D) 조명을 교체하고 있다

해설 3시 20분의 대사 내용을 토대로 정답을 확인할 수 있다. 일을 도와 달라고 했는데 안 되는 이유로 파이프 교체를 언급했기 때문에 노박 씨가 배관 문제를 해결하려고 하고 있음을 알 수 있다. 따라서 정답은 (B)이다.

155-157 회람

수신: 전 직원	9월 30일

서밋 스파의 영업시간 연장 계획과 더불어 관리팀에서는 마사지 치료사를 뽑기 위해 지원자들의 면접을 실시했습니다. ¹⁵⁵우리 팀에 합류할 분으로 안젤라 소프 씨를 구했음을 알려 드리게 되어 기쁩니다.

소프 씨는 국가 자격증을 보유한 마사지 치료사로서 새크라멘토에 있는 그런디 인스티튜트에서 첫 교육을 받았습니다. 그녀는 처음에 산타바바라에 있는 재스퍼 호텔 스파에서 일했으며, 그곳에서 일하는 동안 이완 기법을 통해 치료를 가르치는 자선 단체인 스트레스 줄이기 협회(SRA)를 시작했습니다. ¹⁵⁶그 뒤 오클랜드로 옮겨 로렐 센터에서 일을 시작했으며, 여기에서 '올해의 직원상'을 수상했습니다. 로렐 센터가 곧 문을 닫는 관계로 소프 씨는 비슷한 일을 찾던 중이었습니다. 소프 씨의 기량은 다양한 기법을 ¹⁵⁷망라하고 있어 우리와 함께 하게 되어 기쁩니다. 첫 출근일은 10월 7일 월요일입니다. 따뜻하게 맞아 주시길 바랍니다.

어휘 extend 늘리다, 연장하다 business hours 영업시간 management team 관리팀 conduct 실시하다 applicant 지원자 therapist 치료사 announce 발표하다 state-certified 국가 자격증을 보유한 initial 처음의 reduction 감소 charity 자선 단체 be committed to ~에 전념하다 healing 치유 relaxation 휴식, 이완 upcoming 다가오는 closure 폐쇄 search for ~를 찾다 a wide range of 다양한 make an effort 노력을 기울이다

155 글의 주제 / 목적

번역 회람의 목적은 무엇인가?
(A) 직원 소개
(B) 입사 지원자 비교
(C) 퇴직 축하 행사 홍보
(D) 승진 발표

해설 글의 주제나 목적의 경우 첫 번째 단락에 나올 확률이 높다. 이 문제도 첫 번째 단락 마지막 줄에 보면 새로운 직원이 팀에 합류하게 되었음을 알리는 문장이 나온다. 따라서 정답은 (A)이다.

156 세부 사항

번역 소프 씨는 산타바바라에서 무엇을 했는가?
(A) 사회 봉사 단체를 창립했다.
(B) 직업 관련 자격증을 받았다.
(C) 새로운 치료 기술을 개발했다.
(D) 직장에서 1년에 한 번 주는 상을 받았다.

해설 두 번째 단락 두 번째 문장을 보면 '산타바바라'라는 지명을 언급하는데, 이완 기법을 통한 치료를 가르치는 자선 단체인 스트레스 줄이기 협회 (SRA)를 시작했다고 되어 있다. 따라서 정답은 (A)이다.

▶▶ **Paraphrasing** 지문의 **a charity** → 정답의 **a community service organization**

157 동의어 찾기

번역 두 번째 단락 10행의 "cover"와 의미가 가장 가까운 것은?
(A) 보호하다
(B) 숨기다
(C) 출판하다
(D) 포함하다

해설 cover는 가장 기본적인 뜻으로 뒤에 나올 내용을 '다루다', 또는 '포함시키다'라는 뜻을 가지고 있다. 여기에서는 '포함하다'라는 의미가 적절하다. 따라서 정답은 (D) include이다.

158 -160 기사

크로프트 커피의 식품점용 신제품 라인 고투

내슈빌, 6월 15일 – 크로프트 커피는 부조화를 이루는 소파와 안락의자, 현대 미술품, 잔잔한 민속 음악 등을 내세워 친구들과 아늑한 오후를 즐길 수 있는 완벽한 만남의 장소로 세계적인 명성을 얻었다. 그러나 이제 제품을 소비자의 가정에까지 들여놓으려는 행보에 나섰다. **158최근 이자벨 해먼드의 뒤를 이은 CEO 디에고 카르도소 씨**는 크로프트 커피 제품을 상점에서 판매하고자 하는 비전을 갖게 되었다.

크로프트 커피 익스프레스라는 이름으로 판매되는 신규 음료 제품은 지난주에 출시되어 현재 버치트리 슈퍼마켓 체인에서 독점 판매되고 있다. 해당 제품군에는 크로프트 커피의 라테, 카푸치노, 아메리카노의 냉장 형태가 있다. 카르도소 씨는 "버치트리와 손잡게 되어 기쁘다."고 말하며, **159"버치트리와 저희의 고객이 비슷하니 완벽한 조화라고 생각했다."**고 덧붙였다.

160그러나 크로프트 커피는 지난 한 해 동안 높은 판매량을 기록한 반면 익스프레스 제품군은 지금까지 소비자들의 관심을 거의 끌지 못한 것으로 보인다. 대부분의 매장들은 제품이 공급된 첫 주 동안 음료를 몇 개밖에 판매하지 못했다고 보고했다. 크로프트 커피는 TV와 소셜미디어 마케팅 캠페인에 크게 투자했음에도 불구하고 이러한 부진한 성적을 낸 것이다. 가장 낙관적인 분석가들조차 수개월 내로 제품이 철수될지도 모른다고 말한다.

어휘 grocery store 식품점, 슈퍼마켓 mismatched 부조화의, 어울리지 않는 armchair 안락의자 contemporary 현대의 artwork 미술품 folk music 민속 음악, 민요 cozy 아늑한, 친밀한 make a move 행동에 들어가다 recently 최근 take over for ~를 대신하다 stock (상품 등을) 갖춰 두고 있다 under the name ~라는 이름으로 exclusively 독점적으로 partner with ~와 협력하다 alike 비슷한 despite ~에도 불구하고 investment in ~에 대한 투자 optimistic 낙관적인 analyst 분석가

158 추론 / 암시

번역 크로프트 커피에 대해 추론할 수 있는 것은?
(A) 버치트리 매장 내에 지점이 있다.
(B) 경영진이 바뀌었다.
(C) 계절별로 메뉴를 바꾼다.
(D) 최근 해외로 확장했다.

해설 첫 번째 단락 마지막 줄에서 '이자벨 해먼드의 뒤를 이은 CEO 디에고 카르도소 씨'라는 말이 나온다. 이를 통해 최근에 경영진의 교체가 있었다는 것을 알 수 있다. 따라서 정답은 (B)이다. 나머지 보기들의 내용은 지문에서 언급되지 않았다.

159 세부 사항

번역 기사에 따르면, 크로프트 커피가 버치트리를 선택한 이유는?
(A) 적정한 가격
(B) 브랜드 인지도
(C) 유사한 고객층
(D) 안정적인 유통망

해설 두 번째 단락 마지막 줄 '고객이 서로 비슷하다(Its shoppers and ours are alike)'라는 부분에서 정답 (C)를 확인할 수 있다.

160 문장 삽입

번역 [1], [2], [3], [4]로 표시된 곳 중에서 다음 문장이 들어가기에 가장 적합한 곳은?
"대부분의 매장들은 제품이 공급된 첫 주 동안 음료를 몇 개밖에 판매하지 못했다고 보고했다."
(A) [1]
(B) [2]
(C) [3]
(D) [4]

해설 세 번째 단락 [3]의 앞 문장에 '익스프레스 제품군은 지금까지 소비자들의 관심을 거의 끌지 못한 것으로 보인다'는 내용이 나왔다. 삽입문은 부연 설명을 해 주고 있으므로 [3]번에 들어가는 것이 가장 적절하다. 정답은 (C)이다.

161 -163 정보문

테트렉스 민물 수족관을 구매해 주셔서 감사합니다. **161물고기를 키우는 느긋한 취미를 즐기시려면** 다음 단계를 따라해 보십시오.

1. 수조 내부를 따뜻한 비눗물로 씻어내십시오. 수조 측면을 주의 깊게 헹궈 물고기에게 유독할 수 있는 **162잔여물이 남지 않도록** 하십시오.

2. 수조 바닥을 조약돌이나 장식용 자갈로 덮고 수조의 75% 정도를 물로 채우십시오. 화초 또는 조화를 넣으십시오. 화초의 뿌리를 부드럽게 다루고 뿌리를 완전히 덮으십시오. 수조의 나머지 부분을 물로 채웁니다.

3. 필터가 물에 잠길 수 있도록 수조 측면에 필터를 매다십시오. 펌프를 켜기 전에 최소 20분간 필터를 물에 담가 둡니다.

4. 물이 실온인지 확인하십시오. 물고기를 수조에 한 마리씩 넣습니다.

빠진 부품이 있을 경우 고객 서비스 전화 1-800-555-0166으로 전화하십시오. **163품질 보증서 사본에 관한 사항은 패트릭 데이비스(pdavis@tetrexaq.com)에게 이메일을 주시기 바랍니다.**

어휘 freshwater 민물 aquarium 수족관 purchase 구매하다 relaxing 느긋한 follow the steps 단계를 따르다 interior 내부 soapy water 비눗물 rinse 헹구다 residue 잔여물 remain 남다 toxic 유독성의 pebble 조약돌 decorative 장식용의 gravel 자갈 handle 다루다 completely 완전히 ensure 확실히 하다 submerge 물 속에 넣다, 잠수하다 soak 담그다 at least 최소한 room temperature 실온 one by one 하나씩, 차례로 missing 빠진 duplicate 사본의 warranty card 품질 보증서

161 글의 주제 / 목적

번역 정보문의 주요 내용은 무엇인가?
(A) 물고기를 기르는 설비 설치하기
(B) 애완동물 선택하기
(C) 가정용 수족관 청소하기
(D) 수중 식물 기르기

해설 첫 번째 단락 두 번째 문장에서 정답을 확인할 수 있다. 두 번째 문장은 수족관을 사용하는 방법에 대해 알려 주겠다는 내용이다. 이를 토대로 정답이 (A)라는 것을 알 수 있다.

162 세부 사항

번역 사용자들에게 무엇을 피하라고 하는가?
(A) 수조에 물을 넘치도록 채우는 것
(B) 전기 부품들을 젖게 하는 것
(C) 수조 표면에 비누를 남기는 것
(D) 식물 뿌리를 공기 중에 노출시키는 것

해설 단계 1번에서 물고기에게 유독할 수 있기 때문에 '잔여물을 남기지 말라(no residue remains)'고 했으므로 정답이 (C)라는 것을 알 수 있다.

163 세부 사항

번역 사용자들은 제공된 주소로 이메일을 보내어 무엇을 할 수 있는가?
(A) 특별한 부대 용품 주문
(B) 품질 보증 클레임 걸기
(C) 빠진 부품 요청
(D) 문서 사본 받기

해설 지문 맨 마지막 부분만 보고 실수로 답을 (C)로 고르기 쉽다. 빠진 부품이 있을 때는 이메일이 아니라 전화로 연락을 하라고 했고, 이메일을 보내서 요청할 수 있는 것은 품질 보증서 사본(a duplicate warranty card)이다. 따라서 정답은 (D)이다.

▶▶ Paraphrasing 지문의 **a duplicate warranty card** → 정답의 **a copy of a document**

164 -167 문자 메시지

콜린 그레이 [오후 1:56]
율라 씨, 문제가 있어요. **164,165휴즈 씨가 여권을 못 찾고 있어요.** 위그 씨와 저는 박물관 직원들과 얘기를 나누기 위해 잠시 여기에 더 있어야 할 것 같아요.

율라 워렌 [오후 1:58]
알겠습니다. 저는 나머지 인원과 함께 먼저 출발할게요. 가능할 때 상황을 알려 주세요. **164여권을 찾지 못하면 휴즈 씨가 교체 발급 신청을 해서 예정대로 토요일에 비행기를 탈 수 있도록** 해야 할 겁니다.

콜린 그레이 [오후 1:58]
네. 지금 선물 가게에서 확인 중입니다.

콜린 그레이 [오후 2:24]
운이 좋네요! **165휴즈 씨가 여권을 찾았어요.** 저녁 식사 때 레스토랑에서 뵙겠습니다.

율라 워렌 [오후 2:25]
다행입니다. **166하지만 지금 관광버스가 가벼운 교통 체증에 걸렸어요.** 두 분이 지금 바로 지하철을 탈 수 있다면 저희를 따라잡을 수 있을 거예요.

콜린 그레이 [오후 2:26]
오, 잘됐네요. 그렇게 할게요. 플레밍 어드벤처 담당자에게는 알리셨나요?

율라 워렌 [오후 2:26]
지금 알릴게요.

콜린 그레이 [오후 2:27]
타비사 씨, 오늘은 저희가 늦어지고 있네요. 3시 15분까지 부두에 닿지 못할 것 같아요.

타비사 페리 [오후 2:31]
안녕하세요, 율라 씨. 괜찮습니다. 오늘은 그다지 바쁘지 않습니다. **167저녁에 파도가 거세지기 전에 모든 일정을 마칠 수 있을 정도로만 도착하셨으면 좋겠네요.**

어휘 passport 여권 for a while 잠시 동안 go ahead 앞서 가다 rest 나머지 turn up (잃어버린 물건 등이) 나타나다 apply for ~을 신청하다 replacement 교체[대체]물 relief 안도 run into traffic 교통 체증에 걸리다 catch up with ~를 따라잡다 run late 늦어지다 pier 부두 rough 거친, 파도가 심한

164 세부 사항

번역 휴즈 씨는 토요일에 무엇을 할 예정인가?
(A) 박물관 관람
(B) 숙소 체크인
(C) 수상 스포츠 강좌 참석
(D) 출국

해설 워렌 씨의 첫 대사에서 '휴즈 씨가 예정대로 토요일에 비행기를 탈 수 있도록 해야 한다'고 했다. 따라서 정답은 (D)이다.

어휘 be scheduled to+동사원형 ~할 예정이다 explore 탐험하다
lodging 임시 숙소 depart 떠나다

165 의도 파악

번역 오후 2시 24분에 그레이 씨가 "운이 좋네요"라고 쓸 때, 그 의도는 무엇인가?
(A) 신청 건이 승인됐다.
(B) 상점에서 특정 유형의 상품을 판매한다.
(C) 업체에서 신분증을 받아줄 것이다.
(D) 잃어버렸던 물건을 찾았다.

해설 '운이 좋네요'라고 말한 후 다음 문장에서 '휴즈 씨가 여권을 찾았어요'라고 했다. 여권을 찾아서 다행이라는 의미이므로 정답은 (D)이다.

어휘 application 신청, 지원 grant 승인하다 merchandise 상품
accept 수락하다 a form of identification 신분증 misplaced
제자리에 두지 않아 찾지 못하는 locate 위치를 파악하다

166 세부 사항

번역 휴즈 씨가 오늘 투어 그룹의 나머지 인원과 다르게 할 일은?
(A) 다른 종류의 교통편을 이용할 것이다.
(B) 다음 활동에 참여하지 않을 것이다.
(C) 저녁 식사를 나중에 할 것이다.
(D) 명소를 무료로 관람할 것이다.

해설 2시 25분에 워렌 씨가 '관광버스가 교통 체증에 걸렸으므로 두 사람이 지하철을 탈 것'을 권하고 있다. 2시 26분에 그레이 씨가 그렇게 하겠다고 했으므로 정답은 (A)이다.

어휘 differently 다르게 means of transportation 교통수단
participate in ~에 참여하다 at a later time 나중에
attraction 명소 for free 무료로

167 추론 / 유추

번역 페리 씨는 어떤 업체에서 일하는가?
(A) 해변 호텔
(B) 보트 투어 업체
(C) 캠핑장 운영자
(D) 야외 음식점

해설 대화 마지막 페리 씨의 말에서 '저녁에 파도가 거세지기 전에 모든 일정을 마칠 수 있을 정도로만 도착하셨으면 좋겠다'고 했다. 따라서 정답은 (B)이다.

어휘 seaside 해변 campground 캠핑장 operator 특정한 사업을 하는 사람[회사] outdoor 야외의

168 -171 이메일

수신: 수신자 미공개
발신: 테일러 딜(diehlt@brantleyinc.com)
날짜: 3월 2일
제목: 안녕하세요

브랜틀리 주식회사를 대표하여 여러분의 입사를 환영합니다. **168**우리는 실험실 시료의 시험과 분석에 있어 정확성 및 효율성을 얻고자 노력하고 있습니다. 이런 점에서 여러분은 중요한 역할을 하게 될 것입니다. 각 팀장들이 곧 여러분에게 연락을 취해 추가 오리엔테이션 자료를 제공할 것입니다. 자료는 우리의 정책과 기대를 **169**철저히 이해하는 데 도움이 될 것입니다. 그동안 저는 여러 동으로 구성된 단지의 주요 장소들에 대해 요약해 드리고자 합니다.

여러분 전원은 회사의 중심부인 딜라노 타워에 배치됩니다. 추가 장비는 스토크스 빌딩 창고에서 조달할 수 있지만 미리 요청서를 작성해야 합니다. 안전 문제가 생기면 **170**엘리엇 빌딩에 현장 간호사가 있습니다. 이 건물은 보안 사무실이 있는 곳이기도 합니다. 급여 및 혜택에 관한 문의사항은 바인 홀(내선 번호 300)에 위치한 재무 부서에서 처리합니다.

자차로 출근하려면 부지 내 주차장 중 한 곳에 차량을 세워두기 위한 **171**주차권이 필요합니다. 무료로 이용 가능하며 대기했다가 스티븐 라이터 씨(내선 번호 251)에게서 받을 수 있습니다. 전 직원은 사진이 부착된 신분증을 항상 패용하여야 합니다. **170**첫 출근일에 도착하자마자 보안 사무실에서 신분증을 받아야 합니다.

질문이 있으시면 언제든 저에게 연락하십시오. 여러분 모두에 대해 더 잘 알게 되기를 고대합니다.

테일러 딜
브랜틀리 주식회사 인사부장

어휘 undisclosed 밝혀지지 않은 on board 승선한 strive for ~을 얻고자 노력하다 accuracy 정확성 efficiency 효율성 analysis 분석 laboratory sample 실험용 시료 play an important role 중요한 역할을 하다 in this regard 이런 점에서 individual 각각의 further 추가의 have a sound understanding of ~를 철저히 이해하다 policy 정책 expectation 기대, 예상 in the meantime 그동안 summarize 요약하다 complex 단지 station 배치하다 procure 구하다, 입수하다 make a request 요청하다 in advance 미리 safety issue 안전 문제 on-site 현장의 regarding ~에 관해 payroll 급여 extension number 내선 번호 at no cost 공짜로 pending ~을 기다리는 동안 availability 이용 가능성 obtain 얻다 at all times 항상

168 추론 / 암시

번역 이 이메일의 수신자들은 누구일 것 같은가?
(A) 방문한 감독관
(B) 실험실 기사
(C) 창고 직원
(D) 취업 지원자

해설 두 번째 문장(We strive for ~ in this regard)을 통해 누구를 대상으로 쓴 글인지를 알 수 있다. 내용을 살펴보면 '실험실, 시험과 분석'이라는 말과 '중요한 역할을 하게 될 것'이라는 말을 통해서 정답이 (B)라는 것을 알 수 있다.

169 동의어 찾기

번역 첫 번째 단락 4행의 "sound"와 의미가 가장 가까운 것은?
(A) 긍정적인
(B) 철저한
(C) 오래 가는
(D) 시끄러운

해설 형용사 sound는 의미 중 명사 앞에만 쓰면서 '철저한'이라는 뜻으로 쓰이는 경우가 있다. 여기서처럼 a sound knowledge, a sound understanding으로 쓰이는 경우가 대표적이다. 따라서 정답은 (B)이다.

170 세부 사항

번역 수신자들은 단지에 도착하는 즉시 어디로 가야 하는가?
(A) 딜라노 타워
(B) 스토크스 빌딩
(C) 엘리엇 빌딩
(D) 바인 홀

해설 세 번째 단락 마지막 줄을 보면 첫날 출근하자마자 보안 사무실에 들러야 한다는 말이 있고, 그 보안 사무실의 위치는 두 번째 단락 중간 부분에서 엘리엇 빌딩이라는 사실을 확인할 수 있다. 따라서 정답은 (C)이다.

171 세부 사항

번역 라이터 씨는 무슨 일을 맡고 있는가?
(A) 오리엔테이션 자료 배부
(B) 급여 관련 질문에 응답
(C) 주차권 발행
(D) 안전교육 실시

해설 라이터 씨에 대한 정보는 세 번째 단락 두 번째 줄에서 확인할 수 있다. 자동차를 이용하여 출근할 시 주차권이 필요하며, 이를 라이터 씨에게서 받을 수 있다는 내용이 나온다. 따라서 정답은 (C)이다.

172-175 기사

닐렛 (1월 31일) – **172**밀스 스트리트 중 한 구획의 주민들은 유명 내비게이션 앱인 '나베가'가 인근에 미치는 영향에 대해 불만을 토로하고 있다.

피해 가구 주민 중 한 명인 달린 리드 씨는 어제 시의회 회의에서의 상황에 대해 이야기했다. 리드 씨는 해당 앱이 운전자들에게 혼잡 시간대에 급경사가 있는

가파른 언덕을 지나야 한다는 사실을 고지하지 않은 채 밀스 스트리트 쪽으로 안내하고 있다고 밝혔다.

리드 씨는 그 앱이 11월에 출시된 이래 거의 한 주에 한 번꼴로 밀스 스트리트에서 차량 관련 문제가 발생했다고 주장했다. **173**그녀는 "자동차들이 저희 집 울타리 일부와 이웃의 우편함을 들이받았습니다."라고 말했다.

174밀스 스트리트는 닐렛 시의 가파른 다른 도로인 터커 스트리트나 하웰 드라이브만큼 잘 알려져 있지는 않지만 시에서 가장 경사가 심한 도로로 손꼽힌다. 언덕 꼭대기가 매우 짧기도 해서 꼭대기에 있는 교차로에 멈춰 선 운전자들은 진입하게 될 지역을 잘 볼 수가 없다.

밀스 스트리트 주민들이 해당 문제와 관련해 나베가를 개발한 채비시라는 업체에 연락을 취해 봤지만 그들의 불만 사항이 묵살됐다고 리드 씨는 밝혔다. 이에 따라 리드 씨와 다른 주택 소유주들은 시에 조치를 취해 줄 것을 요청하고 있다.

175리드 씨가 제안한 방안 중 하나는 밀스 스트리트를 서쪽으로 가는 일방통행로로 만들어 뉴먼 애비뉴로 가는 지름길로 사용되는 것을 막자는 내용이다. 또 다른 방안은 출퇴근 혼잡 시간대에는 시더 로드에서 좌회전해 들어오는 것을 금지하는 것이다.

시 의회 의원들은 교통부에서 이 문제를 조사하도록 지시하겠다고 약속했다.

어휘 resident 주민 section 구간 effect 영향 neighborhood 인근 homeowner 주택 소유주 affect 영향을 주다 city council 시 의회 rush hour 혼잡 시간대 steep 가파른 sharp (변화가) 급격한 incline 경사 claim 주장하다 related 관련된 nearly 거의 release 출시하다 fence 울타리 knock down ~를 치다, 때려눕히다 in fact 사실상 crest 산마루 intersection 교차로 peak 꼭대기 contact 연락하다 develop 개발하다 complaint 불평, 항의 ignore 무시하다 therefore 그러므로 take action 조치를 취하다 one-way 일방통행의 head 향하다 thus 그러므로 discourage 막다 shortcut 지름길 direct 지시하다, 명령하다

172 글의 주제 / 목적

번역 기사를 쓴 목적은 무엇인가?
(A) 정치인의 경력을 개괄적으로 설명하기 위해
(B) 곧 있을 시 프로젝트를 설명하기 위해
(C) 지역 문제에 관심을 불러 모으기 위해
(D) 기술적인 진보를 촉진하기 위해

해설 첫 번째 단락에서 주민들이 유명 내비게이션 앱인 '나베가'가 인근에 미치는 영향에 대해 불만을 토로하고 있다고 했다. 따라서 정답은 (C)이다.

어휘 give an overview of ~를 개괄적으로 설명하다 politician 정치인 career 경력 upcoming 곧 있을, 다가오는 bring attention to ~에 관심을 불러오다 local 지역의 promote 촉진하다 technological 기술적인 advance 진보

173 세부 사항

번역 기사에 따르면 리드 씨는 시 의회 회의에서 무엇을 언급했는가?
(A) 채비시 본사에 가 본 적이 있다.
(B) 운전할 때 자주 나베가를 확인한다.
(C) 리드 씨의 이웃들은 교통 제안에 반대한다.
(D) 최근 리드 씨의 사유 재산이 피해를 입었다.

해설 세 번째 단락에서 리드 씨는 집 울타리 일부와 이웃의 우편함을 차가 들이받았다고 했다. 따라서 리드 씨의 재산이 피해를 입었음을 알 수 있으므로 정답은 (D)이다.

어휘 mention 언급하다 headquarters 본사 frequently 자주 oppose 반대하다 proposal 제안, 제의 private property 사유 재산 recently 최근 be damaged 손상되다

174 추론 / 유추

번역 닐렛 시에 대해 암시된 것은?
(A) 여러 개의 언덕이 있는 땅에 건립됐다.
(B) 11월 이후로 교통량이 증가했다.
(C) 일부 주요 도로는 일방통행로이다.
(D) 도시 공공사업이 효율적인 것으로 이름나 있다.

해설 네 번째 단락에서 터커 스트리트와 하웰 드라이브 모두 닐렛 시의 다른 가파른 도로들이고 밀스 스트리트 또한 시에서 가장 경사가 심한 도로로 손꼽힌다고 했다. 그러므로 정답은 (A)이다.

어휘 feature 특징으로 삼다　multiple 다수의　traffic levels 교통량　increase 증가하다　efficient 효율적인

175 문장 삽입

번역 [1], [2], [3], [4]로 표시된 곳 중에서, 다음 문장이 들어가기에 가장 적합한 곳은?
"또 다른 방안은 출퇴근 혼잡 시간대에는 시더 로드에서 좌회전해 들어오는 것을 금지하는 것이다."

해설 Another가 주어로 나왔으므로 해당 문장 앞에서는 한 가지 해결 방안이 언급되어야 한다. [4]번 앞 문장에서 다른 대안은 밀스 스트리트를 서쪽으로 가는 일방통행로로 만들자고 했다. 따라서 이 문장은 [4]번에 위치하는 것이 가장 적절하므로 정답은 (D)이다.

어휘 ban 금지하다　left turn 좌회전

176 -180 웹페이지+이메일

---

http://www.charterantiques.com/aboutus

차터 앤티크

회사소개

176(B)20년 넘게 로저 리치필드가 소유하고 운영해온 차터 앤티크는 경쟁력 있는 가격대의 골동품 가구를 보유한 동부 해안의 최대 업체 중 하나입니다. **176(C)**재고가 계속 변동되므로 정기적으로 매장에 들르실 것을 권장합니다.

골동품 판매: 모든 주문 건에 대해 무료 배송을 해 드립니다. **178**구매가 만족스럽지 않으실 경우 30일 이내에 전액 환불 받으실 수 있습니다. 제품은 고객이 비용을 부담하여 동일한 상태로 반품하셔야 합니다.

176(D)골동품 재단장: 아끼는 낡은 골동품이 있다면 저희가 원래 상태로 되돌려 드립니다.

당신의 골동품을 판매하세요: **177**로저(roger@charterantiques.com)에게 사진과 설명을 보내 주시면 얼마나 가치 있는 물건인지 알려 드립니다. (최종 제안가는 물건을 직접 보고 결정합니다.)

어휘 decade 십 년　competitively priced 경쟁력 있는 가격의　antique 골동품　inventory 재고, 물품 목록　constantly 지속적으로　encourage 장려하다　regularly 정기적으로　free delivery 무료 배송　full refund 전액 환불　in the same condition 똑같은 상태로　at one's expense ~의 비용 부담으로　refurbishment 재단장　description 설명

수신: 차터 앤티크 (inquiries@charterantiques.com)
178발신: 예 차오 <chaoye@premium-inbox.com>
날짜: 5월 20일
제목: 골동품 책상

관계자께,

5월 15일에 귀하의 매장에서 마호가니 책상을 구매했고 어제 집으로 배송되었습니다. 물건도 좋고 제 서재에 딱 맞는 크기라고 생각했었는데 **178**제품을 반품해야 할 것 같습니다. **179**안타깝게도 나무의 색조가 제가 기대했던 바와 달리 마룻바닥과 어울리지는 않는군요.

제가 이제 어떻게 해야 하는지 이메일로 알려 주십시오. 가능하다면 5월 24일까지 반품하고 싶습니다. **180**제가 주문한 교체용 책상이 그날 도착하는데 방에 두 개를 모두 놓을 공간이 없기 때문입니다.

예 차오

어휘 purchase 구매하다　return an item 반품하다　shade 색조　floorboard 마룻바닥　replacement 교체

176 사실 관계 확인

번역 차터 앤티크에 대해 명시되지 않은 것은?
(A) 지역 잡지에 광고한다.
(B) 20년 동안 영업해 왔다.
(C) 재고가 정기적으로 바뀐다.
(D) 가구 복원 서비스를 제공한다.

해설 다른 보기들은 지문에 언급되었는데 (A)만 언급되지 않았다.

177 사실 관계 확인

번역 차터 앤티크 소유주에 대해 명시된 것은?
(A) 물품 사진을 웹사이트에 게시한다.
(B) 다른 누군가로부터 업체를 인수했다.
(C) 가구의 가치를 평가할 수 있다.
(D) 다른 장소에 매장을 열고 싶어한다.

해설 웹사이트 설명 맨 처음에 소유주 이름이 Roger Litchfield라고 나와 있고, 마지막 단락에서 Roger에게 사진과 설명을 보내면 그 골동품의 가치가 어느 정도인지 알려 주겠다는 말이 나오는 것으로 보아 (C)가 정답임을 알 수 있다.

어휘 merchandise 상품, 물품　assess 평가하다

▶▶ Paraphrasing　지문의 he can give you an estimate of its worth → 정답의 He can assess the value of furniture

178 연계

번역 차오 씨에 대해 추론할 수 있는 것은?
(A) 차터 앤티크의 오랜 고객이다.
(B) 얼마간의 배송비를 부담해야 할 것이다.
(C) 전액 환불을 받지 못한다.
(D) 많은 골동품을 소장하고 있다.

해설 '차오'라는 이름이 나오는 곳을 찾아 보면, 이메일의 발신자임을 알 수 있다. 앞부분을 보면, 차오 씨가 구매한 책상을 반품하고 싶다는 내용이 나온다. 15일에 구매한 것을 24일까지 반품하고 싶다고 했으므로, 첫 번째 지문 중간의 규정과 비교해 보아야 한다. 30일 이내 반품 시 전액 환불이 가능하나, 반품 비용은 고객 부담이라고 했으므로 정답은 (B)이다.

179 세부 사항

번역 차오 씨는 구입한 물건의 어떤 부분이 불만족스러운가?
(A) 상태
(B) 모양
(C) 크기
(D) 색상

해설 이메일 첫 번째 단락 마지막 줄에서 '나무의 색조(the shade of the wood)'가 마룻바닥과 어울리지 않는다고 한 것으로 보아 '색상'에 문제가 있음을 알 수 있다. 따라서 정답은 (D)이다.

180 세부 사항

번역 차오 씨는 왜 처리가 빨리 끝나기를 바라는가?
(A) 여행 가기 전에 문제를 해결하기 위해
(B) 새집으로 이사가 용이하게 하기 위해
(C) 몇몇 손님을 위한 공간을 마련하기 위해
(D) 다른 배송품을 받을 준비를 하기 위해

해설 이메일 마지막 부분을 보면 대체 책상이 도착하게 되면 두 책상을 동시에 놓을 공간이 없다는 내용이 언급되어 있다. 즉 다른 배송품이 오기 전에 이전 물품의 반송 처리가 빨리 되길 바라는 것이다. 따라서 정답은 (D)이다.

181 -185 이메일+정보문

수신: 하미드 카선 ⟨h.kasun@fast-mail.com⟩
발신: 라이트 통신 ⟨accounts@wrightcomm.com⟩
날짜: 3월 10일
제목: RE: 계정 #49506

카선 씨께,

181라이트 통신 서비스를 3월 28일자로 프랑코 스트리트 672에서 올리언스 애비뉴 1051로 이전해 달라는 귀하의 요청을 잘 받았습니다. 귀하의 계정에 공식적으로 요청이 이루어졌으므로 고객님께서는 이제 더 이상 조치를 취하지 않으셔도 됩니다.

현 거주지에서의 마지막 서비스일은 3월 27일이며 신규 서비스는 3월 28일부터 시작됩니다. 서비스가 중단되지 않고 제공되는 것이므로 **182**패키지의 평상시 요금(49.99달러)이 청구될 것입니다. 문의해 주신 내용에 관해 답변 드리자면, 요금 청구 주기는 변동이 없습니다. **184**매월 5일부터 익월 4일까지로 동일합니다.

183아울러 회사에 휴대 전화를 반납한 후 다음 달 중으로 패키지에 휴대 전화를 추가하고 싶다고 말씀하셨는데, 이는 처리가 매우 쉽습니다. 참고하실 수 있도록 저희 패키지 목록을 첨부합니다.

라이트 통신을 이용해 주셔서 감사합니다.

난도 딜레온
계정 담당자, 라이트 통신

어휘 transfer 이전하다 officially 공식적으로 account 계정 further 더 이상의 at this time 지금[현재] 시점에서 current residence 현재 거주지 break 휴지 기간, 중단 bill 청구서를 보내다 regarding ~에 관해 inquiry 문의 billing cycle 요금 청구 주기 turn in 반납하다 attach 첨부하다 for your convenience 편의를 위해

라이트 통신 패키지 상품

패키지	서비스	월 이용료
Basic	인터넷	$39.99
T-Basic	인터넷 + 케이블	**182**$49.99
P-Basic	인터넷 + 전화	$54.99
Premium	인터넷 + 케이블 + 전화	$89.99

184청구서는 요금 청구 주기 마지막 날로부터 5일 후 발행됩니다. 고객 여러분은 저희 웹사이트 www.wrightcomm.com에서 신용카드로 요금을 결제하거나 라이트 통신 청구서 발부 사무소 사서함 1385, 블루밍턴, 인디애나주 47408로 수표를 보내 주시면 됩니다. **185**모든 수표 지불에는 2.99달러의 수수료가 추가되어야 함을 유념해 주시기 바랍니다.

어휘 monthly charge 월 사용료 issue 발행하다 make a payment 지불하다 check 수표 processing fee 수수료

181 글의 주제 / 목적

번역 이메일의 목적은 무엇인가?
(A) 체납 요금 지불 요청
(B) 신규 서비스 소개
(C) 정책 변경에 대한 설명
(D) 주소지 변경 확인

해설 이메일 맨 처음에 서비스 주소를 옮겨 달라는 요청을 받았다는 내용이 나온다. 따라서 이를 토대로 정답이 (D)라는 것을 알 수 있다.

어휘 policy 정책 revision 변경, 개정

182 연계

번역 카선 씨는 현재 어떤 패키지를 이용하는가?
(A) Basic
(B) T - Basic
(C) P - Basic
(D) Premium

해설 이메일 두 번째 단락 중간에 보면 평소 대로 49.99달러가 청구될 것이라는 얘기와 두 번째 지문인 정보문에서 49.99달러인 패키지를 찾아보면 카선 씨가 T-basic 패키지를 이용한다는 것을 알 수 있다. 정답은 (B)이다.

183 추론 / 암시

번역 카선 씨에 대해 추론할 수 있는 것은?
(A) 문의에 대한 답변에 만족하지 못했다.
(B) 그와 다른 고객이 공동 계좌를 갖고 있다.
(C) 패키지 축소를 고려하고 있다.
(D) 현재 업무용으로 발급된 전화가 있다.

해설 이메일 세 번째 단락 after you turn in the one from your company를 통해서 회사에서 받은 전화를 사용하다가 이번에 반납하려고 한다는 사실을 알 수 있다. 따라서 정답은 (D)이다.

번역 joint 공동의 downgrade (등급을) 격하시키다 work-issued 직장에서 발급한

184 세부 사항

번역 카선 씨의 다음 청구서는 언제 발급되겠는가?

(A) 3월 31일
(B) 4월 4일
(C) 4월 9일
(D) 4월 30일

해설 이 문제는 이메일과 정보문을 종합적으로 분석해야 문제의 정답에 도달할 수 있다. 우선 이메일 두 번째 단락 마지막 문장에서 청구 주기의 마지막 날이 4일이라는 점을 알 수 있고, 상품 안내 표 밑의 글 초반부에서 청구 주기 마지막 날을 기준으로 5일 후에 다음 청구서를 받게 된다는 것을 알 수 있다. 따라서 다음 청구서는 4월이고 일자는 9일이 된다. 정답은 (C)이다.

185 사실 관계 확인

번역 요금 결제에 관해 명시된 것은?

(A) 수표로 지불하면 더 비싸다.
(B) 처리하는 데 며칠 걸릴 수 있다.
(C) 전자로 환불이 가능하다.
(D) 지불이 늦으면 수수료가 발생한다.

해설 상품 안내 표 아래 제일 마지막 문장에 수표로 지불 시에는 수수료가 추가된다는 내용이 나온다. 따라서 정답은 (A)이다.

어휘 electronically 전자적으로, 컴퓨터로 refund 환불하다 incur (비용을) 발생시키다

186 -190 공지+이메일+기사

직원 공지: 포르투나 레스토랑 개조

3월 5일

포르투나 레스토랑은 건물에 야외 테라스를 만드는 건축 프로젝트를 진행할 예정입니다. 테라스는 레스토랑의 두 면을 둘러쌀 것입니다. 파슨 애비뉴 쪽에는 일반 고객 구역을, **189**캔터베리 호수 전경이 보이는 건물 남쪽에는 VIP 구역을 만들 예정입니다.

공사는 다음 주에 시작되며, **188**테라스 개장은 공사가 진행되는 상황에 따라 변동 가능하지만 잠정적으로 5월 26일로 잡혀 있습니다. 공사는 주로 건물을 둘러싸고 있는 **186(D)**덤불을 뽑고 **186(B)**석조 바닥을 깔며 철제 **186(C)**울타리를 세우는 일이 포함됩니다. 공사가 진행되는 동안 식당 뒤쪽은 폐쇄될 예정입니다.

협조해 주셔서 감사합니다.

어휘 undergo 겪다 construction 건축 outdoor 야외의 patio 테라스 property 건물 wrap 감싸다 regular 보통의, 정규의 with views of ~의 경치가 보이는 grand opening 개장 tentatively 잠정적으로 be scheduled for ~로 예정되다 be subject to change 변경될 가능성이 있다 depending on ~에 따라 progress 진행 (상황) surround 둘러싸다 lay 깔다 erect 세우다 rear 뒤쪽의 dining room 식당 close off 폐쇄시키다 cooperation 협조

수신: 수신자 미공개
발신: 비네이 나랑 〈v.narang@fortunarest.com〉
날짜: 6월 12일
제목: 포르투나 레스토랑

포르투나 레스토랑을 대표하여 여러분을 저희 레스토랑의 야외 테라스 개장에 초대합니다. **187**이번 매장의 변모는 귀사의 독자들의 관심을 끌 것이라 생각합니다. 행사 당일에 투어를 제공하면서 변화에 대해 더 자세히 말씀드리고 싶습니다. **188**행사는 6월 18일 금요일 오전 11시에 열립니다. 무료 음식과 사진 촬영의 기회가 제공될 것입니다. 또한 스테파니 곤잘레스 시장을 비롯해 시 공무원 몇 분이 자리할 예정입니다. 귀하의 좌석을 예약할 수 있도록 본 이메일 주소로 회신 바랍니다. 행사장에서 뵙겠습니다!

비네이 나랑
총지배인, 포르투나 레스토랑

어휘 undisclosed 미공개의 on behalf of ~를 대표[대신]하여 be of interest to ~에게 흥미롭다 take place 열리다 opportunity 기회 appearance 나타남 reserve a seat 좌석을 예약하다

근사하게 식사하기

조엘 고셋

여름이 한창 무르익었다. 도시 곳곳에서 야외 식사를 즐기기에 완벽한 날씨다.

린다스 카페: 잉그램 로드 922, 555-0196
한정된 예산으로 가벼운 식사를 하고 싶다면, 린다스 카페가 여름철을 맞아 훌륭한 장소다. 옥상에서 식사를 했는데 그늘을 드리우는 커다란 파라솔 테이블이 갖춰져 있다.

포르투나 레스토랑: 파슨 애비뉴 613, 555-0122
포르투나 레스토랑의 새로운 테라스에서 식사를 하면서 즐기는 **189**캔터베리 호수의 풍광이 아름답다. 메뉴는 경제적인 가격의 다양한 애피타이저와 주요리로 구성되어 있다.

펄: 엘크 스트리트 1705, 555-0164
훌륭한 서비스와 이국적인 요리가 있어 특별한 날을 위한 멋진 선택이 된다. 세련된 분위기로 **190**고급 식당을 찾고자 할 때 가장 먼저 선택하게 된다.

마르치니스: 16번 스트리트 1806, 555-0134
이탈리아 요리를 전문으로 하는 마르치니스는 저렴한 가격에 양이 푸짐하다. 야외 발코니 테이블은 낭패를 보지 않으려면 미리 예약해야 한다.

어휘 in style 거창하게, 근사하게 in full swing 한창 진행 중인 casual meal 가벼운 식사 on a budget 한정된 예산으로 rooftop 옥상 a wide selection of 다양한 appetizer 전채 요리 entrée 주요리 exotic 이국적인 special occasion 특별한 경우 sophisticated 세련된 atmosphere 분위기 fine dining 고급 식당 specialize in ~를 전문으로 하다 cuisine 요리 in advance 미리

186 사실 관계 확인

번역 리모델링 프로젝트의 일환으로 언급되지 않은 것은?

(A) 건물 지붕 확장
(B) 석조 바닥 설치
(C) 울타리 세우기
(D) 초목 제거

해설 첫 번째 지문 두 번째 단락 후반부에서 (B) 석조 바닥을 깔며 (C) 울타리를 세우고 (D) 덤불을 뽑는 내용은 언급했지만 (A)에 관한 언급은 없었다. 따라서 정답은 (A)이다.

187 추론 / 암시

번역 이메일은 누구에게 보내졌을 것 같은가?

(A) 식당 신규 종업원
(B) 언론사 직원
(C) 지역 시 공무원
(D) 건설 공사 인부

해설 이메일 두 번째 줄에 '독자들이 이 변화에 관심을 가질 것(will be interest to your readers)'이라는 말이 나온 것으로 보아, 독자층을 가질 수 있는 직업을 가진 사람에게 이 이메일이 보내졌을 것이다. 따라서 보기 중에서는 (B)가 가장 적절하다.

188 연계

번역 리모델링 프로젝트에 대해 암시된 것은?

(A) 두 단계로 진행됐다.
(B) 일시적으로 도로 폐쇄를 야기했다.
(C) 다소 지연됐다.
(D) 결과를 인터넷에서 사진으로 볼 수 있다.

해설 첫 번째 지문 두 번째 단락에서 5월 26일에 테라스 개장이 예정되어 있다는 얘기가 있지만, 두 번째 지문에서는 행사가 6월 18일에 열린다고 한 것으로 보아 테라스 개장이 지연되었다는 것을 알 수 있다. 따라서 정답은 (C)이다.

189 연계

번역 고셋 씨에 대해 암시된 것은?

(A) 포르투나 레스토랑의 VIP 구역에 앉았다.
(B) 친구와 함께 포르투나 레스토랑을 방문했다.
(C) 테이블 예약을 위해 555-0122로 전화했다.
(D) 현재 파슨 애비뉴 근처에서 근무한다.

해설 첫 번째 지문 첫 단락 마지막 줄에서 VIP 구역에서 캔터베리 호수가 보인다는 내용과, 세 번째 지문의 포르투나 레스토랑에서 캔터베리 호수의 풍경을 봤다는 내용을 종합해 보면 정답이 (A)라는 것을 유추할 수 있다.

190 추론 / 암시

번역 어느 레스토랑이 가장 비싸겠는가?

(A) 린다스 카페
(B) 포르투나 레스토랑
(C) 펄
(D) 마르치니스

해설 (A)에서는 한정된 예산으로 가벼운 식사(casual meals on a budget)를, (B)에서는 경제적인 가격의 애피타이저와 주요리(economical appetizers and entrées)를, (D)에서는 저렴한 가격(a low price)에 비해서 푸짐한 이탈리아 요리를 먹을 수 있다고 했다. (C)에서는 고급 식당(fine dining)이라고 언급하고 있기 때문에 정답은 (C)가 가장 적절하다.

191 -195 이메일+안내문+서식

발신: 더스틴 페인
수신: 영어학과 교수진
제목: 정보
날짜: 8월 15일
첨부: 설명, 서식 1, 서식 2

교수님들께,

대학 도서관에서 저에게 도서관 자료 구입 명목으로 우리 학과에 할당된 예산 중 몇 백 달러가 남아 있다고 알려 왔습니다. 남은 금액을 회계연도 말(8월 31일)까지 쓰지 않으면 향후 해당 목적으로 우리가 받는 금액이 줄어들게 됩니다.

191 따라서 여러분께서는 연구나 교수 활동에 유용한 자료의 구입을 요청해 주시기 바랍니다. **193** 한 분당 최대 40달러이며 요청서는 8월 28일 오후 5시까지 제출해 주십시오. 안내 및 필요한 서식들(서식 1 - 단행본과 미디어, 서식 2 - 연속 간행물)을 본 이메일에 첨부했습니다.

더스틴 페인
영어학과 관리자
그로리 대학교

어휘 department 학과 faculty 교수진 attachment 첨부 instruction 설명 library 도서관 notify 알리다, 통고하다 remain 남아 있다 budget 예산 allot 할당하다 purchase 구입 material 자료 fiscal year 회계연도 funding 자금 purpose 목적 shrink 줄어들다 therefore 그러므로 request 요청하다 acquisition 획득, 구입 research 연구, 조사 activity 활동 submit 제출하다 serial 연재의 publication 출판물

그로리 대학교 도서관
교수진 자료 구입 요청에 관한 안내

1. **192** 웹사이트에서 카탈로그를 검색하여 구입하기를 원하는 품목이 도서관에 없다는 것을 확인하십시오.

2. www.grawrylibrary.com/acquisitions/forms에서 정확한 요청서를 다운로드하십시오.

3. 서식을 작성하십시오. 원하는 품목에 대해 가능한 한 많은 정보를 적으십시오. 급한 요청 건인 경우 '의견'란에 이유를 설명하십시오.

4. **194** 도서관 연락 담당자로 지명된 학과 직원에게 서식을 제출하십시오. 해당 직원이 도서관으로 전달하기에 앞서 검토할 것입니다.

이 절차와 관련된 문의사항은 도서관 자료 구입 담당자에게 보내 주세요

어휘 confirm 확인하다, 확정하다 possess 소유하다 search 검색하다 correct 정확한, 올바른 request form 요청서 fill out the form 서식을 기입하다 include 포함시키다 rush request 서둘러 하는 요청 designate 지명하다 liaison 연락 담당자 review 검토하다 pass A on to B A를 B로 전하다, 옮기다 inquiry 문의 process 절차 be directed to ~로 보내지다 coordinator 조정자, 진행자

그로리 대학교 도서관
교수진 자료 구입 요청서
서식 1 (단행본과 미디어)

요청자:	오드리 메디나	¹⁹⁴제출처:	진 바우어즈
¹⁹⁴학과:	영어	날짜:	8월 27일
이메일:	a.medina@grawry.edu		

제목*:	시의 심리학적 접근	출판년도:	
저자*:	리 딕슨	출판사:	포테로 북스
판/연재:	초판	¹⁹³정가:	43달러
권수:	1		

급한 요청 건: 예 □ 아니요 ■

의견: ¹⁹⁵www.norris-rare-books.com에서 위의 가격을 찾았습니다. 다른 사이트에서 더 낮은 가격을 찾으실 수도 있습니다.

*필수 작성 항목

어휘 psychological 심리적인 approach 접근 poetry 시 author 저자 publisher 출판사 edition 판

191 글의 주제

번역 이메일을 쓴 목적은?
(A) 문제 해결을 위한 제안을 얻기 위해
(B) 수신인의 직무 책임을 명확히 하기 위해
(C) 수신인의 자원 사용을 독려하기 위해
(D) 절차의 개선 사항을 알리기 위해

해설 첫 번째 지문에서 확인할 수 있다. 두 번째 단락 첫 번째 줄에서 '연구나 교수 활동에 유용한 자료의 구입을 요청해 주시기 바란다'고 했으므로 정답은 (C)이다.

어휘 solicit 간청하다, 구하다 suggestion 제안 resolve 해결하다 clarify 명확히 하다 recipient 수신인 responsibility 책임 encourage 장려하다 resource 자원 announce 알리다, 발표하다 improvement 향상, 개선

192 사실 관계 확인

번역 안내문에서 교수들에게 무엇을 하라고 요청하는가?
(A) 자금 이용이 가능한지 확인하기
(B) 특별 소프트웨어 프로그램 다운로드하기
(C) 서점 여러 곳의 웹사이트 방문하기
(D) 도서관 소장 자료 검색하기

해설 두 번째 지문에서 확인할 수 있다. 웹사이트에서 카탈로그를 검색하여 구입을 원하는 품목이 도서관에 없다는 것을 확인하라고 했으므로 정답은 (D)이다.

어휘 available 이용 가능한 bookseller 서점 conduct (특정한 활동을) 하다 collection 소장품

193 연계

번역 메디나 씨에 대해 암시된 것은?
(A) 마감 시한을 지키지 못했다.
(B) 잘못된 서류를 작성했다.
(C) 서식에 필요한 정보가 빠져 있다.
(D) 요청 건이 지출 한도를 초과한다.

해설 첫 번째 지문 이메일 두 번째 단락 첫 부분에서 비용은 한 사람당 최대 40달러까지라는 내용이 나온다. 세 번째 지문 신청서 내용을 보면 가격이 43달러로 비용이 3달러 초과됐음을 알 수 있다. 따라서 정답은 (D)이다.

어휘 meet a deadline 마감 시한을 지키다 fill out 작성하다 exceed 초과하다 spending limit 지출 한도

194 연계

번역 바우어즈 씨는 누구일 것 같은가?
(A) 영어학과 직원
(B) 도서관 자료 구입 담당자
(C) 서점 영업 사원
(D) 도서 저자

해설 두 번째 지문 4번에서 도서관 연락 담당자로 지명된 학과 직원에게 서식을 제출하라고 하였고, 세 번째 지문 왼쪽에 해당 부서는 '영어'이고, 오른쪽에 제출처는 바우어즈 씨임을 확인할 수 있다. 이를 통해 바우어즈 씨가 영어학과 직원임을 알 수 있으므로 정답은 (A)이다.

어휘 sales associate 영업 사원

195 동의어 찾기

번역 서식에서 두 번째 단락 7행의 "better"와 의미가 가장 가까운 단어는?

해설 앞 문장에서 가격에 대해 언급하였고 다른 사이트에서 'better one'을 찾으실 수도 있다고 하였다. 그러므로 better는 가격이 좀 더 저렴하다는 의미임을 알 수 있다. 따라서 정답은 (A) more affordable이다.

어휘 affordable 가격이 알맞은 skilled 숙련된 tidy 깔끔한

루이 브라이언트 감독의 최신작들

〈바다 건너서〉: 동명의 소설을 원작으로 한 영화 〈바다 건너서〉는 지금까지 가장 돈을 많이 벌어들인 액션 영화 중 하나다. **196**17세기 후반을 배경으로 한 이 영화는 코리 언더우드가 왕의 환심을 사려는 말썽 많은 해적으로 주연을 맡았다.

〈손힐의 동틀 무렵〉: **196**엘리자베스 시대를 배경으로 하여 비평가들의 극찬을 받은 이 조용한 사극은 빈곤에 허덕이는 가족의 모습을 그렸다. 브라이언트 감독은 모든 측면에서 정확성을 기하기 위해 **200**영국 역사에 관해 선두적인 학자들에게 자문을 구했다.

〈얼어붙은 보도〉: 코리 언더우드 주연의 액션 영화로 뉴욕 엘리트 계층을 위협하는 범인을 추적하는 **196,197**1920년대 탐정의 삶을 그렸다. 이 영화는 비평가들로부터 호평을 받았으며 수많은 상을 수상한 작품이다.

〈우리가 그곳에 있었다〉: **196,197**스페인 내전(1936~1939년) 당시 군 생활을 묘사한 〈우리가 그곳에 있었다〉는 시사점이 많은 대사와 더불어 액션이 넘쳐나는 장면들을 보여 준다. 주인공 역할은 코리 언더우드와 팻 애비스가 맡아 능숙란하게 연기했으며 이들에게 각각 남우주연상과 남우조연상을 안겨준 작품이다.

베니토 지오다노, 소유주

어휘 recent 최근의 highest-grossing 돈을 가장 많이 벌어들인 to date 지금까지 mischievous 짓궂은 pirate 해적 win one's favor ~의 환심을 사다 critically acclaimed 비평가들의 극찬을 받은 historical drama 사극 struggle with ~와의 투쟁 poverty 가난 seek advice 조언을 구하다 scholar 학자 accuracy 정확성 in all aspects of ~의 모든 측면에서 pavement 보도 star 주연을 맡다 detective 탐정 criminal 범인 threaten 위협하다 rave review 호평 numerous 수많은 depict 묘사하다 action-packed 액션으로 가득한 alongside ~와 함께 thought-provoking 시사하는 바가 많은, 생각을 하게 하는 lead role 주연 masterfully 능숙란하게 respectively 각각

---

http://www.channel9guide.com

홈	방영 중	편성표	연락처

9번 채널 편성표: 4월 10일

〈세계여 깨어나라!〉   오전 6:30
진행자 제니 커크랜드가 화장품에서 사진에 이르기까지 집에 있는 모든 것의 정리 요령을 살펴본다.

〈뮤직 스포트라이트〉   오전 8:00
198페루의 전통 음악에 관한 방영 시리즈의 최신 회. 이번 주에는 만타로 밸리가 등장한다.

〈맞서는 의견들〉   오전 9:00
새로운 시간대로 옮긴 이 활기찬 토크쇼에서는 최근의 대통령 선거 토론을 다룬다.

〈무대 뒤에서〉   오전 10:00
수상 경력이 있는 루이 브라이언트 감독이 **197**군인에 대한 그의 최신 영화의 기획과 준비 과정을 털어 놓는다.

다음 페이지 →

어휘 explore 탐구하다, 분석하다 organization 정리 feature ~가 나오다 time slot 시간대 presidential debate 대통령 선거 토론 award-winning 상을 받은

수신: 〈feedback@channel9guide.com〉
발신: 러셀 데이븐포트 〈davenportr@bb-inbox.com〉
날짜: 4월 11일
제목: 9번 채널 프로그램 편성

관계자께,

저는 9번 채널 아침 프로그램의 열렬한 시청자라는 사실을 알려 드리고자 이 메일을 씁니다. 프로그램 방영 시 항상 시간이 있지는 않습니다만, 루이 브라이언트 감독 인터뷰에 관심이 있어 어제 프로그램은 필히 시청했습니다. **200**저는 〈손힐의 동틀 무렵〉의 자문위원으로 일할 때 그를 직접 만나볼 기회가 있었는데, 인터뷰 진행자가 그의 개성을 훌륭히 잘 짚어냈더군요.

아울러 제니 커크랜드 씨가 진행하는 쇼에서 유익하고 흥미로운 주제도 항상 즐겨 보고 있습니다. **199**시청자들을 위해 훌륭한 프로그램들을 계속 제공해 주시기 바랍니다.

러셀 데이븐포트

어휘 make a point of 반드시 ~하다 capture 포착하다 personality 개성

196 세부 사항

번역 브라이언트 씨의 최근 영화들은 어떤 공통점이 있는가?
(A) 모두 비평가들에게 호평을 받았다.
(B) 모두 과거를 배경으로 한다.
(C) 모두 같은 배우가 출연한다.
(D) 모두 액션 영화이다.

해설 〈바다 건너서〉는 17세기 후반을 배경으로, 〈손힐의 동틀 무렵〉은 엘리자베스 시대를 배경으로, 〈얼어붙은 보도〉는 1920년대를 배경으로, 〈우리가 그곳에 있었다〉는 1930년대를 배경으로 했다는 공통점을 가지고 있다. 따라서 정답은 (B)이다.

197 연계

번역 9번 채널에서는 4월 10일에 어떤 영화를 언급했는가?
(A) 〈바다 건너서〉
(B) 〈손힐의 동틀 무렵〉
(C) 〈얼어붙은 보도〉
(D) 〈우리가 그곳에 있었다〉

해설 두 번째 지문 오전 10시에 예정된 프로그램(Behind the Scenes) 소개 글에서 루이 브라이언트 감독이 제작한 군인에 대한 영화를 언급했다. 첫 번째 지문에서 *We Were There*를 보면 스페인 내전 당시 군생활을 묘사했다고 나와 있기 때문에 이를 토대로 정답이 (D)라는 것을 알 수 있다.

198 세부 사항

번역 웹페이지에서 9번 채널 프로그램에 대해 명시된 것은?
(A) 〈세계어 깨어나라〉의 진행자가 최근 교체됐다.
(B) 〈뮤직 스포트라이트〉의 최신 방송분들은 모두 하나의 테마를 공유한다.
(C) 〈맞서는 의견들〉에는 초대 손님으로 정치인들이 나온다.
(D) 〈무대 뒤에서〉는 방영 시간이 가장 길다.

해설 〈뮤직 스포트라이트〉는 페루의 전통 음악에 관한 최신 시리즈물을 방영 중이라고 했으므로 정답은 (B)이다.

199 동의어 찾기

번역 이메일에서 두 번째 단락 2행의 "keep"과 의미가 가장 가까운 것은?
(A) 보존하다
(B) 계속하다
(C) 잡다
(D) 통제하다

해설 keep providing은 이 문장에서 '계속해서 제공해 달라'는 의미이기 때문에 continue라는 단어와 동일하게 사용할 수 있다. 따라서 정답은 (B) continue이다.

200 연계

번역 데이븐포트 씨에 대해 무엇이 사실이겠는가?
(A) 이전에 커크랜드 씨를 만난 적이 있다.
(B) 9번 채널을 매일 시청한다.
(C) 영국 역사에 정통하다.
(D) 그의 저서가 영화로 만들어졌다.

해설 이메일의 발신자가 바로 Mr. Davenport인데, 이메일의 중간쯤에서 자신이 Dawn at Sornhill에서 자문위원 역할을 했다는 말을 했다. 그리고 첫 번째 지문에서 Dawn at Sornhill 설명을 보면, 주요 역사학자들에게 영국 역사에 대해 자문을 구했다는 말이 나온다. 따라서 데이븐포트 씨가 영국 역사에 능통한 역사학자일 것임을 유추할 수 있다. 따라서 정답은 (C)이다.

TEST 4

101 (B)	**102** (C)	**103** (B)	**104** (A)	**105** (C)
106 (D)	**107** (C)	**108** (A)	**109** (A)	**110** (D)
111 (B)	**112** (C)	**113** (D)	**114** (B)	**115** (A)
116 (B)	**117** (C)	**118** (D)	**119** (D)	**120** (C)
121 (A)	**122** (A)	**123** (C)	**124** (D)	**125** (B)
126 (B)	**127** (D)	**128** (A)	**129** (B)	**130** (A)
131 (C)	**132** (B)	**133** (A)	**134** (D)	**135** (A)
136 (C)	**137** (C)	**138** (D)	**139** (D)	**140** (A)
141 (A)	**142** (B)	**143** (B)	**144** (A)	**145** (C)
146 (A)	**147** (B)	**148** (B)	**149** (B)	**150** (A)
151 (A)	**152** (C)	**153** (C)	**154** (A)	**155** (D)
156 (C)	**157** (A)	**158** (B)	**159** (A)	**160** (A)
161 (A)	**162** (C)	**163** (D)	**164** (B)	**165** (A)
166 (D)	**167** (B)	**168** (C)	**169** (B)	**170** (D)
171 (C)	**172** (C)	**173** (D)	**174** (A)	**175** (D)
176 (D)	**177** (B)	**178** (A)	**179** (B)	**180** (D)
181 (C)	**182** (D)	**183** (A)	**184** (D)	**185** (B)
186 (A)	**187** (B)	**188** (B)	**189** (C)	**190** (C)
191 (D)	**192** (A)	**193** (B)	**194** (D)	**195** (B)
196 (B)	**197** (D)	**198** (C)	**199** (C)	**200** (C)

PART 5

101 소유격 대명사

해설 'own(형용사) + savings(명사)' 앞에서 수식할 수 있는 대명사의 소유격을 고르는 문제로 (B)가 정답이다. own은 '소유'에 관한 내용을 강조하기 위해 쓰는 표현이므로 his savings와 his own savings는 같은 의미이다. 시험에서도 소유격 his 대신에 his own이 등장하기도 한다.

번역 윌릭 씨는 작년에 자신이 저축한 돈으로 작은 제과점을 열었다.

어휘 bakery 제과점 one's own ~ 자신의 savings 저축, 저금

102 상관접속사 _ either A or B

해설 'mail ~ or send ~'로 연결되어 있는 구조 앞에 나올 수 있는 상관접속사 문제로 정답은 (C) either이다. (A) neither는 nor와 함께 쓰인다는 것도 기억해 두자.

번역 의뢰인이 늦어도 다음 주 수요일까지 계약서를 우편으로 보내거나 스캔한 사본을 보내 주기로 동의했다.

어휘 either A or B A나 B 둘 중 하나 mail 우편으로 부치다 contract 계약(서) scan 스캔하다 copy 사본 at the latest 늦어도

103 전치사 어휘

해설 명사와 또 다른 명사(items) 사이에는 전치사가 필요하다. 주문 제작한 제품을 '제외'한 모든 상품에 대해 할인권을 사용할 수 있다는 의미가 되는 것이 적절하므로 '~을 제외하고'의 뜻을 가진 (B) except가 정답이다.

번역 이 할인권은 주문 제작한 상품을 제외한 모든 크레스트뷰 가정용품을 구입할 때 사용 가능하다.

어휘 coupon 쿠폰, 할인권 housewares 가정용품 merchandise 상품 custom-made 주문 제작한 item 물품, 항목

104 형용사 어휘

해설 Although가 이끄는 부사절에서 주어가 유명한 컬렉션 중에 하나이긴 하지만 주절에서 전시회는 매우 드물다는 내용으로 이어지는 것이 자연스러우므로 '드문'이라는 말이 들어가는 것이 가장 적절하다. 따라서 정답은 (A) rare이다.

번역 정 컬렉션이 그 박물관에서 가장 유명한 컬렉션 중에 하나이지만 작품 전시회는 드물다.

어휘 collection 소장품, 컬렉션 exhibition 전시, 전시회 urgent 긴급한 mistaken 잘못된, 틀린 wide 넓은

105 전치사 어휘

해설 '열차'라는 장소에서 판매한다고 할 때 그 장소에 맞는 전치사를 고르는 문제이다. 보통 자동차처럼 작은 공간에서는 '안쪽'이라는 개념으로 전치사 in을 사용하지만, 기차처럼 큰 공간에서는 그 공간에 '접촉'을 해서 혹은 '위'에서 행위가 일어난다고 생각하기 때문에 전치사 on을 쓴다. 따라서 정답은 (C) on이다.

번역 노스랜드 철도는 대부분의 열차에서 뜨거운 음료와 샌드위치를 판매한다.

어휘 hot drink 뜨거운 음료 most of ~의 대부분

106 동사 어휘

해설 빈칸 뒤의 전치사 with와 결합하여 '제공하다'라는 의미를 나타내는 동사를 선택해야 한다. 따라서 정답은 (D) supply이다. 나머지 보기 outline (개요를 서술하다), remind(상기시키다), introduce(소개하다)는 의미상 적합하지 않다.

번역 첨부된 소책자가 베스크 프린팅의 서비스에 관해 귀하가 요청하신 정보를 제공할 것입니다.

어휘 attached 첨부된 brochure (안내, 홍보용) 소책자, 브로슈어 supply A with B A에게 B를 제공하다

107 부사 자리

해설 빈칸 앞의 주어와 그 다음에 온 동사 사이에 들어갈 수 있는 품사는 부사로 정답은 (C) skillfully이다. 주어와 동사 사이에는 명사 (A) skill(기술), 형용사 (B) skillful(숙련된), 명사 (D) skillfulness(숙련)는 적합하지 않다.

번역 브릿 퍼니처의 최신 제품들은 전통적이면서 현대적인 디자인 요소들을 솜씨 좋게 혼합했다.

어휘 offering (판매하기 위해 생산해) 제공된 것 blend 섞다 element 요소 skillfully 솜씨 좋게, 교묘하게

108 명사 자리 + 수 일치

해설 delicate이라는 형용사의 수식을 받는 자리이기 때문에 빈칸에는 명사가 들어가야 한다. 그리고 문장에서 동사는 brings about이기 때문에 주어는 3인칭 단수 명사가 되어야 한다. 따라서 정답은 (A) balance(균형)이다.

번역 협상에 있어서 힘과 유연함의 섬세한 균형이 최고의 결과를 낳는다.

어휘 negotiation 협상, 교섭 delicate 섬세한 strength 힘 flexibility 유연함 bring about ~을 유발[초래]하다 outcome 결과

109 부사 어휘 _ 미래 시제와 어울리는 부사

해설 빈칸은 동사 무리에 끼어서 동사를 수식해 주는 역할을 하는 부사 자리이다. 따라서 부사가 '미래 시제'와도 어울릴 수 있는 의미를 가져야 한다. soon과 shortly는 '곧, 머지않아'라는 뜻으로 미래 시제 동사와 어울린다. 따라서 답은 (A) soon이다. 참고로 timely의 경우 in a timely manner[fashion](시기적절하게)라는 표현으로 쓰는 형용사이다.

번역 댈턴 보험사의 신규 지점 공사가 곧 완료될 것이다.

어휘 construction 공사, 건설 insurance 보험 complete 완료하다 timely 제때에, 적시에 highly 매우, 몹시

110 effect 관련 관용 표현

해설 effect와 관련된 표현 중에서 시험에 가장 잘 나오는 표현은 go[come] into effect(효력이 발생하다)와 be in effect(시행되다)가 있다. 약간 더 난이도가 높게 나오는 경우 여기서와 같이 '효력을 유지하다'라는 뜻으로 stay[remain] in effect가 나올 수 있다. 따라서 정답은 (D) effect이다.

번역 일기예보에 따르면, 자정까지 심각한 폭풍 경보가 발효 상태를 유지할 것이다.

어휘 according to ~에 따르면 weather report 일기예보 severe 심한, 심각한 storm warning 폭풍 경보 opposition 반대 practice 실행, 실천 contact 접촉

111 형용사 자리 _ 명사 수식

해설 빈칸은 동사 become 뒤에 보어인 형용사가 들어갈 자리이다. '차이가 뚜렷해지다'라는 의미가 가장 적절하기 때문에 (B) noticeable이 정답이다.

번역 분석가들은 두 브랜드의 품질의 차이가 시간이 지날수록 뚜렷해졌다고 말한다.

어휘 quality 품질 notice ~을 알아차리다 noticeable 뚜렷한, 현저한

112 소유격 관계대명사

해설 한 문장에 동사가 두 개 나오기 때문에 접속사가 있어야 한다. 접속사 역할(의문사는 모두 접속사 역할이 가능)을 할 수 있는 (B), (C) 중에서 앞의 선행사(commuters)를 받으면서 뒤의 명사 routes를 수식해 줄 수 있는 관계대명사 소유격이 적절하다. 따라서 정답은 (C) whose이다.

번역 오늘 야구 경기는 경기장을 지나는 통근자들에게 정체를 야기할 것 같다.

어휘 be likely to+동사원형 ~할 것 같다 delay 지체, 정체 commuter 통근자 route 길, 경로 stadium 경기장

113 be + p.p. + to부정사 표현

해설 문장에서 고객(customers)은 뒤에 있는 내용을 하도록 '권고 받는' 입장에 있기 때문에 의미상으로 수동태 표현을 써야 한다. 따라서 정답은 (D)이다. 참고로 'be advised to+동사원형(~하기를 권고 받다)'과 같이 수동태 뒤에서 to부정사를 취하는 표현을 기억하자.

번역 냄봇 전자의 고객들은 제품 보증 기간 동안 모든 영수증을 보관하도록 권고받는다.

어휘 customer 고객 retain 보관하다, 보유하다 receipt 영수증 the life of the warranty 보증 기간

114 부사 어휘

해설 보기의 품사는 모두 부사이다. 빈칸이 부사라면 이 부사의 역할은 앞에 있는 동사(be tracked)를 수식하는 역할을 한다. 따라서 '추적되다'라는 표현과 어울릴 수 있는 부사를 찾으면 된다. '정확하게 추적되어야 한다'는 표현이 가장 적절하기 때문에 (B) accurately가 정답이다.

번역 정확한 급여 지불을 위해 급여 규정은 직원들의 근무 시간을 정확하게 추적해야 한다고 명시한다.

어휘 ensure 확실히 하다 payment 급여 지불 employee 직원 track 추적하다 namely 즉, 다시 말해 enormously 엄청나게, 대단히

115 형용사 자리 _ 명사 수식

해설 정관사(the)와 명사(goal) 사이에 들어갈 수 있는 것은 형용사와 명사이다. 복합 명사가 되려면 의미가 통해야 하는데 (C) admiration이 들어가면 '존경 목표'라는 어색한 말이 되기 때문에 정답이 될 수 없다. 형용사 (A), (B) 중에서 (B) admiring은 '찬양하는, 감탄하는'이라는 뜻이 되기 때문에 어색하다. 따라서 '훌륭한'이라는 뜻을 가진 (A) admirable이 정답이다.

번역 그 자선 단체가 모금하는 자금은 모두 개발 도상국들에게 깨끗한 물을 공급한다는 훌륭한 목표를 위해 쓰인다.

어휘 fund 자금 charity 자선 단체 raise 모금하다 go toward the goal of ~라는 목표에 쓰이다 developing country 개발 도상국 admire 존경하다, 감탄하다 admiration 존경, 감탄 admirably 훌륭하게

116 형용사 어휘

해설 so that이라는 인과 관계를 나타내는 접속사가 이 문제에서 핵심 역할을 한다. 앞 문장과 뒤 문장이 인과 관계로 이어져 있기 때문에 빈칸의 힌트는 뒤 문장에서 찾을 수 있다. withstand는 '버티다, 견디다'라는 뜻으로 빈칸에 들어갈 수 있는 단어를 찾을 수 있는 단서가 된다. 따라서 '내구성이 있는, 오래가는'이라는 뜻의 (B) durable이 정답이다.

번역 이 테이블은 튼튼한 소재로 만들어져 있어 대부분의 일상용품의 무게를 지탱할 수 있다.

어휘 be made from ~로 만들어지다 material 소재, 재료 withstand 지탱하다, 버티다 mandatory 의무적인 durable 튼튼한, 내구성이 있는 grateful 감사하는 frequent 빈번한

117 명사 자리 _ 전치사 뒤

해설 전치사 뒤가 빈칸이므로 전치사의 목적어인 명사가 와야 한다. (D)를 제외하고 다 명사지만, 높은 평가를 줄 수 있는 주체가 나와야 하기 때문에 명사 중에서도 사람을 나타내는 명사가 와야 한다. 따라서 (C) critics(평론가들)가 정답이다.

번역 앨런 코로나도 감독의 코미디 영화 〈미즈 올슨〉이 영화계 평론가들로부터 호평을 받았다.

어휘 director 감독 favorable 호의적인 ratings 평가 the film industry 영화계 criticism 평론, 비평 critical 비판적인, 중대한

118 부사 자리 _ 형용사(분사) 수식

해설 stored(저장된)라는 과거분사를 수식해 주는 부사를 고르는 문제이다. '안전하게 저장된 파일'이라는 의미가 되는 (D) securely가 정답이다.

번역 모든 기밀 정보는 본사 건물에 안전하게 저장된 파일로 보관된다.

어휘 confidential 기밀의 store 저장하다, 보관하다 headquarters 본사 security 보안, 안보 secure 확보하다 securely 안전하게

119 동사 어휘

해설 repair, renovation처럼 '변화'와 관련된 일을 '겪다, 받다'라고 할 때는 동사 undergo를 쓴다. 따라서 정답은 (D)이다. 참고로 '수술을 받는다'고 할 때도 undergo surgery라는 표현을 사용한다. (A) commit은 '저지르다, 헌신하다', (B) establish는 '설립하다', (C) accompany는 '동반하다'라는 의미이다.

번역 시에 프로젝트에 필요한 금액이 충분히 모이면 도서관에 대규모 보수 공사를 하게 될 것이다.

어휘 once 일단 ~하면 set aside (특정 목적을 위해) 따로 떼어 두다 extensive 광범위한, 대규모의 renovation 보수, 수리, 개조

120 명사 어휘

해설 빈칸은 동사 다음에 오는 명사 목적어 자리로, 2억 파운드라는 숫자 표현 다음에 올 수 있는 말로 의미상 '입찰'이 가장 적절하다. 따라서 정답은 (C) bid이다. 또한 bid는 make a bid(입찰하다)라는 관용 표현으로도 쓰인다.

번역 거대 투자사인 베데라 홀딩스는 댄슬리에 있는 콘도미니엄 개발업체인 웨스텔크릭을 사들이기 위해 2억 파운드의 입찰을 했다.

어휘 giant 거인, 거물 make a bid 입찰하다 condominium 콘도미니엄, 아파트 development 개발지

121 전치사 어휘

해설 스프레드시트와 빈칸 뒤에 나오는 일정(a schedule)을 공유 폴더에서 확인할 수 있을 것이라는 의미의 문장이다. 따라서 두 단어를 '~와 함께'라는 표현으로 묶을 수 있는 (A) along with가 정답이다.

번역 수정 스프레드시트들을 소프트웨어 세미나 일정과 함께 화요일에 공유 폴더에서 확인할 수 있을 것이다.

어휘 available 이용할 수 있는, 구할 수 있는 shared folder 공유 폴더 notwithstanding ~에도 불구하고 other than ~ 외에

122 동사 어휘

해설 수익이 많이 나기 때문에 파트너십을 '어떻게' 하기를 꺼려한다는 문장에 적절한 동사를 고르는 문제이다. 문맥상 파트너십을 '끝낸다'는 의미인 (A) terminate가 정답이다. 보통 terminate는 계약을 종결할 때 쓰는 표현으로 자주 등장한다.

번역 메리맥 미디어의 중역들은 동업으로 얻는 수익이 많았기 때문에 동업 관계를 종료하기를 주저하고 있다.

어휘 executive 중역, 임원 hesitant 주저하는 partnership 동업 (관계) profitable 수익성이 있는 enable ~을 할 수 있게 하다 surpass 능가하다, 뛰어넘다 misplace 잘못된 곳에 두다

123 형용사 자리 _ 명사 수식

해설 give는 목적어를 두 개 취하는 4형식 동사로 them과 relief가 목적어 역할을 한다. 빈칸은 그 중간에서 뒤에 있는 relief를 수식해 줄 수 있는 형용사가 와야 하는 자리이다. '상당한 완화'라는 의미로 형용사 (C) significant가 정답이다.

번역 약물 실험에 참여한 많은 환자들이 그 약을 먹고 증상이 현저히 완화됐다고 보고했다.

어휘 patient 환자 drug trial 약물 실험 medicine 약 relief 완화 symptom 증상 signify 의미하다, 나타내다 significant 현저한, 상당한, 중요한 significance 의미, 중요성

124 동사 자리

해설 빈칸은 that 목적절의 동사를 찾는 문제이다. 전치사구 앞에 위치한 복수 명사 retailers의 동사로 (D) expect(예상하다)가 정답이다. 보기의 to부정사 (A) to expect, 명사 (B) expectations, 부사 (C) expectantly(기대하여)는 품사상 적합하지 않다.

번역 비공식 여론조사 결과 전국의 소매업자들은 긴 주말 연휴 동안 큰 매출을 예상하고 있다.

어휘 informal 비공식의 poll 여론조사 retailer 소매상 sales 매출, 매상

125 접속사 자리

해설 한 문장에 동사가 두 개 있기 때문에(is, justify) 접속사가 필요하다. 따라서 빈칸은 접속사 자리이다. (A) 전치사, (D) 부사는 제외된다. 음식이 맛있다는 내용과 양이 적다는 상충되는 내용을 연결해 주는 접속사인 (B) While(~인 반면, 비록 ~지만)이 정답이다. 참고로 while은 보통 '동시 동작'의 의미로 사용하지만, 문장 맨 첫 부분에 쓰는 경우에는 although와 같은 의미를 나타낸다.

번역 가든 비스트로의 음식은 맛은 있지만 양이 적어서 비싼 가격이 정당화되지 않는다.

어휘 delicious 맛있는 portion size 1회 제공량 justify 정당화하다 in spite of ~에도 불구하고 otherwise 그렇지 않으면

126 형용사 어휘

해설 명사 standards를 수식해 주면서 도로 안전에 관한 신뢰를 얻었다는 의미와 연관성을 가질 수 있는 형용사를 고르는 문제. 여기에서는 '엄격한 기준'에 부합했기 때문에 사람들의 신뢰를 얻었다는 것이 가장 자연스럽다. 따라서 정답은 (B) rigorous(엄격한)이다.

번역 펠프스 오토모티브는 엄격한 도로 안전 시험 기준을 따르기 때문에 신뢰할 수 있다는 명성을 얻었다.

어휘 automotive 자동차의 gain a reputation for ~로 명성을 얻다 reliability 신뢰성 standard 기준 road safety testing 도로 안전 시험 contrary 반대의 vague 모호한 fluent 유창한

127 명사 자리 _ 목적어

해설 동사 offers의 목적어로 형용사 generous의 수식을 받을 수 있는 명사를 고르는 문제이므로 정답은 (D) compensation(보상)이다.

번역 해당 분야에서 가장 재능 있는 화학자들을 채용하기 위해 골덱스 제약은 직원들에게 넉넉한 보상을 제공한다.

어휘 in an effort to+동사원형 ~하려는 노력으로 talented 재능 있는 chemist 화학자 pharmaceutical 제약(의) offer 제공하다 generous 후한, 넉넉한 compensation 보상 compensate 보상하다, 보충하다 compensatory 보상의, 보충의

128 전치사 자리 _ 명사 앞

해설 콤마 뒤에 주어와 동사가 나오고, 콤마 앞에 동사가 없는 구 형태이므로 빈칸에는 전치사가 들어가야 한다. 따라서 접속사인 (C) Though(~에도 불구하고)와 (D) In case(~할 경우에)는 제외된다. '짧은 시간을 고려해 보면'이라는 의미가 적절하기 때문에 정답은 (A) Given(~을 고려하면)이다. (B) Prior to는 '~에 앞서'라는 의미이다.

번역 그 광고 캠페인을 만드는 데 주어진 짧은 시간을 감안하면, 결과가 실망스러운 것은 놀랄 일이 아니다.

어휘 allow 허락하다, 용납하다 it is no surprise that ~은 놀랄 일도 아니다 result 결과 disappointing 실망스러운

129 부사 어휘

해설 파커 씨가 한 행동을 다른 관리자들은 할 생각을 하지 않았다는 의미가 들어가야 적절하기 때문에 '똑같이, 비슷하게'라는 의미의 부사 (B) likewise가 정답이다.

번역 파커 씨는 CEO의 생일에 선물을 가져왔지만 다른 관리자들은 그렇게 할 생각을 하지 못했다.

어휘 yet 아직 likewise 마찬가지로 still 여전히 instead 대신에

130 동사의 시제 / 태

해설 문장의 본동사가 와야 할 자리이므로 현재분사인 (B) withdrawing은 제외된다. 일반적인 사실을 제시하는 문장이므로 현재완료 시제인 (D), 주어

가 은행의 고객이므로 수동태 (C)는 적절하지 않다. 정답은 조동사 may와 동사원형을 쓴 (A)이다.

번역 러틀랜드 은행 고객들은 이 기계에서 수수료 없이 최대 1000달러까지 인출할 수 있다.

어휘 patron 고객, 단골 이용자 without -ing ~하지 않고 pay a fee 수수료를 내다 withdraw 인출하다

PART 6

131-134 설명문

> 냅 사의 커피메이커로 완벽한 커피를 끓이시려면 다음과 같이 손쉬운 설명을 따라 주세요. 물통에 원하는 높이까지 옆면에 표시된 컵 수만큼 물을 채워 주세요. **항상 병에 든 생수나 정수된 물을 사용하세요. 131이렇게 해야 불순물을 피하는 데 도움이 되고,** 커피 맛도 좋아집니다. 물이 정확한 온도로 데워질 때까지 초록색 버튼이 **132계속** 깜박일 것입니다. 플라스틱 거름망을 빼서 만들고자 하는 잔 수만큼 가루로 된 커피를 한 잔당 한 스푼씩 넣어 주세요. 그런 다음 거름망을 **133도로 꽂으세요.** 몇 초 **134내로** 우리는 과정이 시작됩니다. 이렇게 되지 않으면 거름망이 제자리에 잘 끼워져 있는지 확인하세요.

> **어휘** instructions 지시, 설명 brew (차나 커피를) 끓이다, 우리다 water reservoir 물통 level 정도, 수준 as indicated by ~에 표시된 대로 avoid 피하다 impurities 불순물 improve 개선하다, 개량하다 blink 깜박이다 bottled water 병에 든 생수 filtered water 정수된 물 heat 데우다 temperature 온도 remove 제거하다 basket 원두를 넣는 바스켓 scoop 한 숟갈[스푼] continuously (끊이지 않고) 계속 continual (끊어졌다 이어졌다) 계속 반복되는 check 확인하다 be clicked into place 제자리에 끼워져 있다

131 문맥에 맞는 문장 고르기

번역 (A) 전선이 젖지 않도록 주의하세요.
(B) 기기를 벽에서 몇 인치 떨어진 곳에 놔주세요.
(C) 항상 병에 든 생수나 정수된 물을 사용하세요.
(D) 두 컵에서 열 컵까지 고르실 수 있습니다.

해설 빈칸 뒤 문장에서 불순물을 피하는(avoid impurities) 데 도움이 된다는 말이 나오므로, 빈칸에는 '깨끗한 것'과 관련된 내용이 오는 것이 문맥상 자연스럽다. 따라서 병에 든(bottled) 생수 혹은 정수 처리가 된(filtered) 물을 사용하라는 (C)가 정답이다.

132 부사 자리 _ 동사 수식

해설 문장 구조상 until이 접속사로 쓰여 이후 새로운 문장을 이끌고 있다. 따라서 의미상 연관은 있지만, 앞 문장만 보고도 답을 찾을 수 있다. blink는 목적어가 필요 없는 자동사이므로 뒤에서 blink를 수식할 수 있는 품사는 부사이다. 따라서 '계속'이라는 의미의 부사 (B) continuously가 정답이다.

133 동사 어휘

해설 거름망을 바깥으로 빼내서 거기에다가 커피를 넣고 원래 있던 자리로 '다시 놓다'라는 의미가 빈칸에 들어가야 한다. 동사 return은 '(원래 있던 자리에) 다시 놓다'라는 의미로 쓰일 수 있다. 따라서 (A) return이 정답이다. (B) label은 '딱지[꼬리표]를 붙이다', (C) discard는 '버리다', (D) empty는 '비우다'라는 의미로 모두 빈칸에 적절하지 못하다.

134 전치사 어휘

해설 보기는 모두 전치사 역할을 할 수 있어서 명사 앞에 쓸 수 있는 단어들이다. 전치사 within은 특정 기간이나 거리 앞에 쓰여 '~ 이내에'라는 뜻을 나타내므로 빈칸에 within이 들어가면 '몇 초 이내로 시작할 것이다'라는 뜻으로 해석이 된다. 따라서 (D) within이 정답이다.

135 -138 편지

> 릭 웹 시장
> 시청 302호실
> 트윌링게이트, NL A0G 4M0
>
> 친애하는 웹 시장님께,
>
> 저는 시장님께 중요한 문제 한 가지를 알려 드리고 싶습니다. 시에서 최근에 벌이고 있는 관광 캠페인이 우리 도시와 아름다운 해안 풍경을 찾도록 많은 사람을 135**끌어들였습니다.** 하지만 해변을 찾는 방문객들이 땅바닥에 쓰레기를 버리고, 허가 없이 모닥불을 피우고, 개똥을 치우지 않는 일이 벌어지고 있습니다. 이런 136**행위들은** 모든 사람에게 이 지역을 불쾌하게 만들고 있습니다. 이 문제들을 해결할 수 있는 방법들을 정리한 목록을 동봉했는데, 137,138**그중 하나는 그저 쓰레기통을 추가로 마련하는 것입니다.** 이렇게 하면 시에도 비용이 많이 들지 않을 것입니다. 사실, 지역 업체들 중 하나가 쓰레기통을 기증할 수도 있을 겁니다, 제 제안을 고려해 주시기 바랍니다.
>
> 트윌링게이트 주민
> 리비 가이거 드림
> 동봉

> **어휘** mayor 시장 bring A to B's attention A가 B의 주목을 받게 하다 recent 최근의 tourism 관광(객) attract 끌어들이다, 유치하다 coastal scenery 해안 풍경 seaside 해변, 해안 throw litter 쓰레기를 버리다 unauthorized 허가받지 않은 build a campfire 모닥불을 피우다 clean up after one's dog 개똥을 치우다 behavior 행위 enclose 동봉하다 resolve 해결하다 trash can 쓰레기통 cost 비용이 들게 하다 donate 기증하다

135 동사 자리

해설 The town's ~ scenery까지 문장에 동사가 없기 때문에 빈칸은 동사가 와야 하는 자리이다. 따라서 동사가 아닌 (B), (C)는 제외. (A)는 능동태 동사, (D)는 수동태 동사이다. 관광 캠페인에서 사람을 '직접' 유치하는 것이기 때문에 능동의 개념이 와야 한다. 따라서 (A) has attracted가 정답이다.

136 명사 어휘

해설 빈칸 앞 These라는 지시형용사를 통해서 앞 문장의 내용을 받는 명사가 빈칸에 와야 함을 알 수 있다. 앞 문장에서는 해변을 찾는 이들의 잘못된 '행동'에 대해서 기술하고 있다. 따라서 (C) behaviors가 정답이다. (A) shortages는 '부족', (B) obligations는 '의무', (D) occupants는 '거주자, 점유인'이라는 의미로 모두 적절하지 못하다.

137 목적격 관계대명사

해설 문장 구조부터 살펴보면 두 개의 문장이 연결되어 있지만 접속사가 없다. 빈칸은 접속사 역할을 하면서 앞의 (a list of) ways를 받을 수 있는 대명사가 들어가야 하는 자리이다. 또한, 전치사 뒤에는 목적격 대명사가 들어가야 한다. 종합해 보면 관계대명사는 '관계'라는 말에서 접속사 역할을 하면서 말 그대로 '대명사' 역할을 겸하는 것이므로 관계대명사 (B), (C) 중에서 답을 찾으면 된다. 전치사 뒤에는 관계대명사 that을 쓸 수 없기 때문에 목적격 관계대명사인 (C) which가 정답이다.

138 문맥에 맞는 문장 고르기

번역 (A) 예를 들면, 깨진 유리병이 해안으로 떠밀려오고 있습니다.
(B) 심지어 몇몇 시 의원들은 그 지역을 방문해오기도 했습니다.
(C) 어느 쪽이든, 그것은 주민들에게 부당한 부담을 지우는 결과를 낳습니다.
(D) 사실, 지역 업체들 중 하나가 쓰레기통을 기증할 수도 있을 겁니다.

해설 앞 문장에서 언급한 그저 쓰레기통만 추가하면 이 문제를 해결할 수 있다는 내용에서 크게 벗어나지 않는 문장이 와야 자연스러운 정답이 된다. 그 방안이 돈이 그렇게 많이 들지 않는다는 내용이 이어졌으므로 '쓰레기통'에 관련된 내용이 나오면서 '비용' 부분에서도 부담이 되지 않는다는 내용을 뒷받침해 주고 있는 (D)가 정답이다.

139 -142 공지

> **새 정책 공지**
>
> 스카울 파이낸셜은 9월 1일자로 업무 공간 개인화에 관한 새로운 정책을 채택하게 됩니다. 정책의 주요 목적은 회사 자산을 보호하고 우리 사무실이 반드시 고객과 기타 방문객들에게 긍정적인 139**인상을** 주도록 하기 위한 것입니다. 140**그러므로,** 직원들은 가구나 벽면을 손상시키는 식으로 자신의 업무 공간을 변경하는 것을 금해 주시기 바랍니다. 141**지저분한 상태를** 최소화하기 위한 조치도 취해져야 합니다. 업무와 관련 있는 물건들은 가능한 깔끔하게 정리되어야 하고, 142**여러분의 사무실이나 칸막이가 공간 중 20% 이상을 개인 물건이 차지하면 안 됩니다.** 여기에는 사진, 장식용 조각상, 포스터 등이 포함됩니다.
>
> 8월 22일에 여러분 회사 이메일 계정으로 전체 정책을 발송했습니다. 그것을 꼼꼼하게 검토해 주세요. 질문 사항은 erika.strong@scoulfinancial.com으로 보내주시면 됩니다.

> **어휘** notice 알림, 공지 policy 정책 adopt 채택하다 work space 작업 공간 personalization 개인화, 인격화 as of ~일자로 property 재산, 부동산 ensure that 반드시 ~하게 하다[보장하다]

positive 긍정적인 **client** 고객 **avoid** 피하다 **modify** 수정하다,
변경하다 **damage** 손상시키다 **take steps** 조치를 취하다
minimize 최소화하다 **material** 자료 **organize** 정리하다,
체계화하다 **neatly** 깔끔하게 **no more than** ~만큼만 **cubicle**
칸막이 공간 **take up** (공간을) 차지하다 **address to** (주소) ~ 앞으로
보내다

139 명사 자리

해설 빈칸 앞에는 형용사 positive가 있고 뒤에는 전치사가 있으므로 빈칸은 명사 자리다. 따라서 정답은 (D) impressions(인상)이다.

어휘 impress 감명을 주다 impressively 감동적으로

140 부사 어휘

해설 빈칸 앞 문장에서 '고객과 방문객에게 좋은 인상을 남겨야 한다'고 했고, 빈칸 뒤 문장에서는 '개인 업무 공간을 변경하는 것을 금해 달라'고 했다. 따라서 두 문장의 의미를 가장 잘 연결하는 접속부사 (A) Therefore(그러므로)가 정답이다.

어휘 nevertheless 그럼에도 불구하고 additionally 덧붙여 rather 다소, 꽤; 오히려

141 명사 어휘

해설 빈칸은 to부정사의 명사 목적어를 찾는 문제로 앞 문장의 내용에 비추어 보면 '지저분한 상태'를 최소화한다는 내용이 가장 적절하므로 정답은 (A) mess(지저분함)이다.

어휘 mess 엉망인 상태 conflict 갈등, 충돌 lateness 늦음, 지각 spending 소비

142 문맥에 맞는 문장 고르기

번역 (A) 일이 잘되면, 올해 말쯤 우리가 30%에 이를 수 있을 것 같습니다.
(B) 여기에는 사진, 장식용 조각상, 포스터 등이 포함됩니다.
(C) 그러면 여러분의 상관이 새로운 업무 공간으로 안내해 줄 것입니다.
(D) 이들 전자 기기를 '절전' 모드로 해놓는 것도 역시 도움이 됩니다.

해설 빈칸 앞 문장을 보면 사무실이나 칸막이 공간 중 '20% 이상을 개인 물건이 차지하면 안 된다'는 내용이 나왔다. 따라서 빈칸에는 개인 물건에 관한 부연 설명이 들어가야 적절할 것이므로 정답은 (B)이다.

어휘 statue 조각상 supervisor 관리자, 상관 electronic device 전자 기기

143-146 이메일

수신: 머피 스위츠 세입자 일동 ⟨alltenants@murphysuites.net⟩
발신: 케빈 요시다 ⟨k_yoshida@murphysuites.net⟩
날짜: 5월 18일
제목: 보수 공사

세입자 여러분께,

머피 스위츠가 여러분의 생활 공간을 더 편안하고 쾌적하게 만들기 위해 이번 여름에 시급히 필요한 보수 공사를 하려 합니다. 저희는 세입자들께서 요청하신 **143**개선 사항 목록에서 몇 가지를 골랐습니다. 주로, 카펫을 바꾸고 벽면에 칠을 해서 공용 휴게실을 **144**보수할 예정입니다. **145**이 작업은 5월 20일부터 23일까지 일정이 잡혀 있습니다. 공사가 진행되는 동안 세입자들께서는 휴게실을 이용하실 수가 없습니다. 여름에 계획된 또 다른 작업은 수영장을 다시 칠하는 것입니다. 다른 회사가 **146**별도로 진행할 예정이라 작업 일정은 아직 잡히지 않았습니다. 참고 기다려 주셔서 감사합니다.

케빈 요시다 배상

어휘 tenant 세입자 renovation 보수, 개조 undertake 착수하다 much-needed 몹시 필요한 comfortable 편안한, 안락한 enjoyable 쾌적한, 즐길 만한 select 선발하다, 고르다 improvement 개선 사항 request 요청하다 community lounge 공용 휴게실 be scheduled for ~로 예정되어 있다 separately 별도로 patience 인내, 참을성

143 명사 어휘

해설 쉽게 생각하면 renovations와 관련해서 적절한 단어를 고르는 것도 문제를 해결하는 방법 중에 하나일 수 있다. 또 다른 방법으로는 뒤 문장을 보면 힌트가 나오기 때문에 이를 통해 유추해 볼 수 있다. 카펫을 바꾸고 벽을 칠하는 작업 등을 아우르는 단어가 빈칸에 들어가야 할 것이다. (B) improvements는 이전보다 더 나아지는 상태를 일컫는 단어로 '개선 사항'이라는 뜻이다. 따라서 정답은 (B)이다. (A) shipments는 '수송품', (C) regulations는 '규정', (D) transactions는 '거래'라는 의미이다.

144 동사 자리 + 시제

해설 주어 바로 다음이 빈칸이며 문장에 동사가 없다. 따라서 빈칸은 동사 자리이다. 그리고 '보수 공사'는 아직 시작되지 않았기 때문에 시제는 '미래'가 적절하다. 따라서 정답은 (D) will upgrade이다.

145 문맥에 맞는 문장 고르기

번역 (A) 이후에 저희에게 의견을 주셔서 감사합니다.
(B) 휴게실은 흔히 단체 모임과 회의를 위해 사용됩니다.
(C) 공사가 진행되는 동안 세입자들께서는 휴게실을 이용하실 수 없습니다.
(D) 따라서 일부 세입자들이 새로운 임대차 계약서에 서명할 예정입니다.

해설 보수 공사가 예정된 날짜가 나오고 곧바로 뒤에 나올 수 있는 내용을 고르는 문제이다. (A)의 '의견'과 관련된 내용은 앞에서 언급되지 않았고, (B) 휴게실의 용도와 현재 보수 공사와는 관계가 없는 내용이고, (D)에서 갑자기 계약서 얘기가 나오는 것은 적절하지 않은 내용이다. 따라서 공사가 진행되면서 발생할 수 있는 상황이 나오는 (C)가 정답이다.

146 부사 어휘

해설 다른 회사에서 '별개로' 진행할 것이라는 의미가 들어가야 문맥에 맞는 문장이 성립된다. 따라서 (A) separately(별개로, 따로)가 정답이다. (B) previously는 '이전에', (C) consistently는 '일관되게', '지속적으로', (D) urgently는 '급히'라는 의미이다.

PART 7

147 -148 안내문

147베프넥스 은행은 다음 조건하에서 미디어의 정보 요청에 협조하게 되어 기쁩니다. 질문은 언론 기관의 피고용인에게서 나와야 하며 제출자, 그리고 그 제출자와 연관되어 있는 기관의 이름이 포함되어야 합니다. 질문은 이메일을 통해 저희 커뮤니케이션부 communications@vepnexbank.com으로 제출해 주십시오. **148**커뮤니케이션부는 은행의 영업 시간(월~금요일 오전 8시~오후 5시)에 직원이 근무하며, 일반적으로 영업일 기준 이틀 이내에 응답할 수 있습니다.

커뮤니케이션에서는 고객 지원은 하지 않는다는 점을 기억해 주세요. 고객 서비스를 받으려면 이 페이지를 방문해 주십시오.

어휘 cooperate with ~와 협력하다 inquiry 질문 media organization 언론 기관 submitter 제출자 be affiliated with ~와 연관되다 submit 제출하다 be staffed 직원이 있다 hours of operation 영업 시간, 운영 시간 business day 영업일, 업무일 note 주목하다 obtain 얻다

147 글의 주제 / 대상

번역 이 안내문은 누구를 대상으로 하는가?
(A) 잠재적인 판매상
(B) 언론사 관계자
(C) 기존 고객
(D) 은행 직원

해설 지문의 첫 문장에서 '베프넥스 은행은 다음 조건으로 미디어의 정보 요청에 협조하게 되어 기쁘다'고 했다. 이 안내문의 대상은 정보 요청에 관한 '언론사 관계자'일 것이므로 정답은 (B)이다.

어휘 potential 잠재적인, (~가 될) 가능성이 있는 vendor 판매상, 판매 회사 the press 언론사 existing 기존의, 존재하는

148 세부 사항

번역 베프넥스 은행에 관해 명시된 것은?
(A) 지역 기관과 동업 관계이다.
(B) 최근에 새 부서를 만들었다.
(C) 실시간 대화 지원 서비스가 된다.
(D) 주말에는 문을 열지 않는다.

해설 첫 번째 단락 후반부에서 '은행 영업시간은 월요일부터 금요일, 오전 8시에서 오후 5시까지'라고 했으므로 주말에는 영업하지 않는다. 따라서 정답은 (D)이다.

어휘 partnership 동업 관계 live chat 실시간 대화, 라이브 채팅

149 -150 온라인 채팅

루이스 샌토스	오후 2:39
149내가 이메일로 보내드린 최신 4월 예산 보고서가 어떤가요? 모든 게 정확해 보이나요?	

젠 타이	오후 2:41
149당신한테서 아무것도 받지 못했는데요. 스팸 메일 폴더를 확인해 볼게요.	

젠 타이	오후 2:45
거기에도 없어요.	

루이스 샌토스	오후 2:46
이상하군요. **149**몇 시간 전에 보냈는데.	

젠 타이	오후 2:48
어떻게 된 영문인지 모르겠네요. 다른 사람들이 보낸 이메일 몇 통은 잘 받았거든요.	

루이스 샌토스	오후 2:49
아… 음, 당신이 언제쯤 그걸 검토할 시간이 있을까요?	

젠 타이	오후 2:50
4시 이후에나 돼요. **150**다가올 프로젝트에 대해 스타일스 씨와 회의를 하기로 해서 지금 나가야 하거든요.	

루이스 샌토스	오후 2:52
알겠어요. 한 부 출력해서 당신 책상 위에 놓아 둘게요.	

젠 타이	오후 2:53
좋아요. 돌아오자마자 살펴볼게요.	

어휘 updated 최신의, 갱신된 budget report 예산 보고서 correct 정확한 check 확인하다 happen 발생하다, 일어나다 have time to+동사원형 ~할 시간이 있다 review 검토하다 not until ~까지 안 되는 a printed copy 출력본 look over 살펴보다 as soon as ~하자마자 get back 돌아오다

149 의도 파악

번역 오후 2시 46분에 샌토스 씨가 "이상하군요"라고 쓴 의도는 무엇이겠는가?
(A) 파일 하나가 왜 삭제되었는지 모른다.
(B) 이메일 메시지가 도착했어야 한다고 생각한다.
(C) 문서의 내용 때문에 혼란스럽다.
(D) 자신의 이메일 계정에 접근하는 데 문제가 있다.

해설 '이상하다'는 말을 하기 바로 직전과 바로 직후의 대화 내용을 살펴보는 것이 이 문제의 핵심이다. 예산 보고서를 보냈지만 받지 못했다는 내용이 바로 직전 내용이고 자신은 보냈다고 말하는 부분이 바로 직후의 내용이다. 따라서 정답은 원래 왔어야 하는 보고서가 오지 않았다는 의미인 (B)가 정답이다.

어휘 delete 삭제하다 be confused by ~에 의해 혼란스러워하다 access 접근하다 account 계정

150 추론 / 암시

번역 타이 씨가 다음에 할 일은 무엇이겠는가?
(A) 회의 참석
(B) 재무 보고서 검토
(C) 책상 서랍 안을 찾아보기
(D) 프린터를 켜기

해설 본문 중간에 샌토스 씨가 '보고서를 살펴볼 시간이 있냐'고 묻는 말에 타이 씨가 4시까지는 안 된다고 하면서 스타일스 씨와 회의하러 가는 길이라는 말을 한다. 따라서 (A)가 정답이다.

▶▶ Paraphrasing 지문의 I'm supposed to sit down ~ need to head out now → 정답의 Go to a meeting

151 -152 회람

발신: 오예원
수신: 전 직원
제목: 공지
날짜: 9월 19일

151루비 밀러가 정보기술부에서 마케팅부로 자원해서 부서가 변경되었음을 전 직원께 알려 드립니다. '마케팅 혁신 전문가'라는 새로운 위치에서 루비는 새로운 마케팅 기술을 연구하고 필요에 따른 기술 채택을 감독하는 일을 책임지게 될 것입니다. 루비는 또한 시장 조사나 제품 출시 캠페인 기획 같은 마케팅 활동을 위해 헌신적으로 기술 지원을 하게 됩니다.

이 같은 변동은 9월 26일에 시행됩니다. 정보기술부는 루비의 후임자를 찾는 일을 이미 시작했고 10월 말까지는 이 자리를 채울 것으로 예상합니다. **152**그때까지는 세스 플레밍이 자신의 현 업무와 더불어 그녀가 했던 일을 맡게 됩니다. 이 변화의 시기에 여러분의 인내와 지원을 요청 드립니다.

어휘 hereby 이에, 이렇게 notify 통지하다 voluntarily 자원해서 reassign 새로 발령 내다 position 직위, 자리, 위치 be responsible for ~을 책임지다[담당하다] research 연구하다, 조사하다 oversee 감독하다 adoption (아이디어, 기술 등의) 채택 as necessary 필요에 따라, 필요한 만큼 dedicated 헌신적인 product launch 제품 출시 take place 일어나다, 발생하다 successor 후임자 fill (일자리에 사람을) 채우다 handle 처리하다 former 예전의 responsibilities 책무, 직무, 업무 patience 인내심 transition period 과도기, 변화 시기

151 글의 주제 / 목적

번역 회람의 주요 목적은 무엇인가?
(A) 부서 이전 공고
(B) 일자리 광고
(C) 우수 사원 수상자 프로필 소개
(D) 마케팅 캠페인 관련 최신 소식 전달

해설 지문의 첫 번째 문장에서 '루비 밀러가 정보기술부에서 마케팅부로 자원해서 발령 받았다'고 했다. 따라서 정답은 (A)이다.

어휘 publicize 알리다 transfer 이전 profile 프로필을 알려 주다

152 세부 사항

번역 회람에 따르면 플레밍 씨는 무엇을 할 것인가?
(A) 신규 채용 과정을 돕는다.
(B) 가끔씩 재택 근무를 하기 시작한다.
(C) 일시적으로 추가 업무를 수행한다.
(D) 10월에 다른 지사로 출장을 간다.

해설 두 번째 단락 후반부에서 '그때까지 세스 플레밍이 자신의 현재 업무와 그녀가 하던 업무를 같이 맡아 하게 된다'고 했다. 따라서 플레밍 씨가 추가 업무를 수행할 것임을 알 수 있으므로 정답은 (C)이다.

어휘 assist with ~하는 것을 도와주다 recruitment 채용 carry out 수행하다 duties 직무

153 -154 광고

아파트 임대

에딩턴 부동산은 크로셋 타워의 **방 3개짜리 널찍한 아파트**를 내놓게 되어 기쁩니다. 이 아파트는 5층에 자리 잡고 있으며 현대식 가전제품과 에어컨, 화상 인터컴 시스템이 갖추어져 있습니다. 크로셋 타워는 인기 있는 교외 지역인 빙엄 하이츠에 자리 잡고 있으며, 아마릴로 역에서 불과 몇 구역밖에 떨어져 있지 않습니다. 건물에는 지하 주차장과 옥상 정원, **153**세입자들을 위한 1층 체육관이 있습니다.

이 아파트는 1년이나 2년 단위로 임대차 계약을 할 수 있으며 추후 갱신이 가능합니다. **154**관심 있으신 분들은 에딩턴 부동산 웹사이트(www.edingtonrealty.com)에서 다운로드 받을 수 있는 신청서를 작성하여 현재 혹은 이전 집주인에서 신청자의 인품을 확인해 주는 문서와 함께 제출해야 합니다.

어휘 for rent 임대용 be pleased to+동사원형 ~해서 기쁘다 offer (매물로) 내놓다 spacious 널찍한 come with ~이 딸려 있다 appliances 가전제품 intercom 인터컴(내부 통화 장치) popular 인기 있는 suburb 교외, 근교 feature ~을 특징으로 하다, 구비하다 underground parking 지하 주차장 rooftop garden 옥상 정원 ground-floor 1층의 gym 체육관 tenant 세입자 lease 임대차 계약 renewal 갱신 interested 관심이 있는 complete an application form 신청서를 작성하다 downloadable 다운로드 받을 수 있는 submit 제출하다 previous 이전의 landlord 집주인

153 사실 관계 확인

번역 크로셋 타워에 관해 명시된 것은?
(A) 기차역 맞은편에 위치해 있다.
(B) 그곳의 아파트들은 크기가 세 가지다.
(C) 현장에 운동 시설이 갖춰져 있다.
(D) 5층짜리 건물이다.

해설 (A) 기차역은 건물에서 멀리 떨어져 있지 않다는 내용만 나오고, (B) 아파트 크기에 대한 내용은 명시되어 있지 않다. (D) 임대하는 아파트가 5층에 있다는 것이지 5층짜리 건물이라는 내용은 지문에 없다. 첫 번째 단락 마지막 줄 a ground-floor gym for tenants에서 정답이 (C)라는 것을 알 수 있다.

154 세부 사항

번역 입주 신청자들은 에딩턴 부동산에 무엇을 보내야 하는가?
(A) 추천서
(B) 입주 보증금
(C) 희망하는 임대료
(D) 은행 계좌의 입출금 내역서

해설 '보낸다'는 말이 질문에서는 send로 나왔고 지문에서는 마지막 문장에서 submit으로 표현했기 때문에 그 이후 내용을 살펴보면 된다. application form과 함께 an accompanying statement ~ verifying the applicant's good character를 보내라고 했으므로 정답이 (A)라는 것을 알 수 있다.

155 -157 일정표

메도우뷰 극장

주간 상영 일정: 4월 14일 금요일 – 4월 20일 목요일

제목	장르	오후 상영 (토/일요일만)	저녁 상영 (매일)	밤 상영 (매일)
조용한 외침*	스릴러	—	7:20	9:35
시카고 추격전*	액션	3:15	7:05	9:20
외계 대모험	가족	3:30	7:10	**156__**
위플 형제	코미디	3:20	—	9:15

155*13세 미만 관람객은 입장할 수 없습니다.

저희 매표소는 주중 오후 6시, 주말 오후 1시 30분에 문을 엽니다. 입장권 예매는 영화 상영 최대 1주일 전부터 하실 수 있습니다. **157**입장권 교환은 영화 상영 24시간까지 하실 수 있습니다. 입장권에 대한 환불은 되지 않습니다.

어휘 cinema 극장 genre 장르 matinee 오후 상영[공연] chase 추격, 추적 alien 외계의 adventure 모험 patron 손님 admit 입장을 허락하다 box office 매표소 weekdays 주중 purchase 구입하다 in advance 미리, 사전에 accept 받다, 수락하다 exchange 교환 refund 환불

155 사실 관계 확인

번역 상영 일정표를 보고 알 수 있는 것은?
(A) 영화 중 두 편은 장르가 똑같다.
(B) 〈위플 형제〉는 매일 상영하지 않는다.
(C) 영화 중 일부는 같은 시간에 시작한다.
(D) 어린이는 〈시카고 추격전〉을 관람할 수 없다.

해설 (A) 상영하는 모든 영화는 장르가 다르다. (B) 〈위플 형제〉는 밤에 매일 상영한다. (C) 동일 시간에 상영하는 영화는 없다. (D) 〈시카고 추격전〉은 표 아래 명시된 내용으로 알 수 있듯이 13세 미만 관람객이 입장할 수 없는 영화이기 때문에 맞는 내용이다. 따라서 정답은 (D)이다.

156 세부 사항

번역 밤에 상영하지 않는 영화는 어떤 것인가?
(A) 〈조용한 외침〉
(B) 〈시카고 추격전〉
(C) 〈외계 대모험〉
(D) 〈위플 형제〉

해설 일정표의 밤 상영 항목을 보면 〈외계 대모험〉을 제외하고는 모두 상영되고 있는 것을 알 수 있다. 따라서 정답은 (C)이다.

157 사실 관계 확인

번역 입장권에 관해 명시된 것은?
(A) 상영 당일에는 교환할 수 없다.
(B) 예매를 해야만 한다.
(C) 관람객의 연령에 따라 가격도 다르다.
(D) 관리자의 승인이 있어야 환불 받을 수 있다.

해설 일정표 마지막 부분에서 알 수 있듯이 상영일 24시간 전까지만 표 교환이 가능하다(up to 24 hours before the show)고 했으므로 정답이 (A)라는 것을 알 수 있다. (B)는 예매를 일주일 전부터 할 수 있다는 의미이지 반드시 해야만 하는 것은 아니다. (C), (D)는 지문에서 언급하지 않았다.

▶▶ **Paraphrasing** 지문의 accept exchanges of tickets up to 24 hours before the show → 정답의 cannot be exchanged on the day of the show

158 -160 이메일

수신: 메리 셸번 〈shelburnem@hilltopmfg.com〉
발신: 데일 캔트렐 〈cantrelld@hilltopmfg.com〉
날짜: 11월 17일
제목: 보건과 안전

셸번 씨께,

우리 시설이 11월 20일, 이번 주 금요일 오전 9시부터 **160**보건안전부의 점검을 받는다는 통지를 방금 받았습니다. 직원들이 모든 규정을 정확히 따르고 있는지 검사관이 확인하게 됩니다. 그래서 **158**모든 직원은 필요한 안전모와 장갑, 보안경을 반드시 착용하고 있기 바랍니다. 또한 파손되었거나 구식인 장비를 지니고 있는 사람들에게는 새로운 물품을 지급해야 합니다.

점검이 진행되는 동안 우리는 기계 일부의 가동을 멈춰야 하겠습니다. **158, 159** 그 시간이 얼마나 걸릴지는 모르지만, 근무를 안 한 시간만큼 나중에 초과 교대 근무를 배정해 주시기 바랍니다.

감사합니다.

힐톱 매뉴팩처링, 시설 관리자
데일 캔트렐 드림

어휘 notify 통보하다, 통지하다 facility 시설 inspect 점검하다, 조사하다 accordingly 그런 이유로, 그래서 make sure that ~ 반드시 ~하다 required 필요한, 필수적인 hard hat 안전모 safety goggles 보안경 issue 지급하다, 발급하다 damaged 망가진, 손상된 outdated 구식의, 낡은 gear 장구, 복장 shut down (기계를) 멈추다 overtime shift 초과 교대 근무 as necessary 필요한 만큼 make up for ~을 보상[벌충]하다

158 글의 주제 / 목적

번역 캔트렐 씨가 이메일을 보낸 이유는 무엇인가?
(A) 안전 기록에 관해 문의하려고
(B) 직원에게 할 일을 부탁하려고
(C) 안전 점검 일정을 잡으려고
(D) 연수 과정을 공지하려고

해설 이메일 내용에 따르면 직원들이 해야 할 일은 1. 안전 장비 착용, 2. 새로운 안전 장비 지급, 3. 초과 교대 근무 배정으로 요약할 수 있다. 이를 토대로 정답은 (B)라는 것을 알 수 있다. (A), (C), (D)는 본문에 나와 있지 않은 내용이다.

159 사실 관계 확인

번역 캔트렐 씨가 잘 모르는 것은 무엇인가?
(A) 점검 소요 시간
(B) 누구에게 문의해야 할지
(C) 일부 상품을 주문할 곳
(D) 발표 예정자

해설 두 번째 단락 두 번째 문장에서 이 문제의 답을 찾을 수 있다. 얼마나 오랫동안 기계 가동을 멈춰야 할지 모르겠다는 내용을 바탕으로 정답이 (A)라는 것을 알 수 있다.

160 문장 삽입

번역 [1], [2], [3], [4]로 표시된 곳 중에서 다음 문장이 들어가기에 가장 적합한 곳은?
"직원들이 모든 규정을 정확히 따르고 있는지 검사관이 확인하게 됩니다."
(A) [1]
(B) [2]
(C) [3]
(D) [4]

해설 검사관이 확인하러 나오는 것과 직원들이 규정을 지켜야 하는 상황이 자연스럽게 이어지려면 [1]이 적절하다. 그 이유는 앞부분에 inspect하러 나올 것이라는 말이 언급되었고 뒤 문장에서 직원들이 이에 따라서 안전 장비를 착용해야 한다는 말이 나오기 때문이다. 따라서 정답은 (A)이다.

161-164 문자 메시지

카푸르, 아밋 [오전 8:14]
나는 리터 애비뉴 구역에 있는 에버그린 공원에 있어요. 트럭의 짐을 어디에다 내려놓을까요?

울프, 일레인 [오전 8:16]
161우리 부스는 공원 반대편에 있어요. 차를 몰고 유니온 스트리트 구역으로 오면 좋겠어요. 우리는 축제 중앙 무대 뒤편에 있어요.

리베라, 프레드 [오전 8:19]
162물건을 내리는 데 도움이 필요한가요? 내가 지금 공원 사무실에서 전시 업체 통행증을 받고 있는데, 이후에 다시 부스에 가 있을 거예요.

카푸르, 아밋 [오전 8:20]
도울 사람이 있어요. 물건을 나르려고 내가 데이브를 데려왔어요.

리베라, 프레드 [8:22 a.m.]:
좋아요. 잘됐네요. 축제 하기 딱 좋은 날씨 같아요. 나는 나폴리 식당의 시연을 정말 고대하고 있어요.

울프, 일레인 [오전 8:23]
그래요. **163설립자인 안젤로 두카가 다양한 소스 조리법을 보여줄 거라고 들었어요.**

카푸르, 아밋 [오전 8:27]
우리가 축제의 나머지 부분도 시간 내서 볼 수 있게 조를 나눠서 교대로 일합시다.

울프, 일레인 [오전 8:29]
좋은 생각이에요. **164프레드, 돌아오는 길에 병에 든 생수를 파는 게 보이거든 좀** 사다 줄래요?

리베라, 프레드 [오전 8:30]
그럴게요.

어휘 lot 부지 unload 짐을 내리다 on the opposite side of ~의 반대편에 be better off -ing ~하는 게 낫다 drive over to 차를 몰고 ~로 오다 main stage 본 무대, 중앙 무대 pick up 받다, 찾다, 사다 exhibitor pass 전시[출품]자 통행증 be covered 필요한 것을 제공받다 carry 운반하다, 나르다 it looks like perfect weather for ~하기에 딱 좋은 날씨 같다 look forward to+명사/-ing ~을 고대하다 demonstration 시연, 시범 founder 설립자, 창립자 a variety of 다양한 work in shifts 교대 근무하다 bottled water 병에 든 생수 for sale 시판용 No problem. 문제없어요., 그러죠.

161 추론 / 암시

번역 부스의 위치에 관해 맞을 것 같은 것은?
(A) 리터 애비뉴 주차 구역에서 멀리 떨어져 있다.
(B) 허가를 받기 어려웠다.
(C) 공원 사무실 뒤편에 있다.
(D) 뜻밖에 변경되었다.

해설 처음 대사를 통해 에버그린 공원이 리터 애비뉴 구역에 위치해 있고 축제 부스는 그 공원 반대편에 위치해 있다는 점을 알 수 있어 정답을 (A)로 유추할 수 있다. 나머지 보기들은 본문에 제시되어 있는 내용과 일치하지 않는다.

162 의도 파악

번역 오전 8시 20분에 카푸르 씨가 "도울 사람이 있어요"라고 쓴 의도는 무엇이겠는가?
(A) 그는 부스가 악천후로부터 안전하다고 생각한다.
(B) 그는 전시 수수료를 이미 지불했다.
(C) 그는 리베라 씨의 도움이 필요 없다.
(D) 그는 교대 근무 일정을 이미 짜놓았다.

해설 바로 앞 문자 메시지에서 리베라 씨가 물건을 내리는 데 도움이 필요한지를 물었고 이에 대한 대답이 도울 사람이 있다는 내용이었다. 따라서 정답은 (C)이다.

어휘 assistance 도움, 지원

163 추론 / 암시

번역 두카 씨에 관해 무엇을 추론할 수 있는가?
(A) 그는 지난해 축제에 참가했다.
(B) 그는 글쓴이들의 동료였다.
(C) 그는 나폴리 식당의 주인이다.
(D) 그는 장식 기법을 시연할 것이다.

해설 8시 23분 문자 메시지에서 두카 씨가 the founder로 언급되는데, 바로 앞 메시지에서 언급한 나폴리 식당의 주인이라는 것을 알 수 있다. 따라서 정답은 (C)이다.

164 세부 사항

번역 리베라 씨는 무엇을 해달라고 요청 받는가?
(A) 트럭 이동
(B) 음료 구입
(C) 몇몇 상자 하차
(D) 지도 수령

해설 마지막 두 대사를 통해서 정답을 도출해 낼 수 있다. 울프 씨가 리베라 씨에게 생수를 사다 달라는 내용이 나오기 때문에 정답은 (B)이다.

165-167 웹페이지

---

http://www.uniquehomeinteriors.co.uk

유니크 홈 인테리어즈

"〈유니크 홈 인테리어즈〉 덕에 리모델링을 재미있고 손쉽게 할 수 있어요!"
– 팸 모건, 전문 디자이너

〈유니크 홈 인테리어즈〉는 전국에서 가장 인기 있는 실내 디자인용 **165계간지입니다**. 저희 잡지에 기고하는 이들은 업계의 전문가들이며, 매 호마다 다른 곳에서는 찾아볼 수 없는 유용한 정보와 창의적인 디자인 아이디어가 가득합니다. 한정된 예산으로 귀하의 공간을 개선할 방법뿐 아니라 **166(B)최신 유행 색상들도 알아볼 수 있습니다**. 매 호마다 인터넷에서 다운로드 받아 출력해서 멋진 DIY 룩을 연출할 수 있는 **166(C)벽화 견본들이 포함되어 있습니다**. 잡지는 또한 가구, 페인트, 가정용 소품 등 **166(A)정기 구독자에게만 제공하는 특가품들도 소개하고 있습니다**.

오늘 1년 정기 구독을 신청하세요!

167디지털 시험판 무료!* [선택]

인쇄판 단독 14.95파운드 [선택]

디지털판 단독 9.95파운드 [선택]

최고의 제안! 인쇄판과 디지털판 16.95파운드 [선택]

167*이달 말까지 다운로드 가능. 유효한 이메일 주소 필수.

어휘 unique 독특한, 특별한 interior 실내, 내부 popular 인기 있는 quarterly magazine 계간지 contributor 기고자 expert 전문가 issue (잡지의) 호 be packed with ~로 가득하다 creative 창의적인 find out about ~에 관해 알아보다 A as well as B B뿐 아니라 A도 upgrade 개선하다, 업그레이드하다 on a budget 한정된 예산으로 come with ~가 딸려 있다 template 견본, 형판 wall painting 벽화 DIY 본인이 직접 만드는(= do-it-yourself) feature 특집으로 싣다 subscriber-only 구독자에게만 제공되는 bargain 싸게 사는 물건, 특가품 home accessories 가정용 소품 subscription 구독 for free 무료로 digital version 디지털판 print version 인쇄판 offer 제안, 매물 available 이용할 수 있는, 구할 수 있는 valid 유효한 require 요구하다, 필요하다

165 세부 사항

번역 〈유니크 홈 인테리어즈〉는 매년 몇 회 발행되는가?
(A) 4회
(B) 6회
(C) 12회
(D) 24회

해설 첫 번째 문장에서 quarterly magazine이라는 표현을 통해 분기별로 출간되는 잡지임을 알 수 있다. 따라서 정답은 (A)이다.

166 사실 관계 확인

번역 〈유니크 홈 인테리어즈〉에서 볼 수 있는 것으로 언급되지 않은 것은?
(A) 단독 할인 판매품
(B) 유행하는 색상 정보
(C) 출력 가능한 문양
(D) 전문가 인터뷰

해설 (A)는 지문 중간의 subscriber-only bargains에서, (B)는 the hottest color schemes에서, (C)는 templates for wall painting that you can download and print에서 확인할 수 있다. (D)는 본문에서 언급하지 않은 내용이다. 따라서 정답은 (D)이다.

167 사실 관계 확인

번역 웹페이지에 따르면, 〈유니크 홈 인테리어즈〉에 대해 사실인 것은?
(A) 언제든지 구독을 취소할 수 있다.
(B) 제한된 시간 동안 견본용 잡지에 접근할 수 있다.
(C) 재구독은 신규 구독보다 저렴하다.
(D) 신규 구독자들은 보너스 선물을 받을 수 있다.

해설 웹페이지 맨 하단을 보면 이번 달 말까지 다운로드를 할 수 있다는 내용에서 제한된 시간 동안 이용할 수 있다는 점을 알 수 있다. 따라서 정답은 (B)이다.

어휘 renewed 갱신[연장]된 be eligible for ~에 자격이 있다

▶▶ Paraphrasing 지문의 **Available for download until the end of this month** → 정답의 **can be accessed for a limited time**

168-171 기사

로세인 (5월 22일)—**168,171로세인 시립 공원 및 오락 관리국에서는 시 청사 종탑 안에서 최근에 태어난 새 두 마리의 이름을 지어주기 위한 대회를 개최합니다**.

169이 새들은 매입니다. 작은 동물을 잡아먹으려고 하늘에서 하강할 때 시속 200마일 이상의 속도를 내는 능력으로 유명한 종입니다. 해로운 농약의 영향 때문에 20세기 중반에 개체수가 위험할 정도로 줄었지만, 환경 단체들이 새들의 수를 안전한 수준으로 끌어올리는 데 성공적인 노력을 기울였습니다. 방법은 새들에게 둥지를 틀 장소를 더 많이 제공하는 것이었습니다.

170종탑 안에 있는 둥지를 짓기 위한 평평한 장소는 이 캠페인이 우리 지역 내에서 새들을 어떻게 보호하고 있는지 보여주는 한 예입니다. 이 단이 설치된 지 수십 년 만에 몇 쌍의 다 자란 매들이 이곳에 둥지를 틀었습니다. 관리국에서 일하는 새 연구가 에이지 나카지마의 말에 따르면, 현재의 두 마리 새는 지난 3년간 해마다 그곳으로 돌아오고 있다고 합니다. 그는 설명합니다. "새들은 여름철에 이곳에서 지내다가 늦가을에 남쪽으로 날아갑니다." '잭'과 '질'이라는 별명으로 불리는 이 쌍은 올해 암컷 새끼 한 마리, 수컷 새끼 한 마리를 낳았습니다.

171주민 여러분들은 www.rosseinfalcons.com에 가셔서 새끼 새들의 사진을 보시고 제안하는 이름을 제출해 주시기 바랍니다. 5월 31일까지 접수를 받으며, 그 후에 최종 결선 다섯 쌍이 선발됩니다. 그런 다음, 주민들께서 6월 3일부터 9일까지 사이트를 다시 방문해 마음에 드는 쌍에 투표해 주시기 바랍니다. 당선된 이름은 6월 10일에 발표됩니다.

어휘 hold a contest 대회를 열다 be born 태어나다 bell tower 종탑 peregrine falcon 매 species 종 drive 돌진하다 population 개체 수 drop (수치, 정도가) 낮아지다, 약해지다 due to ~때문에 harmful 해로운 agricultural chemicals 농약 environmental 환경의 make an effort 노력하다 nest 둥지를 틀다 platform (뭔가를 올려놓을 수 있는) 대, 단, 평평한 장소 decade 10년 install 설치하다 current 현재의 annually 1년에 한 번 nickname 별명을 부르다 produce (새끼를) 낳다 male 수컷의 female 암컷의 chick 새끼 새 submit 제출하다(submission 제출) suggestion 제안 accept 받다, 수락하다 finalist 결승 진출자 cast a vote for ~에 (찬성) 표를 던지다

168 세부 사항

번역 기사에서 말하는 현 프로젝트의 목적은 무엇인가?
(A) 환경 관련 실험실을 현대화하기 위한 재원을 확보하기 위해
(B) 특정 종의 새가 특정 방식으로 행동하는 이유를 배우려고
(C) 새끼 동물들이 어떤 이름으로 불릴지 결정하기 위해
(D) 주민들에게 자연에 대해 교육시키기 위해

해설 첫 번째 단락에서 '최근에 시 청사 종탑 안에서 태어난 새 두 마리의 이름을 지어주기(give names to two birds)' 위한 대회'라고 했다. 따라서 정답은 (C)이다.

169 세부 사항

번역 언급되는 새의 종에 관해 명시된 것은?
(A) 1년 내내 같은 곳에서 산다.
(B) 매우 빨리 움직일 수 있다.
(C) 물속에서 먹이를 찾는다.
(D) 현재 멸종위기 종으로 분류되어 있다.

해설 두 번째 단락 첫 번째 문장에서 이 두 마리의 새에 대한 특징으로 '하늘에서 하강할 때 시속 200마일 이상의 속도를 내는 능력'이 있다고 했다. 따라서 정답은 (B)이다.

어휘 classified 분류된 endangered 멸종위기에 처한

170 세부 사항

번역 기사에 따르면, 오래전에 로세인에는 무슨 일이 있었나?
(A) 프로그램을 감독하기 위해 나카지마 씨가 고용되었다.
(B) 일부 화학약품의 사용이 금지되었다.
(C) 한 도시 건물이 새들에 의해 손상되었다.
(D) 새들을 위한 집이 지어졌다.

해설 세 번째 단락 앞부분에서 '이 단이 설치된 지 수십 년 만에 몇 쌍의 다 자란 매들이 이곳에 둥지를 틀었다'고 했다. 그러므로 오래전에 새들을 위한 둥지가 지어졌음을 알 수 있으므로 정답은 (D)이다.

어휘 oversee 감독하다 forbidden 금지된

171 추론 / 유추

번역 웹사이트에 관해 암시된 것은?
(A) 5월 31일 이후에는 갱신이 되지 않을 것이다.
(B) 홍보 행사 사진들이 나온다.
(C) 지방 자치 단체에서 운영한다.
(D) 대회에 참가하기 위해 선발된 사람들의 팀 명단이 있다.

해설 네 번째 단락 첫 번째 문장에서 '주민 여러분들은 웹사이트에서 새끼 새들의 사진을 보고 제안하는 이름을 제출해달라(Community members are encouraged to go to ~)'고 했다. 그러므로 웹사이트는 지역 정부에서 운영되고 있음을 알 수 있다. 따라서 정답은 (C)이다.

172-175 광고

슈퍼 스핀 빨래방
청결한 의복은 우리의 열정입니다!

슈퍼 스핀 빨래방은 여러분이 세탁을 하기에 가장 좋은 장소입니다. 저희의 세탁기와 건조기들은 첨단 기술을 사용해 **172의류의 마모를 피하고** 기존 세탁기로 세탁할 때보다 의류 수명이 최대 3배까지 늘어나는 방식으로 여러분의 의류를 세탁하고 건조합니다.

급하실 경우 저희에게 풀서비스 세탁으로 세탁물을 맡겨 주시면 세탁과 건조, 의류 개기까지 해 드립니다. 약간의 추가 요금을 내시면 의류를 여러분의 집이나 사무실까지 배달도 해드립니다.

더 경제적인 선택을 원하신다면 본인이 직접 세탁할 수 있는 기계들도 현장에 있습니다. 저희는 또한 매우 다양한 세제와 섬유 유연제, 건조기용 섬유 유연제도 판매합니다. 더 관리에 신경 써야 하는 의복이 있습니까? **173저희 직원들이 음식이나 화장품 등으로 인한 변색을 제거하는 데 필요한 조언을 해드립니다.** 저희는 또 섬세한 의류를 손빨래할 수 있는 개수대도 갖추고 있습니다.

174슈퍼 스핀 빨래방은 이제 여러분의 편의를 위해 하루 24시간 영업하고 있으며, 대기실에는 텔레비전과 자판기, 무료로 읽을 수 있는 잡지들을 구비해 두고 있습니다.

175저희는 도시 전역에 다섯 개의 지점이 있습니다. 여러분이 계신 곳에서 가장 가까운 지점을 찾으시려면 저희 웹사이트 www.s-spin.com을 방문하셔서 전체 목록을 살펴보십시오. 슈퍼 스핀 빨래방에서 곧 만나 뵙기를 바랍니다!

어휘 laundromat 빨래방, 세탁소 passion 열정 laundry 세탁물 washer 세탁기 dryer 건조기 state-of-the-art 최신식, 첨단 technology 기술 avoid 피하다 wear and tear 마모 last 오래가다, 지속되다 up to ~까지 launder 세탁하다 traditional 기존의, 전통적인 in a hurry 급한, 서두르는 full-service wash 풀서비스 세탁 fold 접다, 개다 deliver 배달하다 additional fee 추가 요금 economical 경제적인 option 선택 on site 현장에서 do one's laundry 세탁하다, 빨래하다 a wide variety of 매우 다양한 detergent 세제 fabric softener 섬유 유연제 dryer sheet (종이 형태의) 건조기용 섬유 유연제 an article of clothing 의류 한 점 extra attention 추가적인 관심[관리] available 이용할 수 있는, 만날 수 있는 get rid of ~을 제거하다 discoloration 변색, 퇴색 delicate 섬세한 by hand 손으로 for one's convenience ~의 편의를 위해 waiting area 대기실 vending machine 자판기 location 장소, 위치 throughout ~전역에

172 추론 / 암시

번역 슈퍼 스핀 빨래방에 있는 기기들에 관해 암시된 것은?
(A) 사용이 간편하다.
(B) 동전으로 작동된다.
(C) 의류를 부드럽게 다룬다.
(D) 세탁 시간이 더 오래 걸린다.

Test 4

해설 첫 번째 단락 두 번째 문장에 빨래방 기기들이 첨단 기술을 사용해서 마모를 피할 수 있게 도와준다는 말이 나온다. 의류를 부드럽게 다룬다는 의미와 근접하므로 정답은 (C)가 적절하다. 나머지 보기는 본문에 언급된 내용만으로 유추할 수 없다.

173 세부 사항

번역 고객들은 슈퍼 스핀 빨래방 직원들로부터 무엇을 얻을 수 있는가?
(A) 배달 일정
(B) 손세탁 기술 설명
(C) 인터넷 접속 비밀번호
(D) 얼룩 제거에 관한 조언

해설 질문의 employees라는 표현이 지문에서는 staff로 달리 표현되어 있다. 세 번째 단락 중간 부분을 보면 우리 staff들이 변색 제거에 관한 조언을 준다는 얘기가 나오기 때문에 정답은 (D)이다.

> ▶▶ **Paraphrasing** 지문의 **advice on getting rid of discolorations**
> → 정답의 **Tips on stain removal**

174 세부 사항

번역 슈퍼 스핀 빨래방이 최근에 한 일은 무엇인가?
(A) 영업 시간 연장
(B) 더 많은 기계 추가
(C) 드라이클리닝 서비스 개시
(D) 새로운 지점 개장

해설 네 번째 단락의 now라는 표현에서 예전과는 달리 이제부터는 고객의 편의를 위해 24시간 영업을 하게 되었다는 말이 나온다. 따라서 정답은 (A)이다.

175 문장 삽입

번역 [1], [2], [3], [4]로 표시된 곳 중에서 다음 문장이 들어가기에 가장 적합한 곳은?
"여러분이 계신 곳에서 가장 가까운 지점을 찾으시려면 저희 웹사이트 www.s-spin.com을 방문하셔서 전체 목록을 살펴보십시오."
(A) [1]
(B) [2]
(C) [3]
(D) [4]

해설 가까운 지점의 위치를 알려 주는 내용과 관련된 문장은 마지막 단락에서 찾을 수 있다. 도시 전역에 5개의 지점이 있다는 내용 뒤에 위치하는 것이 가장 적절하다. 따라서 정답은 (D)이다.

176 -180 웹페이지+이메일

http://www.mitchtoncommunity.com/startups

소개	기업 회원	**신생 기업**	연락처

나일스 컨 사는 활발한 신생 기업 문화가 도시의 장기적인 재정 건전성의 열쇠라고 믿고 있습니다. 그런 이유로 저희는 미츠턴 커뮤니티를 설립해 장래가 유

망한 셰나의 선별 신생 기업들에게 매년 지원 서비스를 제공합니다. **177,179저희는** 전문적인 비즈니스 컨설팅, 무료 사무실 공간, 그리고 필요하다면 클라우드 기반 데이터 저장 공간 등을 제공합니다. 그리고 가장 중요한 것은, 셰나에 본사를 둔 주요 기업들과 연결시켜 준다는 점입니다. 설립자인 나일스 컨 이외에, 저희 기업 회원 중엔 도탐 인더스트리즈와 미난드 호텔도 있습니다. 평균적으로, 저희와 거래하는 신생 기업의 거의 3분의 1이 결국은 이들 업체에 서비스와 장비를 제공하는 수익성 있는 계약을 맺게 됩니다.

지원 세부 사항

신청은 매년 12월에 받습니다. **176신청 기관은** 모두 셰나 지역에 위치해야 하며 다음 중 한 분야에서 창조적인 제품이나 서비스를 개발하는 데 종사하고 있어야 합니다.

- **178A – 재무**
- B – 마케팅
- C – 의학
- D – 재생 에너지

내년도 신청서를 다운로드하려면 여기를 클릭하세요.

어휘 corporate member 법인 회원 startup 신생 (벤처) 기업, 스타트업 vibrant 활발한 long-term 장기적인 financial health 재정 건전성 found 설립하다 select 엄선된 promising 장래성 있는 expert 전문적인 office space 사무실 공간 storage 저장 corporation 기업, 법인 headquartered in ~에 본사가 있는 founder 설립자 count A among B A를 B에 포함시키다[B로 여기다] on average 평균적으로 end up -ing 결국 ~가 되다[~로 끝이 나다] make a deal 협상하다, 거래하다 lucrative 수익성이 좋은 equipment 장비 business 기업, 장사 application 신청, 지원(cf. applicant 지원자) details 세부 사항 organization 조직, 기관 be located 위치하다 engaged in ~에 종사하는 innovative 혁신적인 finance 재무 renewable 재생 가능한 upcoming year 다음 해

발신: 저레드 아인스워스〈j.ainsworth@mitchtoncommunity.com〉
수신: 패드미니 미즈라〈padmini@yowenosys.com〉
제목: 축하합니다!
날짜: 12월 28일
첨부: 미츠턴 커뮤니티 신생 기업 합의서

미즈라 씨께,

요우에노 시스템즈가 공식적인 내년도 미츠턴 커뮤니티 신생 기업으로 인정되었음을 알리게 되어 기쁩니다. **178저희 심사위원회는** 귀사의 지불 처리 소프트웨어 시제품을 보고 매우 감명을 받았습니다. 저희는 귀사가 잠재력을 최대한 발휘할 수 있도록 도울 수 있게 되어 매우 흥분됩니다.

신생 기업 대상 표준 합의서 한 부를 첨부합니다. **180귀사의 법정 대리인에게 검토를 하도록 해 주십시오. 179준비가** 되시면, 저희가 만날 약속을 잡아 서류에 서명하고 귀사의 새로운 사무실 공간 배정 논의를 시작할 수 있습니다.

합의서 또는 기타 문제와 관련해 궁금하신 사항은 이 이메일 주소로 제게 연락 주시면 됩니다.

저레드 아인스워스
신생 기업 관련 책임자
미츠턴 커뮤니티

어휘 **notify** 알리다 **selection committee** 심사 위원회 **prototype** 원형, 시제품 **processing** 처리 **realize one's full potential** 잠재력을 최대한 발휘하다 **agreement** 합의, 합의서 **legal representative** 법정 대리인 **review** 검토하다 **assignment** 배정

176 세부 사항

번역 미츠턴 커뮤니티 신생 기업들에 관해 암시된 것은?
(A) 연말에 최종 보고서를 제출한다.
(B) 서로 협력할 것으로 예상된다.
(C) 종종 더 큰 회사에 매입된다.
(D) 특정 지역에 기반을 두고 있다.

해설 웹페이지의 두 번째 단락 지원 세부 사항에 보면 '신청 기관은 모두 셰나 지역(the greater Shenna area)에 위치해야 한다'고 했다. 그러므로 미츠턴 커뮤니티의 지원을 받으려면 특정 지역에 기반을 두어야 함을 알 수 있으므로 정답은 (D)이다.

어휘 **collaborate with** ~와 협력하다 **acquire** 얻다, 인수하다

177 사실 관계 확인

번역 미츠턴 커뮤니티 신생 기업이 되는 것의 혜택으로 언급되지 않은 것은?
(A) 전문가의 지도
(B) 큰 액수의 돈
(C) 무료 디지털 저장 공간
(D) 기존 기업들과의 연계

해설 (A)와 (C)는 웹사이트 첫 번째 단락 중간 부분에서 '저희는 전문적인 비즈니스 컨설팅, 무료 사무실 공간, 그리고 필요하다면 클라우드 기반 데이터 저장 공간 등을 제공한다'에서, (D)는 '그리고 가장 중요한 것은, 셰나에 본사를 둔 주요 기업들과 연결해 준다'고 했다. 따라서 정답은 (B)이다.

178 연계

번역 요웨노 시스템즈는 어떤 분야에 신청을 했겠는가?
(A) A
(B) B
(C) C
(D) D

해설 두 번째 지문 이메일의 첫 번째 문장에서 '요웨노 시스템즈가 신생 기업으로 인정되었다'고 했고, 두 번째 문장에서 '귀사의 지불 처리 소프트웨어 시제품을 보고 매우 감명을 받았다'고 했다. 웹사이트의 '지원 세부사항'에 보면 A 항목이 재무 분야이므로 정답이 (A)임을 알 수 있다.

179 세부 사항

번역 요웨노 시스템즈에 관해 사실일 것은?
(A) 경영진이 바뀌었다.
(B) 현재의 사무실을 떠나고 싶어 한다.
(C) 신청서에 장치 시범 동영상이 포함되었다.
(D) 직원들이 1년 근로계약을 했다.

해설 아인스워스 씨의 이메일 두 번째 단락 세 번째 문장에서 '귀사의 새로운 사무실 공간(new office space) 배정 논의를 시작할 수 있다'고 했다. 그러므로 요웨노 시스템즈가 사무실 이전을 하리라는 것을 알 수 있다. 따라서 정답은 (B)이다.

어휘 **vacate** 비우다, 떠나다 **yearlong** 1년간의

180 세부 사항

번역 미즈라 씨는 무엇을 하라고 설명을 받는가?
(A) 서류 초안 작성 시작하기
(B) 아인스워스 씨와 만날 약속 잡기
(C) 전자 서명을 하기
(D) 회사 변호사에게 연락하기

해설 이메일에서 아인스워스 씨는 미즈라 씨에게 '신생 기업 대상 표준 합의서 한 부를 첨부하니 법정 대리인(legal representatives)이 검토하도록 해 달라'고 했다. 변호사가 법정 대리인의 역할을 담당하므로 정답은 (D)이다.

181 -185 웹페이지+온라인 양식

http://www.customsol.com

커스텀 솔루션즈

당신이 원하는 바로 그것을 얻으세요. 너무 크거나 너무 작은 일은 없습니다!

커스텀 솔루션즈는 분야를 선도하는 주문 제작 의류 공급 업체입니다. **181**저희는 귀하가 사업체를 홍보하고, 독특한 선물을 제작하고, 스포츠 팀의 유니폼을 준비하는 등의 일을 하는 것을 돕기 위해 귀하의 글귀 및 회사 로고를 의복에 인쇄해 드립니다. **182**온라인으로 주문하시고, 623-555-0192번으로 전화하시거나 윌로우 드라이브 226번지, 세인트 클라우드, MN 56303에 있는 매장에 직접 들러 주세요. 복잡한 주문일 경우 직접 방문하실 것을 적극 권장합니다.

저희는 기본적인 흰 티셔츠(품번 #238)에 다음과 같은 선택 사항을 제공합니다. 전체 상품 목록을 보시려면 저희의 가격 페이지를 참고해 주세요.
- 1도 인쇄, 앞면만: 9.50달러
- 2도 인쇄, 앞면만: 10.00달러
- 1도 인쇄, 앞면과 뒷면: 11.50달러
- **184**2도 인쇄, 앞면과 뒷면: 12.00달러

주문 시 가격의 25%를 보증금으로 내셔야 합니다. 전체 금액 중 잔금은 물건을 수령하거나 배송받을 때 결제하시면 됩니다.

어휘 **leading** 선도적인 **provider** 공급 업체, 공급자 **made-to-order** 주문 제작한, 맞춤 제작한 **apparel** 의상 **garment** 의복, 옷 **promote** 홍보하다 **unique** 독특한, 특별한 **prepare** 준비하다 **place an order** 주문하다 **stop by** 잠시 들르다 **in person** 몸소, 직접 **highly recommend** 적극 권장하다 **complicated** 복잡한 **offer** 제공하다 **option** 선택 사항 **basic** 기본적인 **pricing** 가격 책정 **list** 목록 **merchandise** 상품 **one-color printing** 1도 인쇄 **two-color printing** 2도 인쇄 **front** 앞면 **be required to**+동사원형 ~해야만 한다 **deposit** 보증금 **remainder** 나머지, 잔금 **balance** 잔액 **due** 지불 기한이 된 **at the time of pick-up** 물건을 수령할 때, 찾을 때

고객 이름: 에바 퍼거슨	연락 전화번호: 623-555-0127

주문 날짜: 5월 25일　　예상 배송일: 6월 18일

물품 번호: 238

해당 영역들을 전부 기입해 주세요. 필요하지 않은 영역에는 X표 하세요.

앞면	뒷면
1행: 헨드릭스 아동 병원	1행: 동전 한 닢도 소중합니다!
크기: 소	크기: 중
색상: 184감청색	색상: 184짙은 황록색
2행: 183제5회 연례 자선 달리기 대회	2행: 6월 30일, 에이브람스 공원
크기: 대	크기: 소
색상: 184짙은 황록색	색상: 184감청색
이미지: hendrix.jpg	이미지: X
이미지 위치: 중앙, 글귀 아래	이미지 위치: X

특이 사항: 수령하게 될 물품을 참가자들에게 보여 주기 위해, 185가능하면 적어도 배송 일주일 전에 완성된 물품 중 한 개를 사진으로 찍어 주시기 바랍니다.

계속해서 크기 및 배송 정보로 이동 ↻

어휘　customer 고객　contact number 연락 전화번호 expected 예상된　complete 기입하다　applicable 해당하는 field 영역, 필드　front 앞면　instructions 지시 사항　in order to + 동사원형 ~하기 위해　participant 참가자　finished 완성된 at least 적어도　delivery 배송　if possible 가능하면

181 세부 사항

번역　커스텀 솔루션즈는 무엇을 파는가?
(A) 가구
(B) 문구류
(C) 의류
(D) 표지판

해설　첫 번째 단락에서 '주문 제작 의류 공급 업체'라는 말과 그 뒤 문장에서 글 귀와 회사 로고를 의복에 인쇄한다는 내용을 토대로 정답이 (C)라는 것을 알 수 있다.

182 사실 관계 확인

번역　상품 주문에 관해 명시된 것은?
(A) 물품의 최소 주문 수량이 있다.
(B) 배송 전에 전액 선불로 지불해야 한다.
(C) 요금에는 디자인 비가 포함되어 있다.
(D) 몇 가지 다른 방식으로 주문할 수 있다.

해설　주문하는 방법은 1. 온라인 주문, 2. 전화 주문, 3. 직접 방문이 있다. 따라서 (D)가 정답이다. (A), (C)는 본문에서 언급이 없었고 (B)는 웹페이지 마지막 문단에서 주문 시 가격의 25%를 보증금으로 내야 한다는 말이 나오기 때문에 오답이다.

어휘　exceed 초과하다, 넘어서다　full payment 전액　shipment 배송

183 추론 / 암시

번역　퍼거슨 씨는 물품을 어디에 사용할 것 같은가?
(A) 모금 행사
(B) 직원 수련회
(C) 스포츠 훈련 캠프
(D) 개업식

해설　양식에서 Line 2에 Charity라는 단어를 통해 이 문제를 해결할 수 있다. charity는 '자선'을 의미한다. 따라서 정답은 (A)이다.

184 세부 사항

번역　퍼거슨 씨는 물품 한 개당 얼마를 지불하겠는가?
(A) 9.50달러
(B) 10.00달러
(C) 11.50달러
(D) 12.00달러

해설　퍼거슨 씨는 양면에 인쇄하고 색상은 forest green과 navy blue 두 가지(2도 인쇄)를 선택했기 때문에 웹페이지에서 이에 해당하는 상품의 가격은 12달러라는 것을 알 수 있다. 따라서 정답은 (D)이다.

185 세부 사항

번역　퍼거슨 씨가 커스텀 솔루션즈에 특별히 요청하는 것은?
(A) 여러 이미지 결합하기
(B) 사진을 미리 보내 주기
(C) 배송을 신속히 해주기
(D) 남은 재료 보관하기

해설　양식 마지막 부분의 special instructions에서 퍼거슨 씨는 배송 일주일 전에 완성된 물품을 사진으로 찍어 보내 달라고 요청했다. 따라서 정답은 (B)이다.

▶▶ Paraphrasing　지문의 one week before delivery
→ 정답의 in advance

186-190 웹페이지+양식+이메일

http://www.burristhotels.com/search

검색 결과

지역: 린체이　▼	날짜: 9월 23일 – 9월 25일(2박)　▼

버리스트 호텔 린체이

189드러몬드 가 160번지, 린체이

호텔에 관한 자세한 설명

이용 가능한 객실과 숙박료(1박 기준):

186싱글	73달러	선택 ➡
더블	104달러	선택 ➡
디럭스 더블	128달러	선택 ➡
스위트 룸	157달러	선택 ➡

(객실 유형을 클릭해서 사진과 이용 가능한 편의 시설 목록을 확인하세요.)

어휘 available 구할 수 있는 amenities 편의 시설

버리스트 호텔

고객 피드백 양식

체류하신 기간 동안 마음에 드셨던 점과 저희가 어떻게 개선해 나갈 수 있을지 알려 주십시오.

고객 이름: 조디 말로   **연락처:** j.marlow@viopind.com

호텔 소재지: 린체이

의견: 지난달 말에 호텔을 방문했는데 체험은 전반적으로 만족스러웠습니다. **186**1박에 70달러 남짓이면 제 방은 가격에 비해 훌륭했습니다. 저는 특히 프런트 데스크의 프라이타스 씨에게 감사를 표하고 싶습니다. 제가 머무는 동안 작은 건강상의 문제가 생겼는데 그녀가 배달 서비스가 되는 약국을 찾을 수 있도록 친절하게 도와주었어요. 하지만, 언급하고 싶은 문제가 하나 있습니다. **187** 호텔 웹사이트에는 이 호텔이 로이트 컨벤션 센터에서 셔틀 버스로 5분 거리라고 나와 있어요. 하지만 제 셔틀 버스로는 그곳까지 가는 데 거의 25분이 걸렸습니다. 그런 잘못된 광고는 안 내시는 게 좋다고 생각합니다.

어휘 stay 체류 comment 논평, 지적 be satisfied with ~에 만족하다 overall 전반적으로 appreciation 감사 minor 사소한, 가벼운 medical 의학의, 의료상의 issue 문제 pharmacy 약국 engage in ~에 관여하다 false 잘못된, 거짓의

발신: ⟨august.blair@burristhotels.com⟩
수신: ⟨j.marlow@viopind.com⟩
제목: 피드백에 대한 대답
날짜: 10월 4일

말로 씨께,

시간을 내서 피드백 양식을 작성해 주셔서 감사합니다.

188제기하신 문제에 관해 말씀드리겠습니다. **189**고객님께서 이곳에 계셨을 때, 저희 호텔이 위치해 있는 도로가 사실은 노면을 보수하는 중이었습니다. 공사 현장이 길 저편에 있어서 고객님께서 못 보셨을 수도 있습니다. 린체이의 모든 일방통행 도로는 물론이고, 공사로 인해 도로가 폐쇄되는 바람에 셔틀 버스들이 오래 걸리는 우회로를 통해 컨벤션 센터로 가야 했습니다. 셔틀 버스 운전사가 고객님과 다른 승객들에게 이런 상황을 설명하지 않은 점 죄송하게 생각하고, 이로 인해 고객님께서 크게 불편하지 않았기를 바랍니다.

그리고, 프라이타스 씨 얘기를 전해주신 것 정말 감사 드립니다. **190**고객님의 칭찬을 그녀의 직원 기록부에 적어두도록 하겠습니다.

제가 추가로 도울 일이 있다면 주저하지 마시고 연락 주십시오.

어거스트 블레어
고객 서비스 담당, 버리스트 호텔 린체이

어휘 fill out 작성하다 form 양식 address 말하다 raise (문제를) 제기하다 resurface the road 노면을 보수하다 work site 작업 현장 closure 폐쇄 one-way street 일방 통행로 take a ~ route ~길[경로]로 가다 circuitous 우회하는 inconvenience 불편 share 공유하다 make a note of ~을 적어두다[기록하다] employee file 직원 기록 hesitate 망설이다 further 더 이상의 assistance 도움

---

186 연계

번역 말로 씨는 어떤 종류의 객실에 묵었겠는가?
    (A) 싱글
    (B) 더블
    (C) 디럭스 더블
    (D) 스위트룸

해설 두 번째 지문 말로 씨의 고객 피드백 양식에 보면 '1박에 70달러 정도로 객실이 가격 대비 훌륭했다'고 했다. 첫 번째 지문 웹페이지의 객실 요금에 보면 첫 번째 항목에 '싱글 73달러'라고 나와 있으므로 정답은 (A)이다.

187 세부 사항

번역 말로 씨는 무엇에 불만이 있는가?
    (A) 요청하지 않은 서비스에 대해 요금 청구를 받았다.
    (B) 호텔 웹사이트의 정보가 잘못되었다.
    (C) 운송 노동자들이 연달아 실수를 했다.
    (D) 호텔이 기본적인 의료품을 가지고 있지 않다.

해설 두 번째 지문의 후반부에서 말로 씨는 '웹사이트에서 호텔이 로이트 컨벤션 센터에서 셔틀버스로 5분 거리라 했지만 실제로는 거의 25분이 걸렸고 그런 잘못된 광고는 안 내는 게 좋다'고 했다. 따라서 웹사이트의 정보가 잘못되었다고 했으므로 정답은 (B)이다.

어휘 be charged for 요금이 부과되다

188 동의어 찾기

번역 이메일에서, 두 번째 단락 1행의 "raised"와 의미가 가장 가까운 단어는?
    (A) 증가시켰다
    (B) 지적했다
    (C) 보살폈다
    (D) 세웠다

해설 raise의 사전적 의미는 '올리다, 인상하다'의 의미이나 여기서는 앞에 있는 'problem'을 수식하고 있다. 그러므로 이 문장에서는 '(문제를) 지적하다'의 의미가 가장 적절하다. 따라서 정답은 (B)이다.

189 연계

번역 드러몬드 가에 대해 가장 사실일 것은?
    (A) 언제나 주중 특정 요일에는 차량이 진입할 수 없다.
    (B) 큰 회의 공간이 이곳에 있다.
    (C) 최근에 도로 공사를 했다.
    (D) 차량이 한 방향으로만 운행하도록 허용한다.

해설 세 번째 지문인 이메일의 두 번째 단락 두 번째 문장에서 '고객께서 이곳에 계셨을 때, 저희 호텔이 있는 도로가 사실은 노면을 보수(resurfaced)하는 중이었다'고 했다. 그리고 첫 번째 지문 웹사이트 맨 윗부분에 있는 호텔의 주소가 '드러몬드 가 160번지, 린체이'이다. 따라서 정답은 (C)이다.

190 세부 사항

번역 블레어 씨는 무엇을 쓰겠다고 말하는가?
    (A) 일부 고객 대상 정식 사과 편지
    (B) 셔틀 버스 운영자를 위한 지시사항 메모
    (C) 인사 기록에 들어갈 긍정적인 메시지
    (D) 웹페이지에 게시할 경고문

해설 세 번째 지문 블레어 씨의 이메일의 세 번째 단락에서 '고객님의 칭찬을 그녀의 직원 기록부에 적어두겠다(make a note of your praise in her employee file)'고 했다. 따라서 정답은 (C)이다.

191-195 정보문+이메일+이메일

---

http://www.stratfordci.com

| 홈 | 수업 | 사진 갤러리 | 연락처 |

스트랫포드 요리 학원

191스트랫포드 요리 학원은 편리한 시내 중심가에서 매우 다양한 수업을 제공하며, 저희 강사진은 일상적인 식사 만들기부터 특별한 때에 먹는 아주 맛있는 디저트 준비에 이르기까지 모든 것을 가르칠 수 있습니다. 예전에 저희에게 배운 학생들 중 일부는 자신들의 식당을 차리기까지 했습니다. 저희는 주중 저녁 수업과 토요일 종일반 수업을 제공합니다. 아래에서 저희의 가장 인기 있는 수업들을 확인하시거나 www.stratfordci.com에 방문하여 전체 목록을 살펴보세요.

수업 / 시간대 / 강사

이탈리아 요리 / 월요일, 수요일 오후 7시 / 래번 트렌트
195기초 케이크 장식 / 화요일 오후 8시, 토요일 오후 2시 / 돈 스펜서
파티 전채 요리 / 목요일 오후 7시 / 섀런 그랜트
해산물 정복하기 / 수요일, 금요일 오후 8시 / 제니퍼 알바라도

어휘 institute 학원 offer 제공하다 a wide variety of 매우 다양한 downtown 시내의 location 위치, 입지, 장소 instructor 강사 daily meal 일상식 decadent 매우 맛있는 special occasion 특별한 때 former 예전의 go on to+동사원형 (무엇을 끝마친 뒤에) 이어서 ~하기 시작하다 check out 확인하다 a complete list 전체 목록 decoration 장식 appetizer 전채, 에피타이저 seafood 해산물

수신: 크리스토퍼 맥코믹 ⟨c.mccormick@stratfordci.com⟩
발신: 글로리아 영 ⟨younggloria@pinsonconsulting.net⟩
날짜: 4월 5일
제목: 핀슨 컨설팅으로부터
맥코믹 씨께,

저는 핀슨 컨설팅에서 제가 속한 부서의 팀 강화 활동을 계획하는 책임을 맡고 있는데요, **192귀하의 학원에서 우리 그룹만을 위한 요리 수업을 마련해 주실 수 있는지** 궁금합니다. 이와 같이 독특한 활동들을 하면 직원들이 한 팀으로 업무를 더 잘 **193수행하는** 데 도움이 된다고 생각합니다. 저희는 5월 1일부터 5일 사이에 오후에는 언제든지 시간이 있으며, 특별히 선호하는 주제는 없습니다. 만약 이것이 가능하다면 인원이 20명일 때 **194(B)일인당 비용이 얼마나 들며, 194(C)제가 수업료를 어떻게 지불해야 하는지,** 그리고 **194(A)수업이 얼마나 걸리는지** 알려 주시기 바랍니다.

핀슨 컨설팅, 회계 담당 이사
글로리아 영 드림

어휘 be in charge of ~을 책임지다, ~ 담당이다 team-building activities 팀 강화 활동 department 부서 I'm wondering if ~인지 궁금하다 arrange 마련하다, 주선하다 unique 독특한, 특별한 employee 직원 perform 수행하다 available 시간을 낼 수 있는 preference 선호 fee 수수료, 수업료 last 지속되다 accounting director 회계 담당 이사

수신: 글로리아 영 ⟨younggloria@pinsonconsulting.net⟩
발신: 크리스토퍼 맥코믹 ⟨c.mccormick@stratfordci.com⟩
날짜: 4월 6일
제목: RE: 핀슨 컨설팅으로부터

영 씨께,

저희 학원에 관심을 가져 주셔서 감사합니다. 저희가 귀하의 요청을 수용할 수 있다는 말씀을 드리게 되어 기쁩니다. **195저희의 케이크 장식 수업을 담당하는 강사가 5월 3일 수요일 2시부터 4시까지 2시간짜리 수업을 진행할 수 있습니다.** 요금은 일인당 16달러이며, 저희 웹사이트에서 신용카드로 결제하실 수 있습니다. 수업료에는 모든 재료비가 포함되며, 각자가 자신이 작업한 최종 결과물을 집에 가져가게 됩니다. 저희 학원은 보통 주간에는 문을 열지 않기 때문에 정문이 잠겨 있어서 정문을 이용하실 수는 없을 겁니다. 대신에, 강사가 교실을 준비하는 동안 **194제가 현장에 나가 여러분을 옆문으로 들어오시도록 하겠습니다.** 도착하시면 그냥 555-0160으로 제게 전화하시기 바랍니다.

스트랫포드 요리 학원, 입학 담당 이사
크리스토퍼 맥코믹 드림

어휘 be pleased to+동사원형 ~하게 되어 기쁘다 accommodate 수용하다 request 요청 cake decorating class 케이크 장식 수업 available 시간을 낼 수 있는 pay by credit card 신용카드로 결제하다 include 포함하다 ingredient 재료, 성분 material 재료, 소재 finished result 완성된 결과물 main entrance 정문 be locked 잠겨 있다 instead 대신에 on site 현장에 prepare 준비하다 simply 그냥, 단지 admissions director 입학 담당 이사

---

191 사실 관계 확인

번역 스트랫포드 요리 학원에 관해 명시된 것은?
　(A) 동종 업계에서 가장 인기 있는 학원이다.
　(B) 일주일에 7일 수업을 한다.
　(C) 식당과 제휴를 맺고 있다.
　(D) 시내 한복판에 자리 잡고 있다.

해설 웹페이지 첫 번째 문장의 at our convenient downtown location에서 시내 중심가에 요리 학원이 위치한다는 것을 알 수 있다. 따라서 정답은 (D)이다.

▶▶ Paraphrasing　지문의 **at our convenient downtown location** → 정답의 **It is located in the city center**

192 글의 주제 / 목적

번역 영 씨의 이메일은 목적이 무엇인가?
(A) 개인적인 수업을 개설하려고
(B) 단체 할인을 요청하려고
(C) 초청을 수락하려고
(D) 계획에 변경을 확인하려고

해설 이메일 두 번째 줄(I'm wondering if ~)에서 우리 그룹만을 위한 요리 수업을 개설해 줄 수 있는지를 묻고 있다. 따라서 정답은 (A)이다.

▶▶ **Paraphrasing** 지문의 a class at your institute just for our group → 정답의 a private class

193 동의어 찾기

번역 첫 번째 이메일에서 첫 번째 단락 4행의 "perform"과 의미가 가장 가까운 것은?
(A) 관찰하다
(B) 성취하다
(C) 즐겁게 하다
(D) 기능을 발휘하다

해설 perform은 보통 '행하다, 수행하다, 실시하다'라는 뜻으로 사용한다. 여기에서는 팀으로 업무를 더 잘 '수행하다'라는 뜻으로 쓰였다. 즉, 팀으로서 '역할을 잘 해낸다'는 의미로 function이라는 의미와 동일하게 쓰일 수 있다. 따라서 정답은 (D)이다.

194 연계

번역 맥코믹 씨가 주는 정보 중 영 씨가 요청하지 않은 것은?
(A) 수업 소요 시간
(B) 일인당 비용
(C) 지불 수단
(D) 이용할 입구

해설 영 씨가 맥코믹 씨에게 보낸 이메일인 두 번째 지문과 맥코믹 씨가 영 씨에게 보내는 답장인 세 번째 이메일을 비교해 보아야 한다. 종합해보면, (A) 수업 소요 시간, (B) 일인당 비용, (C) 지불 수단에 대해서는 요청한 것에 대해 답변하고 있다. (D)는 영 씨가 요청한 것은 아닌데 추가 정보를 주고 있는 것이므로, 정답은 (D)이다.

▶▶ **Paraphrasing** 지문의 how much it would cost per person → 보기의 The cost per person

지문의 how I should pay the fee → 보기의 The payment method

지문의 how long the class will last → 보기의 The duration of the class

195 연계

번역 누가 5월 3일에 주간 수업을 가르치겠는가?
(A) 트렌트 씨
(B) 스펜서 씨
(C) 그랜트 씨
(D) 알바라도 씨

해설 두 번째 이메일 두 번째 줄에서 5월 3일에 케이크 장식 수업을 하는 강사가 수업을 진행할 것이라고 나온다. 그리고 웹페이지에 기초 케이크 장식 수업을 맡은 강사의 이름이 돈 스펜서라고 나와 있다. 따라서 정답은 (B)이다.

196 -200 보고서+이메일+기사

에너지 효율 감사 개요: 스턴버그 매뉴팩처링
미스트랄 에너지 서비스(MES)가 9월 4일 실시

베드포드에 있는 스턴버그 매뉴팩처링 현장에서 MES 팀이 에너지 효율 감사를 실시했다. **196**이 현장이 전국에 있는 스턴버그의 13개 시설 가운데서 선정된 이유는 이곳이 스턴버그 매뉴팩처링의 최초의 공장이었고 개선될 가능성이 가장 높았기 때문이다.

최적화를 위한 다섯 가지 영역이 밝혀졌고, 각 영역에 대한 구체적인 제안들이 만들어졌다. 첫째, 페랄레스 사의 태양광 패널을 옥상 부분에 추가하고 지속가능한 에너지를 생산해서 현장에서 사용하거나 전력망에 되팔 수 있게 해야 한다. 둘째, 포장 장비를 포시스 사에서 설계한 에너지 효율이 높은 기계로 교체해야 한다. 셋째, 무료로 자연광을 제공하기 위해 번 엔터프라이지즈에 맡겨 채광창을 설치해야 한다. 넷째, **197**열 손실을 줄이기 위해 웹스터 건설에 맡겨 외벽에 단열 처리를 해야 한다. 마지막으로 직원들은 회사가 제공하는 교육을 통해 에너지 사용을 줄이는 데 기여할 수 있는 방법들을 배워야 한다.

어휘 energy efficiency 에너지 효율 audit 감사 carry out 실시하다 site 부지, 장소 facility 시설 factory 공장 optimization 최적화 opportunity 기회 identify 확인하다, 밝혀내다 concrete 구체적인 formulate 만들어 내다 solar panel 태양광 패널 generate 생성하다, 발생시키다 sustainable 지속가능한 grid 전력망 packaging equipment 포장 장비 replace 교체하다, 대신하다 skylight (천장에 낸) 채광창 install 설치하다 provide 제공하다 natural light 자연광 exterior wall 외벽 insulate 단열 처리하다 construction 건설 reduce 줄이다 undergo (변화, 안 좋은 일을) 겪다, 받다 contribute to ~에 기여하다, 공헌하다 reduction 감소 usage 사용(법)

수신: 데브러 라이언 〈d.lyon@sternbergmfg.com〉
발신: 미셸 소프 〈m.thorpe@sternbergmfg.com〉
날짜: 9월 20일
제목: 곧 있을 교육

라이언 씨께,

200저는 다양한 교대조 관리자들이 제시한 교육안들을 검토해 봤는데, 당신의 교육이 회사의 필요에 가장 부합하겠다는 생각이 듭니다. **198**당신이 준비한 자료들은 우리 회사의 목표를 뚜렷이 부각시키며, 직원들이 해야 할 일을 정확히 파악하도록 도움을 줄 것입니다. 우리는 과거에 에너지 절감을 위해 다른 계획들도 시도해 봤습니다. 하지만 이런 조치에도 불구하고 부수적인 일에 사용되는 전력 비율이 여전히 24%를 **199**유지하고 있으며, 이는 업계 평균보다 높은 수치입니다. 함께 협력해서 저는 우리가 이 수치를 줄일 수 있기를 바랍니다.

미셸 소프 드림

어휘 upcoming 다가오는, 곧 있을 training proposal 교육안 present 발표하다, 제시하다 various 다양한 shift manager 교대조 관리자 suitable 적합한, 부합하는 handout 유인물, 자료 highlight 집중 조명하다, 부각하다 exactly 정확히 initiative 계획 energy conservation 에너지 절감 measures 조치 ratio 비율 non-core 비핵심의 steady 꾸준한 industry average 업계 평균 work together 협력하다 reduce 줄이다 figure 수치

스턴버그 매뉴팩처링 월간 소식지
10월 호

진행 중인 새로운 에너지 절감 노력

스턴버그 매뉴팩처링이 간접비와 회사의 환경 영향을 둘 다 줄이기 위해 에너지 사용을 줄이려 애쓰고 있다. 지난달 미스트랄 에너지 서비스(MES)가 권고한 사항들을 기반으로 회사는 네 가지 주요 개선 프로젝트를 실시할 예정이다. 그중 첫 번째가 **197**11월에 웹스터 건설에 의해 시행될 예정이다. 나머지 프로젝트들은 자금 여력에 따라 내년에 그 뒤를 이을 것이다. 이 밖에도, **200**인적자원 담당 이사가 데브라 라이언을 선택해 절감 기술에 관한 직원 교육을 담당하게 했다. 교육 일정은 아직 확정되지 않았다.

어휘 seek to + 동사원형 ～하려고 애쓰다 energy usage 에너지 사용 overhead expenses 간접비 environmental impact 환경 영향 based on ～을 기반으로, ～에 근거하여 recommendation 권고 사항 carry out 실시하다 as funding allows 자금이 허락하는 대로 in addition 이 밖에도, 게다가, 더욱이 human resources 인적자원 employee training 직원 교육 regarding ～에 관하여 set 정하다

196 세부 사항

번역 스턴버그 매뉴팩처링의 베드포드 공장이 감사 대상으로 선정된 이유는?
(A) 검사 점수를 높게 받았다.
(B) 회사에서 가장 오래된 시설이다.
(C) MES 본사와 가깝다.
(D) 회사에서 가장 큰 건물이다.

해설 첫 번째 지문인 보고서 두 번째 문장에 감사 대상으로 선정된 이유가 명시되어 있다. 이 글을 보면 최초의 공장이면서 개선의 여지가 있다는 것이 선정 이유이므로 이를 토대로 회사에서 가장 오래된 시설임을 유추할 수 있다. 따라서 (B)가 정답이다.

197 연계

번역 11월에 무엇이 설치될 것인가?
(A) 태양광 패널
(B) 새로운 포장 장비
(C) 채광창
(D) 벽면 단열재

해설 우선 11월(November)이라는 단어가 있는 곳부터 찾아본다. 소식지 중간 부분에 보면 11월에 웹스터 건설이 4가지 프로젝트 중에서 제일 먼저 시행한다는 내용이 나온다. 이 프로젝트에 관한 내용은 첫 번째 지문(보고서) 두 번째 단락에 언급되어 있는데, 그중에서 네 번째 항목에 웹스터 건설이 외벽에 단열 처리를 한다고 되어 있다. 따라서 정답은 (D)이다.

198 세부 사항

번역 라이언 씨의 교육 자료에 관해 명시된 것은?
(A) 제출된 유일한 자료였다.
(B) 길이를 줄여야 한다.
(C) 이해하기가 쉽다.
(D) 기술적인 정보가 많다.

해설 이메일에서 라이언 씨의 자료에 대한 내용이 나오는데, 두 번째 문장에서 '준비한 자료가 우리 회사의 목표를 분명하게 강조하고 있다'는 내용이 나온다. 이를 토대로 보기에서 가장 유사한 의미를 고른다면 정답은 (C)가 된다.

199 동의어 찾기

번역 이메일에서 첫 번째 단락 6행의 "holds"와 의미가 가장 가까운 것은?
(A) 마련하다
(B) 파악하다
(C) 상태가 지속되다
(D) 점거하다

해설 holds는 이 문맥에서 24%에 '머물러 있다, 지속되다'는 뜻으로 쓰였다. 이와 유사한 의미로는 maintain, retain, remain, continue 등이 있다. 따라서 (C) remains가 정답이다.

200 연계

번역 소프 씨에 관해 암시된 것은?
(A) 라이언 씨에게 몇 가지 지침을 줄 것이다.
(B) MES를 고용하는 것을 추천했다.
(C) 인적자원부의 책임자이다.
(D) 스턴버그 매뉴팩처링의 다른 현장들을 방문할 계획이다.

해설 두 번째 지문이 소프 씨가 작성한 이메일인데, 첫 번째 문장을 살펴보면 '다양한 교대조 관리자들이 제시한 교육안들을 검토해 봤다'는 내용이 나온다. 관리자들보다 직책이 높고 '교육'과 관련된 부서에서 일한다는 것을 유추할 수 있다. 세 번째 지문인 소식지에도 '인적자원 담당 이사가 데브라 라이언을 선택했다'라는 말이 나오므로 소프 씨가 인적자원부의 책임자임을 알 수 있다. 따라서 정답은 (C)이다.

TEST 5

101 (D)	102 (B)	103 (A)	104 (A)	105 (D)
106 (B)	107 (B)	108 (D)	109 (D)	110 (B)
111 (A)	112 (B)	113 (D)	114 (C)	115 (D)
116 (D)	117 (D)	118 (C)	119 (A)	120 (A)
121 (A)	122 (A)	123 (C)	124 (B)	125 (C)
126 (C)	127 (A)	128 (C)	129 (C)	130 (C)
131 (C)	132 (D)	133 (D)	134 (A)	135 (B)
136 (B)	137 (A)	138 (B)	139 (D)	140 (D)
141 (B)	142 (C)	143 (A)	144 (D)	145 (C)
146 (D)	147 (D)	148 (C)	149 (D)	150 (D)
151 (C)	152 (D)	153 (A)	154 (D)	155 (D)
156 (C)	157 (B)	158 (C)	159 (C)	160 (A)
161 (A)	162 (D)	163 (B)	164 (D)	165 (B)
166 (D)	167 (A)	168 (B)	169 (D)	170 (D)
171 (A)	172 (A)	173 (B)	174 (D)	175 (C)
176 (D)	177 (A)	178 (C)	179 (A)	180 (B)
181 (A)	182 (C)	183 (D)	184 (B)	185 (A)
186 (C)	187 (B)	188 (B)	189 (A)	190 (D)
191 (D)	192 (A)	193 (D)	194 (C)	195 (B)
196 (B)	197 (D)	198 (C)	199 (C)	200 (A)

PART 5

101 동사 자리 + 수 일치

해설 빈칸 앞(Health benefits, ~ payments)이 모두 주어인데, 문장에 동사가 없다. 따라서 동사가 들어가야 하는 자리이다. 따라서 준동사나 분사형인 (A) to encourage와 (B) encouraging은 제외된다. 목적어(employees)가 있기 때문에 동사는 능동태로 와야 한다. 또한 주어는 A, B and C로 복수 형태이기 때문에 동사는 (D) encourage(격려하다)가 되어야 한다.

번역 의료 혜택과 휴가, 상여금 지급은 직원들이 열심히 일하게 한다.

어휘 health benefits 의료 혜택 vacation time 휴가 bonus payment 상여금 지급 employee 직원

102 전치사 어휘

해설 오후 5시 '이후'의 주문은 다음날 처리될 것이라는 의미가 가장 적절하기 때문에 (B) after가 정답이다.

번역 오후 5시 이후 접수된 주문은 다음 영업일에 처리될 것이다.

어휘 place an order 주문하다 process 처리하다 business day 영업일

103 부사 어휘

해설 빈칸은 현재완료 동사 사이에 위치하며 not과 함께 쓰는 부사 자리로 정답은 (A) yet(아직)이다. 보기 (B) much는 형용사 수식 부사, (C) always는 not과 함께 부분 부정 의미를 지닌다. (D) either는 앞 문장에 부정의 의미가 있을 때 뒤 문장에서 부정의 의미를 지닌 부사로 쓰일 수 있다.

번역 클라인 씨가 두 달 전에 물러났지만 곤돌 인더스트리즈는 아직 새로운 재무 담당 이사를 임명하지 않았다.

어휘 step down 물러나다 name 임명[지명]하다 finance 재무 either (둘 중) 어느 하나; (부정문에서) 또한, 역시

104 명사 자리 _ 전치사의 목적어

해설 빈칸 앞의 전치사 of 뒤에 올 수 있는 명사이면서, 빈칸 뒤 made와 함께 어울려 '진전을 이루다'라는 뜻으로 쓰일 수 있는 것은 (A) progress(진전)이다.

번역 연례 보고서는 우리의 에너지 절감 목표를 이루기 위한 진전이 부족했음을 설명해야 한다.

어휘 lack 부족 make progress 발전하다, 진전하다 reach one's goal 목표를 달성하다 progressive 진보적인, 점진적인

105 동사 어휘

해설 바로 뒤 목적어(a new CEO)와 의미가 연결되는 동사를 고르는 문제이다. 가장 그럴듯한 오답인 (A) decide도 성립될 것 같지만 정확한 의미를 위해서는 '임명하는 것을 결정하다'라는 식으로 decide to appoint라고 해야 적절하다. 따라서 (A)는 정답이 될 수 없다. 정답은 (D) appoint(임명하다)이다.

번역 휘스턴 엔터프라이지즈는 곧 있을 합병을 지휘하며 회사를 이끌 새 CEO를 임명할 것으로 확인되었다.

어휘 confirm 확인하다 lead 이끌다, 지휘하다 upcoming 다가오는 merger 합병 decide 결정하다 assemble 모으다 establish 설립하다

106 전치사 / 접속사 구분

해설 빈칸 앞뒤를 살펴보니, 동사가 두 개(was, ran) 있음을 알 수 있다. 따라서 빈칸은 접속사가 들어가야 할 자리이다. 문맥을 보면, 뒤 문장이 앞 문장에 대한 이유가 되는 것이 자연스러우므로 정답은 (B) because이다. 다른 보기들은 모두 전치사로 빈칸에 올 수 없다.

번역 어제 방송될 예정이었던 〈도나와의 이야기〉는 바로 앞의 프로그램이 방송 시간을 넘기면서 연기되었다.

어휘 postpone 연기하다 preceding 이전의, 앞선 due to ~ 때문에 following ~ 후에, ~에 따라 by ~에 의해서

107 목적격 대명사

해설 빈칸은 접속사 so 뒤의 절의 목적어로 '어떠한 매체 질의라도 즉시 심 씨에게 전달되어야 한다'는 내용이므로 목적격인 (B) her가 정답이다. 보기 중 재귀대명사 (A) herself, 소유대명사 (C) hers는 해석상으로, 주격 대명사인 (D) she는 문법상 적합하지 않다.

번역 심 씨가 우리의 공식 대변인이므로 어떤 매체의 질의라도 즉시 그녀에게 전달되어야 한다.

어휘 official 공식적인 spokesperson 대변인 inquiry 질문 pass on to ~에게 전하다, 옮기다 immediately 즉시

108 형용사 자리 _ 명사 수식

해설 빈칸은 동사와 명사 사이에서 명사를 수식하는 형용사가 들어갈 자리이다. 가끔 명사가 들어가서 복합명사를 만들기도 하는데, 보기 중에 명사는 (C) cooperator(협력자)가 있으나 연결해 보면 의미상 적절하지 않다. 형용사 (D) cooperative(협동하는)가 정답이다.

번역 제때에 배송하는 것은 생산팀과 배송팀의 협동적인 노력을 필요로 할 것이다.

어휘 timely 시기적절한, 때맞춘 require ~을 필요로 하다 effort 노력 production 생산 distribution 배부, 배급, 유통 cooperatively 협력하여, 합심하여 cooperate 협력하다

109 명사 어휘

해설 여러 차례 성공적이지 못한 '시도'가 있었다는 의미가 가장 적절하다. make attempts(시도하다)라는 표현이 수동태(attempts were made)로 만들어진 문장이라고 보면 된다. 따라서 정답은 (D) attempts(시도)이다.

번역 소포를 수신자에게 배송하려고 몇 차례 시도했지만 실패했다.

어휘 unsuccessful 성공하지 못한, 실패한 deliver 배달[배송]하다 package 소포 intended 의도된, 목표로 하는 recipient 수신자 receipt 영수증 conclusion 결론

110 형용사 / 분사 자리 _ 명사 수식

해설 관사와 명사 사이에서 명사를 수식하는 형용사나 분사가 들어갈 자리이다. 명사가 들어가서 복합명사를 이루기도 하지만, 보기 중 명사인 (D) disappointment의 경우는 연결했을 때 의미상 적절하지 못하다. '실망한, 낙담한'이라는 뜻의 형용사형 분사 (B) disappointed가 정답이다.

번역 실망한 고객을 다루는 최선의 방법은 고객에게 사과하고 문제를 바로잡기 위해 조처하겠다고 확약하는 것이다.

어휘 handle 처리하다 client 고객 apologize 사과하다 assure 확약[확언]하다, 장담하다 take action 조처하다 remedy (문제를) 바로잡다 disappoint 실망시키다 disappointingly 실망스럽게 disappointment 실망

111 접속사 자리 + 접속사 / 전치사 구분

해설 빈칸 뒤에 동사가 나왔으므로 전치사는 들어갈 수 없다. 전치사 뒤에는 동사가 동명사가 되어야 들어갈 수 있으므로 전치사 형태인 (B), (C)는 제외된다. 문맥상 choose 뒤의 동사 to open과 빈칸 뒤의 동사 (to) close를 비교하는 의미가 되어야 하므로 정답은 (A) rather than(~보다는)이 적절하다.

번역 설문 조사는 관리자들이 매장 문을 밤에 더 늦게 닫기보다는 아침에 더 일찍 여는 편을 택하리라는 것을 보여 주었다.

어휘 survey 설문 조사 would choose to+동사원형 ~하는 편을 택하다 earlier in the morning 아침에 더 일찍 later at night 밤에 더 늦게 in spite of ~에도 불구하고 regarding ~에 관해 whereas 반면에

112 형용사 자리 _ become의 보어

해설 become은 보어를 취하는 동사이다. 주어와 동격일 경우에는 명사가, 상태를 설명해 주는 경우에는 형용사를 보어로 취한다. '우리가 가동'이 아니라, '가동하게 되는' 것이므로, 형용사인 (B) operational(가동의, 사용 가능한)이 정답이다.

번역 일단 우리가 장비를 새것으로 바꾸고 나면 완전 가동하게 될 것이라고 직원들에게 알려 주세요.

어휘 inform 알리다 staff 직원들 fully operational 완전 가동 중인 once 일단 ~하면 update 새것으로 바꾸다, 갱신하다 equipment 장비 operate 운영하다, 가동하다 operation 운영, 가동

113 동사 어휘

해설 뒤에 온 전치사 for와 어울릴 수 있는 자동사를 찾는 문제이다. apply for 는 '~에 지원하다'라는 의미로 뒤에 지원하는 '자리(position)'가 나오기 때문에 적절하다. 따라서 정답은 (D) apply이다.

번역 일자리를 찾을 때는 어떤 일자리를 제공하는 회사에 대해 조사하기 전까지 지원하지 마십시오.

어휘 search for work 일자리를 찾다, 구직 활동을 하다 position 직위, 자리 research 조사하다 submit 제출하다 approve 인정하다, 승인하다

114 부사 어휘

해설 문맥을 보면, '(고객의) 불만에 대해 ------ 대응해야 한다'는 말이 되어야 한다. 보기의 부사들의 의미를 살펴보고 가장 자연스러운 것을 찾도록 한다. (A) rarely는 '드물게', (B) namely는 '즉', '다시 말해', (C) promptly는 '즉시', (D) heavily는 '심하게'라는 뜻으로, 이 중 가장 적절한 것은 (C) promptly이다. promptly 외에도 '곧바로, 즉시'라는 의미로 immediately, directly, quickly를 동일하게 사용할 수 있다.

번역 고객의 불만에 신속히 대응하고 전문적으로 처리해 주세요.

어휘 be sure to+동사원형 반드시[꼭] ~하다 respond to ~에 대응하다, 응답하다 complaint 불만, 불평 address 처리하다, 해결하다 in a professional manner 전문적으로, 노련하게

115 부사 자리 _ 동사 수식

해설 증가(increase), 감소(decrease)를 뜻하는 동사 뒤에는 '상당히'라는 의미의 부사가 따라오는 경우가 많은데, significantly, substantially, dramatically 등의 부사들이 있다. 이 문제에서 빈칸도 increased 를 뒤에서 수식해 주는 부사가 들어가야 하는 자리이다. 따라서 정답은 (D) dramatically(극적으로, 상당히)이다.

번역 특히 안전과 관련해 관광 산업을 규제하는 법률의 수가 지난 10년 동안 극적으로 늘어났다.

어휘 regulate 규제[통제, 단속]하다 travel industry 관광 산업 increase 증가하다, 늘다 decade 10년 particularly 특히 in relation to ~과 관련하여 safety 안전 dramatic 극적인 dramatize 각색하다

116 형용사 어휘

해설 주어인 온도계(The X-R70 Thermometer)를 설명하는 형용사를 찾는 문제로, 심지어 약간의 기온 변화에도 '민감한'이라는 말이 가장 적절하다. 따라서 정답은 (D) sensitive이다.

번역 심지어 기온의 미세한 변화에도 민감한 X-R70 온도계는 실험실의 필수품이다.

어휘 thermometer 온도계   slight 약간의, 조금의   temperature 온도   must-have 꼭 가져야 하는   laboratory 실험실   committed 헌신적인, 열성적인   impressive 인상적인   perceptive 통찰력 있는

117 부사 자리 _ 부사구 수식

해설 빈칸은 by 이하의 부사구를 수식하는 부사가 올 자리이다. 따라서 정답은 부사형인 (D) simply(단지)이다. simply by ~ing라는 표현은 '단지 ~하기만 하면'이라는 의미로 자주 쓰인다.

번역 저희 충성 고객 프로그램에 등록하시면 그레그 청과물점의 모든 배달 주문에서 가격의 5%를 빼드립니다.

어휘 save 절약하다   delivery order 배달 주문   green grocer 청과물상   register 등록하다   simplicity 단순성   simplify 단순화하다   simpler 더 단순한

118 동사 시제

해설 if나 when이 이끄는 시간이나 조건 부사절에서는 의미가 미래여도 현재 시제를 사용한다. 하지만 주절에서는 미래 시제를 나타내 주어야 하므로, 이 문장의 빈칸에는 미래 시제가 들어가야 한다. 따라서 정답은 미래 시제인 (C) will arrive이다.

번역 우리가 정오에 사무실을 나서면 시간 넉넉하게 역에 도착해서 시카고행 기차를 잡게 될 것이다.

어휘 at noon 정오에   arrive 도착하다   in plenty of time 시간이 넉넉하게   catch a train 기차를 잡다

119 전치사 어휘

해설 빈칸 뒤의 중심 명사 section 앞에 쓸 수 있는 전치사를 골라야 한다. 구매 내역을 'My History'라는 섹션에서 볼 수 있다'는 의미이므로 정답은 장소나 범위를 나타내는 (A) in이다.

번역 잰트마켓닷컴 쇼핑객들은 이제 자신의 계정에 새로 마련된 '나의 구매 이력' 섹션에서 과거 구매 내역을 볼 수 있다.

어휘 shopper 쇼핑객, 구매자   purchase 구입(품)   section 섹션, 부분   account 계정   among ~ 사이에   except ~을 제외하고   of ~의

120 명사 자리 _ 복합 명사

해설 이 문장에는 이미 동사(has risen)가 있으므로 빈칸에 동사는 들어갈 수 없다. 따라서 (B), (C)는 제외된다. (D) enrolled가 과거분사 형태로 명사 뒤에서 수식하는 것으로 본다면, international student 앞에 관사가 있어야 하므로 역시 오답이다. 따라서 '국제 학생 등록'이라는 복합 명사를 만들어 주는 (A) enrollment(등록)가 정답이다.

번역 뉴잉글랜드 캠퍼스에서는 지난 몇 년 동안 국제 학생 등록이 증가해왔다.

어휘 international student 국제 학생, 유학생   enroll 등록하다

121 동사 어휘

해설 빈칸은 주어인 세부 통계(detailed statistic)가 정기적으로 집계된다는 것을 설명하는 내용으로 정답은 (A) compiled(집계하다)이다. 나머지 보기는 주어와 의미상 적합하지 않다.

번역 다양한 이유로, 해외에서 온 관광객 및 기타 방문객에 관한 세부 통계가 정기적으로 집계된다.

어휘 a variety of 다양한 ~   detailed 자세한   compile statistics 통계를 내다   from abroad 해외에서   on a regular basis 정기적으로   undergo 겪다   attract 끌어들이다   convene 소집하다, 회합하다

122 명사 어휘

해설 이 문제에서는 at a ------- of의 형태로 쓰이는 표현을 생각해 내야 한다. '~의 비율로'라는 뜻으로 at a rate of가 있다. 또는 of 뒤의 10%를 보고 힌트를 얻을 수도 있다. rate가 '비율'이라는 의미이므로 퍼센트로 많이 표현된다. 따라서 정답은 (A) rate(비율)이다.

번역 카 씨가 마케팅 부장이 된 이후로 회사의 수익이 분기마다 거의 10%씩 성장했다.

어휘 head of marketing 마케팅 부장   revenue 수익   grow 성장하다   quarter 분기   height 높이, 키   measurement 치수, 측정   figure 수치

123 동사 자리 + 능동태 / 수동태 구분

해설 The clients가 주어이고 동사가 들어가야 할 자리이다. 그리고 감정을 나타내는 동사(satisfy)는 사람이 주체가 되면 수동태로 써야 한다. 따라서 정답은 (C) were satisfied이다. (B) satisfied와 혼동하기 쉬운데, satisfied가 과거분사여서 clients를 뒤에서 수식하는 것이라면 The clients ~ sketches까지가 주어가 되어야 하고, 뒤에 동사가 연결되어야 가능하다. 그러나 and로 연결된 두 개의 문장이기 때문에 답이 될 수 없다.

번역 고객들은 건축가의 최종 스케치들이 마음에 들어서 즉시 공사를 시작하고 싶어 한다.

어휘 client 고객   be satisfied with ~에 만족하다, 마음에 들어 하다   final 최종적인, 마지막의   construction 공사   right away 즉시, 곧바로

124 접속사 어휘

해설 보기가 모두 접속사이므로 문장과 문장과의 연결 관계를 파악해서 구분한다. 문맥상 앞의 내용이 아니더라도 뒤 내용의 일을 해주었으면 한다는 뜻이므로 '가정'과 '양보'의 의미이다. 따라서 정답은 '만약 ~하더라도'로 해석할 수 있는 (B) Even if가 정답이다.

번역 설령 당신이 컨퍼런스에 참석하지 않더라도 관리자는 당신이 팀을 도와 행사를 준비해 주기를 원한다.

어휘 attend 참석하다   conference 컨퍼런스, 회의   manager 관리자, 경영자   preparations 준비   event 행사   whether ~인지 아닌지   as soon as ~하자마자

125 명사 자리 _ 주어

해설 '관사+형용사' 뒤에 올 수 있는 품사는 명사이므로 (C) translation(번역)이 정답이다.

번역 학자들은 본문을 중국어에서 영어로 직역하여 저자의 의도가 누락되었음을 발견했다.

어휘 scholar 학자 direct 직접적인 result in ~를 야기하다 a loss of ~의 손실 author 저자 intention 의도 translatable 번역할 수 있는

126 부사 어휘

해설 문맥상 7일간의 무료 시험 사용을 신규 고객에게만 제공하겠다는 의미가 자연스럽다. 따라서 신규 고객들에게만 '독점적으로'라는 의미가 되려면 (C) exclusively(독점적으로)가 정답으로 적절하다. (A) expensively는 '비싸게', (B) thoroughly는 '대단히, 철저히', (D) respectively는 '각각'이라는 의미이므로 문장에 어울리지 않는다.

번역 7일 동안의 무료 시험 사용 기간은 사이프러스 TV의 신규 고객들에게만 제공되는 일회성 할인 행사다.

어휘 free 무료의, 공짜의 one-time 한 번뿐인, 일회적인 offer 할인 (행사) available 이용할 수 있는, 입수할 수 있는 new customer 신규 고객

127 관계대명사 _ 선행사

해설 빈칸은 to부정사(to discuss)의 목적어이면서 '주어+동사+형용사'가 꾸며주는 대명사를 찾는 문제다. 또한, 빈칸 다음에는 목적격 관계대명사 that이 생략되어 있으므로 정답은 (A) anything(어떤 것)이다.

번역 회의 참가자들은 그들이 현재 근무 기록 체계에 불편하다고 여기는 어떤 사항이라도 논의하도록 요청받을 것이다.

어휘 participant 참가자 inconvenient 불편한 current 현재의 time sheet 근무시간 기록표 especially 특히

128 전치사 / 부사 구분

해설 빈칸은 앞의 just minutes와 함께 쓰여 '해변으로부터 몇 분만 가면 되는'이라는 의미가 어울리는 뜻의 전치사가 들어가야 할 자리이다. 따라서 정답은 (C) away from(~로부터 떨어져 있는)이다. 보기 (A) further는 부사, (B) besides는 전치사로 문장 전체의 의미를 볼 때 어울리지 않으며, (D) as far는 as far as 형태로 쓰인다.

번역 라요 호텔은 해변에서 몇 분만 가면 되는 적당한 가격의 숙소를 원하는 이들에게 안성맞춤이다.

어휘 perfect 완벽한 affordable (가격이) 알맞은 accommodation 숙소 further 더 이상의 besides ~ 외에

129 부사 어휘

해설 오랫동안 집이 팔리지 않았기 때문에 가격을 낮추는 데 '어쩔 수 없이, 마지못해' 동의했다는 의미가 가장 적절하다. 따라서 정답은 (C) reluctantly이다.

번역 판매자인 톰슨 씨는 집이 오랫동안 시장에 나와 있었기 때문에 더 낮은 제시가를 받아들이는 데 마지못해 동의했다.

어휘 seller 판매자 accept 받아들이다, 수락하다 a lower offer on ~에 대한 더 낮은 제시가 on the market 시장에 나와 있는 for a long time 오랫동안 fluently 유창하게 adversely 불리하게, 반대로 unanimously 만장[전원]일치로

130 형용사 어휘

해설 빈칸 뒤에 온 명사 costumes(의상)를 꾸며주며 의미가 어울릴 형용사를 골라야 한다. 따라서 정답은 (C) elaborate(정교한)이다.

번역 그 연극에는 팀원들이 수 주에 걸쳐 공들여 제작했음이 틀림없는 정교한 의상이 나온다.

어휘 feature 특별히 포함하다 painstaking 공들인 vigorous 활기찬 courteous 공손한, 정중한 eventful 다사다난한

PART 6

131-134 정보문

리노스트 전자 수염 정리기를 구입해 주셔서 감사합니다. 새 정리기를 사용하시기 전에 칼날을 덮고 있는 **131**보호용 플라스틱 피복을 제거해 주십시오. 리노스트 디럭스 세면도구 꾸러미를 구입하셨다면 정리기에 AA 건전지 두 개가 미리 장착되어 있습니다. 꾸러미를 구입하신 게 아니라면 기기 뒤편에 있는 **132**칸 안에 해당 건전지를 삽입하셔야 합니다.

133수염 정리기를 사용하시고 나면 반드시 매번 청소해 주십시오. 제공된 솔을 사용하여 칼날에서 수염을 제거하십시오. 또한, 기기를 건조한 곳에 보관하시고 아이들이 갖고 놀지 **134**못하도록 해 주십시오. 이렇게 하면 수염 정리기를 오랫동안 좋은 상태로 사용하실 수 있습니다.

어휘 purchase 구입[구매]하다 beard trimmer 수염 정리기 remove 제거하다 plastic coating 플라스틱 피복[코팅] cover 덮다 blade 칼날 toiletries 세면 도구 package 꾸러미, 패키지 pre-loaded with ~가 미리 장착된 battery 건전지, 배터리 insert 삽입하다, 끼우다 at the back of ~의 뒤편에 device 기기, 장치 make sure 꼭[반드시] ~하다 clean 청소하다 store 보관하다, 저장하다

131 형용사 자리 _ 명사 수식

해설 관사와 명사 사이에 들어갈 수 있는 것은 명사를 수식하는 형용사이거나 복합 명사를 만드는 명사가 가능하다. 명사 (A), (B)는 의미 연결이 부자연스럽기 때문에 제외된다. 정답은 '보호하는, 보호용의'라는 의미의 형용사 (C) protective이다.

132 명사 어휘

해설 '~ 안에 해당 건전지를 삽입해야 한다'고 말하고 있으므로 건전지를 삽입할 수 있는 '곳, 위치'를 나타낼 수 있는 명사가 들어갈 자리

이다. (A) warranty는 '품질 보증서', (B) description은 '묘사, 기술', (C) power는 '전원, 힘'이라는 뜻이므로 빈칸에 적합하지 않다. compartment는 나뉘어 있는 '구획, 칸'이라는 뜻이므로 의미상 적합하다. 따라서 정답은 (D) compartment이다.

133 문맥에 맞는 문장 고르기

번역 (A) 귀하의 요청이 즉시 처리될 것입니다.
(B) 아래 그림은 다른 인기 있는 스타일들을 보여줍니다.
(C) 결국, 종이 피복이 더 환경친화적입니다.
(D) 제공된 솔을 사용하여 칼날에서 수염을 제거하십시오.

해설 단락이 바뀌고 빈칸 앞의 첫 문장이 문제 해결의 단서이다. 정리기를 사용하고 나면 매번 청소해야 한다고 있는데, 솔(brush)을 사용해서 칼날에 있는 수염을 제거하라는 내용이 문맥상 가장 알맞으므로 정답은 (D)이다.

134 동사 자리 _ 명령문

해설 명령문 구조가 접속사 and로 연결되어 있다. 따라서 동사의 형태도 동일한 동사원형이 되어야 한다. 참고로 prohibit A from -ing(A가 ~하지 못하게 하다)라는 표현을 알고 있으면 좀 더 쉽게 문제를 해결할 수 있을 것이다. 정답은 (A)이다.

135 -138 편지

4월 22일

프레드 씨께,

새로운 식당 슈니첼즈 앤 서치를 개업하신 것을 축하드립니다! 귀하는 이제 홈본트 카운티의 사업주이시니 홈본트 카운티 상공회의소(HCCOC)에 가입하시도록 귀하를 **135**정식으로 초대합니다. **136**HCCOC는 82년 전에 카운티의 사업적 관심을 홍보하기 위해 설립되었습니다. <u>그 이후로 저희는 이 목적을 이루기 위해 노력해왔습니다.</u>

우리 조직은 몇 가지 방법으로 지역 사업체들을 **137**돕고 있습니다. 예를 들면, 회원들은 저희의 월간 소식지로 지역 사회에 알려지는 이점이 있습니다. **138**게다가, 지역 사회의 행사에 참가 초청도 받습니다. 더 알고 싶으시면, 리먼 스트리트에 있는 저희 본부나 웹사이트 www.hccoc.com을 방문해 주시기 바랍니다.

수전 케인
홈본트 카운티 상공회의소

어휘 Congratulations 축하합니다 invite 초대[초청]하다 join 가입하다, 합류하다 chamber of commerce 상공회의소 found 설립하다 benefit from ~로부터 이득을 얻다, 혜택을 누리다 community exposure 지역 사회에 알려짐 headquarters 본부, 본사

135 부사 자리 _ 동사 수식

해설 to부정사 to와 invite 사이에서 invite를 수식하는 부사가 와야 하는 자리이다. '공식적으로' 초대한다는 의미의 부사인 (B) formally(공식적으로)

가 정답이다. 다른 보기 (A) formal(공식적인), (C) formalize(공식화하다), (D) formality(격식)는 품사면에서 어울리지 않는다.

136 문맥에 맞는 문장 고르기

번역 (A) 저희 자문위원회에서 봉사해 주셔서 감사합니다.
(B) 그 이후로 저희는 이 목적을 이루기 위해 노력해왔습니다.
(C) 그래서 저희는 음식 축제를 열기로 결정했습니다.
(D) 우리 회원들 각자가 이러한 규정에 동의해야 합니다.

해설 빈칸 앞에 HCCOC의 82년 전 설립된 목적이 나왔다. 문맥상 그동안 어떻게 해왔다는 말이 나와야 적절하므로 (B)가 정답이다.

137 동사 어휘

해설 목적어(local businesses)와 의미 연결이 긴밀하게 이뤄지면서 앞에서 밝힌 것처럼 상공회의소가 하는 역할을 설명할 수 있는 단어가 들어가야 한다. 지역 사업체를 '지원하는' 역할을 하고 있다는 것이 가장 적절하므로 정답은 (A) assists(지원하다, 돕다)이다.

어휘 investigate 조사하다 reorganize 재편성[재조직]하다 surpass 뛰어넘다, 능가하다

138 부사 어휘

해설 앞 문장에서, 상공회의소에 가입하게 되면 월간 소식지로 지역 사회에 알릴 수 있다는 점을 얘기했는데, 뒤 문장에서 행사에 초청을 받는다는 점을 '추가로' 말한 것이므로 (B) In addition(게다가)가 정답으로 가장 적절하다.

어휘 in contrast 그에 반해서

139 -142 웹페이지

http://www.lattlerapparel.com/recycling

래틀러 어패럴

의복 재활용 프로그램

래틀러 어패럴의 **139**주요 목표 중 하나는 패션업계의 지속가능성에 이바지하는 것입니다. 이에 따라 딜라인 서비시즈와 **140**손잡고 의복 재활용 프로그램을 실행하게 되어 자랑스럽게 생각합니다. 해당 프로그램에 따라 소비자께서는 입었던 래틀러 옷을 저희 매장 어느 곳이든 갖다 주시면 됩니다. 이후 딜라인 서비시즈가 옷을 수거해 상태에 따라 분류합니다. 상대적으로 마모나 손상이 거의 없는 옷은 재판매를 위해 중고 매장으로 **141**유통됩니다. 이와 동시에 재활용 공장에서는 **142**나머지 옷들을 방직 섬유로 변형시킵니다. <u>이것은 가구 완충재와 같은 물품을 만드는 데 사용됩니다.</u> 그러므로 래틀러 어패럴의 소비자는 자신이 더 이상 원치 않는 옷도 다른 소비자들에게 계속 유용하게 쓰이도록 할 수 있습니다.

어휘 clothing 옷, 의복 recycling 재활용 contribute to ~에 공헌하다 sustainability 지속가능성 objective 목표, 목적 proud 자랑스러운 operate 운용하다 customer 소비자 drop off 갖다주다, 내려주다 collect 모으다, 수집하다 sort 분류하다 according to ~에 따라 condition 상태 garment 의복 relatively 상대적으로 wear 마모, 닳음 damage 손상 secondhand 중고의 resale 재판매 at the same time 동시에 turn A into B A를 B로 바꾸다 textile fiber 방직 섬유 thus 그러므로 unwanted 원치 않는 useful 유용한

139 형용사 어휘

해설 빈칸 뒤에 있는 명사 objectives를 꾸며주는 형용사를 고르는 문제다. 주어인 '패션업계의 지속가능성에 이바지하는 것'이 '주된 목표'라는 의미가 가장 어울린다. 따라서 정답은 (A) prime(주된, 주요한)이다.

어휘 fragile 깨지기 쉬운 remote 먼 eligible (자격이 맞아서) ~를 할 수 있는

140 전치사 어휘

해설 빈칸은 명사 목적어 딜라인 서비시즈와 어울리는 '~와 함께'라는 뜻의 전치사구에 들어갈 단어를 골라야 한다. in conjunction with(~와 더불어, 함께)가 적절하므로 정답은 (D) conjunction이다.

어휘 impact 영향 authority 권위, 권한 supplement 보충 conjunction 결합

141 동사의 시제 / 태

해설 빈칸은 주어 Garments와 어울리는 동사 자리로, 뒤에 목적어가 없으므로 수동태이다. 또한, 전체 지문이 '의복 재활용 프로그램'을 현재 시제로 설명하고 있다. 따라서 정답은 (B) are distributed이다.

어휘 distribute 유통시키다

142 문맥에 맞는 문장 고르기

번역 (A) 재활용 방법은 소재에 따라 달라집니다.
(B) 그리고 나서 원치 않는 옷을 문 옆의 녹색 통에 넣어주십시오.
(C) 이것은 가구 완충재와 같은 물품을 만드는 데 사용됩니다.
(D) 현재 저희는 토론토 외부 지역에 새로운 것을 지을 준비를 하고 있습니다.

해설 바로 앞 문장에서 '나머지 옷들을 방직 섬유로 변형시킨다'는 내용이 나왔기 때문에 그 뒤에 이어지는 문장은 '이것은 가구 완충재와 같은 물품을 만드는 데 사용된다'라는 내용이 적절하므로 정답은 (C)이다.

어휘 method 방법 vary 달라지다, 다르다 depending on ~에 따라 material 소재, 재료 place 놓다, 두다 bin 통 padding 완충재, 충전재 currently 현재 prepare 준비하다

143-146 이메일

발신: 도로시 스콰이어스
수신: 루디 나카야마
제목: 로비 디자인 수정
날짜: 9월 17일
첨부: 세트 A, 세트 B

루디 씨께,

143수정된 로비 디자인의 모형 두 세트를 첨부하였습니다. 말씀하신 문제의 대부분이 해결된 것을 확인하실 수 있을 겁니다. 두 세트 모두 요청하신 좌석을 추가하였으며 조명 기구는 눈에 덜 띄는 것으로 교체했습니다.

세트 B에서 **144**요청하신 대로 바닥재를 바꾸지 않은 것을 보실 텐데요. **145**제가 보기엔, 원래 바닥재가 로비 전체 디자인에 훨씬 더 잘 맞을 듯합니다. 물론 결정하시는 바에 따르겠지만 결정을 하실 때 두 가지 세트를 꼼꼼히 비교해 보시기 바랍니다.

본 프로젝트의 디자인 단계를 9월 20일까지 마치도록 계획되어 있습니다. **146**그때까지 답변을 주시기 바랍니다.

도로시 스콰이어스
스콰이어스 인테리어 디자인

어휘 revise 변경하다, 수정하다 attach 첨부하다 mock-up 실제 크기의 모형 seating 좌석, 자리 replace A with B A를 B로 교체하다 light fixture 조명 기구 noticeable 눈에 띄는, 뚜렷한 option 선택 flooring 바닥재 request 요청하다 original 원래의 suited 어울리는, 적당한 overall 전체의 accept 받아들이다 decision 결심, 결정 urge 강력히 권고하다 be scheduled to+동사원형 ~할 예정이다 phase 단계

143 문맥에 맞는 문장 고르기

번역 (A) 말씀하신 문제의 대부분이 해결된 것을 확인하실 수 있을 겁니다.
(B) 개조 과정은 직원과 고객들의 불만을 살 수도 있습니다.
(C) 그로 인해 건물은 지역 건축의 랜드마크가 됐습니다.
(D) 제 웹사이트의 '포트폴리오' 페이지에 추가 디자인이 들어 있습니다.

해설 빈칸의 앞 문장에서 '모형 두 세트를 첨부했다'라는 내용이 나왔고 뒤 문장을 보면 '요청하신 좌석 추가와 조명 기구 교체'라는 내용이 나왔다. 빈칸에는 '문제가 해결되었다'라는 내용이 들어가야 적절하므로 정답은 (A)이다.

어휘 issue 문제 raise 제기하다, 언급하다 resolve 해결하다 renovation 개조 process 과정, 절차 frustrating 불만스러운 cause 일으키다 architectural 건축학의 extra 추가의

144 접속사

해설 as you requested(요청하신 대로)라는 구문을 알고 있다면 쉽게 풀 수 있는 문제이다. 빈칸은 접속사 자리이고 '요청하신 대로 바닥재 또한 바꾸지 않았다'라는 내용이 가장 적절하므로 정답은 (B)이다. (D) beyond는 전치사이므로 정답이 될 수 없다.

어휘 beyond ~ 너머

145 목적격 대명사

해설 빈칸은 앞의 전치사 To와 어울리는 대명사를 고르는 문제다. 빈칸 다음에 바닥재에 관한 자신의 의견을 말하고 있으므로 정답은 (D) me이다.

146 부사 어휘

해설 빈칸은 앞의 전치사 by와 어울리는 부사로 앞 문장에서 날짜를 지정하였고 '그때까지 회신을 바란다'고 했다. 따라서 정답은 (D) then이다.

어휘 quickly 빨리 such 그런 far 먼

PART 7

147-148 회람

> **회람**
>
> **콘웨이 회계**
>
> 수신: 전 직원
>
> 발신: 샌드라 브루나 이사
>
> 날짜: 1월 4일
>
> 제목: 1월 12일 휴무
>
> 시에서 **147**다음 주 화요일에 우리의 수도관을 보수할 예정이라서, 그날 모두에게 물 사용을 자제해 달라고 요청하는 대신 사무실은 문을 닫을 예정입니다. 급여에 관해서는 이 날은 평일 근무일처럼 계산될 것입니다. 여러분은 마감 일자가 있는 프로젝트로 일하지 않는 한 재택근무를 하도록 요청받지 않을 것입니다. 특히 애킨스 건을 맡아 작업하고 있는 **148**팀장들은 보고서 작성을 마치고 제게 이메일로 보내주세요. 저는 수요일 아침 컨퍼런스 전에 그 보고서들이 필요합니다.
>
> 샌드라 브루나

어휘 accounting 회계 conduct 실시하다, 시행하다 repair 수리, 보수 water line 수도관 instead of ~ 대신에 avoid 자제하다, 피하다 close 문을 닫다 call upon ~에게 청하다, 부탁하다 work from home 재택근무를 하다 work on ~에 대한 작업을 하다 deadline 기한, 마감 일자 account 거래선, 거래처 report 보고서

147 세부 사항

번역 사무실은 화요일에 왜 문을 닫을 예정인가?
(A) 애킨스 건에 관한 업무가 완료되어서
(B) 시 축하 행사가 혼란을 일으킬 것이어서
(C) 직원들이 컨퍼런스에 갈 예정이라서
(D) 일부 파이프를 보수할 필요가 있어서

해설 첫 번째 문장을 보면 다음 주 화요일에 수도관을 보수한다는(conducting repairs on our water lines next Tuesday) 내용이 나온다. 따라서 정답은 (D)이다.

▶▶ **Paraphrasing** 지문의 **conducting repairs on our water lines** → 정답의 **Some pipes require maintenance.**

148 세부 사항

번역 브루나 씨는 몇몇 팀장들에게 무엇을 해 달라고 요청하는가?
(A) 물 사용을 자제할 것
(B) 급여를 일찍 지급할 것
(C) 자신에게 이메일을 보낼 것
(D) 사무실 문을 잠글 것

해설 team leaders가 나오는 부문을 찾아보면, 회람 후반부에 '보고서를 나에게 이메일로 보내 달라(e-mail me their reports)'는 내용을 확인할 수 있다. 따라서 정답은 (C)이다.

149-150 광고

> **카를루치스 다이너**
>
> 51번가 55번지, 뉴욕시, 뉴욕주 10019
>
> 카를루치스 다이너에 오셔서 풍성한 정통 이탈리아 요리를 즐기세요. 갓 구운 마늘빵, 올리브 오일 파스타, 씬 크러스트 피자까지 무엇 하나라고 할 것 없이 모두 나폴리에서 온 맛 그대로입니다! 점심 메뉴에는 클래식 델리 샌드위치 특선이 포함됩니다.
>
> **149**화요 특선! 음료와 디저트 값을 절약하세요!
> 모든 라지 사이즈 음료가 단돈 1달러, 모든 디저트 콤비네이션 요리가 3달러입니다. 6세 이하의 어린이는 무료입니다!
>
> 점심 식사
> 오전 11시 ~ 오후 3시
>
> 저녁 식사
> 오후 4시 ~ 오후 10시
> (오후 3시~4시에는 문을 닫습니다.)
>
> **150**"할머니의 손맛 그대로… 별점 5점 중 4점!"
> – 니콜 로시, 유명 음식 블로그 테이스트 오브 뉴욕의 필자
>
> 저녁 식사 예약은 202-555-0189로 전화하십시오.

어휘 diner 작은 식당, (식당에서) 식사하는 사람 authentic 정통의, 진품인 cuisine 요리 feature 특별히 포함하다, 특징으로 삼다 reservation 예약

149 세부 사항

번역 고객들은 일주일에 한 번 무엇을 할 수 있는가?
(A) 무료 디저트 주문
(B) 음료 할인 받기
(C) 저녁 식사 예약
(D) 개인 식사 공간 얻기

해설 Tuesday Special!에서 음료수와 디저트를 할인해 주고 있다는 것을 알 수 있다. 화요일에만 이 행사를 진행하고 있기 때문에 정답은 (B)이다.

▶▶ **Paraphrasing** 지문의 **Save money on drinks and desserts** → 정답의 **Pay a lower price for beverages**

150 사실 관계 확인

번역 비평가가 식당에 대해 언급한 것은?
(A) 식재료를 이탈리아에서 수입한다.
(B) 델리 샌드위치를 주문 조리한다.
(C) 요리가 신속하게 준비된다.
(D) 음식이 가정식과 같은 맛이다.

해설 지문 마지막 부분에서 Nicole Rossi라는 유명 음식 블로그 필자의 언급이 나온다. 할머니가 만들어 주신 음식 맛과 같다는 평에서 (D)가 정답인 것을 확인할 수 있다.

▶▶ **Paraphrasing** 지문의 **tastes like my grandma's cooking** → 정답의 **tastes homemade**

151 -152 문자 메시지

줄리 바유 오후 1:34

전화를 못 받아서 미안하지만, 아무튼 너무 시끄러워서 통화할 수가 없어요. 거의 다 왔어요? 156경기가 2회째인데, 당신은 벌써 홈런 한 개를 못 보고 놓쳤어요.

행크 로 오후 1:38

경기장에 막 도착했어요. 오늘 교통이 혼잡하네요! 입구가 여러 개인 것 같아요. 157어떤 입구로 가야 하죠?

줄리 바유 오후 1:39

입장권 가지고 있잖아요, 그렇죠?

행크 로 오후 1:40

아, 알았어요. 좋아요. 몇 분 뒤에 그곳으로 갈게요. 매점에서 뭐든 원하는 거 없어요? 나는 핫도그를 살 거예요.

어휘 miss one's call ~의 전화를 받지 못하다 loud 시끄러운 anyway 아무튼, 어쨌든 almost 거의 inning (야구에서 9회 중 한) 회, 이닝 already 벌써, 이미 stadium 경기장 traffic 교통(량) entrance gate 입구 in a few minutes 몇 분 뒤에 snack bar 매점, 간이식당

151 추론 / 암시

번역 바유 씨는 어디에 있을 것 같은가?

(A) 버스 투어 중에
(B) 미술 전시회에
(C) 스포츠 행사에
(D) 야외 콘서트에

해설 첫 번째 대화 내용의 the second inning, a home run 등의 표현을 통해서 바유 씨가 야구장에 있다는 것을 알 수 있다. 따라서 정답은 (C)이다.

152 의도 파악

번역 오후 1시 39분에 바유 씨가 "입장권 가지고 있잖아요, 그렇죠?"라고 쓴 의도는 무엇이겠는가?

(A) 로 씨가 입장권을 기념으로 보관해야 한다.
(B) 로 씨가 직접 입장권을 구입했다.
(C) 입장권을 사용해서 할인을 받을 수 있다.
(D) 입장권에 무언가 유용한 정보가 포함되어 있다.

해설 바로 앞 문장에서 입구가 여러 개라는 말을 하고 나서 입장권에 대해 언급한 이유는 입장권에 입구에 대한 정보가 포함되어 있기 때문일 것이다. 따라서 정답은 (D)이다.

153 -154 정보문

알피트 인더스트리즈
셰프스 메이트 480

153알피트 인더스트리즈에서 새로 나온 육류용 온도계 겸 주방 타이머 셰프스 메이트 480은 긴 철망 케이블 옆 견고한 전자 받침대에 부착된 날카로운 6인치 탐침으로 구성된다. 가격은 18.99달러로 패스트푸드 가격으로 미식 요리를 맛보는 셈이다.

기능:

- – 50℃∼300℃의 범위 내 온도 측정
- 일반 육류를 위한 설정 추천 온도 제공
- 받침대의 대형 LCD 디스플레이를 통해 가독성 우수
- 타이머로 최대 50시간까지 계산 가능
- 154탐침 및 케이블은 최대 380℃까지 견딜 수 있는 내열성 있음
- AAA 건전지 한 개로 수 주간 작동 가능

어휘 meat thermometer 육류용 온도계 consist of ~로 구성되다 probe 탐침, 탐색침 attached to ~에 부착된 sturdy 견고한 electronic 전자의 mesh 철망 gourmet 미식가(의) feature 특색, 기능 measure 측정하다 temperature 온도 degrees Celsius 섭씨 온도 offer 제공하다 recommend 추천하다 allow 허락하다 up to ~까지 withstand 견뎌내다

153 세부 사항

번역 셰프스 메이트 480의 기능으로 맞는 것은?

(A) 시간 계산
(B) 음식 데우기
(C) 조리도구 연마
(D) 주방 위생 향상

해설 첫 번째 단락 첫 번째 문장에서 '알피트 인더스트리즈에서 새로 나온 육류용 온도계 겸 주방 타이머 셰프스 메이트 480'을 소개하고 있다. '타이머'라는 말에서 시간을 재어줌을 알 수 있으므로 정답은 (A)이다.

어휘 function 기능 keep track of ~를 계산하다, 기록하다 warm up 데우다 sharpen 날카롭게 하다 tool 도구, 연장 sanitation 위생

154

번역 셰프스 메이트 480의 케이블에 대해 명시된 것은?

(A) 받침대에 전원을 공급한다.
(B) 강한 열에 견딜 수 있다.
(C) 떼어낼 수 있다.
(D) 길이 조절이 가능하다.

해설 두 번째 단락에 언급된 기능(Features)의 다섯 번째 항목에 '탐침 및 케이블은 최대 380℃까지 견딜 수 있는 내열성 있음'이라고 했다. 따라서 정답은 (B)이다.

어휘 supply 공급하다 power 전원, 동력 endure 견디다 intense 극심한, 강렬한 removable 떼어낼 수 있는, 제거할 수 있는 length 길이 adjust 조절하다

155 -157 일정표

메이슨에서 열리는 제5회 미국 접객업소 협회(AHA) 연례 워크숍

올드리치 컨벤션 센터 – 5월 23일

시간	주제
오전 9:30 – 오전 10:45	신기술 활용 – 155주문을 받는 데 활용할 수 있는 태블릿 컴퓨터 등 최신 기기들에 대해 배워 보세요.

오전 11:00~정오	외모 관리 – 155서비스 업계의 일원으로서 전문가답게 보이는 것이 중요합니다. 언제나 가장 멋진 모습을 보여 줄 수 있는 방법을 배워 보세요.
156오후 1:30~오후 3:15	고객 상대하기 – 156불만에 찬 고객들과 대화하는 법을 알아 보세요. 문제를 명확하게 설명하고 해결책을 제안하는 법 등을 배울 수 있습니다.
오후 3:30~오후 4:45	신속한 서비스 – 155서비스의 수준을 낮추지 않고 식당 손님들에게 더 빠른 서비스를 제공하는 법을 배워 보세요.

157참석자들은 컨벤션 센터에 도착하는 즉시 등록 영수증을 제시해서 휴식 시간 동안 구내식당에서 점심 식사로 교환할 수 있는 식권을 받아야 합니다. 주차는 선착순으로 할 수 있습니다. 추가적인 주차 공간은 근처에 있는 윌리스 쇼핑몰 주차장에서 찾으실 수 있습니다.

더 자세한 정보를 원하시면 www.masonaha.com/workshop/info를 방문하세요.

어휘 annual 연례의, 해마다 열리는 hospitality 접대, 환대 association 협회 convention 대회, 회의 session (특정한 활동을 위한) 시간[기간] new technology 신기술 gadget (작고 유용한) 도구, 장치 take an order 주문을 받다 maintain 유지하다 appearance 외모 service industry 서비스업 professional 전문가다운, 전문적인 look one's best 가장 멋있게[매력적으로] 보이다 at all times 항상, 언제나 deal with ~을 다루다, 상대하다 customer 고객 find out 알아내다, 발견하다 dissatisfied 불만에 찬 issue 문제, 사안 solution 해결책 diner 식당 손님 lower 낮추다 standard of service 서비스의 수준 attendee 참가자, 참석자 present 제시하다 registration receipt 등록 영수증 upon arrival 도착하자마자 token 교환권, 식권 redeem for ~로 교환하다 cafeteria 구내식당 break 쉬는 시간 parking 주차 available 이용할 수 있는 on a first-come, first-served basis 선착순으로 additional 추가의 parking space 주차 공간 nearby 근처의, 인근의 parking area 주차장 further information 더 자세한 정보

155 추론 / 암시

번역 워크숍의 대상은 누구일 것 같은가?
(A) 호텔 직원들
(B) 운송 근로자들
(C) 의류 매장 직원들
(D) 음식점 종업원들

해설 첫 세션의 '주문을 받다(taking orders)'나 두 번째 세션의 '서비스 업계의 일원(a member of the service industry)'이나 마지막 세션의 '식당 손님들에게 더 빠른 서비스를 제공하는 법(how to serve diners more qickly)' 등의 표현으로 보아 이 워크숍에 참가하는 대상이 음식점 종업원들이라는 것을 알 수 있다. 따라서 정답은 (D)이다.

156 세부 사항

번역 워크숍 참가자들은 언제 의사소통 기술에 관해 배우겠는가?
(A) 오전 9시 30분
(B) 오전 11시
(C) 오후 1시 30분
(D) 오후 3시 30분

해설 세 번째 세션의 Dealing with Customers에서 보면 how to speak(대화하는 법)이라는 표현이 나온다. 이것이 의사소통 기술을 뜻하므로 정답은 (C)이다.

157 사실 관계 확인

번역 워크숍에 관해 언급된 내용은 무엇인가?
(A) 참석자들은 주차 허가증이 필요할 것이다.
(B) 참석자들에게 식사가 제공될 것이다.
(C) 일정이 변경될지도 모른다.
(D) 쇼핑몰에서 열릴 것이다.

해설 표 바로 밑에 언급된 식사권이 제공된다는 말을 통해서 (B)가 정답임을 알 수 있다. (A) 주차에 대한 내용은 선착순이라는 언급만 있었고, (C) 일정 변경에 관한 내용은 없고, (D) 행사 개최 장소는 컨벤션 센터(the convention center)에서 열린다고 되어 있다.

158 -160 기사

시 당국, 도리스 패션 확장 위해 대출 제공

미라 — 미라 시가 사업 발전 대출 프로그램의 일환으로 도리스 패션이 대출을 받을 수 있게 해 주었다. 이 신규 대출 덕에 도리스는 새로운 일자리 두 개를 만들고, 생산 능력을 확대하며, 판매를 늘릴 수 있게 되었다.

160도리스는 우아한 여성 블라우스와 스커트, 드레스로 미라와 주변 여러 지역에서 유명해졌다. 이 품목들은 사내에서 디자인하고 만든 것들이라 스타일이 독특해서 값어치가 있다. 158경영주 도리 손더스는 반덴 패션 학교 졸업생으로, 2년 전에 이 사업을 시작했다. 그녀는 대출에 감사를 표하며, 그 돈으로 기계를 구입하고 여성복을 만드는 보조 직원과 판매원을 채용해 매장 직원 수를 최대 5명까지 늘리겠다고 밝혔다. "그러면 내가 디자인에 더 많은 시간을 할애할 수 있고 매장에 옷들도 더 빨리 갖다 놓을 수 있게 될 것"이라고 그녀는 설명했다.

사업 발전 대출 프로그램 담당 공무원인 바트 사우스콧은 이렇게 말했다. "우리가 볼 때 도리스 패션은 미라 경제계의 귀중한 일부가 될 수 있는 잠재력이 있습니다. 이 프로젝트의 결과가 우리가 기대하는 만큼 훌륭하다면 159또다시 대출을 받아 공장과 계약을 맺고 대규모 의류 제작을 촉진하는 것이 다음 단계가 될 수도 있습니다." 그는 이 프로그램이 올해 추가 수령자들을 찾고 있다고 덧붙이면서 관심이 있는 사람들은 555-0175번으로 그에게 연락하라고 요청했다.

어휘 provide 제공하다 expansion 확장, 확대 loan 대출(금) available 이용할 수 있는, 입수할 수 있는 as part of ~의 일환으로 development 개발, 발전 allow 허용[허락]하다 create jobs 일자리를 만들다 production capacity 생산 능력 expand 확장하다, 증축하다 increase 늘리다 sales 판매, 매출 famous 유명한, 이름난 surrounding area 주변 지역 elegant 우아한 skirt 치마 design 디자인하다, 설계하다 clothes 옷 item 품목, 물건 prized in-house 사내에서, 조직 내부에서 값어치 있는, 귀한 unique 독특한 express gratitude 감사를 표하다 machinery 기계류 hire 채용[고용]하다 assistant 조수 salesperson 판매원, 영업 직원 employee 직원 up to 최대 ~까지 spend +돈+ on ~에 돈을 쓰다 explain 설명하다 official 공무원 potential 잠재력 valuable 귀중한 business community 경제계, 재계 result 결과 outstanding 뛰어난, 독보적인 expect 기대하다, 예상하다 facilitate 촉진하다 large-scale 대규모의 manufacturing 제작 clothing 의류 contract with

~와 계약하다　factory 공장　add 덧붙이다　seek 찾다, 구하다
recipient 수령자, 수취인　the current year 올해　those interested 관심이 있는 사람들　contact 연락하다, 접촉하다

158　사실 관계 확인

번역　손더스 씨에 관해 명시된 것은?
(A) 미라에서 성장했다.
(B) 남성복을 전문으로 한다.
(C) 대학에서 패션을 공부했다.
(D) 현재 매장의 유일한 직원이다.

해설　두 번째 단락 앞부분에 보면 도리 손더스 씨가 패션 학교를 졸업했다 (Owner Dorry Saunders ~ is a graduate of Vanden Fashion Institute)는 내용이 언급되어 있다. 따라서 정답은 (B)이다.

159　세부 사항

번역　사우스콧 씨는 향후 대출이 어떤 용도로 쓰일 수 있다고 말하는가?
(A) 신규 소매점을 위한 부동산 구입
(B) 마케팅 캠페인 규모 확대
(C) 대량 생산 시설 임대
(D) 온라인 매장 개설 및 유지

해설　도리스 패션이 대출을 받아 사업의 성공을 기대하고 있다는 내용이 지문의 주 핵심인데, 마지막 단락 중간쯤에 another loan 얘기가 나오고 있다. 향후 대출을 또 받아서 공장과 계약을 맺고 대규모로 의류 대량 생산을 촉진하고자 한다는 내용이 나왔으므로 정답은 (C)이다.

160　문장 삽입

번역　[1], [2], [3], [4]로 표시된 곳 중에서 다음 문장이 들어가기에 가장 적합한 곳은?
"이 품목들은 사내에서 디자인하고 만든 것들이라 스타일이 독특해서 값어치가 있다."
(A) [1]
(B) [2]
(C) [3]
(D) [4]

해설　삽입문에 these items라는 표현이 있으므로, 이 물건들의 종류가 언급된 곳을 찾아야 한다. [1]번 바로 앞을 보면, 블라우스, 스커트, 드레스가 언급되어 있는 것을 볼 수 있다. 따라서 정답은 (A)가 가장 적절하다.

161 -163 이메일

발신: 히소카 이토〈hisoka@me-zoom.com〉
수신: 로젠 카운티 동물보호협회〈contact@rcaps.org〉
제목: 웹사이트 문제
날짜: 7월 30일

안녕하세요.

귀사의 웹사이트에 관한 문제를 알려드리려고 메일을 씁니다. **161저는 동물 구호 물품 구매를 위한 모금 운동에 기부하고 싶습니다.** 그래서 RCAPS 사이트에 들어가서 링크를 클릭했습니다. 다음 페이지에서 빈칸에 요청된 결제 정보를 모

두 적었습니다. **162하지만 '제출'을 누르자, 여러 칸 옆에 빨간색으로 '필수 정보 누락'이라는 문구가 떴습니다.** 페이지를 다시 열고 정보를 다시 입력했지만 같은 일이 반복됐습니다.

163저희 동물병원에서 모금 운동 포스터를 보고 매우 감동을 받아 무척 참가하고 싶습니다. 이 문제를 곧 해결해 주실 수 있길 바랍니다.

히소카 이토

어휘　report 보고하다　contribute to ~에 기여하다
fund-raising drive 모금 운동　care supply 보급품　provide 제공하다　requested 요청된　payment details 결제 정보　submit 제출하다　missing 누락된, 빠진　required 필수의　appear 나타나다　next to ~의 옆에　happen 발생하다　veterinarian 수의사　fix 고치다

161　세부 사항

번역　이토 씨는 RCAPS 웹사이트를 왜 방문했는가?
(A) 자선 활동에 기부하기 위해
(B) 수신자 명단에 가입하기 위해
(C) 자원봉사 기회에 대해 알아보기 위해
(D) 반려동물 보급품에 대한 평가를 읽기 위해

해설　첫 번째 단락 두 번째 문장에서 '동물 구호 물품 구매를 위한 모금 운동에 기부하고 싶다(contribute to your fund-rasing drive)'고 했다. 따라서 정답은 (A)이다.

어휘　donate 기부하다　charity 자선　effort 활동　subscribe 가입하다　volunteer 자원 봉사자　evaluation 평가

▶▶ Paraphrasing　지문의 **contribute to your fund-raising drive** → 정답의 **donate to a charity effort**

162　세부 사항

번역　이토 씨는 어떤 문제를 겪었는가?
(A) 컴퓨터 프로그램의 갑작스러운 정지
(B) 이용할 수 없는 웹페이지로 연결
(C) 느린 업로드 속도
(D) 틀린 에러 메시지

해설　첫 번째 단락 후반부에서 이토 씨는 '여러 칸 옆에 필수 정보 누락이라는 빨간색 문구가 떴다'고 했다. 그러므로 정답은 (D)이다.

어휘　encounter 맞닥뜨리다　sudden 갑작스러운　shutdown 정지　unavailable 이용 불가능한　inaccurate 오류가 있는, 부정확한

163　세부 사항

번역　RCAPS에 대해 명시된 것은?
(A) 국가 기관의 지부이다.
(B) 동물병원에 광고를 한다.
(C) 최근에 새 사옥으로 이전했다.
(D) 감사 선물로 포스터를 나눠준다.

해설　두 번째 단락에서 이토 씨는 '저희 동물병원에서 모금 운동 포스터를 보고 매우 감동을 받았다'고 했다. RCAPS가 동물병원에 광고를 한다는 것을 알 수 있으므로 정답은 (B)이다.

어휘 branch 지점 national 국가의 organization 단체 advertise 광고하다 medical clinic 병원 recently 최근 give out 나눠주다

▶▶ Paraphrasing 지문의 my veterinarian's office
→ 정답의 a medical clinic for animals

164-167 웹페이지

http://www.clecknerprinting.com/newsletters

| 홈 | 인쇄물 | 소식지 | 연락처 |

월간 소식지

정기 소식지는 기업과 기타 단체들이 고객, 환자, 회원과 계속 연락을 취하기에 매우 좋은 방법입니다. 최근 몇 년간 이메일 소식지가 인기를 끌었지만 인쇄물로 된 소식지를 선택해야 할 타당한 이유들이 있습니다. **164**이메일 소식지는 수신인이 보기 전에 스팸 필터에 의해 걸러지고 삭제될 수 있지만, 인쇄된 소식지는 확실히 전달됩니다. 또한 인쇄된 내용은 온라인 정보보다 독자들에게 더 강렬한 느낌을 주기 쉽습니다.

소식지 발행을 시작하기로 결정하시거나 현재 간행물에 쏟는 수고가 힘드시다면 저희 클레크너 프린팅이 기꺼이 도와드리겠습니다. **165**저희 소식지 서비스는 다른 업체들이 제공하는 디자인 지원, 출력, 발송 등을 넘어서 실제 소식지 '제작'까지 포함합니다.

진행 방식:
167(C)매월 저희에게 소식지에 넣고 싶은 기사, 쿠폰이나 다른 소재를 보내주십시오. 보내주시는 내용 개수는 하한선이 없지만 최소 한 개 이상 제출해 주실 것을 권장합니다. **166,167(B),(D)**귀사의 업종이 가구점이든 지역 은행이든 관계없이 나머지 부분은 업계 관련 기사, 만화, 퀴즈 등 하렌코와 같은 신뢰할 만한 콘텐츠 작성 업체에서 받은 내용으로 채웁니다. 끝으로 귀사의 소식지는 고급지에 인쇄되어 명시해 주신 날짜에 발송됩니다.

어휘 printing 인쇄 newsletter 뉴스레터, 소식지 monthly 매월의 regular 정규의 business 업체 organization 단체 keep in touch with ~와 연락하다, 접촉하다 recent 최근의 good reason 타당한 이유 deliver 전달하다 unlike ~와 달리 get caught 잡히다, 포착되다 delete 삭제하다 receiver 수신인 moreover 게다가 tend to+동사원형 ~하는 경향이 있다 make an impression 느낌을 주다 issue 발행하다 put effort into ~에 노력을 쏟다 existing 기존의 publication 발행물 go beyond ~를 넘어서다 offer 제공하다 include 포함하다 actual 실제의 article 기사 material 소재 contain ~이 들어 있다 lower limit 하한 provide 제공하다 submit 제출하다 at least 최소한 local 지역의 industry-related 업계와 관련된 cartoon 만화 obtain 얻다, 구하다 trustworthy 신뢰할 만한 be mailed out 발송되다 specify 명시하다

164 세부 사항

번역 이메일 소식지에 관해 언급된 것은?
(A) 가격이 저렴하다.
(B) 빠르게 배포할 수 있다.
(C) 열었을 때 제대로 보이지 않을 수도 있다.
(D) 목표로 하는 수취인에게 전달되지 않을 수 있다.

해설 첫 번째 단락 중간 부분에서 '이메일 소식지는 수신인이 보기 전에 스팸 필터에 의해 걸러지고 삭제될 수 있다.'고 했다. 이메일 소식지는 제대로 전달되지 않을 수 있으므로 정답은 (D)이다.

어휘 inexpensive 비싸지 않은 distribute 배포하다 reach 도달하다 intended 목표로 삼은, 겨냥한 recipient 수취인

165 세부 사항

번역 웹페이지에 따르면 클레크너 프린팅은 경쟁업체와 어떻게 차별화되는가?
(A) 특수 용지를 사용한다.
(B) 추가 서비스를 제공한다.
(C) 실제 매장이 있다.
(D) 수수료를 더 적게 청구한다.

해설 두 번째 단락에서 '클레크너 프린팅의 서비스는 다른 업체들이 제공하는 디자인 지원, 출력, 발송 외에 실제 제작(actual *creation* of newsletters)까지 포함한다'고 했다. 그러므로 추가 서비스를 제공한다는 의미이므로 정답은 (B)이다.

어휘 competitor 경쟁자 charge 청구하다 fee 수수료

166 세부 사항

번역 하렌코는 어떤 업종의 회사인가?
(A) 인쇄
(B) 금융
(C) 콘텐츠 제작
(D) 문구류 제조

해설 세 번째 단락 중반부에서 '진행 방식'의 중간 부분에서 '업계 관련 기사, 만화, 퀴즈 등 하렌코와 같은 신뢰할 만한 콘텐츠 작성 업체(trust worthy writing services like Harenko)에서 받은 내용으로 채운다'고 했다. 그러므로 하렌코는 콘텐츠 제작 업체임을 알 수 있다. 정답은 (C)이다.

어휘 finance 금융 stationery 문구류 manufacturing 제조업

▶▶ Paraphrasing 지문의 writing services → 정답의 content creation

167 사실 관계 확인

번역 소식지의 수취인이 할 수 있는 활동으로 암시되지 않은 것은?
(A) 우편을 통한 콘테스트 참가
(B) 단문 필기시험 응시
(C) 할인 쿠폰 교환
(D) 재미있는 그림 감상

해설 지문의 '진행 방식(How it works)' 부분에서 퀴즈(quizzes)는 (B)로, 쿠폰(coupons)은 (C)로, 만화(cartoons)는 (D)로 paraphrasing된 것임을 알 수 있다. 따라서 정답은 (A)이다.

어휘 mail-in 우편으로 처리되는 contest 대회 written test 필기시험 redeem (현금, 상품권 등으로) 교환하다 drawing 그림

▶▶ Paraphrasing 지문의 quizzes → 보기의 a short written test
지문의 coupons → 보기의 a discount voucher
지문의 cartoons → 보기의 humorous drawings

168-171 온라인 채팅

애브라이벌 사내 메신저

소피아 앨벨로 [오전 9:40]	스탠리가 어디에 있는지 아는 사람 있어요? 전화를 안 받네요.
듀앤 시블리 [오전 9:42]	아, **168**어머님을 도우려고 잠시 휴가를 냈어요. 어머님 건강에 문제가 있대요.
소피아 앨벨로 [오전 9:43]	그렇다니 안됐네요. 그가 언제 복귀하는지 알아요? **170**재맥슨 주식회사와 관련해서 문제가 생겼거든요.
안웨이 차오 [오전 9:44]	그는 적어도 5월 14일까지는 자리를 비울 거예요. 하지만 제가 그의 업무를 많이 담당해왔어요. 무슨 일인데 그러세요?
듀앤 시블리 [오전 9:44]	**169**나는 재맥슨에 관해 아무것도 몰라요. 그 일은 두 사람에게 맡길게요.
	〈듀앤 시블리 님이 대화방에서 퇴장했습니다.〉
소피아 앨벨로 [오전 9:45]	우리가 맡아 놓고 싶어 하는 그 기간에 또 다른 회사가 더 큰 계약을 제안했다는 말을 재맥슨 사로부터 들었어요.
안웨이 차오 [오전 9:46]	그러니까 그들이 다른 회사의 제안을 받아들이고 싶어 한다는 건가요?
소피아 앨벨로 [오전 9:47]	그래요. **171**우리가 더 높은 가격을 제시할 수 있는지 내가 알아야 해요. 할 수 있다면 우리는 그렇게 해야 해요. **170**지금 와서 또 다른 제조업체를 찾기가 어렵기 때문에 그래요.
안웨이 차오 [오전 9:48]	예산을 검토해 봐야 해요.
소피아 앨벨로 [오전 9:49]	알았어요. **171**하지만 그들이 다른 회사와 계약을 마무리하기 전에 우리가 서둘러야 해요. 오늘 중으로 내게 다시 연락해서 결론을 알려 줄 수 있어요?
안웨이 차오 [오전 9:50]	최선을 다할게요.

어휘 company messenger 사내 메신저 answer one's phone 전화를 받다 take some time off 휴가를 내다, 잠시 일을 쉬다 come up with ~에게 (문제가) 생기다 be away 출타 중이다, 부재 중이다 be put in charge of ~을 책임지게[담당하게] 되다 task 업무 leave A to B A를 B에게 맡기다 exit 나가다, 퇴장하다 chat room 대화방 get word 기별[말]을 듣다 offer 제안(하다) contract 계약 time period 기간 reserve 맡아 놓다, 예약하다 make a higher offer 더 높은 가격을 제시하다 manufacturer 제조업체 at this stage 지금에 와서, 현재 단계에서 look over 살펴보다 budget 예산 deal 거래, 계약 finalize 마무리하다, 종결짓다 get back to ~에게 나중에 다시 연락하다 conclusion 결론, 최종 판단 by the end of the day 오늘 중으로 do one's best 최선을 다하다

168 세부 사항

번역 시블리 씨는 스탠리가 무엇을 하고 있다고 말하는가?
(A) 해외로 휴가를 감
(B) 가족 구성원 돌보기
(C) 교육 프로그램 참석
(D) 잠재 고객 방문

해설 오전 9시 42분 대화에서 건강상의 이유로 어머니를 돕고 있다는 내용이 나온다. 따라서 정답은 (B)이다.

▶▶ **Paraphrasing** 지문의 his mother → 정답의 a family member

169 추론 / 암시

번역 시블리 씨는 왜 대화방을 떠나는 것 같은가?
(A) 토론 중인 사안과 관련이 없어서
(B) 앨벨로 씨에게 자료를 가져다주려고
(C) 어떤 소식을 이미 알고 있어서
(D) 스탠리에게 전화를 걸어야 해서

해설 오전 9시 44분 대사에서 시블리 씨는 '자신은 아는 것이 없으니 두 사람에게 맡기겠다'고 말하고 있다. 따라서 정답은 (A)이다.

170 추론 / 암시

번역 재맥슨 주식회사에 관해 암시된 것은?
(A) 본사가 다른 나라에 있다.
(B) 애브라이벌 사와 계약을 완료했다.
(C) 5월 14일에 결정을 내릴 것이다.
(D) 제조업체이다.

해설 오전 9시 43분 대화에서 재맥슨 주식회사와 문제가 생겼다고 했는데, 9시 47분 대화에서 '다른 제조업체를 찾기 어렵다'는 말이 나온다. 이를 종합해 보면 재맥슨 주식회사가 제조업체라는 것을 알 수 있다. 따라서 정답은 (D)이다.

171 의도 파악

번역 오전 9시 48분에 차오 씨가 "예산을 검토해 봐야 해요"라고 쓴 의도는 무엇이겠는가?
(A) 지금 당장은 질문에 답을 줄 수 없다.
(B) 일부 계산이 잘못되었다고 생각한다.
(C) 앨벨로 씨는 업무를 수행할 자격이 없다.
(D) 앨벨로 씨는 그녀 없이 회의를 시작해야 한다.

해설 '우리가 더 높은 가격을 제시할 수 있는지 내가 알아야 해요.'라는 앨벨로 씨의 말에 차오 씨는 알아보려면 시간이 필요하다는 의미로 '예산을 검토해 봐야 한다'는 말을 한 것이라고 볼 수 있다. 따라서 정답은 (A)이다.

172-175 이메일

발신: 사샤 우즈 〈sasha.woods@yoplexholdings.com〉
수신: 전 직원
날짜: 4월 9일
제목: 소셜 미디어 정책

172회사의 소셜 미디어 정책을 위반해서 최근 발생한 문제들 때문에 요플렉스 홀딩스는 중요 사항들에 대해 직원들의 기억을 상기시키고자 합니다. 다음 내용을 찬찬히 읽어 주십시오.

• 여기서 '소셜 미디어'라는 용어는 블로그, 메시지 게시판, 대화방, 소셜 네트워킹 사이트, 그리고 유사한 사이트들과 서비스들을 가리킵니다.

- 회사와 관련된 일로 소셜 미디어를 사용할 때 **173(D)직원들은 직원 편람에 제시된 행동 규범**을 준수해야 합니다.
- **175요플렉스는 직원들이 소셜 미디어에 공개한 글이나 사진이 회사에 해가 되지 않는다는 것을 확인하기 위해 해당 정보를 찾아볼 수 있습니다.** 그런 자료가 발견되면 해당 직원은 그것을 삭제하라는 요청을 받을 수도 있습니다.
- **173(A)회사의 절차, 고객, 재정에 관한 기밀 정보를 공개해서는 안 됩니다.**
- 근무 시간에는 회사 업무가 소셜 미디어 사용보다 우선해야 합니다. 그런 활동으로 하루에 몇 분 이상의 근무 시간을 쓰는 것은 현명하지 못합니다.
- 회사와 관련한 소셜 미디어 교류가 갈등으로 번질 경우 그 상황에서 빠져나와 홍보 부서에 알리십시오. **173(C)소셜 미디어를 통해서 받은 회사에 관한 모든 문의** 역시 홍보 부서에 전달해야 합니다.

전체 규칙 목록은 이곳에서 볼 수 있습니다. 수칙을 따르지 않으면 경영진으로부터 징계를 받는 결과가 생길 수도 있습니다.

174이 사항들에 관해 궁금한 점이 있으면 제게 이메일을 보내셔도 됩니다. 감사합니다.

사샤 우즈
인사 조정관

어휘 recent 최근의 issue 문제, 사안 violation 위반, 위배 policy 정책, 방침 refresh one's memory 기억을 상기시키다[새롭게 하다] main point 요점, 중요 사항 term 용어 refer to 가리키다, 지칭하다 in reference to ~와 관련하여 adhere to ~을 준수하다 code of conduct 행동 규범[수칙] set out 제시되다 employee handbook 직원 편람 seek out 찾아내다, 뒤지다 make public 공개하다 in order to+동사원형 ~하기 위해 ensure 확인하다 harmful to ~에 해로운 disclose 공개하다 confidential information 기밀[비밀] 정보 procedure 절차 client 고객 finance 재정, 재무 duties 업무, 직무 take priority over ~보다 우선하다 usage 사용 working hours 근무 시간(= company time) unwise 현명하지 못한 in the case that ~할 경우 interaction 교류 turn into a conflict 갈등으로 번지다 disengage from ~에서 빠져나오다 notify 알리다, 통지하다 public relations 홍보 inquiry 문의, 질문 refer 맡기다, 회부하다 failure 실패 result in ~ 결과가 생기다 penalty 처벌, 벌칙 impose 부과하다 management 경영진 contact 연락하다, 접촉하다 human resources coordinator 인사 조정관

172 글의 주제 / 목적

번역 이 이메일은 왜 발송되었는가?
(A) 일부 규칙들이 지켜지지 않고 있어서
(B) 정책에 몇 가지 변경 사항이 생겨서
(C) 해마다 이맘때면 비슷한 이메일이 보내져서
(D) 직원들이 정보를 요청하여

해설 첫 번째 문장을 보면 이 이메일을 쓴 이유가 Because of부터 설명이 되어 있다. 회사의 소셜 미디어 정책을 위반하는 문제가 최근에 있었다는 내용을 토대로 정답이 (A)라는 것을 알 수 있다.

173 사실 관계 확인

번역 직원들에게 지시된 것 중 하나가 아닌 것은?
(A) 회사 비밀을 공개하지 말 것
(B) 직장에서 소셜 미디어를 아예 사용하지 말 것
(C) 접수된 문의 사항을 홍보 전문가들에게 보낼 것
(D) 직원 편람에 나온 일반 정책을 준수할 것

해설 (A)는 네 번째 항목에, (C)는 마지막 항목에, (D)는 두 번째 항목에 언급되어 있다. 하지만 (B)처럼 소셜 미디어를 절대로(Never) 사용하지 말라는 언급은 없고, 다섯 번째 항목에서 회사 업무가 우선시 되어야 한다고 했다. 따라서 정답은 (B)이다.

▶▶ Paraphrasing 지문의 Do not disclose confidential information → 보기의 Do not reveal company secrets.

지문의 adhere to the codes of conduct set out in the Employee Handbook → 보기의 Comply with general Employee Handbook guidelines.

174 추론 / 암시

번역 직원이 왜 우즈 씨에게 연락할 것 같은가?
(A) 소셜 미디어 사이트에 발생한 갈등을 보고하려고
(B) 전체 규칙 목록을 얻으려고
(C) 이전에 받은 징계에 이의를 제기하려고
(D) 정책에 관해 확인을 하려고

해설 발신자가 사샤 우즈이고 마지막 문장에서도 알 수 있듯이 본 내용에 관해 궁금한 사항이 생겼을 경우 자신에게 이메일 달라는 말이 나온다. 그러므로 직원들은 소셜 미디어 정책과 관련된 사항이 궁금할 경우 우즈 씨에게 연락을 취할 것이다. 따라서 정답은 (D)이다.

175 문장 삽입

번역 [1], [2], [3], [4]로 표시된 곳 중에 다음 문장이 들어가기에 가장 적합한 곳은?
"그런 자료가 발견되면 해당 직원은 그것을 삭제하라는 요청을 받을 수도 있습니다."
(A) [1]
(B) [2]
(C) [3]
(D) [4]

해설 such material에서 알 수 있듯이 특정 내용에 관한 언급이 앞 문장에 있어야 하고, 그 내용은 회사측에서 없애라고 할 수 있는 민감한 내용이어야 한다. 이를 충족시켜 주는 곳은 [3]이다. 바로 앞 문장에서 소셜 미디어에 공개한 정보가 회사 이미지에 해가 되지 않는지 확인해야 한다는 내용이 나오기 때문이다. 따라서 정답은 (C)이다.

176-180 공지 + 양식

랜치 핸즈가 시식자를 찾습니다

맛있는 요리 재료들로 유명한 랜치 핸즈 식품 회사는 내년 1사분기에 냉동식품 시장에 진출할 예정입니다. **176**랜치 핸즈는 새로운 편의 식품의 풍미와 맛에 관

해 의견을 줄 그룹을 찾고 있습니다. **179**이 편의 식품들은 성인과 십대에게 어필해야 하므로 십대 자녀가 있는 3~4인 가족이 이상적인 시식단이 될 것입니다. 지원을 원하시면 고객 지원 담당관 릭 멀로니에게 (270) 555-0165번으로 연락해 주시기 바랍니다. 그가 여러분에게 작성할 지원서를 드리고 간단한 면접을 **177**실시할 것입니다. **180**저희의 주간 소식지를 구독하시는 지원자들은 자동으로 100달러 상당의 랜치 핸즈 상품권 추첨 대상이 됩니다.

- 시식은 윈스롭 레인에 위치한 **178(B)**랜치 핸즈 시설에서 합니다.
- **178(A)**시식은 1시간이 걸립니다.
- **178**시식 장면이 녹화됩니다.
- **178**해당 녹화 테이프가 홍보에 쓰일 수도 있습니다.

어휘 taster 맛 감식가 famous for ~로 유명한[이름난] delicious 맛있는 cooking ingredient 요리 재료 frozen food 냉동식품 quarter 분기 look for ~을 찾다, 물색하다 give feedback on ~에 관해 의견을[피드백을] 주다 flavor 풍미(냄새로 느끼는 맛) palatability (먹어서 느끼는) 맛 ready-to-eat meal 편의 식품 appeal to ~에게 호소하다, 매력이 있다 adult 성인 ideal 이상적인 apply 지원하다, 신청하다 contact 연락하다, 접촉하다 customer outreach 고객 지원 coordinator 조정자 application form 지원서, 신청서 fill out 기입하다 conduct a brief interview 간단한 인터뷰를 실시하다 applicant 지원자, 신청자 subscribe to ~을 구독하다 weekly newsletter 주간 소식지 automatically 자동으로 be entered into a drawing 추첨 대상이 되다 gift certificate 상품권 tasting 시식, 맛보기 satellite 위성의 videotape 비디오테이프에 녹화하다; 녹화 테이프 for promotional purposes 홍보용으로

시식단 신청서

소속 그룹:
그린 백 대학교에서 마케팅 수업에 함께하고 있음

그룹 구성원:

이름	**179** 나이	직업
피카 쿠알라나	29	대학원생
이블린 라	31	대학원생
마리나 류보프	24	연구 조교
딘 탄	41	교수

랜치 핸즈의 식품들을 정기적으로 드십니까? 드신다면 얼마나 자주 드십니까?
네, 일주일에 약 두 번

연락처 정보:
전화 (270) 555-0106
이메일 kualana@greenbackuniversity.edu
주소 데이비스로 111번지, 오웬스보로, KY 42303

180제공하신 우편 주소로 저희 소식지를 받아 보시겠습니까?
☑ 예 □ 아니오

어휘 affiliation 소속 occupation 직업 graduate student 대학원생 research assistant 연구 조교 professor 교수 regularly 정기적으로 frequently 자주 contact information 연락처 정보 provided 제공된 mailing address 우편 주소

---

176 세부 사항

번역 시식할 제품의 특징은 무엇이겠는가?
(A) 저렴한 가격
(B) 특이한 맛
(C) 건강함
(D) 편리함

해설 공지문의 두 번째 문장에서 새로운 편의 식품(new ready-to-eat meals)에 관해 의견을 줄 그룹을 찾고 있다고 했으므로 정답은 (D)이다.

---

177 동의어 찾기

번역 공고문에서 첫 번째 단락 7행의 "conduct"와 의미상 가장 가까운 것은?
(A) 실시하다
(B) 조종하다
(C) 전송하다
(D) 수집하다

해설 이 문장에서처럼 '인터뷰' 같은 특정한 활동을 할 때 conduct라는 표현을 쓴다. conduct an interview처럼 '인터뷰를 하다'라는 표현을 만들 수 있는 동사는 hold, give, have 등이 있다. 따라서 정답은 (A) hold이다. (B) steer는 '조종하다', (C) transmit은 '전송하다', (D) collect는 '수집하다'라는 의미로 문맥에 어울리지 않는다.

---

178 사실 관계 확인

번역 시식에 관해 사실인 것은?
(A) 저녁 내내 해야 끝이 난다.
(B) 기업 본사에서 할 것이다.
(C) 광고용으로 녹화될 것이다.
(D) 대학교를 위한 자료를 모을 것이다.

해설 공고문 후반부 4개 항목에서 정답을 확인할 수 있다. (A) 시식은 한 시간 정도 걸리고, (B) 시식은 생산 공장에서 실시되고, (D)에 대한 내용은 언급되지 않았다. (C)는 세 번째와 네 번째 항목을 종합한 것으로, 시식은 녹화되고 홍보용으로 사용될 것이라고 했으므로 정답은 (C)이다.

---

179 연계

번역 쿠알라나 씨의 신청서는 왜 제외되었겠는가?
(A) 그룹 구성원들이 모두 성인이라서
(B) 집단의 한 구성원이 랜치 핸즈에서 근무했어서
(C) 몇몇 사람이 음식 알레르기가 있어서
(D) 집단 구성원이 충분히 많지 않아서

해설 첫 번째 지문 세 번째 문장을 보면 이 식품은 성인과 십대에게 어필해야(The meals should appeal to adults and teenagers)하므로, 십대 자녀가 있는 3~4인 가족(a family of 3 to 4 people with teenage children)이 시식단으로 이상적이라고 했다. 하지만, 두 번째 지문에 나온 참가자들의 나이를 보면 십대가 포함되어 있지 않다. 따라서 정답은 (A)이다.

---

180 연계

번역 쿠알라나 씨에 관해 암시된 것은?

(A) 랜치 핸즈의 음식을 한 번도 먹어본 적이 없다.
(B) 상품권 추첨 대상으로 등록될 것이다.
(C) 학술 프로그램의 연구 조교이다.
(D) 전에 시식에 참여했다.

해설 첫 번째 지문 마지막 부분에 보면 주간 소식지를 구독하는 지원자들은 자동적으로 상품권 추첨 대상이 된다는 말이 나왔고, 두 번째 지문 마지막 항목에서 소식지를 받아 보겠다는 곳에 체크한 것을 바탕으로 쿠알라나 씨가 상품권 추첨 대상이 된다는 것을 알 수 있다. 따라서 정답은 (B)이다.

181 -185 이메일+청구서

발신: 셜리 힐

수신: 랜달 곽

제목: 보고

날짜: 11월 6일

랜달 씨께,

휴가를 잘 보내고 계시길 바랍니다. **181매장의 현 상황을 알려드릴게요.**

먼저, 하급 기술직 이메일 지원을 몇 건 더 받았습니다. **182월요일에 살펴보실 수 있게 출력해서 폴더에 넣어 책상 위에 두겠습니다.**

둘째로, 내일 아침에 어빙 홀세일 오토 서플라이에서 일부 물품을 주문할 예정입니다. 광택용 패드와 렌즈 수선 테이프가 다 떨어졌어요. **184그리고 일전에 들었다고 하신 친환경 세척제 한 병을 주문해서 써 보려고 합니다.** 더 필요한 게 있을까요? **183어빙은 원하는 제품은 거의 다 갖고 있으니까요.** 만약 있다면 오늘 퇴근 전까지 알려주세요.

셜리 힐
사무실 관리자
샌디스턴 오토 리페어

어휘 time off 휴식 application 지원 junior 하급의 technician 기술자 position 직위 print out 출력하다 order 주문하다 supply 물품 wholesale 도매 run out of ~를 다 써버리다 polishing 연마, 광내기 repair 수리 environmentally-friendly 친환경적인 try out 시험적으로 써 보다 stock 필요한 상품을 갖추다 by the end of the day 오늘 퇴근 전까지

어빙 홀세일 오토 서플라이

4200 로웰 드라이브   **청구서**
플라스킨, 노스캐롤라이나주 27009
www.irving-was.com

고객: 샌디스턴 오토 리페어   주문 번호: 12773
계정 번호: 340691   주문일자: 11월 7일
청구/배송 주소: 460 팔머 스트리트   예상 배송일자: 11월 9일
        샌디스턴, 미주리주 63030   **결제 예정일: 12월 6일**

품목 #	설명	수량	단가	금액
T3207	자동차 렌즈 수선 테이프	2상자	16.00달러	32.00달러
184F1843	기름 제거 용액	1병	35.00달러	35.00달러
M6215	미끄럼 방지 바닥 매트	1개	57.00달러	57.00달러
P5033	광택용 패드	5묶음	28.00달러	140.00달러

주:		
185요청하신 대로 모든 물품을 하나의 포장으로 묶을 예정입니다. 이로 인해 지연이 발생할 수 있음을 알려드립니다.	소계	264.00달러
	세금	18.48달러
	배송비	13.20달러
	총계	295.68달러

어휘 invoice 청구서, 송장 account 계정 billing 청구서 발부 shipping 배송 estimated 추측의 payment 결제 description 설명 quantity 수량 unit price 단가 grease 기름 removal 제거 fluid 유체 slip 미끄러짐 floor 바닥 be grouped into ~로 묶다, 그룹화하다 shipment 수송품 subtotal 소계

181 글의 주제

번역 이메일을 보낸 목적은?

(A) 최근 상황을 알리기 위해
(B) 비교하기 위해
(C) 직원 관련 문제를 지적하기 위해
(D) 수리에 관한 조언을 요청하기 위해

해설 힐 씨의 이메일 두 번째 문장에서 '매장의 현 상황을 알려드린다'라는 말에서 업무 점검임을 알 수 있다. 따라서 정답은 (A)이다.

어휘 purpose 의도, 목적 make a comparison 비교하다 point out 지적하다 personnel 인사, 직원 request 요청하다 advice 조언

182 세부 사항

번역 이메일에 따르면 곽 씨는 월요일에 무엇을 볼 것인가?

(A) 전자 기기
(B) 탁상 달력
(C) 문서
(D) 제품 견본

해설 이메일의 두 번째 단락 두 번째 문장에서 힐 씨가 곽 씨에게 '이메일 지원서를 월요일에 살펴보실 수 있게 출력해서 폴더에 넣어 책상 위에 두겠다'고 했다. 따라서 정답은 (C)이다.

어휘 have access to ~에 접근 권한을 갖다 electronic 전자의 device 기기 document 문서 sample 견본

183 세부 사항

번역 힐 씨가 어빙 홀세일 오토 서플라이에 대해 명시한 것은?

(A) 처음에 친구에게 추천을 받았다.
(B) 수년간 영업 중이다.
(C) 신속 배송을 선택할 수 있게 해 준다.
(D) 다양한 제품을 판매한다.

해설 이메일 세 번째 단락 후반부에서 '어빙은 원하는 제품은 거의 다 갖고 있다'고 했다. 여러 가지 다양한 제품을 판매함을 알 수 있으므로 정답은 (D)이다.

어휘 recommend 추천하다 be in business 영업하고 있다 expedited 신속 shipping 배송 a wide selection of 다양한 종류의 ~

184 연계

번역 샌디스턴 오토 리페어가 처음으로 주문하는 물품은 무엇이겠는가?
(A) T3207
(B) F1843
(C) M6215
(D) P5033

해설 이메일 세 번째 단락의 세 번째 문장에서 '일전에 들었다고 하신 친환경 세척제 한 병을 주문해서 써 보려고 한다'고 했다. 그리고 샌디스턴 오토 리페어의 주문 청구서의 두 번째 품목이 기름 제거 용액이므로 정답은 (B)이다.

185 세부 사항

번역 주문 건에 대해 청구서에서 언급된 것은?
(A) 모든 물품이 한꺼번에 발송될 것이다.
(B) 은행 자동이체를 통해 결제될 것이다.
(C) 이전 주문 건보다 세금이 더 나왔다.
(D) 일부 물품은 환불이 불가능하다.

해설 청구서의 맨 아래 주를 보면 '요청하신 대로 모든 물품을 하나의 포장으로 묶을 예정이다'라고 했다. 그러므로 주문 물품은 묶음 배송으로 처리됨을 알 수 있다. 따라서 정답은 (A)이다.

어휘 at the same time 동시에 automatic 자동의 previous 이전의 return 반납하다, 되돌려주다

186 -190 웹페이지+기사+이메일

---
www.gerarduniversity.edu/facultyprofiles

교수진

애너벨 파커는 제라드 대학교의 방문 교수이다. **186포트 브라이트 칼리지에서 컴퓨터과학으로 이학석사 학위를 받았으며** 나이츠타운 경영대학원에서 경영학 석사 학위를 받았다.

파커는 현재 스피겔 테크놀로지 사의 최고경영자이다. 그녀는 17년 전 이 회사의 제품개발부에서 근무하기 시작했다. 최고경영자가 된 이후에는 스피겔의 수익을 꾸준히 늘리고 회사를 전국에서 가장 인기 있고 신뢰 받는 기술 기업 중 하나로 만드는 데 기여했다.

스피겔에 입사하기 전 파커 씨는 샌프란시스코에 본사를 둔 스테이머스 앤 컴퍼니에서 근무했다. 회사의 컴퓨터 소프트웨어 프로그램 다수를 만들어 낸 책임자였다. **190그녀는 또한 엑셀 기업가 프로그램(EEP)이라는 인턴십 프로그램도 시작했다.** 이 프로그램은 매년 여름 운영되며 학생들이 실제 스테이머스 앤 컴퍼니 직원들로부터 기술 산업에 관해 배우도록 돕는다.

187파커 씨는 다가오는 가을 학기에 '디지털 시대'라고 하는 12주짜리 과목을 가르칠 예정이다. 이 과목은 석사 과정 학생들만 들을 수 있다.

어휘 visiting professor 방문 교수 computer science 컴퓨터과학 MBA 경영학 석사 school of business 경영대학원 current 현재의 product development department 제품개발부 CEO 최고경영자 be credited with ~한 공로가 있다, ~하는 데 기여하다 steadily 꾸준히 increase 늘리다, 증가시키다 revenue 수익, 수입 popular 인기 있는 trusted 신뢰받는 prior to ~하기 전에, ~에 앞서 -based ~에 본사[본부, 근거지]를 둔 be in charge of ~을 책임지다, 담당하다 internship 인턴십, 실습 훈련 기간 entrepreneur 기업가 run 운영되다 technology industry 기술 산업 employee 직원 course 과정, 과목 upcoming 다가오는 semester 학기 master's program student 석사 과정 학생

제라드 대학 소식지

12월 28일 — 애너벨 파커는 최고경영자를 비롯해 인상적인 긴 직함 목록에 이제 초빙교수라는 직함을 하나 더 얻게 됐다.

파커 씨는 일찍이 자신의 스테이머스 앤 컴퍼니 근무 경력을 바탕으로 **187지난 학기에 이곳 제라드 대학교에서 한 과목을 가르쳤다.** 그녀는 아이디어를 브레인스토밍 및 평가하고, 다른 사람들과 협력하고, 기술적인 한계를 극복하는 등과 같은 컴퓨터 소프트웨어 프로그램 제작의 서로 다른 면들에 관해 주로 이야기했다.

파커 씨는 또한 학생들에게 조언과 영감을 제공하기도 했다. 한 학생은 이렇게 설명했다. "교수님은 처음 일을 시작했을 때 자신이 **188맞닥뜨렸던** 갖가지 어려움 가운데 몇 가지를 함께 나누셨어요. 지금 제가 씨름하고 있는 똑같은 고민들을 극복하셨다는 걸 알고 정말 힘이 났어요."

그렇다면 파커 씨는 또 다른 수업을 가르칠까? 당장은 돌아올 계획이 없지만 가르치는 것을 배제하고 있지는 않다고 그녀는 말한다.

어휘 title 직함 semester 학기 based on ~을 바탕으로[근거로] aspect 양상, 측면 such as ~와 같은 collaboratively 협력하여, 힘을 합쳐 overcome 극복하다 technical limitation 기술적 한계[제약] inspiration 영감 share 공유하다, 함께 나누다 trials and hardships 갖가지 어려움[시련] face 직면하다, 맞닥뜨리다 encouraging 고무적인 struggle 고민 deal with 처리하다, 다루다 immediate 당장의, 즉각적인 rule out 배제하다

수신: 애너벨 파커 ⟨annabelle@spiegeltechnologies.com⟩
발신: 데번 레빗 ⟨dlevitt@gerard.edu⟩
제목: EEP
날짜: 6월 3일

파커 교수님께,

189교수님께서 제가 듣는 수업을 가르치신 후 이렇게 많은 시간이 흘렀다니 믿기지가 않습니다. 제가 EEP에 합격했다는 소식을 알려 드리고 싶었습니다! 아낌없이 조언해 주시고 제 지원서 준비를 도와 주셔서 감사합니다. **190이번 여름에 있을 인턴십이 정말 기대됩니다.** 다시 한 번 감사드립니다.

데번 레빗 올림

어휘 go by 지나가다, 흘러가다 let A(사람) know A에게 알려 주다 get accepted into ~에 합격하다, 받아들여지다 application 지원서 look forward to+명사/-ing ~을 고대하다

186 사실 관계 확인

번역 파커 씨에 관해 명시된 것은?
(A) 여름 인턴십을 마쳤다.
(B) 두 회사의 합병을 감독했다.
(C) 두 개의 대학교 과정에 참가했다.
(D) 연구개발부를 설립했다.

해설 웹페이지 첫 단락의 두 번째 문장에 그녀의 대학교 이상의 고등 교육
(higher education) 학력이 나와 있다. 정답은 (C)이다.

187 연계

번역 '디지털 시대'는 주로 무엇에 초점을 맞추었는가?
(A) 제품의 온라인 마케팅
(B) 소프트웨어 프로그램 개발
(C) 자료 보안 시스템 평가
(D) 신생 기술 기업을 위한 자금 모금

해설 첫 번째 지문 마지막 단락에서 파커 씨가 '디지털 시대'라는 과목을 가르칠
예정이라고 했고, 두 번째 지문에서는 파커 씨가 가르친 '그 과목'이 컴퓨
터 소프트웨어 프로그램 개발에 관한 내용을 다룬 강의였다는 내용이 나온
다. 이를 종합해 보면 정답이 (B)라는 것을 알 수 있다.

188 동의어 찾기

번역 기사에서 세 번째 단락 2행의 "faced"와 의미상 가장 가까운 것은?
(A) 보존했다
(B) 겪었다
(C) 반대했다
(D) 보았다

해설 동사 face가 '어려움', '시련' 등의 목적어와 함께 쓰일 때는 '직면하다', '맞
닥뜨리다'로 해석할 수 있다. 어려움과 시련을 '겪다'라고 표현해도 의미의
차이는 없다. 따라서 (B) experienced(겪다, 경험하다)가 정답이다.

189 추론 / 암시

번역 레빗 씨는 누구일 것 같은가?
(A) 파커 씨가 가르쳤던 학생
(B) 스테이머스 앤 컴퍼니의 최고경영자
(C) 스피겔 테크놀로지의 인턴 사원
(D) 포트 브라이트 칼리지의 교수

해설 세 번째 지문에서 '제가 듣는 수업을 가르쳐 주신 이후(since you taught
my class)'라는 문구를 통해서 파커 씨가 레빗 씨를 가르쳤다는 것을 알
수 있다. 따라서 정답은 (A)이다.

190 연계

번역 레빗 씨는 여름에 무엇을 할 것 같은가?
(A) 새 컴퓨터를 구입할 것이다.
(B) 웹사이트를 개설할 것이다.
(C) 파커 씨를 만날 것이다.
(D) 샌프란시스코에서 일할 것이다.

해설 세 번째 지문 후반부에서 이번 여름에 있을 인턴십이 기대된다는 말이 나
오는데, 이 인턴십에 대한 언급은 첫 번째 지문 세 번째 단락에서도 확인할
수 있다. 샌프란시스코에 있는 스테이머스 앤 컴퍼니에서 인턴십 프로그램
을 진행한다고 했기 때문에 이를 종합해 보면 정답이 (D)라는 것을 알 수
있다.

191-195 웹페이지 + 이메일 + 이메일

http://www.woodisfleetmanagement.com/search

차량 검색

자동차, 밴, 트럭 중 어느 것을 찾으시든, 우디스 플릿 매니지먼트는 귀사에 적합
한 차량을 쉽게 찾을 수 있도록 해드립니다. 차량 유형과 구입 또는 대여 여부로
검색하세요. ¹⁹¹필요하신 사항을 정확히 모르시면 저희에게 연락하셔서 귀사의
업종, 예산, 위치, 기타 주요 요인에 따른 맞춤형 조언을 받아보세요.

검색 결과: 세단 대여 가능

제조업체 및 모델	연비 (시내 / 고속도로)	소매 가격	대여 가격 (월)
해로나 런더너	26 / 36	1만 6,200달러	367달러
젠틀러 아바렉스	28 / 37	1만 7,500달러	482달러
채틀린 RCG 4	29 / 38	1만 8,100달러	526달러
193 무어비 인트리노	32 / 40	1만 8,900달러	570달러

어휘 vehicle 차량 search 검색하다; 검색 lease 대여하다
need 필요성, 요구 personalize (개인의 필요에) 맞추다
according to ~에 따라 budget 예산 location 위치 factor
요인 manufacturer 제조업체 miles per gallon 연비, 갤런 당
마일 수 retail price 소매 가격

발신: 에츠코 사토우 〈e.satou@isiomassociates.com〉
수신: 다니엘 제퍼슨 〈daniel.jefferson@woodisfm.com〉
제목: 문의
날짜: 9월 8일

다니엘 씨,

먼저 우디스의 차량과 차량 관리 서비스에 매우 만족하고 있다는 말씀부터 드립
니다. 우디스에서 차량을 대여하고 거의 6개월간 어떤 주요 문제도 발생하지 않
았습니다. 사실 저는 귀사의 스판과 정비센터를 칭찬하고 싶습니다. ¹⁹⁴저희 영
업사원 중 한 명이 최근 근처에서 경미한 교통사고를 겪었는데 센터 직원들이 매
우 잘 도와주었다고 합니다.

그런데 저희 쪽에 문제가 있어서 도움을 주셨으면 합니다. 저희 직원들이 차마
다 설치된 차량 추적 장치에 대해 알게 됐는데 사생활과 관련하여 우려를 표명
하고 있습니다. ¹⁹²아시는 바와 같이 저희는 실제로 장치를 사용하지 않는데, 직
원들이 제거해 달라고 요청하고 있습니다. 그렇게 해 주실 수 있을까요? 알려 주
십시오.

에츠코 사토우
경영지원 담당자
이시옴 어소시에이츠

어휘 assure 확언하다, 보장하다 fleet 차량군 management
관리 nearly 거의 major 주요한 compliment 칭찬하다
maintenance 유지 보수 sales representative 영업사원
nearby 근처에서 provide 제공하다 on our end 우리 측에
tracking device 추적 장치 install 설치하다 express 표현하다
-related ~에 관련된 concern 우려 actually 사실, 실제로

발신: 트레이시 욘트 ⟨t.yount@isiomassociates.com⟩
수신: 에츠코 사토우 ⟨e.satou@isiomassociates.com⟩
제목: Re: 업데이트
날짜: 9월 21일

에츠코 씨께,

회사 차량 프로그램의 최근 상황에 대해 알려주셔서 감사합니다. **194**보이드 스넬 씨의 사고 차량 수리가 효율적으로 이루어졌고 우디스에서 특별 요청에 빠르게 대응했다고 하니 다행입니다. **193**아울러 개인적으로는 저희 대여 차량으로 인트리노가 결정되어 기쁩니다. 주차장에서 어서 보고 싶군요!

하지만 에츠코 씨와 마찬가지로 저도 일부 운전자들이 제때 주행거리 기록을 제출하지 않는 점을 우려하고 있습니다. **195**업무 용도와 개인 용도의 차량 사용에 대해 신속하고 정확한 정보를 입수해서 출장에 사용된 연료에 대해 적절히 환급해 줄 수 있도록 하는 것이 중요합니다. 이 문제를 만나서 논의하고 싶습니다. 내일 시간이 있으신가요?

트레이시

어휘 repair 수리 take care of ~를 처리하다 efficiently 효율적으로 responsive to ~에 빠른 반응을 보이는 personal 개인적인 parking lot 주차장 be concerned about ~에 대해 우려하다 submit 제출하다 mileage 주행거리 record 기록 on time 제때에, 늦지 않게 prompt 신속한 accurate 정확한 reimburse 변상하다, 환급하다 properly 적절히 business trip 출장

191 세부 사항

번역 웹페이지에 명시된 특별 서비스는 무엇인가?
(A) 운전자 안전 교육
(B) 중고차량 재판매
(C) 현장 정비 작업
(D) 맞춤형 자문

해설 웹페이지의 첫 번째 단락 세 번째 문장에서 '필요하신 사항을 정확히 모르시면 저희에게 연락하셔서 귀사의 업종, 예산, 위치, 기타 주요 요인에 따른 맞춤형 조언(advice personalized)을 받아보라'고 했다. 따라서 정답은 (D)이다.

어휘 safety training 안전 교육 on-site 현장의 customized 개개인의 요구에 맞춘 consulting 자문, 조언

192 세부 사항

번역 사토우 씨가 우디스 플릿 매니지먼트에 요청한 사항은?
(A) 자동차에서 장치 제거하기
(B) 대여 계약기간 연장하기
(C) 보험담보 범위 확대하기
(D) 추적 소프트웨어 업그레이드하기

해설 사토우 씨의 이메일의 두 번째 단락 세 번째 문장에서 '저희는 실제로 장치(devices)를 사용하지 않는데, 직원들이 제거해 달라고 요청하고 있다. 이 장치를 제거해 달라'고 했다. 따라서 정답은 (A)이다.

어휘 remove 제거하다 equipment 장비 automobile 자동차 extend 늘리다, 연장하다 agreement 계약 insurance coverage 보험담보 범위

193 연계

번역 이시옴 어소시에이츠는 차량당 얼마의 대여료를 지불하는가?
(A) 367달러
(B) 482달러
(C) 526달러
(D) 570달러

해설 욘트 씨의 이메일 첫 번째 단락 세 번째 문장에서 '저희 대여 차량으로 인트리노가 결정되어 기쁘다'고 했다. 첫 번째 지문 웹페이지의 네 번째 항목에 인트리노 모델의 대여 가격이 570달러로 나와 있다. 따라서 정답은 (D)이다.

194 연계

번역 스넬 씨는 누구이겠는가?
(A) 우디스 플릿 매니지먼트의 회계 담당자
(B) 우디스 플릿 매니지먼트의 자동차 정비공
(C) 이시옴 어소시에이츠의 영업사원
(D) 이시옴 어소시에이츠의 이사

해설 욘트 씨 이메일 첫 번째 단락 두 번째 문장에서 '이드 스넬 씨의 사고 차량 수리가 효율적으로 이루어졌고 우디스에서 특별 요청에 빠르게 대응했다'고 했다. 사토우 씨의 이메일의 첫 번째 단락 네 번째 문장에서는 '영업사원 중 한 명이 경미한 교통사고를 겪었는데 센터 직원들이 매우 잘 도와주었다'고 했다. 그러므로 스넬 씨는 사토우 씨와 같은 회사의 영업사원임을 알 수 있다. 따라서 정답은 (C)이다

어휘 account manager 회계 담당자, 계정 관리자 mechanic 정비공 salesperson 영업사원 executive 중역, 이사

195 세부 사항

번역 두 번째 이메일에서 이시옴 어소시에이츠에 대해 명시된 것은?
(A) 행정 기록을 디지털화한다.
(B) 직원들에 의해 발생한 유류비를 지불해 준다.
(C) 최근 주차장을 넓혔다.
(D) 해외에 고객들이 있다.

해설 욘트 씨의 이메일 두 번째 단락 두 번째 문장에서 '출장에 사용된 연료(gas used on business trips)에 대해 적절히 환급해 줄 수 있도록 하는 것이 중요하다'고 했다. 그러므로 회사가 직원들에게 연료비를 지급하는 것을 알 수 있다. 따라서 정답은 (B)이다.

어휘 digitize 디지털화하다, 수치화하다 administrative record 행정 기록 fuel cost 유류비 incur (비용을) 발생시키다 expand 확장하다 overseas 해외의

196 -200 웹페이지+영수증+이메일

http://www.wander-tg.nl/eng/day

완더 관광 그룹과 함께하는 당일 여행

이제 암스테르담을 보셨으니 당일 여행으로 네덜란드의 다른 그림 같은 명소들을 구경해 보세요!

자전거 관광: 이 5시간짜리 여행은 **196**암스테르담 교외의 시골 지역에서 진행됩니다. 자전거 여행객들은 습지에서 평원에 이르기까지 아름다운 네덜란드의 다양한 경치를 볼 수 있는 기회를 얻게 될 것입니다. 여행은 성인과 어린이에게 개방되어 있지만 참가자들은 적정한 수준의 체력과 자전거 기술이 필요합니다.

화훼 관광: 700만 개가 넘는 꽃 구근이 심어져 있는 세계 최대의 **196**야외 화원을 거닐어 보세요. 방문객들은 또한 (추가 요금을 내시면) 다채로운 화단 한복판에서 점심으로 소풍 도시락을 즐기실 수 있습니다. **198**이 여행은 꽃이 활짝 피는 봄에만 이용하실 수 있습니다.

196수공예와 풍차 관광: 이 관광은 고풍스러운 시골 마을 두 곳에 들러 방문객들이 네덜란드의 전통 생활을 느낄 수 있게 해 줍니다. 방문객들은 네덜란드의 수공예품을 구입하고 직접 만드는 것을 배울 수 있습니다. 그런 다음, 오늘날에도 여전히 돌아가고 있는 오래된 풍차들을 구경하게 됩니다.

555-0122번으로 전화하거나 reservations@wander-tg.nl로 이메일을 보내셔서 오늘 관광 상품 중 한 **197**자리를 예약해 보세요.

어휘 now that 이제 ~이니까(= since) take a day trip 당일 여행을 하다 picturesque 그림 같은 sight 명소, 관광지 take place 일어나다, 발생하다 rural 시골의 have a chance to+동사원형 ~할 기회를 얻다 a range of 다양한 Dutch 네덜란드의 landscape 경치, 풍경 wetland 습지 plain 평원, 평야 be open to ~에게 개방되어 있다 adult 성인 be required to+동사원형 ~해야 한다, ~할 필요가 있다 reasonable 적정한, 합당한 fitness 건강 상태, 체력 open-air 야외의, 옥외의 flower garden 화원 bulb 구근, 알뿌리 for an additional fee 추가 요금을 내면 in the middle of ~한가운데, 한복판에 colorful 다채로운, 화려한 flower bed 화단 available 이용할 수 있는 be in bloom 활짝 피어 있다 windmill 풍차 make a stop 들르다, 멈추다 quaint 고풍스러운, 예스러운, 진기한 get a feel for ~을 느껴보다, ~에 대한 감을 익히다 reserve a spot 자리를 예약하다

예약 영수증 #4623

이름: 캐롤라인 브랙스턴
구입일: 3월 3일

관광	날짜	손님	가격
198화훼 관광 (중식 포함)	4월 18일	1명	40유로
수공예와 풍차 관광	4월 20일	1명	80유로
		지불 합계:	120유로

여행 시작 1주일 이상 전에 취소된 예약에 대해서는 80%를 환불해 드립니다. 여행 시작 1주일 미만 전에 취소된 예약은 50%를 환불해 드립니다. **200**여행 시작 하루 전에 취소된 예약은 10%를 환불해 드립니다.

어휘 receipt 영수증 booking 예약 cancel 취소하다 prior to ~전에, ~에 앞서 refund 환불 less than ~미만

수신: ⟨customersupport@wander-tg.nl⟩
발신: ⟨caroline22@jrmail.com⟩
날짜: 4월 19일
제목: 취소

안녕하세요.

우선, 어제 완더 투어 그룹 여행은 몹시 즐거웠음을 알려드립니다. 우리가 방문한 곳들은 참으로 아름다웠고, **199**제 안내인인 알렉스는 아는 게 많았으며 네덜란드어와 영어로 관광을 인솔했는데 그의 안내를 듣는 것은 즐거웠습니다.

하지만 안타깝게도 오늘 아침 병이 나고 말았습니다. **200**내일 관광을 할 수 없게 되어서 환불을 받고 싶습니다. 제 예약 번호는 4623입니다.

캐롤라인 브랙스턴 드림

어휘 cancellation 취소 thoroughly 철저히, 아주, 대단히 guide 안내인 knowledgeable 박식한, 아는 것이 많은 conduct 인솔하다, 지휘하다 get sick 병이 나다

196 사실 관계 확인

번역 웹페이지에 따르면, 당일 여행에 관해 사실인 것은?
(A) 암스테르담에서 진행된다.
(B) 야외 활동을 중심으로 이루어져 있다.
(C) 최소 연령 제한이 있다.
(D) 일요일에는 운영되지 않는다.

해설 첫 번째 지문에 소개된 당일 관광 세 종류의 내용을 보면 모두 야외에서 이뤄지는 여행이라는 점을 알 수 있다. 따라서 정답은 (B)이다. (A)는 웹페이지의 첫 문장에서 암스테르담을 봤으니 네덜란드의 다른 곳을 보라는 말에서 오답임을 알 수 있고, (C)는 Bike Tour에서 성인과 어린이들에게 개방되어 있다(the tour is open to adults and children)는 내용만 있을 뿐 나이에 대한 언급은 없으므로 오답이다. (D)의 요일에 관한 내용도 언급되어 있지 않다.

197 동의어 찾기

번역 웹페이지에서 다섯 번째 단락 1행의 "spot"과 의미상 가장 가까운 것은?
(A) 지점
(B) 얼룩
(C) 전망
(D) 자리

해설 이 문장에서 spot은 관광을 할 때 '정해진 인원'에 해당하는 '자리 혹은 좌석'을 뜻하는 의미로 사용되었으므로, seat와 바꿔 쓸 수 있다. 따라서 정답은 (D) seat(자리, 좌석)이다.

198 연계

번역 브랙스턴 씨에 관해 암시된 것은?

(A) 일시적인 가격 할인을 이용했다.
(B) 네덜란드 전통 문화에 관심이 없다.
(C) 계절 여행을 신청했다.
(D) 자전거를 자주 탄다.

해설 두 번째 지문을 보면 브랙스턴 씨가 Flower Tour를 신청한 것을 알 수 있는데, 첫 번째 지문에서 Flower Tour 소개를 보면, 마지막 문장에 이 관광은 '봄에만 가능하다(only available in the spring)'라고 되어 있다. 이를 토대로 정답은 (C)라는 것을 알 수 있다.

199 추론 / 암시

번역 완더 관광 그룹에 대해 브랙스턴 씨가 암시하는 것은?

(A) 웹사이트의 정보가 잘못되었다.
(B) 관광 집단의 인원수가 너무 많다.
(C) 이중언어를 쓰는 관광 안내인이 있다.
(D) 설문 조사를 실시한다.

해설 세 번째 지문 중간을 보면, 가이드인 알렉스가 네덜란드어와 영어(in Dutch and English)를 구사할 줄 안다는 내용을 확인할 수 있다. 따라서 정답은 (C)이다.

▶▶ **Paraphrasing** 지문의 **conducted the tour in Dutch and English** → 정답의 **bilingual tour guides**

200 연계

번역 브랙스턴 씨는 투어 가격의 몇 퍼센트를 환불 받을 것인가?

(A) 10%
(B) 50%
(C) 80%
(D) 100%

해설 세 번째 지문에서 브랙스턴 씨가 내일 관광을 할 수 없다는 것을 확인할 수 있고, 두 번째 지문 마지막 줄에서 전날 취소할 경우 10%를 환불해 준다는 것을 알 수 있다. 따라서 정답은 (A)이다.

TEST 6

101 (D)	**102** (A)	**103** (C)	**104** (C)	**105** (A)
106 (B)	**107** (C)	**108** (D)	**109** (B)	**110** (C)
111 (C)	**112** (A)	**113** (A)	**114** (A)	**115** (D)
116 (B)	**117** (B)	**118** (C)	**119** (B)	**120** (D)
121 (D)	**122** (D)	**123** (B)	**124** (B)	**125** (D)
126 (C)	**127** (C)	**128** (A)	**129** (B)	**130** (A)
131 (D)	**132** (C)	**133** (D)	**134** (B)	**135** (C)
136 (A)	**137** (A)	**138** (D)	**139** (D)	**140** (B)
141 (D)	**142** (B)	**143** (B)	**144** (A)	**145** (C)
146 (C)	**147** (B)	**148** (D)	**149** (D)	**150** (B)
151 (A)	**152** (C)	**153** (D)	**154** (B)	**155** (D)
156 (B)	**157** (A)	**158** (C)	**159** (C)	**160** (D)
161 (A)	**162** (B)	**163** (D)	**164** (C)	**165** (D)
166 (B)	**167** (A)	**168** (C)	**169** (A)	**170** (D)
171 (A)	**172** (B)	**173** (C)	**174** (B)	**175** (D)
176 (A)	**177** (C)	**178** (A)	**179** (C)	**180** (C)
181 (C)	**182** (D)	**183** (B)	**184** (A)	**185** (D)
186 (C)	**187** (A)	**188** (B)	**189** (D)	**190** (A)
191 (D)	**192** (C)	**193** (B)	**194** (A)	**195** (D)
196 (C)	**197** (B)	**198** (A)	**199** (B)	**200** (C)

PART 5

101 전치사 어휘

해설 '8킬로그램 미만으로'라는 뜻이 되어야 하므로 '(양, 나이가) ~ 미만의'라는 뜻의 (D) under가 정답이다. (A) on(~ 위에)과 (B) across(~을 가로질러)는 의미상 어색하고, (C)의 between은 'between A and B(A와 B 사이에)'라는 형태로 쓰이므로 답이 될 수 없다.

번역 라번 항공은 무게가 8킬로그램 미만인 가방은 휴대 가능 수하물로 비행기에 반입이 되도록 허용한다.

어휘 weigh 무게가 ~이다 carry 가지고 타다 aircraft 항공기 hand luggage 휴대 가능[기내 반입] 수하물

102 수량 형용사 _ 단수 가산명사 수식

해설 candidate는 단수 가산명사로 형용사의 수식을 받는다. (B) Especially (특히), (D) Almost(거의)는 부사이기 때문에 올 수 없다. 나머지 보기는 모두 형용사로 쓰일 수 있지만 (C) Few(몇몇의)는 뒤에 가산명사가 오는 경우에 복수 명사가 와야 한다. 따라서 단수 가산명사가 올 수 있는 (A) Neither(둘 다 ~ 아닌)가 정답이다.

번역 두 지원자 다 필수 소프트웨어 프로그램 사용법에 대해 잘 알고 있음을 보여 주지 못했다.

어휘 candidate 지원자 demonstrate 보여 주다 required 필수의

103 부사 자리 _ 동사 수식

해설 수동태 형태인 동사구 will be shared를 수식하는 부사 자리이다. 따라서 부사 형태인 (C) openly(공개적으로)가 정답이다.

번역 회사의 전 분기 판매 실적은 일반에 공개될 것이다.

어휘 previous quarter 이전 분기

104 명사 자리 _ 전치사의 목적어

해설 전치사 뒤에 오면서 형용사의 수식을 받는 명사 자리이다. 따라서 명사형인 (C) impressions(인상)가 정답이다. leave A with B(A에게 B를 남기다)라는 표현도 기억해두자.

번역 경제 발전에 대한 바브 살로넨의 연설은 지속적으로 청중에게 좋은 인상을 남긴다.

어휘 speech on ~에 관한 연설 consistently 일관하여, 지속적으로 audience 청중 favorable 호의적인 impress 감명을 주다

105 동사 어휘

해설 빈칸 뒤에 전치사 to가 있다는 점이 중요한 힌트가 된다. 주로 to와 함께 쓰는 동사는 (A) commit과 (C) lead이다. commit to는 '~에 헌신하다, 전념하다', lead to는 '~로 이어지다'라는 의미이다. 여기서 문맥상 더 어울리는 것은 commit이므로, (A) commit(헌신하다, 전념하다)가 정답이다. (B)는 주로 participate in(~에 참가하다), (D)는 주로 'afford to+동사원형(~할 형편이 되다)'으로 쓰인다는 점도 기억해두자.

번역 직원들은 연간 한 개 이상의 자원 봉사 프로젝트에 전념해서는 안 된다.

어휘 volunteer 자원 봉사

106 명사 어휘

해설 서비스가 무료로 제공되는 기간 동안 계속될 '추세'라는 말이 가장 적절하다. 따라서 정답은 (B) trend(추세, 경향)이다. (A) setting은 '환경', (C) record는 '기록', (D) quote는 '인용구'라는 의미이다.

번역 국제전화 모바일 앱의 사용은 서비스가 무료인 한 계속될 듯한 추세다.

어휘 international call 국제전화 be likely to+동사원형 ~할 것 같다

107 대명사 _ 소유 형용사

해설 지역 테니스 애호가들(local tennis enthusiasts)이 '그들 자신들만의 공간'을 갖게 되었다는 의미다. 'of one's own(~자신(만)의)'의 활용을 묻는 문제이다. one's는 소유 형용사이므로 (C) their own이 정답이다.

번역 공원 개조 공사로 마침내 지역 테니스 애호가들이 농구 코트와 분리된 자신들만의 공간을 가지게 되었다.

어휘 renovation 수리, 개조 enthusiast 열광적인 팬, 애호가 space 공간 separate from ~와 분리된

108 형용사 자리 _ 명사 수식

해설 빈칸 뒤에 온 명사(efforts)를 수식하는 형용사를 찾는 문제이다. 따라서 형용사 (D) collaborative(공동의)가 정답이다.

번역 커뮤니티 집단들의 공동의 노력으로 시의회는 조각상 건립을 승인했다.

어휘 effort 노력 town council 시의회 statue 조각상 collaborate 협력하다

Test 6

109 명사 어휘

해설 문맥상 a three-year-long과 함께 쓰이려면 '3개년 계획'이라는 표현이 가장 어울린다. plan이나 act와 같은 뜻으로 사용할 수 있는 (B) initiative(계획)가 정답이다. 나머지 보기의 의미를 보면 (A) election은 '선거', (C) comment는 '언급', (D) industry는 '산업'으로 이 문장에는 어울리지 않는다.

번역 카슨 시는 도시 건물 전체에 태양 전지판을 설치하는 3개년 계획을 시작하겠다고 발표했다.

어휘 announce 발표하다 install 설치하다 solar panel 태양 전지판

110 동사 자리 _ 수동태

해설 빈칸 앞의 부사가 명사를 수식할 수 없으므로 (A) enforcement(집행)는 정답이 될 수 없고, 앞에 be동사 are가 있으므로 또 다른 동사 (D) enforce(집행하다)도 올 수 없다. 규정이 '적용되는' 것이므로 수동태 'be + p.p.'의 형태가 되어야 한다. 따라서 과거분사 (C) enforced가 정답이다.

번역 비스크 야생동물 보호지역에서는 주 어업 규정이 엄격하게 적용되어 방문객들에게 한 번에 물고기 10마리씩으로 제한한다.

어휘 regulation 규정, 규칙 strictly 엄격하게 limit 제한하다
enforce (법을) 집행하다[시행하다]

111 접속사 어휘

해설 문맥상 '날씨가 나빠지지 않는 한 기념 파티는 야외에서 열릴 것이다'라는 의미가 되어야 하므로, '~하지 않는 한'이라는 의미의 '조건' 부사절 접속사인 (C) unless가 정답이다. 참고로, 문장의 시제가 미래(will be held)일 경우 시간이나 조건을 나타내는 부사절 접속사가 포함된 절에서는 미래 시제 대신 현재 시제(becomes)를 사용한다는 것도 알아두자.

번역 20주년 기념 파티는 날씨가 나빠지지 않는 한 허친슨 가든의 야외에서 열릴 것이다.

어휘 anniversary 기념일[식] inclement (날씨가) 궂은

112 부사 자리 _ 동사 수식

해설 동사(impacted)를 수식하는 부사 자리이다. 합병이 투자자들에게 '긍정적으로' 영향을 주었다는 의미이므로, 정답은 (A) positively(긍정적으로)이다.

번역 밸류트 사와 스탠포드 파트너스의 합병은 투자자 대다수에게 긍정적인 영향을 주었다.

어휘 merger 합병 impact 영향을 주다 majority of 다수의 ~
investor 투자자 positive 긍정적인 positivity 확신

113 명사 어휘

해설 동사 obtain의 목적어로 의미가 통하는 명사를 고르는 문제이다. 자동차 정비공이 차 수리에 앞서 차 주인에게서 '(수리할) 권한'을 얻는다는 뜻이 되어야 하므로 (A) authorization(공식적인 허가, 권한 부여)이 정답이다. (B) opportunity(기회), (C) supervision(감독), (D) demand(수요; 요구)는 의미상 어색하다.

번역 비니스 자동차 정비소의 정비공들은 정비 작업을 수행하기 전에 손님들에게 승인을 받는다.

어휘 auto shop 자동차 정비소 mechanic 정비공 obtain 획득하다
perform 수행하다 repair 수리, 정비

114 명사 자리 _ 주어

해설 동사 앞 주어 자리에 들어갈 수 있는 명사를 고르는 문제이다. 동사가 fail인 것으로 보아, 주어인 명사는 복수형이 되어야 한다는 것을 알 수 있다. 따라서 정답은 (A) registrants(등록자)이다.

번역 등록자가 이주 한 달 이내에 주소 변경을 알리지 못할 경우, 과태료가 부과될 것이다.

어휘 notify A of B A에게 B를 알리다 fine 벌금 register 등록하다; 기록부

115 대명사 / 명사 자리 _ 선행사

해설 tour participants will need는 '투어 참가자들이 필요로 할'이라는 뜻의 문장으로 앞에 목적격 관계대명사 that이 생략된 형용사절이다. 따라서 빈칸은 그 수식을 받는 선행사 자리이므로 명사 또는 대명사가 와야 한다. (D) everything(모든 것)이 정답이다. (A) most(대부분의), (B) much(많은, 많이), (C) anywhere(어디서나)는 모두 어색하다.

번역 꾸러미 안에 투어 참가자들이 필요로 할 모든 것의 목록이 들어 있다.

어휘 packet 꾸러미 participant 참가자

116 형용사 어휘

해설 문맥상 '상당한' 연금을 보장해 준다는 뜻을 완성하는 (B) substantial(상당한)이 가장 적절하다. (D) numerous(많은)는 many와 마찬가지로 복수형의 가산명사를 수식해 주어야 하기 때문에 여기에는 올 수 없다. (A) skillful은 '숙련된', (C) loyal은 '충성된'이라는 의미로 문맥상 어울리지 않는다.

번역 왕 씨가 하포드원 타이어 회사에서 보낸 수십 년은 그녀에게 상당한 연금을 보장해 준다.

어휘 guarantee 보장하다 pension 연금

117 형용사 자리 _ 명사 수식

해설 명사(inspections)를 앞에서 수식해주는 형용사를 고르는 문제이다. 보기에서 품사가 형용사인 것은 (B) random(무작위의)이므로 정답은 (B)이다.

번역 윌트셔 타워는 신규 안전 기준이 시행된 이래 무작위로 실시되는 점검을 몇 차례 받았다.

어휘 implementation 실행 standard 기준 undergo 겪다
inspection 점검 randomly 임의로 randomize 임의로 추출하다, 무작위로 순서를 정하다

118 부사 어휘

해설 빈칸 뒤의 형용사 high와 어울리는 부사여야 하고, 뒤에 compared to(~와 비교하여)가 나온 것으로 보아 비교하는 표현과 관련이 있어야 한다. 따라서 (C) relatively(비교적)가 가장 적절하다. (A) diligently는 '부지런히', (B) productively는 '생산적으로', (D) tightly는 '단단히, 꽉'이라는 의미로 빈칸에는 어울리지 않는다.

번역 비라프테크의 최신 고화질 캠코더는 유사 모델에 비해 비교적 높은 가격에 첫선을 보였다.

어휘 latest 최신의 high-definition 고화질 debut (물건이) 시장에 처음 나오다 compared to ~와 비교하여

119 전치사 어휘

해설 문맥상 세미나가 열리는 '동안 내내' 간식이 제공된다는 의미가 가장 자연스럽다. 따라서 정답은 (B) throughout(~ 동안 내내)이 적절하다. (A) along은 '~를 따라서', (C) such as는 '예를 들어', (D) among은 '~ 사이에'라는 뜻으로 의미상 어울리지 않는다.

번역 오늘 세미나 동안 내내 참가자들에게 간단한 간식과 음료가 제공될 것이다.

어휘 beverage 음료 attendee 참가자

120 명사 자리 _ 형용사 뒤

해설 빈칸은 형용사(initial)가 수식할 수 있는 명사 자리이다. 따라서 정답은 명사형인 (D) analysis(분석)이다.

번역 외부 실험실이 실시한 비타민제 실험 결과는 찬 박사의 초기 분석에 부합한다.

어휘 outcome 결과 external 외부의 laboratory 실험실 vitamin formula 비타민제 match ~와 부합하다 analytical 분석적인 analyze 분석하다

121 동사 시제 + 능동태 / 수동태 구분

해설 시제를 알 수 있는 힌트가 되는 표현이 딱히 없기 때문에 assign이라는 동사의 쓰임을 아는 것이 중요하다. assign은 주로 수동태 형태로 '~로 배치하다, ~을 맡다'라는 의미로 쓰인다. 따라서 보기 중에서 유일한 수동태형인 (D) has been assigned가 정답이다.

번역 수딥 바네르지는 인도의 새 직책에 임명되어 우리의 사업 네트워크를 성장시킬 것으로 기대된다.

어휘 post 지위, 직 be expected to+동사원형 ~할 것으로 기대되다

122 전치사 자리 _ 명사 앞

해설 빈칸 뒤에는 명사구만 있고, 콤마(,) 뒤에 완전한 문장이 있다. 따라서 빈칸은 명사 앞에 들어갈 전치사 자리이다. (A) Although는 접속사이기 때문에 제외되며, (B) Until(~까지)과 (C) Except(~은 제외하고)는 의미상 맞지 않는다. 내용상 (D) Unlike(~와 달리)가 적절하므로 정답은 (D)이다.

번역 많은 고위 임원들과는 달리, 응구엔 씨는 조사 부문에서 경력을 쌓기 시작했다.

어휘 senior director 고위 임원 start one's career 경력을 쌓기 시작하다 research 조사, 연구

123 부사 자리 _ 동사 수식

해설 빈칸은 일반동사(carries) 앞에서 동사를 수식하는 부사가 들어갈 자리이다. 따라서 정답은 (B) actually(실제로)이다. (A) actual은 형용사로 '실제의', (C) actuality는 명사로 '실제, 현실', (D) actualize는 동사형으로 '실현하다'라는 의미이므로 품사 면에서 어울리지 않는다.

번역 화장품으로 유명한 로잘리타스 네세서리즈는 실제로 약용 및 치료용 피부관리 제품도 갖추고 있다.

어휘 cosmetic 화장품 medicinal 약효가 있는 therapeutic 치료적인

124 전치사구 자리

해설 빈칸 뒤에 명사(your letter of request)가 나왔기 때문에 전치사(구)가 들어가야 할 자리이다. 뒤에 '주어+동사' 절이 와야 하는 (C) Now that, (D) In case는 제외된다. '요청서에 대한 응답으로 할인을 해주겠다'는 의미가 자연스러우므로 정답은 (B) In response to(~에 대한 응답으로)이다.

번역 노스리지 스위트는 요청서에 대한 응답으로, 이두베 협회에 할인된 금액으로 주 연회장을 제공하게 되어 기쁘게 생각합니다.

어휘 letter of request 요청서 offer 제공하다 at a reduced rate 할인된 금액으로 on behalf of ~을 대표하여

125 동사 어휘

해설 매입 동기를 정확히 모르지만 '추측하는' 상황이므로 (D) speculating(추측하는)이 정답이다. (A) attributing(탓하는)은 'attribute A to B(A를 B의 탓으로 돌리다)'로 많이 쓰인다. (B) investigating(조사하는)도 어색하다. (C)의 동사 convince는 '확신시키다'라는 뜻이며 '확신하다'는 뜻이 되려면 'be convinced' 형태가 되어야 한다.

번역 잘비가 립챗을 매입하는 동기를 밝히지 않고 있지만 전문가들은 후자의 회사가 가지고 있는 많은 양의 소비자 데이터와 관련 있는 것으로 추측한다.

어휘 reveal 밝히다 motive 동기, 이유 acquire 인수하다, 매입하다 be related to ~와 관련이 있다 latter 후자의 firm 회사 collection 수집, 수집품 speculate 추측하다

126 부사 어휘

해설 보기의 의미를 보면, (A) unusually는 '대단히, 몹시', (B) slightly는 '약간', (C) rarely는 '거의 ~ 않는', (D) sparsely는 '드문드문, 성기게'이다. 초콜릿을 받을 만큼의 포인트를 '거의 적립하지 못한다'는 의미가 가장 자연스러우므로, 정답은 (C) rarely(거의 ~ 않는)가 된다.

번역 스테이시 캔디 가게 고객들은 초콜릿 한 상자를 공짜로 받는 데 충분한 연간 포인트를 거의 적립하지 못한다.

어휘 accumulate 모으다, 축적하다 reward 보상 earn 받다

127 접속사 자리 + 접속사 / 부사 구분

해설 동사가 두 개(will receive, is approved)가 나왔기 때문에 빈칸에는 두 문장을 연결할 접속사가 들어가야 한다. (C) once를 제외한 나머지는 모두 부사나 전치사구이다. 따라서 접속사인 (C) once(일단 ~하면)가 정답이다.

번역 이미지 쉐어 신규 회원들은 신청이 승인되면 이메일로 확정을 받는다.

어휘 confirmation 확인 application 신청 approve 승인하다 thereby 그렇게 함으로써 at least 최소한 regardless of ~에 상관없이

128 분사 자리 _ 명사 수식

해설 'Exhibitors ~ the fair'가 문장의 주어, may contact가 동사이다. 빈칸에는 동사가 올 수 없으므로 (C) concern(우려하게 하다)은 정답이 될 수 없다. 명사인 (B) concerns(우려)도 의미상 어색하다. 'be concerned about(~을 우려하다)'이 적용되므로 (A) concerned가 정답이다. concerned 앞에 'who are'가 생략되었다. (D) concerning은 '~에 관해'라는 뜻의 전치사이다.

번역 박람회의 보안이 우려되는 출품 업체들은 555-0162번으로 전시 서비스 팀에 연락하십시오.

어휘 exhibitor 전시회 출품자[기업] security 보안 fair 박람회

129 부사 어휘

해설 대중의 이해를 돕기 위해서 과학 용어들이 '의도적으로' 삭제됐다는 의미가 가장 자연스럽다. 따라서 정답은 (B) intentionally(의도적으로)이다. 나머지 보기인 (A) enormously는 '대단히', (C) domestically는 '국내에서', (D) alternatively는 '그 대신에'로 의미상 어울리지 않는다.

번역 일반 대중이 더 쉽게 이해할 수 있도록 기사에서 많은 과학 용어들이 의도적으로 삭제됐다.

어휘 term 용어 delete 삭제하다 article 기사 general public 일반 대중

130 형용사 어휘

해설 빈칸 뒤의 전치사 to가 힌트가 된다. to와 함께 잘 쓰이는 형용사는 (A) essential(필수적인)과 (C) accustomed(익숙한)이다. 문맥상 직책에 '필수적'이라고 여겨지는 것만 구인광고에 언급된다는 의미가 더 적절하므로, 정답은 (A) essential이다. (B) flexible은 '융통성 있는', (D) competent는 '능숙한'이라는 의미로 문맥에 어울리지 않는다.

번역 정책에 따라 구인광고에는 해당 직책에 필수적이라고 여겨지는 책무와 자격 요건만 언급된다.

어휘 credential 자격 (증명서) deem 여기다, 간주하다 job posting 구인광고

Part 6

131-134 웹페이지

http://www.rhodes-mr.com

로즈 마운틴 휴양지

로즈 마운틴 휴양지는 멋진 산 전망을 자랑하는 **131**아늑한 호텔이면서 스파입니다. 이곳은 스키나 스노보드를 타는 사람들, 그리고 그냥 느긋하게 쉬고 싶은 사람들에게 정말 완벽합니다. 25개 객실이 딸린 저희 호텔은 우아한 실내장식을 뛰어난 방문객 서비스**132**와 결합시켰습니다. 저희 휴양지는 〈로즈 마운틴 저널〉에서 선정한 지역 내 최우수 **133**묵을 만한 장소 목록에 자주 등장합니다. 마찬가지로, 저희 스파에서도 미용 및 건강 처방과 관련해 최고의 서비스를 제공합니다. **134**여러분은 산 비탈에서 긴 하루를 보낸 후 간단한 스포츠 마사지를 받으실 수 있습니다. 아니면 얼굴 마사지나 발 관리 같은 추가 서비스가 포함된 일괄 패키지를 선택하실 수도 있습니다.

저희 스파에서 제공하는 것을 보다 자세히 확인하시려면 이 페이지를 방문하시고, 예약을 하시려면 저희에게 연락하세요.

어휘 retreat 휴게처, 안식처 cozy 아늑한 boast 자랑하다 spectacular (경치가) 장관인 combine A with B A를 B와 결합시키다, A와 B를 겸비하다 artful 기교적인, 우아한 décor 실내 장식 regularly 규칙적으로, 자주 appear (글 속에) 나오다, 언급되다 likewise 마찬가지로 wellness 건강 treatment 치료, 처치 mountain slope 산비탈 inclusive 포괄적인, (가격에) 모든 경비가 포함된 additional 추가적인 facial 얼굴 마사지 pedicure 발톱[발] 관리, 페디큐어 offering (상품으로) 제공하는 것 make a reservation 예약하다

131 문맥에 맞는 문장 고르기

번역 (A) 최근 몇 년간 점점 더 많은 사람들이 산을 방문하고 있습니다.
(B) 상공회의소에서 유용한 사업체 목록을 발행합니다.
(C) 12세 미만 어린이는 특별 할인 요금을 이용할 수 있습니다.
(D) 이곳은 스키나 스노보드를 타는 사람들, 그리고 그냥 느긋하게 쉬고 싶은 사람들에게 정말 완벽합니다.

해설 로즈 마운틴 휴양지를 소개하는 도입부이다. 바로 앞에서 이곳이 아늑한 호텔이면서 스파라고 했으므로, 이어서 이곳이 겨울 스포츠와 휴식을 즐기기에 완벽하다고 말하는 (D)가 오는 게 자연스럽다.

어휘 publish 발표하다 business directory (분야별로 분류된) 사업체 목록 special rate 특별 할인 요금

132 전치사 어휘

해설 '우아한 실내장식과 뛰어난 방문객 서비스를 결합시켰다'는 뜻이다. 동사 combine은 'combine A with B(A와 B를 결합하다)'의 형태로 쓰이므로 정답은 (C) with이다.

133 동사 어휘

해설 to부정사가 앞의 top places를 수식한다. 의미상 '묵을' 만한 최고의 장소라는 말이 가장 자연스러우므로 (D) stay(묵다)가 정답이다. (A) work(일하다), (B) dine(식사하다), (C) shop(쇼핑하다)는 다소 어색하다.

어휘 dine 식사하다 stay 묵다

134 주격 대명사

해설 리조트 호텔을 소개하는 광고문이므로 말하는 주체는 호텔 측(we, our), 대상은 광고를 읽는 사람(you)이다. '스포츠 마사지를 즐길 수 있다'고 했으므로 빈칸에 광고 주체인 (C) We는 들어갈 수 없다. 광고를 읽는 '여러분'이 되어야 하므로 (B) You가 정답이다.

135-138 기사

당신의 이력서에 생명을 불어넣으세요

구직자들에게 어려운 시기다. 경쟁이 치열해서 같은 일자리에 똑같이 **135자격을 갖춘** 지원자 수백 명이 이력서를 보낸다.

이러한 상황에서는 조직이 당신을 알아보도록 하는 비결은 당신이 돋보이도록 하는 것이라고 진로상담가 히로시 타나카는 말한다. "구직자는 더 이상 지원서를 소박한 성과의 나열로 여겨서는 안 됩니다." 그는 설명한다. "**136그 대신에** 이러한 과정을 자신만의 독특한 이야기를 할 기회로 보아야 합니다." 인사 담당자에게 단순히 당신이 '훌륭한 조직화 기술'을 갖췄음을 알리려고 하지 말라. 일에서 자신이 겪은 어려움과 이를 해결하기 위해 그런 능력을 어떻게 **137성공적으로** 활용했는지 설명하라. 읽는 사람에게는 이것이 더 기억에 남는다.

어휘 job hunter 구직자 competition 경쟁 stiff 심한
applicant 지원자 résumé 이력서 key to ~의 핵심
organization 단체, 조직 stand out 두드러지다 job applicant
구직자 no longer 더 이상 ~ 않다 achievement 성취, 업적
process 절차 opportunity 기회 merely 단순히
organizational skill 조직화 기술 describe 기술하다, 설명하다
utilize 활용하다 ability 능력

135 형용사 어휘

해설 문맥상 동등하게 '자격을 갖춘' 지원자라는 의미가 가장 적절하기 때문에 정답은 (C) qualified(자격을 갖춘)이다. 나머지 보기를 보면 (A) extensive는 '대규모의', (B) unbiased는 '선입견 없는, 편파적이지 않은' (D) beneficial은 '유익한'이라는 의미로 문맥에 어울리지 않는다.

136 부사 어휘

해설 이력서를 쓸 때 꾸밈 없는 성과의 나열에 초점을 맞추지 말고, 자신의 독특한 이야기를 할 기회로 삼아야 한다는 내용 사이에 두 문장을 연결해줄 수 있는 연결고리를 찾는 문제다. '그 대신에'라는 뜻을 가진 (A) Instead가 가장 적절하다. (B) Similarly는 '비슷하게' (C) Nevertheless는 '그럼에도 불구하고', (D) Finally는 '마침내'라는 의미로 문맥에 어울리지 않는다.

137 부사 자리

해설 빈칸에는 뒤에 있는 동사 utilized를 수식할 부사가 와야 한다. 따라서 정답은 (A) successfully(성공적으로)이다.

138 문맥에 맞는 문장 고르기

번역 (A) 무엇보다, 그런 어려움은 매우 흔하다.
(B) 그러면 진로상담가가 필요한 부분은 편집할 것이다.
(C) 그것들은 증명서 발급 기관에 의해 확인되어야 한다.
(D) 읽는 사람에게는 이것이 더 기억에 남는다.

해설 빈칸 앞에서 이력서를 쓸 때 바람직한 서술 방향을 설명해 주고 있기 때문에 이 내용을 자연스럽게 받을 수 있는 문장이 나와야 한다. (D)처럼 이력서를 보게 되는 사람에게 인상을 심어줄 수 있다는 내용이 나오는 것이 가장 적절하다. 따라서 정답은 (D)이다.

139-142 이메일

수신: 토스티 오츠 광고팀
발신: 잰 오르테가
날짜: 10월 29일
제목: 추가 회의

안녕하세요, 팀원 여러분.

예기치 못한 변동사항으로 인해, 토스티 오츠 시리얼의 겨울철 광고 캠페인에 관해 추가 회의가 있을 예정입니다. 모든 팀원들은 내일 아침 9시 30분에 회의실로 **139와야** 합니다.

다음의 두 가지 항목이 **140안건**이 될 것입니다. 첫째로, TV 방송국 광고 비용이 현저히 증가했습니다. 둘째로, 토스티 오츠 마스코트 사용에 관한 저작권 위반 가능성이 있습니다. 광고 패키지를 런칭하기 전에 이러한 문제들을 논의하고 해결해야 합니다.

142회의는 세 시간이 소요될 것임을 141알려드립니다. 이보다 더 길어지면 점심 식사가 제공됩니다.

감사합니다.

잰

어휘 advertising 광고 additional 추가의 due to ~ 때문에
unexpected 예기치 못한 conference room 회의실 following
다음의 dramatic 극적인 copyright 저작권 violation 위반
involving ~을 포함하여 complication 문제 resolve (문제를)
해결하다

139 동사 어휘

해설 빈칸 뒤의 전치사 to와 함께 회의실에 '도착하다'는 뜻을 지닌 동사가 와야 한다. 정답은 (A) report(도착을 알리다)이다. (B) accompany는 '수반하다', (C) consolidate는 '강화하다', (D) seek는 보통 to부정사와 함께 '추구하다'는 의미로 문맥상 어울리지 않는다.

140 명사 어휘

해설 빈칸 뒤의 내용으로 보아 회의의 '안건'을 뜻하는 말이 빈칸에 와야 하므로 정답은 (B) agenda이다. (A) invoice는 '송장', (C) questionnaire는 '설문지', (D) cover는 '표지'라는 의미로 문맥상 적절치 않다.

Test 6

141 동사 어형 _ 명령문

해설 주어가 없는 문장 구조이면서 앞에 please라는 말이 나왔으므로 뒤에는 명령문 형태인 동사원형으로 시작해야 한다. '권고된다'는 말에 해당하는 수동태의 동사원형 형태인 (D) be advised가 정답이다.

142 문맥에 맞는 문장 고르기

번역 (A) 여러분은 그날 중 나중 시간으로 연기할 수도 있습니다.
(B) **이보다 더 길어지면 점심식사가 제공됩니다.**
(C) 이번의 큰 성공을 축하해야 합니다.
(D) 대부분의 시간은 시음을 위해 사용됩니다.

해설 회의가 세 시간 소요될 것으로 예상된다(is expected to take three hours)는 앞 문장과 자연스럽게 연결될 문장을 골라야 한다. (C), (D)는 회의 소요 시간과 관련이 없고, (A)는 문맥상 적절하지 않다. 따라서 정답은 (B)이다.

143 -146 편지

4월 4일

페트리샤 쉐퍼
더든 웨이 450번지
아르티스, 조지아주 39851

쉐퍼 씨께.

아시겠지만, 아르티스 주민 센터에서 현재 수영장 시설 보수 공사를 하고 있습니다. 계획 중인 **143개선 사항**은 보다 나은 여과 장치와 탈의실 추가 등입니다. 유감스럽게도, 이 사업이 **144원래** 예상했던 것보다 **145더 많은 작업이 필요하다**는 걸 발견했습니다. 수영장 덱 받침 부분이 교체돼야 하는 게 드러났습니다. 이 비용을 충당하기 위해 여러분의 지원을 **146부탁드립니다.** 주민 센터 모든 회원 분들이 오늘 100달러씩 기부해 주신다면 우리 지역의 이 멋진 자원을 큰 지체 없이 재개장할 수 있을 것입니다. 기부를 하시려면 동봉한 양식을 작성하셔서 기부금과 함께 저희에게 보내주세요. 감사합니다.

앨런 케니
아르티스 주민 센터 책임자

동봉

어휘 currently 현재 renovate 보수하다 facilities 시설, 설비 filtration system 여과 장치 additional 추가적인 changing room 탈의실 donate 기부하다(donation 기부금) reopen 재개장하다 resource 자원 major 중대한, 심각한 delay 연기, 지체 contribute 기여하다, 기부하다 fill out (양식을) 작성하다 enclosed 동봉된(줄임말은 encl) form 양식

143 명사 자리 _ 주어

해설 include가 문장의 동사이며 빈칸이 주어 자리이다. 과거분사 planned (계획된)의 수식을 받는 명사가 와야 하므로 (B) improvements(개선, 개선 사항들)가 정답이다. (C) 동명사 improving(개선하는[되는] 것)도 주어가 될 수 있지만 과거분사의 수식을 받을 수 없고, 뒤의 동사도 단수형인 includes가 되어야 한다.

144 부사 어휘

해설 과거분사 expected(예상된)를 수식해 의미가 통하는 부사를 찾는 문제이다. 처음에 예상됐던 것보다 많은 작업이 필요하다는 뜻이므로 (A) originally(원래)가 정답이다. (B) considerably(상당히), (C) separately(별개로), (D) gradually(점진적으로)는 의미상 어색하다.

145 문맥에 맞는 문장 고르기

번역 (A) 수영장 이용자 다수가 아르티스의 주민 어르신들입니다.
(B) 수영장은 공사가 시작될 때까지는 개장을 할 예정입니다.
(C) **수영장 덱 받침 부분이 교체돼야 하는 게 드러났습니다.**
(D) 젠크 주민 센터에서 저희 고객들이 수영장을 이용하도록 하는 데 의견이 일치했습니다.

해설 바로 앞 문장에서 '작업 시간이 더 필요하다는 걸 발견했다'라고 했다. 그 뒤에는 시간이 더 필요한 이유를 설명하는 게 자연스러우므로 (C)가 정답이다.

어휘 majority 대다수 elderly 나이든 resident 주민 be scheduled to+동사원형 (일정상) ~할 예정이다 turn out 결국 ~로 밝혀지다 foundation 토대, 기반부 pool's deck 수영장 덱(풀 가장자리에 발을 디딜 수 있게 마루 등을 깔아놓은 부분) replace 교체하다 patron 고객 access 접근하다, 이용하다

146 동사시제 _ 현재진행형

해설 문맥상 '요청드립니다'라는 뜻이 어울리므로 현재진행형인 (C) are asking이 정답이다. (A) would have asked는 가정법 과거완료로 '~ 요청했을 텐데'라는 뜻이고, (B) asked는 과거 시제이고, (D) will be asked는 수동태이므로 모두 정답이 될 수 없다.

어휘 ask for ~을 요청하다

PART 7

147-148 안내판

건물 안내판	
1층 안내데스크 건물 관리실 메인 로비 카페	**4층** 네라 마케팅 어드밴티지 라피도 퍼스널 트레이너즈 GSB 필름
2층 **147로빈토 약국** **휘틀리 보건 서비스** **오레아 그로서즈 앤 비타민즈**	**5층** 웨스턴 루프탑 휘틀리 바인 아자니스 캐리비언 키친 메리스 버거스 앤 프라이즈
3층 스미스 앤 헤슨 법률사무소 옴스 컨설팅 미셸 글로벌 트레이딩 사 프레튼 프레스	엘리베이터는 로비 북쪽 출입문에서 탑승 가능합니다.

148휘틀리 스퀘어에서 임대 서비스 제공 (202) 555-0198

어휘 information desk 안내데스크 pharmacy 약국 law office 법률사무소 trading 거래, 교역 press 출판사 rooftop 옥상 access 접근하다, 이용하다 leasing service 임대 서비스

147 세부 사항

번역 방문객들은 몇 층에서 개인 관리용품을 살 수 있겠는가?
(A) 1층
(B) 2층
(C) 3층
(D) 4층

해설 personal care products는 개인 미용 및 위생 용품을 말한다. 대다수가 Pharmacy(약국)에서 판매되는 것들이므로 2층 Robinto Pharmacy에서 구매할 수 있다. 따라서 정답은 (B)이다.

148 세부 사항

번역 방문객들이 사무 공간을 임대하려면 누구에게 연락해야 하는가?
(A) 미셀 글로벌 트레이딩 주식회사
(B) 옴스 컨설팅
(C) 건물 관리실
(D) 휘틀리 스퀘어

해설 지문 마지막 줄에 임대 서비스를 누가 제공하는지 전화번호와 함께 명시되어 있다. 정답은 (D)이다.

149 -150 안내문

고객 여러분, 주목해 주세요.

1493월 1일부터 그레고렐 마켓에서는 계산대에서 나눠주는 1회용 비닐 봉지 하나에 0.10달러를 부과할 예정입니다. **150**새로운 시 조례에서 명한 이 청구는 어떤 상황에서도 예외일 수 없습니다.

비용을 내지 않으려면 손님 여러분께서 구입한 물건을 담을 수 있는 재사용 가능한 가방을 가지고 오시거나 구입하시기 바랍니다. 각 계산대 앞에 천 가방을 구입할 수 있게 이미 마련해 놓았습니다.

돈을 받는 것은 킬링 시에서 발생되는 재활용 불가능 폐기물의 양을 줄이기 위한 것입니다. 그레고렐 마켓과 킬링 시는 이 가치 있는 명분을 위해 여러분의 지지를 부탁 드립니다.

어휘 charge for ~에 비용을 청구하다(charge 청구, 요금) single-use plastic carrier bag (쇼핑용) 1회용 비닐 봉지 issue 지급하다 checkout (슈퍼마켓) 계산대(= checkout counter) mandate 지시하다, 명령하다 ordinance 법령, 조례 waive (법 집행 등을) 중단하다, 포기하다 under any circumstances 어떤 상황에서도, 무슨 일이 있어도 be encouraged to+동사원형 ~하도록 권유받다 reusable 재사용할 수 있는 purchase 구입(한 것) cloth 천 available 손에 넣을[이용할] 수 있는 be intended to+동사원형 ~할 의도이다 waste 폐기물 worthy 가치 있는 cause 대의명분

149 글의 주제 / 목적

번역 안내문의 주요 목적은 무엇인가?
(A) 재활용 프로젝트를 발표하려고
(B) 신상품 출시를 알리려고
(C) 일부 계산대 폐쇄에 대해 해명하려고
(D) 쇼핑객에게 새로 도입된 요금을 알리려고

해설 '앞으로는 계산대에서 1회용 비닐 봉지를 나눠줄 때 돈을 받겠다'는 내용이므로 (D)가 정답이다.

150 사실 관계 확인

번역 변화에 관해 명시된 것은?
(A) 일시적으로만 효력이 있을 것이다.
(B) 지방 법규에서 요구한다.
(C) 고객 피드백이 동기가 되었다.
(D) 그레고렐 마켓 모든 지점에 영향을 미치지는 않는다.

해설 첫 번째 단락에서 '이 청구는 새로운 시 조례에서 명한 것이다(is mandated by a new city ordinance)'라고 했으므로 (B)가 정답이다.

▶▶ Paraphrasing   지문의 mandated → 정답의 required
지문의 a new city ordinance
→ 정답의 a local law

151 -153 이메일

발신: 리드스루 고객 서비스부 〈service@readthrough-app.com〉
수신: 치부초 이헤메 〈grover123@aeg-mail.com〉
날짜: 3월 30일
제목: 계정 확인

이헤메 씨께,

리드스루에 오신 것을 환영합니다! **151**저희 계정을 만드셨으므로 이제 고객께서는 리드스루 앱을 통해 완전 무료로 저희 방대한 목록의 소설과 비소설 오디오북을 대여해 들으실 수 있습니다.

152리드스루를 처음 사용하신다면 저희가 앱의 특징들을 설명하기 위해 만든 짧은 동영상을 먼저 보시면서 시작해 주세요. 앱을 열면 자동으로 나옵니다. 그렇지 않은 경우에는 '도움' 메뉴를 통해 동영상을 찾아 보실 수 있습니다.

153또한, 고객께서는 홍보용 이메일 알림을 수신하지 않는 것으로 확인됩니다. 이 선택은 존중될 것이므로 안심하시기 바랍니다. 지금부터, 저희는 고객의 계정과 관련해 중요한 안내사항이 있을 때 이메일만 보내드리겠습니다. 아니면, 새로운 서비스와 책이 나오자마자 이들에 관해 알 수 있도록 이 설정을 변경하실 수도 있습니다.

즐겁게 들어보세요!

-리드스루 팀

어휘 confirmation 확인 now that ~이므로 account 계정 borrow 빌리다 vast 막대한 absolutely 전적으로 clip 동영상,

클립(영화 등의 일정 부분) feature 특징 pop up 불쑥[자동으로] 나타나다 promotional 홍보용의 notification 알림 from now on 지금부터 (계속해서) alternatively 아니면 setting 설정 as soon as ~하자마자 available 손에 넣을 수 있는

151 세부 사항

번역 이헤메 씨는 등록을 해서 무엇을 이용할 수 있는가?
(A) 오디오 자료
(B) 최신 소식
(C) 서평
(D) 언어 번역 서비스

해설 첫 번째 단락에서 '리드스루 계정을 만들었기 때문에 소설과 비소설 오디오북(fiction and nonfiction audiobooks)을 대여해 들을 수 있다'라고 했다. 따라서 (A)가 정답이다.

▶▶ Paraphrasing 지문의 fiction and nonfiction audiobooks → 정답의 Audio content

152 세부 사항

번역 이메헤 씨는 앱에서 무엇을 하라고 권유받는가?
(A) 화면 설정 조정
(B) 도움 요청 제출
(C) 비디오 사용 지침서 보기
(D) 새로운 기능 테스트

해설 두 번째 단락에서 '앱의 특징들을 설명하기 위해 만든 짧은 동영상을 봐 줄 것(viewing the short clip we made to explain the app's features)'을 권유했으므로 (C)가 정답이다.

▶▶ Paraphrasing 지문의 viewing the short clip we made to explain the app's features → 정답의 Watch a video tutorial

153 문장 삽입

번역 [1], [2], [3], [4]로 표시된 곳 중에서 다음 문장이 들어가기에 가장 적합한 곳은?
"이 선택은 존중될 것이므로 안심하시기 바랍니다."
(A) [1]
(B) [2]
(C) [3]
(D) [4]

해설 해당 문장 앞에는 고객의 선택 내용이 언급되어야 한다. [4]번 바로 앞에서 '고객이 홍보용 이메일 알림을 수신하지 않는 것을 확인했다'라고 했으므로 주어진 문장은 [4]에 들어가는 것이 자연스럽다.

어휘 rest assured 확신하다, 믿고 안심하다 preference 선호 respect 존중하다

154-155 문자 메시지

앤디 마우로	오전 10:08
방금 체크인했어요. 스토펠 일은 어떻게 되어 가죠?	
브래드 던랩	오전 10:09
준비가 됐어요. ¹⁵⁴그 집의 현관등을 계속 나가게 만든 낡은 배선을 모두 교체해야 했어요.	
앤디 마우로	오전 10:10
와, 알았어요. 그럼 문제가 해결됐네요, 그렇죠?	
브래드 던랩	오전 10:10
네. 새 붙박이 설비와 에너지 절약형 전구도 끼워 넣었어요.	
앤디 마우로	오전 10:11
좋아요. 언제 이스트 플라자로 넘어갈 수 있는 거죠?	
브래드 던랩	오전 10:12
주말까진 확실히 돼요.	
앤디 마우로	오전 10:13
¹⁵⁵그럴 수 있기를 바랍니다. 그 일을 끝마쳐야 해요.	
브래드 던랩	오전 10:14
물론입니다. 제가 오늘 건축자재 매장에 달려가서 이 프로젝트에 필요한 자재들을 사 올게요.	
앤디 마우로	오전 10:15
좋아요. 고마워요. 나중에 다시 얘기해요.	

어휘 be set 준비되다 replace 교체하다 wiring 배선 porch 현관 fixture 붙박이 세간 energy-saving 에너지를 절약하는 go over to ~로 넘어가다 building supply 건축자재 material 자재, 재료

154 세부 사항

번역 던랩 씨에 따르면, 문제점은 무엇이었는가?
(A) 건축자재가 품절이었다.
(B) 등이 제대로 작동하지 않았다.
(C) 주방에 한 가전 기기가 없었다.
(D) 빌딩 출입 코드가 사용 불가능했다.

해설 10시 9분 대화를 통해 정답을 확인할 수 있다. '낡은 배선으로 인해 현관등이 계속 나간다(causing house's porch light to keep going out)'는 내용을 통해 정답이 (B)라는 것을 알 수 있다.

▶▶ Paraphrasing 지문의 keep going out → 정답의 not functioning properly

155 의도 파악

번역 오전 10시 11분에 마우로 씨가 "언제 이스트 플라자로 넘어갈 수 있는 거죠?"라고 쓴 의도는 무엇이겠는가?
(A) 던랩 씨의 일 처리를 칭찬하고 싶다.
(B) 어떤 장소로 가는 길 안내가 필요하다.
(C) 자재 구매를 위한 허락을 요청하고 있다.
(D) 던랩 씨에게 일의 긴급함을 일러두고 있다.

해설 10시 12분과 13분에 이루어진 대화에서 이 말의 의도를 파악할 수 있다. 던랩 씨가 '주말까지는 확실히 된다'고 했고, 마우로 씨가 I hope so.라고 말하면서 그 일을 끝내야 한다고 부탁하고 있는 것으로 보아 그 일이 긴급함을 알 수 있다. 따라서 정답은 (D)이다.

156 -157 회람

회람

2월 4일

수신: 전 부서
발신: 재무 회계부
제목: 비용과 환급

지출품의서가 기한을 넘겨 제출되는 경우가 잦아, **156제출 기일을 바꾸려고 합니다.** 2월 20일부터 모든 개인 지출품의서는 지출일로부터 영업일 기준 3일 이내에 접수되어야 합니다. 여러분의 지출 일지에 환급받고자 하는 경비 전액을 각 지출이 발생된 시간 및 날짜와 함께 적으십시오.

157같은 날부터 지출품의서는 회사 이메일로만 받겠습니다. 모든 종이 영수증은 다음 근무일에 주셔야 합니다.

한 가지 상기시켜 드릴 것은, 환급이 가능한 개인 지출은 고객과의 저녁식사, 출장, 회사에 관련된 기타 예기치 못한 비용 등입니다. 개인 지출 정책에 관해 질문이 있으면 세필드 씨에게 연락하시기 바랍니다.

어휘 financing and accounts 재무 회계 expense 비용, 지출 reimbursement 상환, 변제 due to ~ 때문에 frequency 빈발, 잦음 expense report 지출품의서 submit 제출하다 beyond the deadline 마감기한을 넘겨 due date 기일 submission 제출 business day 영업일 expenditure 지출 incur 발생하다 from the same date onward 같은 날 이후로 receipt 영수증 reminder 상기시키는 것 spending 지출 related to ~에 관련된

156 글의 주제 / 목적

번역 회람의 주목적은 무엇인가?
(A) 직원들에게 지출을 제한하라고 촉구하기 위해
(B) 직원에게 정책 변경을 고지하기 위해
(C) 한 부서의 새로운 임무를 설명하기 위해
(D) 최근의 지출 경비의 개요를 설명하기 위해

해설 첫 단락 첫 번째 문장에서 글의 목적을 확인할 수 있다. '제출 기일을 변경하겠다(will be changing the due date for submission)'는 말을 통해 정답이 (B)라는 것을 알 수 있다.

157 추론 / 암시

번역 지출품의서에 대해 암시된 것은?
(A) 현재는 실제 서류를 받는다.
(B) 종종 계산 착오가 있다.
(C) 영수증은 동시에 제출해야 한다.
(D) 분기에 한 번 제출해야 한다.

해설 두 번째 단락을 보면, '앞으로는 지출품의서를 이메일로만 받을 것(we will accept ~ e-mail only)'이라는 내용이 나온다. 이를 통해서 기존에는 다른 방식으로도 받고 있었다는 것을 유추할 수 있다. 따라서 정답은 (A)이다.

158 -160 광고

에브리 카 클럽

에브리 카 클럽은 전국에서 으뜸가는 차량 공유 클럽 중 하나로, 20년 이상 고객의 신뢰를 받아 왔습니다. 아침, 점심, 저녁에 대여할 수 있는 800대 이상의 차량을 보유하여, 고객은 필요하실 때 언제나 차량을 구할 수 있습니다. 세단, 트럭, 하이브리드, 기타 차량 중 선택하십시오. **159(C)어떤 종류의 차량이 필요하든지 연중 무휴 사용 가능합니다.**

* **159(A)전국의 공항, 도시 등에 30개 이상의 지점이 있습니다.** 여러분이 현재 계신 곳에서 대여 차량을 반납, 픽업하세요. **160스마트폰에서 카파인더 앱을 사용하시면** 판매 대리인과 얘기하지 않고도 가장 가까운 픽업 지점을 찾거나 어떤 차량을 언제 사용 가능한지 확인하실 수 있습니다. 이보다 더 쉬울 수는 없습니다!

* **158월 이용료를 납부하세요.** 회비는 월 10달러에서 시작합니다. **159(B)보험 및 서비스 비용이 포함된 금액입니다.** 1년에 수백 달러에 달하는 자동차 소유 비용을 절약하세요!

이동 한 시간 전에 전화하시거나 온라인으로 예약하세요.
전화: 503-555-0194
www.everycarclub.com

어휘 car sharing 차량 공유 trust 신뢰하다 vehicle 차량, 탈것 available 이용 가능한 24/7 하루 24시간 일주일 내내, 연중 무휴의 drop off 갖다 놓다 locate 정확한 위치를 찾아내다 representative 판매 대리인 monthly fee 월 이용료 insurance 보험 charge 요금 ownership 소유권 reserve 예약하다

158 세부 사항

번역 에브리 카 클럽에 가입하려면 무엇이 필요한가?
(A) 기존 회원의 추천
(B) 특별 운전자 보험
(C) 회비 납부
(D) 새 차의 구입

해설 세 번째 단락에서 월 회비가 있고 1개월에 10달러부터 시작한다는 내용(Pay ~ $10/month)을 통해 이 클럽에 가입하려면 회비를 내야 한다는 것을 알 수 있다. 따라서 정답은 (C)이다.

▶▶ Paraphrasing 지문의 a simple monthly fee → 정답의 a membership charge

159 사실 관계 확인

번역 에브리 카 클럽 고객이 할 수 있는 것으로 언급되지 않은 것은?
(A) 여러 지역에서 차량 대여
(B) 유지보수 비용 절감
(C) 단거리 여행을 위한 운전자 고용
(D) 주중 언제나 차량 이용

해설 두 번째 단락 첫 번째 문장에서 (A) 30개 이상의 지역에서 대여 가능하다는 것(We have ~ across the country)을 알 수 있고, 세 번째 단락 마지막 문장에서 (B) 비용 절감(Save ~ year!)을 확인할 수 있고, 첫 번째 단락 마지막 문장에서 (D) 연중 무휴(24/7)를 확인할 수 있다. 정답은 본문에 언급되지 않은 (C)이다.

160 세부 사항

번역 광고에 따르면, 에브리 카 클럽을 이용하는 가장 효율적인 방법은?

    (A) 차량 소유주에게 연락하기
    (B) 웹사이트에 방문하기
    (C) 대여 사무소에 가기
    (D) 모바일 앱 활용하기

해설 두 번째 단락 중간 부분에 스마트폰에서 카파인더 앱을 사용하는 것이 가장 쉬운 방법이라는 내용이 나온다. 따라서 정답은 (D)이다.

161-163 설문지

토베코 시 연구

크리설리스 야외 수영장 및 인접한 공원이 철거 중이며, 현재 신규 시설에 대한 여러 제안들이 검토되고 있습니다. 저희가 신규 시설을 통해 지역사회에 최상의 서비스를 제공하는 방법을 찾을 수 있도록 돕는 차원에서, 지역 주민 여러분께서는 다음의 질문에 답해 주셨으면 합니다.

1. **161실내 수영장을 선호하십니까, 야외수영장(6, 7, 8월에만 운영)을 선호하십니까?**

    (a) 실내 수영장 ☐　　　　　(b) 야외 수영장 ■

2. **161다음 시설들 중 해당 시설에 포함되었으면 하는 것 두 개를 표시해 주십시오.**

    (a) 축구장 ☐　　　　　(b) 야구장 ■
    (c) 미식축구장 ☐　　　(d) 농구 코트 ☐
    (e) 테니스 코트 ■

3. 어느 시간대에 시설을 이용하시겠습니까?

    (a) 새벽 (오전 6시~9시) ☐　　(b) 아침 (오전 9시~11시) ☐
    (c) 오후 (정오~오후 5시) ☐　　**162(d) 저녁 (오후 6시~9시) ■**

4. 회비를 내는 시민들에게 우선 주차권이 제공되어야 한다고 생각하십니까?

    (a) 예 ☐　　　　　(b) 아니오 ☐
    (c) 기타 (의견을 명시해 주십시오) ■

의견: 저는 사무실에서 주간 근무를 하고, 주중에 시설을 이용할 계획을 하고 있습니다. 그곳은 제가 사는 지역이지만 이미 혼잡한 지역입니다. **163시설 이용을 위해 방문객들이 더 많이 찾아오면 이 지역에 운전자들이 대거 몰려들 텐데요. 이 문제는 어떻게 처리하시겠습니까?**

어휘 adjoining 인접한　demolish 철거하다　facility 시설
resident 주민　indicate 명시하다　priority 우선권　specify
명시하다　day shift 주간 근무　influx 밀어닥침, 유입　account for
~을 처리하다

161 글의 주제 / 목적

번역 어떤 종류의 시설에 대한 설문 조사인가?

    (A) 공공 스포츠 종합단지
    (B) 지방 관청
    (C) 역사 박물관
    (D) 소매 센터

해설 항목 1, 2번을 살펴보면 수영장, 축구장, 테니스 코트 등 운동시설에 관해서 조사를 하는 것을 알 수 있다. 따라서 정답은 (A)이다.

162 추론 / 암시

번역 조사 응답자는 언제 시설을 방문할 것 같은가?

    (A) 출근 전
    (B) 퇴근 후
    (C) 점심 시간
    (D) 주말

해설 지문의 3번 항목은 어느 시간대에 이 시설을 방문하겠는지 물어보는 질문이다. 저녁 시간대에 체크가 되어 있으므로 정답은 (B)이다.

163 세부 사항

번역 조사 응답자는 무엇에 대해 걱정하는가?

    (A) 공사 소음
    (B) 교통 체증
    (C) 짧은 운영 시간
    (D) 시야 방해

해설 마지막 의견(Comments) 부분을 보면 '이미 혼잡한 지역인데, 앞으로 더 많은 운전자들이 대거 몰려들 것(a serious influx of drivers)'을 우려하고 있음을 알 수 있다. 따라서 정답은 (B)이다.

> ▶▶ **Paraphrasing**　지문의 **a serious influx of drivers**
> → 정답의 **Traffic congestion**

164 -167 문자 메시지

진저 심스 [오전 11:23]	헤롤드, 난 고객이 불러서 사무실 밖에 나와 있어요. 오늘 오후로 예정된 인터뷰에 참가하지 못할 것 같습니다.
헤롤드 버드 [오전 11:24]	알겠습니다. **164**음, 인터뷰를 미루고 싶지는 않은데, 나 혼자 그 인터뷰를 해낼 만큼 컴퓨터 프로그래밍을 잘 아는 게 아닌 거 같아요. 좋은 생각 있어요?
진저 심스 [오전 11:25]	네. 딱 이런 상황을 위해 구스타프를 예비 면접관으로 교육시키고 있어요. 그가 시간이 되는지 알아 볼게요.
진저 심스 [오전 11:26]	구스타프, **165** 오늘 오후 2시부터 5시까지 프로그래머 지원자를 인터뷰 하는데 헤롤드 좀 도와줄 수 있을까요? 지원자들 코딩 테스트 결과를 논의하면 돼요. 우리들이 얘기했던 것처럼요.
구스타프 액슬슨 [오전 11:26]	좋아요. 지금 당장 급하게 해야 할 일은 없어요.
진저 심스 [오전 11:27]	좋습니다. 지금 바로 테스트 파일을 이메일로 보낼게요. **166**거기에 내 의견은 이미 적어놨으니까, 그걸 기반으로 질문을 하시면 됩니다. 그리고 물론 필요에 따라 후속 질문도 하시면 되고요.
구스타프 액슬슨 [오전 11:27]	알겠습니다.
헤롤드 버드 [오전 11:28]	**167**고마워요, 구스타프. 정말 고맙습니다.

구스타프 액슬슨 [오전 11:29] 음, 숙련된 프로그래머를 고용하는 게 중요하죠! 그 밖에 사전에 알고 있어야 할 게 있으면 알려주세요.

어휘 out of the office 사무실 밖의 client 고객 take part in ~에 참여하다 scheduled for ~로 예정된 avoid 피하다 postpone 미루다 feel like ~한 느낌이 든다, ~인 것 같다 manage 해내다 backup 예비[대체]의, 지원하는 interviewer 면접관 available 만날 수 있는, 시간이 되는 assist 도와주다 candidate 후보자, 지원자 urgent 급박한 base on ~을 기반으로 하다 follow-up 후속의 appreciate 고마워하다 hire 고용하다 skilled 숙련된 be aware of ~을 알다 beforehand 사전에

164 세부 사항

번역 버드 씨가 혼자서 인터뷰 진행하는 것을 주저하는 이유는?
(A) 회사에 새로 들어왔기 때문에
(B) 직책이 다소 낮기 때문에
(C) 기술적인 전문지식이 부족하기 때문에
(D) 개인적으로 입사 지원자 몇 명을 알기 때문에

해설 오전 11시 24분에 버드 씨는 '스스로 인터뷰를 감당할 만큼 컴퓨터 프로그래밍을 잘 아는 것 같지 않다(I don't feel like I know enough about ~ by myself)'라고 했다. 따라서 (C)가 정답이다.

▶▶ Paraphrasing 지문의 **don't ~ know enough about computer programming**
→ 정답의 **lacks some technical expertise**

165 세부 사항

번역 심스 씨가 액슬슨 씨에게 언급한 숫자는 무엇인가?
(A) 방 번호
(B) 단체 인원
(C) 시험 점수
(D) 시각

해설 오전 11시 26분에 심스 씨는 '오늘 오후 2시부터 5시까지(from two to five this afternoon) 프로그래머 지원자를 인터뷰 하는 데 도와줄 수 있는지' 물었다. 여기서 언급한 숫자는 하루 중 특정 시각을 말하므로 (D)가 정답이다.

166 세부 사항

번역 심스 씨는 일부 컴퓨터 파일에 대해 무엇을 언급하는가?
(A) 액슬슨 씨가 이것을 버드 씨와 공유해야 한다.
(B) 자신이 안에 메모를 해 놓았다.
(C) 자신이 그것을 인쇄해 놓았다.
(D) 이메일로 보내기에는 용량이 너무 크다.

해설 오전 11시 27분에 심스 씨는 '파일을 이메일로 보낼 텐데, 그 안에 내 의견을 이미 적어놨으므로(I've already written my comments in them) 그걸 기반으로 질문하라'고 말했다. 따라서 (B)가 정답이다.

▶▶ Paraphrasing 지문의 **written my comments**
→ 정답의 **made notes**

167 의도 파악

번역 오전 11시 29분에 액슬슨 씨가 "숙련된 프로그래머를 고용하는 게 중요하죠"라고 쓸 때 그 의도는 무엇인가?
(A) 버드 씨가 감사할 필요는 없다.
(B) 버드 씨가 신중하게 준비해야 한다.
(C) 추가적인 테스트를 하기를 원한다.
(D) 심스 씨에게 조언을 구할 것이다.

해설 프로그래머 선발을 위한 인터뷰를 진행해야 하는 상황에서 액슬슨 씨가 버드 씨에게 도움을 주겠다고 했다. 버드 씨가 이를 고마워하자 액슬슨 씨는 '숙련된 프로그래머 고용하는 게 중요하다'고 했다. 좋은 프로그래머를 고용하기 위해 마땅히 도움을 주는 것이므로 굳이 고마워할 필요는 없다는 의도이므로 (A)가 정답이다.

168-171 보도 자료

즉시 배포용   3월 5일

콜머 시 – 콜머 시의 역사적으로 가치가 있는 단일 스크린 할레딕 극장이 2개월의 보수 작업을 거쳐 3월 13일 금요일에 다시 문을 연다. 새롭게 리모델링한 극장은 **168**더 커진 스크린과 새 디지털 영사 및 음향 시스템을 자랑한다. **177**내부 보수 작업으로 통로를 넓히고 좌석을 더 크고 편안하게 만들었다. 이러한 개선에 보완하여 구내 매점도 확장했다.

열성적인 영화 팬들은 극장이 유서 깊은 영화 영사기 중 한 대를 계속 유지해 오래된 영화들을 계속 상영할 수 있다는 소식을 들으면 기쁠 것이다. **169**한 달에 두 번 목요일 저녁, 극장은 대중에게 콜머 아트 칼리지 학생들이 제작한 영화를 볼 수 있는 흔치 않은 기회도 제공한다. 과거와 같이 매주 일요일에는 외국 영화가 공개될 것이다.

극장주인 돈 그레쉬 씨는 올해 한 주간 열리는 고전영화 축제를 특히 기대하고 있다. 고전영화 축제는 5월 첫 번째 월요일에 시작될 예정이다. 행사는 대중의 요구에 부응하여 장편 서사 영화 〈칸푸르의 보물〉을 완벽히 복원한 버전을 상영하면서 다시 그 막을 연다.

170또한 올해부터 이 축제의 이름은 '클래식 시네마 위크'가 되어 프로그램 내용을 더 잘 반영하게 된다. 이전의 이름은 '할레딕 필름 소사이어티 페스티벌'이었다. 올해 14주년을 맞는 이 행사는 매년 5000여 명의 방문객을 끌어들인다.

어휘 immediate 즉각적인 historic 역사적 가치가 있는 renovation 개조, 보수 boast 자랑하다 projection 영사 devoted 헌신적인 vintage 유서 깊은, 고전적인 screen 상영하다 rare 드문 showcase 공개하다 weeklong 일주일 간의 be scheduled to+동사원형 ~하도록 예정되다 popular demand 대중의 요구 fully-restored 완벽히 복원된 epic 서사적인 reflect 반영하다 patron 손님

168 추론 / 암시

번역 할레딕 극장에 대해 암시된 것은?
(A) 새로운 경영진으로 바뀌었다.
(B) 극장표 가격을 올릴 계획이다.
(C) 새로운 장비를 설치했다.
(D) 한 개 이상의 스크린을 보유하고 있다.

해설 첫 번째 단락 두 번째 문장에서 새롭게 단장한 극장은 더 커진 스크린(a larger screen)과 새 디지털 영사 및 음향 시스템(an all-new digital projection and sound system)을 자랑한다고 했다. 이를 통해 새로운 장비를 갖춘 것을 확인할 수 있으므로 정답은 (C)이다.

169 세부 사항

번역 할레딕 극장 손님은 한 달에 두 번 무엇을 할 수 있는가?
(A) 아마추어 영화 제작자의 작품 감상
(B) 학술적 분석 듣기
(C) 야간 상영 참석
(D) 어린 자녀 데려오기

해설 두 번째 단락 중간에 학생들이 만든 영화(films made by students)를 한 달에 두 번 목요일 저녁에 상영한다는 내용이 있다. 따라서 정답은 (A)이다.

▶▶ Paraphrasing 지문의 see films made by students
→ 정답의 View amateur filmmakers' work

170 세부 사항

번역 보도자료에 따르면, 새 이름을 갖게 된 것은?
(A) 장편 극영화
(B) 극장
(C) 도시의 거리
(D) 영화 축제

해설 마지막 단락에서 페스티벌의 이전 이름이 '할레딕 필름 소사이어티 페스티벌'이었고 올해부터 '클래식 시네마 위크'가 되었다는 것을 확인할 수 있다. 따라서 정답은 (D)이다.

171 문장 삽입

번역 [1], [2], [3], [4]로 표시된 곳 중에서 다음 문장이 들어가기에 가장 적합한 곳은?
"이러한 개선에 보완하여 구내 매점도 확장했다."
(A) [1]
(B) [2]
(C) [3]
(D) [4]

해설 삽입문의 내용이 개조에 대한 것인데, 지문 전체를 볼 때, 이 극장의 보수 작업이나 개조 등에 관련한 내용이 나오는 곳은 첫 번째 단락이다. 따라서 이 문장이 들어가기에는 [1]이 가장 적절하므로 정답은 (A)이다.

172 -175 편지

스틸 앤 콘크리트

7월 12일

도리안 헤링
이슨 레이크 건설
4번가 756번지
이슨 레이크, 애리조나 주 87524

헤링 씨께,

〈스틸 앤 콘크리트〉는 독자들에게 지난 40년간 상업용 건물 업계에 관한 최신 소식과 사려 깊은 통찰을 제공해 온 월간 잡지입니다. **175**저희는 슬로스텐 엔지니어링, 크레스비스트 같은 최고의 건축, 공학, 건설, 그리고 부동산 개발 회사들을 저희 열렬한 구독자로 포함하고 있습니다.

172, 173 귀하가 최근 건설 회사를 설립한 것을 저희가 알게 되어, 연락을 드려서 귀하와 귀하의 협력업체들에게 〈스틸 앤 콘크리트〉 구독의 수많은 혜택을 알려 드리고자 합니다. 신속하게 확장을 하실 생각이든, 단순히 고객들에게 우수하면서 비용 효율성 높은 서비스를 제공하고 싶으시든, 저희가 도움을 드릴 수 있습니다.

〈스틸 앤 콘크리트〉는 인쇄본과 디지털 방식으로 나오며, 디지털 단독 그리고 인쇄본 플러스 디지털 방식으로 정기 구독을 제공합니다. **174, 175**두 방식 모두, 저희가 건설 업계 연간 수치 자료를 편집한 〈수치로 본 한 해〉 한 부가 포함됩니다. S&C 나이츠 입장 할인도 포함되는데요, 저희가 올해 전국 도시에서 주최하기 시작한 업계 관련 강좌입니다.

신규 구독자로서 귀하는 연간 인쇄본 플러스 디지털 구독(136달러 상당)을 99달러라는 놀라운 가격으로 받으실 자격이 있습니다. 이 특별 가격을 활용해 귀중한 정보와 의견을 얻기 시작하시려면, 간단히 동봉한 구독 신청 카드를 작성해 보내 주시거나, sandc-mag.com/subscribe에서 NEWSUMMER 코드를 입력하시면 됩니다.

대니타 올랜도
편집장

동봉

어휘 monthly 월간의 provide A with B A에게 B를 제공하다 latest news 최신 소식 thoughtful 사려 깊은 insight 통찰(력) commercial 상업의 industry 산업, 업계 count A among B A를 B에 포함시키다, A를 B에 속한 것으로 간주하다 architectural 건축의 property 부동산 loyal 충성스러운 subscriber 구독자(subscribe to ~을 구독하다; subscription 구독, 가입) come to one's attention ~의 눈에 띄다, ~가 알게 되다 establish 설립하다 firm 회사 reach out (잡으려고) 손을 뻗다 benefit 이득, 혜택 expand 확장하다 rapidly 신속하게 superior 우수한 cost-effective 비용 효율성이 높은 format 구성 방식 copy 한 권 figure 수치 yearly 1년에 한 번의 compilation 편집본, 모음집 numerical 숫자의 as well as ~에 더해, 게다가 admission 입장(료) lecture 강의 host 주최하다 be eligible to+동사원형 ~할 자격이 있다 yearlong 1년간의 enclosed 동봉된(= encl) take advantage of ~을 이용하다 offer (일시적인) 할인, 할인가 access 접근하다, 이용하다 invaluable 귀중한 editor-in-chief 편집장

172 글의 주제 / 목적

번역 올랜도 씨가 헤링 씨에게 편지를 쓰는 이유는?
(A) 프리랜스 원고 업무를 요청하려고
(B) 잡지 구독 시작을 요청하려고
(C) 잡지 내 광고의 이점을 설명하려고
(D) 구독 갱신을 설득하려고

해설 두 번째 단락에서 '귀하가 최근 건설 회사를 설립한 것을 알게 되어 우리 잡지 구독의 혜택을 알려 드리고자' 편지를 쓴다고 했다. 그러면서 뒷부분에서 잡지의 내용과 가격, 신청 방식을 알려주고 있다. 잡지 구독을 권하는 편지임을 알 수 있으므로 (B)가 정답이다.

173 사실 관계 확인

번역 헤링 씨에 관해 명시된 것은?
(A) 업계 단체의 구성원이다.
(B) 인터넷을 통해 질의를 했다.
(C) 최근에 사업을 시작했다.
(D) 동료들이 그를 올랜도 씨에게 보냈다.

해설 두 번째 단락에서 '귀하가 최근 건설 회사를 설립한(established a construction firm) 것을 저희가 알게 되었다'라고 말했으므로 (C)가 정답이다.

▶▶ **Paraphrasing** 지문의 **established a construction firm**
→ 정답의 **started a business**

174 세부 사항

번역 편지에 따르면, 올랜도 씨 회사는 최근에 무엇을 제공하기 시작했는가?
(A) 잡지의 디지털 판
(B) 일련의 라이브 강연
(C) 몇몇 도시의 정보 책자
(D) 유명 상표 의류

해설 세 번째 단락에서 잡지사가 고객에게 'S&C 나이츠 입장 할인'을 제공한다고 했다. 그러면서 S&C Nights를 '저희가 올해 전국 도시에서 주최하기 시작한 업계 관련 강좌'라고 부연 설명했다. 잡지사가 S&C Nights를 시작했고, 이는 지속적인 강좌이며, 사람들이 입장해서 들을 수 있는 것임을 파악할 수 있다. 따라서 (B)가 정답이다.

175 추론 / 암시

번역 크레스비스트에 관해 암시된 것은?
(A) 건축 회사이다.
(B) 제품 할인을 받을 수 있다.
(C) 예전에 〈스틸 앤 콘크리트〉를 발행했다.
(D) 통계 보고서를 받았다.

해설 첫 번째 단락에서 잡지사는 '크레스비스트 같은 최고의 회사들을 구독자로 포함하고 있다'고 말했다. 세 번째 단락에서는 잡지사에서 모든 구독자에게 '건설 업계 연간 수치 자료'를 제공한다고 했다. 따라서 구독자인 크레스비스트가 연간 수치 자료를 받았을 것으로 추론할 수 있으므로 (D)가 정답이다.

▶▶ **Paraphrasing** 지문의 **compilation of numerical data**
→ 정답의 **a statistical report**

176 -180 공지+편지

공지

1801월 4일부터, 위플 애슬레틱 클럽의 모든 고객과 회원은 수중 활동 참여 시 손목 밴드를 착용하여야 합니다.

- 파란색 밴드는 18세 이상 성인이 착용합니다.
- 노란색 밴드는 5세 미만의 모든 어린이가 착용합니다.
- 5세 이상 어린이는 파란색 밴드 착용을 위해 수중 안전 시험을 치러야 합니다.

176영구적으로 사용 가능한 손목 밴드는 프런트 데스크에서 5달러에 구입하실 수 있습니다. 이러한 신규 정책은 다운타운 지점과 크로스로즈 지점에 모두 적용됩니다. 더 큰 지역사회의 편의를 위해 진행되는 일이므로 이 조치가 회원 및 직원 여러분에게 마음의 평안을 드릴 수 있기를 바랍니다.

177지금 춘계 라켓볼 토너먼트에 참가를 신청하세요! 동계 시합 결과는 근력 운동실 옆에 있는 회원 게시판에 게시되어 있습니다.

어휘 be required to+동사원형 ~하도록 요구되다 wristband 손목 밴드 engage in ~에 참여하다 aquatic 물과 관련된 take a test 시험을 치르다 safety 안전 apply to ~에 적용되다 move forward 전진하다 serve the community 지역사회를 위해 일하다 sign up 등록하다 bulletin board 게시판 weightlifting 근력 운동

위플 애슬레틱 클럽

회원 여러분께,

저희가 최근 시행한 새 수중 안전 조치에 관해 몇 가지 질문을 받았습니다.

이러한 조치를 취하게 된 배경을 말씀드리겠습니다. 저희는 위험 관리 전문가 및 조사관들로부터 좀 더 엄격한 수중 안전 정책을 개시하고 보안카메라 시스템을 설치하며 직원 채용을 늘려야 한다는 권고를 받았습니다. 변화는 어렵고 힘들다는 점을 잘 알고 있습니다. 그러나 이를 통해 여러분께 제공하는 서비스를 향상시킬 수 있습니다.

180이러한 정책을 꼬박 한 달 동안 시험해 보았으므로 이제 여러분의 피드백에 답변을 드리고자 합니다. 가장 중요한 문제는 수영장에서 왕복 수영 시 어떤 **178**형태로든 실리콘 밴드를 착용하는 것이 어렵다는 게 분명합니다. **179**아울러 학생이 8명을 넘기지 않고 강사가 있는 수업을 제외하고는, 밴드를 항상 착용하지 않으면 안전 목적이 위태로워질 것이라는 점도 분명합니다.

이에 따라 저희는 첫 번째 밴드에 더 이상 요금을 부과하지 않고 두 가지 크기를 제공하는 것으로 결정했습니다. 이 필요조건은 회원 여러분에게 부담을 주기 위한 일이 아니라 향후 모든 수중 관련 시설에 일반적인 관행이 될 계획임을 양지해 주시기 바랍니다.

위플 애슬레틱 클럽 운영진

어휘 measure 조치 implement 실행하다 background 배경 install 자리잡게 하다 recommend 권고하다 risk management 위험 관리 inspector 조사관 initiate 개시하다 stringent 엄중한 staffing 직원 채용 frustrating 좌절감을 주는, 불만스러운 test out 시험해 보다 respond to ~에 응답하다 overriding 무엇보다 가장 중요한, 우선시되는 lap swimming 수영장을 왕복해서 도는 것 compromise 타협하다, 위태롭게 하다 determine 결정하다 burden 부담을 지우다 common practice 일반적인 관행

176 추론 / 암시

번역 공지에 따르면, 사람들은 왜 프런트 데스트에 가겠는가?
(A) 물건을 구매하기 위해
(B) 강좌를 신청하기 위해
(C) 장비를 반납하기 위해
(D) 정책을 보기 위해

해설 첫 번째 지문 중간에 손목 밴드는 프런트 데스크에서 5달러에 구입할 수 있다는 내용이 나온다. 따라서 정답은 (A)이다.

177 사실 관계 확인

번역 공지에서 위플 애슬레틱 클럽에 대해 명시한 것은?
(A) 수중 시설이 하나뿐이다.
(B) 로고의 색을 바꾸었다.
(C) 계절별 경기를 개최한다.
(D) 무료 수영 강좌를 제공한다.

해설 첫 번째 지문 마지막 단락에서 춘계 라켓볼 토너먼트(the spring racquetball tournament)에 참가 신청하라고 했으며, 동계 시합 결과는(Winter results) 회원 게시판에 게시되어 있다는 말을 통해서 (C)가 정답인 것을 알 수 있다.

178 동의어 찾기

번역 편지에서 세 번째 단락 2행의 "form"과 의미가 가장 가까운 것은?
(A) 방식
(B) 서류 작업
(C) 통증
(D) 물건

해설 form은 여기에서 '형태'라는 의미로 해석할 수 있다. 선택지에서는 '방식'이라고 해석할 수 있는 (A) style이 가장 가까운 의미를 가진 단어다.

179 추론 / 암시

번역 수영 중에 누가 손목 밴드 착용을 하지 않아도 될 것 같은가?
(A) 시험을 통과한 성인
(B) 5세 미만 어린이
(C) 단체 수업을 듣는 사람들
(D) 클럽의 모든 장기 회원

해설 두 번째 지문의 세 번째 단락 마지막 부분을 보면, 8명 이하이면서, 강사가 진행하는 수업을 제외하고(except in a class setting ~ eight students)는 착용을 해야 한다는 내용이 나오기 때문에 정답이 (C)라는 것을 알 수 있다.

180 연계

번역 편지는 언제 발송됐을 것 같은가?
(A) 12월
(B) 1월
(C) 2월
(D) 3월

해설 첫 번째 지문 첫 문장에서 1월 4일자로 손목 밴드를 착용하는 정책을 시행한다고 했고, 두 번째 지문 세 번째 단락을 보면 이 정책을 꼬박 한 달 동안 시행해봤다고 했다. 이 정책을 시행한지 한 달이 지난 시점이므로, 이를 바탕으로 이 편지는 2월에 보낸 것이라는 것을 알 수 있다. 따라서 정답은 (C)이다.

181-185 지원서 + 이메일

자원봉사 지원서

주니퍼 커뮤니티 어시스턴스 센터를 위한 자원봉사 활동에 관심을 가져 주셔서 감사합니다. 저희의 자원봉사자들은 매년 저희를 찾아오는 수천 명의 새 주민들에게 고품질 서비스를 제공하는 일을 돕고 있습니다. 본 지원서를 작성하시어 여러분에 대해 말씀해 주셨으면 합니다. 자원봉사 지원서는 1월 15일 시작하는 세션을 위해 채용 심사를 할 수 있도록 **181 12월 10일까지 접수되어야 합니다.**

지원일자: 10월 15일

개인정보
이름: 싱   그레고리   F.
　　　(성)　　　　　(이름)　　　(중간 이니셜)
우편주소: 크레센트 대로 203   주니퍼   MD   48392
　　　　(도로명 또는 사서함)　　(시)　(주)　(우편번호)
전화번호: 321-555-0182   283-555-0169
　　　　　(자택)　　　　　　(휴대전화)
이메일 주소: gregory.singh@rpoglobal.com

자원봉사에 대한 관심
이전 자원봉사 경험에 대해 말씀해 주십시오 (있는 경우).
저는 주니퍼 의료센터에서 자원봉사 통역사로 일했으며 주니퍼 공공도서관에서 10주짜리 영어회화 그룹 프로그램을 진행했습니다.

저희 센터에서 자원봉사를 하고 싶은 이유는 무엇입니까?
182 제가 10년 전 처음 미국에 왔을 때 이 센터에서 서비스를 받은 적이 있어 이를 지역사회에 환원하고 싶습니다. **185 회계사로 6년간 일한 경력이 있어, 세무 서식에 관해 고객을 돕는 데 특히 관심이 있습니다.**

제공된 봉투에 추천서와 함께 본 자원봉사 지원서를 넣어 다시 보내 주십시오.

어휘 volunteer 자원봉사(하다) application 지원서 resident 주민 complete 기입하다 interpreter 통역사 decade 10년 accountant 회계사 particularly 특히 tax form 세무 서식

수신: 그레고리 싱 〈gregory.singh@rpoglobal.com〉
발신: 라제시 아미르 〈ramir@communityasst.org〉
날짜: 10월 17일
제목: 귀하의 자원봉사 지원서

싱 씨께,

커뮤니티 어시스턴스 센터의 자원봉사에 지원해 주셔서 감사합니다.

다음 주에 자원봉사자들이 자신의 경험을 최대한 활용할 수 있는 방법을 파악하기 위해 면접을 실시합니다. **183,184 다음 주 어느 요일에 오전 10시에서 오후 2시 사이에 시간이 되시는지 알려주십시오.** 귀하가 저희 재무서비스 코디네이터(FSC)인 제사 플린트 씨와 15분간 얘기를 나눌 수 있도록 일정을 잡고자 합니다. **185 귀하의 근무 경력을 근거로 판단하면, 플린트 씨는 귀하가 보조하게 될 가능성이 가장 높은 분입니다.**

답변 주시기를 고대합니다. 지원해 주셔서 다시 한 번 감사드립니다!

라제시 아미르
자원봉사 코디네이터
주니퍼 커뮤니티 어시스턴스 센터

어휘 conduct 시행하다 determine 알아내다, 밝히다 leverage 활용하다; 지렛대 사용 financial 재정의

181 세부 사항

번역 지원서는 지원자들에게 무엇을 알려주는가?
(A) 잠재적인 비용
(B) 필요한 교육
(C) 제출 기한
(D) 봉사자의 부족

해설 첫 번째 지문 첫 단락 마지막 문장에 자원봉사 지원서는 12월 10일까지 접수되어야 한다(must be received by December 10)는 말이 있으므로 정답이 (C)라는 것을 알 수 있다.

182 사실 관계 확인

번역 싱 씨에 대해 언급된 것은?
(A) 의사이다.
(B) 휴대전화가 없다.
(C) 센터를 방문한 적이 없다.
(D) 과거에 다른 나라에 살았었다.

해설 첫 번째 지문 마지막 질문에 대한 대답에서 싱 씨가 10년 전 처음 미국에 왔다(I first moved to the United States a decade ago)고 말한 것으로 보아 그가 이전에 다른 나라에서 살았었다는 것을 알 수 있다. 따라서 정답은 (D)이다.

> ▶▶ **Paraphrasing** 지문의 **moved to the United States a decade ago** → 정답의 **used to live in another country**

183 세부 사항

번역 아미르 씨는 싱 씨에게 무엇을 하라고 요청하는가?
(A) 증명서 송부
(B) 가능한 시간 알려 주기
(C) 지침 읽기
(D) 계약서에 서명

해설 두 번째 지문 두 번째 단락에 있는 언제 면접을 볼 수 있는지 가능한 시간을 알려달라(Please let me know if you are free any day ~)는 내용을 통해 정답이 (B)라는 것을 확인할 수 있다.

184 추론 / 암시

번역 다음 주에 어떤 일이 일어날 것 같은가?
(A) 싱 씨가 센터 직원을 만날 것이다.
(B) 싱 씨가 자원봉사 일을 시작할 것이다.
(C) 아미르 씨가 짧은 시연을 할 것이다.
(D) 플린트 씨가 사임할 것이다.

해설 두 번째 지문 두 번째 단락에서 자원봉사에 지원한 사람들을 대상으로 면접을 실시한다는 내용이 나온다. 싱 씨도 자원봉사를 신청했기 때문에 다음 주에는 인터뷰를 보기 위해 재무서비스 코디네이터인 제사 플린트 씨를 만날 것이다. 따라서 정답은 (A)이다.

185 연계

번역 FSC가 도와줄 활동 중 하나는 무엇일 것 같은가?
(A) 근로 비자 갱신
(B) 은행에서 대출 받기
(C) 의료보험료 요청하기
(D) 세무 서류 준비

해설 첫 번째 지문의 마지막 질문에 대한 대답을 보면, 싱 씨는 6년간 회계사로 일했고, 특히 세무 서식에 관해 고객을 돕는 일에 관심이 있다고 했다. 두 번째 지문에서는 싱 씨의 경력을 근거로 판단하면, 재무서비스 코디네이터를 보조하게 될 것이라는 말이 언급되어 있다. 이를 종합해 보면 재무서비스 코디네이터는 '세무 서류'와 관련된 업무를 제공할 것으로 보인다. 따라서 정답은 (D)이다.

186 -190 이메일 + 공지 + 이메일

발신: 로이드 킴
수신: 나오미 터너
제목: 변경 사항
날짜: 8월 13일
첨부: 안내문

나오미 씨께.

186컨벤션 센터 직원이 지금 전화해서 얘기하는데, 2층 일부분의 에어컨이 고장 나서 내일 정오가 돼야 정상으로 돌아온다고 합니다. 더운 날씨를 고려할 때, 학회 오전 시간 일부를 옮겨야 할 것 같습니다. 다행히, 그때 진행되는 다른 행사가 많지는 않아요. 그래서 그 직원이 같은 층 내에서 영향을 받지 않는 몇 개 방을 배정해 줄 수 있었습니다.

발표자들에게는 제가 공지를 하겠지만, 당신이 두 가지를 해 주셨으면 합니다. 첫째, 변경 사항을 설명하는 첨부 안내문을 인쇄하셔서 참가자들을 위한 안내 자료집 앞쪽에 하나씩 넣어 주세요. **187**둘째, 그 직원 말에 의하면 때때로 방문객들이 207호실을 찾는 데 애를 먹는다고 합니다. 그러니까 내일 근처 복도에 서서 사람들을 그리로 안내해 주셨으면 합니다. 그 방 강연이 시작되기 10분 전에 그곳에 도착하도록 해 주세요.

고맙습니다.

로이드

어휘 representative (회사, 기관을 대표하는) 직원 break down 고장 나다 in working order 제대로 작동하는 given ~을 고려하면 conference 학회 session (회의, 강의 등의) 기간 assign 배정하다 affect 영향을 미치다 notify 고지하다 speaker 발표자, 연사 print out 인쇄하다 attached 첨부된 packet 자료집 attendee 참가자 have trouble -ing ~하는 데 애를 먹다 locate (위치를) 찾다 hallway 복도 direct (길을) 안내하다

186 세부 사항

번역 회의실이 변경된 이유는?
(A) 2층에서 다른 행사가 있을 예정이어서
(B) 한 발표자가 회의실 배정에 불만이 있어서
(C) 컨벤션 센터에 기술적인 문제가 생겨서
(D) 많은 사람들이 학회에 등록해서

해설 첫 번째 이메일 첫 단락에서 '에어컨 일부가 고장 나서(has broken down) 학회 시간 일부를 옮겨야 하고, 다행히 다른 방을 배정 받았다'고 했다. 회의실이 변경된 이유가 '에어컨 고장' 때문이므로 (C)가 정답이다.

▶▶ Paraphrasing 　지문의 has broken down
　　　　　　　　　　→ 정답의 a mechanical problem

187 연계

번역 터너 씨는 몇 시에 복도에 서 있었을까?
(A) 오전 9시 45분 직전
(B) 오전 11시 직전
(C) 오전 11시 15분 직전
(D) 오후 12시 30분 직전

해설 첫 번째 이메일 두 번째 단락에서 '207호를 찾기 어렵기 때문에 강연 시작 10분 전에 복도에 서서 안내를 해 달라'고 부탁했다. 안내문 시간표에서 보면 207호로 변경된 강의는 오전 9시 45분에 시작한다. 따라서 (A)가 정답이다.

▶▶ Paraphrasing 　지문의 about ten minutes before
　　　　　　　　　　→ 정답의 Shortly before

188 세부 사항

번역 안내문에서는 읽는 사람들에게 무엇을 하라고 요청하는가?
(A) 약간의 소음 견디기
(B) 너무 많은 공간을 차지하지 않기
(C) 회의실을 청결하게 유지하기
(D) 약간의 지체를 예상하기

해설 표 아래에서 '강연이 명시된 것보다 조금 늦게 시작할 수도 있으므로(may begin slightly later than stated) 불편함을 참아달라'고 덧붙이고 있다. 따라서 (D)가 정답이다.

▶▶ Paraphrasing 　지문의 begin slightly later than stated
　　　　　　　　　　→ 정답의 some delays

189 연계

번역 해리슨 씨는 어떤 방에서 열린 학회 강연에 참석했는가?
(A) 202호실
(B) 203호실
(C) 205호실
(D) 206호실

해설 두 번째 이메일에서 해리슨 씨는 훌륭한 강의를 들었다며 '발표자 브리짓 폴락은 빅데이터 전문가이고, 빅데이터를 고용 과정에 활용하는 방안을 설명했다'라고 말했다. 안내문 시간표에서 보면 브리짓 폴락의 빅데이터 관련 강연은 206호실에서 있었다. 따라서 (D)가 정답이다.

190 사실 관계 확인

번역 해리슨 씨가 학회 발표자를 칭찬한 이유가 아닌 것은?
(A) 발표자의 강연에 포함된 그룹 활동
(B) 발표자의 제시 자료
(C) 발표자의 주제 선택
(D) 발표자의 연설 능력

해설 해리슨 씨는 브리짓 폴락의 강의를 칭찬하면서 그 이유로 '주제가 유익했고(C)', '관객들을 주의를 사로잡았기(D)' 때문이라고 했다. 또한 강의에서 얻은 '아주 유용한 배포 자료(B)'도 가지고 있다고 했다. 그룹 활동과 관련된 언급은 없으므로 (A)가 정답이다.

191-195 요약 + 이메일 + 뉴스레터 기사

기록 관리 문제에 대한 응답: 요약

194본 보고서는 오가닉 모어 푸즈의 요청으로 디노백 비즈니스 컨설턴트(DBC)가 수행한 조사 결과를 자세히 기술하고 있다. 본 연구의 목적은 회사의 인사 서류를 간소화하고 더 효율적으로 관리할 수 있는지 여부를 알아보기 위한 것이다. 조사는 통계 분석 및 관련 직원들과의 인터뷰를 통해 수행되었다. **191**직원들에 관한 기록이 매일 지역 책임자들의 손을 거치므로, 이들의 응답은 시기 적절한 해결책이 필요함을 시사한다. 두 가지 주요 결론은 다음과 같다.

- 응답자의 82%는 직원 기록 관리에 시간이 많이 든다고 보고했다.
- 응답자의 74%는 직원 기록 관리에 관한 비용 부담에 관한 우려를 표했다.

이 보고서는 **192**전략적 합병과 지역적 확장을 비롯한 고객사의 사업 전략에 대한 상세 개요, DBC 조사 결과의 심층 발표, 고객사의 경영진이 실행해야 할 해결안 등 세 부분으로 나누어져 있다.

어휘 respond to ~에 응답하다 detail 열거하다, 상세히 알리다 inquiry 조사 at the request of ~의 요청으로 determine 알아내다 personnel 직원 streamline 간소화하다 effectively 효율적으로 carry out 수행하다 statistical 통계의 analysis 분석 relevant 관련된 timely 시기 적절한 on a daily basis 매일 finding 결론, 결과 respondent 응답자 time consuming 시간이 많이 드는 cost burden 비용 부담 related to ~에 관련된 be divided into ~로 나누다 overview 개요 strategy 전략 involve ~을 포함하다 merger 합병 expansion 확장 in-depth 심층 implement 실행하다 management 관리; 경영진

수신: 칼 브랜슨 <cbranson@organicmorfoods.com>
발신: 재니스 고레츠키 <jgorecki@organicmorfoods.com>
날짜: 11월 11일
제목: 제안

브랜슨 씨께,

마침내 지역 관리자들 모두와 이야기를 나눴으며 이들은 저, 그리고 프로젝트 상의 판매업체들과 협력하기 위해 함께 하고 있습니다. 이와 관련하여, 도움을 받기 위해 **193**리콜 팩을 요청해 주실 것을 제안하고자 합니다. 평판이 좋으며 저희 본사 근처 델프 시에 위치하고 있습니다.

재니스 고레츠키

어휘 suggestion 제안 regional 지역의 vendor 판매업체 regarding ~에 관해 enlist 요청하여 얻다 have a good reputation 평판이 좋다

내추럴 푸드 리테일러를 위한 리콜 팩 솔루션

200개에 달하는 매장과 1만 5000명의 직원을 보유한 오가닉 모어 푸즈는 주요 천연 식품 소매점으로 자리잡았습니다. 그러나 신규 매장을 열면서 **195**상당한 양의 종이로 된 인사 기록이 나왔습니다. 이 서류 관리 업무는 다시 운영비를 상승시켰습니다. 컨설팅 업체의 권고에 따라 오가닉 모어 푸즈는 문서를 디지털화하기로 결정했습니다. 그 과정이 복잡한 결정을 수반한다는 것을 알게 된 오가닉 모어 푸즈 경영진은 **193**프로젝트 전체를 감독하는 리콜 팩으로 방향을 틀었습니다. 저희 전문가들은 이 업체를 도와 **194**종이 인사 서류를 없앴고, 이제 관리자들이 컴퓨터를 통해 동료의 파일에 접근할 수 있게 되었습니다. 이 조치로 궁극적으로 시간과 귀중한 자원을 아낄 수 있었습니다.

어휘 retailer 소매점 associate 직원, 동료 significant 상당한, 중요한, 의미 있는 in turn 다시 operational cost 운영비 complex 복잡한 supervise 감독하다, 지휘하다 eliminate 없애다, 제거하다 via ~을 통하여 ultimately 궁극적으로

191 세부 사항

번역 DBC가 지역 책임자들에게 이야기한 이유는 무엇이겠는가?
(A) 그들이 새로운 직원 교육 프로그램을 시행한다.
(B) 그들이 컨설팅 업체의 고용을 담당한다.
(C) 그들이 회사 매장을 위한 전시품을 선정한다.
(D) 그들이 인사 기록을 직접 다루며 일한다.

해설 첫 번째 지문의 중간 부분을 보면, '직원들에 관한 기록이 매일 지역 책임자들의 손을 거친다(as employee records pass ~ on a daily basis)'는 말이 나오는데, 이 '기록'은 지문 앞의 내용을 통해 '인사 기록(personnel records)'이라는 것을 알 수 있다. 따라서 이를 통해서 지역 책임자들이 인사 기록을 직접 담당한다는 것을 알 수 있다. 따라서 정답은 (D)이다.

192 세부 사항

번역 DBC 보고서에 포함되었을 것 같은 내용은 무엇인가?
(A) 직원 승진 기준
(B) 소비자 설문 조사 고안에 대한 조언
(C) 합병 건에 대한 세부 사항
(D) 유기농 음식 가격의 비교

해설 첫 번째 지문 세 번째 단락에 있는 '전략적 합병(strategic mergers)'에 관한 내용이 포함되어 있다는 말을 토대로 정답이 (C)라는 것을 알 수 있다. 다른 보기의 내용은 찾아볼 수 없다.

193 연계

번역 브랜슨 씨에 대해 암시된 것은?
(A) 뉴스레터 기사를 위해 인터뷰를 했다.
(B) 고레츠키 씨의 제안을 따랐다.
(C) 더 이상 델프 시에 본거지를 두지 않는다.
(D) 이전 지역 관리자이다.

해설 두 번째 지문에서 고레츠키 씨는 브랜슨 씨에게 리콜 팩을 제안했고, 세 번째 지문에서 경영진이 프로젝트 전체를 감독하는 리콜 팩으로 결정했다고 했으므로, 종합해보면 브랜슨 씨는 고레츠키 씨의 제안을 받아들였다고 볼 수 있다. 따라서 정답은 (B)이다.

194 세부 사항

번역 DBC는 아마도 오가닉 모어 푸즈에 무엇을 하라고 권장했을 것 같은가?
(A) 종이 문서를 전자파일로 변환하기
(B) 특정 지점에서 직원 채용 줄이기
(C) 컴퓨터 시스템의 보안 높이기
(D) 저장 시설에 자금을 더 할당하기

해설 DBC는 첫 번째 지문에 소개된 컨설팅 회사이다. 첫 번째 지문에서 'DBC는 오가닉 모어 푸즈의 요청으로 인사 서류를 간소화하고 효율적으로 관리할 수 있는지 여부를 알아보기 위해 조사했다'는 내용이 나온다. 세 번째 지문에서는 오가닉 모어 푸즈에서 그 결과 어떤 일이 있었는지의 내용이 나온다. 세 번째 지문 후반부에 보면 '종이 서류를 없애고 컴퓨터로 파일을 확인할 수 있게 되었다'는 말이 나온다. 따라서 정답은 (A)이다.

195 동의어 찾기

번역 뉴스레터 기사에서 첫 번째 단락 5행의 "significant"와 의미가 가장 가까운 것은?
(A) 동시대의
(B) 의미 있는
(C) 필요한
(D) 상당한

해설 significant는 여기에서처럼 amount와 함께 쓰여 '상당한 양의 ~'라는 의미로 자주 사용된다. 비슷한 의미를 가진 단어로는 sizable, considerable 등이 있다. 따라서 정답은 (D) sizable이다.

196 -200 보도자료+이메일+온라인 게시판

즉시 배포용 (4월 9일) — 구역 예술 협회(DAC)는 7월 7일 토요일 **196벨튼 시립 공원에서** 타운 아트 페스티벌을 개최하기 위해 준비 중이다. 베스트 로컬 아티스트 상을 놓고 경합을 벌이는 예술가들이 낸 참가비로 페스티벌 개최 비용을 일부 충당하지만 DAC는 여전히 기업의 후원금을 구하고 있다. 선택할 수 있는 네 가지 후원 형태가 있다.

헤드라인 – 타운 아트 페스티벌 웹사이트의 홈페이지와 페스티벌에서 판매하는 **198티셔츠 일체에 회사명과 로고가 표시된다.** 5,000달러

플래티넘 – 페스티벌에서 전시하는 모든 포스터에 회사명과 로고가 들어간다. 3,000달러

어피어런스 – 페스티벌의 48페이지짜리 기념 잡지에 회사 개요가 실린다. 1,000달러

서포터 – 후원자는 타운 아트 박물관의 평생 회원권을 위한 4개의 바우처를 받는다. 500달러

연락처: 555-0108 –루 케너, DAC 기금 모금 책임자

어휘 district 구역, 지구 gear up 준비하다 entry fee 참가비 compete for ~를 놓고 경쟁하다 stage 개최하다 corporate 기업의 funding 자금 제공 sponsorship 후원 overview 개요 souvenir 기념품 lifetime membership 평생 회원

발신: 디나 팰런 〈fallon@bilesky-designstudio.com〉
수신: 아미트 모하일 〈mohile@bilesky-designstudio.com〉
날짜: 6월 23일
제목: 기부

아미트 씨께,

DAC가 저희의 후원 기부금을 방금 받았습니다. 장부 기입 목적으로 "아트 페스티벌"이라고 기록해 두십시오.

저는 회사 로고의 디지털 사본을 DAC에 제출하여 **198공식 행사 티셔츠에 인쇄할 수 있도록 하겠습니다.** DAC의 디자이너들은 광범위한 서체를 **197수용할 수** 있어 저희 것도 문제가 되지 않습니다.

소식이 더 있습니다. **200저는 페스티벌에서 베스트 로컬 아티스트 상을 시상해 달라는 DAC의 초청을 수락했습니다.** 바일스키 디자인 스튜디오 전 직원을 대표할 좋은 기회가 될 것입니다.

회장 디나 팰런

어휘 donation 기부 bookkeeping 부기 accommodate 수용하다, 맞추다 a wide range of 광범위한 present an award 상을 주다 represent 대표하다

---

http://www.townartsfestival.com/forum

홈	아티스트	방문객	언론	게시판

가장 최근 후기

➤ "**199DAC가 준비한 요리대회**는 페스티벌 마지막에 추가된, 재미있는 행사였다." – 프랭크 아이오리오, 7월 10일

➤ "우리 모두 멋진 시간을 보냈다. 내게 미술을 배우는 학생은 베스트 로컬 아티스트 경연대회에서 2등을 차지했고 상을 모두 준 뒤 **200시상자와 즐거운 대화를 나눴다.**" – 칼라 데이비스, 7월 10일

더 많은 후기가 여기에 있습니다.

후기를 입력하시려면 여기를 클릭하세요.

어휘 put together 준비하다, 만들다 last-minute addition to ~에 마지막으로 추가된 runner-up 2위, 차점자 award presenter 시상자 hand out 나눠 주다

196 사실 관계 확인

번역 타운 아트 페스티벌에 대해 명시된 것은?
(A) 연례 축하 행사다.
(B) 이틀 동안 계속되었다.
(C) 시립 공원에서 열렸다.
(D) 참가자는 무료 입장이었다.

해설 첫 번째 지문 첫 문장에 벨튼 시립 공원에서(at Belten City Park) 행사가 개최된다는 말이 나왔으므로 정답은 (C)이다. (A)의 경우, 매년 열리는 행사인지 알 수 없기 때문에 오답이며, (B)는 7월 7일 하루만 페스티벌이 열린다고 했으므로 오답, (D)는 행사에서 경합을 벌이는 예술가들로부터 참가비(entry fees)를 받는다는 말이 나왔으므로 역시 오답이다.

197 동의어 찾기

번역 이메일의 두 번째 단락 2행의 "accommodate"와 의미가 가장 가까운 것은?
(A) 포함하다
(B) 다루다
(C) 규제하다
(D) 빌리다

해설 accommodate은 '수용하다'라는 의미로 가장 많이 쓰인다. 본문에서처럼 '다양한 서체를 수용할 수 있다'는 말은 '다양한 서체를 다룰 수 있다'는 말로 바꿔 쓸 수 있다. 따라서 정답은 (B) handle이다.

198 연계

번역 바일스키 디자인 스튜디오는 어떤 후원 옵션을 선택했을 것 같은가?
(A) 헤드라인
(B) 플래티넘
(C) 어피어런스
(D) 서포터

해설 두 번째 지문 두 번째 단락의 공식 행사 티셔츠에 로고가 인쇄된다는 내용(print it onto ~ event T-shirts)과 첫 번째 지문에 있는, Headline 옵션은 모든 티셔츠에 회사명과 로고가 보일 수 있게 한다는 점을 종합해 보면 이 회사는 Headline 옵션을 선택했다는 것을 알 수 있다. 따라서 정답은 (A)이다.

199 추론 / 암시

번역 온라인 게시판에 DAC에 대해 언급된 것은?
(A) 지역 기업가에 의해 설립됐다.
(B) 최근 요리 경연대회를 준비했다.
(C) 행사 시작일을 연기했다.
(D) 매주 예술 강좌를 열기 시작했다.

해설 세 번째 지문의 첫 번째 후기를 보면 DAC가 요리 경연대회를 연 사실을 확인할 수 있다. 따라서 정답은 (B)이다.

▶▶ **Paraphrasing** 지문의 **The cooking competition**
→ 정답의 **a cooking contest**

200 연계

번역 데이비스 씨에 대해 사실일 것 같은 것은?
(A) 신문 기사에 소개됐다.
(B) 인쇄 업무에 책임이 있다.
(C) 시상식 이후 팰런 씨를 만났다.
(D) 회계 업체에 고용되었다.

해설 두 번째 지문은 팰런 씨가 쓴 이메일인데, 세 번째 단락을 보면 시상자로 와달라는 초청을 수락했다(I accepted ~ at the festival)는 내용이 나온다. 그리고 세 번째 지문의 두 번째 후기에서 데이비스 씨가 '시상이 끝나고 나서 시상자와 즐거운 이야기를 나눴다'고 했다. 이 두 가지 내용을 종합해보면 팰런 씨가 시상을 한 후 데이비스 씨와 이야기를 한 것을 알 수 있다. 따라서 정답은 (C)이다.

TEST 7

101 (B)	102 (C)	103 (D)	104 (B)	105 (A)
106 (B)	107 (C)	108 (B)	109 (A)	110 (D)
111 (D)	112 (B)	113 (C)	114 (C)	115 (A)
116 (B)	117 (C)	118 (D)	119 (A)	120 (A)
121 (C)	122 (D)	123 (B)	124 (C)	125 (A)
126 (C)	127 (D)	128 (A)	129 (D)	130 (B)
131 (D)	132 (B)	133 (A)	134 (D)	135 (B)
136 (B)	137 (C)	138 (C)	139 (D)	140 (A)
141 (D)	142 (D)	143 (A)	144 (A)	145 (D)
146 (B)	147 (A)	148 (C)	149 (D)	150 (A)
151 (B)	152 (B)	153 (A)	154 (A)	155 (D)
156 (A)	157 (C)	158 (C)	159 (D)	160 (A)
161 (C)	162 (A)	163 (D)	164 (D)	165 (A)
166 (C)	167 (A)	168 (A)	169 (D)	170 (B)
171 (C)	172 (B)	173 (D)	174 (A)	175 (C)
176 (B)	177 (D)	178 (A)	179 (D)	180 (B)
181 (A)	182 (B)	183 (B)	184 (D)	185 (D)
186 (C)	187 (C)	188 (D)	189 (D)	190 (D)
191 (A)	192 (C)	193 (B)	194 (D)	195 (D)
196 (A)	197 (C)	198 (B)	199 (C)	200 (D)

PART 5

101 동사의 형태 _ 조동사 뒤

해설 조동사 뒤에 동사가 원형의 형태로 오는 자리이기 때문에 준동사인 (A)는 올 수 없다. 주어(Comments)가 '남겨지는 것'이므로 동사가 수동태로 와야 한다. 따라서 정답은 (B) be left이다.

번역 질러 슈퍼마켓 관리에 관한 의견은 계산대에 남겨 주십시오.

어휘 comment 논평, 의견 management 관리 checkout counter 계산대

102 접속사 자리

해설 excited 앞에 'Ms. Irving is'가 생략되어 있으며 빈칸에는 두 문장을 연결하는 접속사가 필요하다. 따라서 부사인 also와 전치사인 like는 정답이 될 수 없다. 아쉬워하는(sorry) 것과 기뻐하는(excited) 것은 서로 반대되므로 (C) but(그러나, 하지만)이 정답이다. (A) nor는 '~ 또한 아니다'라는 뜻으로 앞에 부정어가 나왔을 때 쓰인다.

번역 어빙 씨는 가멜 인더스트리즈를 떠나게 되어 아쉬워하면서도 새로운 도전을 하게 된 것을 기뻐한다.

어휘 depart 떠나다 excited 신이 난, 들뜬, 흥분한 take on 맡다 challenge 도전

103 대명사 _ 소유격

해설 빈칸 뒤의 복합명사(score report)를 수식할 수 있는 대명사는 소유격이다. 따라서 정답은 (D) your이다. 다른 보기는 품사 면에서 모두 적절하지 못하다.

번역 성적표 사본을 받으려면 서면으로 요청서를 제출해 주십시오.

어휘 a copy of ~의 사본 score report 성적표 submit 제출하다 request 요청 in writing 서면으로

104 형용사 / 한정사 어휘

해설 빈칸에는 that절의 주어인 명사 information을 수식하는 말이 필요하므로 '모든'을 뜻하는 (B) all이 정답이다. information은 불가산명사이기 때문에 all information 다음에 단수동사(is)를 썼다. (D) every는 가산 단수 명사와만 함께 쓰여서 '하나하나의'라는 뜻이므로 information을 수식할 수 없다. (A) total은 '(합산한) 전체의', (C) full은 '(정해진 양 등이) 꽉 찬'을 뜻하므로 의미상 부자연스럽다.

번역 이 문서에서 제공된 모든 정보가 사실이며 정확하다는 것을 증명하려면 이곳에 서명하십시오.

어휘 sign 서명하다 certify 증명하다 information 정보 provide 제공하다 correct 정확한

105 명사 자리

해설 부정관사(a)와 전치사구(of ~ head) 사이에 있으므로 빈칸에는 명사가 와야 한다. 따라서 (B) 과거분사 profiled와 (C) to profile은 답이 될 수 없다. (D) profiler(범죄 분석관)는 의미상 적절하지 않다. (A) prpfile(신상 명세, 프로필)이 정답이다.

번역 저희 회사 웹사이트의 '회사 소개' 페이지에는 각 부서장의 프로필이 포함되어 있습니다.

어휘 corporate 회사의 include 포함하다 department 부서 profile 개요, 신상 명세, 프로필; 프로필을 작성하다

106 부사 어휘 _ 동사 수식

해설 동사 be examined를 수식해 의미가 통하는 부사를 찾아야 한다. (A) commonly(보통, 흔히), (C) eventually(결국), (D) fortunately (다행스럽게도)는 모두 의미상 부적절하다. '철저하게 검토되는'이라는 뜻이 자연스러우므로 (B) thoroughly(철저히)가 정답이다.

번역 조사관은 전문가가 더욱 철저하게 검토해야 하는 구조상의 모든 문제를 지적할 것이다.

어휘 inspector 조사관, 감독관 point out 지적하다 structure 구조 examine 검토하다, 시험하다 specialist 전문가

107 동사 어휘

해설 뒤의 명사(a spot)를 목적어로 취하여 적절한 의미를 완성할 수 있는 동사를 고르는 문제이다. 강좌에서 자리를 '확보하다'는 뜻이 가장 적절한 의미이다. 따라서 정답은 (C) secure(확보하다)이다. (A) compete는 '경쟁하다'라는 의미의 자동사, (B) surround는 '둘러싸다', (D) remain은 자동사로 '남다'나 형용사 보어를 받아 '계속 ~이다'라는 뜻으로 빈칸에 적절하지 않다.

번역 강좌에서 자리를 확보하려면 납입금을 수요일까지 본점에 납입해야 한다.

어휘 payment 납입금 spot 자리, 장소, 위치

108 형용사 자리 _ 명사 수식

해설 관사(a)와 명사(discount) 사이에 들어가서 명사를 수식하는 형용사를 고르는 문제이다. 부사인 (C)와 (D)는 제외되고, (A)는 최상급이기 때문에 앞에 정관사가 붙어야 한다. 이 문제에서는 '큰 할인 폭'이라는 의미를 만들어 줄 (B) steep(가파른, 급격한)이 적절하다.

번역 불량 상품은 대폭 할인되어 중고용품점에 팔리고, 그 상품은 그곳에서 새것이라고 광고된다.

어휘 imperfect 결함이 있는, 불완전한   merchandise 상품   at a steep discount 대폭 할인해서   secondhand store 중고용품점   advertise 광고하다   steeply 가파르게

109 전치사 어휘

해설 'from A to[until] B(A부터 B까지)' 구문이다. 따라서 (A) until(~까지)이 정답이다. (B) across(~을 가로질러), (C) into(~ 안으로), (D) by(~ 옆에)는 의미상 적절하지 않다.

번역 던 씨는 개업 때부터 2년 전 문을 닫을 때까지 레이크사이드 그릴에 고용되어 일했다.

어휘 employ 고용하다   launch 개시   closure 폐쇄, 종결

110 명사 어휘

해설 판매되기 전에 90일 정도 '시장'에 머무른, 즉 매물로 나와 있다는 뜻이 되어야 적절한 의미가 전달된다. 따라서 정답은 (D) market(시장)이다. (A) industry는 '산업', (B) neighborhood는 '이웃', (C) utility는 '(수도, 전기, 가스 같은) 공익사업'이라는 의미이다.

번역 램실 대도시권에 있는 주택들은 평균 90일 동안 시장에 매물로 나와 있다가 팔린다.

어휘 metropolitan area 대도시권   stay on the market 시장에 매물로 나와 있다   average 평균

111 접속사 자리 _ 두 문장 연결

해설 빈칸에는 2개의 문장을 연결하는 접속사가 와야 하므로 전치사인 (A) According to(~에 따르면), (B) On top of(~ 위에, ~외에)는 답이 될 수 없다. Should가 '주어 + 동사' 앞에 오는 것은 if가 생략되어 도치되는 경우이나, 이 때는 뒤에 동사원형이 와야 하므로 (C) 또한 정답이 아니다. 의미상 서로 반대되는 상황이므로 (D) Whereas(~인 반면에)가 자연스럽다.

번역 트리트 씨는 성적이 훌륭한 반면, 마 씨는 귀중한 실무 경험이 있다.

어휘 excellent 훌륭한   academic record 성적표   valuable 귀중한   hands-on experience 직접 경험

112 형용사 / 분사 자리 _ 명사 수식

해설 소유격과 명사 사이로, 명사를 수식하는 형용사가 들어갈 자리이다. 보기에 형용사가 없으니 형용사 역할을 하는 분사형을 찾도록 한다. 따라서 과거분사인 (B) revised(개정된)가 정답이다.

번역 버팔로 수족관은 야생동물위원회의 개정된 권고 사항에 맞춰 바다사자 서식지를 개조할 것이다.

어휘 aquarium 수족관   renovate 개조하다   sea lion 바다사자   habitat 서식지   in keeping with ~에 맞추어, ~에 따라   wildlife 야생동물   council 위원회   recommendation 권고, 추천   revise 개정하다, 수정하다

113 전치사 어휘

해설 빈칸 뒤의 month는 셀 수 있는 가산명사인데, 앞에 관사도 없고 복수형도 아니라는 점에서 힌트를 얻을 수 있다. per 뒤의 명사는 관사 없이 쓰여, '~당, ~마다'의 뜻을 갖기 때문에 정답은 (C) per이다.

번역 헤이즈 클럽의 회원은 한 달에 한 번 손님 한 명을 피트니스 센터에 데려올 수 있는 권리가 있다.

어휘 be entitled to + 동사원형 ~할 권리가 있다   guest 손님   per month 한 달에 (한 번)   except ~을 제외하고

114 동사 자리 / 시제

해설 한 문장에는 동사가 하나 있어야 하는데 이 문장에는 없다. 따라서 빈칸에는 동사가 들어가야 할 자리이므로, 일단 (A) increasing은 제외된다. 나머지 보기의 차이는 시제인데, 시제를 알 수 있는 힌트는 over the past year이다. 따라서 과거 시제가 되어야 하므로 정답은 (C) increased이다.

번역 페이버퀵 기술을 채택한 덕에 지난해 동안 파밍엄 공장의 생산이 9% 가까이 늘었다.

어휘 adoption 채택; 입양   nearly 거의(= almost)   increase 증가시키다, 늘리다

115 명사 자리 _ 전치사의 목적어

해설 any paint의 수식을 받을 명사가 와야 한다. 따라서 정답은 (A) choices (선택)이다.

번역 브론티가의 유서 깊은 주택들의 소유주들은 어떤 페인트 칠 선택에 있어 보존위원회의 승인을 받아야 한다.

어휘 historic 역사적으로 중요한   preservation 보존   approval 승인

116 to부정사 자리

해설 빈칸 뒤에 동사원형(meet)이 나오는 것으로 보아 빈칸은 to부정사가 들어가야 할 자리임을 알 수 있다. (A)는 전치사구이기 때문에 뒤에 오는 동사의 형태는 동명사가 되어야 하므로 오답이며, (C) As soon as는 접속사이기 때문에 뒤에 주어, 동사가 포함된 완벽한 문장이 와야 하므로 오답이다. (D) Not only는 보통 뒤에 but (also)와 함께 '~뿐만 아니라 …도'라는 뜻으로 쓰인다. 정답은 (B) In order to(~하기 위하여)이다.

번역 수요를 충족시키기 위해 알리안투스 디자인 사는 인테리어 디자인 전문가를 채용하기 시작했다.

어휘 meet demand 수요를 충족시키다   recruit 채용하다   as soon as ~하자마자

117 동사 어휘

해설 '기술적인 문제(technical difficulties)'를 '겪은, 마주친' 것에 대해 사과하는 상황이므로 '(반갑지 않은 일을) 맞닥뜨리다'를 뜻하는 encounter의 과거형인 (C) encountered가 정답이다. (A), (B), (D)는 의미상 적절하지 않다.

번역 던래스 어패럴은 저희 모바일 앱을 사용하면서 여러분이 겪으신 기술적 문제에 대해 진심으로 사과드립니다.

어휘 sincerely 진심으로   apologize for ~에 대해 사과하다
technical 기술의   undertake 착수하다   surrender 항복하다, 굴복하다   accompany 동반하다, 동행하다

118 부사 자리 _ 동명사 수식

해설 processing은 동명사이므로 동사의 성격을 갖는다. 따라서 부사인 (D) rapidly(빠르게)의 수식을 받아야 한다. (A) rapid(빠른)가 답이 되려면 'rapid process of large ~'가 되어야 한다. (B) rapider(더 빠른), (C) rapidness(빠름)는 답이 될 수 없다.

번역 우리가 개발한 소프트웨어 프로그램은 대용량 통계 데이터를 빠르게 처리할 수 있다.

어휘 develop 개발하다   be capable of ~를 할 수 있다   process 처리하다   quantity 양   statistical 통계적인

119 명사 어휘

해설 'the ------- of ~'의 형태로 쓰는 명사는 (A) majority와 (B) amount가 있다. the majority of는 '대다수의', the amount of는 '~의 양'이라는 의미로, 여기서는 문맥상 '대다수의' 인터넷 신생 기업들이 실패한다는 의미가 가장 적절하다. 따라서 정답은 (A) majority이다. 참고로 (C) variety는 주로 a variety of(다양한 ~)의 형태로 많이 쓰인다.

번역 언론 보도가 인터넷 신생 기업들의 얼마 안 되는 성공 신화에 초점을 맞추는 경향이 있긴 하지만 대다수의 인터넷 신생 기업들은 망한다.

어휘 media coverage 언론 보도   tend to+동사원형 ~하는 경향이 있다
start-up company 신생 기업   the majority of ~의 대다수, 과반수   amount 양, 액수   variety 다양성   extent 정도, 규모

120 부사 어휘

해설 빈칸 앞(lively atmosphere)과 뒤(boring)가 상반되는 의미로 이루어져 있음을 알 수 있다. 문맥상 화초들이 생기를 가져다 주는데 '그렇지 않았으면' 지루했을 장소라는 의미가 되면 연결이 자연스럽다. 따라서 (A) otherwise(그렇지 않으면)가 정답이다.

번역 화분에 심은 야자수 같은 식물들은, 식물이 없었다면 지루했을 사무용 건물들에 활기를 불어 넣어 줄 수 있다.

어휘 plant 식물   such as ~ 같은   potted palm 화분에 심은 야자수
lively 활기[생기] 넘치는   else 또 다른

121 형용사 어휘

해설 'be worth+비용[액수] (~의 값어치가 있는)'라는 표현을 알고 있으면 쉽게 답을 찾을 수 있다. (C) worth가 정답이다. (A) designated(지정된), (B) related(관련된), (D) due(지불 기한이 된)는 적절하지 않다.

번역 우리가 시바타 솔루션즈에서 구입한 고효율성 기계는 지불한 상당한 금액만큼의 가치가 있다.

어휘 efficiency 효율성   machinery 기계   substantial sum 상당한 금액

122 형용사 자리 _ 명사 수식

해설 명사(feedback)를 수식하는 형용사가 들어갈 자리이다. instead of 뒤의 general과 상반되는 의미의 형용사 (D) specific(구체적인)이 정답이다. 다른 보기들은 품사 면에서 적절하지 않다.

번역 연구 결과 어린이들은 전반적인 칭찬 대신에 구체적인 피드백을 받으면 더 잘한다는 것을 보여준다.

어휘 research 연구   do better 더 잘하다   general 일반적인   praise 칭찬   specifically 구체적으로   specify 구체적으로 명시하다

123 부사 자리

해설 '주어(one indicator)+동사(suggests)+목적절(that 이하)'로 되어 있는 하나의 문장이다. 따라서 빈칸에는 전치사인 (A) Apart from(~ 이외에), 그리고 접속사인 (C) Even if(비록 ~일지라도)와 (D) Now that(~이므로)은 올 수 없다. (B) At least(적어도, 최소한)가 정답이다.

번역 경제가 최근 침체에서 회복되기 시작했다는 사실을 적어도 한 개의 지표가 시사한다.

어휘 indicator 지표   suggest 시사하다, 암시하다   recover 회복하다
recent 최근의   downturn 침체, 하락

124 동사 시제 _ 시간 부사절

해설 문장 맨 뒤를 보면 when it opens라고 나와 있는데, 시간을 나타내는 부사절에서는 미래 의미일 때 현재 시제를 사용한다. 내용상 문장 전체의 의미는 미래이므로, 미래 시제인 (C) will visit가 정답이다.

번역 운동선수 모리스 비커스는 트로이에 새로 생긴 지역생활복지관이 개관할 때 개관식에 참석할 것이다.

어휘 athlete 운동선수   community activity center 지역 생활복지관
ribbon-cutting ceremony 개관식

125 주격 관계대명사

해설 문장에 동사가 두 개(wish, must notify) 나왔기 때문에 빈칸에 접속사 역할을 하는 것이 들어가야 한다. 따라서 (B)와 (C)는 제외된다. (A)와 (D)는 접속사 역할을 하는 관계대명사인 (A) who와 (D) whose가 가능한데 선행사가 사람(Employees)이고 관계대명사절에서 동사 wish의 주어 역할을 해야 하므로 주격 관계대명사인 (A) who가 정답이다.

번역 휴가 일정을 잡고 싶은 직원들은 2주 전에 인사과에 알려야 한다.

어휘 employee 직원   schedule vacation time 휴가 일정[계획]을 잡다   notify 알리다, 통지하다   Human Resources 인사과, 인력관리부

126 명사 자리 _ 목적어

해설 동사 requires의 목적어이자, 형용사 basic이 수식하는 명사가 들어갈 자리이다. 따라서 정답은 명사형인 (C) knowledge(지식)이다.

번역 레이크햄 웹디자인 세트는 사용자들에게 인상적인 웹사이트를 만들 수 있는 도구를 제공하며 기초적인 컴퓨터 지식만을 요구한다.

어휘 suite (가구, 용품) 세트   tool 도구   craft 만들다   require 요구하다, 필요로 하다   basic 기초적인, 기본적인   knowingly 다 알고도, 고의로

127 형용사 어휘

해설 주절의 목적어 a third party(제3자)라는 표현이 힌트가 된다. '제3자로부터의 평가'라는 말은, 즉, '외부의 평가'라는 의미가 되므로, 정답은 (D) external(외부의)이 된다. (A) ambiguous는 '애매모호한', (B) occupied는 '사용 중인, 점령된', (C) abundant는 '풍부한'이라는 의미로, 문맥상 적절하지 않다.

번역 결함에 관한 보도가 걱정되어, 시 정부는 제3자에게 새 다리 건설 계획에 대한 외부 평가를 시행해 달라고 요청했다.

어휘 flaw 결함   third party 제3자   external review 외부 평가[감사]

128 전치사 어휘

해설 those(= benefits) 이하를 목적어로 취해 의미가 통하는 전치사를 찾아야 한다. '~보다 많은, ~ 이상의'라는 뜻의 전치사가 와야 하는데, (D) than은 앞에 비교급이 있어야 하므로 답이 될 수 없다. (B) since(~이래로), (C) through(~ 동안 내내)는 의미상 어색하다. '~ 이상의, ~를 초과하는'을 뜻하는 (A) beyond가 정답이다.

번역 코락 어소시에이츠는 재능 있는 직원을 영입하고 보유하기 위해 다른 회사들에서 얻을 수 있는 것 이상으로 직원 혜택을 제공한다.

어휘 attract 끌어들이다   retain 보유하다, 유지하다   employee benefit 복리후생, 직원 혜택   available 이용 가능한, 손에 넣을 수 있는

129 명사 어휘

해설 회의에 참석할 수 있고 권한이 있는 주체여야 하므로 (D) delegates(대표)가 정답이다. (A) patents(특허권), (B) debate(토론), (C) expenditures(지출)는 모두 의미상 어색하다.

번역 대회 중 이 부분에 대한 참석은 회원 단체에서 중요한 권한을 가진 대표에게로 국한된다.

어휘 attendance 참석   convention 대회   be limited to ~로 제한되다, ~에 국한하다   significant 중요한   authority 권한   organization 단체

130 부사 자리 _ 동사 수식

해설 조동사(will)와 동사(improve) 사이에서 동사를 수식해 줄 수 있는 부사를 찾는 문제이다. 품사가 부사인 (B) assuredly(분명히)가 정답이다.

번역 조수를 채용하는 것의 경제적 가치는 논란의 여지가 있지만 추가적인 도움이 있으면 사기는 분명히 높아질 것이다.

어휘 economic value 경제적 가치   hire 채용[고용]하다   assistant 조수   disputable 논란의 여지가 있는   extra 추가적인   improve 향상시키다, 개선하다   morale 사기, 의욕   assure 장담하다, 확언하다   assurance 확언, 자신감   assured 자신감 있는, 확실한

PART 6

131-134 편지

레지나 아라미드
마샬 레인 907번지
가본, OK 73415

아라미드 씨께

지난번 시력 검사를 받으신 후 1년이 지났습니다. 검안사협회에서는 모든 성인이 시력 교정이 필요한지 여부와 상관없이 **131**1년에 한 번 검사를 받도록 권장하고 있습니다. 귀하의 **132**시력 건강을 확실히 지키시도록 곧 저희 병원을 방문해 주시기를 바랍니다.

또한, 저희가 6월에 사우스 메도우 가 38번지에 두 번째 지점을 개점한 것을 모르실 것 같습니다. 만일 이 지점이 귀하의 거주지에서 **133**더 가까우시면 그 지점으로 오기 시작하시기를 권해드립니다. **134**동봉한 카드에 저희 두 지점 연락처가 적혀 있습니다. 둘 중 한 곳에서 곧 진료 예약을 하시기 바랍니다.

기억해주세요. 저희는 귀하의 눈 건강에 관심을 갖고 있습니다!

의사 제인 웨더롤

어휘 eye exam 시력 검사   Association of Optometrists 검안사협회   recommend 권장하다, 추천하다   adult 성인   checkup 검사   regardless of ~에 상관없이   correction 교정   ensure 확보하다, 보증하다   vision 시력   branch 지점   location 지점, 위치   residence 거주지

131 형용사 어휘

해설 앞 문장에서 시력 검사한 지 1년(one year)이 지났다는 말이 나온 것으로 보아 정기적인 검진을 '1년에 한 번씩' 하라는 의미가 들어가야 적절하다. 따라서 '1년에 한 번의, 연례의'라는 뜻의 (D) annual이 정답이다. (A) fluent는 '유창한', (B) grateful은 '감사한', (C) vacant는 '비어 있는'이라는 의미이다.

132 명사 어휘

해설 첫 문장에서 eye exam이라는 단어가 나왔기 때문에 '눈'의 건강이라는 의미가 자연스럽다. 따라서 정답은 '시력'이라는 뜻의 (B) vision이 정답이다. (A) diet는 '식습관, 규정식', (C) hearing은 '청력', (D) breathing은 '호흡, 숨쉬기'라는 뜻으로 문맥상 어울리지 않는다.

133 형용사 자리

해설 빈칸 앞의 be동사 is와 뒤의 전치사 to로 보아 형용사가 와야 할 자리다. 보기 중 형용사의 비교급인 (A) nearer(더 가까운)가 정답이다.

어휘 nearly 거의 near 가까운; 가까워지다

134 문맥에 맞는 문장 고르기

번역 (A) 유효 기간은 월말까지입니다.
(B) 귀하의 진료 기록과 함께 안전하게 보관될 것입니다.
(C) 이 실수를 친절히 지적해주셔서 감사합니다.
(D) 둘 중 한 곳에서 곧 진료 예약을 하시기 바랍니다.

해설 바로 앞에 원래 방문했던 지점 이외에 또 다른 지점을 열었다(we opened a second branch at ~)는 내용이 나오기 때문에 둘 중 한 곳에서 진료 예약을 하라는 (D)가 정답이다.

어휘 schedule an appointment 진료 예약을 잡다 either 둘 중 하나의

135 -138 이메일

> 발신: 〈jhartmann@molinacity.gov〉
> 수신: 〈nskeane@molinacity.gov〉
> 날짜: 7월 28일
> 제목: 2사분기 보고서
> 첨부: 4월 보고서; 5월 보고서; 6월 보고서
>
> 키니 씨 께,
>
> 여기 요청하신 보고서들 보내드립니다. 다른 필요한 것이 있으시면 저에게 알려 주십시오.
>
> --------------------------------
> 이 이메일과 첨부 파일에는 **135**기밀 정보가 담겨 있을 수 있습니다. 이러한 이유로 기재된 수신자만 읽으실 수 있습니다. 만약 당신이 이 이메일이 의도한 수신자가 아니라면 여기에 포함된 어떤 정보의 배포도 **137**시 규례 3조 4.1항에 의해 **136**철저히 금지되어 있다는 것을 양지하시기 바랍니다. www.molinacity. gov/code에서 조항을 보실 수 있습니다. 착오로 이 이메일을 받으셨다면 이 메시지에 답신을 보내어 발신자에게 그 사실을 알려 주시고, 이 이메일을 즉시 **138**삭제해 주시기 바랍니다.
>
> 감사합니다.
>
> 제이슨 하트만

> **어휘** address 주소를 쓰다, ~ 앞으로 보내다 intended 의도된 recipient 수신자, 수취인 distribution 배포 be prohibited 금지되다 section 항 city code 시 규례 in error 실수로, 착오로 reply 답장을 보내다 immediately 즉시

135 형용사 어휘

해설 바로 뒤 문장에서 힌트를 찾을 수 있다. 이 정보를 사용할 수 있는 대상을 only로 한정하기 때문에 이를 설명해줄 수 있는 형용사가 빈칸에 와야 한다. '기밀의'라는 뜻의 (B) confidential이 가장 적절하다. (A) predictable은 '예측 가능한', (C) outdated는 '오래된', (D) diverse는 '다양한'이라는 의미이다.

136 부사 자리

해설 빈칸에는 뒤의 prohibited(금지된)를 꾸며줄 부사가 와야 할 자리이다. 보기 중 부사인 (C) expressly(분명히, 명확히)가 정답이다.

137 문맥에 맞는 문장 고르기

번역 (A) 웹사이트에서 간단히 '공유' 아이콘을 클릭하십시오.
(B) 건설 관련 규제는 4조에 있습니다.
(C) www.molinacity.gov/code에서 조항을 보실 수 있습니다.
(D) 시에서는 회의에 사본을 가져오시도록 권합니다.

해설 빈칸 앞에 있는 city code와 연관이 있는 문장이 나오면 연결이 자연스러울 것이다. 따라서 정답은 (C)이다.

138 동사 어휘

해설 지문 내용상 이 이메일에 기밀 정보가 담겨 있을 수 있으니 잘못 받은 사람은 즉시 이메일을 '삭제해 달라'는 내용이 오는 것이 적절하다. 정답은 (C) delete(삭제하다)이다.

어휘 interrupt 방해하다 withdraw 철수하다; 빼내다 waive (세금을) 탕감해 주다; (권리 등을) 포기하다

139 -142 이메일

> 발신: 에이브 퍼거슨
> 수신: 관리자들
> 제목: 공지
> 날짜: 1월 29일
>
> 안녕하세요 관리자 여러분,
>
> **139**최고경영자 펄 그리피스 씨께서 다음 주 후반에 우리 사무실을 방문하신다는 소식을 방금 들었습니다. 그리피스 씨는 고위 관리자들을 만나 경영에 관한 사항을 살펴볼 것입니다. 이에 대비하기 위해 다음의 정보를 동료 직원들에게 전달해 주십시오.
>
> 첫째, 그리피스 씨는 방문 중 어느 시점에 사무실을 둘러볼 예정입니다. **140**따라서 직원 여러분께서는 최고경영자분의 방문 내내 업무 공간을 깔끔하게 유지해야 합니다. 둘째, 그리피스 씨를 **141**환영하기 위해 목요일 오후 5시에 대회의실에서 연회가 있을 것입니다. 연회는 업무 시간 이후이므로 직원 여러분의 참석은 **142**의무사항이 아닙니다. 그러나 많은 분들이 참석하시길 바랍니다.
>
> 저는 이번 방문 건에 더 관여할 예정인 분들께 앞으로 며칠간 개별 메시지를 보내 드릴 것입니다.
>
> 에이브

> **어휘** inform 알리다 in preparation for ~의 준비로 relay 전달하다 following 다음에 나오는 at some point 어느 시점에 throughout ~ 내내 reception 환영 연회 be held 개최되다 business hours 업무 시간, 영업 시간 presence 참석 attend 참석하다 be scheduled to+동사원형 ~하기로 예정되어 있다 involved 관여하는

139 문맥에 맞는 문장 고르기

번역 (A) 그리피스 씨를 보내야 한다는 것이 아쉽지만, 그녀는 훌륭한 경력을 쌓았습니다.
(B) 그리피스 씨는 고위 관리자들을 만나 경영에 관한 사항을 살펴볼 것입니다.
(C) 우리는 그리피스 씨의 이러한 업적을 축하할 방법을 찾아야 합니다.
(D) 제가 읽은 바에 따르면 그리피스 씨는 그 직책에 매우 적합한 지원자입니다.

해설 바로 다음에 '이에 대비하기 위해(In preparation for this)'라는 말이 나오므로, 빈칸에는 this에 해당하는 내용이 들어가야 한다. 또한 바로 앞에서 최고경영자가 방문한다는 말을 전했으므로 방문에 따른 구체적 일정을 설명한 (B)가 정답이다.

어휘 career 경력, 직장생활 senior management 간부직, 고위 관리자 look over 살펴보다 congratulate 축하하다 achievement 업적 candidate 지원자, 후보자

140 부사 어휘

해설 앞뒤 문장의 문맥을 보면 최고경영자가 사무실을 둘러볼 예정이고, 그 때문에 업무 공간을 정돈해야 하는 것이므로 빈칸에는 (A) accordingly(따라서)가 오는 것이 자연스럽다.

어휘 nevertheless 그럼에도 불구하고 furthermore 게다가 rather 오히려

141 부사구 자리 _ to부정사

해설 '주어(a reception)+동사(will be held)'가 이미 들어간 완전한 문장이므로 또 다른 동사인 (A) welcomes, (B) welcomed, (C) should welcome은 들어갈 수 없다. 부사구인 (D) to welcome(환영하기 위해서)가 정답이다.

142 형용사 어휘

해설 주어 employees' presence를 설명하는 주격 보어로 의미가 통하는 형용사를 찾아야 한다. 업무 시간 이후의 행사이기 때문에 행사 참여에 강제성은 없다는 내용이므로 (D) mandatory(의무적인, 강제적인)가 정답이다.

어휘 costly 비싼 allowed 허용되는 particular 특정한

143 -146 광고

인포보
구직자들을 위한 유용한 도구

인포보는 홍보 부서가 아닌 일반 직원 및 구직자로부터 수집한 수만 개의 회사 관련 정보를 공유합니다. 이것이 바로 수백 만 명의 전문 인력들이 직업 관련 결정을 내리기 위해 저희 사이트를 이용하는 **143이유**입니다. 사용자는 어느 회사에 지원할지 고려할 때 업체들의 기업 문화에 대한 솔직한 후기를 읽을 수 있고 면접을 보기 **144전에** 예상 문제를 찾아볼 수 있습니다.

또한 데이터 분석을 기반으로 **145폭넓은** 통찰력을 제공합니다. **146일자리를 제안받았지만 제시된 급여가 합리적인지 잘 모르시나요? 귀하의 분야 내 유사한 일자리의 일반적인 급여 범위를 보여드립니다.**

무엇을 망설이십니까? 오늘 www.infovo.com에 들러 귀하의 경력을 향상시키세요.

어휘 invaluable 매우 귀중한, 유용한 tool 수단, 도구 jobseeker 구직자 share 공유하다 collect 수집하다 ordinary 보통의 job applicant 구직자 public relations 홍보 professional 전문가, 전문직 종사자 corporate 회사의 apply 지원하다 go in for (시험, 경쟁 등에) 참가하다 insight 통찰력 analysis 분석 offer a position 일자리를 제안하다 reasonable 합리적인 on the fast track 출세가도를 달리는

143 관계부사 _ why

해설 첫 문장에서는 인포보가 관계자로부터 수집한 수많은 기업 정보를 가지고 있다고 했고, 두 번째 문장에서는 전문 인력들이 인포보를 많이 사용한다고 했다. 첫 문장이 두 번째 문장 내용에 대한 이유가 되므로, 'That's (the reason) why ~'(그것이 바로 ~한 이유이다)라는 표현이 되는 것이 좋다. 따라서 정답은 (A) why이다.

144 전치사 어휘

해설 예상 문제를 찾아보는 것과 면접을 보러 가는 것은 시간상 전후 관계로 연결할 수 있으므로 (A) before(~ 전에)가 정답이다.

어휘 despite ~에도 불구하고 plus ~도 또한

145 형용사 자리 _ 명사 수식

해설 빈칸은 목적어인 명사 insights를 수식하는 자리이므로 형용사가 와야 한다. 따라서 (D) broad(폭넓은, 전반적인)가 정답이다.

어휘 broaden 넓히다 broadly 대략 broadness 넓음

146 문맥에 맞는 문장 고르기

번역 (A) 잠재적인 고용주가 귀하를 발견할 수 있도록 이력서를 업로드하세요.
(B) 귀하의 분야 내 유사한 일자리의 일반적인 급여 범위를 보여드립니다.
(C) 저희는 그 후기들이 현재 또는 이전의 실제 직원들이 올린 것인지 검증합니다.
(D) 저희 목록은 구직 사이트 중 가장 자주 업데이트됩니다.

해설 바로 앞 문장에서 급여가 적절한지 궁금했던 적이 없냐고 물었다. 따라서 우리 사이트에서 유사한 직종의 급여 범위를 보여준다고 말하는 (B)가 정답이다.

어휘 potential 잠재적인 typical 일반적인, 전형적인 range 범위 verify 확인하다, 검증하다 former 이전의 jobseeking 구직(의)

PART 7

147-148 공지

> **에너지와 물을 절약하도록 도와 주세요!**
>
> **147**저희는 손님이 머무시는 동안 매일 아침 손님의 침구류를 갈아드릴 것입니다. 침구류를 세탁하는 데 필요한 자원을 절약하기 위해 덜 자주 갈기 원하시면 이 카드를 침대 위에 남겨 주십시오.
>
> **148**손님이 출타 중이라 안 계실 때는 자동온도조절기가 감지하고 히터나 에어컨의 전원을 끌 것입니다. 히터나 에어컨을 그대로 두기를 원하시면 나가시면서 초록색 버튼을 눌러 주십시오.
>
> 애용해 주셔서 감사합니다! 더 그랜드는 뛰어난 고객 서비스를 제공하는 데 매진하고 있습니다. 머무시는 것과 관련해 무엇이든 훌륭하지 못한 부분이 있다면 프런트 데스크에 연락해 주시기 바랍니다.

> **어휘** linen (침대 시트와 베갯잇 같은) 침구류, 리넨 제품 stay 숙박 frequently 자주 thermostat 자동온도조절기 sense 감지하다 be away 출타 중이다, 부재 중이다 switch off 끄다 heater 히터, 온열기 air conditioning 에어컨 press 누르다 stay on 켜진 상태를 계속 유지하다 patronage 애용, 단골 거래 be dedicated to ~에 헌신하다, 매진하다 provide 제공하다 excellent 탁월한, 뛰어난 customer service 고객 서비스 contact 연락하다, 접촉하다 less than exceptional 뛰어나지 않은

---

147 추론 / 암시

번역 더 그랜드는 무엇일 것 같은가?
(A) 극장
(B) 미술관
(C) 식당
(D) 호텔

해설 첫 문장만 보더라도 알 수 있다. 'change your linens, during your stay' 등의 표현을 통해서 이 시설이 호텔인 것을 알 수 있다. 따라서 정답은 (D)이다.

---

148 사실 관계 확인

번역 자동온도조절기에 관해 명시된 것은?
(A) 지원 데스크 뒤에 있다.
(B) 난방에만 영향을 미친다.
(C) 자동 제어 장치를 지니고 있다.
(D) 매일 아침 재설정해야만 한다.

해설 두 번째 단락 첫 번째 문장에서, 투숙객이 없을 때 자동온도조절기가 히터나 에어컨을 끈다는 내용을 통해서 (C)가 정답임을 알 수 있다.

149-150 광고

> **제14회 레이크타운 화장품 박람회**
>
> 레이크타운 화장품 박람회가 **150**6월 27-28일 오전 9시부터 오후 4시까지 센터 스트리트 1145번지에 있는, 레이크타운 컨벤션 센터에서 열립니다. 업계 전문가들을 위한 이 연례 행사는 레이크타운에서 가장 큰 행사 중 하나입니다!
>
> • **149**화장품의 역사를 다룬 다큐멘터리를 관람하세요.
> • 최신 경향의 제품들을 눈으로 보고 시험 삼아 써 보세요.
> • 모든 주요 화장품 회사들뿐 아니라 독립 개발 업체들의 직원들과 직접 이야기를 나눠보세요.
> • 레이크타운 카운티 박물관 및 개인 소장가들에게서 빌려 온 고전적인 화장품들을 살펴보세요.
>
> 행사는 **150**6월 28일 일요일 하루 동안 일반 대중에 공개됩니다. 입장권은 성인 7달러, 어린이 4달러입니다. 입장권을 구입하시면 이 지역의 고품질 화장품 및 피부 보호 제품 회사인 폴리아즈에서 사용할 수 있는 100달러 상당의 상품권을 받으실 수 있는 경품 추첨권을 드립니다.
>
> 더 자세한 정보를 원하시면 저희 웹사이트 www.laketowncosmeticsexpo.com을 방문하시기 바랍니다.

> **어휘** cosmetics 화장품 industry professional 업계 전문가 try out 시험 삼아 써보다 trendy 최신 유행[경향]의 directly 직접 representative 직원 major 주요한 independent developer 독립 개발자 explore 탐구하다 display 전시 vintage 빈티지[고전적, 유서 깊은] private collector 개인 소장가 the public 일반인, 대중 purchase 구입(하다) raffle 경품 추첨 gift certificate 상품권 local 지역의, 현지의 source 원천 high-quality 품질 좋은, 고품질의

---

149 사실 관계 확인

번역 광고에는 어떤 활동이 언급되는가?
(A) 역사적 건물 탐방
(B) 논픽션 영화 관람
(C) 강연 청취
(D) 특별한 음식 먹기

해설 중간 부분에 열거된 항목 중 첫 번째 항목(Watch a documentary)을 통해서 정답이 (B)라는 것을 확인할 수 있다. (C)의 내용과 세 번째 항목이 혼동될 수 있는데, 주요 회사 및 독립 업체 직원들과 직접 이야기를 나눈다는 내용이지, 강연(lecture)을 듣는 것은 아니므로 오답이다.

▶▶ **Paraphrasing** 지문의 **Watch a documentary**
→ 정답의 **Seeing a nonfiction film**

---

150 추론 / 암시

번역 레이크타운 화장품 박람회에 대해 암시된 것은?
(A) 2년에 한 번씩 열린다.
(B) 업계 회원사들에게만 개방된다.
(C) 두 곳에서 열린다.
(D) 토요일에 시작한다.

해설 첫 번째 단락에서 6월 27-28일(June 27-28) 이틀 동안 열린다는 말과 세 번째 단락에서 28일(on Sunday, June 28)이 일요일이라는 사실을 바탕으로 박람회가 27일 토요일에 시작함을 알 수 있다. 따라서 정답은 (D)이다.

151-152 초대장

초대합니다!

서부 펜실베이니아의 스윈턴 클럽이 **151**지역 사업자들을 위한 사교 행사에 귀하를 진심으로 초대합니다. 오셔서 이웃들을 알아가세요! 참석자들에게는 또한 스윈턴 클럽을 더 잘 알고, 지난 주말의 하천 청소같이 곧 있을 봉사활동들에 참여하는 방법을 알 수 있는 기회가 될 것입니다.

날짜: 2월 27일 금요일

시간: 오후 5:30 – 7:30

장소: 스프링필드, 엘머가 431, 스위트 라이프 제과 앤 델리

2월 23일 월요일까지 줄리 워커에게 j.walker@swintonclub.com으로 이메일을 보내어 자리를 예약하십시오. 일반적인 문의 사항이 있으시면 **152**몰리 필즈 부대표에게 m.fields@swintonclub.com으로 이메일을 보내주시기 바랍니다.

어휘 cordially 진심으로 get to know 알게 되다 attendee 참석자 have the change to+동사원형 ~할 기회를 얻다 become involved in ~에 참여[관여]하다 service projects 봉사 활동 river cleanup 하천 청소 reserve 예약하다 vice president 부대표

151 추론 / 암시

번역 이 초대장을 받게 될 사람은 누구일 것 같은가?

(A) 프로 운동선수
(B) 상점 주인
(C) 대학생
(D) 지역 정치인

해설 첫 번째 문장을 보면 초대하는 대상이 지역 사업가들(for local business owners)이라는 것을 확인할 수 있다. 따라서 정답은 (B)이다.

▶▶ **Paraphrasing** 지문의 **local business owners**
→ 정답의 **A store owner**

152 추론 / 암시

번역 필즈 씨에 관해 암시된 것은?

(A) 스위트 라이프 제과 앤 델리를 운영한다.
(B) 스윈턴 클럽에서 직책을 맡고 있다.
(C) 하천 청소 작업을 조직할 것이다.
(D) 예약 처리를 책임지고 있다.

해설 마지막 문장에서 필즈 씨가 부대표(Vice President Moly Fields)를 맡고 있다는 것을 알 수 있다. 즉 스윈턴 클럽에서 부대표를 맡고 있다는 뜻이기 때문에 정답은 (B)이다.

153-155 이메일

수신: 토마스 건터 〈thomas_gunther@gmsmail.com〉
발신: 수전 궈 〈susan.guo@boardgamesunltd.com〉
제목: 귀하의 질문
날짜: 5월 13일

건터 씨 귀하,

안녕하세요! **153**저희 웹사이트의 연락처 양식에 기입하신 정보에 근거하여 귀하가 저희 회사와 친숙해지시도록 하기 위해 연락을 드립니다.

155(C)보드게임즈 무한책임회사는 중국 광저우에 본사를 두고 10년 넘게 다양한 회사들을 위해 보드게임을 인쇄하고 포장한 경험이 있는 보드게임 제작업체입니다. 인쇄와 조립이 모두 사내에서 이루어지며, 카드와 주사위, 동전, 그리고 무엇이든 고객이 원하는 재료로 주문 제작하는 부품들을 포함해 최고 품질의 액세서리들을 찾아드리는 저희 조달팀은 믿어도 좋습니다. **155(D)**이미 방문하셔서 아시겠지만 저희 웹사이트에서 저희 게임의 견본들을 보실 수 있습니다. **155(A)**많은 게임들이 팬작 메달을 비롯해 수많은 찬사와 상을 받아 왔습니다.

154저희는 품질과 비용을 조합해 귀하가 정한 예산 내에서 최선의 게임을 출시할 수 있도록 제안서를 마련하는 일에 만전을 기하고 있습니다. 귀하가 원하시는 바를 더 자세히 상의하기 위해 전화 통화하고자 하는 시간을 제게 알려 주시기 바랍니다.

수전 궈 드림

보드게임즈 무한책임회사

주소: 중국 광둥성 광저우시
     농종산 6로 1500번지 802–804호 (우편번호: 102108)
휴대전화: +86 555 1609 4291
전화: +86 55 51696158

어휘 contact form 연락처 양식 reach out 연락하다 familiarize 친숙[익숙]해지게 하다 manufacturer 제작업체, 제조업체 based in ~에 본사를 둔 decade 10년 printing 인쇄 packaging 포장 a range of 다양한, 폭넓은 assembly 조립 do in-house 사내에서 하다 rely on ~에 의지하다 sourcing team 조달팀 customized 주문 제작한 material 재료, 자재 earn 얻다 accolade 찬사 award 상 prestigious 권위 있는, 명망 있는 be committed to ~에 전념하다, 매진하다, 몰두하다 craft a proposal 제안서를 마련하다[만들다] combination 조합, 결합 cost 비용 enable 가능하게 하다 launch 출시하다 budget 예산 schedule a phone call 전화 통화 일정을 잡다

153 글의 주제 / 목적

번역 이 이메일의 주목적은 무엇인가?

(A) 회사를 소개하려고
(B) 계약을 마무리하려고
(C) 일정을 수정하려고
(D) 새로운 서비스를 홍보하려고

해설 지문 전체가 보드게임즈 무한책임회사라는 회사에 대한 소개를 하고 있으므로 정답은 (A)이다.

154 추론 / 암시

번역 건터 씨에 관해 암시된 것은?

(A) 보드게임을 만들고 싶어 한다.
(B) 보드게임즈 무한책임회사의 직원이다.
(C) 전에 궈 씨를 만난 적이 있다.
(D) 곧 중국에 갈 것이다.

해설 이메일을 쓴 측은 보드게임 제작업체이고, 수신자는 건터 씨이다. 세 번째 단락에 '귀하가 예산 내에서 게임을 출시할 수 있도록 해주겠다'는 내용이 나온 것으로 보아 건터 씨는 보드게임을 출시하고 싶어 한다는 것을 알 수 있다. 따라서 정답은 (A)이다.

155 사실 관계 확인

번역 보드게임즈 무한책임회사에 관해 언급되지 않은 것은?
(A) 수상 경력이 있는 제품들을 만들었다.
(B) 사내에서 액세서리들을 생산한다.
(C) 창립한 지 10년이 넘었다.
(D) 웹사이트에서 그 회사 제품 견본들을 보여준다.

해설 (A)는 두 번째 단락 마지막 문장에서 많은 상을 수상했다는 내용을 토대로 확인이 가능하고, (C)는 두 번째 단락 첫 번째 문장에서 10년 넘게 인쇄하고 포장한 경험이 있다는 내용을 확인할 수 있고, (D)는 두 번째 단락 중간 부분에서 웹사이트에서 여러 견본을 확인할 수 있다는 내용으로 확인이 가능하다. (B)는 두 번째 단락 중간 부분을 보면 조달팀에서 최고 품질의 액세서리를 찾아준다(find the highest-quality accessories)고 했기 때문에 맞지 않다. 따라서 정답은 (B)이다.

▶▶ Paraphrasing 지문의 **You can see samples of our games on our Web site**
→ 선택지의 **Its Web site shows examples of its work.**

156-157 문자 메시지

빅터 머노즈 [오전 9:42]
안녕하세요, 베스. 아직 연구실에 있어요?

베스 시릴로 [오전 9:43]
지금 안내 데스크로 돌아왔어요. 그쪽에서 파일들이 필요해요?

빅터 머노즈 [오전 9:44]
아뇨, 하지만 인쇄소에서 현재 우리의 훈련 교본을 배송 중이라고 방금 전화가 왔어요.

베스 시릴로 [오전 9:44]
잘됐네요. 156내가 여기 로비에 있다가 수령하고 서명할게요.

빅터 머노즈 [오전 9:45]
고마워요. 한 가지만 더요. 물품 보관실에 오래된 컴퓨터 부품으로 가득 찬 통이 있어요. 그것에 관해 아는 바가 있나요?

베스 시릴로 [오전 9:46]
그래요? 물품 보관실이 두 개인데요.

빅터 머노즈 [오전 9:47]
157자료 분석팀이 사용하는 보관실이에요. 아마 재활용하기 위한 부품들이겠죠?

베스 시릴로 [오전 9:48]
아마도요. 제가 내일 살펴볼게요. 지금은, 제가 여기 안내 데스크에 앉아 있잖아요. 배송품이 도착하면 알려드릴게요.

어휘 print shop 인쇄소 training manual 훈련 교본, 교육 안내서 reception area 로비, 안내실 bin 통 part 부품 supply closet 비품실, 물품 보관실 analysis 분석 recycling 재활용 look into 살펴보다, 조사하다

156 세부 사항

번역 시릴로 씨는 무엇을 하겠다고 제안하는가?
(A) 배송품을 수령한다.
(B) 파일을 프린트한다.
(C) 설명서를 교정본다.
(D) 시설 견학을 인도한다.

해설 9시 44분 대화 내용에서 교본이 도착하는 대로 서명하겠다(sign for them)는 내용을 토대로 정답이 (A)라는 것을 알 수 있다.

157 의도 파악

번역 오전 9시 46분에 시릴로 씨가 "물품 보관실이 두 개인데요"라고 쓴 의도는 무엇이겠는가?
(A) 부서에서 물품을 너무 많이 주문했다.
(B) 어떤 업무가 걸릴 시간이 걱정된다.
(C) 추가적인 설명이 필요하다.
(D) 일부 품목을 넣을 공간이 충분하다.

해설 물품 보관실이 하나만 있으면 이렇게 물어 볼 필요가 없었을 것이다. 어느 물품 보관실을 의미하는지 추가적인 설명을 원하는 것이다. 당연히 이어지는 문장도 어떤 물품 보관실인지 알려주는 문장이 나온다. 따라서 정답은 (C)이다.

158-160 회람

알린 플라자

발신: 알린 플라자 관리부
수신: 모든 입주자
제목: 중요: 주차 정책
날짜: 2월 3일

158저희 쇼핑몰의 실제 고객들을 위해 항상 충분한 주차 공간을 확보할 수 있도록 새로운 주차 정책을 도입하기로 결정했습니다. 160더 읽으시기에 앞서, 새 정책을 알리는 공식 보도 자료는 내일 내보낼 것임을 알려드립니다. 발표 이전에 귀하의 직원 및 다른 사람과 이 문제에 대해 이야기하지 마십시오.

1593월 1일부터 쇼핑몰 주차장 이용은 최초 1시간 30분 동안만 무료이며 이후에는 방문객에게 시간당 2달러의 요금이 부과됩니다. 본 정책을 실시하기 위해 할로웨이 주차업체에서 운영하는 주차 부스가 주차장 입구와 출구에 세워질 예정입니다.

159물론 알린 플라자 전 직원 및 입주업체는 여전히 무료로 주차할 수 있습니다. 이를 위해 전 직원께서는 www.hollowayparking.com/arlin에 방문하셔서 주차 허가증을 신청해 주시기 바랍니다. 변경 사항이 시행되기 한참 전에 신청해 주셔야 합니다.

어휘 tenant 임차인, 세입자 policy 정책 sufficient 충분한
patron 고객, 후원자 at all times 항상, 언제나 institute 도입하다,
시작하다 prior to ~ 전에 charge 요금을 부과하다 enforce
실시하다, 집행하다 operate 운영하다 construct 건설하다
entrance 입구 exit 출구 be allowed to+동사원형 ~하는
것이 허용되다 enable 가능하게 하다 register for ~를 등록하다
permit 허가증 implement 시행하다

158 추론 / 암시

번역 알린 플라자의 주차장에 대해 암시된 것은?
(A) 최근에 두 번째 출구가 추가되었다.
(B) 한 신문에서 이 주차장의 보안에 관한 문제를 보도했다.
(C) 손님이 아닌 사람들이 사용한다.
(D) 운영 시간이 연장될 예정이다.

해설 회람 도입 문장에서 '저희 쇼핑몰의 실제 고객들(actual patrons)'을 위해
충분한 주차 공간을 확보하겠다'고 한 것으로 보아, 실제 손님이 아닌 사람
들도 주차장을 사용한다고 추측할 수 있다. 따라서 (C)가 정답이다.

어휘 security 보안 be extended 연장되다

▶▶ Paraphrasing 지문의 patrons → 정답의 customers

159 세부 사항

번역 회람에 따르면, 알린 플라자 입주업체 직원들은 2월에 무엇을 해야 하는가?
(A) 시 공무원에게 양식 제출하기
(B) 전 직원 교육 시간에 참여하기
(C) 건설 현장에 가지 않기
(D) 주차권 신청하기

해설 마지막 단락에서 알린 플라자 전 직원은 새로운 정책 시행 한참 전에 웹사
이트를 방문해 주차증을 신청하라(register for a permit)고 당부했다.
새로운 정책이 3월 1일부터 시작되므로 직원들은 2월에 주차권을 신청할
것이다. 따라서 정답은 (D)이다.

어휘 submit 제출하다 city official 시 공무원 avoid 피하다 parking
pass 주차권

▶▶ Paraphrasing 지문의 register for a permit
→ 정답의 Sign up for a parking pass

160 문장 삽입

번역 [1], [2], [3], [4]로 표시된 곳 중에서, 다음 문장이 들어가기에 가장 적합한
곳은?

"발표 이전에 귀하의 직원 및 다른 사람과 이 문제에 대해 이야기하지 마십시오."

(A) [1]
(B) [2]
(C) [3]
(D) [4]

해설 [1]번 빈칸 바로 앞에서 공식 보도 자료는 내일 내보낸다(an official
press ~ tomorrow)고 했다. 따라서 '발표 이전에는 이 내용을 남에게
알리지 말라'고 한 해당 문장은 [1]에 들어가야 한다.

어휘 matter 문제, 사안 publication 발표, 공개

161 -163 정보문

로우랜트 어소시에이츠 직원을 위한 스타글린트 관련 정보

스타글린트는 회사의 생산성을 높이고 긍정적인 환경을 조성하기 위한 혁신적
수단입니다. 자신이 저평가를 받는다고 느끼는 직원들은 병가를 더 많이 내고
동료들과 소통에 있어 덜 효율적입니다. 161로우랜트 어소시에이츠는 다른 직원
들에게 감사를 표하고 감사를 받기 위한 쉬운 방법을 제공함으로써 이러한 문제
들을 해결하고자 스타글린트에 투자를 했습니다.

스타글린트는 사용하기에 매우 간단합니다. 다른 사람에게 '최고의 별점'을 주려
면 '별점 주기'라고 적힌 빨간 버튼을 클릭하여 필요한 정보를 입력하세요. 162
별점을 받는 사람의 칭찬할 만한 행동을 간략하게 기술하셔서 인사부에서 이해할
수 있도록 해 주시기 바랍니다. 그리고 나서 '보내기' 버튼을 눌러 제출하세요.

본인이 받은 최고의 별점을 확인하시려면 '내 별점 보기'라고 적힌 파란 버튼을
클릭하세요. 163최고의 별점 10개를 획득하면 '교환하기'를 클릭해 로우랜트 어
소시에이츠의 지역 내 제휴 매장이나 음식점의 상품권으로 교환하십시오.

모든 로우랜트 어소시에이츠 가족 여러분이 스타글린트를 자주, 그러면서도 현
명하게 사용해 서로를 격려해 주시기를 바랍니다.

어휘 innovative 혁신적인 productivity 생산성 positive
긍정적인 atmosphere 분위기 undervalued 저평가된
effectively 효율적으로 incredibly 놀라울 정도로 label (표 같은
것에) 적다 make certain 확실히 하다 description 기술, 서술
recipient 수혜자, 받는 사람 praiseworthy 칭찬할 만한 earn
벌다, 받다 redeem (상품과 현금 등을 서로) 교환하다 exchange
교환하다 gift certificate 상품권

161 세부 사항

번역 스타글린트의 용도는 무엇인가?
(A) 휴가 신청
(B) 공유 파일 원격 수정
(C) 동료에게 감사 표시
(D) 기계 문제 보고

해설 첫 번째 단락에서 스타글린트를 통해 '다른 직원들에게 감사를 표하고 감
사를 받기 위한(to thank and receive thanks from others) 쉬운 방
법을 제공함으로써'라고 언급했다. 스타글린트가 동료 간에 서로 감사를
표시하는 역할을 할 것임을 알 수 있으므로 (C)가 정답이다.

어휘 time off 휴식, 휴가 remotely 원격으로

▶▶ Paraphrasing 지문의 thank and receive thanks from
others → 정답의 Expressing appreciation
to coworkers

162 세부 사항

번역 제출 시 직원들이 특히 해야 하는 일은?
(A) 설명 쓰기
(B) 기록 저장하기
(C) 목록에서 카테고리 선택하기
(D) 받는 사람의 이름 재확인하기

해설 두 번째 단락에서, 별점 주기를 할 때는 별점을 받는 사람의 칭찬 받을 행동을 간략히 기술해 달라고(write a short description) 했다. 따라서 정답은 (A)이다.

어휘 make a submission 제출하다 double-check 확인하다

▶▶ Paraphrasing 지문의 write a short description
→ 정답의 Include an explanation

163 사실 관계 확인

번역 로우랜트 어소시에이츠에 대해 명시된 것은?
(A) 가족 소유 회사이다.
(B) 직원들에게 교육 수료증을 발급한다.
(C) 인사부를 확장하고 있다.
(D) 소매업체들과 특별한 제휴 관계가 있다.

해설 세 번째 단락에서, 별점이 쌓이면 '지역 내 제휴 매장이나 음식점의 상품권으로 교환하라'고 했다. 회사가 소매업체들과 제휴를 맺고 있음을 알 수 있으므로 (D)가 정답이다.

▶▶ Paraphrasing 지문의 shops and restaurants
→ 정답의 retail businesses

164-167 서신

스타넬로 로지스틱스
오스틴가 3400번지
미어 파크, 코네티컷주 06002

1월 12일

과달루페 마르티노
모반 솔루션즈
그린 애비뉴 1650번지
밴슨, 코네티컷주 06016

마르티노 씨께,

귀사의 창고 관리자 자리 지원자인 스튜어트 글로버 씨에 대한 추천서 요청에 답변 드립니다.

164저 자신도 창고 관리자로서, 4년 전 글로버 씨가 신입 포장물류 담당자로 입사했을 때 저는 그와 많은 접촉이 없었습니다. 하지만 1년 후 관리 직책에 공석이 있을 때 글로버 씨의 상사가 그를 그 자리에 승진시킬 것을 강력히 추천했습니다. 저는 그 제안을 수락했고 그렇게 한 것에 만족하고 있습니다.

지난 3년간 글로버 씨는 자신이 관리하는 사람들을 훌륭히 돕고 지도하는 타고난 지도자라는 점을 **165목격해왔습니다.** 글로버 씨는 종종 운영을 개선할 수 있는 방법을 찾았습니다. **166일례로, 직원들을 위해 기존 작업대를 높이 조정이 가능한 작업대로 교체할 것을 제안했습니다. 그렇게 했더니 생산성이 8% 상승했습니다.**

167글로버 씨와의 업무 경험과 보내주신 구인 광고를 살펴봤을 때, 글로버 씨를 채용하실 것을 자신 있게 추천합니다.

폴린 매시

미어 파크 지점 창고 관리자
스타넬로 로지스틱스

어휘 reference 신원 보증, 추천 applicant 지원자 warehouse 창고 entry-level 신입직의 handler 담당자 supervisory 감독의, 관리의 strongly recommend 강력히 추천하다 promote 승진시키다 observe 주시하다, 목격하다 deliver support 지원을 제공하다 guidance 지도 replace 교체하다 workbench 작업대 height-adjustable 높이 조절이 가능한 accommodate (요구에) 부응하다 in light of ~에 비추어 job listing 채용 공고 confidently 자신 있게

164 사실 관계 확인

번역 매시 씨가 스타넬로 로지스틱스에서 글로버 씨가 한 업무에 대해 언급한 것은?
(A) 세 개의 직책을 맡았다.
(B) 추천을 받아 채용됐다.
(C) 처음에는 글로버 씨의 업무 수행에 대해 큰 감흥이 없었다.
(D) 처음에는 글로버 씨와 가까이에서 일하지 않았다.

해설 두 번째 단락에서, 글로버 씨가 입사했을 당시를 얘기하며 '그와 많은 접촉을 하지 않았다(did not have much contact with Mr. Glover)'라고 말하고 있다. 따라서 (D)가 정답이다.

어휘 job title 직책 hire 채용하다 initially 처음에 unimpressed 대단하다고 생각되지 않는 performance 성과, 수행

▶▶ Paraphrasing 지문의 have much contact with
→ 정답의 work closely with

165 동의어 찾기

번역 세 번째 단락 1행의 "observed"와 의미가 가장 가까운 것은?
(A) 알았다
(B) 조사했다
(C) 기념했다
(D) 따랐다

해설 여기서 observe는 '주시하다, (봐서) 알다'라는 뜻이다. notice가 '보거나 듣고 알다, 주목하다'라는 뜻이므로 정답은 (A) noticed이다. (B) investigated(조사했다), (C) commemorated(기념했다), (D) obeyd(복종했다)는 모두 어울리지 않는다.

166 세부 사항

번역 스타넬로 로지스틱스는 창고의 생산성을 어떻게 향상시켰는가?
(A) 오래된 소프트웨어를 교체해서
(B) 직원들에게 장려금을 제공해서
(C) 맞춤형 장비를 제공해서
(D) 보관 창고의 배치를 바꿔서

해설 세 번째 단락에서, '기존 작업대를 높이 조정이 가능한(height-adjustable) 작업대로 교체해 생산성이 8% 상승했다'고 언급했으므로 (C)가 정답이다.

어휘 out-of-date 구식의, 낡은 incentive 장려책 customizable 맞춤형인 equipment 장비 layout 배치

▶▶ Paraphrasing 지문의 height-adjustable ones
→ 정답의 customizable equipment

167 사실 관계 확인

번역 매시 씨는 자신이 무엇을 검토했다고 명시하는가?
(A) 직책에 대한 설명
(B) 검사 결과
(C) 문서 포맷에 관한 지침
(D) 생산 관련 수치 요청

해설 마지막 단락에서 '귀하가 제공한 채용 공고(job listing)를 잘 살펴보건대'라고 말한 것으로 보아 채용 공고를 검토했음을 알 수 있다. 따라서 (A)가 정답이다.

어휘 description 기술, 서술 inspection 검사, 검토 guideline 지침 figure 수치

▶▶ **Paraphrasing** 지문의 **the job listing**
→ 정답의 **A description of a position**

---

168 -171 온라인 채팅

제프 놀런 [오후 2:44]	여기 있어요! 드디어 우리의 조립식 완구 세트에 관한 설문 자료를 입수했어요.
도나 호블랜드 [오후 2:45]	표적 집단들이 작성한 것이에요? **168잘됐네요. 제품 개발의 선임 디자이너인 로라**가 그 결과들을 간절히 알고 싶어 해요. 그녀를 대화에 초대할게요.
로라 테이텀 [오후 2:46]	안녕하세요 제프. 조사 결과가 나왔다니 기쁘네요. 부정적인 의견은 없었나요?
제프 놀런 [오후 2:47]	부모들이 반복해서 낸 의견이 하나 있었어요. "장난감을 담은 상자의 판지가 얇아서 장난감 조각들을 보관하기가 힘들다."
로라 테이텀 [오후 2:49]	문제가 될 수도 있겠네요. 어떻게 생각하세요?
도나 호블랜드 [오후 2:50]	마케팅 관리자로서, 포장이 좋아지면 브랜드 이미지가 높아질 거라는 데 동의해요. **169상자 디자인을 바꿀 수 있을까요?**
로라 테이텀 [오후 2:51]	아마도요. 사일레시의 팀이 그것을 처리할 수 있어요. 다른 문제들은 없었나요?
제프 놀런 [오후 2:53]	네, 실은 어린이들로부터 무작위로 받은 의견들이 있어요. "이 장난감은 가지고 놀기에 재미있다"―92%가 동의했어요. "나는 이 장난감을 원한다"―91%가 동의했어요. 대다수의 수치들이 이와 같았어요.
로라 테이텀 [오후 2:54]	오! 그래요? **170예상했던 것보다 훨씬 좋군요!**
도나 호블랜드 [오후 2:55]	정말 좋은 소식이네요. 자, 저는 이만 나갈게요.
로라 테이텀 [오후 2:56]	나중에 얘기해요, 도나. 제프? **171지금 제가 당신 사무실에 방문해도 될까요?** 우리 팀 회의를 하기 전에 설문 결과들을 살펴보고 싶어요.
제프 놀런 [오후 2:57]	물론이죠. 곧 봅시다.

어휘 survey data 설문 자료 construction toy 조립식 완구 focus group 표적 집단 senior designer 선임 디자이너

---

product development 제품 개발 be eager to+동사원형 ~하기를 고대하다, 갈망하다 result 결과 add 추가하다, 더하다 negative feedback 부정적인 의견[피드백] recurring 되풀이되는, 거듭 발생하는 comment 논평, 의견 cardboard box 판지 상자 store 보관하다, 저장하다 boost the brand's image 브랜드 이미지를 높이다[제고하다] handle 처리하다, 다루다 random 무작위의 indeed 정말로, 실제로

---

168 추론 / 암시

번역 테이텀 씨는 누구일 것 같은가?
(A) 제품 개발자
(B) 마케팅 관리자
(C) 웹디자이너
(D) 경리 임원

해설 2시 45분 대화 내용을 보면 제품 개발팀의 선임 디자이너인 로라(Laura, our senior designer ~ team) 씨를 대화에 초대하겠다는 말이 나온다. '제품 개발팀 디자이너'라는 직책과 가장 유사한 표현인 (A)가 정답이다.

---

169 세부 사항

번역 호블랜드 씨는 무엇을 하자고 제안하는가?
(A) 제품 가격을 인하하기
(B) 포장을 재디자인하기
(C) 질문을 다시 쓰기
(D) 추가 면접하기

해설 2시 50분 대사의 마지막 부분에서 상자 디자인을 바꿀 수 있을지(Could we change the box's design?)에 대해서 묻고 있다. 따라서 정답은 (B)이다

▶▶ **Paraphrasing** 지문의 **change the box's design**
→ 정답의 **Redesigning some packaging**

---

170 의도 파악

번역 오후 2시 54분에 테이텀 씨가 "그래요?"라고 쓴 의도는 무엇이겠는가?
(A) 일부 설문 절차를 잘 모르겠다.
(B) 몇몇 설문 결과가 놀랍다.
(C) 일부 자료가 부정확한 게 틀림없다고 생각한다.
(D) 일부 참가자의 연령을 확인하고 싶다.

해설 바로 뒤 문장의 '예상했던 것보다'라는 말을 통해서 기대했던 것보다 훨씬 긍정적인 결과가 나와서 놀랐다는 것을 알 수 있다. 정답은 (B)이다.

---

171 추론 / 암시

번역 놀런 씨는 다음에 무엇을 하겠는가?
(A) 표적 집단 회의 주재
(B) 보도 자료 검토
(C) 테이텀 씨와 만남
(D) IT 팀에 연락

해설 마지막 두 개의 대사를 살펴보면 테이텀 씨가 놀런 씨에게 사무실을 방문해도 되는지 물었을 때 놀런 씨가 곧 보자고 말한다. 놀런 씨와 테이텀 씨가 이 대화 이후에 만날 것이라는 것을 알 수 있으므로 정답은 (C)이다.

Test 7

172-175 기사

도시 소식   12월 22일

일하기 좋은 직장 명단에 오른 식료품 업체

멜뷰—지역 슈퍼마켓 체인인 데일샛 주식회사가 다시 한 번 일하기 좋은 직장으로 인정받았다.

이 회사는 올해의 일하기 좋은 직장 명단에서 지난해보다 두 단계 오른 3위를 차지했다.

멜뷰에 본사를 둔 데일샛 주식회사는 루미세도 지역 전역에서 107곳의 슈퍼마켓을 운영하고 있다. **172매장들은 '데일샛' 브랜드로 시판되는 견과류, 크래커류, 말린 과일류를 포함해 다양하게 엄선된 자연식품들을 제공한다.**

일하기 좋은 직장 시상 프로그램은 경제 전문 잡지들을 발행하는 대형 출판사 톱 컴퍼니즈 그룹이 운영한다. 인정을 받으려면 참여 회사들은 두 단계로 된 평가 과정을 거쳐야 한다. **175직원 만족도 조사 결과로 최고 80점까지 배점하는 한편, 직장 정책과 경영 철학을 검토해 최고 20점까지 채점한다. 합산된 점수로 최종 순위가 정해진다.** **173현재 대부분의 지역 회사들이 이 평가 프로그램에 참여하고 있지만, 소수의 작은 회사들은 아직 참여하지 않고 있다.**

톱 컴퍼니즈 그룹은 보고서에서 데일샛 주식회사가 직원들의 아이디어에 "따라 행동하는 것"을 칭찬했다. 부분적으로 자사 직원들의 의견을 토대로 이 체인 업체는 최근 개점한 브랜든 로드 매장에서 새로운 개념을 선보였다. 이 매장의 특징은 따뜻한 샌드위치와 차가운 샌드위치, 샐러드 바, 그리고 고객들이 쟁반에 음식을 담아가서 **174매장 내 테이블에서 먹을 수 있는 트레이 서비스 등이다.** 데일샛 주식회사의 에밀리 왕 부사장은 "이러한 변화는 우리 직원들의 개척 정신을 나타낸다"고 말했다.

어휘 grocery store 식료품점 be recognized as ~으로 인정받다 a wide selection of 다양하게 엄선된 ~ natural foods 자연식품 recognition 인정 go through 거치다, 겪다 evaluation process 평가 과정 earn (점수를) 따다 employee satisfaction survey 직원 만족도 조사 be based on ~에 근거[기초]하다, ~을 토대로 하다 workplace policy 직장 정책[방침] management philosophy 경영 철학 as of now 현재로선 participate in ~에 참여[참가]하다(= take part in) assessment program 평가 프로그램 praise 칭찬하다 act on ~에 따라 행동하다 unveil 베일을 벗다, 선보이다, 밝히다 concept 개념 feature ~을 특징[특색]으로 하다 tray service (쟁반에 음식을 담아가서 먹는) 트레이 서비스 pioneering spirit 개척 정신

---

172 사실 관계 확인

번역 데일샛 주식회사에 관해 언급된 것은?
(A) 100년이 넘었다.
(B) 자체적으로 만든 간식류를 판매한다.
(C) 잡지 회사가 인수했다.
(D) 본사를 이전할 계획이다.

해설 세 번째 단락 마지막 문장의 "'데일샛' 브랜드로 시판되는 견과류, 크래커류, 말린 과일류를 포함해 다양하게 엄선된 자연식품"이라는 부분을 통해서 정답이 (B)라는 것을 알 수 있다.

---

173 추론 / 암시

번역 일하기 좋은 직장 프로그램에 관해 암시된 것은?
(A) 분기마다 한 번씩 시상한다.
(B) 소기업들을 위한 별도의 카테고리가 있다.
(C) 최고의 회사들에게 상금을 준다.
(D) 프로그램 참여는 자발적이다.

해설 프로그램을 언급한 부분은 네 번째 단락에서 확인할 수 있는데, 마지막 문장에 대부분의 회사들은 참가를 하지만 참가하지 않는 회사들도 있다고 했으니 이 프로그램의 참여는 자유라는 것을 알 수 있다. 따라서 정답은 (D)이다.

---

174 세부 사항

번역 기사에 따르면, 데일샛이 최근에 선보인 새로운 특징은 무엇인가?
(A) 매장 내 식사 선택
(B) 가정 배달 서비스
(C) 셀프 계산대
(D) 직원 유니폼

해설 마지막 단락에서 정답을 확인할 수 있다. 최근 개점한 브랜든 로드 매장에서 새로운 개념을 선보였다고 하는데, 그것은 고객들이 '매장 내'에서 식사를 할 수 있도록 하는 서비스를 제공한다(The store features ~ inside the store.)는 것이다. 따라서 정답은 (A)이다.

---

175 문장 삽입

번역 [1], [2], [3], [4]로 표시된 곳 중에서 다음 문장이 들어가기에 가장 적합한 곳은?

"합산된 점수로 최종 순위가 정해진다."

(A) [1]
(B) [2]
(C) [3]
(D) [4]

해설 이 삽입문이 들어가려면, 그 앞에 점수 배점에 대한 언급이 필요하다. 그래야 '합산된 점수(The combined scores)'라는 말을 사용할 수 있기 때문이다. [3]번 바로 앞부분에서 평가 방식과 배점에 대한 설명이 나오고 있는 것으로 보아 (C)가 정답이다.

176-180 차트 + 편지

**올리바드 아파트 단지
쓰레기 처리 지침**

소재 종류	쓰레기통 색깔	내용
178종이	노란색	– 미용 티슈를 넣지 마십시오. – 마른 것이어야 하며 음식물 등을 넣지 마십시오.
플라스틱	파란색	– 스티로폼을 넣지 마십시오. – 지나친 물기나 음식물 같은 물질이 들어가면 안 됩니다. – 라벨은 떼지 않아도 됩니다.

177금속	보라색	– 소형 가전이나 배터리를 넣지 마십시오. – 지나친 물이나 음식물 같은 물질이 들어가면 안 됩니다. **– 금속 뚜껑은 캔 안에 넣어 주십시오.**
유리	하얀색	– 거울이나 도자기를 넣지 마십시오. **– 176쓰레기통에 넣기 전에 헹구어 주십시오.** – 라벨은 떼지 않아도 됩니다.
음식물 쓰레기	녹색	– 뼈다귀나 딱딱한 껍질을 넣지 마십시오.
기타	검은색	– 기타 위험하지 않은 소형 쓰레기를 넣어 주십시오.

어휘 waste 쓰레기, 폐기물 disposal 처리, 처분 excess 초과의 liquid 액체 remove 제거하다 appliance 가전제품 lid 뚜껑 rinse 헹구다 place 놓다, 두다 shell (달걀, 견과류 등의) 딱딱한 껍질 non-hazardous 위험하지 않은

올리바드 아파트 단지

1786월 1일

주민 여러분께,

단지 내 쓰레기 처리와 관련하여 다음 변경 사항을 안내해 드립니다.

→ 6월 10일부로, 특별 수거가 필요한 폐기물(가구 및 가전제품 등)은 서쪽 출입구 바로 옆이 아니라 북쪽으로 200야드 떨어진 곳에 두어야 합니다. '대형 물품 처리'라고 쓰인 표지판을 찾으십시오.

→ 178,179시민들의 쓰레기 재활용을 간소화하기 위한 시의 노력에 힘입어 이번 달부터는 종이와 플라스틱을 따로 재활용하지 않아도 됩니다. 종이 재활용에 사용했던 쓰레기통에 두 가지 소재를 모두 넣으십시오.

180아울러 단지 소유주들은 놀이터에 정기적으로 버려지는 쓰레기의 양이 지나치게 많아졌다는 결론을 내렸습니다. 소유주들은 단지 내에 쓰레기를 버리는 행위에 벌금을 25달러로 올리는 것을 고려하고 있습니다. 6월 30일 전까지 이 문제에 대한 의견을 관리사무소에 알려 주십시오.

데이먼 브룩스
아파트 단지 관리인

어휘 following 다음에 나오는 related to ~에 관해 as of ~일자로 entrance 입구 streamline 간소화하다 separately 별도로, 따로 recyclables 재활용품 in addition 게다가, 덧붙여 trash 쓰레기 regularly 정기적으로 playground (야외) 놀이터 excessive 지나친 fine 벌금 litter 쓰레기를 버리다 property 건물, 재산, 구내 register 표명하다

---

176 세부 사항

번역 표에 따르면, 사람들은 유리를 재활용 쓰레기로 버리기 전에 무엇을 해야 하는가?
(A) 물기 제거하기
(B) 제품에서 스티커 떼기
(C) 물로 씻어내기
(D) 색깔별로 분류하기

해설 표에서 유리 항목을 보면 '쓰레기통에 넣기 전에 헹구어 주십시오(Rinse before ~)'라는 말이 나온다. 따라서 (C)가 정답이다.

어휘 eliminate 제거하다 cleanse 세척하다 sort 분류하다

▶▶ **Paraphrasing** 지문의 Rinse
→ 정답의 Cleanse them with water

---

177 사실 관계 확인

번역 보라색 쓰레기통에 넣을 수 있는 것은?
(A) 납작하게 편 종이 상자
(B) 고장 난 밥솥
(C) 다 쓴 건전지
(D) 빈 음료수 캔

해설 보라색 쓰레기통인 '금속(Metal)' 항목에서 '금속 뚜껑을 캔 안에 넣으라'고 말한 것으로 보아, 캔을 보라색 쓰레기통에 넣을 수 있음을 알 수 있으므로 (D)가 정답이다. 소형 가전이나 건전지는 넣지 말라고 했다.

어휘 flattened 납작해진 cardboard 판지 rice cooker 밥솥 battery cell 전지 beverage 음료

---

178 연계

번역 6월부터 재활용 가능한 플라스틱은 어떤 색깔 쓰레기통에 넣어야 하는가?
(A) 노란색
(B) 파란색
(C) 하얀색
(D) 검은색

해설 편지에서 '이번 달부터 종이와 플라스틱을 분리하지 않으므로 종이 재활용 쓰레기통에 플라스틱까지 넣으라'고 안내했다. 표로 돌아가 보면 종이 재활용 통은 '노란색(Yellow)'이라고 되어 있다. (A)가 정답이다.

---

179 추론 / 암시

번역 재활용 정책이 변경된 이유는 무엇이겠는가?
(A) 단지 주민들이 불만을 제기해서
(B) 단지 소유주들이 비용 감축을 희망해서
(C) 신 기술을 이용할 수 있게 되어서
(D) 지역 정부 당국이 규제를 완화해서

해설 편지에 보면 '시의 노력에 힘입어(Thanks to the city's efforts)' 종이와 플라스틱을 분리하는 기존 방침이 변경되었다고 했다. 따라서 (D)가 정답이다.

어휘 lower 낮추다 available 이용 가능한 authority 정부 당국 relax (규정, 규칙을) 완화하다 regulation 규정, 규제

▶▶ **Paraphrasing** 지문의 the city → 정답의 A local authority

---

180 사실 관계 확인

번역 올리바드 아파트 단지에 대해 명시된 것은?
(A) 주요 출입구가 네 개 있다.
(B) 야외 놀이 시설이 갖춰져 있다.
(C) 가구 기부 프로그램을 운영한다.
(D) 쓰레기통에 재활용품을 넣는 행위에 대해 벌금을 부과한다.

해설 편지 마지막 단락에서 '놀이터(playground)'에 버려지는 쓰레기에 관해 언급했다. 놀이터는 야외 놀이 시설이라고 할 수 있으므로 (B)가 정답이다.

어휘 recreational 오락의, 여가의 donation 기부 impose 부과하다
trash bin 쓰레기통

▶▶ Paraphrasing 지문의 **the playground**
→ 정답의 **an outdoor recreational facility**

181-185 웹페이지 + 회의록

> http://www.marblerock.city.gov/council
>
> ### 마블록 시의회 회의
>
> 시의회는 매월 첫째, 셋째 화요일에 소집됩니다. 모든 회의는 클로버 스트리트 E. 93번지에 있는 시청에서 열립니다.
>
> **181**회의는 오후 6시 30분에 일반에 공개되지 않는 집행위원회 회의를 열면서 시작됩니다. 하지만 비공개 회의록은 회의가 끝난 후 열람할 수 있습니다.
>
> 출입문이 지역 주민들에게 7시 15분에 개방되며, 오후 7시 30분에 공개 회의 개회가 선언됩니다. **184**각각의 공개 회의는 지역 주민들이 각각 5분 이내로 발언할 수 있는 **182**의견 발표 시간과 함께 시작할 것입니다.
>
> 각 회의의 의제는 이 웹사이트에 게시되고 회의에 앞서 일요일에 〈클로버 스트리트 헤럴드〉 지에 발표될 것입니다.
>
> 시의회 회의록

어휘 city council 시의회 convene 모이다 town hall 시청
executive committee 집행위원회 closed 비공개의 minutes
회의록 community 지역사회, 주민 be called to order 개회가
선언되다 comment portion 의견 제시[논평] 시간 no more
than ~ 이내로 agenda 의제, 안건 post 게시하다 publish
발표하다, 출판[출간]하다 prior to ~에 앞서

> ### 시의회 회의록
>
> **날짜:** 6월 14일
>
> **참석 의원:** 테드 런스트, 캐리 호니그봄, 필 프레스턴, 조지 매스터즈
>
> **비공개 회의**
> 오후 6시 30분에 개회
>   1. **회의록 승인.** 회의록 정정 및 승인. 기권: 필 프레스턴
>   2. **예산 논의.** 시 재무관이 예산안을 제출함. 예산이 논의되었고 몇 가지 바꿀 내용이 제안되었음. **183**재무관이 예산안을 수정하기로 동의함. 심의를 위해 7월 27일로 특별 회의 일정이 잡힘.
> 오후 7시 10분에 산회.
>
> **공개 회의**
> 오후 7시 30분에 개회
>   1. 회의록 승인
>   2. **184**빌 브래디가 폴스 리버 지역의 보도 교체 현황에 대한 최신 정보를 요청함. 의회가 웹사이트에 최신 정보를 발표하는 데 동의함.

> 3. 건축 개발 회사 세 곳이 카토가 스트리트의 빈 학교 건물에 대한 제안서를 제출함. 제안서들은 시청 로비에 3주 동안 게시된 후 그것에 대해 주민 투표를 하기로 함.
>   4. 의회가 체스넛 스트리트와 메이플 스트리트 사이에 있는 메인 스트리트를 10월 3일 금요일, 오후 6시 30분부터 오후 9시 30분까지 **185**가을의 빛 등불 축제를 위해 차량 통제하는 것을 승인함.
> 오후 8시 15분에 산회

어휘 present 출석한, 참석한 meeting called to order 개회
선언 approval 승인 abstention 기권 city treasurer 시 재무관
propose 제안하다 agree 동의하다, 찬성하다 revise 수정하다 be
scheduled for+날짜 ~로 일정이 잡히다 meeting dismissed
산회 open session 공개 회의 request 요청하다 update 최신
정보 status 상황, 현황 sidewalk replacement 보도 교체
present 제출하다 proposal 제안서 empty 빈 post 게시하다
vote 투표하다 ban 금지하다 autumn 가을 lantern festival
등불 축제

181 세부 사항

번역 웹페이지에 따르면, 집행위원회 위원들은 언제 도착해야 하는가?
  (A) 오후 6시 30분까지
  (B) 오후 7시 15분까지
  (C) 오후 7시 30분까지
  (D) 오후 8시까지

해설 첫 번째 지문 두 번째 단락을 살펴보면 집행위원회 회의를 오후 6시 30분부터 시작한다는 말이 나온다. 집행위원회 위원들은 이 시간까지는 도착을 해야 회의에 참석을 할 수 있다는 것을 알 수 있다. 따라서 정답은 (A)이다.

182 동의어 찾기

번역 웹페이지에서 세 번째 단락 2행의 "portion"과 의미상 가장 가까운 것은?
  (A) 부문
  (B) 시간
  (C) 배경
  (D) 지문

해설 여기에서 portion은 전체 회의 시간에서 발언을 할 수 있는 '일정 시간'을 의미한다. 전체 시간에서 의견을 개진할 수 있는 '일부분, 시간'이라는 의미로 본다면 period와 동일한 의미라고 볼 수 있다. 따라서 정답은 (B) period이다.

183 세부 사항

번역 집행위원회의 특별 회의에서 논의될 내용은 무엇인가?
  (A) 정정된 회의록
  (B) 수정된 재정 계획
  (C) 빈 건물에 대한 제안서
  (D) 투표 결과

해설 두 번째 지문의 비공개 회의 항목 중 2번 내용을 보면 특별 회의(special meeting)에 대한 내용이 나오는데, 이 회의의 목적은 예산을 수정하기로 합의를 본 것에 대한 심의이므로, 정답은 (B)라는 것을 알 수 있다.

184 연계

번역 브래디 씨는 누구일 것 같은가?
(A) 건축 개발 회사 직원
(B) 〈클로버 스트리트 헤럴드〉의 기자
(C) 시 재무관
(D) 마블록 시의 주민

해설 빌 브래디(Bill Brady)라는 이름을 먼저 찾아보자. 두 번째 지문인 회의록의 Open Session 2번에 나온다. 그가 보도 교체에 대한 최신 정보를 요청했다고 했는데, 첫 번째 지문의 세 번째 단락을 보면, '각각의 회의에서 지역 주민들이 발언할 수 있는 기회가 5분씩 주어진다'고 언급하고 있다. 따라서 빌 브래디 씨가 마블록 시의 주민인 것을 확인할 수 있다. 따라서 정답은 (D)이다.

▶▶ **Paraphrasing** 지문의 **community members**
→ 정답의 **A resident of Marble Rock**

185 세부 사항

번역 시의회는 축제를 위해 무엇을 하기로 동의하는가?
(A) 보안 인력 추가 제공
(B) 소음 규제 해제
(C) 웹사이트에 광고
(D) 한 도로의 차량 통행 폐쇄

해설 두 번째 지문 후반부에서 정답을 확인할 수 있다. 축제(the Lights of Autumn lantern festival)로 인해 일정 시간 동안 거리의 차량 통제를 한다는 내용을 토대로 정답이 (D)라는 것을 알 수 있다.

▶▶ **Paraphrasing** 지문의 **the banning of vehicles**
→ 정답의 **Close a roadway to traffic**

186-190 회람+이메일+청구서

에니스 앤 레온 회계

발신: 션 구스타프슨
수신: 전 직원
제목: 청소 알림 공지
날짜: 4월 17일

3월에 공지한 바와 같이, 4월 25일 토요일과 **186**4월 27일 월요일에 사무실 대청소를 예약했습니다. 예약 날짜가 **187**가까워지고 있으므로 계획을 설명해 드리고자 합니다. 전날 금요일 오후에는 사무실 한쪽의 가구를 다른 한쪽으로 옮겨 사무실 일부가 토요일에 청소되도록 할 것입니다. 월요일에는 반대쪽이 진행됩니다. **186**따라서 월요일 아침 사무실에 보고한 다음 점심 이후 집에서 평소 업무를 완료해 주기 바랍니다.

188여러분이 미리 해 주어야 할 유일한 일은 청소부들이 제거해 줬으면 하는 얼룩에 대해 세부 사항(위치, 물질 등)을 저에게 알려 주는 것입니다. 청소부들이 4월 23일 오후 5시까지 그 정보를 전달받아 필요한 물품을 준비해야 합니다. 4월 24일, 27일, 28일에는 편한 복장으로 출근해서 가구를 옮기거나 다른 필요한 부분을 도와주십시오.

어휘 notify 알리다 appointment 예약, 약속 draw near 다가오다 preceding 바로 전의 reverse the process 과정을 거꾸로 하다 therefore 그러므로 complete 완료하다 beforehand 사전에 substance 물질 stain 얼룩 prepare 준비하다 supplies 용품

발신: 매들린 베이 〈m.bey@porcaro-cc.com〉
수신: 션 구스타프슨 〈sean.gustafson@ennis-leone.com〉
제목: 청소 서비스
날짜: 4월 28일
첨부: 청구서

구스타프슨 씨께,

4월 25일과 27일에 시행된 서비스에 관한 청구서를 첨부했습니다.

189아울러, 귀하의 사무실에 보냈던 청소부장이 저에게 전달해 달라고 부탁한 사항들이 있습니다. **188**첫째, 청소부장은 칸 씨가 책상 근처 커피 얼룩 제거 작업에 만족하셨기를 바랍니다. 그렇지 않을 경우 한 번 더 무료로 해 드리겠다고 제안했습니다. **190**둘째, 휴게실 의자 전체에 세탁 가능한 커버를 구입하시면 전문 청소를 다시 맡기지 않아도 된다고 합니다.

저희 포카로 커머셜 클리너스를 이용해 주셔서 다시 한 번 감사드립니다.

매들린 베이
고객 서비스 담당자

어휘 invoice 청구서, 송장 render 하다 offer 제안하다 for free 무료로 avoid 피하다 break room 휴게실 professionally 전문적으로 washable 세탁이 가능한

포카로 커머셜 클리너스
갈랜드가 602번지
페어팩스, 버지니아주 22030
(571) 555-0182

고객: 에니스 앤 레온 회계
서비스 일자: 4월 25일, 4월 27일　　　　　**지불 기한: 5월 31일**

서비스	개수 또는 제곱피트	단가	소계
카펫 세척	1450	0.40달러	580달러
창문 청소	14	3.00달러	42달러
190가구 청소	4	15.00달러	60달러
천장 청소	1850	0.40달러	740달러
		합계	1422달러

어휘 payment due 지불 기한

186 세부 사항

번역 구스타프슨 씨는 회람 수신인들에게 4월 27일에 무엇을 하라고 요청하는가?
(A) 오전에 청소 과정 감독
(B) 오전에 회의 참석
(C) 오후에 사무실 밖에서 근무
(D) 오후에 가구 비치 구역 청소

해설 회람 시작 부분을 보면 4월 27일은 월요일이다. 첫 번째 단락에서 '월요일 아침에 사무실에 보고하고 이후에는 집에서 업무를 완료하라고 (complete your regular tasks from home after lunch)' 요청했다. 따라서 (C)가 정답이다.

어휘 recipient 수신인 oversee 감독하다 off-site 부지 밖에서 furnishing 가구

▶▶ **Paraphrasing** 지문의 **complete your regular tasks from home after lunch**
→ 정답의 **Work off-site during the afternoon**

187 동의어 찾기

번역 회람의 첫 번째 단락 2행의 "drawing"과 의미가 가장 가까운 것은?
(A) 스케치하는
(B) 끄는
(C) 다가오는
(D) 어울리는

해설 draw near가 '다가오다, 접근하다'라는 뜻이므로 질문의 drawing은 (C) coming과 의미가 가장 가깝다.

어휘 sketch 스케치하다 attract 마음을 끌다 match 어울리다; 연결시키다

188 연계

번역 칸 씨에 대해 암시된 것은?
(A) 3월에 공지를 받지 않았다.
(B) 칸 씨의 책상을 베이 씨가 옮겼다.
(C) 칸 씨의 업무 공간은 4월 25일에 청소했다.
(D) 그는 구스타프슨 씨에게 문제를 미리 알렸다.

해설 구스타프슨 씨가 전 직원에게 보낸 회람에 보면 두 번째 단락에서 '제거해야 할 얼룩에 대해 자신에게 미리 알려주면 청소부들이 제거하도록 하겠다'는 내용이 나온다. 그런데 청소 업체에서 보낸 이메일에 보면 '칸 씨가 커피 얼룩 제거 작업에 만족했기를 바란다'는 언급이 있다. 따라서 칸 씨는 얼룩에 대해 사전에 구스타프슨 씨에게 알렸을 것으로 짐작할 수 있으므로 (D)가 정답이다.

어휘 notification 공지 alert 알리다 in advance 미리

189 추론

번역 베이 씨가 포카로 커머셜 클리너스에 대해 암시한 것은?
(A) 한 명 이상의 청소부가 있다.
(B) 신용카드로만 지불할 수 있다.
(C) 에니 앤 레온 회계에 정기적으로 서비스를 제공하기 시작할 것이다.
(D) 바닥 보호 깔개를 설치할 수 있다.

해설 베이 씨가 보낸 이메일을 보면 두 번째 단락 첫 문장에서 '귀하의 사무실에 보낸 청소부장이(the leader of the crew)'라는 언급이 나온다. 청소 작업원이 여러 명임을 알 수 있으므로 (A)가 정답이다.

어휘 install 설치하다 protective 보호하는

190 연계

번역 베이 씨는 청구서의 어떤 금액을 향후 아낄 수 있다고 언급하는가?
(A) 42달러
(B) 60달러
(C) 580달러
(D) 740달러

해설 이메일에서 '휴게실 의자 전체에 세탁 가능한 커버를 구입하면 전문 청소를 다시 맡기지 않아도 된다'고 말했다. 송장을 보면 '가구 청소(furniture cleaning)' 항목에 들어간 돈이 60달러이다. 따라서 60달러가 절약 가능하므로 정답은 (B)이다.

191-195 웹페이지 + 회람 + 후기

www.gosilconationalpark.com/info/trails

| 홈 | 정보 | 뉴스 | 연락처 |

정보 〉 트레일

고실코 국립공원의 등산로들은 쉬운 길부터 어려운 길, 스스로 찾아가는 길부터 안내인이 인솔하는 길, 반나절부터 이틀에 걸쳐 가는 코스까지 다양합니다. 여러 날 동안 이어지는 등산에 참여하는 방문객들은 모두 등산을 하기 전에 **191야영지 숙박 시설을 예약해야 합니다.** 또한, 모든 등산로는 기상 조건 때문에 사전 공지 없이 폐쇄될 수도 있습니다.

실반 트레일: 이 24km의 산책로는 고실코의 아름다운 자연을 구경하기에 더할 나위 없이 좋은 길입니다. 이 도보 여행은 등산객들을 인도해 숲을 통과하고 강가를 지나 실반 폭포에서 끝납니다. 등산객들은 안내인이 동반해야 합니다.

펩 호숫길: 펩 호수 남쪽 가를 따라 여유롭게 걸어 보십시오. 이 8km 구간 길은 평탄하고 평평합니다. 들어가고 나오는 길이 많아서 방문객들은 한 지점에서 시작하고 끝내지 않아도 됩니다.

카비 언덕길: 스스로 찾아가는 이 등산로는 카비 언덕 꼭대기에서 끝나며, 그곳에서 **192(D)펩 호수의 아름다운 광경을 볼 수 있습니다.** 등산객들은 **192(B)이 11km 구간의 오르막길을 걷기 위해 192(A)등산화를 착용해야 합니다.** 카비 언덕길은 성수기에만 이용할 수 있습니다.

데이지 레인: 이 중급 수준의 14km 등산로를 따라가면 등산객들은 데이지 숲을 통과하게 될 것입니다. 이 숲은 고실코에서 사람들이 희귀조인 **195재니토 새**를 얼핏 볼 수 있는 유일한 장소입니다. 이 등산로는 홀로 또는 안내인과 함께 걸을 수 있습니다.

어휘 trail 등산로, 산길 range from A to B 범위가 A에서 B까지 이르다 self-guided 스스로 찾아가는 participate in ~에 참여[참가]하다 be required to + 동사원형 ~해야 한다, ~할 필요가 있다 book 예약하다 campsite 야영지 accommodations 숙박 시설 hike 하이킹, 도보 여행 without prior notice 사전 공지[안내] 없이 due to weather conditions 기상 조건 때문에 the perfect way to + 동사원형 ~하기에 딱 좋은 방법 waterfall 폭포 accompany 동반하다 take a leisurely walk 여유롭게 걷다 smooth 매끄러운 flat 평평한 entrance 입구 exit 출구 at one point 한 지점에서 at the top of ~의 꼭대기에 stunning views 눈부시게 아름다운 경치 hiking boots 등산화 uphill 오르막의 peak season 성수기 intermediate 중급의 catch a glimpse of ~을 어렴풋이 보다 rare 희귀한

회람

수신: 부서 관리자들

발신: 포티야 우더드

제목: 산행

날짜: 4월 14일

허칭스 제약의 연례 산행을 5월 18일에 고실코 국립공원으로 **193**가려고 합니다. 오늘 밤에 제가 이메일로 행사에 관해 모든 사람에게 자세히 설명하겠습니다. 관심 있는 모든 사람이 함께하도록 독려해 주시기 바랍니다. **194**20명 이상이 신청하면 허칭스 제약은 전속 안내인 두 명이 동행하는 대규모 집단에 맞도록 구성된 특별 단체 등반 자격을 얻게 됩니다. 4월 28일까지 제게 참가자 명단을 보내 주시기 바랍니다.

어휘 pharmaceutical 제약회사 yearly 1년에 한 번 하는 head to ~로 가다, 향하다 detailed 자세한, 상세한 description 설명, 묘사 encourage 장려하다, 권장하다 join 함께하다, 합류하다 sing up 참가하다, 등록하다, 가입하다 qualify for ~할 자격을 얻다 private guide 전속 안내인 participant 참가자

---

www.gosilconationalpark.com/info/trails/reviews

| 홈 | 정보 | 뉴스 | 연락처 |

후기 작성자: 줄리엣 캠포스

날짜: 5월 21일

★★★★☆

며칠 전에 허칭스 제약의 동료들과 함께 고실코 국립공원을 방문해서 아주 즐거운 시간을 보냈다. 우리는 인원이 많아서 특별 단체 등반에 참여했다. **194**우리의 안내인인 켄과 리사는 자생식물들을 지목해서 알려 주고 땅의 지질학적 특성도 설명해 주었다. 우리는 운 좋게 **195**재니토 새도 두 마리나 보았다! 나는 고실코에 여행해 볼 것을 강력히 추천한다.

어휘 coworker 직장 동료 participate in ~에 참여[참가]하다 point out 가리키다, 지목하다 native plant 자생식물 geology 지질학(적 특성) highly recommend 강력히 추천하다

---

191 사실 관계 확인

번역 고실코 국립공원에 관해 명시된 것은?
(A) 1박을 할 수 있는 야영지들이 있다.
(B) 겨울철에는 들어갈 수 없다.
(C) 공원 직원들이 멸종 위기종에 관한 연구를 한다.
(D) 방문객들이 등산로를 도보 여행하려면 등록해야 한다.

해설 웹페이지 첫 번째 단락 후반부에서 야영지를 예약해야 한다(are required to book campsite accommodations)고 했으므로 고실코 국립공원에 야영지가 있다는 것을 알 수 있다. 따라서 정답은 (A)이다.

---

192 사실 관계 확인

번역 카비 언덕길에 관해 주어지지 않은 정보는?
(A) 권장되는 복장
(B) 등산로의 길이
(C) 시작 지점
(D) 등산객에게 보이는 전망

해설 웹페이지의 카비 언덕길을 설명하는 단락에서 답을 확인할 수 있다. (A)는 '등산화(hiking boots)를 착용하라'는 말에서, (B)는 '11km 오르막길(uphill 11-kilometer track)'이라는 말에서, (D)는 '펩 호수의 아름다운 광경(stunning views of Lake Pep)을 볼 수 있다'는 말에서 확인할 수 있다. 따라서 주어지지 않은 정보는 (C)이다

---

193 동의어 찾기

번역 회람에서 첫 번째 단락 2행의 "head"와 의미상 가장 가까운 것은?
(A) (길을) 안내하다
(B) 가다
(C) 연기하다
(D) 생각하다

해설 head는 특정 방향으로 '향하다, 이동하다'라는 의미의 단어이다. 따라서 head to 대신에 go to라고 바꿔도 같은 의미이다. 정답은 (B) go이다.

---

194 연계

번역 허칭스 제약의 산행에 관해 사실일 것 같은 것은?
(A) 사진 찍기를 좋아하는 사람들을 대상으로 했다.
(B) 며칠 연기되었다.
(C) 캄포스 씨가 구성했다.
(D) 참가 인원이 20명이 넘었다.

해설 두 번째 지문에서 참가 인원이 20명이 넘으면 전속 안내인 두 명이 동행한다고 했고, 세 번째 지문에서 '우리의 안내인이었던 켄과 리사(Our guides, Ken and Lisa)'라는 말이 나왔다. 이를 통해 허칭스 제약의 산행이 20명이 넘은 특별 단체 등반이었던 것을 알 수 있다. 따라서 정답은 (D)이다.

---

195 연계

번역 캠포스 씨는 어느 등산로를 도보 여행했을 것 같은가?
(A) 실반 트레일
(B) 펩 호숫길
(C) 카비 언덕길
(D) 데이지 레인

해설 세 번째 지문에서 캠포스 씨는 재니토 새를 두 마리나 보았다고 했다. 첫 번째 지문에서 재니토 새가 나오는 부분을 찾아보니, 마지막에 소개된 데이지 레인(Daisy Lane)에서 볼 수 있다는 말이 나온다. 따라서 정답은 (D)이다.

196-200 웹페이지 + 온라인 양식 + 일정

http://www.safa.org/events/conference

홈	소개	회원제도	자료	행사

항공 승무원 남부 협회
제25차 컨퍼런스
페리에타 컨벤션 센터, 10월 5-6일

196항공 승무원 남부 협회(SAFA)에서는 유익하고 고무적인 모임의 25주년을 기념하여, 항공 승무원을 위한 최초의 교육 센터가 있었던 곳 중 하나인 페리에타에서 올해 회의를 개최함으로써 우리 직업의 지난날을 기념하기로 결정했습니다. **197(B)**아울러 오랫동안 SAFA의 중책을 맡아온 베시 앨런 씨가 지난 경력을 거치며 목도한 변화에 대해 기조 연설을 해 주실 예정입니다.

하지만 컨퍼런스에는 우리 업계의 현재와 미래에 큰 관심을 갖는 분들께 제공해 드릴 많은 내용이 있습니다. **197(A),(D)**참가자분들은 고무적인 발표, 즐거운 만남의 기회, 최신 기내용 제품을 구비한 업체 부스 등을 접하실 수 있습니다.

198조식, 중식, 석식이 포함된 컨퍼런스 2일 참석권, 또는 일정을 자유롭게 조정할 수 있는 1일 참석권을 구입하시려면 여기를 클릭하세요. SAFA 회원은 두 가지 참석권 모두 20% 할인을 받으실 수 있습니다.

어휘 association 협회 flight attendant 항공 승무원 celebrate 기념하다, 축하하다 quarter 1/4 informative 유익한, 유용한 정보를 주는 inspiring 고무적인 gathering 모임, 집회 profession 직업 long-time 오랜 give a keynote address 기조 연설을 하다 stimulating 자극이 되는, 고무적인 meet-and-greet 만나는 stocked with ~가 구비된 cutting-edge 최신의 in-flight 기내의 flexibility 융통성

http://www.safa.org/events/conference/reg

제25차 회의
신청서

이름: 히스 와이스
소속단체: 와스켄 항공
직급: 일반 승무원
SAFA 회원이십니까? 예 ☒ 아니오 ☐
회원 ID: 04329
주소: 아파트 202호, 샌드가 5660번지, 털사, OK, 74120
연락처: (918) 555-0174
이메일: h.weiss@waskenair.com

198참석권 유형: 2일 참석권 ☒ 1일 참석권 ☐ (10/5 ☐ 10월 6일 ☐)

저희가 향후 행사를 준비하는 데 도움이 될 수 있도록 본 회의 참석 목적을 말씀해 주십시오. **200**이 분야에 막 발을 들여놓은 사람으로서, 향후 선택 사항에 대해 더 알아보고 직업상의 인맥을 쌓고 싶습니다.

제출 →

(다음 페이지에서는 결제 관련 사항을 입력하셔야 합니다.)

어휘 registration form 신청서 start out 시작하다 make connections 인맥을 쌓다

항공 승무원 남부 협회
제25차 컨퍼런스
10월 5일 일정

시간	행사	장소
오전 8-9시	조식	카페테리아
오전 9 -10:30	'상대방의 입장에서' (한나 새들러, 드본 대학교) - 승객 체험에 대한 연구를 바탕으로 기대 서비스 향상을 위한 조언 제공	102호
오전 10:45 -오후 12:15	'준비가 되셨나요?' (차오 양, 앨그레인 컨설팅) - 비행 중 겪는 일반적 의료 상황 소개 및 조치법 설명	104호
오후 12:15 -1:15	중식	카페테리아
오후 1:30 -3시	'최고의 음식' (카일 잔, 구스티나 이벤츠) - **199**수십 년간 모든 곳에서 최고의 요리를 만들고 싶어나르고 제공하면서 얻은 비결 전수	103호
오후 3:30 -5시	'여정을 계획하며' (디드러 피츠제럴드, 링크웨스트 항공) - **200**항공 승무원들에게 열려 있는 직업적 계발 기회 및 진로 논의	104호
오후 6-8시	마무리 연회	대연회장

어휘 based on ~에 기반하여 passenger 승객 improve 향상시키다 medical situation 의료 상황 deal with ~를 다루다, 처리하다 fare 식사, 음식 pass on 전수하다 gain 얻다 decade 10년 professional 전문적인, 직업의 career path 진로

196 세부 사항

번역 컨퍼런스는 왜 페리에타에서 개최되는가?
(A) 페리에타가 가진 역사적 의의 때문에
(B) 페리에타가 중심지에 위치하고 있어서
(C) 페리에타에 훌륭한 운송 서비스가 있어서
(D) 페리에타는 SAFA의 새로운 본부가 있는 곳이기 때문에

해설 웹페이지 첫 부분에 보면 페리에타에서 올해 회의를 개최한다고 알리면서 '최초의 항공 승무원 교육 센터가 있었던 곳 중 하나(the location of one of the first training centers for flight attendants)'라고 페리에타를 설명하고 있다. 따라서 (A)가 정답이다.

어휘 significance 중요성, 의의 headquarters 본사, 본부

197 사실 관계 확인

번역 웹페이지에서 컨퍼런스의 일부로 언급되지 않은 것은?
(A) 인적 네트워크 형성 행사
(B) SAFA 간부의 연설
(C) 인근 현장 견학
(D) 진열된 상품

해설 컨퍼런스에서 오랫동안 SAFA의 중책을 맡아온 베시 앨런 씨의 기조 연설 (B), 즐거운 만남의 기회(A), 최신 기내용 제품을 구비한 업체 부스(D) 등을 접할 수 있다고 소개했다. 현장 견학에 대한 언급은 없으므로 (C)가 정답이다.

어휘 networking 인적 네트워크 형성 field trip 현장학습 nearby 인근의 merchandise 상품

198 연계

번역 와이스 씨에 대해 암시된 것은?
(A) 신청 할인을 받을 자격이 없다.
(B) 회의 전에 식사 비용을 치를 것이다.
(C) 숙소가 필요하지 않을 것이다.
(D) 회사에서 경비를 환급해 줄 것이다.

해설 신청서 양식을 보면 와이스 씨는 '2일 참석권'을 선택했다. 웹페이지 마지막 단락을 보면 '조식, 중식, 석식이 포함된 회의 2일 참석권(a two-day conference pass that includes breakfasts, lunches, and dinners)을 구입하려면 클릭해 신청하라'는 말이 나온다. 사전에 신청하면서 식사 비용을 미리 치르는 것이 되므로 (B)가 정답이다.

어휘 be eligible for ~할 자격이 있다 accommodations 숙소 reimburse 변상하다, 배상하다

199 추론 / 암시

번역 잔 씨는 누구이겠는가?
(A) 전문 의료인
(B) 수하물 담당자
(C) 행사 음식 제공업자
(D) 비행기 조종사

해설 행사 일정표 중 '최고의 음식' 강연 항목을 보면 연사가 카일 잔으로 되어 있고, '수십 년간 다양한 곳에서 최고의 요리를 만들고 실어나르고 제공하면서(making, transporting, and serving) 얻은 비결 전수'라는 설명이 나온다. 이는 행사 음식 제공업자가 하는 일이므로 (C)가 정답이다.

어휘 handler 담당자

200 연계

번역 와이스 씨는 누구의 연설에 가장 흥미를 느끼겠는가?
(A) 새들러 씨
(B) 양 씨
(C) 잔 씨
(D) 피츠제럴드 씨

해설 와이스 씨는 신청서 맨 아래, 회의 참석 목적을 밝히는 부분에서 '향후 선택 사항에 대해 더 알아보고 직업상의 인맥을 쌓고 싶다'고 밝혔다. 일정표를 보면 디드러 피츠제럴드의 연설 '여정을 계획하며'가 '항공 승무원에게 열려 있는 직업적 계발 기회 및 진로를 논의한다'고 설명되어 있다. 와이스 씨는 피츠제럴드 씨의 연설에 흥미를 가질 것으로 추측할 수 있으므로 (D)가 정답이다.

어휘 presentation 발표

101 (A)	102 (B)	103 (C)	104 (C)	105 (B)
106 (A)	107 (C)	108 (B)	109 (D)	110 (D)
111 (A)	112 (B)	113 (C)	114 (D)	115 (C)
116 (A)	117 (B)	118 (C)	119 (C)	120 (C)
121 (A)	122 (D)	123 (B)	124 (D)	125 (D)
126 (A)	127 (D)	128 (B)	129 (A)	130 (A)
131 (A)	132 (D)	133 (C)	134 (B)	135 (D)
136 (B)	137 (D)	138 (A)	139 (B)	140 (D)
141 (C)	142 (A)	143 (D)	144 (A)	145 (B)
146 (A)	147 (D)	148 (A)	149 (A)	150 (B)
151 (D)	152 (B)	153 (C)	154 (D)	155 (A)
156 (A)	157 (C)	158 (C)	159 (D)	160 (D)
161 (C)	162 (B)	163 (B)	164 (C)	165 (A)
166 (B)	167 (D)	168 (D)	169 (D)	170 (D)
171 (B)	172 (B)	173 (C)	174 (C)	175 (D)
176 (B)	177 (A)	178 (D)	179 (C)	180 (C)
181 (C)	182 (C)	183 (D)	184 (A)	185 (D)
186 (D)	187 (A)	188 (C)	189 (A)	190 (C)
191 (C)	192 (B)	193 (C)	194 (B)	195 (C)
196 (C)	197 (D)	198 (D)	199 (B)	200 (C)

PART 5

101 명사 어휘

해설 빈칸 앞 shipping이라는 말과 함께 쓰기 적합한 단어가 들어가야 한다. 제품의 적절한 배송 '요금'이라는 말이 가장 자연스러우므로, 정답은 (A) rates(요금)이다. (B) facilities는 '시설' 또는 '기능', (C) supervisors는 '상사, 관리자', (D) evaluations는 '평가'라는 의미이다.

번역 불안정한 연료 가격은 우리 제품의 적절한 운송료 책정을 어렵게 만든다.

어휘 unstable 불안정한 fuel price 연료비 appropriate 적절한 shipping 배송

102 명사 자리 _ 관사와 형용사 뒤

해설 관사와 형용사가 수식해줄 수 있는 명사가 들어가야 하는 자리이다. 보기 중에서 품사가 명사인 것은 (B) correction(수정, 정정)이다.

번역 편집자는 그 기사의 인터넷 판을 즉시 수정할 수 있었다.

어휘 editor 편집자 immediate 즉각적인 make a correction 고치다 article 기사 correctly 바르게

103 부사 어휘

해설 VIP석이 다 차면 일부 사람들은 '다른 어딘가'에 앉아야 한다는 의미가 가장 적절하다. '다른 곳'이라는 뜻의 (C) elsewhere가 정답이다. (A) otherwise는 '그렇지 않으면', (B) instead는 '대신에', (D) even은 '~조차, 심지어'라는 의미이다.

번역 앞 줄에 있는 VIP석이 이미 다 찼기 때문에, 일부 존경받는 귀빈들은 다른 곳

에 앉아야 할 것이다.

어휘 row 줄, 열 occupy 차지하다 esteemed 존중받는, 존경받는

104 소유대명사

해설 빈칸은 부사절 접속사(after)가 이끄는 부사절 내 동사(were cancelled)의 주어 역할을 하는 자리이므로, 정답은 소유대명사 (C) theirs이다. 참고로 소유대명사 theirs는 their flights를 대신한다.

번역 승객 수백 명이 자신들의 항공편이 컴퓨터 시스템 오류로 인해 취소된 이후 항공편을 다시 예약하려고 기다리고 있다.

어휘 rebook 다시 예약하다 flight 항공편 cancel 취소하다 due to ~ 때문에 error 오류, 실수 themselves 그들 자신

105 형용사 자리 _ 명사 수식

해설 빈칸은 뒤의 명사를 수식해주는 형용사가 들어갈 자리이다. '특별한, 뛰어난'이라는 뜻으로 뒤에 있는 '음식 서비스'를 수식할 수 있는 형용사인 (B) exceptional이 적절하다. 따라서 정답은 (B)이다.

번역 클라크 케이터링은 25년간 지역사회에 뛰어난 음식 서비스를 제공했다.

어휘 local community 지역사회 exceptionally 특별히, 예외적으로 exception 예외 excepting ~을 제외하고

106 동사 시제

해설 문장 맨 뒤의 yesterday(어제)가 힌트가 된다. 과거 시제를 나타내는 부사이므로, 동사도 과거형을 써야 한다. 따라서 정답은 (A) departed이다.

번역 레인타운으로 가는 마지막 기차는 어제 오후 11시 17분에 도심에서 출발했다.

107 전치사 어휘

해설 move는 동사의 의미상 '움직임'이 있는 전치사와 어울린다. '~ 안으로 이동하다, 이사하다'라는 의미를 완성하는 전치사 (C) into가 정답이다. into 대신 to를 써도 된다.

번역 제프리즈 씨가 동쪽 사무실로 이동하면 모든 기술자가 같은 층에서 일할 수 있는 공간이 있을 것이다.

어휘 room for ~를 위한 공간 engineer 기술자, 엔지니어, 기사

108 동사 어휘

해설 자신의 연구 결과(his findings)를 이사회에 '발표하다, 알리다'라는 의미가 문맥상 가장 적절하다. 공식석상에서 어떤 사실을 알린다고 할 때 announce(발표하다)라는 단어를 사용하므로 정답은 (B) announced이다. (A) collaborated(협력했다)는 자동사이기 때문에 뒤에 목적어가 나오려면 with로 연결해야 한다. (C) invested는 '투자했다', (D) acquired는 '습득[획득]했다'라는 의미로 문맥상 어색하다.

번역 이시다 씨는 10월에 열린 정기 회의에서 이사회에 자신의 연구 결과를 발표했다.

어휘 findings 연구 결과 board 이사회

109 부사 어휘

해설 뒷부분의 prompt라는 단어가 이 문장에서 정답을 고르는 열쇠이다. 모든 직원들이 빠른 피드백을 받기 위해서 인사고과서를 쓸 때 '어떻게' 써야 하는지를 묻고 있는 문제다. (D) quickly(빨리)가 정답이다.

번역 관리자들은 연례 인사고과서를 빨리 작성하여 직원들이 신속한 피드백을 받을 수 있도록 해야 한다.

어휘 annual review 연례 인사고과서 prompt 신속한 suddenly 갑자기 rather 꽤, 약간 forward 앞으로

110 형용사 자리 _ 목적보어

해설 5형식 〈make + 목적어 + 목적보어〉 구문으로 빈칸에는 형용사 보어가 와야 한다. 빈칸 뒤 전치사 to와 함께 '~에게 소중한, 귀중한'이라는 뜻을 지닌 형용사 (D) valuable이 정답이다.

번역 헨더슨 씨의 이전의 회계 부문 경험은 그를 팀의 귀중한 존재로 만들어 준다.

어휘 previous 이전의 accounting 회계 value 가치

111 접속사 자리

해설 콤마(,)로 연결된 두 개의 문장을 연결하는 접속사가 들어갈 자리이다. (A) When(~할 때)과 (C) Whether(~인지 아닌지)가 접속사인데, (C) Whether는 '~인지 아닌지' 불확실성을 설명할 때 쓰기 때문에 이 문장에서는 어색하다. 기록을 세웠을 때 보너스를 받았다는 '시기'에 관한 의미가 들어가야 하기 때문에 정답은 (A) When이다.

번역 생산부가 분기 기록을 세웠을 때 팀 전원은 상여금을 받았다.

어휘 set a record 기록을 세우다 quarterly 분기의 earn a bonus 상여금을 받다

112 형용사 어휘

해설 현재분사(holding)의 목적어 역할을 하는 명사(passport)를 수식할 가장 알맞은 형용사를 고르는 문제다. 문맥상 '유효한 여권을 소지한'이라는 의미가 자연스러우므로 정답은 (B) valid(유효한)이다. (A) sizable(크기가 상당한), (C) willing(기꺼이 하는), (D) steady(꾸준한)은 모두 의미상 적절하지 않다.

번역 유효한 여권을 소지한 모든 시민은 정부의 여행자 안전 경보 프로그램에 등록할 자격이 있습니다.

어휘 citizen 시민 hold 지참하다 eligible to + 동사원형 ~할 자격이 있는 alert 경계 태세[경보]

113 전치사 자리

해설 빈칸 뒤 명사구(this wonderful series of paintings)를 목적어로 취하는 전치사 자리로, 빈칸을 포함한 전치사구는 앞에 있는 명사(artist)를 수식한다. 따라서 정답은 전치사 (C) behind(~ 뒤의)이다. 수량형용사 (A) both(둘 다)는 복수명사를 한정 수식하고, 접속부사 (B) therefore (그러므로)는 명사를 목적어로 취할 수 없다. 또한, 부사절 접속사 (D) while(~하는 동안) 뒤에는 완전한 절이 나와야 하므로 품사상 적합하지 않다.

114 부사 자리

번역 이 팜플릿은 미술관 방문객들에게 이 훌륭한 그림 시리즈의 배후에 있는 화가를 접하게 해줄 것이다.

어휘 pamphlet 팜플릿, 소책자 introduce A to B A를 B에 접하게 하다 gallery 화랑, 미술관 artist 화가 painting 그림

해설 자동사로 끝났고 뒤에 곧바로 전치사구가 이어지기 때문에 빈칸은 시각과 함께 쓰이며 동사를 수식할 수 있는 부사 (D) exactly(정확히, 틀림없이)가 와야 가장 적절하다.

번역 방산 기술 분야 선도자들의 연설이 있을 올해 세계기술정상회의는 정확히 정오 12시에 시작할 예정이다.

어휘 summit 정상회담 defense technology 방산 기술 exact 정확한 exactness 정확함

115 전치사 어휘

해설 빈칸은 명사구(serious attempts)를 목적어로 취하는 전치사 자리로, 빈칸을 포함한 전치사구는 동사(failed)를 수식한다. 문맥상 '진지한 노력에도 불구하고 실패했다'라는 양보의 의미가 자연스러우므로 (C) despite(~에도 불구하고)이 정답이다. (A) by(~ 옆에; ~에 의해), (B) against(~에 반하여), (D) regarding(~에 관해)는 모두 의미상 적절하지 않다.

번역 팔리암 사와의 계약 갱신 협상은 타협에 이르고자 하는 진지한 노력에도 불구하고 실패했다.

어휘 contract renewal 계약 갱신 negotiation 협상, 협의 serious 진지한 attempt 시도, 노력 reach ~에 이르다[도달하다] compromise 타협

116 부사 어휘

해설 빈칸 뒤에 5월에 열어서 9월에 닫는다는 말이 나오기 때문에 '계절적으로, 정기적으로'라는 뜻의 (A) seasonally가 적절하다. (B) gradually는 '점진적으로', (C) especially는 '특히', (D) absolutely는 '전적으로'라는 의미로 문맥상 어색하다.

번역 롤랜드 월드 놀이공원은 해당 연도의 5월에 개장하고 9월에 폐장하여 계절별로 운영한다.

어휘 amusement park 놀이공원 operate 영업하다

117 명사 자리 _ 목적어

해설 동사 allow의 목적어이면서, 형용사(commercial)가 수식해 줄 수 있는 명사가 들어가야 하는 자리이다. (A)와 (B)가 명사인데 둘 다 가산명사이기 때문에 (A)가 정답이 되려면 commercial 앞에 관사가 있거나 또는 builders가 되어야 한다. 따라서 정답은 (B) buildings이다.

번역 지역 주민들의 반대에도 불구하고 체리 스트리트의 북쪽 끝 지역은 상업용 건물이 허가되도록 재구분되었다.

어휘 notwithstanding ~에도 불구하고 opposition 반대 rezone 지역을 재구분하다 commercial 상업의 builder 건축업자

118 형용사 자리 _ 명사 수식

해설 financing은 '융자'라는 뜻의 명사이다. 따라서 소유격과 명사 사이에 들어갈 수 있는 형용사를 고르는 문제이다. 문맥상 '적정한 융자'라는 의미가 되는 (C) reasonable(적정한, 타당한)이 정답이다.

번역 구매자들은 웨스트 노리치 자동차의 적정한 융자와 경쟁력 있는 가격에 분명히 만족하며 차를 가져갈 것입니다.

어휘 drive away 차를 타고 떠나다 financing 자금 조달, 융자 competitive 경쟁력 있는 reason 이유; 이성 reasoning 추리, 추론

119 주격 관계대명사

해설 앞의 사물 선행사(a social media campaign)를 받으면서 동사 tripled의 주어 역할까지 겸할 수 있는 주격 관계대명사를 고르는 문제이다. 정답은 (C) that이다.

번역 마케팅 부사장인 박 씨는 온라인 참여를 거의 세 배로 만든 소셜 미디어 캠페인을 시작했다.

어휘 launch 시작하다 nearly 거의 triple 세 배로 만들다 engagement 참여

120 명사 어휘

해설 빈칸 앞의 sales와 어울려 쓸 명사가 들어가야 한다. 목적어를 보니 새로운 관리자가 필요하다는 내용이므로, 문맥상 '영업 부서'라는 말을 만들어줄 (C) division(부서)이 정답이다. (A) illustration은 '삽화', (B) pressure은 '압박', (D) outcome은 '결과'라는 의미로 문맥상 적절하지 않다.

번역 영업 부서에 새 관리자가 필요함에도 불구하고 인사부장은 아직 그 공석을 충원하지 않았다.

어휘 human resources (회사의) 인사부 fill the job opening 공석을 충원하다

121 동사 어휘

해설 항공사에서 수하물 가방에 25달러씩 수수료를 부과하기로 했다는 말이 가장 자연스러우므로, (A)의 instituted(도입했다, 시작했다)가 정답으로 적합하다. (B) patterned는 '무늬를 만들었다', (C) dominated는 '～을 지배했다', (D) motivated는 '동기를 부여했다'라는 의미이다.

번역 크로스컨트리 항공은 수하물 가방마다 25달러의 수수료와, 무게가 50파운드가 넘는 가방에는 추가로 5달러를 부과하기 시작했다.

어휘 check (비행기를 탈 때 수하물로) 부치다

122 명사 자리 _ 전치사의 목적어

해설 빈칸은 소유격 인칭대명사(its)와 형용사(in-depth)의 수식을 받는 명사 자리로, 빈칸을 포함한 명사구는 전치사(for)의 목적어 역할을 한다. 명사 (A) cover(덮개; 표지)와 (D) coverage(보도) 중에 문맥상 '깊이 있는 보도에 대해'라는 의미가 자연스러우므로 정답은 (D) coverage이다. 과거 시제 동사/과거분사인 (B) covered와, 형용사 (C) coverable은 품사상 적합하지 않다.

번역 〈루핀 트리뷴〉 직원들은 루핀 지역 농업 분야의 변화에 관한 깊이 있는 보도로 언론 상을 수상했다.

어휘 win a prize 상을 타다 journalism 저널리즘, 언론 in-depth 깊이 있는, 면밀한 farming industry 농업 cover 덮개; 표지; 보도하다; 덮다 coverable 덮을 수 있는 coverage 보도; 보상 범위

123 접속사 자리

해설 콤마(,)로 연결된 두 개의 문장을 연결해야 하는 접속사 자리이다. (A) Including(～을 포함하여)과 (D) From은 전치사, (C) However(하지만)는 부사이기 때문에 제외된다. (B) Since는 '～ 이후로'라는 의미일 때는 전치사와 접속사가 다 가능하지만, 접속사로 쓸 때는 '～ 때문에'라는 의미도 있다. 여기서는 '이유'를 의미하는 접속사가 자연스러우므로 (B) Since가 정답이다.

번역 오늘 아침 전기 기사들이 로비의 스위치를 고치러 올 것이기 때문에 안내원들은 회의실에서 일하고 있다.

어휘 electrician 전기 기사 conference room 회의실

124 능동태 / 수동태 구분

해설 빈칸이 be동사 뒤에 있으므로 형용사나 분사가 올 수 있는 자리이다. direct A to B는 'A를 B에게 보내다[돌리다]'라는 의미로 쓰인다. 모든 약속과 문의는 비서에게 '보내진다'는 의미가 되어야 하므로 동사는 수동태여야 한다. 따라서 정답은 (D) directed이다.

번역 주 씨는 일정이 바빠서 모든 약속 요청과 문의는 그의 비서에게 해야 한다.

어휘 appointment 약속 inquiry 문의 direct 직접적인; ～로 향하다; ～을 지휘하다 directly 곧장; 직접적으로

125 형용사 어휘

해설 명사를 수식하는 형용사의 어휘를 구분하는 문제이다. (A) unequal(불공평한), (B) honorary(명예의), (C) resolved(단호한), (D) urgent(급한) 중에서, 문맥상 휴가 중에도 '급한' 문의는 이메일로 답해줄 수 있다는 말이 가장 자연스럽다. 따라서 정답은 (D) urgent이다.

번역 제품개발 부서장인 케네스 페이지는 휴가 중이지만 급한 문의는 이메일로 답변할 수 있다.

어휘 be on vacation 휴가 중이다

126 명사 어휘

해설 빈칸은 부정관사(a)와 형용사(remarkable)의 수식을 받는 명사 자리로, 〈a + remarkable + 빈칸 + of〉는 명사구(talented performers)를 한정 수식한다. 문맥상 '주목할 만한 일련의 재능 있는 연주자들'이라는 의미가 자연스러우므로 정답은 (A) array이다. an array of는 '다수의, 일련의'라는 의미의 관용적인 표현으로 기억하자.

번역 사이펠 음악 축제의 주최자들은 주목할 만한 일련의 재능 있는 연주자들을 집합시켰다.

어휘 organizer 주최자 assemble 모으다, 집합시키다 remarkable 놀라운, 주목할 만한 talented 재능 있는 performer 연주자; 연기자 pace 걸음; 속도 role 역할 option 선택, 옵션

127 부사 자리 _ 동사 수식

해설 수동태 동사 사이에 끼어서 동사를 수식해주는 부사를 고르는 문제이다. 부사인 (D) completely(완전히, 전적으로)가 정답이다.

번역 지역의 기업체들이 도시 공원을 위한 기금으로 큰 돈을 모금하였기 때문에 그 정원은 향후 3년 동안 완전히 유지될 수 있다.

어휘 raise money 돈을 마련하다 fund 기금 maintain 유지하다 complete 완전한; 완료하다

128 형용사 어휘

해설 우선 보기의 의미를 살펴보자. (A) persistent(끈질긴, 지속되는), (B) obsolete(더 이상 쓸모없는, 한물간), (C) separate(분리된), (D) crucial(중대한) 중에서, 문맥상 빠른 속도로 기술이 '쓸모없어진다'는 의미가 적절하므로 정답은 (B) obsolete이다.

번역 기술이 노후화되는 속도가 빨라서 구식 전자제품을 재활용할 비용효율적인 방법을 찾는 일이 훨씬 더 중요해진다.

어휘 cost-effective 비용효율적인 recycle 재활용하다 outdated 구식의 electronic device 전자제품

129 동사의 수 / 태

해설 빈칸은 주어(the link to the page ~ contact details) 뒤에 나오는 동사로, 수동태 동사 (A)와 (C), 능동태 동사 (D) 중에 하나를 선택해야 한다. 주어(the link)가 단수이고, '링크는 가까이에 놓여져야 한다'라는 수동의 의미가 자연스러우므로 정답은 (A) should be placed이다.

번역 더 나은 접근성을 위해 우리 회사의 연락처 정보가 담긴 페이지의 링크는 홈페이지 가장 윗부분 가까이에 놓여져야 한다.

어휘 accessibility 접근성 contain 포함하다 contact details (자세한) 연락처 정보 close to ~에 가까운 place 놓다, 두다

130 동사 어휘

해설 제품이 주어이고 목적어로 나오는 특징들을 '자랑한다'는 의미가 들어가야 가장 적절하다. 따라서 정답은 (A) boasts(자랑하다)이다. (B) aims는 '목표하다', (C) excels는 '뛰어나다', (D) appeals는 '매력적이다'라는 의미이다.

번역 하이뷰의 곡선형 모니터 제품군 중 최신 제품은 고화질과 70인치 디스플레이를 자랑한다.

어휘 entry 출품작, 등재된 것 curved 곡선의 high-definition 고화질

PART 6

131-134 편지

고객님,

134저희 피트니스 언리미티드의 메이플 스트리트점이 그린데일 지역사회에서 15년간의 영업을 마치고 **131**문을 닫을 것임을 알려드리게 되어 죄송합니다. 마지막 영업일은 다음 주 금요일인 3월 31일로 예정되어 있습니다.

저희는 기쁜 마음으로 지역 행사들을 후원했고 우리 지역사회가 신체 단련의 목표를 이루도록 도와왔으며 이 변화가 가능한 한 쉽게 되기를 바랍니다. 구내에 있는 물품 보관함에 개인 소지품을 보관하고 **132**계시다면 3월 31일까지 치워주시기 바랍니다. 3월 말 이후의 회비를 납부하신 분은 프런트 데스크에 연락해 회원권을 루트 7 지점으로 **133**이관하는 일을 의논해 주십시오.

<u>지난 15년간 성원해 주셔서 감사합니다.</u>

밥 잭슨, 사장

어휘 serve the community 지역사회를 위해 일하다 notify 알리다, 통지하다 sponsor 후원하다 meet a goal 목표를 달성하다 store 보관하다 personal belongings 개인 소지품 locker 물품 보관함 premises 구내 pay for a membership 회비를 납부하다

131 동사 시제

해설 바로 다음 문장을 살펴보면 문을 닫게 되는 시점이 미래인 것을 알 수 있다. 선택지에서 미래 시제를 나타내는 것은 (A), (B) 두 개인데, (B)의 미래완료 시제는 '과거에서 시작하여 미래까지 영향'을 미쳐야 한다. 즉, 미래 '언제쯤이면 ~가 완료될 것이다'라는 의미가 되어야 한다. 하지만, 여기서는 단순한 미래의 의미이므로, 정답은 (A) will be shutting이 적절하다.

132 접속사 자리

해설 콤마(,)로 연결된 두 개의 문장을 연결해주는 접속사가 들어가야 하는 자리이다. 따라서 전치사 (A) Among은 불가능하다. '소지품이 있다면 특정 일자까지 치워라'라는 의미가 되는 것이 가장 자연스러우므로, 접속사 (D) If가 정답이다.

133 동명사 자리 _ 전치사 뒤

해설 전치사 뒤가 빈칸이므로 전치사의 목적어인 명사나 동명사가 들어가는 자리이다. (C) transferring과 (D) transfers가 후보가 될 수 있는데, 빈칸 뒤에 their membership이라는 목적어가 있는 것으로 보아 빈칸에는 동명사가 들어가야 한다. 따라서 정답은 (C) transferring이다.

134 문맥에 맞는 문장 고르기

번역 (A) 이 목표들을 달성하신 분은 상을 받게 됩니다.
(B) **지난 15년간 성원해 주셔서 감사합니다.**
(C) 마지막으로, 수건들은 소정의 비용으로 대여할 수 있습니다.
(D) 곧 방문하셔서 스스로 시험해 보십시오.

Test 8

해설 지문 전체가 피트니스 센터가 문을 닫는 것에 대해 양해를 구하는 글이다. 단락이 바뀌고 마지막 한 문장으로 글을 마무리하기에 적절한 문장을 골라야 한다. 여기서는 그동안의 성원에 감사하는 문장이 가장 적절하므로 정답은 (B)이다.

135 -138 기사

도넛 광고가 시청자의 마음을 사로잡다

에젤 도넛의 최근 TV 광고 시리즈는 전국적으로 많은 시청자의 호응을 얻었다. 이 광고에는 여배우 버지니아 콘티가 프랜차이즈 한 지점의 제빵사 '세럴' 역으로 출연한다. 광고 속에서 세럴은 독창적인 **135다양한 종류의** 새 도넛 아이디어로 동료들과 상점의 고객들을 기쁘게 한다. 이 **136호감 가는** 광고가 방송되기 시작하자 에젤 도넛은 소셜 미디어를 통해 쇄도하는 칭찬을 받았고 매출액에서도 현저한 신장을 누렸다. **137그 결과,** 에젤 도넛은 **138콘티 씨가 출연하는** 추가적인 광고 몇 편을 내년에 제작할 계획을 밝혔다. <u>첫 번째 광고는 3월 초에 방송될 예정이다.</u>

어휘 latest 최근의 advertisement 광고(= ad) win over 호응[지지]를 얻다, 자기 편으로 끌어들이다 viewer 시청자 star (영화 등의) 주역을 맡다 actress 여배우 baker 제빵사 franchise 프랜차이즈, 가맹점 location 지점 delight 기쁘게 하다 coworker 동료 once 일단 ~하면 appear 나타나다, 방송되다 flood 쇄도, 홍수 praise 칭찬 noticeable 현저한 boost 신장 sales 매출, 매출액 reveal 밝히다 feature 등장시키다 over the coming year 내년에

135 명사 어휘

해설 빈칸은 형용사(creative new)와 전치사구(of donuts)의 수식을 받는 명사 자리로, 전치사 for의 목적어 역할을 한다. 또한 빈칸을 포함한 전치사구는 명사(ideas)를 수식한다. 문맥상 '독창적이며 다양한 종류의 새 도넛에 대한 아이디어'라는 의미가 자연스러우므로 정답은 (D) varieties(종류, 다양성)이다. (A) phases(단계, 국면), (B) approaches(접근 방식), (C) majorities(다수)는 모두 의미상 적절하지 않다.

136 형용사 자리 _ 명사 수식

해설 빈칸 뒤 명사(ads)를 수식하는 형용사 자리이므로, 형용사 (B) likable (좋아할 만한)과 전치사, 접속사, 동사 외에 형용사로도 쓰일 수 있는 (D) like(비슷한) 중에 선택해야 한다. 문맥상 '좋아할 만한 광고'라는 의미가 자연스러우므로, 정답은 (B) likable(호감이 가는)이다. 부사 (A) likably와 명사 (C) liking(좋아함)은 품사상 적합하지 않다.

137 부사 어휘 _ 문장 수식

해설 빈칸에는 앞뒤 문장을 자연스럽게 이어줄 접속부사가 필요하다. 빈칸 앞 문장에서 광고의 성과를 언급하고 있고, 빈칸 뒤 문장에서 그 성과에 따른 추가 광고 제작이라는 결과를 밝히고 있으므로 정답은 (B) As a result(그 결과)이다. (A) nevertheless(그럼에도 불구하고), (C) For example(예를 들어), (D) In other words(다시 말해)는 모두 문맥상 적절하지 않다.

138 문맥에 맞는 문장 고르기

번역 (A) 첫 번째 광고는 3월 초에 방송될 예정이다.
(B) 모든 에젤 도넛 방문자가 하나씩 받게 될 것이다.
(C) 팬들은 변화에 대해 우려를 나타내고 있다.
(D) TV 광고의 효과는 비슷했다.

해설 빈칸 앞 문장 '콘티 씨가 출연하는 추가적인 광고 몇 편을 내년에 제작할 계획을 밝혔다'에서 추가적인 광고 제작 계획을 언급하고 있다. 따라서 빈칸에는 광고와 관련된 구체적인 계획 및 일정을 제시하는 것이 문맥상 자연스러우므로 정답은 (A)이다.

어휘 expect 예상하다 air 방송되다 express 표현하다 concern 우려 effect 효과, 영향 similar 유사한

139 -142 광고

너낼리 산업의 루프 5는 농장주 및 기타 농업 분야 종사자들이 사용할 수 있게 **139특별히** 고안된 고정 날개 드론입니다. 넓은 지역에 퍼져 있는 농작물이나 가축들의 상태를 추적 관찰하는 것이 이렇게 수월했던 적은 없습니다. 고성능 배터리 덕분에 루프 5는 1회 충전에 55분간 **140날** 수 있습니다. 공중에 떠 있는 동안 드론의 카메라와 기타 센서들이 다양한 자료를 포착하고, 그 데이터는 착륙 즉시 모든 FMIS(농업 관리 정보 시스템) 소프트웨어의 모든 **141주요** 브랜드에 업로드됩니다. **142간단하고, 신속하면서, 믿을 수 있는** 루프 5는 여러분의 농장을 위한 완벽한 선택이 될 것입니다. <u>가격, 설치 시기, 기타 명세 사항을 알고 싶으시면 555-0176번으로 전화 주십시오.</u>

어휘 fixed-wing 날개가 고정된 drone 드론, 무인 항공기 designed for ~을 위해 설계된[만들어진] agriculture industry 농업 monitor 감시하다, 추적 관찰하다 crop 농작물 livestock 가축 spread out 널리 퍼진 high-powered 강력한, 고성능의 charge 충전 in the air 공중에 sensor 센서, 감지 장치 capture 포착하다 a range of 다양한 upload 업로드하다 upon -ing ~하자마자 land 착륙하다 management 운영, 관리 reliable 믿을 수 있는

139 부사 자리 _ 동사 수식

해설 빈칸은 수동의 현재완료시제 동사를 이루는 has been과 designed 사이에서 과거분사(designed)를 수식하는 부사 자리이므로, 정답은 (B) specially(특별히)이다. 형용사 (A) special, 명사 (C) specialty, 동사의 과거 시제나 과거분사형인 (D) specialized는 모두 품사상 적합하지 않다.

어휘 specialty 특선, 특산품 specialized 전문화된

140 동사 어휘

해설 빈칸은 조동사(can) 뒤에 나오는 동사원형 자리로, 전치사구(for 55 minutes on a single charge)의 수식을 받는다. 빈칸이 설명하는 주어(the Rupp 5)는 '고정 날개 드론(a fixed-wing drone)'이므로, '루프 5는 1회 충전에 55분간 날 수 있다'는 의미가 되어야 문맥상 자연스럽다. 따라서 정답은 (D) fly(날다)이다. (A) ring(소리가 울리다), (B) roll(구르다), (C) dig(파다)는 모두 의미상 적절하지 않다.

141 형용사 어휘

해설 빈칸은 한정사(any)와 명사(brand) 사이에서 명사를 수식하는 형용사 자리이다. 또한 빈칸을 포함한 전치사구가 동사(can be uploaded)를 수식하므로, 빈칸에는 명사 및 동사와 가장 잘 어울리는 형용사가 들어가야 한다. 문맥상 '(FMIS 소프트웨어의) 모든 주요 브랜드에 업로드될 수 있다'라는 의미가 자연스러우므로, 정답은 (C) major(주요한)이다. (A) ideal (이상적인), (B) repeated(반복되는), (D) eager(열심인)는 모두 의미상 적절하지 않다.

142 문맥에 맞는 문장 고르기

번역 (A) 가격, 설치 시기, 기타 명세 사항을 알고 싶으시면 555-0176번으로 전화 주십시오.
(B) 청소 및 복원 서비스는 포함되지 않는 점을 기억해 주십시오.
(C) 저희 웹사이트에서 식물들 사진을 다운로드할 수 있습니다.
(D) 이 제안은 규모가 500에이커 이하인 농가 자산에만 적용됩니다.

해설 빈칸 앞 문장은 광고하는 제품의 장점을 강조하고 있다. 따라서 빈칸에는 광고하는 제품의 추가 정보(pricing, set-up times, and other specifications) 문의 및 제품 구매와 관련된 내용이 이어지는 것이 문맥상 자연스러우므로 정답은 (A)이다.

어휘 pricing 가격 (책정) set-up 설치의 specifications 명세(서)
cleanup 청소 restoration 복원, 복구 offer 제안, 할인가
holdings 자산, 재산

143-146 이메일

발신: 잭 롤러 (j.lawler@fivelive-software.com)
수신: 에벌린 모레츠 (e.moretz@addigitalware.com)
날짜: 4월 17일
제목: 요청

모레츠 씨께,

저는 파이브라이브 소프트웨어의 채용 담당 인사부장입니다. 최근 귀하의 **144**이전 직원이었던 **143**앨런 네일러 씨의 면접을 기쁘게 진행했습니다. 그는 자기가 AD 디지털웨어 주식회사에서 근무할 때 귀하가 팀장이었다고 말했습니다.

네일러 씨는 저희 회사의 수석 프로그래머 직에 지원했으며, 귀하를 이력서상의 추천인 중 한 명으로 올렸습니다. 이 전도유망한 지원자에 대해 귀하의 피드백을 주시면 **145**감사하겠습니다. 특히 귀하 밑에서 일할 때 맡았던 다양한 프로젝트에 앨런 씨가 기여한 **146**바에 대해 관심이 있습니다.

이 점에 대해 다음 주에 15분 동안 저와 전화 통화를 하실 수 있는 일시를 몇 개 알려 주시기 바랍니다. 배려해 주셔서 감사합니다.

잭 롤러
파이브라이브 소프트웨어

어휘 have the pleasure of ~하는 것을 기쁘게 여기다 apply
for ~에 지원하다 reference 추천인, 신원보증인 résumé 이력서
regarding ~에 관한 promising 전도유망한 candidate 지원자
in particular 특히 contribution 기여

143 문맥에 맞는 문장 고르기

번역 (A) 귀사의 디자인 서비스를 고용할 가능성에 대해 메일을 씁니다.
(B) 저희 프로젝트가 지연되었음을 알리게 되어 죄송합니다.
(C) 저는 프로그래밍 분야에 대해 더 배우고 싶은 학생입니다.
(D) 저는 파이브라이브 소프트웨어의 채용 담당 인사부장입니다.

해설 빈칸 뒤에서 수신자의 이전 직원이었던 사람을 인터뷰한 내용을 이야기하고 있다. 첫 문장은 자신의 소속이나 소개에 관한 내용을 먼저 밝히는 것이 적절할 것이다. 따라서 (D)가 정답이다.

144 형용사 어휘

해설 뒤의 문장을 보니, you were his team leader라는 말이 나온다. 이를 바탕으로 인터뷰한 사람이 '예전 직원'이었다는 것을 알 수 있으므로, 정답은 (A) former(이전의)이다.

145 동사 시제

해설 '지원자에 대한 피드백을 주시면 감사하겠다'는 말이 들어가야 한다. '~하면 …할 것이다'라는 말은 일종의 가정법으로, 상상하는 일의 결과에 대해 말할 때 would(~할 것이다)를 사용한다. 따라서 조동사 would를 포함한 (B)가 가장 적절하다.

146 명사절 접속사

해설 전치사 뒤에는 명사가 와야 하는데 곧바로 뒤에 문장이 왔기 때문에 이 문장이 명사 역할을 할 수 있도록 만들어 줄 명사절 접속사가 와야 한다. 또한 was 뒤에 주어(Alan's contribution)와 동격으로 와야 하는 보어가 없다. 따라서 명사절 접속사 역할을 하면서 보어 역할을 동시에 할 수 있는 (C) what(~하는 것)이 정답이다.

PART 7

147-148 광고

신입생 특별 행사

6월 한 달간, 아다스 로터스 **147**요가에 처음 오는 학생 여러분께 첫 강좌를 무료로 제공합니다! 또한 할인된 가격에 강좌 패키지를 구매하실 수 있습니다.

• 3회 수업: 45달러
• 5회 수업: 60달러
• 12회 수업: 100달러

저희 웹사이트 www.adahlotusyoga.com/newstudent에 등록하여 이 혜택을 누려보세요. 이 할인 행사는 저희 스튜디오를 방문한 적이 없는 학생에게만 적용됩니다. **148**할인 가격은 학생 일인당 하나의 패키지만 허용됩니다.

어휘 discounted price 할인 가격 register 등록하다 offer
(짧은 기간의) 할인 (행사) good 유효한 be allowed 허용되다

147 글의 주제 / 목적

번역 무엇을 광고하는가?
(A) 언어 강좌
(B) 운동 강좌
(C) 요리 강좌
(D) 음악 강좌

해설 앞 부분의 Adah's Lotus Yoga get their first class free라는 표현에서 요가 수업에 대한 광고임을 알 수 있다. 따라서 정답은 (B)이다.

148 세부 사항

번역 신규 학생 한 명은 몇 개의 할인 패키지를 구매할 수 있는가?
(A) 1
(B) 3
(C) 5
(D) 12

해설 마지막 문장에서 정답을 확인할 수 있다. 할인 행사의 대상은 신규 학생들로 한정을 지었고, 일인당 하나의 패키지만 허용된다고 나와 있다. 따라서 정답은 (A)이다.

149 -150 문자 메시지

> **머틀 콜먼, 오후 12:08**
> 레비, 보고서 작업하는 거 시간이 많이 더 걸려요? **149그렇다면,** 난 먼저 아래 층으로 내려가 로비에서 기다릴게요.
>
> **레비 하인스, 오후 12:09**
> 아, 아니요! 난 이미 나왔어요. 오늘 점심 같이 먹기로 한 거 깜박 잊었네요. 정말 미안해요, 머틀.
>
> **머틀 콜먼, 오후 12:09**
> 괜찮아요. **150그럼 우리 약속 취소해야 될까요?**
>
> **레비 하인스, 오후 12:10**
> **150음, 지금 막 레비스 그릴에 앉았는데, 아직 주문은 안 했어요.** 어떻게 할까요?
>
> **머틀 콜먼, 오후 12:11**
> 레비스를 좋아하지는 않는데, 하지만 옆집 멕시코 레스토랑에 가는 건 괜찮아요.
>
> **레비 하인스, 오후 12:11**
> 좋아요. 거기서 봅시다.

어휘 work on ~에 대해 작업하다 head downstairs 아래층으로 향하다 be supposed to+동사원형 ~하기로 되어 있다 cancel 취소하다 order 주문하다 mind -ing ~하기를 꺼리다 next door 옆집에

149 사실 관계 확인

번역 콜먼 씨에 관해 아마도 무엇이 사실이겠는가?
(A) 하인스 씨와 같은 건물에서 일한다.
(B) 오늘 아침에 대중교통을 이용했다.
(C) 멕시코 음식을 좋아하지 않는다.
(D) 보고서를 읽으려고 기다리고 있다.

해설 콜먼 씨가 오후 12시 8분 메시지에서 먼저 아래 층으로 내려가 로비에서 기다린다고 했으므로, 두 사람이 같은 건물에서 일한다는 것을 유추할 수 있다. 따라서 정답은 (A)이다.

150 의도 파악

번역 오후 12시 10분에 하인스 씨가 "아직 주문은 안 했어요"라고 쓸 때 그 의도는 무엇인가?
(A) 예정보다 늦어졌다.
(B) 아직 계획을 변경할 수 있다.
(C) 콜먼 씨가 음식을 추천해 주기를 원한다.
(D) 레비스 그릴이 매우 붐빈다는 것을 강조한다.

해설 콜먼 씨가 오후 12시 9분 메시지에서 하인스 씨와의 약속을 취소해야 할지 물었고, 이에 대해 하인스 씨가 지금 막 레비스 그릴에 앉았지만 아직 주문은 안 했다고 했으므로, 하인스 씨의 계획이 변경 가능하다는 것을 유추할 수 있다. 따라서 정답은 (B)이다.

151 -152 공지

> ### 아이보리 세레니티가 우드필드 몰에서 개점합니다.
>
> 우드필드 몰은 복합쇼핑몰 서쪽 끝에 새 매장의 개장을 알리게 되어 자랑스럽게 생각합니다. **151이 매장은 지난봄 메가북스가 나가고 비어 있던 자리를 채우게 됩니다.**
>
> 아이보리 세레니티는 10월 15일 토요일에 개점하며 지역사회를 보살피고 평화롭게 유지하기 위해 광범위한 서비스를 제공할 예정입니다. **152미용 서비스는 헤어컷, 염색, 매니큐어, 페디큐어 등을 포함하며 모든 서비스는 자격증을 소지한 미용사가 제공합니다.** 고객들은 매장 안에 있는 스파에서 마사지, 얼굴 마사지, 몸의 각질 제거 등을 받으실 수 있습니다.
>
> 서비스 전체 메뉴는 아이보리 세레니티 웹사이트 www.ivoryserenity.com/services에서 확인할 수 있습니다.

어휘 grand opening 개점 complex 복합 건물 addition 추가된 것 fill the vacancy 공석을 메우다 departure 떠남 a wide range of ~ 매우 다양한 pamper 소중히 보살피다 certified 면허증을 가진, 증명된 aesthetician 미용사 facial 얼굴 마사지 body scrub 보디 스크럽(몸의 각질 제거) entire 전체의 available 이용 가능한

151 사실 관계 확인

번역 메가북스에 관해 명시된 것은?
(A) 10월에 새 지점을 개점한다.
(B) 아이보리 세레니티 옆에 위치해 있다.
(C) 소유주가 아이보리 세레니티도 운영하고 있다.
(D) 더 이상 우드필드 몰의 일부가 아니다.

해설 첫 번째 단락 두 번째 문장에서 아이보리 세레니티가 메가북스가 나간 자리를 채운다(fills the vacancy left by ~ last spring)고 했으므로 더 이상 메가북스가 우드필드 몰에서 영업을 하지 않는다는 것을 알 수 있다. 따라서 정답은 (D)이다.

▸▸ Paraphrasing 지문의 the vacancy left by the departure of MegaBooks → 정답의 no longer part of Woodfield Mall

152 세부 사항

번역 손님은 왜 아이보리 세레니티에 방문하겠는가?
(A) 미술 기법을 배우기 위해
(B) 미용 서비스를 받기 위해
(C) 장식용 제품을 얻기 위해
(D) 건강에 좋은 간식을 구입하기 위해

해설 두 번째 단락 중간에 아이보리 세레니티의 서비스 종류가 나열되어 있다. 헤어컷, 염색, 매니큐어 등의 미용 서비스를 제공한다고 하므로 정답은 (B)이다.

▸▸ Paraphrasing 지문의 **Salon services** → 정답의 **beauty treatments**

153 -155 웹페이지

http://www.moyandville-ha.org/internships

모얀드빌 주택 관리국 인턴 과정

모얀드빌 주택 관리국(MHA)의 인턴십 프로그램은 참여하는 학생들과 MHA 둘 다에게 이익이 되도록 설계되었습니다. **153MHA 직원들의 지도하에 프로젝트에 참여하는 동안, 인턴 사원들은 적정 가격의 주택 서비스를 제공하는 분야에서 경험을 쌓으며 후한 시급도 받게 됩니다.** MHA는 젊고 다양한 여러 목소리와의 접촉, 그리고 졸업 후 이 분야에 발을 디딜 때 교육이 덜 필요하게 될 숙련 근로자의 향후 증가로 인해 이득을 얻게 됩니다.

인턴 과정은 6월 초에 시작해 약 3개월간 지속되며, 이 기간 중에 인턴 사원들은 주 20시간 근무합니다(월~금요일, 오전 8시~정오 12시, 또는 오후 1시~5시). **154모얀드빌 대학교, 또는 모얀드빌 주립대학교에 정식 등록한 사람만 신청할 수 있습니다.** 하지만, 몇 개 부서에 자리가 있기 때문에 어떤 학과 학생이라도 환영합니다. **155각 자리는 적격 대학교의 온라인 채용 게시판에 개별적으로 광고됩니다.** 따라서 지원에 관심 있는 분은 관련 서비스를 수시로 확인하시기 바랍니다.

어휘 internship 인턴직, 인턴 과정(intern 인턴 사원) structure 체계화[구조화]하다, 설계하다 advantage 이점, 유리한 점 participate in ~에 참여하다 under the guidance of ~의 지도하에 affordable (가격이) 알맞은 generous 후한 hourly wage 시급 benefit from ~에서 득을 보다[혜택을 입다] contact 접촉 skilled 숙련된 require 필요로 하다 graduation 졸업 last 지속하다 approximately 대략 enroll 등록하다 full-time 전일제의, 정식의 apply 지원하다 academic discipline 학과 position (일)자리 available 이용할 수 있는, 유효한 advertise 광고하다 separately 별개로 job board 채용 게시판 eligible 자격이 있는, 적격인 interested in ~에 관심이 있는 regularly 수시로, 정기적으로

153 사실 관계 확인

번역 MHA 인턴 과정에 관해 명시된 것은?
(A) 저렴한 숙소가 포함된다.
(B) 기간은 20주이다.
(C) 탄력적인 근무 시간제가 있다.
(D) 유급직이다.

해설 첫 번째 단락에서 인턴 사원들은 적정 가격의 주택 서비스를 제공하는 분야에서 경험을 쌓으며 후한 시급도 받게 된다(earn a generous hourly wage)고 했으므로 정답은 (D)이다. 반면에 인턴 사원들은 적정 가격의 주택 서비스를 제공하는 분야에서 경험을 쌓는 것이지 저렴한 숙소를 제공받는 것은 아니므로 (A)는 적절하지 않다.

▸▸ Paraphrasing 지문의 **earn a generous hourly wage** → 정답의 **paid positions**

154 세부 사항

번역 웹페이지에 따르면, 누가 인턴 과정에 자격이 있는가?
(A) 특정 과목을 공부하는 학생들
(B) 특정 기관에 다니는 학생들
(C) 평균 학점이 높은 학생들
(D) 대학 2년 과정을 마친 학생들

해설 두 번째 단락에서 모얀드빌 대학교 또는 모얀드빌 주립대학교에 정식 등록한 사람만 신청할 수 있다고 했으므로 정답은 (B)이다.

▸▸ Paraphrasing 지문의 **Only those enrolled full-time at the University of Moyandville or Moyandville State University** → 정답의 **Students who attend certain institutions**

155 세부 사항

번역 예비 신청자들은 무엇을 하라고 지시받는가?
(A) 웹사이트 게시물 보기
(B) 대학교 내 학과에 연락하기
(C) 공식 서류 준비
(D) MHA 발간물 읽기

해설 두 번째 단락에서 각 자리는 적격 대학의 온라인 채용 게시판에 개별적으로 광고가 되므로, 지원에 관심 있는 사람은 관련 서비스를 수시로 확인할 것을 요청하고 있다. 따라서 정답은 (A)이다.

▸▸ Paraphrasing 지문의 **those interested in applying** → 질문의 **potential applicants** 지문의 **check those services** → 정답의 **Monitor postings**

156 -157 이메일

발신: 코르미 〈customerservice@cormi-co.com〉
수신: 클린트 볼드윈 〈drbaldwin@pv-dc.com〉

날짜: 1월 27일

제목: 코르미에서 보내드리는 코드

볼드윈 씨께,

귀하의 승인 코드는 06178입니다. **156**귀하의 코르미 계정에 로그인하셔서 파스크 밸리 치과의 소유주 또는 관리자임을 증명하라는 말이 나오면 이 승인 코드를 입력하세요.

일단 이것을 마치면, 귀하의 업체를 위한 코르미 명단을 통제할 수 있게 됩니다. **157**귀하는 코르미 방문자들이 귀하의 도시에서 적절한 서비스 제공자를 찾을 때 그들에게 제시되는 정보의 대부분을 추가, 갱신, 삭제하실 수 있습니다. 잠재 고객들의 편리함을 위해 가능한 한 상세한 정보를 포함시킬 것을 권해드립니다.

변경 사항이 귀하의 목록에 나타나려면 최대 48시간이 걸릴 수 있다는 점을 기억해 주십시오. 또한, 코르미 사용자가 귀하의 업체에 대해 게시한 후기는 수정하거나 삭제하실 수 없습니다. 후기들에 짧은 답변을 다실 수는 있습니다.

코르미를 사용하는 데 도움이 필요하시면 저희 웹사이트의 '도움' 페이지를 먼저 방문해 주세요.

코르미 고객 서비스부

어휘 authentication 인증, 확인 sign in to one's account ~의 계정에 로그인하다 enter 입력하다 prompt ~하라고 유도하다[촉발하다] prove 증명하다 dental clinic 치과 once 일단 ~하면 gain 얻다 control over ~에 대한 통제(력) listing 명단 update 갱신하다 search for ~을 찾다 relevant 관련 있는 service provider 서비스 제공자[제공 업체] recommend 추천하다 as much ~ as possible 가능한 많은 ~ detail 세부 사항 convenience 편리함 potential 잠재적인, 가능성 있는 change 변경 (사항); 변경하다 take up (시간, 공간을) 쓰다[차지하다] review 후기, 논평 post 게시하다 assistance 도움

---

156 주제 / 목적

번역 이 이메일의 목적은 무엇인가?
(A) 한 개인의 신분 확인을 가능하게 하려고
(B) 주문이 접수되었음을 확인해 주려고
(C) 이용자의 불만에 응답하려고
(D) 계정 비밀번호를 재설정하려고

해설 첫 번째 단락에서 코르미 계정에 로그인하여 파스크 밸리 치과의 소유주 또는 관리자임을 증명하라는 말이 나오면 코드를 입력하라고 했으므로, 신분 확인을 가능하게 하기 위한 이메일임을 알 수 있다. 따라서 정답은 (A)이다.

▶ **Paraphrasing** 지문의 **to prove that you are the owner or manager of Pask Valley Dental Clinic** → 정답의 **verification of a person's identity**

---

157 세부 사항

번역 코르미는 무엇을 하는 곳인가?
(A) 병원에 장비 공급
(B) 광고주들이 사용할 이메일 리스트 관리
(C) 일반 대중에게 사업체 정보 제공
(D) 단기 근로자 채용 지원

해설 두 번째 단락에서 코르미 방문자들이 귀하의 도시에서 적절한 서비스 제공자를 찾을 때 그들에게 제시되는 정보의 대부분을 추가, 갱신, 삭제할 수 있다고 했으므로, 코르미가 사업체에 관한 정보를 대중에게 제공한다는 것을 알 수 있다. 따라서 정답은 (C)이다.

158-160 기사

시 소식

이스트시티 (9월 2일) – 이스트시티 파머스 마켓이 하다 플라자에서 거의 15년 전 영업을 시작했던 **158**코트웨이 스퀘어에 있는 이전 자리로의 복귀하자 방문자 수가 "꾸준히 증가했다"고 시장 조직위원인 린다 리 씨는 밝혔다.

"시장이 없는 동안 코트웨이 스퀘어 주변에 많은 주택 건설이 이뤄졌습니다." 리 씨는 설명한다. "이러한 개발은 더 많은 고객을 불러왔습니다." 시장은 5월부터 11월까지, 매주 토요일 아침 7시부터 오후 4시까지 영업한다. 방문객 숫자는 특정 날짜에 따라 다를 수 있지만 6월에서 8월까지 전체 방문자는 지난해 대비 27% 상승했다. 8월의 어느 화창한 날에는 600명이라는 기록적인 인파가 시장을 방문했다.

조직위원들은 장소 자체에 대해 대부분 고무적인 피드백을 받았다. **159"**손님들은 시장의 테라스가 있는 곳을 무척 좋아합니다. 그늘에 앉을 수 있는 장소가 많거든요." 리 씨가 말한다. 그러나 그녀의 팀이 현재 주차 장소 부족 문제를 적극 해결하고 있다는 점도 언급한다. **160**시장이 문을 연 코트 스트리트 근처는 길거리 주차 장소가 종종 부족하다. 당분간 방문객들이 해당 지역에서 두어 블록 서쪽에 있는 곳에 주차하도록 할 것이다.

시장은 자체 웹사이트가 없지만 인근 지역의 사이트인 www.courtway-sq.com에 올라가 있다.

어휘 operation 영업 nearly 거의 steadily 꾸준히 increase 증가하다 attendance 참석, 참석자 수 organizer 조직자 residential construction 주택 건설 take place 일어나다, 발생하다 development 개발 vary 달라지다 given (이미) 정해진, 특정한 overall 전체적인 encouraging 힘을 북돋아 주는 patio 테라스 plenty of 많은 note 언급하다 address the issue of ~라는 문제를 해결하다 shortage 부족 scarce 드문 neighborhood 인근, 근처

---

158 사실 관계 확인

번역 이스트시티 파머스 마켓에 대해 언급된 것은?
(A) 부동산 회사가 후원한다.
(B) 몇 년간 영업을 중단했다.
(C) 원래 위치로 다시 이전했다.
(D) 6월에 기록적으로 많은 방문객들이 찾았다.

해설 첫 번째 단락 첫 문장을 보면 '하다 플라자에서 이전 자리로의 복귀 (return from Hardar Plaza to its old site)'는 말이 나온다. 이를 통해 정답이 (C)라는 것을 알 수 있다.

▶ **Paraphrasing** 지문의 **return ~ to its old site** → 정답의 **moved back to its original location**

159 세부 사항

번역 방문객들이 시장에서 좋아하는 것으로 리 씨가 언급한 것은?
(A) 영업시간
(B) 배달 서비스
(C) 온라인 홈페이지
(D) 야외 좌석

해설 세 번째 단락에서 리 씨가 말한 부분을 통해서 정답을 확인할 수 있다. '손님들이 시장의 야외에 있는 테라스가 있는 곳(the market's patio area)를 좋아한다'고 한 말을 통해서 (D)가 정답임을 알 수 있다.

▸▸ **Paraphrasing** 지문의 **the market's patio area**
→ 정답의 **Its outdoor seating**

160 문장 삽입

번역 [1], [2], [3], [4]로 표시된 곳 중에서 다음 문장이 들어가기에 가장 적합한 곳은

"당분간 방문객들이 해당 지역에서 두어 블록 서쪽에 있는 곳에 주차하도록 할 것이다."

(A) [1]
(B) [2]
(C) [3]
(D) [4]

해설 주차에 관한 내용은 세 번째 단락 후반부에 언급이 되어 있다. 따라서 문장이 들어가기에 가장 적절한 곳은 (D)이다.

161 -164 회람

> 발신: 사무실 관리자
> 수신: 전 직원
> 제목: 공지 및 정책
> 날짜: 5월 22일
>
> 본 메시지는 **161 2층 휴게실이 5월 29일 월요일부터 개조에 들어간다는 사실을** 여러분께 알리기 위한 것입니다. 이 작업은 5일이 소요될 예정이며 고급 바닥재 및 현대적인 조리대의 설치와 싱크대, 전자레인지, 냉장고의 교체가 포함됩니다.
>
> 휴게실 준비를 위해 냉장고에 보관한 것을 모두 치워 주시기 바랍니다. **162남아 있는 것은 모두 5월 26일 금요일 오후 5시에 버릴 예정입니다.** 공사 중 직원들은 5층에 있는 냉장고에 점심 도시락을 보관할 수 있으나, 공간이 **164제한되어 있**음을 유념하시기 바랍니다.
>
> 다음의 휴게실 정책을 상기시켜 드립니다.
>
> * 냉장고에 보관된 모든 음식물에는 주인의 이름과 날짜를 붙여 두어야 합니다.
> * 모두에게 본인의 쓰레기 또는 기한이 지난 음식을 버릴 책임이 있습니다.
> * 그러나 각 부서는 이 정책을 시행할 책임이 있는 휴게실 대표를 지명해야 합니다.
> * 전자레인지 내부는 사용 후 세정제로 꼼꼼히 닦아야 합니다.
> * 지저분한 그릇을 싱크대 안에 남겨 두어서는 안 됩니다.
> * 세척한 그릇은 일과 종료 시 건조대에서 치워야 합니다.
> * **163싱크대는 사용 후 철저하게 닦아야 합니다. 주: 이는 신규 정책입니다.**

여러분 모두가 새 휴게실을 잘 사용하며, 이러한 정책으로 향후 몇 년간 휴게실을 깨끗하고 유용하게 유지할 수 있기를 바랍니다.

어휘 policy 정책 alert 알리다 break room 휴게실 undergo 겪다 renovation 개조, 보수 process 과정, 절차 be scheduled to + 동사원형 ~할 예정이다 involve 포함하다 installation 설치 deluxe 고급의 flooring 바닥재 countertop 조리대 replacement 교체 microwave 전자레인지 refrigerator 냉장고 leave behind 두고 가다 discard 버리다 reminder 상기시키는 것 label 표를 붙이다 expired 기한이 지난 designate 지명하다 representative 대표 enforce 시행하다 thoroughly 철저히 cleaning agent 세정제 drying rack 건조대 for years to come 앞으로 몇 년간

161 글의 주제 / 목적

번역 회람의 한 가지 주제는 무엇인가?
(A) 직원 휴게 시간
(B) 일부 자원 아껴 쓰기
(C) 사무실 편의 시설의 개선
(D) 청소부에 대한 불만

해설 첫 번째 단락 첫 문장에서 이 글의 목적을 알 수 있다. '휴게실 보수공사가 있다(break room will undergo renovations)는 것을 알려주기 위해 이 메시지를 쓴다'는 내용을 토대로 (C)가 정답임을 알 수 있다.

▸▸ **Paraphrasing** 지문의 **renovations**
→ 정답의 **Improvements**

162 세부 사항

번역 5월 26일에 어떤 일이 일어날 것인가?
(A) 식사 시간이 평소보다 짧을 것이다.
(B) 가전제품의 속이 비워질 것이다.
(C) 일부 정책이 발효될 것이다.
(D) 대표가 선출될 것이다.

해설 5월 26일은 두 번째 단락에 나오는데 냉장고에 남아 있는 것들을 모두 버릴(will be discarded) 것이라는 내용이 나온다. 따라서 정답은 (B)이다.

▸▸ **Paraphrasing** 지문의 **Anything left behind will be discarded**
→ 정답의 **An appliance will be emptied.**

163 세부 사항

번역 휴게실 정책에 추가된 권장 행동은?
(A) 전자레인지를 정기적으로 닦기
(B) 싱크대 사용 후마다 치우기
(C) 매일 건조대에서 그릇 치우기
(D) 냉장고에 보관한 항목에 표 붙이기

해설 항목별로 열거된 마지막 부분에서 '이것은 신규 정책입니다(This is a new policy.)'라는 부분을 보면 싱크대 사용 후 깨끗이 닦아야 한다는 내용이 나온다. 따라서 추가된 정책은 (B)가 정답이다.

번역 두 번째 단락 4행의 "limited"와 의미가 가장 가까운 것은?

(A) 제한된
(B) 주의하는
(C) 불완전한
(D) 비밀의

해설 limited는 '제한된, 한정된'이라는 의미이다. 이와 비슷하게 크기나 양, 범위 등을 한정시킬 때 쓸 수 있는 표현은 (A) restricted(제한된)이다.

165-168 웹페이지

www.kendellpark.org/news

| 방문자 정보 | 행사 | **뉴스** | 연락처 |

5월 27일 주간

지난달 **165**켄델 파크 활동위원회(KPAC)가 실시한 조사에서는 응답자의 거의 **85%가 켄델 파크의 편의시설에 만족하는 것으로 나타났습니다.** "우리는 정말 자랑스럽지만, 그 수치를 100%까지 끌어올리고 싶습니다." KPAC의 에드 마크슨 이사가 말했습니다.

그는 그 목적을 이루기 위해 KPAC가 취하고 있는 몇 가지 방법을 설명했습니다. **166(A),(B)** "저희는 시설 업체를 고용해 공원의 피크닉 테이블에 접이식 양산을 설치하고 있으며, 공원의 장식용 조각상과 분수의 균열 수리 공사는 7월 말에 완료될 예정입니다." 분수의 기증자인 짐 랜더스를 기념하는 기념 명패도 복원되어 다시 바닥에 고정시킬 예정입니다.

한편 프렌즈 오브 켄델 파크(FKP)의 카렌 빅스비 회장은 연못 수위가 균형 잡힌 생태계를 지지하기에 너무 낮아진다고 우려를 표명했습니다. KPAC는 현재 이 문제에 대해 공원의 네이처 센터에 있는 생명과학자 티나 베키오와 협의 중입니다. **167**"연못에 물을 대기 위해 공원의 목초지에 대한 접근을 막는 것에 대해 그녀가 최종 결정을 내릴 것입니다." 마크슨 씨의 설명입니다. 폐쇄가 이뤄질 경우 목초지에는 울타리를 치게 됩니다.

다른 소식으로, KPAC는 지난 토요일 청소의 날을 대성공으로 이끄는 데 도움을 준 모든 사람에게 감사를 전하고 싶습니다. 자원봉사자들은 **166(C)**공원의 하이킹 도로망에서 시작해 낮은 나뭇가지를 제거하고 잡초를 제거하면서 하루를 보냈습니다.

마지막으로, 향상된 쓰레기 관리 프로그램의 진전에 대해 말씀 드리게 되어 기쁘게 생각합니다. **168**새로운 녹색 쓰레기통들이 공원 전역의 편리한 위치에 설치됐습니다. 그중 두 개는 공원 서문 근처에 눈에 잘 띄도록 설치됐습니다.

공원을 깨끗하게 유지하는 데 도움을 주셔서 감사합니다.

어휘 survey 조사 carry out 시행하다 respondent 응답자 amenities 편의 시설 attach 붙이다 folding 접이식 crack 균열 decorative 장식의 sculpture 조각상 fountain 분수 memorial 기념비 plaque 명패 donor 기증자 restore 복구하다 meanwhile 한편 voice a concern 우려를 표하다 balanced 균형 잡힌 ecosystem 생태계 consult ~와 상의하다 life scientist 생명과학자 issue 문제 make a decision 결정하다 ultimate 궁극적인 meadow 목초지 in the event

of ~의 경우 closure 폐쇄 fence off 울타리를 치다 set out 출발하다, 시작하다 low-hanging 낮은 tree limb 나뭇가지 trim 잘라내다, 다듬다 weed 잡초 convenient 편리한

165 추론 / 암시

번역 KPAC는 최근 무엇을 했을 것 같은가?

(A) 설문 조사를 실시했다.
(B) 새 이사를 임명했다.
(C) 입장료를 인상했다.
(D) 과학 컨퍼런스를 주최했다.

해설 첫 번째 단락 첫 문장에서 KPAC는 켄델 파크 편의 시설 만족도에 대한 설문 조사를 실시했다는 내용이 나온다. 따라서 (A)가 정답이다.

166 사실 관계 확인

번역 공원의 어느 요소가 웹페이지에 언급되지 않았는가?

(A) 공공 미술작품
(B) 피크닉 시설
(C) 하이킹 코스
(D) 주차 공간

해설 (A)와 (B)는 두 번째 단락에서, (C)는 네 번째 단락의 '공원의 하이킹 도로망(park's network of hiking paths)'에서 확인할 수 있다. 언급되지 않은 (D)가 정답이다.

167 추론 / 암시

번역 공원의 폐쇄 부분에 대해서는 누가 결정을 내릴 것 같은가?

(A) 마크슨 씨
(B) 랜더스 씨
(C) 빅스비 씨
(D) 베키오 씨

해설 세 번째 단락 마지막 부분의 마크슨이 말한 내용에서 공원 목초지에 대한 접근을 막는 것은 생명과학자인 티나 베키오 씨가 결정할 것이라는 내용이 나온다. 따라서 정답은 (D)이다.

▸▸ **Paraphrasing** 지문의 **the ultimate decision**
→ 질문의 **a final decision**

168 문장 삽입

번역 [1], [2], [3], [4]로 표시된 곳 중에서 다음 문장이 들어가기에 가장 적합한 곳은?

"그중 두 개는 공원 서문 근처에 눈에 잘 띄도록 설치됐습니다."

(A) [1]
(B) [2]
(C) [3]
(D) [4]

해설 삽입문의 Two of them이라는 말이 힌트가 된다. 이 삽입문 앞에는 뭔가 두 개 이상 설치한다는 말이 나와야 한다. 따라서 녹색 쓰레기통의 설치에 대해 언급한 뒤인 [4]에 들어가는 것이 가장 자연스러우므로 정답은 (D)이다.

169-171 회람

> ### 회람
>
> 수신: 서튼티 은행 직원들
> 발신: 제시 오듀본, 인사부장
> 제목: 직원 표창장
> 날짜: 12월 1일
>
> 서튼티 은행에서 또 한 해를 성공적으로 마무리하며, 인사부에서는 다음의 직원 표창장에 대해 곧 추천을 받기 시작할 것입니다.
>
> - **169**올해의 지점장
> - 올해의 창구 직원
> - 올해의 지역사회 자원봉사자
>
> 자신의 정상 업무를 넘어서서 고객과 지역사회를 위해 봉사한 직원을 표창하는 것이 목표입니다. **170**누군가를 추천하고자 할 경우, 서튼티 은행 웹사이트의 홈 화면에서 "직원 표창" 링크를 클릭하십시오. 뛰어난 직원에 대해 고객들의 피드백도 받고자 하오니, 이 기회를 서튼티 은행 고객분들에게도 홍보해 주십시오.
>
> **171**추천은 12월 14일부터 12월 31일까지 받습니다. 1월 31일에 수상자들을 발표하려고 하며 그다음 주에 있는 연회에서 시상이 이뤄질 것입니다. 이 중요한 계획에 협조해 주셔서 감사합니다.

어휘 recognition award 표창장 bring ~ to a close ~을 끝내다 human resources department 인사부 nomination 지명, 추천 teller 창구 직원 recognize 알아보다, 인정하다 go above and beyond ~를 넘어서다, ~ 밖의 일을 하다 normal duty 정상 책무 advertise 광고하다 patron 고객 outstanding 뛰어난 banquet (공식) 연회, 만찬 initiative 계획

169 사실 관계 확인

번역 직원 표창장에 대해 명시된 것은?
(A) 회사 전체 투표로 선정된다.
(B) 두 개의 범주로 나뉜다.
(C) 수상자는 상여금을 지급받는다.
(D) 매년 시상된다.

해설 표창장의 명칭을 보면 모두 of the Year로 끝난다. 즉, 이 상은 매년 시상하는 상이라는 것을 알 수 있다. 따라서 정답은 (D)이다. (A)의 투표 방식에 관한 언급은 없었고, (B) 두 개가 아니라 세 개의 범주로 나눴고, (C) 상여금에 관한 내용도 본문에서 찾을 수 없다.

170 세부 사항

번역 회람에 따르면, 수신자들은 직원을 추천하기 위해 무엇을 해야 하는가?
(A) 저녁식사에 참석하기
(B) 의견서 제출하기
(C) 이메일 보내기
(D) 웹페이지 방문하기

해설 두 번째 단락 두 번째 문장을 보면 추천하고 싶으면 웹사이트를 방문하라는 내용을 확인할 수 있다. 따라서 정답은 (D)이다.

▶ **Paraphrasing** 지문의 **go to the main page of the Certainty Bank Web site** → 정답의 **Visit a Web page**

171 세부 사항

번역 추천서는 언제 제출할 수 있는가?
(A) 12월 1일
(B) 12월 14일
(C) 1월 31일
(D) 2월 7일

해설 마지막 단락 첫 문장에서 12월 14일부터 12월 31일까지 추천을 받는다고 했다. 따라서 선택지 중에서 해당 기간 내에 포함된 것은 (B)이다.

172-175 문자 메시지

> **아리아나 체하브, 오전 10:42**
> 팀, 작업 반이 유리 섬유 수영장 설치를 위해 땅 파는 거 마쳤나요?
>
> **팀 나이트, 오전 10:43**
> 사실, 막 전화 드리려던 참이었어요. **172,173**흙바닥 일부에서 지하수가 나왔어요. 그래서 자갈이 추가로 한 집 더 필요할 것 같습니다.
>
> **아리아나 체하브, 오전 10:44**
> 제가 공급 업체에 연락할게요.
>
> **팀 나이트, 오전 10:44**
> 고맙습니다.
>
> **아리아나 체하브, 오전 10:50**
> **173**됐어요, 1시까지 그쪽으로 가져다 줄 수 있을 겁니다. 운 좋게도 두 번째 덤프트럭이 오늘은 다른 작업에 쓰이지 않네요.
>
> **팀 나이트, 오전 10:51**
> 잘됐네요. 그럼 수영장 틀을 오늘 저녁 때까지 바닥에 깔 수 있겠네요.
>
> **아리아나 체하브, 오전 10:53**
> 에반스 씨한테 이 문제에 대해 알리셨어요? **174**추가 자갈 때문에 비용이 발생하지는 않는다고 안심시켜 주는 게 좋겠어요.
>
> **팀 나이트, 오전 10:54**
> 네, 얘기했습니다. 괜찮아요. **175**아, 그리고 풀장 주변에 어떤 울타리를 원하는지 에반스 씨한테 다시 물어봤어요. 하지만 목재하고 알루미늄 울타리 중에서 그가 아직 결정을 못하고 있습니다.
>
> **아리아나 체하브, 오전 10:55**
> 시간 있어요. 울타리 설치는 최소한 두 주 있어야 하거든요.

어휘 crew (함께 일하는) 팀, 조 excavate (구멍을) 파다 fiberglass 유리 섬유 swimming pool 수영장 installation 설치 be about to+동사원형 막 ~하려는 참이다 run into ~와 마주치다 groundwater 지하수 foot (길이 단위) 피트 extra 추가의 a load of gravel 자갈 한 짐(차) contact 연락하다 supplier 공급자, 공급 회사 get 가지고 오다, 가져다 주다 dump truck 덤프트럭 mold 틀, 주형 ground 지면, 바닥 notify 통지하다 reassure 안심시키다 cost 비용이 들다 fencing 울타리 be torn between A and B A와 B 사이에서 갈피를 못 잡다 wooden 나무로 된 aluminum 알루미늄(의) at least 적어도 be away 떨어져 있다

172 세부 사항

번역 나이트 씨가 언급하는 문제는 무엇인가?
(A) 수영장에 물이 샌다.
(B) 흙 일부가 자연발생적으로 물을 포함하고 있다.
(C) 작업 현장에 현재 비가 내린다.
(D) 굴착기 때문에 일부 파이프가 손상되었다.

해설 나이트 씨가 오전 10시 43분 메시지에서 흙바닥 일부에서 지하수가 나오는(We ran into some groundwater in the last foot or so of dirt) 문제점을 언급하고 있으므로 정답은 (B)이다.

▸▸ **Paraphrasing** 지문의 ran into some groundwater → 정답의 contains water

173 사실 관계 확인

번역 체하브 씨는 오후 1시까지 무슨 일이 있을 거라고 언급하는가?
(A) 발송품이 배달된다.
(B) 차량이 수리된다.
(C) 계약서를 작성한다.
(D) 변경된 일정표가 발표된다.

해설 나이트 씨가 오전 10시 43분 메시지에서 흙바닥 일부에서 지하수가 나오는 문제로 인해 추가로 자갈 한 짐이 필요할 거 같다는 의견을 밝혔고, 이에 대해 체하브 씨가 오전 10시 50분 메시지에서 1시까지 그쪽으로 가져다 줄 수 있다고 응답하고 있으므로, 정답은 (A)이다.

▸▸ **Paraphrasing** 지문의 get it to you → 정답의 A shipment will be delivered

174 추론 / 암시

번역 에반스 씨는 누구이겠는가?
(A) 건설 작업반원
(B) 주택 배관공
(C) 건물 주인
(D) 공급 업체 대표

해설 체하브 씨가 오전 10시 53분 메시지에서 추가 자갈로 인해 비용이 발생하지는 않는다고 에반스 씨를 안심시켜 줄 것을 건의하고 있다. 이를 통해 에반스 씨가 비용을 부담하는 건물 주인임을 유추할 수 있으므로, 정답은 (C)이다.

175 의도 파악

번역 오전 10시 55분에 체하브 씨가 "시간 있어요"라고 쓸 때, 그 의도는 무엇인가?
(A) 에반스 씨가 일을 도울 수 있을 것이다.
(B) 조금만 가면 목적지에 도착한다.
(C) 에반스 씨가 자신에게 연락을 하지 않아서 실망했다.
(D) 아직 결정을 내리지 않아도 된다.

해설 나이트 씨가 오전 10시 54분 메시지에서 풀장 주변에 어떤 울타리를 원하는지 에반스 씨한테 다시 물어봤지만 아직 결정을 못하고 있다고 했고, 이에 대해 체하브 씨가 시간이 있다(He has time)는 응답을 했으므로, 결정을 서두르지 않아도 된다는 것을 유추할 수 있다. 따라서 정답은 (D)이다.

176 -180 송장 + 이메일

어더 네트워킹

패튼슨 스트리트 99	날짜: 12월 10일
보스턴, MA 20039	송장번호: 1122334
전화: (222) 555-0199	고객 ID: 4532
팩스: (222) 555-0167	

청구지
176앤드류스 헤어케어 서플라이즈
폰 스트리트 22
오타와, ON, 캐나다 K2L 1B6

설명	세금	금액
기본요금		$0.10
광고 크기: 중		$0.03
177광고 유형: 팝업		$0.10
추가 요구사항		$0.04
	클릭당 합계:	$0.27

178$0.27 x 2만 5304회 클릭 = $6,832.08
총 지불액: $6,832.08

주:
1. 전액 지불은 30일 안에 이뤄져야 합니다.
2. 인쇄된 영수증은 요청하신 경우에만 발부됩니다.
3. 영수증에는 '온라인 마케팅 서비스'라고 표시됩니다.
4. 문의사항이 있는 경우, 퍼트리샤 호크 (pathawk@adurnet.com)에게 이메일을 보내 주십시오.
5. **179**우선 노출을 받으시려면 2150달러를 포함하여 지불하십시오. (귀하의 현재 광고 기준에 의거하여 계산)
6. 광고는 자동으로 갱신됩니다.

어휘 invoice 송장, 청구서 base rate 기본요금 additional 추가의 request 요청; 요청하다 charge per click 클릭당 지불 due (돈을) 지불해야 하는 receipt 영수증 issue 발부하다 priority 우선순위 criteria 기준 automatically 자동으로 renew 갱신하다

수신: 퍼트리샤 호크 (pathawk@adurnet.com)
발신: 제이슨 앤드류스 (jandrews23@jeetmail.com)
날짜: 12월 20일
제목: 송장번호 1122334

호크 씨께,

저희의 현 광고 캠페인에 대한 송장번호 1122334를 잘 받았습니다. 두 장의 수표를 보냈습니다. 하나는 6832.08달러짜리이고, **179**다른 하나는 2150달러 짜리입니다.

그런데 저는 **180(B)**"추가 요청사항"의 의도를 명확히 하고 싶습니다. 저희가 18~35세 사이의 여성 인터넷 사용자들을 겨냥해 달라고 한 요청을 뜻하는 것입니까?

아울러 다음 달 여러 개의 신규 광고와 함께 저희 광고 캠페인을 확대하려고 합니다. **180(C)**이렇게 하면 가격이 얼마나 높아지는지, **180(D)**주문을 넣기 위해 콘텐츠를 얼마나 미리 준비해야 하는지 알려 주시겠습니까?

감사합니다.

제이슨 앤드류스
오가닉 헤어 케어

> **어휘** ad campaign 광고 캠페인 clarify 명확하게 하다 purpose 의도, 목적 refer to ~을 나타내다 expand 확장[확대]하다 multiple 다수의 advertisement 광고 in advance 미리

176 추론 / 암시

번역 광고에 포함된 것은 무엇이겠는가?
(A) 미용사 교육 프로그램
(B) 헤어 제품
(C) 미용실 서비스
(D) 헤어스타일링 잡지

해설 어더 네트워킹이 송장을 보내는 곳(BILL TO)을 보면, 앤드류스 헤어케어 서플라이즈라는 회사이다. 그리고, Description을 살펴보면 Ad(광고)라는 말이 등장한다. 따라서 이 회사가 어더 네트워킹에 헤어 제품 광고를 요청했음을 알 수 있다. 정답은 (B)이다.

177 추론 / 암시

번역 고객이 주문한 광고 유형에 대해 암시된 것은?
(A) 갑자기 화면에 나타난다.
(B) 동영상 광고를 포함한다.
(C) 가능한 최대 크기이다.
(D) 한 달 후 만료된다.

해설 송장 Description 부분의 세 번째 항목 광고 유형으로 "Pop-up"이 나와 있다. 따라서 정답은 (A)이다.

▶ **Paraphrasing** 지문의 Pop-up
→ 정답의 appears on-screen suddenly

178 사실 관계 확인

번역 청구 방식에 대해 명시된 것은?
(A) 광고회사가 요금을 낮췄다.
(B) 클릭 수에 따라 고객에게 청구한다.
(C) 지불 금액은 매월 동일하다.
(D) 총 송장 금액은 주 단위로 계산된다.

해설 송장 중간 부분에서 '클릭당 지불(charge per click)'이라는 말이 나온다. 이를 통해 (B)가 정답인 것을 알 수 있다.

▶ **Paraphrasing** 지문의 charge per click → 정답의 is billed by the number of clicks

179 연계

번역 앤드류스 씨는 왜 두 장의 수표를 보내는가?
(A) 다음 달 기본요금을 내기 위해
(B) 두 번째 마케팅 노력 비용을 대기 위해
(C) 광고가 눈에 더 잘 띄도록 하기 위해
(D) 지불 기일이 지난 청구서를 해결하기 위해

해설 이메일 첫 단락에서 2150달러의 수표를 보냈다는 내용이 나오는데 이 숫자에 주목할 필요가 있다. 송장에서 Comments 5번을 살펴보면 이 가격을 지불하는 이유는 '우선 노출(priority placement)'을 받기 위해서다. 따라서 광고가 상위에 노출되어 눈에 더 잘 띄게 하려 한다는 목적인 (C)가 정답이다.

180 연계

번역 앤드류스 씨가 질문하지 않는 것은?
(A) 캠페인의 성공률
(B) 특정 소비자를 목표로 할 때의 수수료
(C) 추가 광고 비용
(D) 신규 광고 처리에 필요한 시간

해설 (B)는 송장 Description 부분의 추가 요청 금액(Additional Requests)에 대해 이메일 두 번째 단락에서 묻고 있고, (C), (D)는 이메일 마지막 단락에서 각각 확인할 수 있다. 따라서 언급되지 않은 (A)가 정답이다.

181 -185 기사+이메일

카운티 교통위원회 이사 은퇴

글 엘렌 깁슨

미나한(9월 8일)—보이빈 카운티 교통위원회(BCTC)를 11년간 이끌어 온 안드레아 루이즈가 올해 말에 직책에서 물러날 의향을 밝혔다. 그의 후임자를 위한 탐색이 현재 진행 중이다.

루이즈 씨는 로어 하이츠 교통부에서 경력을 시작해, 그곳에서 근무하며 프로젝트 딜리버리 그룹 수장까지 올랐다. **184**그는 23년간의 재직 기간 중 수 마일의 자전거 전용도로를 설치한 것을 가장 중요한 순간으로 여긴다. 시내 도로에서 오염을 일으키는 차량 수를 줄인다는 목표를 달성해낸 사업이었다.

BCTC 이사로 임명된 후 루이즈 씨는 주로 이 기관의 기존 서비스를 향상시키는 데 주력해 왔다. **182**그는 카운티의 혼잡 시간대에 일부 버스를 고속버스로 전환하고 테버네트에 환승역을 건설했으며, 모든 버스 노선의 주말 운행 시간을 확장했다. **181**그뿐 아니라, 65세가 넘는 주민들에게 인기 있는 무료 교통 서비스 등 새로운 제안들도 맡아 했다.

루이즈 씨는 자신의 재임 기간 중에 BCTC가 이루어 낸 것들에 자부심을 느낀다고 하면서 이렇게 설명했다. "우리는 보이빈 주민들의 삶의 질을 개선해 왔다고 생각합니다." **185**웨스트 서멜의 자택에서 가족과 함께 시간을 보내는 것 외에, 그는 은퇴 후 기간에도 자문 역할을 통해 지역사회를 계속 도울 수 있기를 희망한다.

> **어휘** director 이사, 책임자 transportation commission 교통위원회 retire 은퇴하다 head 이끌다; 책임자 reveal 밝히다 intention 의도, 의사 step down from ~에서 물러나다 position 직책 conduct 수행하다 successor 후임자 highlight 가장 좋은 부분 installation 설치 bicycle lane 자전거 전용 도로 decrease 줄이다 pollution-causing 오염을 야기하는 appoint 임명하다 existing 기존의 convert 전환시키다 rush hour 혼잡 시간대 transfer station 환승역 offering 제공(되는 것) accomplish 성취하다 tenure 재임 기간 retirement 은퇴, 은퇴 생활 consulting 자문의, 상담의

발신: 펠리시아 페리스 〈felicia.parris@shaltfoundation.org〉
수신: 안드레아 루이즈 〈a.ruiz@bc-tc.org〉
제목: 기회
날짜: 9월 19일

루이즈 씨께,

〈보이빈 헤럴드〉에서 귀하의 은퇴에 관한 기사를 읽었습니다. 우선, 쉘트 재단을 대표해 축하를 드립니다. 귀하가 저희 재단 및 기타 비영리 단체와 협력해 주신 데 대해 항상 감사하고 있습니다.

하지만 둘째로, 귀하가 지역 사회에서 계속 활동하는 데 관심을 보여주셨다는 사실에 감동을 받았습니다. **183**사실 저희 단체는 새 이사회 임원을 찾고 있는데, 귀하께서 그 역할을 맡아주신다면 정말 좋을 것 같습니다. **184**귀하의 전문 지식이 재단의 효율성을 상당히 높여줄 수 있을 것이고, 로어 하이츠 프로젝트에 자부심을 가지신 것으로 보아 저희와 동일한 목표를 가지신 것으로 보입니다. **185**또한 기사에서 보니, 저희 본사가 귀하의 도시에 있는 것 같습니다. 정말 우연의 일치죠!

관심 있으시면, 한번 뵙고 이야기를 나눌 수 있을까요? 답신을 기다리겠습니다.

펠리시아 페리스
쉘트 재단 책임자

어휘 on behalf of ~을 대신[대표]해서 appreciate 감사하다 cooperation 협력, 협조 nonprofit 비영리 단체 be struck by ~에 감명 받다 interest in ~에 대한 관심 active 활동적인 board member (이사회) 임원 fill (빈자리를) 채우다 role 역할 expertise 전문 지식 effectiveness 효과, 효율성 share 공유하다 be headquartered in ~에 본사를 두다 coincidence 우연의 일치 get together 만나다 await 기다리다

181 사실 관계 확인

번역 BCTC에 관해 언급된 것은?
(A) 11명의 임명된 공직자로 구성되어 있다.
(B) 루이즈 씨의 후임자를 지명했다.
(C) 노인들을 위해 특별한 서비스를 제공한다.
(D) 모든 보이빈 카운티 주민들은 BCTC 회의에 참석할 수 있다.

해설 기사의 세 번째 단락에서 65세가 넘는 주민들에게 인기 있는 무료 교통 서비스를 제공한다고 했으므로 정답은 (C)이다. (B)는 기사의 첫 번째 단락에서 후임자를 위한 탐색이 현재 진행 중이라고 했으므로 답이 될 수 없다.

▶▶ **Paraphrasing** 지문의 a popular free transportation service for residents over the age of 65 → 정답의 a special service for the elderly

182 세부 사항

번역 루이즈 씨의 업적 중 하나로 열거된 것은?
(A) 일부 버스 노선 확장
(B) 여객 운임 인상 억제
(C) 버스 승객들의 보다 빠른 통근 실현
(D) 한 건축물의 환승역 전환

해설 기사의 세 번째 단락에서 루이즈 씨가 카운티의 혼잡 시간대에 일부 버스를 고속버스로 전환했다고 했으므로, 버스로 통근하는 시간이 줄었다는 것을 알 수 있다. 따라서 정답은 (C)이다. 모든 버스 노선의 주말 운행을 확장하고, 테버네트에 환승역을 새로 건설했다는 말은 있지만 (A)와 (D)는 적절하지 않다.

183 글의 주제 / 목적

번역 이메일을 보낸 목적에 해당하는 것은?
(A) 루이즈 씨에게 조직 구성원이 되어 달라고 요청하려고
(B) BCTC를 위한 새 사업을 제안하려고
(C) 지역 사회 서비스의 문제점을 보고하려고
(D) 쉘트 재단이 마련한 파티에 루이즈 씨를 초대하려고

해설 이메일의 두 번째 단락에서 단체가 새 임원을 찾고 있고 루이스 씨가 그 역할을 맡아준다(fill that role)면 좋을 것 같다고 했으므로 정답은 (A)이다.

▶▶ **Paraphrasing** 지문의 fill that role → 정답의 become part of an organization

184 연계

번역 쉘트 재단에 관해 무엇이 사실이겠는가?
(A) 환경 친화적인 교통을 장려한다.
(B) 대중 교통의 적정 요금에 관심이 있다.
(C) 장애인들에게 지원을 제공한다.
(D) 도로 안전을 향상시키기 위해 노력한다.

해설 이메일의 두 번째 단락에서 루이즈 씨의 로어 하이츠 프로젝트에 대한 자부심을 보아 쉘트 재단과 목표를 공유하는 것으로 보인다고 했다. 기사의 두 번째 단락에서 수 마일의 자전거 전용도로를 설치하여 시내 도로에서 오염을 일으키는 차량 수를 줄인다는 목표를 달성해낸 사업으로 로어 하이츠 프로젝트를 설명하고 있다. 따라서 쉘트 재단 또한 환경 친화적인 교통을 장려하는 기관임을 유추할 수 있으므로, 정답은 (A)이다.

▶▶ **Paraphrasing** 지문의 decreasing the number of pollution-causing vehicles → 정답의 environmentally-friendly transportation

185 연계

번역 쉘트 재단의 본사는 어디에 있는가?
(A) 미나한
(B) 로어 하이츠
(C) 테버네트
(D) 웨스트 서멜

해설 이메일의 두 번째 단락에서 쉘트 재단이 루이즈 씨의 도시에 본사를 두고 있는 것 같다고 했고, 기사의 마지막 단락에서 루이스 씨가 웨스트 서멜의 자택에서 가족과 함께 시간을 보낼 것이라고 했으므로 정답은 (D)이다.

186-190 회람+이메일+양식

회람

수신: 전 직원

발신: 헨리에타 드레이크, 인사부 이사

제목: 직원 동호회

날짜: 3월 20일

아글란 메디컬 테크놀로지스는 직원 동호회에 대한 지원을 시작하기로 결정했습니다. **186(A)(B)(C)**이 같은 지원을 제공함으로써 우리는 사회적 관계를 돈독히 하고, 건강을 증진하고, 직원들이 서로에게서 배울 수 있는 기회를 향상시키기를 희망합니다.

동호회를 만들기 원하신다면 첨부된 신청서를 작성해서 저희 부서로 보내주세요. **187**동호회 운영을 도울 최소한 다른 한 명의 직원을 찾으셔야 한다는 점 기억해 주십시오. **190**신청서를 검토한 후, 필요하다면 회계부나 법률팀에 보내 각각 예산 및 법적인 책임 문제를 검토하도록 할 예정입니다. 일단 신청서가 승인되면 회사 소통 채널을 통해 회원 모집을 시작하실 수 있습니다.

어휘 sponsor 후원하다 provide 제공하다 support 지원, 후원 foster 조성하다 social relationship 사회적[사교적] 관계 wellness 건강, 안녕 fill out (서식 등을) 작성하다 application form 신청서 return 돌려주다 note 주목하다 assist with ~을 돕다 operation 운영 review 검토하다; 검토 if necessary 필요하다면 budget 예산 liability 법적 책임 issue (해결해야 할) 문제 respectively 각각 once 일단 ~하면 approve 승인하다 recruit 모집하다

발신: 코너 헤이즈

수신: 헨리에타 드레이크

제목: 직원 동호회

날짜: 6월 2일

드레이크 씨께,

직원 동호회 프로그램에 대한 공지를 매우 관심 있게 보았습니다. 그리고 동호회 개설을 신청하고 싶습니다. 하지만 공지가 있은 이후부터 제가 어떤 프로젝트로 바빠서 이 기회를 놓치게 된 것은 아닐지 걱정이 됩니다. **188**새 동호회를 위한 자금이 아직도 남아 있는지 확인해 주실 수 있을까요? **189**또한, 저는 농구 동호회를 시작하는 데 가장 관심이 있습니다. 그래서 이미 누가 농구 동호회를 신청한 것은 아닌지 확인하고 싶습니다. 만약 그렇다면 저는 다른 활동을 알아보겠습니다.

감사합니다

코너 헤이즈

어휘 be busy with ~로 바쁘다 worried 걱정하는 miss (기회를) 놓치다 confirm 확인하다 funding 자금 (지원) left 남아 있는 whether ~인지 아닌지 apply to ~을 신청하다 look into ~을 조사하다

직원 동호회 개설 신청서

신청자 정보

이름: 코너 헤이즈   부서: 영업부   직책: 판매 컨설턴트

내선 번호: 493   이메일 주소: c.hayes@aglanmt.com

제2 지원자 이름: 카미유 잉그럼   내선 번호: 448

동호회 정보

189이름: 하이킹 동호회

제안하는 활동: 지역 산길 주말 하이킹, 한 달에 한 번

제안하는 예산: 월 50달러

의견: 비용은 간식, 물, 휘발유 구입에 쓸 예정

인사부 전용

신청서 접수 일자: 6월 3일

검토자: 하치로 카토

승인 여부: 승인 __ 비승인 __ **190**추가 검토 필요 x (예산 __ 법적 책임 x)

서명 (승인될 경우):

어휘 applicant 신청자, 지원자 position 직책 secondary 부차적인, 제2의 proposed 제안된 hike 하이킹 trail 오솔길, 산길, 트레일 snack 간식 gas 휘발유 approve 승인하다 require 필요로 하다 further 더 이상의 signature 서명

---

186 사실 관계 확인

번역 직원 동호회 프로그램의 목적으로 언급되지 않은 것은?

(A) 직원의 건강 증진

(B) 직원들간의 우정 함양

(C) 직원들의 지식 공유 장려

(D) 직원들에게 새로운 경험 제공

해설 회람의 첫 번째 단락에서 동호회를 지원함으로써 직원들의 사회적 관계를 돈독히 하고, 건강을 증진하고, 서로 배울 수 있는 기회를 향상시키기를 희망한다고 했으므로, (A), (B), (C)가 직원 동호회 프로그램의 목적임을 확인할 수 있다. 따라서 정답은 (D)이다.

▶▶ **Paraphrasing** 지문의 **foster social relationships** → 보기의 **stimulate friendships between employees**
지문의 **improve wellness** → 보기의 **enhance employees' health**
지문의 **increase opportunities for employees to learn from each other** → 보기의 **encourage employees to share knowledge**

---

187 세부 사항

번역 회람에 따르면, 직원이 동호회를 시작하기 위해 필요한 것은?

(A) 동료의 운영 지원

(B) 부서장의 승인

(C) 잠재적인 동호회 회원의 명단

(D) 관련 활동에 관한 배경 지식

해설 회람의 두 번째 단락에서 동호회를 만들기 원하면 운영을 도와줄 다른 직원을 최소 한 명 이상 찾아야 한다고 했으므로, 정답은 (A)이다.

▶▶ **Paraphrasing** 지문의 **one other staff member to assist with the club's operation** → 정답의 **The administrative support of a coworker**

188 글의 주제 / 목적

번역 헤이즈 씨가 이메일을 쓴 이유는?
(A) 거절된 것에 대해 물어보려고
(B) 절차를 확인하려고
(C) 최신 정보를 알아보려고
(D) 문제점을 지적하려고

해설 이메일의 중반부에서 새 동호회를 지원해줄 자금이 아직 남아 있는지 확인해 줄 것을 요청하고 있으므로, 동호회 신청 가능성에 대한 최신 정보를 확인하기 위한 이메일임을 알 수 있다. 따라서 정답은 (C)이다.

189 연계

번역 직원 동호회 프로그램에 관해 암시된 것은?
(A) 농구 동호회 시작 신청을 이미 받았다.
(B) 영업부 직원들 사이에 가장 인기가 있다.
(C) 동호회 활동은 항상 주말에 한다.
(D) 모든 예산을 이미 사용했다.

해설 이메일에서 헤이즈 씨가 농구 동호회를 시작하는 데 가장 관심이 있다고 한 후, 이미 다른 사람이 신청했다면 다른 활동을 알아보겠다고 했다. 헤이즈 씨가 작성한 신청서의 동호회 정보 중 '이름: 하이킹 동호회(Hiking Club)'를 통해 농구 동호회는 다른 사람이 이미 신청했다는 것을 유추할 수 있으므로, 정답은 (A)이다.

190 연계

번역 신청서는 다음에 어느 부서로 보내질 것인가?
(A) 인사부
(B) 회계부
(C) 법률팀
(D) 영업부

해설 신청서의 '인사부 전용' 밑에 있는 항목에 '추가 검토 필요'와 '법적 책임(Liability)' 부분에 체크 표시가 돼 있다. 회람의 두 번째 단락에서 신청서를 검토한 후, 필요하다면 회계부나 법률팀에 보내 각각 예산 및 법적 책임 문제를 확인한다고 했으므로, 정답은 (C)이다.

191 -195 웹페이지 + 이메일 + 이용자 후기

---

http://www.schumofffurniture.com

슈모프 퍼니처

191앨턴 스트리트에 한 세기 이상 자리를 지켜 온 슈모프 퍼니처는 이 지역에서 가장 신뢰받는 소매 수공 목재 가구점이라는 점을 자랑스럽게 생각합니다. 본 웹사이트에 모든 품목을 다 보여드리지 않으니 저희 전시관을 방문하셔서 현재 가구 모음을 살펴보시기 바랍니다.

특별 품목 할인 – 6월 4일부터 6월 21일까지

- SKU#122 4개의 보관 서랍이 있는 디럭스 목재 컴퓨터 책상 – 685달러
- **192가능한 색깔: 검은색, 갈색, 체리색**
- 업그레이드 옵션:
  - **193접이식 테이블과 조정 가능한 선반 3개가 달린 책장**– 865달러
  - 패브릭 안락의자가 딸린 2개 세트 – 895달러
  - 가죽 등받이 중역용 의자가 딸린 2개 세트 – 935달러

지역 목공예 스튜디오에서 나온 특별판입니다.

마지막 업데이트: 6월 1일

어휘 fixture 고정, 붙박이 region 지역 trusted 신뢰받는 retailer 소매업자 handmade 수공의 deluxe 고급의 drawer 서랍 storage 보관 fold-out 접는 방식의 adjustable 조정 가능한 armchair 안락의자 leather-backed 등 부분이 가죽 재질인 woodwork 목공예

수신: 영업팀
발신: 줄리아 코너스
제목: 특별 품목
날짜: 6월 3일

팀원 여러분께,

애펠리 스튜디오의 톰 챔버스 씨로부터 우리 웹사이트 상에서 고급 목재 컴퓨터 책상(SKU#122)의 설명이 잘못되었다고 들었습니다. **192생산 문제로 인해 갈색과 체리색 옵션은 현재 이용할 수 없습니다, 매력적인 흰색이 있습니다.**

고객을 응대할 때 이러한 변경사항을 언급해 주십시오. IT팀에서 업데이트를 할 수 있게 되면 웹사이트에 수정된 정보가 올라갈 것입니다.

줄리아 코너스
매장 영업팀장

어휘 description 기술, 설명 inaccuracy 부정확 production 생산 currently 현재 available 이용 가능한 appealing 매력적인 corrected 수정된

고객 리뷰 플러스
리뷰된 업체: 슈모프 퍼니처   작성자: 매기 클락슨   날짜: 7월 12일

저는 특별판 목재 컴퓨터 책상을 사기 위해 '특별 품목' 세일 첫날에 슈모프 퍼니처에 갔습니다. 정말 마음에 듭니다. **193편리한 접이식 테이블과 책꽂이 덕분에** 일체형 작업장과 같은 기능을 합니다. 사실 제가 원했던 홈오피스의 모습을 **195정확히** 얻을 수 있었습니다. 이보다 더 잘 어울리는 걸 요구할 수 없었을 정도입니다. **194제 구매를 담당한 직원 제리 힌데 씨는** 전시관의 수공예 가구 전체에 대해 무척 많이 알고 있었습니다. 대체로 책상과 매장 모두 강력 추천합니다.

어휘 purchase 구매하다 handy 편리한, 유용한 bookshelf 책꽂이 function 기능을 하다 all-in-one 일체형 workstation 작업공간 handle 다루다 knowledgeable 아는 것이 많은 all in all 대체로 recommend 추천하다

191 사실 관계 확인

번역 슈모프 퍼니처에 대해 명시된 것은?
(A) 수공예 가구를 생산한다.
(B) 종이 카탈로그에 제품 목록을 실었다.
(C) 100년 이상 영업해 왔다.
(D) 한 해의 일부는 영업하지 않는다.

해설 첫 번째 지문 첫 문장에서 앨턴 스트리트에 한 세기가 넘는(for more than a century) 세월 동안 자리해 있었다는 내용을 토대로 정답 (C)를 고를 수 있다. 참고로, 다른 업체들에서 생산한 가구를 판매하는 소매점이므로 (A)는 답이 될 수 없다.

192 연계

번역 책상은 현재 어떤 색상을 구입할 수 있는가?
(A) 황갈색과 체리색
(B) 검은색과 흰색
(C) 갈색과 검은색
(D) 흰색과 황갈색

해설 첫 번째 지문 중간에, 가능한 색상(Colors available)이 검정, 갈색, 체리색이라고 되어 있는데, 두 번째 지문 첫 단락 후반부를 보면 생산 문제로 인해 현재 갈색과 체리색은 없고, 대신 흰색이 있다고 했다. 따라서 검은색과 흰색이 가능하므로 정답은 (B)이다.

어휘 tan 황갈색(의)

193 연계

번역 클락슨 씨는 책상 값으로 얼마를 지불했을 것 같은가?
(A) 685달러
(B) 865달러
(C) 895달러
(D) 935달러

해설 세 번째 지문에서 클락슨 씨는 접이식 테이블(handy folding table)과 책꽂이(bookshelf)를 구입했다는 말이 나온다. 이를 토대로 첫 번째 지문 Upgrade options에서 찾아보면, 첫 번째 항목에 접이식 테이블(fold-out table)과 책장(bookcase)이 나와 있다. 따라서 클락슨 씨가 지불한 비용은 865달러라는 것을 알 수 있다. 따라서 정답은 (B)이다.

194 추론 / 암시

번역 힌데 씨에 대한 설명으로 사실일 것 같은 것은?
(A) 클락슨 씨의 리뷰를 읽었다.
(B) 클락슨 씨를 직접 만났다.
(C) 콜센터에서 일한다.
(D) 책상을 하나 조립했다.

해설 세 번째 지문에서 클락슨 씨는 힌데 씨가 자신의 구매를 담당(handled my purchase)했다고 했으므로 힌데 씨는 클락슨 씨를 직접 만났다는 사실을 알 수 있다. 정답은 (B)이다.

195 동의어 찾기

번역 이용자 후기에서 첫 번째 단락 3행의 "just"와 의미가 가장 가까운 것은?
(A) 간신히
(B) 아마
(C) 정확히
(D) 최근에

해설 just는 흔히 알고 있는 '막, 방금'이라는 뜻도 있지만 본문과 같이 '딱, 바로'처럼 '정확히'라는 뜻으로도 사용할 수 있다. 따라서 가장 가까운 의미는 (C) precisely(정확히)이다.

어휘 barely 간신히; 거의 ~ 없다[않다]

196-200 이메일+이메일+일정표

수신: 지나 레트 〈glett@rendec-tech.com〉
발신: 미아 오티즈 〈mortiz@rendec-tech.com〉
날짜: 4월 17일
제목: 카드

레트 씨께,

회사 신용카드인 RCT 페이먼트 카드에 대한 귀하의 신청을 저희 회계팀에서 처리하고 있습니다. 저희가 처리해 드리기 위해서는 다음 증빙 자료 중 하나가 필요합니다.

* 뉴저지주 로디에 있는 테크 캠퍼스로 최소한 5개월 이상 통근한 자료
* **196**총 400달러 이상의 회의 또는 워크숍 비용 지불 내역
* 타지에서 온 고객 접대 목적으로 최소 200달러 이상 사용한 비용에 대한 관리자의 승인 내역

또한, 카드를 발급 받으시면, 다음의 RCT 출장 정책을 따르도록 하십시오.
– 차량 대여는 사내 출장부서를 통해 예약해야 합니다.
– 숙소는 지정된 여행사인 **200(C)**TZAD 트래블을 통해 구해야 합니다.
– 공항을 오가는 택시비는 종이 영수증을 받아야 합니다.
– 일일 최대 75달러의 현금 선지급은 **200(D)**5일 이상의 출장에만 받을 수 있습니다.

미아 오티즈, 회계팀, 렌덱 센터 오브 테크놀로지(RCT)

어휘 accounting 회계 process 처리하다 application 신청 proof 증명 commute 통근 conference 회의 approval 승인 entertain 접대하다 out-of-town 타지에서 온 corporate travel 출장 reserve 예약하다 in-house (회사) 내부의 lodging 임시 숙소 designated 지정된 obtain 구하다, 입수하다 cash advance 현금 선지급

수신: 지나 레트 〈glett@rendec-tech.com〉
발신: DTEC 〈workshop@dtec.com〉
날짜: 4월 19일
제목: 확정

레트 씨께,

196델포드 테크놀로지 에듀케이션 센터(DTEC)의 5월에 있을 3일짜리 워크숍에 대한 450달러의 등록비를 받았습니다. **197**이로써 귀하는 DTEC 웹사이트상의 주별 강좌도 이용하실 수 있음을 주지해 주십시오.

예전과 마찬가지로 DTEC은 샬롯 공항에서 워크숍 장소인 샤르비아 호텔까지 무료 셔틀버스 서비스를 제공합니다. 또한, 라라 이아로치의 기조 연설은 오전 10시가 아닌 10시 20분에 시작함을 알려드립니다.

198이 워크숍이 귀하와 다른 참석자분들이 유용한 새 지식을 많이 얻을 기회가 되기를 바랍니다. 5월에 뵐 날을 고대하겠습니다.

DTEC 워크숍

어휘 registration 등록 grant 부여하다, 승인하다 lecture 강좌 as in the past 전처럼 complimentary 무료의 keynote speech 기조연설 attendee 참석자 take in 흡수하다

```
                    일정표: 지나 레트

5월 2일
 • 오전 9시 DTEC 셔틀로 샤르비아 호텔까지 이동 200(C)(예약#181, TZAD
   트래블)

 •199오후 2시~5시 론 윤 박사가 주재하는 워크숍 참석

5월 3일
 • 오전 10시~오후 3:40 그룹 토의
 •199오후 4시 호텔 회의실에서 론 윤 박사 면접

5월 4일
 • 오전 10시~오후 5시 실무 시간
 • 오후 5:30 폐회사 및 연회

5월 5일
 • 오전 8시 DTEC 셔틀로 공항까지 이동
```

어휘 transfer 이동하다 booking 예약 attend 참석하다 job
interview 면접 hands-on 직접 해 보는 closing remarks
맺음말 reception (환영, 축하) 연회

196 연계

번역 레트 씨는 왜 RCT 페이먼트 카드를 받을 것 같은가?
(A) 자주 테크 캠퍼스로 통근한다.
(B) 5월에 고객들을 만나 접대할 예정이다.
(C) 산업 행사로 400달러 이상 지불했다.
(D) 관리직으로 승진했다.

해설 첫 번째 지문에서 RCT 페이먼트 카드를 받기 위해서는 세 가지 요건 중
하나를 충족시켜야 한다고 했는데, 두 번째 지문에서 레트 씨는 워크숍 비
용을 450달러 지불하였다는 점을 바탕으로 이 요건을 충족시켰기 때문에
카드를 발급 받을 수 있을 것이다. 따라서 정답은 (C)이다.

197 사실 관계 확인

번역 DTEC에 대해 명시된 것은?
(A) RCT 직원에게 할인을 제공한다.
(B) 자체 호텔 체인을 운영한다.
(C) 이아로치 씨가 설립했다.
(D) 자사의 웹사이트에 강연을 공유한다.

해설 두 번째 지문 첫 단락 마지막 문장에 DTEC 웹사이트에서 주별 강좌
(weekly lectures)를 볼 수 있다는 말이 나온다. 이를 토대로 정답 (D)를
고를 수 있다.

▸▸ Paraphrasing   지문의 **weekly lectures via the DTEC
                 Web site** → 정답의 **talks on its Web site**

198 동의어 찾기

번역 두 번째 이메일에서 세 번째 단락 1행의 "take in"과 의미가 가장 가까운
것은?
(A) ~에게 주택을 제공한다
(B) ~로 구성되어 있다
(C) 단축하다
(D) 받아들이다

해설 take in은 음식과 같은 경우에는 '섭취하다'라는 의미로, 지식의 경우에는
'받아들이다, 이해하다' 정도로 해석할 수 있다. 이와 유사한 뜻을 가진 단
어는 absorb이다. 마찬가지로 '(정보를) 받아들이다'라는 의미로 동일하
게 해석할 수 있다. 따라서 정답은 (D)이다.

199 추론 / 암시

번역 레트 씨에 대해 암시된 것은?
(A) 다른 일터로 이동할 것이다.
(B) 워크숍 강사를 면접할 것이다.
(C) 폐회사를 듣지 못할 것이다.
(D) 공항에서 연착 시간이 길 것이다.

해설 세 번째 지문 5월 3일 오후 4시에 있는 일정을 살펴보면 론 윤 박사와 면접
(Job interview)이 예정되어 있는데 5월 2일 일정에서 론 윤 박사는 워크
숍을 주재하는 것을 알 수 있다. 이 두 가지를 고려해보면 레트 씨가 워크숍
강사인 론 윤 박사를 면접할 것임을 알 수 있으므로 정답은 (B)이다.

200 연계

번역 레트 씨의 출장에 어떤 출장 정책이 적용될 것 같은가?
(A) 차량 대여에 관한 정책
(B) 택시 영수증에 관한 정책
(C) 호텔 마련에 관한 정책
(D) 현금 선지급에 관한 정책

해설 레트 씨가 첫 번째 지문 두 번째 단락에서 명시된 정책 어느 부분에 해당되
는지를 묻는 문제이다. 세 번째 지문 첫 줄에서 예약을 TZAD 트래블을 통
해서 했다는 부분에서 숙박에 관한 정책이 적용된 것을 알 수 있다. 따라
서 정답은 (C)이다. 두 번째 지문 마지막 단락에서 공항에서 호텔까지 무
료 서틀 서비스를 제공한다는 점을 바탕으로 (A), (B)는 해당이 되지 않는
다는 것을 알 수 있다. 그리고 두 번째 지문 첫 단락에서 워크숍이 3일 동
안 이뤄지는 점과 네 번째 정책에서 5일 이상 지속되는 출장에서 선지급이
가능하다는 점을 종합해보면 (D)도 적용되지 않는 것을 알 수 있다.

101 (D)	**102** (B)	**103** (B)	**104** (D)	**105** (A)
106 (D)	**107** (D)	**108** (A)	**109** (C)	**110** (D)
111 (B)	**112** (C)	**113** (A)	**114** (B)	**115** (C)
116 (B)	**117** (C)	**118** (A)	**119** (A)	**120** (D)
121 (C)	**122** (D)	**123** (A)	**124** (D)	**125** (B)
126 (C)	**127** (C)	**128** (B)	**129** (A)	**130** (B)
131 (C)	**132** (B)	**133** (C)	**134** (A)	**135** (B)
136 (C)	**137** (A)	**138** (D)	**139** (C)	**140** (A)
141 (B)	**142** (D)	**143** (A)	**144** (D)	**145** (C)
146 (D)	**147** (C)	**148** (C)	**149** (D)	**150** (D)
151 (A)	**152** (B)	**153** (D)	**154** (D)	**155** (B)
156 (A)	**157** (D)	**158** (A)	**159** (D)	**160** (C)
161 (C)	**162** (A)	**163** (C)	**164** (B)	**165** (C)
166 (B)	**167** (B)	**168** (B)	**169** (A)	**170** (C)
171 (C)	**172** (C)	**173** (B)	**174** (D)	**175** (A)
176 (D)	**177** (C)	**178** (A)	**179** (D)	**180** (C)
181 (D)	**182** (B)	**183** (D)	**184** (D)	**185** (C)
186 (B)	**187** (A)	**188** (A)	**189** (C)	**190** (D)
191 (A)	**192** (B)	**193** (B)	**194** (C)	**195** (D)
196 (B)	**197** (D)	**198** (C)	**199** (B)	**200** (D)

PART 5

101 명사 자리 _ 전치사 뒤

해설 빈칸 앞에 전치사(in)가 있으므로 명사나 동명사가 올 자리이다. 여기서는 동사 (A) observe를 제외하고는 모두 명사나 동명사이다. (B) observers(관찰자)는 내용상 맞지 않고, (C) observing(준수하기)은 타동사이기 때문에 뒤에 목적어가 반드시 나와야 하므로 오답이다. 따라서 정답은 (D) observance(준수)이다. 참고로 in observance of(~을 기념하여, 준수하여)라는 표현을 기억해두도록 하자.

번역 청소 직원들은 국경일을 기념하여 오늘 일찍 근무를 마칠 것이다.

어휘 cleaning staff 청소 직원들 observe 준수하다; 관찰하다

102 목적격 대명사

해설 전치사 on 뒤에 빈칸이 있으므로 앞에 언급된 the firm을 받는 대명사의 목적격이 와야 한다. 따라서 (B) it이 정답이다.

번역 그 회사에서의 면접을 잘 준비하기 위해 애덤스 씨는 그 회사에 관해 미리 조금 조사를 했다.

어휘 in order to + 동사원형 ~하기 위해 be well-prepared for ~에 잘 준비하다 firm 회사 do research 조사하다 in advance 미리, 사전에 on one's own 혼자서, 단독으로

103 동사 시제

해설 tomorrow라는 시제 힌트를 보고 미래 시제를 고를 수 있어야 한다. 문을 닫는 시점이 내일이기 때문에 미래 시제인 (B) will close가 정답이다.

번역 카운티 법원 청사는 히스토릭 홈즈 축제 때문에 내일 오후 2시에 문을 닫을 것이다.

어휘 courthouse 법원 청사 due to ~ 때문에 close 문을 닫다

104 전치사 어휘

해설 빈칸 뒤의 from과 어울리는 전치사를 찾아야 하는데, 휴게실(break room)의 '바로 맞은편에서' 오리엔테이션이 열린다는 의미가 가장 적절하다. 정답은 (D) across이다.

번역 신입사원 예비 교육이 4월 26일 일요일에 휴게실 맞은편에 있는 사무실에서 열릴 예정이다.

어휘 orientation 예비 교육[오리엔테이션] new employee 신입사원 across from ~ 맞은편에 break room 휴게실 inside ~ 안에 above ~ 위에 beside ~ 옆에

105 명사절 접속사 자리

해설 as to는 regarding과 마찬가지로 '~에 대하여'라는 의미의 전치사로 뒤에 명사가 와야 한다. 하지만 빈칸 뒤에 주어, 동사로 시작하는 문장이 나왔기 때문에 빈칸 이후를 명사절로 만들어 줘야 한다. 따라서 빈칸에는 명사절 접속사가 와야 한다. (B) everything(모든 것)은 대명사, (D) merely(단지)는 부사, (A) whether와 (C) since는 접속사인데, whether가 '~인지 아닌지'라는 의미의 명사절 접속사이고, 뒤쪽에 or라는 힌트를 통해 정답임을 알 수 있다. 따라서 정답은 (A) whether이다.

번역 우리가 예산을 지금 수정해야 하는지, 아니면 권 씨의 보고서를 기다려야 하는지를 놓고 약간의 논란이 있다.

어휘 debate 논쟁, 논란 revise 수정하다 budget 예산 since ~이니까; ~ 이래

106 부사 자리 _ 형용사 수식

해설 be동사와 형용사 available 사이가 빈칸이므로, 형용사를 수식하는 부사가 들어가야 한다. (D) exclusively가 '오직, 독점적으로'라는 뜻으로 뒤에 있는 available을 수식하는 부사이므로 정답은 (D)이다.

번역 스태빌리티 리클라인 안락의자 제품군은 오로지 퀸 백화점에서만 구입할 수 있다.

어휘 lounge chair 안락의자 exclusion 배제, 제외 exclusive 배타적인, 독점적인 exclude 배제하다, 제외하다

107 부사 어휘

해설 보기가 모두 부사이므로, 문맥상 바로 뒤에 나오는 동사 avoid와 가장 자연스러운 것을 골라야 한다. 행진 때문에 발생한 교통 체증을 '완전히' 피하다라는 의미가 가장 적절하다. 따라서 정답은 (D) fully(완전히)이다.

번역 WXI 통신원들은 운전자들에게 행진으로 인한 교통 혼잡을 완전히 피하려면 딜 코트 고속도로를 타라고 권했다.

어휘 reporter 통신원, 기자 recommend 권하다 expressway 고속도로 avoid traffic 교통 혼잡을 피하다 newly 새로 heavily 무겁게 loudly 시끄럽게

108 동사(과거분사) 어휘

해설 서비스 중단으로 인해 '영향을 받은' 고객들이라는 의미가 가장 자연스러우므로, 정답은 (A) affected(영향을 받은)이다. 참고로 who were affected에서 주격 관계대명사(who)와 함께 be동사가 생략된 채 affected만 남은 구조이다.

번역 해피 밸리지 은행은 서비스 중단으로 영향을 받은 고객들께 사과드리고 싶습니다.

어휘 apologize 사과하다 customer 고객, 손님 outage 공급 정지, 사용 불능 classify 분류[구분]하다 refer 위탁하다, 맡기다 prevent 막다, 방지하다

109 부사 어휘

해설 문맥상 '이미' 판매되고 있다는 뜻이 가장 적절하다. 따라서 정답은 (C) already(이미, 벌써)이다. 참고로 already는 과거나 현재완료 시제와 많이 사용하지만 현재 시제도 가능하다. 하지만 의미상 (B) previously(예전에는)는 과거 시제에서만 써야 한다.

번역 신형 스마트폰이 네 가지 다른 색상으로 이미 판매되고 있다.

어휘 version ~판, 형태 be on sale 판매 중이다 extremely 매우, 극도로 highly 매우

110 전치사 자리 _ 명사구 앞

해설 바로 뒤에 명사구 urban planners' efforts가 왔으므로 빈칸에는 전치사가 와야 한다. (A) steadily와 (C) far enough는 부사로 일단 제외되고, 빈칸 앞뒤가 서로 반대되는 내용이므로 전치사구 (D) in spite of(~에도 불구하고)가 가장 어울린다. 정답은 (D) in spite of이다.

번역 공공 레크리에이션 공간을 더 만들려는 도시 계획자들의 노력에도 불구하고 카스타르 시 전역에서 아파트 건설이 계속 증가해왔다.

어휘 construction 건설, 건축 increase 증가하다 throughout ~ 전역에서 urban planner 도시 계획자[설계자] recreation 레크리에이션, 오락, 휴양 steadily 꾸준히 except ~을 제외하고 enough 충분히

111 명사 어휘 _ 복합 명사

해설 상품권(Gift certificate)과 어울릴 수 있는 명사를 찾아서 복합 명사를 완성하는 문제이다. 보어를 취하는 be동사 뒤의 형용사(refillable)가 이 명사의 상태를 설명해 주고 있다. '충전을 할 수 있다'고 했으므로 빈칸에 어울리는 것은 (B) balances(잔액)이다.

번역 상품권 잔액은 스완크슨 웹사이트를 통해 재충전할 수 있다.

어휘 gift certificate 상품권 refillable 재충전할 수 있는, 다시 채울 수 있는 via ~을 통해 market 시장 balance 잔액, 잔고 description 묘사, 설명 regulation 규정, 규제

112 분사 자리 _ 명사 뒤에서 수식

해설 빈칸 앞에 명사가 있고 빈칸 뒤가 by로 연결되는 것으로 보아 과거분사(p.p.)가 들어갈 자리임을 알 수 있다. 원래 문장은 price points which are determined by ~로 주격 관계대명사와 be동사가 생략된 형태이다. 따라서 정답은 (C) determined(결정된)이다.

번역 무게와 배송 속도, 보험 액수에 따라 정해진 다양한 가격으로 해외 운송을 이용할 수 있다.

어휘 overseas 해외의 shipping 운송 multiple 다양한 price point 가격점 weight 무게 delivery 배송, 배달 insurance 보험 amount 액수, 금액 determine 정하다 determination 결심

113 전치사 어휘

해설 빈칸 뒤 명사구와 주절을 가장 잘 어울리게 하는 전치사를 찾는 문제이다. '환경 전문가의 조언'과 '골프 코스를 만들자는 제안을 승인하는 것'은 서로 반하는 내용이므로, 정답은 (A) Against(~에 반대하여, ~에 맞서)이다. (B) Until(~까지), (C) Among(~ 중에, ~ 사이에), (D) Near(~ 가까이에)는 모두 의미상 적절하지 않다.

번역 시에서는 환경 전문가들의 조언과 반대로 웬드 힐스에 골프 코스를 만들자는 제안을 승인했다.

어휘 environmental 환경의 expert 전문가 approve 승인하다 proposal 제안

114 등위접속사

해설 빈칸 앞뒤에 완전한 절이 있으므로, 빈칸에는 완전한 절을 연결하는 등위접속사 (B) so(그래서)와 부사절 접속사 (C) in that(~라는 점에서)이 들어갈 수 있다. 빈칸 앞뒤 절이 원인과 결과의 의미를 나타내고 있으므로 정답은 (B) so이다. 명사절 접속사 (A) how와 전치사구 (D) depending on(~에 따라)은 품사상 적합하지 않다.

번역 휴즈 씨가 장기간 휴가를 쓸 계획이라, 도웰 씨는 휴즈 씨의 리셉션 업무를 처리하도록 교육받고 있다.

어휘 long-term 장기간의 leave of absence 휴가 handle 다루다, 처리하다

115 명사 어휘

해설 형용사(poor)와 어울릴 수 있는 명사를 고르는 문제이다. 장마가 길어져서 '흉작'으로 수출이 감소한다는 내용이다. 따라서 '수확'이라는 의미의 (C) harvest가 정답이다.

번역 유난히 긴 장마 탓에 흉작을 거둔 다음이라 과일과 여타 식품의 수출이 감소할 것으로 예상된다.

어휘 export 수출(품) be expected to + 동사원형 ~할 것으로 예상되다 decline 감소하다 poor harvest 흉작 due to ~탓에[때문에] unusually 유난히, 이례적으로 region 지역 fuel 연료 resource 자원

116 형용사 자리 _ 명사 수식

해설 빈칸은 소유격 인칭대명사(their)와 명사(remarks) 사이에서 명사를 수식하는 형용사 자리이므로, 형용사 (B) useful(유용한)과 과거분사 (C) used(중고의) 중에 하나를 선택해야 한다. 문맥상 '그들의 유용한 의견'이라는 의미가 자연스러우므로 정답은 (B) useful이다. 부사 (A) usefully(유용하게), 명사/동사 (D) use(사용; 사용하다)는 품사상 적합하지 않다.

번역 논평자들이 이야기를 마쳤을 때, 후지이 씨는 자신의 연구에 대한 유용한 의견에 감사를 표현했다.

어휘 commenter 논평가 remark 발언, 언급

117 명사 자리 _ 동사의 목적어

해설 빈칸은 'grants + 간접 목적어(the holder) + 직접 목적어'의 구문에서 직접 목적어 역할을 하는 명사 자리로, 전치사구(to all of Maddrington's major museums)의 수식을 받는다. 따라서 정답은 명사 (C) admission(입장)이다. 부사 (A) admittedly(인정하건대), 동명사/현재분사 (B) admitting, 동사 (D) admit은 모두 품사상 적합하지 않다.

번역 '플래티넘 패스'는 소지자들이 매드링턴의 모든 주요 박물관에 입장할 수 있도록 해준다.

어휘 grant 승인하다, 허락하다 holder 소지자 admit 들어가게 하다; 인정[시인]하다

118 형용사 어휘

해설 문맥상 좀 더 '저렴한' 농산물이라는 뜻이 가장 적절하다. affordable이라는 단어는 원래 대부분의 사람들이 충분히 살 수 있는 상태를 뜻하므로 정답은 (A) affordable(저렴한, 가격이 알맞은)이다.

번역 더 저렴한 유기농산물을 원하는 최근의 수요는 유기농 농부들에게 대량 생산의 기회로 이어졌다.

어휘 recent 최근의 demand 수요 organic 유기농의 produce 농산물 mass-production 대량 생산의 organic farmer 유기농 농부 accurate 정확한 enthusiastic 열렬한 effective 효과적인

119 동사 어휘

해설 빈칸은 명사구(our brand)를 목적어로 취하는 타동사 자리로, 전치사구(with the positive values)의 수식을 받는다. 따라서 목적어 및 전치사구와 가장 잘 어울리는 타동사를 선택해야 한다. 문맥상 '우리 브랜드에 긍정적인 가치를 결부시키다'라는 의미가 자연스러우므로, 정답은 (A) associate이다. 자동사 (C) cooperate(협력하다)는 전치사(with/on)와 결합하여 목적어를 취할 수 있고, 타동사 (B) gain(얻다)과 (D) emphasize(강조하다)는 의미상 적절하지 않다.

번역 타치바나 협회의 공식 협력업체가 되면 우리 브랜드에 그 자선 단체가 보여주는 긍정적 가치를 결부시킬 수 있다.

어휘 official 공식적인 associate A with B A와 B를 결부시키다 positive 긍정적인 charity 자선 단체 represent 나타내다, 보여주다

120 형용사 어휘

해설 명사(devices)를 자연스럽게 수식하는 형용사를 고르는 문제이다. '어떤' 기기는 교체될 수 있다는 의미가 되어야 하므로, '제대로 작동하지 않는'이라는 (D) Malfunctioning이 가장 잘 어울린다.

번역 불량 기기들은 구입일로부터 2년 이내에 판매점에서 교체할 수 있다.

어휘 device 기기 exchange 교환하다 point of sale 판매점, 매장 purchase date 구입일 ambitious 야심 찬 prospective 유망한 intermittent 간헐적인, 간간이 일어나는

121 동사 시제 + 능동태 / 수동태 구분

해설 next year라는 표현이 뒤에 있는 것으로 보아 미래 시제임을 알 수 있다. 주어인 glass는 자신이 직접 교체할 수 있는 존재가 아니기 때문에 '교체되다'라는 수동태 동사가 와야 한다. 따라서 정답은 (C) will be replaced이다.

번역 단열을 더 잘하기 위해 이 창문의 단판 유리는 내년에 이중 유리로 교체될 것이다.

어휘 in order to + 동사원형 ~하기 위해 insulation 단열 single-pane glass 단판 유리 replace 교체하다 double-glass pane 이중 유리, 겹유리

122 주격 관계대명사

해설 선행사(The cafeteria)가 사물이면서 빈칸 뒤에 주어가 없기 때문에 사물 주격 관계대명사인 (D) which가 정답이다. (C) where는 관계부사로 '장소'와 관련된 선행사를 받을 수 있지만 뒤에 완벽한 문장이 와야 하기 때문에 정답이 될 수 없다.

번역 직원들이 선택할 수 있는 저렴한 점심 식사와 저녁 식사를 제공하는 구내식당은 2층에 있다.

어휘 cafeteria 구내식당 offer 제공하다 inexpensive 저렴한 option 선택 be located on[in, at] ~에 위치하다 second floor 2층

123 부사 어휘

해설 빈칸 뒤 형용사 noticeable(눈에 띄는)를 수식해 줄 알맞은 부사를 찾는 문제이다. 문맥상 '현재 있는 금은 거의 눈에 띄지 않는다'라는 의미가 자연스러우므로, 정답은 (A) seldom(거의 ~ 않는)이다. (B) exactly(정확히, 꼭)와 (D) hard(열심히)는 의미상 적절하지 않다.

번역 헨드릴러 조리대에 사용된 돌은 금이 거의 가지 않고, 현재 있는 금은 최종 제품에서는 거의 눈에 띄지 않는다.

어휘 crack (갈라져서 생긴) 금 countertop 조리대

124 형용사 / 분사 자리 _ 명사 수식

해설 technical problems를 수식하는 형용사가 들어갈 자리이다. 보기 중에 형용사는 없고 형용사 역할을 하는 현재분사 형태인 (D) lasting(지속되는)이 있으므로 정답은 (D)이다.

번역 회사 지침에 원인 미상으로 지속되는 기술적 문제들만 정보기술부에 요청하도록 쓰여 있다.

어휘 technical 기술적인 unknown causes 원인 미상 IT department 정보기술부 last 지속하다 lastly 끝으로

125 명사 자리 _ 복합명사

해설 과거분사(written)과 명사(exam) 사이에는 명사를 수식하는 형용사와, 복합명사를 이루는 명사가 들어갈 수 있으므로, 형용사 (A) enterable(입장할 수 있는; 입력 가능한), 명사 (B) entrance(입학; 입장; 입구), 과거분사 (C) entered(가입이 끝난) 중에 하나를 선택해야 한다. 문맥상 '입학 필기 시험'이라는 의미가 자연스러우므로 정답은 (B) entrance이다.

Test 9

번역 우편 집배원 지망생들은 우체국 취업 자격을 얻기 위해 입학 필기 시험에 합격해야 한다.

어휘 aspiring 장차 ~가 되려는 mail carrier 우편 집배원 pass an entrance exam 입학 시험에 합격하다 qualify for ~에 대한 자격을 얻다 postal 우편의

126 부사절 접속사

해설 빈칸 뒤에 '주어+동사(they arise)'가 있으므로, 빈칸에는 완전한 절을 이끌 수 있는 접속사가 들어가야 한다. 또한 빈칸을 포함한 절이 앞에 있는 주절을 수식하므로, 정답은 부사절 접속사 (C) as soon as(~ 하자마자, 하는 즉시)이다. 명사절/부사절 접속사 (D) whatever 뒤에는 불완전한 절이 오고, 부사 (A) at first(처음에)와 전치사구 (B) because of(~ 때문에) 뒤에는 절이 올 수 없으므로, 적합하지 않다.

번역 공장의 생산성을 떨어뜨리는 공급망을 중단시키는 일은 발생 즉시 보고되어야 한다.

어휘 supply chain 공급 interruption 중단(시키는 것) reduce 감소시키다 productivity 생산성 arise 발생하다, 생기다

127 부사 자리 _ 동사 수식

해설 빈칸은 현재진행형 동사구 뒤에서 동사를 수식할 부사가 와야 할 자리이다. 정답은 부사인 (C) patiently(참을성 있게)이다.

번역 론드스톤 파이낸셜은 딱 맞는 지원자가 지원서를 제출하기를 참을성 있게 기다리고 있다.

어휘 perfect candidate 딱 맞는 지원자[후보] submit 제출하다 application 지원서 patient 환자; 참을성 있는 patience 인내, 끈기, 참을성

128 형용사 어휘

해설 얼룩(stains)을 수식하면서 연결이 자연스러운 형용사를 고르는 문제이다. stubborn은 원래 '완고한, 고집센'이라는 뜻인데 '얼룩'과 연결되면 '없애기 힘든'이라는 뜻으로 쓸 수 있다. 정답은 (B) stubborn이다.

번역 클래리펜트 표백제 펜은 넥타이와 여타 섬세한 직물들에서 가장 지우기 힘든 얼룩들까지 제거할 것을 약속한다.

어휘 bleach pen 표백제 펜 remove 제거하다 stain 얼룩 stubborn 좀처럼 지워지지 않는, 찌든

129 동사 시제

해설 if 절의 동사(had notified)를 통해 과거 사실에 대한 반대 의미를 나타내는 가정법 과거완료 문장임을 알 수 있으므로, 정답은 (A) could have sent이다. 'If+주어+had p.p. ~, 주어+would/could/might have p.p. ~'의 가정법 과거완료 문장의 형태를 기억해 두자.

번역 도급업체에서 우리에게 건설 관련 문제를 알렸다면, 해결책 모색을 돕도록 우리 엔지니어들을 보낼 수 있었을 텐데요.

어휘 contractor 계약자, 도급업자 notify 알리다, 통고하다 assist with ~를 돕다 find a solution 해결책을 찾다

130 동사 어휘

해설 목적어(a smooth transition)와 잘 어울릴 수 있는 동사를 고르는 문제이다. 문맥상 '이전이 순조롭게 이뤄지기 위해서'라는 의미가 자연스러우므로 '용이하게 하다, 가능하게 하다'라는 뜻의 (B) facilitate가 정답이다.

번역 새 사무실로 순조롭게 이전하기 위해 각 부서에 이사 전문가가 배치되었다.

어휘 smooth 순조로운, 매끄러운 transition 이동, 변천, 전환 relocation specialist 이사 전문가 assign 배정하다, 할당하다 assume 추정하다; (책임을) 맡다 encompass (많은 것을) 포함하다, 아우르다 distribute 배포하다, 유통시키다

PART 6

131-134 웹페이지

벨포트 온라인 숍 → 일시 품절 상품들

벨포트 숍은 제품의 재고를 확보하기 위해 최선을 다합니다. 하지만, 어떤 인기 품목들은 동이 날 수도 있습니다. **131**제품이 '일시 품절'로 표시되면 해당 품목을 현재 구입할 수 없습니다. 저희는 해당 제품을 신속히 더 주문하려고 노력하기 때문에 **132**주기적으로 저희의 웹사이트에 들러 해당 물품이 재입고되었는지 확인해 보시기를 권합니다. 또한, 때때로 결제 과정에서 제품 **133**수량을 늘리지 못합니다. 이는 저희가 여러분께 배송할 수 있는 특정 물품의 개수에 현재 제한이 있다(예를 들어, 4개 이내)는 뜻입니다. 이런 경우에 귀하는 이 **134**한도보다 더 많이 구매할 수 없을 것입니다.

어휘 out of stock 재고가 없는, 일시 품절된 do one's best to+동사원형 최선을 다해 ~하다 ensure 확보하다, 보증하다 product availability 제품 가용성, 재고 unavailable 구입할 수 없는 check 확인하다 back in stock 재입고된 check-out process 결제 과정 restriction on ~에 대한 제한 number of units 개수 no more than ~ 이내 ship 배송하다 at present 현재

131 문맥에 맞는 문장 고르기

번역 (A) 게다가, 이 쿠폰들은 실제 가치를 제공합니다.
(B) 그 결과, 그것은 사전에 철저히 검증되었습니다.
(C) 하지만, 어떤 인기 품목들은 동이 날 수도 있습니다.
(D) 특히, 생산 비용은 중요한 요인입니다.

해설 앞부분에는 제품의 재고(product availability)에 대해 언급되어 있고 뒤 부분은 품절(out of stock)에 관해서 이야기하고 있다. 따라서 그 사이에 들어갈 내용도 마찬가지로 제품의 재고 현황을 알 수 있는 내용이어야 한다. 따라서 정답은 (C)이다.

어휘 run out of ~이 동나다

132 부사 어휘

해설 물건이 다시 입고되었는지를 확인하기 위해서 웹사이트를 '주기적으로' 방문하라는 의미가 가장 적절하다. 따라서 정답은 (B) periodically(주기적으로)이다. (A) consecutively는 '연속적으로', (C) formerly는 '이전에', (D) briefly는 '잠시'라는 의미이다.

133 명사 어휘

해설 바로 다음 문장에서 힌트를 얻을 수 있다. 상품 개수에 제한(a restriction on the number of units)이 있다는 말을 통해서 제품의 '수량'을 늘릴 수 없다는 말이 들어가야 문장이 자연스럽게 이어진다는 것을 알 수 있다. 따라서 정답은 (C) quantity(수량)이다. (A) discount는 '할인', (B) manual은 '사용 설명서'라는 의미이다.

134 명사 자리

해설 빈칸 앞의 지시형용사 this가 수식해줄 수 있는 단수 명사가 들어가야 하는 자리다. 부사인 (C) limitedly는 '제한되어, 한정적으로', 형용사인 (D) limited는 '한정된'이라는 의미로 답이 될 수 없다. 품사가 명사인 (A) limit(한도, 제한)이 정답이다. (B) limits가 명사의 복수형일 수 있지만, 그럴 경우 앞에 these가 와야 하므로 답이 될 수 없다.

135 -138 공지

전 직원을 대상으로 한 휴일 에너지 절약 프로그램에 관한 중요 공지

앨더릭 인더스트리즈 주식회사는 다가오는 연휴 기간**135동안에** 에너지 사용을 최소화하기 위해 노력할 것입니다. 직원 식당 주방에서는 전자레인지, 커피 메이커, 토스터와 같은 소형 가전을 모두 끄고 플러그를 뽑아야 합니다.

또한, 저희 경영진에서는 직원 여러분께 각 사무실에 있는**136공유** 장비를 **138끄고** 플러그를 뽑는 것을 도와주기를 요청합니다. 여기에는 여러분의 근무 구역에 있는 모든 직원들이**137일상적으로** 사용하는 프린터, 스캐너, 복사기가 포함됩니다. 이 일은 한 직원을 지정하여 맡겨도 됩니다. 마찬가지로, 창문과 출입문을 모두 닫고 잠가 주시기 바랍니다.

어휘 energy conservation 에너지 절약 minimize 최소화하다 usage 사용 appliance 가전 제품 turn off 끄다 unplug 플러그를 빼다 management 경영진 equipment 장비 work section 근무 구역

135 전치사 자리

해설 빈칸 뒤에 기간을 나타내는 명사구 the upcoming holiday season이 있으므로 시간과 함께 쓰이는 during(~ 동안), over(~에 걸쳐) 같은 전치사가 와야 할 자리이다. 따라서 정답은 (B) over이다.

어휘 only 오직 then 그리고 나서

136 형용사 어휘

해설 장비를 끄고 플러그를 뽑으라고 말하고 있는데, 뒷문장에 그 장비의 종류가 나열되어 있다. 프린터, 스캐너, 복사기 등을 포함할 수 있는 의미인 '공유하는(shared)' 장비라는 말이 적절하므로 정답은 (C) shared이다.

어휘 portable 휴대가 쉬운 safety 안전(의) defective 결함이 있는

137 부사 자리

해설 빈칸 앞뒤로 'be동사+과거분사'가 있으므로 빈칸은 부사가 와야 할 자리이다. 보기 중 유일한 부사인 (A) normally(일상[통상]적으로)가 정답이다.

어휘 normalize 정상화하다 normality 정상 상태 normal 보통의, 정상적인

138 문맥에 맞는 문장 고르기

번역 (A) 각 구역에는 보통 다섯 명에서 열 명의 직원이 있습니다.
(B) 이 업그레이드들은 에너지 소모량을 현저히 줄일 것입니다.
(C) 창고에 환경친화적인 잉크가 있습니다.
(D) 이 일은 한 직원을 지정하여 맡겨도 됩니다.

해설 두 번째 단락의 첫 문장에서 여러 기기의 전원을 끄고 플러그를 뽑는 업무를 경영진이 지시했다. 각 구역의 모든 직원이 공유하는 기기들인데, 그 업무를 This task로 받은 (D)가 문맥상 가장 어울린다.

139 -142 기사

딘저 (9월 12일) – 홀터 항공은 이제 딘저 공항과 리브턴 국제공항을 **139연결하는** 비행 노선을 제공할 것이다.

딘저의 글로리아 루고 항공 담당 이사는 이러한 결정이 항공사 통계에 의해 이뤄졌다고 밝혔다. "홀터 항공은 많은 승객들이 웬워터를 경유해 딘저와 리브턴 사이를 이동한다는 사실을 알았습니다. 그들은 저희에게 **140직항편**을 대신 제공하겠다고 했습니다."라고 설명했다. 루고 이사는 **141경제적 유사성**으로 인해 두 도시 간 이동이 많을 것이라는 지적도 덧붙였다. 두 도시 모두 주요 보험회사의 지점들이 자리잡은 곳이다.

첫 항공편은 10월 15일에 이륙한다. 처음에는 **141각 노선별로** 1일 1회 운항되다가 향후 운항 횟수가 늘어날 전망이다.

어휘 flight route 항공 노선 aviation 항공 prompt 촉발하다 statistics 통계 approach 접근하다, 다가오다 direct flight 직항 instead 대신에 point out 지적하다 volume of traffic 교통량 similarity 유사성 take off 이륙하다 initially 처음에 direction 방향 frequency 빈도

139 주격 관계대명사 + 동사

해설 문맥상 빈칸 앞 명사구(a flight route)가 공항과 공항을 연결하는 (connect) 주체이므로, 빈칸을 포함한 절은 명사구를 수식하는 형용사 절이 되어야 한다. 따라서 동사 connect(연결하다)의 주어 역할을 하면서 형용사절을 이끄는 주격 관계대명사도 빈칸에 들어가야 하므로, 정답은 (C) that connects이다.

140 형용사 어휘

해설 빈칸 뒤 명사(flights)를 수식할 형용사를 고르는 문제다. 앞 문장에서 많은 승객들이 웬워터를 경유해 딘저와 리브턴 간을 이동한다고 했으므로, 그대신에(instead) '직항편을 제공하겠다'는 의미가 되어야 문맥상 자연스럽다. 따라서 정답은 (A) direct(직항의; 직접적인)이다. 보기 (B) night (야간의), (C) international(국제적인), (D) commercial(상업의)는 모두 의미상 적절하지 않다.

Test 9

141 문맥에 맞는 문장 고르기

번역 (A) 교통 혼잡은 주말과 공휴일에 지연으로 이어졌다.
(B) 두 도시 모두 주요 보험회사의 지점들이 자리잡은 곳이다.
(C) 차로 약 8시간 떨어진 거리다.
(D) 그러나 리브턴의 재정 상황은 최근 몇 년간 나아졌다.

해설 앞 문장에서 경제적 유사성으로 인해 두 도시 간에 이동이 많다고 했으므로, 빈칸에는 두 도시의 경제적 유사성과 관련된 구체적인 예를 제시하는 것이 문맥상 자연스럽다. 따라서 정답은 (B)이다.

어휘 congestion 혼잡 lead to ~로 이어지다 delay 지연
insurance 보험 roughly 대략 finance 재정, 재무

142 전치사 어휘

해설 빈칸 뒤 명사구(each direction)를 목적어로 취하는 전치사 자리로, 빈칸을 포함한 전치사구는 명사(flights)를 수식한다. 문맥상 '각 방향의 비행기'라는 의미가 자연스러우므로, 정답은 (D) in(~에)이다. (A) aboard (~을 타고), (B) under(~ 아래에), (C) with(~와 함께, ~을 가진)는 모두 의미상 적절하지 않다.

143-146 이메일

발신: 델로라 스톡턴 <d.stockton@nqy-mail.com>
수신: <jobs@rendonsystems.com>
제목: 입사 지원
날짜: 4월 17일

메서 씨께,

렌던 시스템즈의 독일어 전문가 직책에 지원하고자 이 메일을 씁니다.

www.language-jobs.com에 게시된 귀사의 광고를 보고 제가 해당 직책을 성공적으로 수행하는 데 필요한 역량과 경험을 **143**갖추고 있다고 확신합니다. 첨부한 이력서에 기술한 바와 같이 저는 영어 원어민이며 독일어 번역 석사 학위를 받았습니다. 지난 3년간 계속 프리랜서 번역가로 일했습니다. 그 기간 동안 귀사의 일자리와 같은 여러 건의 앱 번역과 현지화 작업을 **144**수행했습니다. **145**요청하신다면 관련 고객으로부터 받은 추천서를 드릴 수 있습니다.

저의 자질에 관해 더 이야기를 나누고 싶습니다.**146**이 이메일 주소나 555-0198번으로 연락 주시면 됩니다. 고려해 주셔서 감사합니다.

델로라 스톡턴

어휘 apply for ~에 지원하다 specialist 전문가 confident 자신 있는, 확신하는 succeed in ~에 성공하다 master's degree 석사 학위 continuously 계속해서 localization 현지화 letter of reference 추천서 involved 관련된

143 동사 어휘

해설 빈칸 뒤 명사구(the abilities and experience ~ in the role)를 목적어로 취할 가장 적절한 동사를 선택해야 한다. 문맥상 '해당 직책을 성공적으로 수행하는 데 필요한 역량과 경험을 갖추고 있다'라는 의미가 자연스러우므로, 정답은 (A) possess(갖추고 있다, 지니다)이다. (B) resemble(닮다), (C) occupy(점유하다, 차지하다), (D) fulfill(이행하다)은 모두 의미상 적절하지 않다.

144 동사 시제

해설 빈칸 앞쪽의 전치사구(During that time)는 앞 문장에서 언급한 '지난 3년간(for the past three years)'을 의미하므로, 정답은 동사의 과거시제인 (D) contributed이다.

어휘 contribute 공헌하다

145 가정법 미래 _ 도치

해설 빈칸 뒤에 주어(you)와 동사의 원형(request)이 있다. 빈칸에는 접속사 (A) Unless(만약 ~이 아니라면)와, 가정법 미래 절 'If you should request them'에서 접속사 If가 생략되고 도치된 'Should you request them'의 조동사 (C) Should가 들어갈 수 있다. 문맥상 '요청하신다면 관련 고객으로부터 받은 추천서를 드릴 수 있다'는 긍정의 의미가 자연스러우므로 정답은 (C) Should이다.

어휘 regarding ~와 관련하여 shortly 곧

146 문맥에 맞는 문장 고르기

번역 (A) 렌던 시스템즈는 평판이 훌륭한, 업계의 선도 업체입니다.
(B) 끝으로, 저는 해당 언어를 자유자재로 구사할 수 있습니다.
(C) 외국 업체가 독일어를 사용하는 나라들에서 경쟁하기는 어렵습니다.
(D) 저의 자질에 관해 더 이야기를 나누고 싶습니다.

해설 입사 지원 메일로 빈칸 뒤 문장에서 자신에게 연락할 수 있는 방법을 제시하고 있다. 문맥상 면접의 기회를 달라는 관용적인 표현이 적절하므로 (D)가 정답이다.

어휘 reputation 평판 have a good command of ~를 자유자재로 구사하다 compete 경쟁하다 qualification 자질, 자격

PART 7

147-148 문자 메시지

발신: 제프 밀턴, 555-0194

수신: 나나 드라고티

안녕하세요, 나나. 우리는 작은 고전적인 분수대를 구매자인 유 씨에게 보내려고 준비하고 있어요. 분수대의 조각품 부분과 물 펌프 부분을 따로 분리해서, 운송 중에 서로 부딪혀 훼손되지 않도록 각각 포장하고 배송해야 할 것 같아요. **147**당신이 유 씨에게 이메일을 보내서 물건이 그렇게 나갈 거라고 알려 주겠어요? 고마워요! **148**나는 이제 창고를 떠나 차를 몰고 본사로 복귀하려는 참이에요.

> 어휘 vintage 고전적인, 유서 깊은 fountain 분수(대) shipment 배송, 선적 pack 포장하다, 짐을 싸다 ship 배송하다, 선적하다 sculpture 조각품 separately 따로따로, 각기, 별도로 damage 손상을 주다, 훼손하다 item 물건, 물품 be about to + 동사원형 막 ~하려고 하다 warehouse 창고 drive back to ~에 차로 복귀하다 main office 본사

147 세부 사항

> 번역 드라고티 씨는 무엇을 하라고 요청받는가?
> (A) 직원들에게 곧 있을 정책 변화를 알릴 것
> (B) 일부 품목들의 가격 목록을 수정할 것
> (C) 포장용품을 추가로 구입할 것
> **(D) 고객에게 배송 방법을 알려줄 것**

> 해설 이메일에서 요청하는 문장은 물음표로 끝나는 경우가 많다. 이 글에서도 고객인 유 씨에게 상품이 나가는 방법을 알려 주라는 말이 나오는데 그 앞을 보면 상품이 어떻게 포장되고 배송될지에 대한 것임을 알 수 있다. 정답은 (D)이다.

148 추론 / 암시

> 번역 밀턴 씨는 아마 다음에 무슨 일을 하겠는가?
> (A) 배관 수리
> (B) 몇몇 선반 설치
> **(C) 사무실 복귀**
> (D) 배송 운전자와 통화

> 해설 마지막 문장의 본사로 복귀한다(drive back to the main office)는 표현에서 정답 (C)를 고를 수 있다.

▸▸ Paraphrasing   지문의 **drive back to the main office**
→ 정답의 **Return to an office**

149-150 광고

브린든 디저트 축제가 돌아왔습니다!

지난해 첫 행사의 성공에 이어 브린든 디저트 축제가 브린든 공원에 돌아옵니다. 5월 9일 금요일부터 5월 11일 일요일까지 매일 오후 2시부터 오후 8시까지 열립니다.

- 입장료(1인당 8달러)에는 **150**기념 음료수 잔, 캔버스 천으로 만든 토트백, 두 가지 후식 샘플 무료 시식권이 포함되어 있습니다!
- 현지에서 만든 케이크, 타르트, 페이스트리, 파이 등 많은 음식을 시식해보세요!
- 날마다 라이브 공연을 하는 최고의 출연진!

브린든 공원의 정문은 웰드 드라이브 맞은편에 있습니다. 인근 시립 주차 시설에 넓은 주차 공간이 있을 겁니다. **149**요금을 내지 않으려면 입장권 반쪽을 주차 요원에게 보여 주시기만 하면 됩니다.

> 어휘 dessert 디저트, 후식 inaugural 최초의, 첫 admission 입장료 souvenir 기념품 drinking glass 음료수 잔 canvas 캔버스 천 tote bag 토트백 voucher 쿠폰, 상품권 sample 시식[시음]하다 locally 지역[현지]에서 pastry 페이스트리 lineup 출연진 live entertainment 라이브 공연 main entrance 정문 be located across form ~의 맞은편에 위치하다 ample 넓은, 풍부한 vehicle 탈것, 자동차 city parking facilities 시립 주차 시설 pay a fee 요금을 내다 ticket stub 입장권의 남은 반쪽 parking attendant 주차요원

149 사실 관계 확인

> 번역 축제에 관해 언급된 것은 무엇인가?
> (A) 이제 세 번째로 열리는 것이다.
> **(B) 무료 주차 공간을 이용할 수 있다.**
> (C) 주최측이 공연자들을 물색하고 있다.
> (D) 일요일 시간이 연장되었다.

> 해설 지문 하단의 Brindon Park's main entrance로 시작하는 부분에 주차에 대한 언급이 있다. 마지막 문장에서 요금을 내고 싶지 않으면 입장권을 보여주면 된다는 내용을 통해 무료 주차할 수 있는 방법을 알려 주고 있다. 정답은 (B)이다.

150 사실 관계 확인

> 번역 입장료에 포함되지 않은 것은 무엇인가?
> (A) 유리잔
> (B) 가방
> (C) 음식 쿠폰
> (D) 음료수

> 해설 두 번째 단락 첫 항목에 입장료에 포함된 것들이 나열되어 있다. (A)는 souvenir drinking glass에서, (B)는 canvas tote bag에서, (C)는 a voucher for two sample desserts에서 각각 확인할 수 있다. 따라서 언급되지 않은 (D)가 정답이다.

▸▸ Paraphrasing   지문의 **a voucher for two sample desserts** → 보기의 **A food coupon**

151-152 문자 메시지

마르셀리나 에스퀴벨 [오전 8:52]

클라크 씨, 로라 씨가 아직 교대 근무를 하러 오지 않았어요. 개장 시간이 거의 다 됐는데요. 카운터에 저 혼자 있습니다.

플로이드 클라크 [오전 8:52]

전화해 보셨나요? 직원 전화번호부는 안쪽 사무실에 있어요.

마르셀리나 에스퀴벨 [오전 8:53]

휴대폰으로 두 번 전화해 봤는데 받지 않았어요. 어떻게 해야 할까요? **151저는 아직 특선 커피 만드는 법을 다 알진 못하거든요.**

플로이드 클라크 [오전 8:54]

내가 처음 한 시간은 갈 수 있어요. 하지만 그 후엔 가족 행사 때문에 나가야 해요. 나머지 시간에 일할 사람이 있는지 단체 문자를 보내 볼게요.

마르셀리나 에스퀴벨 [오전 8:54]

그게 좋겠네요. **152하지만 오시기 전에 어떤 손님이 제가 못 만드는 음료를 주문하면 어쩌죠?**

플로이드 클라크 [오전 8:55]

10분 거리에 있어요. 하지만 만약 누가 주문하면 그 음료는 일시적으로 제공할 수 없다고 하고 20% 할인 쿠폰을 주세요. 금전 등록기 아래 서랍에 몇 장 있어요.

어휘 show up (예정된 곳에) 나타나다 shift 교대 근무 specialty 특별, 특선 send out 발송하다 temporarily 일시적으로 unavailable 이용할 수 없는 discount 할인 cash register 금전 등록기

---

151 세부 사항

번역 메시지 작성자들은 어디에서 일하는가?
(A) 카페
(B) 도서관
(C) 공장
(D) 의류 매장

해설 에스퀴벨 씨가 오전 8시 53분 메시지에서 아직 특선 커피 만드는 법을 다 알진 못한다고 했으므로 두 사람이 카페에서 일한다는 것을 알 수 있다. 따라서 정답은 (A)이다.

152 의도 파악

번역 오전 8시 55분에 클라크 씨가 "10분 거리에 있어요"라고 쓸 때, 그 의도는 무엇인가?
(A) 에스퀴벨 씨는 휴식을 취하려면 기다려야 한다.
(B) 에스퀴벨 씨는 문제에 맞닥뜨릴 것 같지는 않다.
(C) 클라크 씨는 매장에 오는 것을 개의치 않는다.
(D) 클라크 씨는 일을 빨리 끝마쳐야 한다.

해설 에스퀴벨 씨가 오전 8시 54분 메시지에서 클라크 씨가 오기 전에 자신이 만들지 못하는 음료를 주문하면 어떻게 해야 할지 우려를 표했고, 이에 대해 클라크 씨가 인용문을 썼으므로, 그 사이 에스퀴벨 씨가 우려하는 문제가 일어나지 않을 것이라는 의도로 쓴 말임을 유추할 수 있다. 따라서 정답은 (B)이다.

어휘 take a break 휴식을 취하다 encounter 맞닥뜨리다

153 -155 공지

주말 지하철 지연

앞으로 두 주 동안 C선과 F선 건설 공사로 인해 일정에 연착이 있을 예정입니

다. **153**이 공사로 노후 철로를 교체하고 특수 비상등을 설치하여 교통 안전이 향상될 것입니다.

C선 열차: 5월 1일 토요일 새벽 2시부터 5월 3일 월요일 새벽 4시까지, C선은 북행 선로에서 작업이 이루어지는 동안 밴 후튼과 뉴베리 정거장 사이의 남행 선로만 사용하게 됩니다.

154F선 열차: 5월 8일 토요일 새벽 2시부터 5월 10일 월요일 새벽 4시까지, F선은 서행 선로에서 작업이 이루어지는 동안 화이트허스트와 캔베리 정거장 사이의 동행 선로만 사용하게 됩니다.

155모든 역 역 플랫폼에서 우회로 지도를 구할 수 있습니다. 저희가 모든 선로를 안전하게 유지하기 위해 작업하는 동안 참고 기다려 주셔서 감사합니다.

어휘 delay 연착 construction work 건설 공사 project 프로젝트, 건설 사업 transport safety 교통 안전 replace 교체하다 old track 노후 철로 install 설치하다 special emergency lights 특수 비상등 -bound ~행 track 선로, 철로 stop 정거장 undergo 겪다, 경험하다 rerouted service map 우회로 지도 available 구할 수 있는

---

153 세부 사항

번역 왜 지연 운행이 예정되어 있는가?
(A) 터미널을 확장하고 있어서
(B) 신규 노선을 건설하고 있어서
(C) 손상된 것을 수리하고 있어서
(D) 향상을 위한 작업을 하고 있어서

해설 제목이 '주말 지하철 지연'이고 첫 단락의 내용을 살펴보면 건설 공사가 있을 예정인데 이 공사가 교통 안전 향상(improve transport safety)을 위해서 한다는 것을 알 수 있다. 따라서 정답은 (D)이다.

154 세부 사항

번역 F선에 대한 작업은 언제 끝날 것인가?
(A) 5월 1일
(B) 5월 3일
(C) 5월 8일
(D) 5월 10일

해설 세 번째 단락에 F선 열차에 대한 내용이 나오는데 이 공사가 5월 8일에 시작해서 10일에 끝나는 것을 알 수 있다. 따라서 정답은 (D)이다.

155 세부 사항

번역 공지에 따르면, 어디에서 특별 지도를 얻을 수 있는가?
(A) 열차에서
(B) 역에서
(C) 인터넷에서
(D) 신문 가판대에서

해설 '지도'와 관련된 내용은 마지막 단락 첫 번째 문장에서 언급된 것이 유일하다. 모든 역 플랫폼에서 우회로 지도(Rerouted service maps)를 구할 수 있다고 했으므로, 이를 토대로 정답 (B)를 고를 수 있다.

▸▸ Paraphrasing 지문의 **Rerouted service maps**
→ 질문의 **special maps**

156-158 이메일

발신: 알렉시스 쿠르츠

수신: 에릭 구오

제목: 조사 결과

날짜: 10월 5일

첨부: 보고서

안녕하세요, 에릭 씨.

저희 팀은 데리시 스낵 크래커의 포장지 디자인에 관한 포커스 그룹 테스트를 완료했습니다. 모든 결과가 담긴 보고서를 첨부했습니다만, 여기에 주요 사항들을 요약해 드립니다.

기억하시겠지만, 저희는 포장 디자인을 두 가지로 압축했습니다. **157**1안은 녹색이고 앞면에 농장 그림이 있는 반면에, 2안은 파란색이고 접시에 담긴 크래커 사진이 있습니다. 포커스 그룹은 매력도 부문에서 두 안에 똑같이 높은 점수를 주었지만 실제로 크래커를 먹어보고 난 후엔 80%가 넘는 참여자가 1안이 맛을 더 잘 표현하고 있다고 말했습니다. **158** 저희 크래커가 카피엑 푸드의 템토스 제품군을 본떠 만들었다는 사실을 알고 나서 포장지도 그렇게 해야 한다고 느끼는 듯했습니다.

그래서 저희는 1안을 권해드립니다.**156**생산 단계로 진행할지 귀사의 승인 여부를 알려 주십시오.

감사합니다.

알렉시스

어휘 complete 완료하다 focus group 포커스 그룹(시장 조사나 여론 조사를 위해 각 계층을 대표하도록 뽑은 소수의 사람들로 이뤄진 그룹) packaging 포장재, 포장 summarize 요약하다 recall 기억해 내다 narrow down 좁히다 drawing 그림 equally 똑같이, 동일하게 attractiveness 매력 represent 나타내다, 보여주다 be modeled after ~를 본뜨다 authorization 승인 proceed 진행하다

---

156 글의 주제 / 목적

번역 쿠르츠 씨가 구오 씨에게 이메일을 보낸 이유는?

(A) 승인을 요청하기 위해

(B) 구오 씨가 회의 준비를 할 수 있도록 하기 위해

(C) 구오 씨에게 계획 수정안을 알려 주기 위해

(D) 구오 씨에게 실수를 사과하기 위해

해설 세 번째 단락에서 생산 단계로 진행해도 될지 승인 여부를 알려 달라고 했으므로, 승인을 요청하기 위한 이메일임을 알 수 있다. 따라서 정답은 (A)이다.

어휘 revision 수정 apologize for ~에 대해 사과하다

▶ **Paraphrasing** 지문의 **let me know if we have your authorization**
→ 정답의 **To request his approval**

---

157 세부 사항

번역 포장 선택안에 대해 어떤 정보가 주어졌는가?

(A) 디자인이 완성된 날짜

(B) 포장 생산의 예상 비용

(C) 포장재의 재료

(D) 포장에 나온 그림

해설 두 번째 단락에서 1안은 녹색이고 앞면에 농장 그림이 있는 반면, 2안은 파란색이고 접시에 담긴 크래커 사진이 있다고 했으므로, 두 선택안 다 그림을 포함하고 있는 것을 알 수 있다. 따라서 정답은 (D)이다.

▶ **Paraphrasing** 지문의 **a drawing of a farm / a photograph of the crackers on a plate**
→ 정답의 **The images**

---

158 추론 / 암시

번역 데리시 스낵 크래커에 대해 암시된 것은?

(A) 한 경쟁업체 제품과 유사하다.

(B) 오랫동안 개발하는 중이다.

(C) 청소년을 겨냥한 제품이다.

(D) 두 가지 맛이 있다.

해설 두 번째 단락의 후반부에 '데리시 크래커가 카피엑 푸드의 템토스 제품군을 본떠 만들었다'고 했으므로, 경쟁업체 제품과 유사하다는 것을 유추할 수 있다. 따라서 정답은 (A)이다.

어휘 competitor 경쟁자 young adult 10대 후반의 청소년

▶ **Paraphrasing** 지문의 **modeled after Karpiec Foods' Temptos line**
→ 정답의 **similar to a competitor's product**

159-160 웹페이지

칼댁 공구 주식회사   홈 ≫ 지원 ≫ 보증

보증 및 반품 정책

159저희의 보증 조건은 귀하가 어떤 종류의 칼댁 제품을 가지고 있느냐에 따라 다릅니다. 특정한 보증 내용을 살펴보시려면 제품 종류별 보증으로 가셔서 지시를 따라 주시기 바랍니다. 모든 보증 반환은 보증서 인증 번호(WAN)가 수반되어야 합니다. WAN은 service@kaldac.com으로 이메일을 보내어 획득할 수 있으며 귀하의 물품을 보내는 데 필요한 반품 전표가 포함되어 있을 것입니다. 제품을 다시 귀하에게 배송하기 위한 배송료가 있다는 점에 유의하시기 바랍니다. 보증 범위에 관해 특정 문의 사항이 있으면 555-0135번으로 저희 고객 지원부에 연락하시기 바랍니다.

소비자를 위한 특기 사항: **160**'공구 날' 보증에 의거하여, 칼댁 공구 주식회사는 보증서가 있든 없든 모든 절삭 공구의 날을 무료로 날카롭게 만들어 드릴 것입니다. 이 서비스를 요청하시려면 support@kaldac.com으로 평생 제품 지원 센터(LPSC)에 이메일을 보내시기 바랍니다.

어휘 warranty 품질 보증서 return 반품 terms and conditions 약관, 조건 vary depending on ~에 따라 다르다 view 보다 specific 특정한 follow the prompts 지시를 따르다 warranty return 보증 반환 be accompanied by ~을 수반[동반]하다 Warranty Authorization Number 보증 인증 번호 return packing slip 반환 전표 package 패키지, 포장된 물건 note 유의하다 warranty coverage 보증 범위 Customer Service Department 고객지원부 special note 특기 사항 cutting edge 칼날 sharpen 날카롭게 만들다 blade 날 cutting tool 절삭 공구 for free 무료로

159 사실 관계 확인

번역 칼댁 공구 주식회사의 제품 보증에 관해 명시된 것은?

(A) 제품에 따라 다르다.
(B) 제품과 별도로 판매된다.
(C) 한 나라에서만 유효하다.
(D) 모든 배송비를 부담한다.

해설 첫 번째 단락 첫 문장에서 제품에 대한 보증 조건은 제품의 종류에 따라 달라진다(The terms and conditions of our warranties ~ you own.)고 했으므로 정답은 (A)이다.

▸▸ Paraphrasing 지문의 **vary depending on which type of Kaldac product**
→ 정답의 **differ according to the product**

160 추론 / 암시

번역 고객은 왜 LPSC에 연락할 것 같은가?

(A) 하자 보증에 관해 자세한 내용을 알아보려고
(B) 대량으로 구입하려고
(C) 무료 서비스를 주선하려고
(D) 어떤 결정에 논쟁하려고

해설 두 번째 단락에서 정답을 확인할 수 있다. LPSC로 연락하는 이유는 날을 날카롭게 만들어주는(sharpen the blades) 무료 서비스를 이용하기 위해서이다. 따라서 정답은 (C)이다.

161 -163 이메일

발신: 에이프릴 맥키 〈a.mackey@lawning.edu〉
수신: 조셉 위트 〈joseph.witt@jwittauthor.com〉
제목: 로닝 대학교 PSP
날짜: 6월 30일

위트 씨께,

안녕하세요. 저는 에이프릴 맥키라고 합니다. 로닝 대학교의 정치 사회 프로그램(PSP) 조직위원회에 있습니다. 최근 귀하의 저서 〈디지털 시민〉을 읽고 논점이 매우 흥미롭다고 생각했습니다. **161**다음 학기에 PSP 행사로 저희 학교에 방문하셔서 연구 내용에 대한 강연을 해 주셨으면 합니다.

162 PSP는 저희 대학교의 사회과학 대학원에서 기금을 조달하며, 정치학 연구원들과 타 학과 연구원들 간의 학술적 교류를 촉진하는 사명을 지니고 있습니다.

현대의 기술이 시민의 존재 의미를 변화시키는 방식에 대한 분석인 귀하의 저서가 저희에게 왜 그토록 흥미롭게 느껴졌는지 아시게 될 것입니다.

귀하의 방문 일정을 10월 11일로 잡았으면 합니다. 강연은 한 시간으로, 그 후 30분간 질의응답 시간을 가지려 합니다. **163**강연료를 드리지는 못하지만 여행 경비는 지급해 드릴 수 있습니다. 여기에는 공항에서 이동하는 택시비와 학교 근처 호텔 숙박료가 포함됩니다. 요청하시면 더 자세한 내용을 알려드리겠습니다. 답신을 기다리겠습니다.

에이프릴 맥키
정치학 교수

어휘 organizing committee 조직위원회 argument 주장, 논거 fascinating 대단히 흥미로운 semester 학기 give a talk 강연하다 fund 자금을 대다 promote 촉진하다 academic 학문의 exchange 교환 political science 정치학 discipline 학과목 analysis 분석 appealing 흥미로운, 매력적인 cover 대다 request 요청, 신청 look forward to -ing ~하기를 고대하다

161 글의 주제 / 목적

번역 이메일을 쓴 목적은?

(A) 위원회 설립을 알리기 위해
(B) 책을 공저하는 것을 제안하기 위해
(C) 강연 초청을 하기 위해
(D) 연구 기금을 신청하기 위해

해설 첫 번째 단락에서 다음 학기에 PSP 행사로 로닝 대학교를 방문하여 연구 내용에 대한 강연을 해줄(give a talk) 것을 요청하고 있으므로, 강연 초청을 위한 이메일임을 알 수 있다. 따라서 정답은 (C)이다.

어휘 establishment 설립 collaborate 협력하다, 공동 작업하다

▸▸ Paraphrasing 지문의 **come to our campus ~ to give a talk** → 정답의 **a speaking invitation**

162 사실 관계 확인

번역 맥키 씨가 PSP의 목표로 명시한 것은?

(A) 서로 다른 분야의 학자들 간의 소통을 장려하는 것
(B) 기존 연구 기법의 문제를 발견하는 것
(C) 대중의 정치 참여도를 높이는 것
(D) 미래 기술 동향을 확실하게 예측하는 것

해설 두 번째 단락에서 PSP가 정치학 연구원들과 타 학과 연구원들 간의 학술적 교류를 촉진하는 사명을 지니고 있다고 했으므로 정답은 (A)이다.

어휘 scholar 학자 existing 기존의, 존재하는 reliably 믿을 수 있게, 확실히 predict 예측하다

▸▸ Paraphrasing 지문의 **our mission**
→ 질문의 **the goal of the PSP**

지문의 **to promote academic exchange between ~ other disciplines**
→ 정답의 **To encourage communication among scholars in different fields**

163 문장 삽입

번역 [1], [2], [3], [4]로 표시된 곳 중에서 다음 문장이 들어가기에 적합한 곳은?
"여기에는 공항에서 이동하는 택시비와 학교 근처 호텔 숙박료가 포함됩니다."

(A) [1]
(B) [2]
(C) [3]
(D) [4]

해설 삽입 문장에서 '여기에는 교통비와 숙박료가 포함된다'고 했으므로, 이들을 포함할 수 있는 여기(These)에 해당하는 것을 밝혀야 한다. [3]번 앞에서 '여행 경비(your travel costs)는 지급해 드릴 수 있다'고 했으므로 정답은 (C)이다.

어휘 lodging 숙박

164 -167 뉴스레터 기사

창고 회사가 스페이시즈-플러스 박람회에서 전시하다

로데포르트—**164**지난주에 스토리지-테크 주식회사가 일반인에게 공개된 연례 무역 박람회인 스페이시즈-플러스 박람회에서 전시회를 연 첫 창고 회사가 되었다.

164(A)호라이즌 컨벤션 센터에서 열린 이번 박람회는 8월 11일부터 14일까지 진행됐으며 내부 공간 장식 동향을 중심으로 했다. **167**박람회 안내 책자에 따르면, 이 행사에는 실내장식 전문가, 개보수 도급업체, 장식품 공급업체 등 600개가 넘는 참가 업체들이 함께했다. 유인물의 온라인 소식에는 5만 명이 넘는 사람들이 이 행사에 참여했다고 나온다.

164(C)스토리지-테크 주식회사의 전시관에는 회사 시설에서 대여하는 것과 비슷한 너비 3.3m의 서서 들어갈 수 있는 창고 유닛이 포함되었다. **165**박람회 기간 동안 스토리지-테크 주식회사는 냉장고와 전자레인지를 포함하여 진열해 놓은 경품들을 매일 추첨했다. 전시관을 찾은 모든 방문객이 회사의 보관 서비스 할인권을 받았다.

더반에 본사를 둔 스토리지-테크 주식회사는 남아프리카공화국의 7개 도시에서 32개의 자가 보관 시설을 운영하고 있다. 최근에는 웁살 셀프-스토리지의 여섯 개 시설을 인수했으며, 이 시설들을 스토리지-테크 이름으로 바꾸어 브랜드 이미지를 쇄신할 계획이다. 회사의 웹사이트 www.storage-tec.com을 찾는 방문객들은 모든 종류의 창고 유닛들의 크기를 살펴보고, 가격 정보를 얻고, **166**고객들의 추천 내용을 읽을 수 있다.

어휘 annual 연례적인 trade fair 무역 박람회 the public 일반인, 대중 decorate 장식하다 interior space 내부 공간 feature ~의 특징으로 하다, ~을 주연으로 하다 exhibitor 참가자, 전시업체 décor specialist 실내장식 전문가 contractor 도급업자 booth 부스, 전시관 walk-in 서서 들어갈 수 있는 rent 대여하다 drawing 추첨, 제비 뽑기 on display 진열 중인 operate 운영하다 self-storage facilities 자가 보관 시설 rebrand 브랜드 이미지를 쇄신하다 properties 부동산, 건물 browse 둘러보다, 훑어보다 a full range of 전반적인 storage unit size 창고 유닛 크기 pricing information 가격 정보 customer testimonial 고객 추천, 사용자 후기

164 사실 관계 확인

번역 올해의 스페이시즈-플러스 박람회에 관해 암시되지 않은 것은?

(A) 특정한 테마에 초점을 맞추었다.
(B) 행사인들에게 보관 공간 사용료를 추가로 물렸다.
(C) 적어도 3미터 너비의 전시관을 갖추었다.
(D) 새로운 유형의 전시 업체를 포함했다.

해설 (A)는 두 번째 단락에 박람회가 '내부 공간 장식 동향(trends in decorating interior spaces)을 중심으로 했다'고 나왔고, (C)는 세 번째 단락에 3.3미터 창고 유닛(a 3.3-meter wide walk-in storage unit)이 전시관(booth)에 포함되어 있다고 얘기하고 있고, (D)는 첫 번째 단락에 전시를 한 첫 번째 창고 회사가 되었다(became the first storage company to exhibit)라는 말을 통해서 확인할 수 있다. 따라서 언급되지 않은 (B)가 정답이다.

165 사실 관계 확인

번역 스토리지-테크 주식회사에 관해 사실일 것 같은 것은?

(A) 본사가 로데포르트에 있다.
(B) 이사 업체를 인수했다.
(C) 무역 박람회에서 가전제품들을 나눠 주었다.
(D) 미래에 회사 이름을 바꾸려 한다.

해설 세 번째 단락에 매일 진열된 경품을 증정하는 추첨 행사를 했다(During the expo, ~ a refrigerator and a microwave.) 내용을 통해 정답 (C)를 확인할 수 있다. 참고로 (A)는, 본사는 더반에 있다고 했으니 (Headquartered in Durban) 오답이고, (B)에 대한 언급은 없었고, (D)의 경우 인수한 회사의 이름을 자사 이름으로 바꿨다(It recently acquired Upsal Self-Storage's ~)는 것이므로 오답이다.

▸▸ **Paraphrasing** 지문의 **a refrigerator and a microwave**
→ 정답의 **appliances**

166 추론 / 암시

번역 뉴스레터 기사에 따르면, 스토리지 테크 사의 웹사이트에 올라 있는 내용은 무엇인가?

(A) 시설물 가상 견학
(B) 고객들의 논평
(C) 회사의 역사에 관한 세부 기록
(D) 사용할 수 있는 창고 유닛 목록

해설 지문의 마지막 문장을 보면 고객들이 웹사이트를 방문하면 고객들의 추천 내용(customer testimonials)을 확인할 수 있다고 했다. 따라서 정답은 (B)이다.

▸▸ **Paraphrasing** 지문의 **customer testimonials**
→ 정답의 **Comments from customers**

167 문장 삽입

번역 [1], [2], [3], [4]로 표시된 곳 중에서 다음 문장이 들어가기에 가장 적합한 곳은?

"유인물의 온라인 소식에는 5만 명이 넘는 사람들이 이 행사에 참여했다고 나온다."

(A) [1]
(B) [2]
(C) [3]
(D) [4]

해설 삽입문의 '유인물(the handout)'이라는 단어와 비슷한 의미가 있는 어휘가 나오는 부분을 찾아본다. [2]번 앞쪽에 '안내 책자(its brochure)'라는 단어가 바로 유인물을 뜻하므로 정답은 (B)이다.

168-171 온라인 채팅

마이클 매노 [오전 10:11]	다들 안녕하세요. 오늘 내가 가져온 스카프들을 봤어요? 잠재 공급업체인 중국 선전의 텍스-감에서 내가 얻어온 제품 견본들이에요.
톰 로페즈 [오전 10:12]	**168**네. 너무 멋있어서 놀랐어요.
수 댈하트 [오전 10:13]	저도요. 제 동료들도 다양한 색상이 정말 마음에 든대요.
마이클 매노 [오전 10:14]	나도 같은 생각이에요! 직물이 두툼하게 짜여 있는 것도 장점이고요.
톰 로페즈 [오전 10:15]	제조 비용은 어떤가요?
마이클 매노 [오전 10:15]	개당 5달러예요. 그러니, 맞아요, 텍스-감이 다른 공급업체들보다 비쌀 거예요.
톰 로페즈 [오전 10:16]	음…**169**우리가 예상했던 것보다 높네요.
수 댈하트 [오전 10:17]	맞아요. 하지만 제품이 매력적이에요. 마케팅 계획을 잘 세우면 그것들로 이윤을 낼 수 있을 거예요.
톰 로페즈 [오전 10:18]	텍스-감의 최소 주문 합계 수량이 얼마나 되나요?
마이클 매노 [오전 10:19]	스카프500개예요. **170**그 물량만큼 주문을 넣어볼까요? 그런 다음 매장에서 한정판 물품으로 시험 삼아 판매해 보는 거예요.
수 댈하트 [오전 10:20]	좋아요. 오후 회의 때 우리 팀원들한테 마케팅 아이디어를 생각해 보라고 할게요. **171**톰? 우리가 회의할 때 당신도 참석했으면 좋겠는데요.
톰 로페즈 [오전 10:21]	물론이죠.
마이클 매노 [오전 10:22]	훌륭한 계획이네요. 그럼 서로 계속 진행 상황을 알려줍시다.

어휘 bring in 가져오다, 들여오다 product sample 제품 견본 pick up 얻어오다 potential 잠재적인 supplier 공급업체 good-looking 잘생긴, 보기 좋은 colleague 동료 a plus 장점, 좋은 점 thick-knit 두툼하게 짜인 manufacturing cost 제조 비용 anticipate 예상하다 make a profit on ~으로 이윤을 내다 minimum order total 최소 주문 합계 수량 put in an order for ~을 주문하다 amount 물량, 수량 test-market 시험 판매하다 limited edition item 한정판 물품 sit in on ~에 참석하다 keep+사람+updated ~에게 계속 최신 정보를 알려 주다

168 사실 관계 확인

번역 제품 견본에 관해 언급된 내용은 무엇인가?

(A) 다양한 크기로 나온다.
(B) 외관이 보기 좋다.
(C) 방수 직물로 만들어졌다.
(D) 빠르게 생산됐다.

해설 10시 12분에 견본이 멋졌다(good-looking)는 말과, 이어지는 두 개의 대사에서 다양한 색상(their variety of colors)과 두툼히 짠 직물(thick-knit fabric)을 종합해 보면 외관에 대한 칭찬을 하고 있는 것을 알 수 있다. 따라서 정답은 (B)이다.

> **▸▸ Paraphrasing** 지문의 good-looking
> → 정답의 a pleasing appearance

169 의도 파악

번역 오전 10시 17분에 댈하트 씨가 "맞아요"라고 쓴 의도는 무엇이겠는가?

(A) 비용에 대한 다른 사람들의 우려를 이해한다.
(B) 마감 시한이 불합리하다는 것에 동의한다.
(C) 한 공급업체가 제안을 수락해주기를 기대한다.
(D) 자기 회사의 최근 매출에 실망했다.

해설 바로 앞 대화에서 로페즈 씨가 가격이 예상한 것보다 높다고 한 말에 동의한 말이다. 따라서 정답은 (A)이다.

170 세부 사항

번역 매노 씨는 무슨 제안을 하는가?

(A) 직원 수 감축
(B) 공단 방문
(C) 허용된 최소량 주문
(D) 해외에서 일부 매장 개점

해설 10시 18분과 10시 19분 대화 내용을 보면, 스카프의 최소 주문량이 500개라고 하면서, 그만큼 주문해 보는 게 어떠냐고 제안하고 있다. 따라서 정답은 (C)이다.

> **▸▸ Paraphrasing** 지문의 put in an order for that amount
> → 정답의 Placing the smallest order allowed

171 세부 사항

번역 댈하트 씨는 로페즈 씨에게 무엇을 하라고 요청하는가?

(A) 현장 시찰을 취소할 것
(B) 프로젝트 팀을 꾸릴 것
(C) 아이디어 회의에 함께할 것
(D) 마케팅 보고서를 작성할 것

해설 10시 20분 대화 내용에서 댈하트 씨가 로페즈 씨도 회의에 참석하길(sit in on our discussion) 원한다고 했다. 따라서 정답은 (C)이다.

> **▸▸ Paraphrasing** 지문의 sit in on our discussion
> → 정답의 Join a brainstorming meeting

172-175 기사

> 보너스란 직원들이 **173**고정 급여 이외에 받는 돈이지만, 그렇다고 해서 보너스를 받을 자격이 있는 직원들이 이를 중시하지 않는다는 의미는 아니다. **172**이러한 사실은 이번 주 골릿 호텔 주식회사가 20년 만에 처음으로 보너스 체계를 변경할 것이라고 발표하자 전국의 직원들이 강력한 반응을 보이면서 다시 한 번 확실해졌다.
>
> 현재 골릿 호텔의 정규직 직원 중 부문별로 30%의 실적 우수자가 최대500 달러의 분기별 보너스를 받고 있다. 그러나 새로운 보너스 체계가 시행되면 골릿 호텔은 복권 추첨을 통해 무작위로 선출된 10%의 직원에게만 연간 보너스를 지급한다. 지급액은 5000달러~2만 달러로 훨씬 높아질 것이다. **174**회사 경영진은 이러한 계획에 따라 보너스 수여 절차가 더욱 흥미로워질 것이라고 주장한다. 그러나 비평가들은 이는 주로 비용을 절감하려는 의도라고 말한다.
>
> 새로운 계획은 월요일 아침 회사 전체 회람을 통해 직원들에게 전달됐다. 소식이 전해지자 골릿 호텔 내부 포럼에 게시글이 쇄도했고, 그날 오후 개별 직원들이 소셜 미디어에 이를 언급하자 공개 토론의 주제로 등극했다. **175**전에 보너스를 받은 적이 없는 직원들이 보너스를 탈 수 있다는 점에서 소수의 직원들과 외부 논객들이 복권 시스템을 지지하지만, 대다수는 보너스 지급이 실적과 연계되지 않는다는 점에서 불공평하다는 데 의견을 모으고 있다.
>
> 이러한 논란으로 결국 결정이 번복될 것으로 예상된다.

어휘 in addition to ~에 더해, ~ 외에 eligible for ~할 자격이 있는 react 반응하다 highest-performing 실적이 우수한 quarterly 분기의 on a yearly basis 1년 단위로 at random 무작위로 lottery 복권 range 범위가 ~다 critic 비평가 intend 의도하다 cut costs 비용을 절감하다 surge 급증, 급등, 밀려듦 commentator 논평가 unfair 불공평한 be tied to ~와 관련되다 controversy 논란 reverse 뒤집다, 번복하다 eventually 결국.

172 글의 주제 / 목적

번역 기사의 목적 중 하나는 무엇인가?
(A) 직원 채용 전략을 제안하기 위해
(B) 서비스업의 특성을 설명하기 위해
(C) 회사가 직면한 어려움을 설명하기 위해
(D) 새로운 유형의 인센티브 체계를 칭찬하기 위해

해설 첫 번째 단락에서 골릿 호텔 주식회사가 20년 만에 처음으로 보너스 체계를 변경할 것이라고 발표하자 전국의 직원들이 강력한 반응을 보였다고 했으므로, 보너스 체계의 변경을 시도하는 회사가 직면한 어려움을 설명하기 위한 기사임을 알 수 있다. 따라서 정답은 (C)이다.

어휘 strategy 전략 recruit 채용하다 hospitality industry 서비스업 face 직면하다 praise 칭찬하다

▸▸ **Paraphrasing** 지문의 **Gollit Hotels, Inc.** → 정답의 **a corporation**

173 동의어 찾기

번역 첫 번째 단락 2행의 "regular"와 의미가 가장 가까운 것은?
(A) 자연 발생적인
(B) 되풀이해 발생하는
(C) 평균의
(D) 최고 수준의

해설 해당 문장은 '보너스란 직원들이 고정 급여 이외에 받는 돈이다'라는 의미로 해석되므로, 여기서 regular는 '고정적인, 정기적인'이라는 의미가 자연스럽다. 따라서 정답은 반복의 의미를 나타내는 (B) recurring(되풀이하여 발생하는)이다.

174 추론 / 암시

번역 비평가들이 골릿 호텔 사의 경영진에 대해 암시하는 것은?
(A) 그 구조가 비효율적이다.
(B) 일부 포럼을 폐쇄하려고 한다.
(C) 직원 보상에 대한 접근 방식이 구식이다.
(D) 비용을 절감하기를 원한다.

해설 두 번째 단락의 후반부에서 비평가들은 회사 경영진이 주로 비용을 절감하려는 의도로 본다고 했으므로 정답은 (D)이다. 다른 보기들은 모두 지문의 내용과 맞지 않는다.

어휘 inefficient 비효율적인 shut down 폐쇄하다 outdated 구식인 expense 경비, 비용

▸▸ **Paraphrasing** 지문의 **cut costs** → 정답의 **lower expenses**

175 세부 사항

번역 기사에 따르면, 대다수의 사람들이 복권 시스템을 싫어하는 이유는?
(A) 직원들에게 좋은 실적에 대해 보상하지 않는다.
(B) 직원들은 참여를 위해 참가 신청서를 작성해야 한다.
(C) 다른 체계에 비해 보너스를 주는 횟수가 적다.
(D) 보너스 수여자 이름이 공개적으로 발표된다.

해설 마지막 단락에서 대다수는 보너스 지급이 실적과 연계되지 않는다는 점에서 불공평하다는 데 의견을 모으고 있다고 했으므로, 정답은 (A)이다.

어휘 reward 보상[보답]하다 entry form 참가 신청서 publicly 공개적으로

▸▸ **Paraphrasing** 지문의 **most agree that it is unfair** → 질문의 **most people dislike**

지문의 **are not tied to employee performance** → 정답의 **not reward employees for doing good work**

176-180 공지 + 편지

디소토 펠로십

179로스앤젤레스에 위치한 디소토 재단 미디어 센터는 기술과 인문학을 결합하는 연구 과제를 추진하는 **176**미술 및 미디어 분야 중간 경력의 전문가들로부터 지원서를 모집한다.

이 펠로십은 매년 최대 7만 달러까지 수혜자가 받는 봉급의 80%에 해당하는 급료와 함께 2년 동안 주거비를 제공하는 상이다. 이것은 2년 동안 수상자의 봉급을 대신하여, 수상자가 펠로십 연구 과제를 완수하는 동안 수상자의 고용인이 임시 대체 인력을 채용할 수 있게 하려는 것이다.

지원자는 다음을 제출해야 한다.

- **177(B)**1,500단어로 된 연구 제안서
- **177(D)**500단어로 된 자기소개서 및 약력
- **177(A)**추천서 3장
- 관련 연구의 포트폴리오(선택)

지원 마감일은 10월 12일이다. 최종 후보자들은 1월 1일까지 통지를 받게 되며, 그 시점에 면접 일정이 잡힐 것이다. 면접은 덴버와 뉴욕 시에서 실시될 것이다.

지원서는 업계 전문가들과 대학 교수들로 구성된 독자적인 위원회가 심사한다. 예전 수혜자들과 그들의 펠로십 연구 과제를 보려면 www.desotofellowship.com/recipients를 방문하면 된다.

어휘 fellowship 펠로십[연구 장학금] foundation 재단 solicit 간청하다, 얻으려고 하다 application 지원서, 신청서 mid-career 중간 경력의 professional 전문가 media 매체 pursue a project 연구 과제를 추진[계속]하다 combine 결합하다 humanities 인문학 residential 주거의 stipend 급료 equal to ~과 같은 recipient 받는 사람, 수혜자 replace 대체하다, 대신하다 awardee 수상자 employer 고용인 hire 채용하다 temporary replacement 임시 대체 인력 complete 완수하다 proposal 제안서 profile 프로필, 신상 명세 letter of recommendation 추천서 optional 선택적인 deadline 마감 시한 finalist 최종 후보 notify 통지하다, 알리다 arrange 마련하다, 준비하다 board 위원회, 이사회 previous 예전의

디소토 재단 미디어 센터

3월 23일

그레이스 선 씨
오렌지 그로브 레인 302번지
올랜도, 플로리다주 29438

선 씨께,

축하합니다! 우리는 귀하가 올해의 디소토 펠로십 수상자로 선정되었다는 소식을 전하게 되어 기쁩니다. 우리의 면접관들은 결정을 하는 데 있어서 특히 귀하가 영화를 이용해 기술 산업과 일반 대중 사이에서 접점을 마련하려는 **178**열정과 헌신을 언급했습니다.

179알다시피 이 펠로십은 디소토 재단 미디어 센터에서 2년간 거주할 것을 요구합니다. 이사하는 과정에서 귀하와 가족을 도와줄 이사 대행업자들을 이용할 수 있습니다. 우리는 귀하를 엄선된 특별 집단의 일원으로 맞이하게 되어 진심으로 기쁩니다. **180**9월에 만나 보게 되기를 고대합니다.

피터 갤런트
디소토 재단 미디어 센터
펠로십 조정관

어휘 Congratulations! 축하합니다! be delighted to+동사원형 ~하게 되어 기쁘다 inform 알리다 select 선발하다, 뽑다 interviewer 면접관 cite 인용하다 enthusiasm 열정 commitment 헌신, 전념, 몰두 interface 접점을 마련하다, 원활히 상호 작용하다 residency 거주 relocation agent 이사 대행업자 process 과정 be pleased to+동사원형 ~하게 되어 기쁘다 select 엄선된, 정선된

---

176 세부 사항

번역 디소토 펠로십을 받을 자격이 있는 사람은 누구인가?
(A) 컴퓨터 프로그래머
(B) 의사
(C) 구조 공학자
(D) 영화감독

해설 첫 번째 지문 첫 문장을 보면, '미술 및 미디어 분야(the arts and media fields)의 중간 경력 전문가들'로부터 신청을 받는다는 말이 나온다. 보기 중에 나온 직업 중 이에 해당하는 것은 영화감독뿐이다. 따라서 정답은 (D)이다.

177 사실 관계 확인

번역 지원서의 필수 부분으로 열거되지 않은 것은?
(A) 추천서
(B) 제안 설명서
(C) 연구 견본
(D) 약력

해설 첫 번째 지문 중간 부분에 지원자들이 제출해야 할 것들을 명시하고 있는데 (A)는 세 번째 항목에서(Three letters of recommendation), (B)는 첫 번째 항목에서(A 1,500-word project proposal), (D)는 두 번째 항목에서(A 500-word personal/professional profile) 확인할 수 있다. 따라서 열거되지 않은 (C)가 정답이다.

178 추론 / 암시

번역 이메일에서, 선 씨에 관해 암시된 것은?
(A) 자신의 일에 열정적이다.
(B) 올해 펠로십의 유일한 수혜자이다.
(C) 봉급을 많이 받는 전문직 종사자이다.
(D) 펠로십에 여러 번 신청했다.

해설 두 번째 지문 첫 단락에서 면접관들이 선 씨를 선발한 이유로 영화를 이용해 기술 산업과 일반 대중 사이에서 접점을 마련하려고 한 '열정과 헌신(your enthusiasm for and commitment to)'을 언급했다고 했다. 따라서 선 씨가 자신의 일에 매우 열정적이었다는 것을 알 수 있다. 정답은 (A)이다.

▶ **Paraphrasing** 지문의 **your enthusiasm for and commitment to**
→ 정답의 **passionate about her work**

179 연계

번역 선 씨는 어디로 이사하게 되는가?
(A) 로스앤젤레스
(B) 덴버
(C) 뉴욕
(D) 올랜도

해설 첫 번째 지문 첫 문장에서 디소토 재단 미디어 센터가 로스앤젤레스에 위치한 것을 확인할 수 있고, 두 번째 지문 두 번째 단락에서 이 펠로십은 2년간 디소토 재단 미디어 센터에서 근무할 것을 요구한다는 것을 알 수 있다. 따라서 선 씨는 로스앤젤레스로 이사해야 한다. 따라서 정답은 (A)이다.

180 세부 사항

번역 선 씨는 언제 펠로십을 시작하게 되는가?
(A) 1월
(B) 3월
(C) 9월
(D) 10월

해설 두 번째 지문 마지막 문장에서 선 씨에게 9월에 만나기를 고대한다(We look forward to seeing you in September)고 했으므로 정답은 (C) 이다.

181 -185 보도자료+이메일

즉시 배포

연락처: 딘 스미스,
d.smyth@burleys.com.au

시드니 (3월 1일) – 벌리스 피자는 매장 내 식사 고객에게 더 이상 플라스틱 음료 빨대를 자동으로 제공하지 않습니다. **181**이러한 변화를 통해 벌리스 피자에서 배출하는 쓰레기 양을 줄일 수 있기를 바랍니다.

빨대는 재활용 가능한 플라스틱으로 만들어졌으나 크기가 작아 재활용 공장에서 분류할 수가 없습니다. 거의 매립되거나 하수도를 통해 바다로 흘러 들어가 생태계에 해를 끼칩니다.

182매장 음료 목록에 스티커를 부착하여 고객들이 요청할 때에만 직원들이 플라스틱 빨대를 제공한다는 사실을 알려 드리게 할 예정입니다. **183, 185**아울러 남동부 지역 매장에서는 재사용 가능한 크레블 인더스트리즈에서 만든 금속 빨대를 판매할 것입니다. 호주 전역의 벌리스 피자 매장들도 빨대가 대량 제조되는 즉시 똑같은 정책을 시행할 것입니다.

이러한 실천은 벌리스 피자가 최근 진행하는 친환경 운동으로, 여기에는 식재료 대부분을 국내에서 조달하는 것과 음식물 쓰레기의 비료 처리도 포함됩니다. 시에라 크라우스 최고경영자는 "지구촌의 일원으로서 저희의 책임은 지구의 지속 가능성에 공헌하는 것이라고 확신합니다."라고 밝혔습니다.

어휘 no longer 더 이상 ~ 않다 automatically 자동으로 decrease 줄이다, 감소시키다 trash 쓰레기 generate 발생시키다, 만들어 내다 recyclable 재활용이 가능한 sort 분류하다 landfill 쓰레기 매립지 sewer system 하수도 ecosystem 생태계 affix 부착하다, 붙이다 upon request 요청 시 additionally 게다가 reusable 재사용이 가능한 manufacture 생산하다 on a large scale 대량으로, 대규모로 practice 실천, 관행 environmentally-friendly 친환경적인 initiative 운동, 계획 sourcing 조달 ingredient 성분, 재료 domestically 국내에서 compost 퇴비를 주다 contribute to ~에 공헌하다 sustainability 지속가능성

발신: 마크 듀란
수신: 전 종업원
제목: 회의
날짜: 3월 2일

안녕하세요, 여러분.

여러분께 영향을 미칠 사항을 회사가 방금 공개 발표했다는 사실을 들으셨을 겁니다. (무슨 이야기인지 모르시는 분은 이 보도자료를 참조하십시오.) **184,185**이번 주에 최소 한 번은 근무 시간 15분 전에 매장에 도착하여 근무 중인 관리자가 여러분께 그것에 대해 설명하고 고객 문의 처리 및 신제품 홍보에 관한 지시사항을 전달할 수 있도록 해 주십시오. 질문이 있으시면 교대 근무 관리자가 답변해 드릴 것입니다.

감사합니다.

마크 듀란
니글 지점 수석 관리자
벌리스 피자

어휘 corporate 기업, 회사 make a public announcement 대중에게 발표하다 press release 보도자료 on duty 근무 중인 instruction 지시, 설명 deal with 다루다 inquiry 문의 promote 홍보하다

181 글의 주제 / 목적

번역 이 보도 자료는 주로 무엇에 관한 것인가?
(A) 회사의 중요한 시점 기념 행사
(B) 두 업체 간 협력 관계
(C) 식당 안전에 관한 정책
(D) 쓰레기 배출량을 줄이기 위한 노력

해설 보도 자료 첫 번째 단락에서 매장 내 식사 고객에게 더 이상 플라스틱 음료 빨대를 자동 제공하지 않는다는 변경 사항을 통해 벌리스 피자에서 나오는 쓰레기의 양을 줄일 수(decrease the amount of trash) 있기를 바란다고 했으므로, 쓰레기 배출량을 줄이기 위한 회사의 노력을 알리기 위한 보도 자료임을 알 수 있다. 따라서 정답은 (D)이다.

어휘 milestone 중요한 시점

▸▸ Paraphrasing 지문의 **decrease the amount of trash**
→ 정답의 **reduce waste production**

182 추론 / 암시

번역 보도자료에 따르면, 고객들에게 변경사항을 어떻게 알리겠는가?
(A) 전면 창에 표지판 내걸기
(B) 메뉴판에 메모 붙이기
(C) 직원이 이야기하기
(D) 대기실에서 팸플릿 제공하기

해설 보도 자료의 세 번째 단락에서 요청 시에만 직원들이 플라스틱 빨대를 제공한다는 사실을 고객들에게 알리기 위해 매장 음료 목록에 스티커를 부착할(A sticker will be affixed to ~ beverages list) 예정이라고 했으므로, 음료 메뉴에 메모를 붙여 알릴 예정이라는 것을 유추할 수 있다. 따라서 정답은 (B)이다.

어휘 notify 알리다, 통지하다 attach 붙이다 statement 진술, 서술

▸▸ Paraphrasing 지문의 **inform**
→ 질문의 **be notified**

지문의 **A sticker will be affixed to the restaurants' beverages list**
→ 정답의 **a note attached to a menu**

183 사실 관계 확인

번역 크레블 인더스트리즈에서 만든 빨대에 대해 명시된 것은?
(A) 국내에서 제조됐다.
(B) 특별한 형태를 갖췄다.
(C) 재활용한 플라스틱으로 만들어졌다.
(D) 반복해서 사용할 수 있도록 만들어졌다.

해설 보도 자료의 세 번째 단락에서 남동부 지역 매장에서는 재사용 가능한 (reusable) 크레블 인더스트리즈의 금속 빨대를 판매할 것이라고 했으므로, 정답은 (D)이다.

어휘 domestically 국내에서 repeatedly 되풀이하여, 여러 차례

> ▸ Paraphrasing   지문의 reusable
> → 정답의 be used repeatedly

184 세부 사항

번역 듀란 씨가 직원들에게 일찍 오라고 요청한 이유는?
(A) 교육을 받기 위해
(B) 장식물을 달기 위해
(C) 교대 근무 일정을 확인하기 위해
(D) 관리자에게 문서를 제출하기 위해

해설 이메일에서 근무 중인 관리자가 고객 문의 처리 및 신제품 홍보에 관한 지시사항을 전달할 수 있도록 이번 주에 최소 한 번은 15분 일찍 매장에 도착하라고 했으므로, 교육 때문에 일찍 올 것을 요청했음을 알 수 있다. 따라서 정답은 (A)이다.

어휘 submit 제출하다

> ▸ Paraphrasing   지문의 arrive 15 minutes early
> → 질문의 come in early
> 지문의 some instructions on dealing with customer inquiries and promoting our new product → 정답의 some training

185 연계

번역 벌리스 피자의 니글 지점에 대해 암시된 것은?
(A) 최근에 개점했다.
(B) 크라우스 씨가 방문할 예정이다.
(C) 호주 남동부 지역에 있다.
(D) 본사로부터 특별 공로를 인정받았다.

해설 이메일에서 근무 중인 관리자가 고객 문의 처리 및 신제품 홍보에 관한 지시사항을 전달할 것이라고 했고, 보도 자료의 세 번째 단락에서 남동부 지역 매장(the chain's southeastern locations)에서는 재사용 가능한 크레블 인더스트리즈의 금속 빨대를 판매할 예정이라고 했으므로, 니글 지점이 신제품인 금속 빨대를 판매할 남동부 지역에 있는 매장임을 유추할 수 있다. 따라서 정답은 (C)이다.

어휘 receive recognition 공로를 인정받다

186-190 이메일+광고+후기

수신: 앨비 트랜 〈atran@castlerockelectronics.com〉
발신: 도로시 코너스 〈dconnors@castlerockelectronics.com〉
날짜: 10월 3일
제목: 요청 사항

앨비씨,

187스토리 가전이 지난달에 출시한 신형 시스템맥스 7 배송 물량이 우리 창고에 도착했어요. 제 생각엔 인기 있을 것 같아서, **186**우리 전자 매장에 현재 진열되어 있는 세탁기를 이것들 중 하나로 교체하고 싶어요. 9번 통로 앞쪽에 설치해야 해요. 다음 주 수요일까지 이것들 좀 준비해 주시겠어요? 고마워요.

도로시
관리자, 캐슬 록 전자

어휘 shipment 배송 물량 appliances 가전제품, 전자기기 release 출시하다 warehouse 창고 replace 교체하다 on display 진열되어 있는 set up 설치하다 aisle 통로 make the arrangements 준비하다, 마련하다

캐슬 록 전자
-11월 추천 세탁기들-

XM332
가장 큰 세탁기 중 하나인 XM332는 담요나 기타 부피 큰 물품들을 수용할 수 있습니다. 또한 세탁하려는 다양한 종류의 직물에 맞게 수온을 조절할 수 있습니다.
188가격: 475달러

시스템맥스 7
LED 디스플레이와 터치스크린 제어판을 갖춘 시스템맥스 7은 날렵한 현대적 외관을 지니고 있습니다. **187**현재 짙은 초록색으로 제공되는데, 이것이 이 세탁기를 일반적인 흑백 세탁기들과 한층 더 구별되게 합니다.
가격: 425달러

워셴 3.0
워셴 3.0은 다른 세탁기들이 소음을 일으키는 진동을 줄이는 데 특화된 세탁기입니다. 아주 조용하게 작동해서 세탁기가 정말 켜져 있는지 사용자들이 의아하게 여길 정도입니다.
정상가: 425달러
189할인가: 350달러 (11월 30일까지 유효)

트론 T40
트론 T40이 여러분의 세탁물을 즉시 끝내 드릴 것입니다! 이 세탁기의 회전 주기로 세탁물이 무겁든 섬세하든 30분 만에 옷을 깨끗이 빨 수 있습니다.
가격: 375달러

이 달 한정!
캐슬 록 전자는 **186**450달러 이상 되는 세탁기에 대해 무료 배송 및 설치 서비스를 제공합니다.

소비자 후기 온라인

후기 작성자: 캐럴라인 애클리
날짜: **189**11월 11일

189어제 캐슬 록 전자에서 워셴 3.0 세탁기를 구입했어요. 판매원이 매우 많은
도움을 주었고, 아주 싸게 샀어요. 대체로 저는 세탁기가 아주 조용해서 인상이
깊었어요. 옛날 세탁기는 **190**돌아가는 소리가 아파트 전체에 들리곤 했는데, 이
세탁기는 소음이 거의 나지 않아요.

186 세부 사항

번역 코너스 씨는 트랜 씨에게 무엇을 하라고 요청하는가?
(A) 차에서 배송 물품을 내릴 것
(B) 제품을 전시할 것
(C) 고장 난 기계를 교체할 것
(D) 매장 통로를 철저하게 청소할 것

해설 첫 번째 지문이 코너스 씨가 트랜 씨에게 보내는 이메일인데, 후반부를 보
면 시스터맥스 7의 진열 준비를 해달라는 내용을 확인할 수 있다. 따라서
정답은 (B)이다.

▶▶ **Paraphrasing** 지문의 **set up**
→ 정답의 **Put merchandise on display**

187 연계

번역 스토리 가전의 한 세탁기에 대해 강조한 점은?
(A) 새로운 색상
(B) 대용량
(C) 조용함
(D) 속도

해설 첫 번째 지문 맨 앞부분에 지난달 스토리 가전에서 시스터맥스 7을 출시했
다는 얘기가 나왔는데, 두 번째 지문에서 시스터맥스 7의 특징 중 하나가
색상이 '짙은 초록색(dark green)'인 것을 확인할 수 있다. 따라서 정답은
(A)이다.

188 세부 사항

번역 캐슬 록 전자는 어느 세탁기를 무료로 설치해 주는가?
(A) XM332
(B) 시스터맥스 7
(C) 워셴 3.0
(D) 트론 T40

해설 두 번째 지문 마지막 문장에서 450달러 이상의 세탁기는 배송과 설치가
무료라고 했는데, 제품 항목을 보면 450달러가 넘는 제품은 처음에 소개
된 XM332이다. 따라서 정답은 (A)이다.

189 연계

번역 애클리 씨의 세탁기에 관해 사실일 것 같은 것은?
(A) 수온 조절기가 있다.
(B) 12월에 판매 중지될 것이다.
(C) 특별가로 구입했다.
(D) 스크린을 눌러서 작동할 수 있다.

해설 세 번째 지문에서 애클리 씨가 어제(11월 11일) 워셴 3.0 세탁기를 구매
한 것을 확인할 수 있고, 두 번째 지문에서 워셴 3.0은 11월 30일까지 할
인 행사를 진행하는 것을 알 수 있다. 따라서 애클리 씨는 할인된 세탁기를
구입했다. 정답은 (C)이다.

▶▶ **Paraphrasing** 지문의 **Sale price**
→ 정답의 **a special price**

190 동의어 찾기

번역 후기에서 첫 번째 단락 3행의 "running"과 의미상 가장 가까운 것은?
(A) 질주하는
(B) 감독하는
(C) 퍼뜨리는
(D) 작동하는

해설 run은 기계를 설명하는 동사로 사용될 때에는 '작동하다'의 의미를 나타낼
수 있다. 마찬가지로 동사 function도 기계를 설명할 때는 '작동하다'의 의
미를 나타낼 수 있다. 따라서 동의어는 (D) functioning이다.

191 -195 기사+달력+웹페이지

12월 12일—5년간의 공백 후 가수 타티아나 뉴턴이 마침내 신보 〈강물은 흐른
다〉를 내놓았다. 이 앨범은 열광적인 평을 얻고 있으며 음반 판매량이 많을 것으
로 기대된다.

그 로스앤젤레스 토박이는 이 앨범의 곡을 쓰는 데 시간이 많이 걸렸다고 말한
다.**191**그녀가 3년 전에 내슈빌에 본사를 두고 시작한 음반 회사 핑크 아티스츠
주식회사를 경영하느라 바빴기 때문이다. 뉴턴 씨는 "내 자신의 음반회사를 시작
하는 것은 어렵지만 아주 보람 있는 일이었다"면서 "음악계의 사업적인 면에 대
해 아주 많은 것을 배웠다"고 밝힌다.

뉴턴 씨는 비록 현재 음반회사 사장이지만 성공적인 가수로서도 계속 활동하고
싶어 한다. 그래서 전국 순회 공연을 준비 중이다. 그녀는 5월에 로스앤젤레스의
193자처 경기장에서 한 차례 공연을 하는 것으로 순회 공연을 시작할 계획이다.
"지난 2, 3년 동안 내슈빌에 살았는데, 고향에 돌아와 하룻밤 공연을 하게 되면
특별할 것 같다"고 뉴턴 씨는 말했다.

Test 9

어휘 release 발표하다, 발매하다, 출시하다 receive rave reviews 극찬을 받다, 열광적인 반응을 얻다 high record sales 높은 음반 판매량 native 토박이 be busy +-ing ~하느라 바쁘다 -based ~에 본사를 둔 record label 음반회사 launch 시작하다, 출범하다 rewarding 보람 있는 share 나누다 head 수장, 우두머리 as well 또한, 역시 in the middle of ~하는 도중에 nationwide tour 전국 순회 공연[투어] performance 공연 arena 경기장 hometown 고향

자처 경기장						
주간 행사						
5월 23일 오후 6:00	5월 24일 오후 7:00	5월 25일 오전 9:00	5월 26일 오전 9:00	5월 27일 오후 8:00	5월 28일 오후 7:00	5월 29일 오후 7:00
라이트닝 대 글래디 에이터즈	바이크 월드	타이스페스트	타이스페스트	미아 웨이드 라이브	193타티아나 뉴턴	193타티아나 뉴턴
행사 종류: 스포츠	행사 종류: 기타 라이브 공연	194행사 종류: 전시회	행사 종류: 전시회	행사 종류:192코미디	행사 종류: 음악	행사 종류: 음악

어휘 weekly 한 주간의, 주례의 lightning 번개 gladiator 검투사 exhibition 전시회

www.jarcherarena.com/guestservices/FAQ

자처 경기장

자주 묻는 질문들

Q: 카메라를 가져가도 되나요?
A: 네, 소형 카메라와 휴대폰이 허용됩니다. 하지만 19435mm가 넘는 렌즈가 장착된 모든 전문가용 카메라는 허용되지 않습니다. 전시 행사에 참가하는 분들은 이런 제한에 해당되지 않습니다. 더 자세한 내용은 여기를 클릭해 주세요.

Q: 음식과 음료수를 가져갈 수 있나요?
A: 아니요. 음식과 음료수는 자처 경기장 안의 매점에서 구입하실 수 있습니다. 195특별한 식이 요법이 필요한 손님들에게 예외가 적용될 수 있습니다. 이메일 guestservices@jarcherarena.com으로 하라다 마사오에게 문의하시기 바랍니다.

Q: 가방을 가져가도 되나요?
A: 네, 하지만 모든 가방은 좌석 밑에 들어갈 정도로 작아야 합니다. 너무 큰 가방과 배낭, 옷가방 등은 허용되지 않습니다. 크기에 대한 자세한 내용을 보려면 여기를 클릭해 주세요.

어휘 allow 허용[허락]하다 professional camera 전문가용 카메라 permit 허가[허용]하다 exhibition event 전시 행사 exempt 면제된 details 자세한 내용, 세부사항 beverage 음료수 exception 예외 dietary 식이 요법의 fit 꼭 맞다 oversized 너무 큰 suitcase 옷가방

---

191 사실 관계 확인

번역 뉴턴 씨에 대해 언급된 것은?
(A) 회사를 설립했다.
(B) 다섯 번째 앨범을 발표했다.
(C) 로스앤젤레스로 이사할 것이다.
(D) 세계 순회 공연을 마쳤다.

해설 첫 번째 지문 두 번째 단락에서 뉴턴 씨가 3년 전에 회사를 설립해서 바쁜 시간을 보냈다는 내용을 토대로 정답 (A)를 고를 수 있다.

192 사실 관계 확인

번역 일정표에서 자처 경기장에 대해 명시된 것은?
(A) 야외 공간이 있다.
(B) 코미디 공연을 개최한다.
(C) 오전 8시에 사무실 문을 연다.
(D) 2만 명이 앉을 수 있다.

해설 두 번째 지문인 주간 행사표를 보면 5월 27일의 공연 종류는 '코미디'라는 것을 알 수 있다. 따라서 자처 경기장에서 코미디 공연을 하는 것을 알 수 있으므로, 정답은 (B)이다.

193 연계

번역 자처 경기장에서 열리는 뉴턴 씨의 공연에 무엇이 변경되었을 것 같은가?
(A) 2시간 이상 공연할 것이다.
(B) 원래 계획보다 공연이 더 많다.
(C) 이제는 투어의 첫 번째 장소가 아니다.
(D) 입장권 가격을 인상했다.

해설 첫 번째 지문 세 번째 단락을 보면, 뉴턴 씨는 자처 경기장에서 한 차례 공연(one performance)을 계획하고 있었다. 하지만 두 번째 지문인 일정표를 살펴보면 5월 28일, 29일 두 차례 공연이 예정되어 있다. 따라서 뉴턴 씨의 공연이 원래 계획보다 늘어난 것을 알 수 있다. 따라서 정답은 (B)이다.

194 연계

번역 손님이 전문가용 카메라를 가져올 수 있는 행사는 어떤 것인가?
(A) 라이트닝 대 글래디에이터즈
(B) 바이크 월드
(C) 타이스페스트
(D) 미아 웨이드 라이브

해설 세 번째 지문 첫 번째 단락에서 전문가용 카메라는 허용되지 않지만 전시회는 예외(Those attending exhibition events are exempt)라는 내용을 확인할 수 있다. 두 번째 지문인 행사 일정표에서 타이스페스트의 종류가 전시회라는 것을 알 수 있으므로 정답은 (C)이다.

195 세부 사항

번역 웹페이지에 따르면, 어떤 사람이 하라다 씨에게 연락해야 할 이유는 무엇인가?
(A) 경기장의 상인이 되기 위해
(B) 큰 가방을 가져오는 것을 허락 받기 위해
(C) 분실물을 찾기 위해
(D) 음식물 관련 요청을 하기 위해

해설 하라다 씨가 나오는 부분은 세 번째 지문의 두 번째 질문에 대한 답변인데 특별한 식이 요법이 필요한 예외적인 경우에 연락을 취하라는 말이 나온다. 따라서 음식물 관련 요청인 (D)가 정답이다.

196-200 이메일 + 안내책자 발췌 + 이메일

발신: 제이 러셀
수신: 클라우디아 산체즈, 더스틴 버틀러, 엘라나 틴슬리
제목: 회사 안내책자
날짜: 1월 10일

안녕하세요 여러분,

여러분께서 만들어 달라고 요청하신 회사 안내책자에 필요한 정보를 수집하고 있습니다. **196**이를 위해 고위 임원이신 여러분을 설명할 짧은 단락 안에 포함하고 싶은 직책이나 경력 세부 사항을 각자 보내주셔야 합니다. 혹은 원하신다면 50단어 미만으로 문구를 각자 작성하셔도 됩니다. 필요한 문구를 받는 대로 템플릿에 함께 넣어 승인을 위해 여러분께 보내드리겠습니다.

감사합니다.

197제이 러셀
마케팅 커뮤니케이션 관리자
레바 주식회사

어휘 brochure 안내책자, 소책자 gather 모으다, 수집하다 to that end 그러한 목적을 위해 executive 임원, 간부 paragraph 단락, 절 as long as ~하는 한 approve 승인하다

경영진

클라우디아 산체스
199사장
산체스 사장은 블래킨 인더스트리즈에서 나와 레바 주식회사를 설립했으며, 10년간 사업부장을 역임했다. 현재 레바의 전반적인 사업 전략을 결정하며 부사장 및 수석 이사들에게 지침을 제공한다.

197더스틴 버틀러
영업 마케팅 부사장
버틀러 씨는 레바 창립 당시부터 중요한 회사의 일원이었다. 새로운 유통업체를 발굴하고 기존 소매 고객을 개발함으로써 사업 확장 계획을 수립하고 실행하는 일을 맡고 있다.

엘라나 틴슬리
사업운영 부사장
198틴슬리 씨는 주식회사 레바의 혁신적인 바닥용 스탠드, 탁자용 스탠드, 책상용 스탠드 개발 및 생산을 관리한다. 하급 엔지니어로 입사한 후, 품질을 위한 노력과 헌신에 힘입어 승진을 거듭했다.

3쪽

어휘 management 경영진 operation 운영 determine 결정하다 overall 전반적인 strategy 전략 guidance 지침 senior executive 고위급 이사, 중역 vice president 부사장 valued 귀중한 establishment 설립 formulate 만들어 내다 implement 시행하다 expand 확장하다 distributor 유통업체 existing 기존의, 존재하는 retail 소매 account 고객; 계정 oversee 감독하다, 관리하다 innovative 혁신적인 rise through the ranks 승진하다 dedication 헌신

발신: 클라우디아 산체스
수신: 제이 러셀
제목: Re: 회사 안내책자 견본
날짜: 1월 22일

안녕하세요 제이 씨,

회사 안내책자 견본을 보내주어 고맙습니다. 확인해 보니 대부분 마음에 들었습니다. 선택한 깔끔하고 간결한 디자인이 좋습니다. 사실, 스타일 관련해 작은 변경 요청 사항이 하나 있습니다. **199**'경영진' 페이지에서 각 단락의 두 번째 줄은 이탤릭체를 사용해서, 이어지는 부분과 더 대조를 이룰 수 있도록 해 주십시오.

그런데 2쪽('레바 주식회사 소개'로 시작하는 페이지)의 내용에 관해 몇 가지 우려 사항이 있습니다. 불필요해 보이는 우리 회사 업무 절차 관련 세부 사항이 많이 있네요. **200**이 정보가 안내책자에 들어가야 할 이유가 무엇인지 설명해 줄 수 있나요? 딱히 그럴 만한 이유가 없다면 삭제하고 대신 그래픽을 하나 넣는 것이 한결 나을 것 같습니다.

– 클라우디아

어휘 mock-up 모형 look over 살펴보다 mostly 주로 request 요청하다 as far as ~에 관한 한 contrast 대조 concern 우려 process 과정, 절차 unnecessary 불필요한 particularly 특히, 특별히 delete 삭제하다 insert 삽입하다

196 글의 주제 / 목적

번역 첫 번째 이메일의 주목적은 무엇인가?
(A) 기회를 준 것에 감사를 표하기 위해
(B) 개인 정보를 요청하기 위해
(C) 수신자들에게 제한 사항을 상기시키기 위해
(D) 제안에 대한 반응을 수집하기 위해

해설 첫 번째 이메일에서 회사 안내책자를 각 고위 임원인 세 사람을 설명하는 짧은 단락 안에 포함하고 싶은 직책이나 경력 세부 사항을 보내 달라고 했으므로, 임원의 개인 정보를 요청하기 위한 이메일임을 알 수 있다. 따라서 정답은 (B)이다.

어휘 gratitude 감사 restriction 규제, 제한

▸▸ **Paraphrasing** 지문의 **any details about your position or career** → 정답의 **some personal information**

197 연계

번역 버틀러 씨에 대해 암시된 것은?

(A) 산체스 씨보다 먼저 레바 사에 입사했다.
(B) 자신에 관한 문구를 작성하지 않기로 결정했다.
(C) 새로 생긴 직책을 맡고 있다.
(D) 러셀 씨의 상관이다.

해설 안내책자에서 버틀러 씨를 '영업 마케팅 부사장(Vice President of Sales and Marketing)'이라고 소개하고 있고, 첫 번째 이메일의 후반부에서 발신인인 러셀 씨가 자신을 '마케팅 커뮤니케이션 관리자'라고 밝히고 있으므로, 버틀러 씨가 러셀 씨의 상관임을 유추할 수 있다. 따라서 정답은 (D)이다.

198 세부 사항

번역 레바 주식회사는 어떤 업체인가?

(A) 조명 설치 업체
(B) 가구 유통 업체
(C) 가전제품 제조업체
(D) 건축 자재 공급 업체

해설 안내책자의 마지막 부분에서 틴슬리 부사장은 회사의 혁신적인 바닥용 스탠드, 탁자용 스탠드, 책상용 스탠드 개발 및 생산을 관리한다고 했으므로, 정답은 (C)이다.

어휘 installation 설치 appliance 가전제품 manufacturer 제조업체

> ▸▸ **Paraphrasing** 지문의 **floor, table, and desk lamps** → 정답의 **appliance**

199 연계

번역 안내책자의 어떤 문구에 산체스 씨의 변경 요청 사항이 반영될 것인가?

(A) '클라우디아 산체스'
(B) '사장'
(C) '레바 주식회사'
(D) '10년'

해설 두 번째 이메일의 첫 번째 단락에서 산체스 씨가 '경영진' 페이지에서 각 단락의 두 번째 줄에 이탤릭체를 사용해, 이어지는 글과 더 대조를 이룰 수 있도록 할 것을 요청했고, 산체스 씨가 글씨체 변경을 요청한 안내책자 각 단락의 두 번째 줄은 직책 부분이므로, 정답은 (B)이다.

200 세부 사항

번역 산체스 씨는 러셀 씨에게 안내책자의 2쪽과 관련해 무엇을 요청하는가?

(A) 그래픽에 대한 설명 추가하기
(B) 제목을 다시 고려하기
(C) 편집 속도를 높이기
(D) 어떤 콘텐트를 포함한 타당한 이유를 설명하기

해설 두 번째 이메일의 두 번째 단락에서 수신인(you)인 러셀 씨에게 업무 절차 관련 상세한 정보가 안내책자에 들어가야 할 이유를 설명해 달라고 요청했으므로, 정답은 (D)이다.

어휘 reconsider 재고하다 wording 단어 선택 justify 정당화하다 inclusion 포함

> ▸▸ **Paraphrasing** 지문의 **explain why you thought this information should be in the brochure** → 정답의 **Justify the inclusion of some content**

TEST 10

101 (A)	**102** (A)	**103** (C)	**104** (C)	**105** (D)
106 (C)	**107** (C)	**108** (A)	**109** (D)	**110** (D)
111 (B)	**112** (A)	**113** (B)	**114** (C)	**115** (D)
116 (C)	**117** (A)	**118** (C)	**119** (D)	**120** (B)
121 (D)	**122** (A)	**123** (B)	**124** (A)	**125** (C)
126 (D)	**127** (D)	**128** (A)	**129** (B)	**130** (B)
131 (A)	**132** (B)	**133** (C)	**134** (A)	**135** (D)
136 (A)	**137** (B)	**138** (B)	**139** (B)	**140** (D)
141 (C)	**142** (A)	**143** (C)	**144** (B)	**145** (C)
146 (D)	**147** (D)	**148** (B)	**149** (C)	**150** (A)
151 (A)	**152** (B)	**153** (C)	**154** (A)	**155** (B)
156 (D)	**157** (A)	**158** (C)	**159** (B)	**160** (C)
161 (A)	**162** (C)	**163** (B)	**164** (C)	**165** (C)
166 (D)	**167** (C)	**168** (B)	**169** (D)	**170** (C)
171 (A)	**172** (D)	**173** (B)	**174** (D)	**175** (C)
176 (B)	**177** (A)	**178** (D)	**179** (B)	**180** (A)
181 (C)	**182** (C)	**183** (B)	**184** (D)	**185** (B)
186 (D)	**187** (B)	**188** (A)	**189** (B)	**190** (C)
191 (A)	**192** (D)	**193** (A)	**194** (D)	**195** (C)
196 (D)	**197** (A)	**198** (D)	**199** (A)	**200** (C)

PART 5

101 동사 시제

해설 과거 10년 전부터 지금까지의 기간을 나타내는 전치사구(Over the past decade)가 있으므로 현재완료시제인 (A) has engaged가 정답이다.

번역 지난 10년 동안 센케 재단은 지속가능한 발전을 촉진하기 위한 다양한 활동에 관여해 왔다.

어휘 decade 10년   a variety of 다양한   promote 촉진하다   sustainable (환경을 파괴하지 않고) 지속가능한   engage in ~에 관여하다

102 전치사 어휘

해설 빈칸 뒤 명사(the waste bins)를 목적어로 취하는 전치사 자리로, 빈칸을 포함한 전치사구는 주어인 '가구와 같은 큰 물건들(Large items ~ furniture)'의 위치를 설명한다. '쓰레기통 옆에 두어야 한다'라는 의미가 자연스러우므로 정답은 (A) beside(~ 옆에)이다.

번역 가구와 같은 큰 물건들은 처리 서비스 팀의 편리한 수거를 위해 쓰레기통 옆에 두어야 한다.

어휘 item 물건, 품목   such as ~와 같은   furniture 가구   leave 놓다, 두다   waste bin 쓰레기통   convenient 편리한   pick-up 집어 감, 수거; 태워 줌   disposal (폐기물) 처리   until ~까지

103 동사 어휘

해설 정보를 한 곳에 모아 놓으면 '비교하기' 쉽다는 의미가 가장 자연스럽다. 따라서 정답은 (C) compare(비교하다)이다. (A) argue는 '논하다, 논쟁

하다', (B) resume은 '다시 시작하다, 재개하다', (D) determine은 '결정하다'라는 의미이다.

번역 모든 제품에 대한 정보를 한 곳에 모아 두면 비교하기가 쉬워진다.

어휘 gather 모으다   product 제품

104 부사 어휘

해설 과거 한때(used to)는 기업 고객들이 많았지만 '최근에는' 없었다는 의미가 가장 적절하다. 과거(used to)와 대비되는 의미의 부사 어휘가 들어가야 한다. 따라서 정답은 (C) lately(최근에)이다. (A) nearly는 '거의', (B) primarily는 '주로', (D) personally는 '개인적으로'라는 의미이다.

번역 질라스 케이터링은 예전에는 많은 기업 고객들을 위해 일했지만 최근에는 기업 고객이 전혀 없었다.

어휘 catering 연회   used to ~하곤 했다   serve ~을 위해 일하다, (음식 등을) 제공하다

105 명사 자리 _ 주어

해설 빈칸에는 문장의 주어 역할을 할 명사가 와야 할 자리이다. 보기 중 명사인 (D) prediction(예측, 예보)이 정답이다.

번역 이번 주 날씨에 대한 오카다 씨의 예측은 대부분 정확했다는 것이 드러났다.

어휘 weather 날씨   turn out ~인 것으로 드러나다[밝혀지다]   mostly 대부분   accurate 정확한   predict 예측하다   predictably 예상대로

106 소유대명사

해설 빈칸은 using의 목적어가 될 대명사를 고르는 문제이다. 앞 절의 headphones를 받아서 'our headphones'를 뜻할 소유대명사는 ours(우리의 것)이다. 정답은 (C) ours이다.

번역 아엘트 사의 시올론 스마트폰은 대부분의 헤드폰과 호환이 되지만, 저희 회사의 헤드폰을 쓰는 것이 최고의 음질을 보장합니다.

어휘 compatible 호환이 되는   ensure 보장하다

107 등위접속사

해설 빈칸은 동명사(adding)의 목적어 역할을 하는 명사구(a row of trees)와 명사구(several planters)를 연결하는 등위접속사 자리로, '나무 한 줄이나 화분 몇 개를 추가할 것'이라는 의미가 자연스러우므로, 정답은 (C) or(또는, ~이나)이다. 참고로, (A) so(그래서)는 절과 절을 연결할 수 있고, 전치사/접속사인 (D) since(~ 이래로)는 의미상 적절하지 않다.

번역 그 도급업자는 앞쪽 보도를 따라 나무를 한 줄 심거나 화분 몇 개를 추가할 것을 제안했다.

어휘 contractor 도급업자   suggest 제안하다   a row of 한 줄의, 일련의   planter (잘 가꾸어 놓은) 화분   along ~을 따라[끼고]   walkway 보도   yet 그렇지만

108 형용사 자리 _ 명사 수식

해설 빈칸이 관사와 명사 사이에 있기 때문에 명사를 수식할 수 있는 형용사를 고르는 문제이다. 형용사인 (A) energetic(활동적인, 정력적인)이 정답이다.

번역 유람선에서 공연했던 주인공 연예인은 무대에 올랐을 때 활기찬 태도를 보였다.

어휘 entertainer 연예인 perform 공연하다 cruise ship 유람선 attitude 태도 take the stage 무대를 차지하다 energetically 활동적으로, 정력적으로

109 부사 자리 _ 동사 수식

해설 앞의 동사 fill out(작성하다)을 수식하는 부사 자리이다. 양식을 '주의 깊게' 또는 '조심해서' 작성해야 한다는 의미를 만들어주는 (D) carefully(주의 깊게)가 정답이다. (A) careful은 '조심하는', (B) carefulness는 '조심, 용의주도'라는 의미이다.

번역 환불 요청 시 처리 지연을 막기 위해 양식을 주의 깊게 작성하십시오.

어휘 avoid 피하다 delay 지연 processing 처리 fill out the form 양식을 작성하다 make a request 요청하다 refund 환불

110 전치사 어휘

해설 빈칸 앞의 동사가 수동태(will be taken)이고 뒤에 장소가 나왔으므로, '~로 보내진다'는 의미가 가장 자연스럽다. 따라서 방향을 나타내는 전치사 (D) to가 정답이다.

번역 소포 주소란에 특정 직원의 이름이 적혀 있지 않으면 우편물실로 보내어질 것이다.

어휘 state (문서에) 명시하다 specific 특정한

111 형용사 어휘

해설 빈칸 뒤의 명사구 overtime pay rate을 수식할 적절한 형용사를 고르는 문제이다. 앞에 양보/대조의 전치사 Despite(~에도 불구하고)가 있으므로, 전치사구와 문장은 서로 대조적인 의미가 되어야 한다. '후한 초과 근무 수당에도 불구하고 직원들을 설득하기 어렵다'라는 의미가 자연스러우므로, 정답은 (B) generous(후한, 관대한)이다. (A) lengthy(긴), (C) infrequent(드문), (D) intensive(집중적인)는 모두 의미상 적절하지 않다.

번역 후한 초과 근무 수당에도 불구하고, 근로자들이 바쁜 시기에 추가 교대 근무를 하도록 설득하는 것은 종종 어렵다.

어휘 overtime 초과 근무 pay rate (단위 시간당 받는) 임금 (액수) persuade A(사람) to+동사원형 A가 ~하도록 설득하다 accept 수락하다 additional 추가의 shift 교대 근무[조]

112 동사구 어휘

해설 빈칸 뒤의 one another와 함께 쓰여 '서로 협력하다'는 의미가 적절하므로 (A) cooperate with(~와 협력하다)가 정답이다.

번역 서로 협력하는 직원을 둔 부서들이 대체로 생산성 수준이 높다.

어휘 one another 서로 productivity 생산성 qualify for ~의 자격을 얻다 refrain from -ing ~하는 것을 삼가다 contribute to ~에 공헌하다

113 전치사 자리 _ 명사 앞

해설 명사 the break 앞에 들어갈 전치사 자리이다. 유일한 전치사 (B) during(~ 동안)이 정답이다. (C) while은 '~하는 동안'의 의미이나, 접속사이므로 while 뒤에는 주어와 동사를 갖춘 절이 온다.

번역 행사 진행자는 두 차례의 회의 사이에 있는 휴식시간에 몇 가지 공지를 했다.

어휘 coordinator 진행자, 조정자 make an announcement 공표하다, 발표하다 break 쉬는 시간 whenever ~할 때마다 then 그때; 그리고 나서

114 부사 자리 _ 분사 수식

해설 빈칸 뒤 과거분사(included)를 수식하는 부사 자리이므로, 정답은 부사 (D) Increasingly(점점 더, 점차)이다. 명사/동사인 (A) Increases, 동명사/현재분사인 (B) Increasing, to부정사인 (C) To increase는 모두 품사상 적합하지 않다.

번역 시의 최고 관광지 목록에 점점 오르는 램버트 지역은 아름답고 다양한 건축물을 보여준다.

어휘 included 포함되는 list 목록 tourist site 관광지 neighborhood 지역, 동네 diverse 다양한 architecture 건축(물), 건축 양식 increase 증가; 증가시키다

115 명사 자리 _ 관사 뒤

해설 관사 뒤에 명사가 와야 하는 자리이다. 빈칸 뒤에는 전치사구가 시작되기 때문에 반드시 관사 a를 받는 명사가 와야 한다. 보기에서 명사는 (A), (D)이지만, 관사 a가 있으므로 단수형인 (D) dispute(논쟁)가 정답이다.

번역 드레이크 씨는 동료 두 명 사이의 논쟁을 능숙하게 처리한 후, 승진을 제안 받았다.

어휘 expertly 능숙하게 handle 다루다, 처리하다 colleague 동료 offer 제공하다, 제안하다 promotion 승진 disputable 논란의 여지가 있는

116 동사 시제

해설 보기의 모든 동사가 능동태이기 때문에 '시제'만 파악하면 되는 문제이다. last weekend를 통해서 시제가 과거가 되어야 함을 알 수 있다. 따라서 정답은 과거완료 시제인 (C) had slowed이다.

번역 쿠퍼 씨는 지난 주말 내내 거래 속도를 늦추게 했던 컴퓨터 문제를 해결했다.

어휘 fix a problem 문제를 해결하다 transaction 거래, 매매

117 명사 어휘

해설 보기 중에서 전치사 on과 어울리는 명사를 먼저 골라본다. 그리고 해석상 적절한 조합을 찾아본다. 해석을 해보면 풍력 공급을 늘리고 반대로 해외 석유에 대한 '의존'을 낮춘다는 내용이다. 따라서 빈칸에 적절한 것은 (A) reliance(의존)이다. (B) congestion은 '혼잡', (C) dissatisfaction은 '불만족', (D) attendance는 '출석'을 의미한다.

번역 정부 관리들은 국가의 풍력 공급을 두 배로 늘리고 해외 석유 의존도를 낮추는 조치를 지지한다.

어휘 government official 정부 관리 measures 방안, 조치 supply
공급 wind power 풍력 reduce 감소시키다

118 형용사 자리 _ 주격 보어

해설 빈칸은 that절의 주어(our office electronics)를 보충 설명하는 주격 보어 자리이고, 뒤에 전치사 for가 있으므로, 형용사 (C) affordable(가격이 적당한, 감당할 수 있는)이 가장 적절하다. 정답은 (C) affordable이다.

번역 앞으로 홍보 자료에서는 우리 사무용 전자 기기들이 작은 업체들도 구매할 만하다는 것을 강조해야 한다.

어휘 emphasize 강조하다 office electronics 사무용 전자 기기
affording 제공하는 affordability 적절한 가격; 구매 가능성
afford (구입할 만한 경제적) 여유가 있다

119 부사 어휘

해설 '흠이 있다(be bruised)'는 의미를 가장 잘 수식해줄 수 있는 부사 어휘를 고르는 문제이다. '조금, 약간'이라는 의미의 (C) slightly가 가장 적절하다. (A) closely는 '접근하여, 밀접하게', (B) actively는 '활발히', (D) briefly는 '잠시'라는 의미이다.

번역 메이에스 씨는 농산물 직판장에서 산 농작물에 약간 흠이 있었기 때문에 할인을 받았다.

어휘 give a discount 할인해 주다 produce 농산물 farmer's
market 농산물 직판장 bruised 멍든, 흠이 있는

120 명사 자리 _ 전치사 뒤

해설 빈칸은 맨 앞의 전치사구 In accordance with(~을 따라, ~에 부합되게)의 영향을 받아 명사가 들어가야 하는 자리이다. noise와 함께 복합 명사를 이뤄야 한다. 동사인 (A), (D)는 불가능하고, (C) regulator는 가산 명사이기 때문에 단수로 쓰인 경우 앞에 관사가 와야 하는데 없으므로 적절하지 않다. 따라서 (B) regulations(규정)가 정답이다.

번역 자치주 소음 규정에 따라 콜드크릭 파빌리온에서 열리는 야외 콘서트는 밤 10시까지 마쳐야 한다.

어휘 outdoor 실외의 regulate 규제하다, 단속하다 regulator 규제 기관, 단속 담당자

121 형용사 어휘

해설 허브와 향신료의 '섬세한' 또는 '미묘한' 혼합이 있는 요리라는 의미가 가장 적절하다. 따라서 정답은 (D) delicate(섬세한, 미묘한)이다. (A) remote는 '외진, 외딴', (B) countless는 '무수한', (C) wealthy는 '부유한, 재산이 많은'이라는 의미이다.

번역 인도의 맛의 수석 주방장은 허브와 향신료가 섬세하게 섞인 요리를 만든다.

어휘 flavor 맛, 풍미 blend 혼합, 조합 herb 약초 spice 향신료

122 부사 어휘

해설 문맥상 '예정된 완성일이 2개월 지났는데도, 여전히 진행 중이다'라는 의미가 자연스러우므로, 정답은 (A) still(여전히)이다. (B) far(훨씬)은 주로 비교급 형용사를, (C) well(잘)은 주로 동사를 수식하고 (D) soon(곧)은 의미상 적절하지 않다.

번역 예정된 완성일이 2개월 지났는데도, 2번 출구 에스컬레이터 건설은 여전히 진행 중이다.

어휘 projected 계획된, 예상된 completion 완성 escalator
에스컬레이터 exit 출구 ongoing 진행 중인

123 동사 자리 + 능동태 / 수동태 구분

해설 한 문장에 동사는 꼭 하나 있어야 하는데 없기 때문에 빈칸은 동사 자리이다. 따라서 to부정사구인 (D) to be generated는 제외된다. 주어인 interest(관심)는 '생겨지는' 것이기 때문에 동사의 형태는 수동태가 되어야 한다. 따라서 정답은 (B) was generated이다.

번역 어제 감독이 소셜 미디어에 의견을 남기자 그 영화에 대해 많은 관심이 생겨났다.

어휘 a great deal of 많은 generate 발생시키다, 만들어 내다

124 부사 자리 _ 동사 수식

해설 빈칸 앞의 접속사 but 앞뒤로 주격 관계대명사 that의 동사들(describe, do not ~ appear)이 있다. 빈칸에는 뒤의 동사를 수식할 부사가 와야 하므로 정답은 (A) preferably(가급적이면)이다.

번역 당신의 연구를 묘사하되, 가급적이면 논문 제목에 이미 나오지는 않은 세 개의 핵심어를 제시해 주십시오.

어휘 suggest 제시[제안]하다 keyword 핵심어 describe 서술하다, 묘사하다 appear (글 속에) 나오다 paper 논문, 리포트 preferred 선호되는 preferable 선호할 만한, 더 좋은 preference 선호

125 접속사 어휘

해설 콤마(,) 앞의 '도로의 눈을 치웠다'는 문장과 콤마(,) 뒤의 '자동차 운전자들은 천천히 운전하도록 권고받는다'는 문장은 서로 상반되는 내용이기 때문에 '대조'를 의미하는 접속사가 와야 한다. 따라서 (C) Even though(비록 ~일지라도)가 정답이다.

번역 도로에서 눈을 치웠지만 자동차 운전자들은 오늘 아침 천천히 운전하도록 권고받는다.

어휘 motorist 자동차 운전자 ahead of ~보다 빨리 in case ~할 경우에 대비하여

126 관용 표현

해설 of와 함께 쓰여 '~에 관계없이'라는 의미를 갖는 관용표현 전치사구를 묻는 문제이다. '차의 상태와 상관없이'라는 의미로 해석이 되어야 하기 때문에 (D) regardless가 정답이다.

번역 빈스 오토는 차의 상태와 관계없이 모든 차량에 적정한 보상판매 가격을 제공할 것을 약속합니다.

fair price 적정 가격 trade-in 보상판매 regardless of ~에 상관없이 regarding ~에 관하여

127 부사절 접속사

해설 빈칸 뒤에 완전한 절이 있으므로, 정답은 부사절 접속사인 (D) now that(~이니까, ~이므로)이다. 부사 (A) after all(결국), 전치사구 (B) instead of(~ 대신에)와 (C) due to(~ 때문에) 뒤에는 완전한 절이 올 수 없으므로 품사상 적합하지 않다.

번역 조디 신이 부상에서 회복했기 때문에 그 팀은 선수권 대회에서 우승할 좋은 기회를 갖고 있다.

어휘 excellent 훌륭한 chance 기회 win the championship 선수권 대회에서 우승하다 recover from ~에서 회복하다 injury 부상, 상처

128 전치사(구) 어휘

해설 빈칸 앞뒤로 긴 주어가 있다. '빨간 스티커로 표시된 것들을 제외하고'라는 의미가 가장 자연스러우므로, 정답은 (A) except(~을 제외하고)이다. (B) apart는 apart from(~을 제외하고)이라고 해야 전치사구가 될 수 있다.

번역 창고에 있는 모든 물건은 빨간 스티커로 표시된 상자들을 제외하고 점심시간까지 풀어 놓아야 한다.

어휘 warehouse 창고 crate 상자 mark with ~로 표시하다 prior to ~에 앞서, 먼저

129 형용사 / 분사 어휘

해설 빈칸에는 모두 -ed 형태로 앞의 명사 expenses를 수식하는 분사형 형용사가 들어가야 한다. 의미상 '발생된 비용'이라는 말이 가장 자연스러우므로, 정답은 (B) incurred(발생된)이다. 보통 '발생 비용'을 incurred expense라고 한다. (A) proceeded는 '진행된', (C) nominated는 '지명된, 임명된', (D) attained은 '얻은'이라는 의미이다.

번역 아미다 인터내셔널의 직원들은 업무 중에 발생한 모든 지출에 대해 환급을 받는다.

어휘 reimbursement 갚음, 환급 expense 지출 in the course of ~ 동안 duty 업무, 직무

130 명사 어휘

해설 빈칸 앞의 take의 목적어로 올 알맞은 명사를 고르는 문제이다. '생산 작업 공간에 들어서기 전에 예방 조치를 취해야 한다'라는 의미가 자연스러우므로, 정답은 (B) precautions(예방 조치)이다. (A) accomplishments(성취, 업적), (C) malfunctions(고장), (D) incidents(사건)는 모두 의미상 적절하지 않다.

번역 방문객들은 공장 생산 작업 공간에 들어가기 전에 예방 조치를 취하는 게 중요하다.

PART 6

131-134 기사

베를린 (9월 5일) – VCF 오토모티브는 자동차 생산공장을 더욱 친환경적으로 만들려는 계획을 추진 중이다.

회사 대변인은 이 **131목표가** 몇 가지 주요 변화를 통해 달성될 수 있다고 밝혔다. 첫째, 옥상 태양전지판을 **132설치하여** 외부 전력 수요를 줄일 수 있을 것이다. 전지판은 공장이 스스로 클린 에너지를 생성하게 만들 것이다. 또한 이 회사는 대기에 방출하는 물질의 양을 **133급격히** 낮추고자 한다. 이에 따라 모든 외부 환기구에 필터를 추가할 예정이다. **134끝으로, 유통센터를 대리점과 더 가까운 위치로 이전할 계획도 있다.** 이는 교통수단으로 인한 오염을 줄이는 결과를 낳을 것이다.

소비자들은 이 소식에 긍정적인 반응을 보였고 환경 피해를 최소화하려는 VCF의 노력을 칭찬하고 있다.

어휘 move forward with ~을 추진하다 manufacturing plant 생산공장 environmentally-friendly 환경 친화적인 spokesperson 대변인 need 필요, 수요 electricity 전력 reduce 감소시키다 rooftop 옥상 solar panel 태양 전지판 enable ~을 할 수 있게 하다 generate 생성하다 clean energy 클린 에너지(태양열이나 전기처럼 대기를 오염시키지 않는 에너지) exterior 외부 vent 환기구, 통풍구 distribution 유통 dealership 대리점 react to ~에 반응하다 favorably 호의적으로 environmental 환경의 impact 영향, 피해

131 명사 어휘

해설 우선 빈칸은 앞 문장의 내용을 하나의 단어로 설명할 수 있는 명사여야 한다. 그리고 공장 내 몇 가지 변화를 통해서 달성할 수 있는 것이어야 한다. 앞 문장에서 말한, 공장을 친환경적으로 만들려는 계획이 바로 '그 목표(the objective)'라고 하는 것이 자연스러우므로 정답은 (A) objective(목표)이다. 참고로 objective는 형용사로는 '객관적인'이라는 의미도 있다. (B) revenue는 '수익', (C) technique은 '기술', (D) facility는 '시설'이라는 의미이다.

132 명사 / 동명사 자리 _ 전치사 뒤

해설 빈칸 앞에 by가 있으므로 명사나 동명사가 와야 한다. 의미상 '옥상 태양 전지판을 설치함으로써'라는 말이 되어야 한다. 따라서 동명사 형태인 (B) installing이 정답이다.

133 부사 자리

해설 빈칸 앞에는 to부정사구의 to가 빈칸 뒤에는 동사원형이 왔다. 따라서 빈칸에는 동사를 수식해 줄 부사만 들어갈 수 있다. 보기 중 유일한 부사인 (C) sharply(급격히)가 정답이다.

134 문맥에 맞는 문장 고르기

번역 (A) 이는 교통수단으로 인한 오염을 줄이는 결과를 낳을 것이다.
(B) 그렇지 않으면 피해는 훨씬 더 커질 것이다.
(C) 센터들은 복잡한 장비를 사용해 재고를 추적한다.
(D) 이렇게 하여 고객은 스스로 이익을 경험할 수 있다.

해설 이 지문의 마지막 문장은 이 글 전체에 대한 정리 문장이기 때문에 바로 앞 문장에서 힌트를 찾는 것이 좋다. 앞 문장에서 가까운 위치로 이전할 계획이라는 말이 나오고 있기 때문에 이전해서 어떤 결과가 있을 것인지에 대한 이야기가 나오는 것이 자연스럽다. 따라서 정답은 (A)이다.

135 -138 정보

커닝햄 도서관은 지역사회에 인상적인 도서 및 정기 간행물 모음을 제공합니다. **135원래의** 상태로 복원시키기 위해 대대적으로 보수한 이 역사적 건물은 아름다운 목공예술, 고전적인 디자인, 아늑한 분위기로 인정받고 있습니다. 이용객들은 연구자료실에서 희귀하고 절판된 도서들을 **136훑어볼** 수 있으며 동시대 도서들을 한 번에 2주까지 대여할 수 있습니다. 도서관 방문자들을 위한 행사도 많이 있습니다. **137화요일 저녁마다 주간 강좌가 열립니다. 주제는 경제학부터 문학까지 모두 아우릅니다.**

작가들만을 위한 특별 **138자료**도 있습니다. 여기에는 학술지, 교과서, 문법 검사용 소프트웨어 등이 포함됩니다. 도서관은 평일 오전 10시부터 오후 8시 30분까지 문을 엽니다.

어휘 impressive 인상적인 collection 모음 periodical 정기 간행물 renovate 개조하다, 보수하다 restore 복원하다 condition 상태 appreciate 인정하다 cozy 아늑한 atmosphere 분위기 patron (도서관 등) 이용객 out-of-print 절판된 borrow 빌리다, 대여하다 contemporary 동시대의 plenty of ~ 많은 lecture 강좌 academic journal 학술지

135 형용사 자리

해설 빈칸에는 뒤에 있는 명사 condition을 수식해 줄 형용사나 복합 명사로 함께 쓰일 명사가 올 수 있다. '원상태'는 original condition이라고 하므로 정답은 (D) original(원래의)이다.

136 동사 어휘

해설 도서관 이용객들(patrons)이 희귀하고 절판된 책을 '볼 수 있다'는 말이 들어가는 것이 가장 자연스럽다. (A) browse(훑어보다)가 정답으로 가장 적절하다. (B) publish는 '출판하다', (C) conserve는 '보존하다', (D) edit는 '편집하다'라는 의미이다.

137 문맥에 맞는 문장 고르기

번역 (A) 시간제 도서관 사서 보조 자리가 몇 개 비어 있습니다.
(B) 주제는 경제학부터 문학까지 모두 아우릅니다.
(C) 이를 위해 여러분의 조리법을 미리 준비해 두세요.
(D) 우리와 같은 규모의 지역사회 대부분은 도서관이 더 작습니다.

바로 앞 문장에서 주간 강좌가 열린다는 말이 나오므로 이 강좌(lecture)에 대한 추가 설명을 하는 문장이 들어가는 것이 자연스럽다. (B)가 그 강연의 '주제'에 대해서 언급하고 있기 때문에 적절하므로 정답이다.

138 명사 어휘

해설 학술지, 교과서, 문법 검사용 소프트웨어 등이 포함될 수 있는, 작가를 위한 '무엇'이 이 빈칸에 들어갈 말이다. 보기 중에서는 (B) resources(자료)가 가장 적절하다. (A) awards는 '상', (D) organizations는 '조직, 단체'라는 의미이다.

139 -142 이메일

수신: 제프리 커티스 〈jeffrey@jcurtisdesign.com〉
발신: 에드워드 윌콕스 〈e.wilcox@conceptmedia.com〉
날짜: 11월 20일
제목: 컨셉트 미디어 제출물

커티스 씨께,

컨셉트 미디어 웹사이트를 다시 여는 데 귀가 제출하신 배경화면이 들어갔음을 알리게 되어 기쁘게 생각합니다. 첨부된 동의서에 서명하셔서 **139즉시** 보내 주십시오. 아시는 바와 같이 제출품에 대해 돈을 지급하지 않습니다. **140그러나** 귀하의 웹사이트로 연결되는 링크를 제공하고 있어, 귀하의 사업을 위한 훌륭한 노출 기회가 될 수 있을 것입니다. 저희의 꾸준한 성장이 지속되면 올해 말쯤이면 일일 순방문자가 800명에 **141이를 것입니다. 142웹사이트 재오픈 디자인을 마무리하게 되면 알려드리겠습니다. 귀하가 저희 메일 수신자 명단에 있으시면 재오픈 알림을 받으실 겁니다.**

에드워드 윌콕스

어휘 relaunch 다시 선보임 background image 배경화면 submit 제출하다 consent form 동의서 submission 제출(물) exposure 노출 steady 꾸준한 unique visitor 순방문자 finalize 마무리짓다

139 부사 어휘

해설 빈칸 앞에 '첨부된 동의서에 서명하여 보내달라'는 요청의 말을 수식할 부사를 고르는 문제이다. 문맥을 고려할 때 (B) promptly(즉시)가 가장 적절하므로 정답이다.

어휘 strictly 엄격히 consistently 일관하여, 지속적으로 largely 대부분, 주로

140 부사 어휘

해설 빈칸에는 접속사나 부사가 들어갈 수 있다. 앞 문장과 빈칸이 있는 문장이 내용상 서로 대조를 이루므로 정답은 (D) However(그러나)이다.

어휘 besides 게다가 in other words 다시 말해서 for instance 예를 들어

141 동사 시제

해설 문장 끝의 by the end of the year(올해 말까지)라는 말이 중요한 단서가 된다. 과거에서부터 일일 방문객이 늘어나고 그 결과, 미래의 그때쯤이면 800명에 이르게 될 것이라는 말이므로 미래완료 시제(will have p.p.)가 되어야 한다. 따라서 정답은 (C) will have reached이다.

142 문맥에 맞는 문장 고르기

번역 (A) 귀하가 저희 메일 수신자 명단에 있으시면 재오픈 알림을 받으실 겁니다.
(B) 귀하가 우리 팀에 합류하게 되어 모두가 기뻐하고 있습니다.
(C) 귀하의 색상 배합 추천이 특히 유용했다고 생각합니다.
(D) 귀하에게 가장 좋은 날짜와 시간을 선택해 주십시오.

해설 앞 문장에서 '재오픈(relaunch)'과 관련된 언급이 있었기 때문에 이것을 다시 한 번 받고 추가적인 설명을 해주는 (A)가 가장 적절하다. (B)처럼 회사에 입사한다든가, (C)의 색상 배합(color scheme)이나, (D)의 만날 일시 약속과 같은 내용은 앞부분에서 언급되지 않았다.

143 -146 공지

이전합니다!

록클리어 치과 센터가 새로운 장소로 이전합니다. 6월 13일 월요일부터 저희 주소는 록클리어 버드 가 1200번지가 됩니다. 영업 시간을 비롯해 모든 연락처 정보는 **143**변하지 않을 것입니다.

이 이전 결정을 하게 된 주요 이유는 버드 가의 공간이 현재 병원보다 더 넓기 때문입니다. 그곳에서 저희가 환자들께 보다 나은 서비스를 제공해 **144**드릴 수 있을 것입니다.

유감스럽지만, 이 이전으로 일부 고객분들**145**에게는 불편함이 없을 수 없습니다. **146**이사는 6월 6일에서 11일까지 진행될 예정입니다. 이 날들에는 저희가 환자를 볼 수 없습니다. 이 기간에 예약이 되어 있으시면, 저희가 전화를 드려 다른 주로 일정을 조정하겠습니다. 이 같은 혼란을 참아 주시기를 부탁드립니다.

어휘 move 이전[이사]하다 dental 치과[치아]의 contact details 연락처 정보 as well as ~뿐만 아니라 hours of operation 운영[영업] 시간 remain ~인 상태로 있다 major 주요한 space 공간 occupy 점유하다, 차지하다 serve 서비스를 제공하다 patient 환자 transition 이행, 변화 inconvenience 불편(함) appointment 예약, 약속 reschedule 일정을 조정하다 patience 인내심 disruption 혼란

143 형용사 어휘

해설 주어를 보충 설명할 형용사를 고르는 문제이다. 앞 문장에서 이전으로 주소가 변경될 것이라고 했으므로, 그것을 제외한 '모든 연락처 정보 및 영업 시간은 변하지 않을 것이다'라는 의미가 되어야 문맥상 자연스럽다. 따라서 정답은 (C) unchanged(변하지 않는)이다. (A) competitive(경쟁력 있는, 경쟁적인), (B) confidential(기밀의), (D) visible(눈에 보이는, 볼 수 있는)은 모두 문맥상 적절하지 않다.

144 동사 시제

해설 빈칸은 주어 Occupying it(버드 가의 공간을 점유하는 것)의 동사 자리이다. 앞 문장에서 이사할 그곳이 현재 병원보다 더 넓다고 했다. '그곳으로 이사를 하면'과 같은 뜻이므로 미래를 나타내는 (B) should allow가 정답이다.

어휘 allow A to+동사원형 A가 ~할 수 있게 하다

145 전치사 어휘

해설 빈칸 앞뒤의 명사들을 가장 잘 연결해 줄 전치사를 고르는 문제다. 문맥상 '일부 고객에게 불편함이 없을 수 없다'는 의미가 자연스러우므로 빈칸에는 for(~에게, ~을 위해)나 to가 알맞다. 따라서 정답은 (C) for이다.

어휘 through ~을 통해서 about ~에 대해 of ~의, ~ 중에

146 문맥에 맞는 문장 고르기

번역 (A) 저희 의사들의 근무 일정은 매주 똑같습니다.
(B) 지난해의 경우, 그 시간은 상당히 짧았습니다.
(C) 직원들은 이 시기 동안 일정한 간격으로 임금을 받게 됩니다.
(D) 이 날들에는 저희가 환자를 볼 수 없습니다.

해설 빈칸 앞 문장에서 이사가 6월 6일에서 11일까지 진행될 예정이라고 했고, 빈칸 뒤 문장에서 이 기간에 예약이 되어 있으면 다른 주로 일정을 조정하겠다고 했다. 문맥상 빈칸에는 이사가 진행되는 기간 동안에는 환자 진료가 불가능하다는 내용을 언급하는 것이 자연스러우므로 정답은 (D)이다.

어휘 physician 의사 shift schedule (시간대별) 근무[교대] 일정 duration 지속 시간 considerably 상당히 at regular intervals 일정한 간격[기간]을 두고 throughout ~ 동안 내내

PART 7

147-148 쿠폰

어메이징 미술용품점
쿡 스트리트 889번지

147토요일에 저희 그림 그리기 강좌가 즐거우셨기를 바랍니다. 향후 또 다른 학습 기회를 위해 방문해 주십시오. 그 동안에, 이 쿠폰을 이용해 집에서 쓸 미술용품을 사 두세요.

수채화 물감 10% 할인
그림붓 20% 할인

한 번 구매할 때 사용하시면 두 가지 할인 모두 적용될 수 있습니다. **148**할인은 4월 1일까지 유효합니다. 구매 시 상점 안에 있는 제품에만 쿠폰을 사용하실 수 있습니다. 현금 가치는 없습니다.

어휘 art supplies 미술용품 in the meantime 그 사이에 stock up on ~를 비축하다 discount 할인 apply 적용하다 offer (짧은 기간 동안의) 할인 valid 유효한 purchase 구매 cash value 현금 가치

147 추론 / 암시

번역 어메이징 미술용품점에 대해 암시된 것은?
(A) 그림에 대한 서적을 판매한다.
(B) 고객의 미술 작품을 전시한다.
(C) 최근 이전했다.
(D) 주말에 강좌를 연다.

해설 첫 문장 중 '토요일 강좌에서(at our Saturday session)'라는 말을 통해서 정답 (D)를 확인할 수 있다.

> ▸▸ **Paraphrasing** 지문의 **our Saturday session**
> → 정답의 **a class on the weekend**

148 사실 관계 확인

번역 쿠폰에 대해 언급된 것은?
(A) 다른 할인과 함께 사용할 수 없다.
(B) 유효 기간이 있다.
(C) 한 가지 물품에만 적용된다.
(D) 특정 상표에만 제한된다.

해설 마지막 단락 중 '할인은 4월 1일까지 유효하다(Offer valid until April 1.)'는 문장에서 유효기간이 있는 것을 알 수 있다. 따라서 정답은 (B)이다.

149-150 웹페이지

```
http://www.canhetgroup.com/mm

                    캔헷 그룹

미디어 감시 서비스

기업들은 미디어와 기타 영향력 있는 인물들이 자사에 대해 뭐라고 말하고 쓰는
지에 대해 알고 있어야 합니다. 캔헷 그룹의 미디어 감시 전문가들은 최신 디지
털 도구를 이용해 영어를 사용하는 모든 주요 채널을 대상으로 캔헷의 고객사들
에 대한 언급을 탐지합니다. ¹⁴⁹그런 다음 해당 기사와 동영상 클립, 소셜 미디어
게시글, 기타 내용을 검토하고, 고객사들에 유용한 정보인지 확인합니다. 이 같은
2단계 접근 방식은 고객이 중요한 정보를 놓치지 않고, 또한 불필요한 자료에
압도되지 않도록 보장해 줄 것입니다.

¹⁵⁰나아가, 다른 미디어 감시 서비스와 달리 캔헷 그룹은 수집한 모든 자료를 저
희 서버에 보관합니다. 고객께서는 자사의 정보를 체계적으로 정리하고, 검색하
며, 언제든 다운로드할 수 있는 편리함을 누리실 수 있습니다.
```

어휘 media 언론, 매체 monitoring 감시, 관찰 influencer 영향력 있는 사람[것] specialist 전문가 latest 최근의, 최신의 detect 알아내다, 감지하다 review 검토하다 post 게시글 content (책 등의) 내용 ensure 보장하다, 확실하게 하다 guarantee 보장하다 miss 놓치다 overwhelmed 압도된 collect 수집하다 organized 체계화된, 정리된

149 사실 관계 확인

번역 캔헷 그룹 직원들에 관해 명시된 것은?
(A) 새로운 디지털 검색 도구를 개발했다.
(B) 미디어 분야에 연줄이 있다.
(C) 수집된 정보의 가치를 판단한다.
(D) 각각 서로 다른 산업을 전문적으로 감시한다.

해설 첫 번째 단락에서 '캔헷 그룹의 미디어 감시 전문가들은 해당 기사와 동영상 클립, 소셜 미디어 게시글 등을 검토하고, 고객사들에 유용한 정보인지 확인한다'고 했으므로, 수집된 정보의 가치를 판단한다는 것을 알 수 있다. 따라서 정답은 (C)이다.

> ▸▸ **Paraphrasing** 지문의 **review these articles, ~ find them useful**
> → 정답의 **judge the value of collected information**

150 사실 관계 확인

번역 캔헷 그룹 미디어 감시 서비스의 특징으로 언급된 것은?
(A) 파일의 전자식 저장
(B) 빠른 자료 전송
(C) 외국어 번역
(D) 오프라인 뉴스 보도

해설 두 번째 단락에서 다른 미디어 감시 서비스와 달리 캔헷 그룹은 수집한 모든 자료를 자체 서버에 보관하고 있다고 했으므로, 정답은 (A)이다.

> ▸▸ **Paraphrasing** 지문의 **keeps all of the materials it collects on our own servers**
> → 정답의 **Electronic storage of files**

151-152 문자 메시지

테사 커크랜드	오후 2:23

제가 록몬드 센터에서 있을 강좌에 당신과 같이 차를 타고 갈 시간에 맞춰 사무실에 돌아갈 수 있을 것 같지 않아요. 어쨌든 가려고 생각 중이에요.

제이슨 용	오후 2:25

지금 어디예요?

테사 커크랜드	오후 2:26

하트포드 빌딩에 있어요. ¹⁵¹에이브릴 커뮤니케이션즈와의 계약을 협상 중이에요. 지금 잠깐 쉬는 시간인데 한 시간은 더 걸릴 것 같아요. 지금쯤이면 끝날 줄 알았거든요.

제이슨 용	오후 2:27

제가 차를 갖고 하트포드 빌딩으로 당신을 데리러 가도 괜찮은데요.

테사 커크랜드	오후 2:27

고맙지만 가는 길이 아니잖아요. ¹⁵²대신 제가 대중교통을 타고 가서 거기서 뵐게요.

제이슨 용	오후 2:28

그래요. 그 편이 더 쉽겠어요. 제가 먼저 도착하면 자리를 잡아둘게요.

테사 커크랜드	오후 2:29

고마워요. 도착하면 문자 메시지 보낼게요.

어휘 in time to+동사원형 ~할 시간에 맞춰 negotiate 협상하다 contract 계약 take a short break 잠깐 휴식을 취하다 public transportation 대중교통 instead 대신 save a seat 자리를 마련해 두다

151 사실 관계 확인

번역 커크랜드 씨는 어떤 문제를 언급하는가?
(A) 논의가 예상보다 길어지고 있다.
(B) 차가 고장 났다.
(C) 건물이 찾기 어려웠다.
(D) 협상에 도움이 필요하다.

해설 2시 26분 대사에서 원래는 지금쯤이면 계약 협상이 끝날 줄 알았는데 한 시간 더 해야 할 것 같다고 말하고 있다. 협상이 예상보다 길어질 것이라는 뜻이므로 정답은 (A)이다.

> ▸▸ **Paraphrasing** 지문의 **negotiating the contract**
> → 정답의 **A discussion**

152 의도 파악

번역 오후 2시 28분에 용 씨가 "그 편이 더 쉽겠어요"라고 쓴 의도는 무엇이겠는가?
(A) 용 씨가 대중교통을 타고 하트포드 빌딩에 갈 것이다.
(B) 록몬드 센터에서 만나는 데 동의한다.
(C) 커크랜드 씨를 대신해 강좌에 참석하고 싶다.
(D) 커크랜드 씨를 한 시간 안에 차에 태울 것이다.

해설 원래 용 씨와 커크랜드 씨는 록몬드 센터에서 있을 강좌에 같이 차를 타고 가려고 했지만, 여의치 않아서 커크랜드 씨가 대중교통을 이용해서 도착지에 가겠다고 한 말에 동의한 문장이다. 따라서 정답은 (B)이다.

153 -154 공지

공지

153달튼빌 우체국은 휠체어 이용자분들이 건물에 좀 더 쉽게 출입할 수 있도록 하기 위해 외부 경사로를 추가할 예정입니다. 공사는 6월 4일에 시작해 6월 5일에 종료됩니다. 현재 **154**홀리 스트리트 출입구로 이어지는 계단의 일부를 철거하고 경사로 및 철제 난간으로 대체합니다. 공사 기간 중 가드니아 몰을 마주보는 베네트 애비뉴 출입구는 계속 일반에게 개방됩니다. 계획된 건물 변경에 관한 전체 목록은 저희 웹사이트를 방문하시거나 엘리베이터 근처에 있는 게시판을 확인하십시오.

어휘 in an effort to + 동사원형 ~하기 위한 노력으로 accessible 접근 가능한 exterior 외부의 ramp 경사로 a portion of ~의 일부 current 현재의 entrance 입구 remove 제거하다 replace 대체하다 railing 난간 remain 여전히 ~이다 open to the public 일반에 개방된 complete 완전한 bulletin board 게시판

153 추론 / 암시

번역 공지는 누구를 위한 것이겠는가?
(A) 아파트 단지 세입자
(B) 쇼핑몰 방문객
(C) **우체국 고객**
(D) 호텔 고객

해설 우체국에서 외부 경사로 공사가 있는 것을 공지하는 글이기 때문에 이 글을 읽는 대상은 우체국을 이용하는 고객이라고 할 수 있다. 따라서 정답은 (C)이다.

154 세부 사항

번역 공사는 어디서 이뤄질 것인가?
(A) **홀리 스트리트 출입구**
(B) 베네트 애비뉴 출입구
(C) 엘리베이터 주변
(D) 건물 내부 계단

해설 지문 중간에 보면 홀리 스트리트 출입구(Holly Street entrance)로 이어지는 현재 사용 중인 계단 일부를 철거하고 그 부분에 공사를 한다는 내용이 나오기 때문에 (A)가 정답이다.

155 -157 광고

빅 엠 투어와 함께 미시시피강 유람선 여행을 즐기세요!

미시시피강 여행으로 다음번 특별한 날을 기억에 남도록 만들어 보세요. 빅 엠 투어는 지난 15년간 사적인 파티에 보트를 대여해 왔습니다. 우리는 뛰어난 안전 기록을 보유하고 있으며 선장 전원은 10~20년의 경험을 갖고 있습니다. **155**고객께서는 각각 독특한 외관과 특색을 갖춘 세 척의 호화 유람선 중 하나를 선택하면 됩니다. 저희 유람선은 매일 이용 가능하며 최대 80명의 단체를 수용할 수 있습니다. **156**적절한 기본 요금에는 노련한 선원, 가벼운 간식, 선착장 근처 주차장 이용비 등이 포함돼 있습니다. 아울러 추가 요금을 지불하면 다음과 같은 서비스를 제공합니다.

- 식사 제공
- 라이브 음악 연주
- 무선 인터넷 서비스

157예약하시려면 555-0113으로 전화하세요. 몇 명이 보트 여행에 참가할지 알려 줄 준비를 해 주세요. 주말은 예약이 빨리 차니 서둘러 예약하실 것을 권장합니다.

어휘 cruise 유람 항해하다 special occasion 특별한 날[경우] memorable 기억할 만한 safety record 안전 기록 distinct 뚜렷한, 분명한 feature 특징 accommodate 수용하다 reasonable 적당한, 비싸지 않은 basic rate 기본요금 experienced 경험이 풍부한, 노련한 docking site 선착장 additional fee 추가 요금 fill up 가득 차다

155 사실 관계 확인

번역 빅 엠 투어에 대해 언급된 것은?
(A) 주말에만 운영한다.
(B) **모든 보트가 서로 다르다.**
(C) 일부 선원은 역사 전문가이다.
(D) 육지 여행도 운영한다.

해설 첫 번째 지문 중간쯤의 '각각 독특한 외관과 특색을 갖춘(with a distinct appearance and features) 세 척의 호화 유람선'이라는 언급을 통해 정답 (B)를 고를 수 있다.

156 세부 사항

번역 기본 요금에 포함된 것은?
- (A) 음악가의 공연
- (B) 무선 인터넷 접속
- (C) 주차장 간 셔틀 버스 운행
- (D) 약간의 다과

해설 첫 번째 지문 후반부에 보면 '기본 요금(basic rate)'에는 노련한 선원, 가벼운 간식, 선착장 근처 주차장 이용비 등이 포함된다'고 했다. '가벼운 간식'을 다르게 표현한 (D)가 정답이다.

▸▸ **Paraphrasing** 지문의 light snacks
→ 정답의 **A small amount of refreshments**

157 세부 사항

번역 광고에 따르면, 사람들은 전화를 걸어 어떤 정보를 제공해야 하는가?
- (A) 탑승 인원
- (B) 선호하는 지불 방식
- (C) 추천인 이름
- (D) 원하는 출발 지점

해설 마지막 단락에서 예약할 수 있는 전화번호를 알려주고, 보트 여행 참가 인원수를 알려 줄 준비를 해달라고 한다. 따라서 정답은 (A)이다.

▸▸ **Paraphrasing** 지문의 how many people will be taking the boat trip
→ 정답의 **The number of passengers**

158 -160 양식

말론 은행 신용카드 서비스 조사

본 설문지를 작성해 주셔서 감사합니다. 귀하의 피드백은 저희에게 소중합니다. 시간을 내 주신 데 감사의 뜻을 표하기 위해, **158**비바뮤직에서 나온 최신 소음 차단 헤드폰을 받을 기회를 드리겠습니다. 당첨되실 경우 연락을 받을 수 있도록 이메일 주소를 꼭 기입해 주십시오.

이름: 앤서니 조던   이메일 주소: _ajordan@quickmail.net_

신용카드를 얼마나 자주 사용하십니까?
[X] 매일 [ ] 1주에 한 번 [ ] 1개월에 한 번 [ ] 1개월에 1회 미만

신용카드로 주로 무엇을 구입하십니까? (해당하는 것 모두 표시)
[ ] 온라인 상품 [X] 식료품 [X] 주유 [X] 기타 의류

다음의 신용카드 특징 중 가장 중요한 것(1)에서 가장 덜 중요한 것(5)까지 순위를 매기십시오.

  _2_   연회비
  _5_   연결된 휴대전화 앱
  _3_   신용카드 한도
159 _1_ 이율
  _4_   포인트/리워드 획득 기회

저희가 알아야 할 다른 유용한 정보가 더 있습니까?
제가 신용카드를 선택할 때는 제 자료의 안전 또한 저에게 중요합니다. 이 문제에 대한 우려가 있어서 귀사의 휴대전화 앱을 사용하지 않고 있습니다. **160**이것과 기타 보안 위험을 막을 수 있는 더욱 강력한 보안 장치를 제공해 주었으면 합니다.

어휘 survey 설문 조사 valuable 귀중한 appreciation 감사 state-of-the-art 최신의 noise-cancelling 소음 차단의 groceries 식료품 rate 평가하다, 순위를 매기다 annual fee 연회비 interest rate 이율 reward 리워드, 보상금 safeguard 보호[안전]장치

158 세부 사항

번역 말론 은행은 설문 조사 참여자들에게 무엇을 제공하는가?
- (A) 상품 추첨에 응모
- (B) 무료 상품권
- (C) 음악 상점의 이용 금액
- (D) 전자제품 할인

해설 첫 단락 두 번째 문장에서 최신 소음 차단 헤드폰 추첨에 응모할 수 있는 기회(you will be entered to win ~ from Viva Music)를 준다는 내용을 토대로 정답 (A)를 고를 수 있다.

159 사실 관계 확인

번역 조던 씨에 대해 명시된 것은?
- (A) 더 좋은 보상 프로그램에 신청하기를 원한다
- (B) 자신이 지불하는 이자의 액수에 가장 관심이 있다.
- (C) 보통 식료품을 온라인으로 산다.
- (D) 신용카드를 그다지 자주 사용하지 않는다.

해설 세 번째 항목을 보면 신용카드의 특징들을 중요성에 따라 순위를 매기도록 돼 있는데 여기에서 조던 씨가 이자(Interest rate)에 가장 관심 있어 한다는 것을 확인할 수 있다. 따라서 정답은 (B)이다.

▸▸ **Paraphrasing** 지문의 **Interest rate**
→ 정답의 **how much interest he pays**

160 세부 사항

번역 조던 씨는 말론 은행이 무엇을 제공해 주기를 원하는가?
- (A) 교육이 잘 된 고객 서비스 팀이 제공하는 전화 상담 서비스
- (B) 신용 한도를 자주 변경할 수 있는 옵션
- (C) 신용카드의 보안 향상
- (D) 휴대전화로 계좌를 확인할 수 있는 기능

해설 마지막 질문의 답변으로 조던 씨는 신용카드와 관련해 더욱 강력한 보안 장치를 제공해 주면 좋겠다고 썼다. 따라서 (C)가 정답이다.

▸▸ **Paraphrasing** 지문의 **stronger safeguards**
→ 정답의 **Improved security protections**

Test 10

161 -163 회람

회람

발신: 니아 개스킨
수신: 모든 실험실 직원
제목: 피펫팅 로봇
날짜: 2월 22일

많이 아시겠지만, 연구소 안에서 피펫 사용과 관련된 대부분의 문제는 사람의 실수로 인한 것입니다. 게다가, 오랜 시간 동안 손으로 피펫팅하면 직원들이 긴장 장애로 인해 의학 치료를 받아야 할 수도 있습니다. **163**이 같은 문제를 해결하기 위해, 저는 '사르피네' 몇 개를 주문했는데요, 핼컴 바이오사이언스에서 만든 새로운 피펫팅 로봇입니다. 이것들은 자동으로 용기 채우기, 연속 희석 같은 과제를 수행하도록 프로그래밍 할 수 있습니다. **162**이것들을 사용하면 우리가 새로운 가정용 청소 세제를 더욱 빠르고 편안하게 고안하고 개선하는 데 도움을 줄 것이라고 확신합니다.

161하지만, 사르피네는 복잡한 소프트웨어가 딸려 나오기 때문에 여러분 모두 사용 방법을 배우기 위해 온라인 교육을 받으셔야 합니다. 그렇게 하려면, 연구소 웹사이트에 접속하여 오른쪽 상단에 있는 '사르피네 교육' 버튼을 클릭하십시오. 교육은 약 한 시간 걸립니다. 3월 5일 금요일까지 마쳐 주시기 바랍니다.

어휘 majority 대다수 pipette 피펫(실험실에서 소량의 액체를 옮길 때 쓰는 도구) research laboratory 연구소 error 실수 manual 손으로 하는 seek 찾다, 구하다 treatment 치료 strain (반복 사용으로 인한 근육의) 긴장 injury 부상, 상처 resolve (문제를) 해결하다 devise 고안하다 refine 개선하다, 개량하다 household 가정의 cleaner 청소기; 청소용 세제 log on to ~에 접속하다 complete 완료하다

161 글의 주제 / 목적

번역 회람의 목적은 무엇인가?
(A) 수신자에게 요구사항을 알리려고
(B) 수신자에게 불편을 끼친 것을 사과하려고
(C) 거절 사유를 설명하려고
(D) 문제의 해결책을 찾으려고

해설 두 번째 단락 첫 문장에서 사르피네는 복잡한 소프트웨어가 딸려 나오기 때문에 직원들 모두 사용 방법을 배우기 위해 온라인으로 교육을 받아야 한다고 했으므로, 수신자인 직원들에게 요구사항을 알리기 위한 회람임을 알 수 있다. 따라서 정답은 (A)이다.

▸▸ **Paraphrasing** need to take a training session online
→ 정답의 a requirement

162 추론 / 암시

번역 개스킨 씨의 연구소는 무엇을 하는 곳이겠는가?
(A) 대학생들의 연구 촉진
(B) 진료소를 위한 테스트 수행
(C) 상품 개발
(D) 실외 환경 관찰

해설 첫 번째 단락의 후반부에서 로봇을 사용하면 새로운 가정용 청소 세제를 더욱 빠르고 편안하게 고안하고 개선하는 데 도움을 줄 것을 확신한다고 했으므로, 가정용 청소 세제와 같은 상품을 개발하는 연구소임을 유추할 수 있다. 따라서 정답은 (C)이다.

▸▸ **Paraphrasing** 지문의 devise and refine new household cleaners
→ 정답의 Develop commercial products

163 문장 삽입

번역 [1], [2], [3], [4]로 표시된 곳 중에서 다음 문장이 들어가기에 가장 적합한 곳은?

"이 것은 자동으로 용기 채우기, 연속 희석 같은 과제를 수행하도록 프로그래밍 할 수 있습니다."

(A) [1]
(B) [2]
(C) [3]
(D) [4]

해설 삽입 문장에서 이것들이 자동으로 과제를 수행하도록 프로그래밍 할 수 있다고 했으므로, 앞에서 먼저 프로그래밍 될 수 있는 이것들(They)에 해당하는 것을 밝혀야 한다. [2]번 앞에서 '사르피네'라는 핼컴 바이오사이언스에서 만든 새로운 피펫팅 로봇(pipetting robots)을 주문했다고 했으므로, 정답은 (B)이다.

164 -167 편지

로렌 탤버트
브라이어힐 레인 2147
킨스턴, 노스캐롤라이나주 28501

탤버트 씨께,

저는 원예와 식물 관리에 힘쓰는 우스터 가드닝 협회(WGA) 회장입니다. 저희는 1년에 4회 정도 지역사회를 위한 사업을 하는데요, 귀하가 시의 공원 및 휴양지 관리국의 책임자이기 때문에 **164**혹시 저희 단체가 밸리 파크에서 도울 일이 있을지 문의하고자 편지를 씁니다. **165**이 지역에 폭풍이 지나간 후 몇 주간 공원이 폐쇄된 사실을 알고 있습니다. 공원이 다시 문을 열었을 때 방문했는데, 쓰러진 나무와 기타 다른 문제들뿐 아니라 화단 여러 곳이 망가진 것을 볼 수 있었습니다. 이 꽃들을 옮겨 심어서 공원이 예전 상태로 회복되는 데 도움이 될 기회를 주시면 기쁘겠습니다.

166저희 프로젝트의 정기 기부자인 우스터 그린하우스의 데릭 나바 씨가 공원 북쪽 끝에 있는 화단 세 곳을 채우기에 충분한 꽃, 식물, 작은 관목을 기부하겠다고 구두로 동의했습니다. 물론 인건비는 일체 청구하지 않을 것입니다. **167**따라서 시에 비용을 전혀 부담시키지 않고 프로젝트를 마칠 수 있습니다.

이 일을 추진하는 데 관심이 있으시면 555-0185로 전화해 알려 주십시오. 답변 기다리겠습니다.

매튜 할로웨이

어휘 dedicated to ~에 전념하는, 헌신하는 gardening 원예 recreation 휴양 flower bed 화단 be torn up 망가지다, 갈기갈기 찢어지다 in addition to ~에 더해, ~뿐만 아니라 replant 옮겨 심다 restore to former condition 이전 상태로 회복시키다 donor 기부자 shrub 관목 charge 요금을 청구하다 at no cost 무상으로 go forward with ~을 진행시키다

186

164 글의 주제 / 목적

번역 편지를 쓴 목적은 무엇인가?
(A) 프로젝트에 대한 기부금을 요청하기 위해
(B) 탤버트 씨가 동호회에 가입하도록 장려하기 위해
(C) 자원봉사 활동을 제의하기 위해
(D) 모금 행사를 위한 아이디어를 제공하기 위해

해설 첫 번째 단락의 두 번째 문장이 이 글을 쓰게 된 이유를 설명해 주고 있다. WGA가 밸리 파크에서 도울 일이 있는지를 (I am writing to you to ask if our group can assist ~) 물어보고 있다. 그리고 두 번째 단락에서도 살펴볼 수 있듯이, 인건비는 청구하지 않을 것이다(we wouldn't charge anything for the labor)는 내용을 토대로 자원봉사의 개념인 것을 확인할 수 있다. 따라서 정답은 (C)이다.

165 추론 / 암시

번역 밸리 파크에 대해 암시된 것은?
(A) 이 지역에서 가장 큰 공원이다.
(B) 현재 안전상 이유로 폐쇄됐다.
(C) 날씨로 인해 피해를 입었다.
(D) WGA의 행사 장소이다.

해설 첫 번째 단락 세 번째 문장에 폭풍이 지나간 후 공원이 몇 주 동안 폐쇄되었으며, 쓰러진 나무와 망가진 화단 등을 봤다는 내용을 바탕으로 정답이 (C)라는 것을 추론할 수 있다.

> ▸▸ Paraphrasing 지문의 **the storm**
> → 정답의 **weather conditions**

166 추론 / 암시

번역 할로웨이 씨에 대해 암시된 것은?
(A) 밸리 파크 근처에 산다.
(B) 최근 시청을 방문했다.
(C) 우스터 그린하우스에서 일한다.
(D) 나바 씨와 대화를 나누었다.

해설 두 번째 단락의 첫 번째 문장을 보면, 데릭 나바 씨가 꽃과 식물 등을 기부하겠다고 구두로 약속했다(has verbally agreed)는 말이 나온다. 따라서 정답은 (D)이다.

167 사실 관계 확인

번역 할로웨이 씨는 계획에 대해 무엇을 강조하는가?
(A) 실현 가능 속도
(B) 시 규례 준수
(C) 시에 비용이 안 든다는 점
(D) 변경의 용이성

해설 두 번째 단락의 후반부를 보면 인건비를 일제 청구하지 않을 것이고, 시에 비용을 전혀 부담시키지 않는다고 하므로, 정답은 (C)이다.

168-171 온라인 채팅

인디라 상카르 [오전 11:13]	방금 섬터의 매릴린 카셀 씨에게서 메시지를 받았어요. 신문 오늘 판에 우리가 잘못된 광고를 인쇄했다고 하더군요. **168그 말이 사실인지 확인하려 하는데 둘 중 한 사람이 저 좀 도와줄래요?**
드웨이 챔 [오전 11:15]	**171패트릭 오데트가 섬터 사를 관리해서** 저는 잘 모르겠어요. 그는 오늘 아침 사무실에 없는데, 오후가 되면 돌아올 거예요.
우베르토 피치오 [오전 11:16]	제가 그쪽 광고의 그래픽 일부를 도왔는데요. 제 기록을 살펴볼게요.
인디라 상카르 [오전 11:17]	고마워요, 우베르토.
우베르토 피치오 [오전 11:19]	됐어요. **170우리 쪽 문제가 아니었어요.** 카셀 씨가 요청한 이미지가 들어 있는 최근 이메일을 갖고 있습니다. **169우리는 그걸 인쇄한 거고요.** 그녀의 매장에서 판매하는 새로운 전동 공구 광고죠. 그 이메일을 전달해 드릴게요.
인디라 상카르 [오전 11:20]	예, 한번 보고 싶어요.
인디라 상카르 [오전 11:26]	당신 말이 맞아요. 그걸 보니 다행이군요.
드웨이 챔 [오전 11:28]	원하시면 제가 카셀 씨에게 전화할게요. 카셀 씨와 과거에 같이 일한 적이 있거든요.
인디라 상카르 [오전 11:29]	고맙지만 **171해당 고객 담당자가 처리하도록 하는 게 더 낫겠어요.** 그 사람한테 그렇게 해야 한다고 말할게요.

어휘 figure out ~을 알아내다, 이해하다 account 고객, 거래처, 광고주 end 부분, 몫, 편 power tool 전동공구

168 세부 사항

번역 상카르 씨가 도움을 요청하는 것은?
(A) 광고를 수정하기
(B) 항의 받은 것을 조사하기
(C) 메시지를 전달하기
(D) 제안서 준비하기

해설 11시 13분 대사 내용을 살펴보면 신문에 잘못된 광고를 내보내 고객이 항의해서, 진위를 파악하려고 도움을 요청하는 것을 알 수 있다. 정답은 (B)이다.

어휘 complaint 불평, 항의 relay 전달하다, 중계하다

169 추론 / 암시

번역 카셀 씨는 어디에서 일할 것 같은가?
(A) 그래픽 디자인 회사
(B) 홍보 대행사
(C) 신문사
(D) 철물점

해설 11시 19분 대사를 살펴보면 카셀 씨의 매장에서 전동 공구(power tools)를 판매한다는 것을 확인할 수 있다. 따라서 정답은 (D)이다.

170 의도 파악

번역 오전 11시 26분에 상카르 씨가 "그걸 보니 다행이군요"라고 쓴 의도는 무엇이겠는가?
(A) 제안된 인쇄 레이아웃을 승인한다.
(B) 챔 씨가 만든 이미지가 마음에 든다.
(C) 자신의 회사가 잘못하지 않아서 기쁘다.
(D) 프로젝트가 제때 완료되어 안심이다.

해설 11시 19분 대사에서, 요청한 이미지를 그대로 인쇄했을 뿐 우리 잘못이 아님(the problem wasn't on our end)을 확인해 주기 위해, 받은 메시지를 전달해주겠다는 말에 대한 답변으로 한 말이다. 즉, 상카르 씨가 그 메시지가 담긴 이메일을 확인하고 자신의 회사 잘못이 아니라는 걸 알았기 때문에 한 말이므로, 정답은 (C)이다.

> ▶▶ Paraphrasing　지문의 **the problem wasn't on our end**
> → 정답의 **her company is not at fault**

171 추론 / 암시

번역 카셀 씨에게 누가 연락할 것 같은가?
(A) 오데트 씨
(B) 챔 씨
(C) 피치오 씨
(D) 상카르 씨

해설 11시 29분 대사에서 '고객 담당자(account manager)'가 처리하는 게 낫다고 언급했는데 11시 15분 대사에서 패트릭 오데트 씨가 섬터 사의 담당자(the one managing the Sumter account)임을 알 수 있다. 따라서 정답은 (A)이다.

172 -175 기사

> 필라델피아 (12월 29일) —¹⁷²근래 들어 가장 인기 있는 한 액세서리 계열의 배후에 있는 인물임에도 불구하고, 왕지애 씨는 자신을 패션 전문가라고 여기지 않는다. "이건 제가 훈련 받은 분야가 아니어서, 지금도 배울 게 아주 많죠." 그녀는 공동 창업한 회사 포셀렛의 필라델피아 사무소에 앉아 웃으며 말한다.
>
> 왕 씨는 4년 전까지만 해도 기업 변호사였다. 당시 병원을 방문하고는 한쪽 어깨에 있던 통증이 들고 다니는 무거운 서류 가방 때문에 생겼을 가능성이 높다는 것을 알게 되었다. 의사는 대신 배낭을 매 볼 것을 그녀에게 권유했다. 하지만 왕 씨는 자신의 보수적인 직업에 적합한 배낭을 찾아 보고는 선택의 여지가 별로 없다는 것을 알게 되었다.
>
> 바로 이 시점에 그녀의 예전 학교 친구이자 현재의 사업 파트너인 아이라 더글라스 씨가 등장한다. ^{173,175}왕 씨가 사무직 여성들을 위한 배낭 제품들을 공동 작업하자는 제안을 가지고 더글라스 씨에게 연락했을 때 그는 카타네오 그룹에서 디자이너로 일하고 있었다. 그는 이 아이디어를 즉시 마음에 들어했다. 이들은 디자인과 기획에 착수했고, 포셀렛은 얼마 안 있어 첫 번째 배낭을 온라인으로 판매하기 시작했다.
>
> ^{174(A),(B),(C)}질 좋은 가죽으로 만들어지고, 우아한 디자인과 편안한 끈을 자랑하는 이 제품들은 즉각적인 성공을 거두었다. 포셀렛은 현재 여섯 가지 스타일로 배낭을 내놓는데, 왕 씨는 더 여러 가지를 만들지는 않을 것이라고 말한다. 그 대신 이 회사는 벨트 같은 다른 종류의 유용한 액세서리를 생산할 것 같다.

어휘 mind (지적이거나 상상력이 뛰어난) 인물, 지성　line (계열이 비슷한 상품의) 종류　accessory 액세서리　expert 전문가　co-found 공동 설립하다　corporate 기업의　attorney 변호사　likely ~할 것 같은　briefcase 서류 가방　carry 가지고 다니다　recommend 추천하다　backpack 배낭　look around 둘러보다　suitable for ~에 적합한　conservative 보수적인　profession 전문직업　few 거의 없는　former 예전의　collaborate 공동 작업하다　white collar job 사무직　get to work 착수하다　made of ~로 만들어진　leather 가죽　boast 자랑하다　elegant 우아한　strap 끈, 줄　instant 즉각적인　hit 성공, 히트

172 사실 관계 확인

번역 왕 씨에 대해 명시된 것은?
(A) 디자인 조언을 위해 의료 전문가와 상담했다.
(B) 곧 오프라인 매장을 열 계획이다.
(C) 더글라스 씨를 4년 전에 처음 만났다.
(D) 패션 분야에 경험이 없다.

해설 첫 번째 단락에서 "이건 제가 훈련 받은 분야가 아니어서, 지금도 배울 게 아주 많죠"라는 왕 씨의 말을 인용하며 왕 씨가 자신을 패션 전문가라고 생각하지 않는다고 했으므로 정답은 (D)이다.

173 세부 사항

번역 포셀렛 배낭은 누구를 대상으로 하는가?
(A) 학생
(B) 사무직 근로자
(C) 도보 여행자
(D) 관광객

해설 세 번째 단락에서 왕 씨가 사무직 여성들을 위한 배낭 제품들을 공동 작업하자는 제안을 가지고 더글라스 씨에게 연락했다고 했으므로, 정답은 (B)이다.

> ▶▶ Paraphrasing　지문의 **women in white collar jobs**
> → 정답의 **Office workers**

174 사실 관계 확인

번역 포셀렛 배낭의 장점으로 언급되지 않은 것은?
(A) 매력적인 외관
(B) 착용자에게 주는 물리적인 편안함
(C) 사용된 고급 재료
(D) 제품의 다양한 스타일

해설 마지막 단락의 '고급스러운 가죽으로 만들어지고, 우아한 디자인과 편안한 끈을 자랑하기 때문에 이 제품들은 즉각적인 성공을 거두었다'를 통해 (A), (B), (C)를 배낭의 장점으로 확인할 수 있다. 반면 포셀렛 배낭이 현재 여섯 가지 스타일로 판매되지만, 왕 씨가 더 여러 가지 스타일을 만들지는 않을 것이라고 했으므로, 제품으로 나온 다양한 스타일은 장점으로 볼 수 없다. 따라서 정답은 (D)이다.

▸ Paraphrasing 지문의 elegant designs
→ 보기의 The attractiveness of their appearance
지문의 comfortable straps
→ 보기의 The physical comfort
지문의 Made of fine leather
→ 보기의 The high-quality material they are made of

175 문장 삽입

번역 [1], [2], [3], [4]로 표시된 곳 중에서 다음 문장이 들어가기에 가장 적합한 곳은?
"그는 이 아이디어를 즉시 마음에 들어했다."
(A) [1]
(B) [2]
(C) [3]
(D) [4]

해설 삽입 문장에 나온 그(He)와 아이디어(the idea)에 해당하는 내용이, 앞 문장에 나와야 할 것이다. [3]번 앞 문장에 왕 씨가 사무직 여성들을 위한 배낭 제품들을 공동 작업하자는 제안을 가지고 더글러스 씨에게 연락했다고 나오므로 정답은 (C)이다.

176 -180 기사+편지

플랜셀 고교 산업 예술 프로그램이 정상화되다

글: 호프 오르테가, 기자

플랜셀 (3월 2일)—플랜셀 고등학교 산업 예술 과정을 살려내기 위한 일부 플랜셀 주민들의 노력이 성공을 거두었다. **176**학교 측에 따르면 목수일과 자동차 기술 입문 수업이 두 학기 연속으로 정원이 다 찼다고 한다.

하지만 1년 전만 해도 이 프로그램은 장기간 담당했던 교사 새뮤얼 리브스가 은퇴를 발표하면서 거의 없어질 뻔했다.

179다행히도, 리브스 씨는 이 프로그램의 앞날이 위태롭다는 것을 플랜셀 고등학교 졸업생이자 브라우어스 자동차 정비소의 소유주인 빈스 브라우어에게 얘기했다. "자동차 정비 수업은 학생들이 생각해 보지 못했던 직업 진로를 보여줍니다. 저는 다년간 이 프로그램 이수자를 고용해왔습니다. 그래서 그냥 문을 닫게 놔둘 수는 없었던 거죠." 브라우어 씨는 말한다. **177**그는 이 프로그램이 처한 어려움에 대해 인식을 높이고 지지를 모으기 위해 소셜 미디어 그룹을 시작했다.

180이 그룹의 캠페인의 최고의 순간은 회원 40명이 지난해 4월 학교 이사회에 참석한 때였다. 이들은 열정적인 주장으로 이사회를 설득해 그 프로그램을 지속하고 심지어 예산을 늘리도록 했다. 학교 측에서는 리브스 씨를 대신해 레슬리 그린을 고용할 수 있었고 새로운 장비도 구입했다. 또한, 브라우어 씨와 기타 지역 업체 지도자들이 교실을 방문해 학생들에게 산업 예술을 홍보하기도 했다.

어휘 industrial arts 산업 예술 back on track 정상 궤도로 다시 돌아온 introductory 입문 과정의 carpentry 목공일 automotive technology 자동차 기술[공학] at (full) capacity 전면 가동 중인 semester 학기 in a row 연달아 nearly 거의 eliminate 없애다 uncertainty 불확실성 graduate 졸업자

수료자 potential 장래의 career path 진로 consider 고려하다 hire 고용하다 stand back 물러서다 shut down 문을 닫다, 폐쇄하다 raise awareness 의식을 일깨우다 gather 모으다 support 후원, 지지 peak 절정 school board meeting 학교 이사회 passionate 열정적인 argument 주장; 논의 convince 확신시키다 replacement 후임자 promote 홍보하다, 장려하다

편집장에게 보내는 편지
〈키워드 헤럴드〉
피셔 레인 3011번지
키워드, 노스다코타주 58003

3월 4일

편집장께,

호프 오르테가 씨의 기사 '플랜셀 고교 산업 예술 프로그램이 정상화되다'를 읽고 편집장님과 기자분께 감사 드립니다. **180**저는 지난해 그 프로그램을 살리기 위해 나섰던 40명 중 하나로, 우리의 노력이 인정 받게 되어 기쁩니다.

179또한, 브라우어 씨의 현 직원인 저는 산업 예술 프로그램이 직업적인 관점에서 중요하다는 그의 의견에 동의합니다. **178**하지만, 그 프로그램이 꼭 필요한 또 다른 이유를 말씀드리고 싶습니다. 10년 전 플랜셀 고등학교 학생이었을 때, 저는 산업 예술 수업을 통해 손재주가 좋다는 건 소중한 기술일 뿐 아니라 또 다른 형태의 지능이라는 걸 배웠습니다. 이 수업들을 통해 제가 얻은 자신감과 극기는 다른 수업에서도 더 잘 할 수 있도록 도와 주었습니다. 독자분들도 이런 유익을 생각해 주셨으면 합니다.

앨런 머레이

어휘 editor 편집장; 편집자 gratitude 감사 step forward 나서다 recognize 인정하다 vocational 직업의 perspective 관점 necessary 꼭 필요한 be good with one's hands 손재주가 좋다 intelligence 지능 valuable 소중한 self-confidence 자신감 discipline 규율, 극기 gain 얻다 perform 수행하다 keep ~ in mind ~을 명심하다 benefit 이익, 혜택

176 사실 관계 확인

번역 기사에서, 산업 예술 프로그램에 대해 명시된 것은?
(A) 세 과목으로 나눠진다.
(B) 수업이 현재 꽉 차 있다.
(C) 참가자들은 교외 현장 학습을 나간다.
(D) 이수하는 데 두 학기가 걸린다.

해설 기사의 첫 번째 단락에서 학교 측에 따르면 목공일과 자동차 기술 입문 수업이 현재 두 학기 연속으로 정원이 다 찼다고 했으므로, 수업이 현재 꽉 차 있다는 것을 확인할 수 있다. 따라서 정답은 (B)이다.

▸ **Paraphrasing** 지문의 at capacity
→ 정답의 full

Test 10

177 세부 사항

번역 기사에 의하면, 소셜 미디어 그룹이 만들어진 이유는?

(A) 한 교육 프로그램을 살리려고
(B) 한 고등학교의 졸업생들을 연결해 주려고
(C) 기술 업계의 추세를 논의하려고
(D) 한 교사의 은퇴 기념 파티를 준비하려고

해설 기사의 세 번째 단락 후반부에서 산업 예술 프로그램이 처한 어려움에 대해 인식을 높이고 지지를 모으기 위해 소셜 미디어 그룹을 시작했다고 했으므로, 정답은 (A)이다.

▶▶ **Paraphrasing** 지문의 to raise awareness of ~ support for it → 정답의 To save an educational program

178 글의 주제 / 목적

번역 편지의 목적은 무엇인가?

(A) 의견에 대해 반대 의사를 표현하려고
(B) 잘못된 정보를 바로잡으려고
(C) 다른 기사를 위한 주제를 제안하려고
(D) 주장에 대해 추가적인 지지를 표현하려고

해설 편지의 두 번째 단락에서 산업 예술 프로그램이 꼭 필요한 또 다른 이유를 제시하고자 한다고 했으므로, 추가적인 지지 이유를 밝히기 위해 쓴 편지임을 알 수 있다. 따라서 정답은 (D)이다.

▶▶ **Paraphrasing** 지문의 to offer another reason why it is necessary → 정답의 to provide additional support for an argument

179 연계

번역 머레이 씨는 누구이겠는가?

(A) 기자
(B) 자동차 정비공
(C) 교사
(D) 목수

해설 편지의 두 번째 단락에서 머레이 씨는 자신을 '브라우어 씨의 현 직원(a current employee of Mr. Brower's)'이라고 소개했고, 기사의 세 번째 단락에서 브라우어 씨가 '브라우어스 자동차 정비소 소유주(the owner of Brower's Auto Repair)'라고 했으므로, 머레이 씨가 자동차 정비공임을 유추할 수 있다. 따라서 정답은 (B)이다.

180 연계

번역 머레이 씨에 대해 암시된 것은?

(A) 학교 이사회에 갔다.
(B) 그린 씨의 제자였다.
(C) 현재의 학생들에게 연설을 했다.
(D) 학교에 일부 장비를 판매했다.

해설 편지의 첫 번째 단락에서 머레이 씨는 자신을 작년에 프로그램을 살리기 위해 나섰던 40명 중 하나라고 언급했고, 기사의 마지막 단락에서 소셜 미디어 그룹 회원 40명이 지난해 4월 학교 이사회에 참석했다고 했으므로, 머레이 씨가 학교 이사회에 참석했음을 유추할 수 있다. 따라서 정답은 (A)이다.

---

181 -185 이메일 + 보고서

수신: 케이시 어빈 〈casey@bluewavespa.co.uk〉
발신: 릴리안 블라이스 〈lillian@bluewavespa.co.uk〉
날짜: 1월 10일
제목: 읽어 주십시오.

케이시 씨께,

181귀하가 저희 스파의 연례 기획회의에서 놓친 부분을 설명해 드립니다. 우리는 더 많은 관리를 제공하는 것과 특히 어떤 관리가 가장 나은지 파악하는 방법에 관한 굴드 씨의 아이디어에 대해 주로 논의했습니다. 저는 회의를 준비하면서 전문 조사 회사를 고용하는 일에 대해 잘 살펴보았습니다. **182**제가 캘빈 호텔에서 함께 근무했던 아이리스 켈름은 스탁스 리서치를 이용해 보라고 제안했습니다. 하지만 결국 그 회사의 높은 서비스 가격을 고려할 때, 우리 스스로 조사를 수행하는 것이 더 낫다고 결정했습니다.

이를 위해 저희는 2월 2일부터 8일까지 '탐색 주간'이라는 행사를 열기로 결정했습니다. **183**우리는 특별히 단골 고객들이 그 기간에 오도록 초청하여 무료로 외부 전문가들의 특별 관리를 받게 할 것입니다. 고객들은 그 대신 관리법들에 대한 의견을 줄 것입니다. **185**그러고 나서 가장 인기 있는 관리법을 계속 이용할 수 있게 할 것입니다. **184**굴드 씨가 추가 자금을 지원하지 않는 한, 최대 40명까지 행사에 참여할 수 있습니다.

이 계획에 문의 사항이 있으시면 알려 주십시오.

릴리안

어휘 fill someone in on ~에게 지금까지 있었던 일을 설명하다 determine 알아내다, 밝히다 look into ~을 조사하다 professional 전문적인 given ~을 고려해 볼 때 to that end 그 목적을 달성하기 위하여 exploratory 탐사의, 탐구의 regular customer 단골 고객 specialist 전문가 at no charge 무료로 in exchange 그 대가로 permanently 영구히 release 풀어놓다 fund 자금

블루웨이브 스파의 탐색 주간 요약 보고서

조사 준비자: 레이먼드 비스코   수신: 마야 굴드 (소유주)

184총 63명의 고객(여성 44명, 남성 19명)이 행사에 참여했습니다. 각 참가자는 본인의 일정 및 기호에 따라 1~3개의 관리를 받았습니다. 관리법에 대한 그들의 평가는 다음과 같이 요약됩니다.

관리	고객 평균 점수 (1=매우 나쁨, 5=훌륭함)
셀 리쥬버네이션 페이셜	4.2
185크리스털 바디 마사지	4.8
옥시전 부스트	3.9
휩트 코코아 바스	3.7

어휘 participant 참가자 depending on ~에 따라 preference 선호 rating 평가, 순위

181 글의 주제 / 목적

번역 블라이스 씨가 이메일을 보낸 이유는?
(A) 질문에 대답하기 위해
(B) 의견을 요청하기 위해
(C) 최근 정보를 알려주기 위해
(D) 회의 일정을 잡기 위해

해설 이메일 첫 문장에서 회의 때 놓쳤던 정보를 알려주겠다는 내용(Let me fill you in on what you missed ~ meeting.)이 나온다. 따라서 정답은 (C)이다.

182 세부 사항

번역 블라이스 씨는 처음에 스탁스 리서치에 대해 어떻게 알게 됐는가?
(A) 우편으로 책자를 받았다.
(B) 직원들과의 논의 중 언급한 것을 들었다.
(C) 이전 동료의 추천을 받았다.
(D) 온라인 검색을 했다.

해설 이메일 첫 번째 단락의 중간쯤에 전에 함께 일했던 동료 아이리스 켈름이 스탁스 리서치를 이용해 보라고 제안해서 알게 되었다(Iris Kelm, whom I used to ~)는 말이 나온다. 따라서 정답은 (C)이다.

> ▶▶ **Paraphrasing** 지문의 **whom I used to work with**
> → 정답의 **a former coworker**

183 사실 관계 확인

번역 '탐색 주간'에 대해 사실이 아닌 것은?
(A) 무료 서비스를 포함한다.
(B) 해마다 열리는 행사이다.
(C) 단골 고객만을 위한 것이다.
(D) 임시 근로자들이 관여할 것이다.

해설 이메일 두 번째 단락의 두 번째 문장에서 (A), (C), (D)와 일치하는 내용을 확인할 수 있다. 따라서 언급되지 않은 (B)가 정답이다.

> ▶▶ **Paraphrasing** 지문의 **at no charge**
> → 보기의 **free**
>
> 지문의 **regular customers**
> → 보기의 **frequent clients**
>
> 지문의 **outside specialists**
> → 보기의 **Temporary workers**

184 연계

번역 블루웨이브 스파에 대해 암시된 것은?
(A) 스탁스 리서치와 컨설팅 계약에 서명했다.
(B) 캘빈 호텔 안에 있다.
(C) 고객들이 더욱 다양한 관리를 요청했다.
(D) 소유주가 행사를 위해 추가 기금을 할당했다.

해설 이메일 마지막 문장에서 굴드 씨가 추가 자금을 지원하지 않는다면 최대 40명이 참석할 수 있다고 했지만, 두 번째 지문 첫 문장에서 확인할 수 있듯이 실제로 참석한 인원은 63명이다. 추가 자금을 지원해서 더 많은 인원이 참석했음을 알 수 있으므로 정답은 (D)이다.

> ▶▶ **Paraphrasing** 지문의 **releases some extra funds**
> → 정답의 **allotted additional funds**

185 연계

번역 블루웨이브 스파는 어떤 관리를 계속 제공하기 시작할 것 같은가?
(A) 셀 리쥬버네이션 페이셜
(B) 크리스털 바디 마사지
(C) 옥시전 부스트
(D) 휩트 코코아 바스

해설 이메일의 두 번째 단락 중간에 보면 스파에서 가장 인기 있는 관리법을 계속 이용할 수 있게 할 것이라고 했다. 두 번째 지문 표를 보면 고객 평균 점수가 높은 (B)를 추가할 것으로 보인다.

186-190 정보 + 이메일 + 후기

8월 9일-15일 발도스타 플라자 행사

8월 9일 일요일 오전 9시 - 오후 4시 - 플라워 스펙태큘러
당신의 정원에 아름다운 꽃을 더하기에 그다지 늦지 않았습니다! 지역 자연협회는 지역 공원들을 위한 기금 조성을 위해 이 판매를 후원합니다.

187 8월 11일 화요일 오후 8시 - 오후 10시 - 시티 글로우
이 등불 행렬의 경로는 벡커 파크에서 시작해 상업 지구를 지나 플라자에서 끝납니다. 플라자에서 등불을 구매할 수 있습니다.

190 8월 14일 금요일 오전 10시 - 오후 5시 - 워크 스루 타임
190 여러분은 가구, 접시, 예술품 등이 있는 지역 최대의 골동품 시장을 놓치고 싶지 않으실 겁니다. 집의 실내장식을 보완해 줄 독특한 물건들을 구입하세요.

186 8월 15일 토요일, 오전 8시 - 오전 11시 - 대출 대시
10킬로미터 단축 경주 대회의 참가자와 관중은 가장 밝은 의상을 입습니다. 행사 티셔츠는 참가자분들에게는 무료로 드리고 관중분들에게는 8달러에 판매합니다. **186 참가를 원하시는 분은 시 웹사이트에서 8월 12일까지 등록하셔야 합니다.**

어휘 bloom 꽃 sponsor 후원하다 raise a fund 기금을 조성하다 parade 행렬 district 지구 miss 놓치다 antique 골동품 artwork 예술품 one-of-a-kind 독특한 complement 보완하다, 덧붙이다 décor 실내장식 spectator 관중 race 달리기, 경주 sign up 등록하다

수신: 수신자 비공개
발신: 모리 아카네
날짜: 8월 4일
제목: 플라자 보안

여러분 안녕하세요.

187 다음 주에 있을 플라자의 보안과 관련해 혼선이 빚어진 것 같습니다. 우리는 행사별로 보안팀장을 지명하는 새 시스템을 시도하고 있습니다. 교대시간을 변

경해야 할 경우 저에게 이메일을 보내지 마십시오. 행사 책임자에게 이메일을 보내셔야 하며 대체 교대 근무자도 직접 **188찾으셔야** 합니다. 다음 주 임무 배정 현황은 아래와 같습니다.

날짜	보안팀장	보안팀 직원 수
8월 9일	마티 해리스	3
1878월 11일	에드거 포스터	18
8월 14일	헬렌 클라크	3
8월 15일	대니얼 램스턴	10

모리 아카네
운영 관리자, 발도스타 보안 서비스

어휘 undisclosed 미공개의 recipient 수신자 confusion 혼동 appoint 임명하다, 지정하다 security 보안 shift 교대 근무 replacement 대체자 assignment 임무

---

www.rateyourvacation.net

목적지: 발도스타   *8월 20일 베서니 엥겔에 의해 게시됨*
점수: 별점 5/5   **190여행 기간: 8월 9일–14일**

저는 최근에 남편과 딸과 함께 발도스타로 여행을 가서 멋진 시간을 보냈답니다. 저는 특히 발도스타 플라자에서 조직적인 시티 글로우 행렬에 감동을 받았습니다. **189그 지역이 매우 혼잡해서 저는 손가방을 잃어버렸습니다.** 다행히도 행사 보안 요원이 도와주어 거의 즉시 가방을 찾을 수 있었습니다. **190여행 마지막 날 다른 특별 행사를 보러 플라자에 들렀는데, 집으로 가져올 멋진 기념품을 구입했습니다.** 저는 확실히 발도스타에 다시 갈 겁니다!

어휘 be impressed with ~에 감명받다 organization 조직적임 crowded 혼잡한 end up -ing 결국 ~하게 되다 fortunately 다행히 locate 찾아내다 immediately 즉시 stop by 잠시 들르다 souvenir 기념품 definitely 분명히

---

186 세부 사항

번역 대즐 대시에 대해 언급된 것은?
(A) 우승자는 트로피를 받는다.
(B) 참가비를 지불해야 한다.
(C) 수천 명의 관중이 몰린다.
(D) 사전 등록을 요한다.

해설 정보문 맨 하단에 '참가를 원하는 분은 8월 12일까지 등록해야 한다'고 나와 있다. 이 행사는 8월 15일에 열리므로 미리 등록해야 함을 알 수 있다. 따라서 정답은 (D)이다.

187 연계

번역 어떤 행사에 가장 많은 보안 요원이 할당되었는가?
(A) 플라워 스펙태큘러
(B) 시티 글로우
(C) 워크 스루 타임
(D) 대즐 대시

해설 이메일 안의 표를 보면 8월 11일 행사에 보안 요원이 가장 많이 투입됨을 알 수 있다. 정보문을 보면 8월 11일에 열리는 행사는 시티 글로우이므로 정답은 (B)이다.

---

188 동의어 찾기

번역 이메일에서 첫 번째 단락 4행의 "find"와 의미가 가장 가까운 것은?
(A) 공급하다
(B) 관찰하다
(C) 발견하다
(D) 성취하다

해설 해당 문장은 대체 인력(replacement)을 '찾다'는 의미이다. (A) supply 는 '공급하다, 제공하다'라는 의미로, 좀 더 확장해서 생각하면, 자신을 대체할 수 있는 인력을 구해서 '공급한다'는 의미로 생각해볼 수 있다. 따라서 정답은 (A) supply이다.

189 세부 사항

번역 엥겔 씨가 보안 요원의 도움이 필요했던 이유는?
(A) 몸이 아팠다.
(B) 개인 소지품을 잃어버렸다.
(C) 명소가 어디에 있는지 찾을 수 없었다.
(D) 가족 한 명과 떨어지게 됐다.

해설 세 번째 지문 중간 부분에 손가방을 잃어버렸는데 보안 요원이 도와주어 금방 찾았다고 했다. 정답은 (B)이다.

▸▸ **Paraphrasing**   지문의 accidentally getting separated from my handbag
→ 정답의 lost a personal item

190 연계

번역 엥겔 씨는 기념품으로 무엇을 구입했을 것 같은가?
(A) 화초
(B) 등불
(C) 골동품
(D) 의류

해설 세 번째 지문 마지막 부분에 여행 마지막 날에 기념품을 구매했다는 언급이 있었고 여행 마지막 날이 '14일인 것을 확인할 수 있다. 그리고 첫 번째 지문의, 14일에 최대 골동품 시장이 열린다는 내용을 종합해보면 엥겔 씨는 기념품으로 골동품을 구입했을 것이라고 추론할 수 있다. 따라서 정답은 (C)이다.

---

191 -195 회람+일정표+이메일

회람

발신: 올리버 러셀

수신: 헤스닉 테크놀로지 전 직원

제목: 소프트웨어 교육

날짜: 11월 25일

안녕하세요, 여러분.

191인사부 책임자로서 우리가 헤스닉 테크놀로지의 휴가 일정 관리 절차를 보다 쉽고 빠르게 해줄 새 소프트웨어인 스위처 싱크를 구입했음을 알려드리게 되어 기쁩니다.

우리는 1월 1일에 스위처 싱크를 전사적으로 채택하기를 희망합니다. 이를 위해서는 직원들이 교육을 받아야 합니다. 정보기술부의 랜달 그랜팀이 이끄는 2시간 교육이면 기능들을 모두 습득하는 데 충분할 것으로 보입니다.

첨부된 일정표에서 여러분 부서의 교육 시간을 확인해 주십시오. **192다른 교육에 참석해야 할 경우 여러분의 관리자가 12월 3일까지 제게 통지해야 합니다. 193또한, 교육 받은 다음 날 제가 피드백 요청을 드리게 될 것입니다.** 시간을 내어 답변해 주시기 바랍니다.

올리버 러셀
인사부 부장

첨부: 스위처 싱크 교육 일정표

어휘 training 교육, 연수 head 책임자 human resources department 인사부 acquire (사서) 취득하다 scheduling 일정 관리 adopt 채택하다 companywide 전사적으로 session 수업 시간 lead 이끌다 feature 기능: 특징 look up 찾아보다, 확인하다 notify 알리다, 통지하다 feedback (결과에 대한) 의견, 피드백

스위처 싱크 교육 일정표

교육은 오전 10시부터 오후 12시까지 제1 회의실에서 열립니다.

날짜	부서
12월 8일	정보기술부
12월 9일	인사부
195 12월 10일	**생산부**
193 12월 11일	**회계부**
12월 12일	영업 마케팅부

발신: 달라 애드킨스
수신: 올리버 러셀
제목: Re: 소프트웨어 교육
날짜: 12월 15일

안녕하세요 러셀 씨.

지난주 제가 받은 교육은 좋았습니다. 저는 실습 부분이 특히 훌륭했다고 봅니다. 스위처 싱크를 직접 사용해 보고 나니, 설명만으로는 기능들을 충분히 이해하지 못했다는 걸 깨달았습니다. 나중에 혼자서 소프트웨어 사용을 시도할 때가 아니라, 강사님이 옆에서 저를 도와줄 수 있을 때 문제점들을 파악할 수 있어서 좋았습니다.

동시에, 이 소프트웨어에 관해서는 덜 긍정적인 의견을 가지고 있습니다. **194,195프로그램 자체는 좋지만, 사실 생산부 직원들에게는 어떤 컴퓨터 기반 시스템이든 어려울 수 있습니다. 저희에게는 회사 컴퓨터에 접근하는 것도 쉽지 않습니다. 교육 후에 저희 부서 사람들과 얘기를 하면서 우리는 회사에서 앞으로는 이 요인을 고려해 주면 좋겠다는 데 동의했습니다.**

달라 애드킨스

어휘 especially 특히 appreciate 진가를 알다 practice 실습 once ~하자(마자) realize 깨닫다 function 기능 catch 알아채다, 포착하다 by oneself 혼자서 positive 긍정적인 access (컴퓨터에) 접속하다 rest 나머지 take ~ into account ~을 고려[참작]하다 factor 요인

---

191 사실 관계 확인

번역 스위처 싱크에 대해 언급된 것은?
(A) 직원 휴가를 계획하는 데 사용될 것이다.
(B) 절차를 보다 안전하게 하기 위한 것이다.
(C) 그랜텀 씨의 팀에서 개발했다.
(D) 이제 몇 가지 새로운 기능이 포함된다.

해설 회람의 첫 번째 단락에서 휴가 일정 관리 절차를 보다 쉽고 빠르게 해 줄 새로운 소프트웨어인 스위처 싱크를 구입했다고 했으므로, 정답은 (A)이다.

▸▸ **Paraphrasing**   지문의 vacation scheduling process
→ 정답의 plan employee leave

192 사실 관계 확인

번역 일정표에 관해 회람에 명시된 것은?
(A) 부서 관리자들에게는 적용되지 않는다.
(B) 두 번의 교육 중에 첫 번째 것만 보여준다.
(C) 러셀 씨는 날짜 중 하나를 아직 확정하지 못했다.
(D) 직원들은 다른 부서 교육에 참여할 수도 있다.

해설 회람의 세 번째 단락에서 부서 교육 시간의 확인을 요청한 후, 다른 교육에 참석해야 할 경우 관리자가 12월 3일까지 자신에게 통지해야 한다고 했으므로, 정답은 (D)이다.

▸▸ **Paraphrasing**   지문의 attend a different one
→ 정답의 go to another department's session

193 연계

번역 러셀 씨는 12월 12일에 무엇을 했을 것 같은가?
(A) 회계부에 요청서를 보냈다.
(B) 영업 마케팅부에 연설을 했다.
(C) 회의실에 무언가 상기시키는 공지를 붙였다.
(D) 오전 정기 모임에 빠졌다.

해설 회람의 마지막 단락에서 러셀 씨는 부서 교육을 받은 다음 날 피드백을 요청할 수 있다는 것을 언급했고, 일정표를 통해 러셀 씨가 12월 12일에 전날인 12월 11일 있었던 회계부 교육에 대한 피드백을 요청했을 것으로 유추할 수 있다. 따라서 정답은 (A)이다.

194 세부 사항

번역 애드킨스 씨는 헤스닉 테크놀로지가 무엇을 해주기를 원하는가?
(A) 다른 시스템을 향상시킬 방법을 찾아보는 것
(B) 강사에게 긍정적인 피드백을 전할 것
(C) 어떤 소프트웨어 사용을 실습할 시간을 더 줄 것
(D) 자기 부서의 상황을 참작해 줄 것

해설 이메일의 두 번째 단락에서 애드킨스 씨가 생산부 직원들에게는 컴퓨터에 접근하는 점이 힘들다고 말한 후, 회사에서 앞으로 생산부의 이러한 요인을 고려해 줄 것을 요청했으므로, 정답은 (D)이다.

▸▸ **Paraphrasing**   지문의 take that factor into account
→ 정답의 Show consideration for her department's situation

195 연계

번역 애드킨스 씨는 어느 날짜에 교육에 참가했는가?
(A) 12월 8일
(B) 12월 9일
(C) 12월 10일
(D) 12월 11일

해설 이메일의 두 번째 단락에서 애드킨스 씨가 생산부의 컴퓨터 기반 시스템 사용과 관련한 어려운 상황과 생산부 교육 후 부서의 다른 직원들과 논의했던 내용을 언급했으므로, 그녀가 생산부 소속임을 알 수 있다. 일정표를 보면 생산부 교육이 12월 10일에 진행되었을 것임을 알 수 있으므로, 정답은 (C)이다.

196-200 공지+이메일+기사

쉬머 주얼리 고객 여러분께 알려드립니다

197쉬머 주얼리는 거의 20년 가까이 파울리 스트리트 지점에서 헌츠빌 지역에 서비스를 제공한 끝에, 4월 30일에 폐업할 예정입니다. 오랫동안 여러분께 서비스를 제공할 수 있어 기쁨이었고, 수많은 결혼식, 기념일, 생일, 기타 축하 행사에 함께할 수 있어 영광이었습니다. 보석 수리 서비스는 더 이상 제공하지 않지만 저희 보석 디자이너들의 제품 스타일 일부는 여전히 구매하실 수 있습니다. 수전 말로우는 자신의 보석 웹사이트를 열 계획이며 에이미 사보는 커스터 애비뉴에 작은 매장을 열 예정입니다. 이들의 노력을 지원해 주시기 바랍니다.

성원해 주셔서 감사합니다.

196머세이디스 체노웨스
쉬머 주얼리 소유주

어휘 jewelry 보석 nearly 거의 decade 10년 go out of business 폐업하다 be honored 영광스럽다 anniversary 기념일 celebration 축하 행사 no longer 더 이상 ~ 않다 endeavor 노력 patronage 후원

수신: 마크 리즈 〈reesem@stylerealty.net〉
발신: 애론 살라자르 〈asalazar@bid-co.com〉
197날짜: 5월 4일
제목: 둘러보기

리즈 씨게,

197오늘 예전의 쉬머 주얼리 매장 공간을 보여 주셔서 감사합니다. 확실히 제가 지난주에 본 메이필드 스트리트 매장보다 훨씬 크군요. 그런데 그 위치에서 제 매장이 얼마나 수익성이 있을지 염려스럽습니다. **198**그 지역은 유동인구가 훨씬 더 많을 것이라고 생각했는데 아니더군요. 라이트 애비뉴에 다음 달부터 이용 가능한 다른 곳이 있다고 말씀하셨는데요. 함께 그곳을 볼 일정을 잡을 수 있을지 알고 싶습니다.
감사합니다.

애론 살라자르

어휘 definitely 분명히 property 부동산, 건물 be concerned about ~에 대해 우려하다 profitable 수익성이 있는 foot traffic 유동인구

도심 매장들, 파산 막으려 몸부림치다

5월 25일 – 한때 북적거리는 활동 지역이었던 그랜드 시티의 도심 쇼핑 지구는 치솟는 임대료 때문에 고전 중이다. **199**이 지역의 임대료는 지난 몇 년간 거의 30% 상승해 소규모 업체들을 사라지게 만들었다. 일례로, **196**지역의 사업주 머세이디스 체노웨스 씨는 이러한 상황 때문에 가게를 폐업했다고 밝혔다. 또 다른 매장 소유주 글로리아 로맨 씨는 클리프턴 몰로 이전했는데 이곳의 임대료는 거의 절반 수준이라고 말했다.

한편, 시 행정 담당관 카일 트레비노 씨는 "임대료와 세금은 문제의 일부일 뿐"이라고 말했다. 그는 지난가을 투표로 통과된 매출세 2% 인상 역시 업체들에게 부담을 주고 있다고 말했다. **200**또한 "이 지역에서 더 많은 활동을 계획한다면 더 많은 업체를 불러들일 수 있다"고 그는 생각한다. 이 구역에서 열리던 축제, 라이브 공연 등 기타 행사의 횟수도 최근 몇 년간 급격히 감소했다. 지역 사업 공동체는 그랜드 시티 중심가의 경제를 활성화시키기 위해 이를 포함한 다른 문제들의 해결책을 모색하고 있다.

어휘 struggle 고투하다, 몸부림치다 stay afloat 빚지지 않고 있다 district 지구 bustling 분주한 skyrocketing 치솟는 rental fee 임대료 drive out 몰아내다, 사라지게 하다 relocate 이전하다 equation 복잡한 상황, 문제 sales tax 매출세 voter 투표자, 유권자 put pressure on ~에 부담을 주다 decline 하락하다, 감소하다 dramatically 극적으로 address (문제 등을) 다루다, 처리하다

---

196 연계

번역 쉬머 주얼리 소유주에 대해 암시된 것은?
(A) 20년 넘게 사업을 해오고 있다.
(B) 자신의 매장을 쇼핑몰로 이전했다.
(C) 보석을 온라인으로 판매할 것이다.
(D) 임대료 인상에 영향을 받았다.

해설 공지 마지막 부분에서 머세이디스 체노웨스 씨가 쉬머 주얼리 소유주라는 것을 확인할 수 있고, 기사 첫 단락 중간에서 체노웨스 씨가 임대료 때문에 폐업했다는 것을 알 수 있다. 따라서 정답은 (D)이다.

197 연계

번역 살라자르 씨는 5월 4일에 어디에서 건물을 보았는가?
(A) 파울리 스트리트
(B) 커스터 애비뉴
(C) 메이필드 스트리트
(D) 라이트 애비뉴

해설 공지 첫 문장에서 쉬머 주얼리의 위치가 파울리 스트리트라는 것을 확인할 수 있고, 이메일에서 오늘(5월 4일) 쉬머 주얼리 예전 매장을 보여줘서 감사하다는 내용을 확인할 수 있다. 따라서 이를 종합해 보면 살라자르 씨가 본 건물은 파울리 스트리트에 있음을 알 수 있다. 정답은 (A)이다.

198 사실 관계 확인

번역 무엇이 살라자르 씨에게 5월 4일에 본 매장에 대해 걱정하게 만드는가?
(A) 주변 주차 공간의 부족
(B) 안 좋은 바닥 상태
(C) 전시장의 협소함
(D) 유동인구가 적은 점

해설 살라자르 씨의 이메일 중간 부분에 '그 지역은 유동인구가 훨씬 더 많을 것이라고 생각했었는데 아니더군요'라고 쓴 것을 통해 정답은 (D)임을 알 수 있다.

199 동의어 찾기

번역 기사에서 첫 번째 단락 6행의 "driving"과 의미가 가장 가까운 것은?
(A) 강요하다
(B) 촉구하다
(C) 수송하다
(D) 동력을 공급하다

해설 drive는 극단적인 상황으로 '몰아가다'라는 의미를 나타낼 때 쓰인다. 이 문장에서도 폐업으로 몰고 갔다는 의미이다. '강제적으로 하게 만든다'는 의미인 (A) forcing이 가장 비슷하다.

200 사실 관계 확인

번역 트레비노 씨는 무엇에 대해 지지를 표하는가?
(A) 비즈니스 협회를 만드는 것
(B) 제안에 대해 재투표하기
(C) 도심에서 더 많은 행사 열기
(D) 시 소유 건물을 임대해 주는 것

해설 기사의 두 번째 단락에 트레비노 씨가 "더 많은 활동을 계획하면 더 많은 업체를 유치할 수 있을 것으로 생각한다"는 말이 나온다. 그랜드 시티 도심 쇼핑 지구에서 더 많은 행사를 여는 것을 지지하는 것임을 알 수 있다. 따라서 정답은 (C)이다.

▸▸ Paraphrasing 지문의 **plan more activities in the area**
→ 정답의 **Hosting more events downtown**